BLACK AMERICANS

THE FBI FILES

Also by Kenneth O'Reilly
  *Hoover and the Un-Americans: The FBI, HUAC, and the Red
    Menace*
  "Racial Matters": The FBI's Secret File on Black America

Also by David Gallen
  Malcolm A to X
  Malcolm X: As They Knew Him
  Remembering Malcolm
    with Benjamin Karim and Peter Skutches
  Thurgood Marshall: Justice for All
    with Roger Goldman

BLACK AMERICANS

THE FBI FILES

KENNETH O'REILLY

Edited by David Gallen

Carroll & Graf Publishers, Inc.
New York

First Carroll & Graf edition 1994

Carroll & Graf Publishers, Inc.
260 Fifth Avenue
New York, NY 10001

Library of Congress Cataloging-in-Publication Data

O'Reilly, Kenneth.
    Black Americans : the FBI files / Kenneth O'Reilly ; edited by
David Gallen.—1st Carroll & Graf ed.
        p.   cm.
    Includes index.
    ISBN 0-7867-0010-6 : $24.95—ISBN 0-7867-0027-0 (pbk.) : $14.95
    1. Afro-Americans—Civil rights—History—Sources.   2. Civil
rights movements—United States—History—20th century—Sources.
3. Afro-Americans—History—1877–1964—Sources.   4. United States.
Federal Bureau of Investigation—Archives.   5. Hoover, J. Edgar
(John Edgar), 1895–1972.   I. Gallen, David.   II. Title.
E185.615.O73   1994
323.1'196073—dc20   93-33870
                                                                CIP

Manufactured in the United States of America

CONTENTS

HOOVER'S FBI AND BLACK AMERICA

I told the Senator [Birch Bayh] that you have an intense demoralizing situation where they [Negroes] cry 'police brutality' on the slightest provocation and the newspapers serve no useful purpose in printing the picture . . . of a Negro on the ground with officers above. . . . I stated that now they [Supreme Court justices] have gone into the field where police officers must address them in courteous language, particularly in the case of Negroes as instead of saying, 'Boy, come here,' they want to be address[ed] as 'Mr.'

J. Edgar Hoover on *Miranda* (July 6, 1966)[1]

When my previous book, *"Racial Matters,"* was released, I received invitations to speak in African-American communities from Roxbury to Compton.[2] During the question-and-answer sections of those engagements, members of the audience inevitably asked, "Why did the FBI kill Martin Luther King?" and "Why did the FBI kill Malcolm X?" Not *whether* J. Edgar Hoover's federal bureaucracy did in fact kill King and/or Malcolm, but *why*. Being a historian with traditional academic credentials, I did my best to answer as trained in graduate school—with emphasis on facts that can be verified as opposed to ideas that remained mere speculation or extrapolation due to lack of evidence. My view, simply put, is that Hoover targeted both King and Malcolm for what he called "neutralization," and his men, in effect, did their best to incite the killings short of actually pulling triggers.

Harris Wofford, formerly President John F. Kennedy's civil rights adviser and now a United States senator from Pennsylvania, concluded in his book, *Of Kennedys and Kings,* that "Hoover and the FBI" certainly helped "create the climate that invited King's assassination."[3] In Malcolm's case, the bureau egged on his feud with Nation of Islam leader Elijah Muhammad and certainly suspected that the worst was possible. "It's time to close his eyes," Muhammad said of Malcolm in a conversation picked up by electronic surveillance experts.[4] The bureau knew it was playing with fire long before February 21, 1965, when self-appointed assassins from the Nation's Newark Mosque gunned down Malcolm X in Harlem's Audubon Ballroom.

It made no difference that King advocated nonviolence and Malcolm resistance at any cost. Hoover's FBI maintained that black leadership had to be destroyed. Despite Malcolm's angry stance and his bloody death, physical violence (as opposed to the rhetoric of violence) was never more than a peripheral part of the struggle for racial justice. However, political violence *was* a central part of the FBI's response to that struggle.

We sometimes forget that the chilling videotape of the beating of Rodney Glenn King didn't start anything new. In the ten-year period (1955–1965) between Rosa Parks's silent courage on a Birmingham bus to the "Bloody Sunday" charge of mounted troopers on Selma's Edmund Pettus Bridge, turn-the-other-cheek gospel ruled the movement for civil rights. Martin Luther King and other advocates of nonviolence hoped their tack would provide a wholesome dignity, and it did to a degree not seen in this country on the race-relations front before or since. To present the movement as a domestic morality play, Dr. King not only counted on the southern resistance's visceral reactions and plain stupidity but the northern media's endless search for dramatic images. What could be more riveting than newspaper photographs and television news footage of Ku Klux Klan thugs with their lead pipes and chains and southern law enforcement officials with their nightsticks and dogs charging peaceful protestors? In Birmingham, Police Commissioner Theophilus Eugene "Bull" Connor even sent his minions to attack black children. Had the Rodney King beating occurred in the 1960s and been captured on film, it would have competed for air time with thousands of like images.

Like those Simi Valley jurors, J. Edgar Hoover stood with the officer above, not with the Negro on the ground. His special agents were on hand during virtually every civil rights demonstration, including ones in which Klan members and police officers turned violent and demonstrators remained nonviolent. Some of the most powerful images from that time, in fact, were captured in photographs of FBI agents standing by with pencils and notebooks in hand, observing the assaults. The agents simply watched and scribbled notes; they sometimes even took their own photographs with spy gear hidden in lunch pails and necktie clasps. Although bureau agents in the 1930s walked through Thompson submachine gun firestorms when going after John Dillinger, agents in the 1960s would not take a baseball bat away from a Klansman even as the bat turned red with the blood of the person being beaten.

If the FBI began the 1960s by passively observing racist violence against civil rights workers, it ended the decade by egging on the racists. Actions against "targets" such as Chicago Black Panther leader Fred Hampton, a charismatic young man of twenty-one, approached the level of planned political assassinations. Hampton ended up dead, shot and killed while sleeping in his bed during a bureau-orchestrated raid carried out by Chicago police assigned to the state's attorney's office. FBI money (that is, tax-payer money) was paid when Hampton died—with Hoover signing off on a $300 bonus to the informant within the Chicago Panthers who had helped with pre-raid logistics.[5]

The actions taken in the name of the nation's security were bad enough and wild enough to make understandable the equally wild speculation and extrapolation. If so many people in Roxbury and Compton *know* that the bureau killed Martin Luther King and Malcolm X and continue to regard the nation's only national police agency with complete distrust, the bureau has only itself to blame.

FBI words and deeds before and on the sad occasion of Fred Hampton's death make it hard to remember that there was (and is) something more to the bureau's relationship with black America than dossiers and COINTELPRO (counterintelligence program) assaults that conjure up images of the previous century's slave patrols. Still, the other image persists—the image of bureau agents taking notes while cops or Klan members beat black Americans in the manner that Rodney King would be beaten decades later. The FBI is linked forever with black history through surveillance/counterintelligence *and* civil rights law enforcement. Hoover spent his decades as director ignoring or minimizing the enforcement of civil rights law, managing as much or more harm by that strategy than the feral aggression elsewhere. With his agents utterly dependent upon local police cooperation to solve more conventional crime in any given community (kidnapping, auto theft, etc.), Hoover was reluctant to jeopardize relationships with those officers by opening brutality cases (now generally called "excessive force" incidents), by far the most common type of civil rights complaint filed by African Americans.

Hoover's avoidance and minimization of civil rights law enforcement is even more repugnant when contrasted with the FBI's red-hot surveillance and counterintelligence pursuit of "communists"—a category less ideological than convenient and elastic. (Hoover defined Reds broadly enough to include anyone interested in racial justice.) Civil rights law, in contrast, was inconvenient and inflexible, so Hoover constructed an elaborate and fairly sophisticated argument based on principles of federalism to explain why his men had no constitutional authority to enforce such statutes. When spying on or harassing blacks, he did not bother with a serious justification at all. He simply cited communist intent to infiltrate the struggle for racial justice and his responsibility to follow the Red kite's tail wherever it led and by any means necessary. The story of Hoover's FBI and black civil rights is thus largely the story of a powerful police agency's reluctance to enforce the law and the willingness of its members to break it.

In Roxbury and Compton, many people seemed surprised to learn that the FBI's civil rights law enforcement mandate dates from this century's first decade when President Theodore Roosevelt turned his attention to the involuntary servitude of African Americans in the turpentine camps of Florida and other southern states. Convinced that peonage represented a "partially successful movement to bring back slavery," Roosevelt nonetheless refused to mobilize his "bully pulpit" against this evil for fear of "embitter[ing] the people." ("People" meant white southerners.) Instead, he urged the historian and scourge of Black Reconstruction, James Ford Rhodes, to rally opposition. In another quiet move, he had Attorney General Charles J. Bonaparte, nephew of Napoleon III, look into peonage. If Roosevelt and Bonaparte had other reasons for creating a Bureau of Investigation within the Department of Justice, the desire to send federal agents south to gather the evidence needed to prosecute involuntary servitude and slavery cases lay near or at the top of the list.[6]

This was 1908, eight years before J. Edgar Hoover entered the Justice Department as a clerk during the Woodrow Wilson administration, sixteen years before he got the directorship under Calvin Coolidge, and twenty-seven years before the old Bureau of Investigation added the word "Federal" to its name under Franklin D. Roosevelt. No matter how limited, a mandate to investigate violations of federal civil rights law existed before Hoover came on board and continued in greatly expanded form after his death, seven presidents later, in the last year of Richard M. Nixon's first term. Another four presidencies later, bureau agents opened an investigation of the Los Angeles police officers who beat Rodney King. The post-Hoover FBI entered the case on the grounds that the officers may have violated federal civil rights law by pounding King to a pulp—in the same manner that Hoover's men moved into the Martin Luther King assassination case, even though murder is not a federal crime, on the grounds that the murderer may have deprived King of his civil rights by killing him. The FBI got into the Fred Hampton killing in the same manner.

Hoover's Racial Domain, 1895–1960

Whether pre- or post-Hoover, the FBI is better known for fighting communists and more conventional criminals than racists. While initial civil rights cases under the peonage heading remained mere sideshows, the early bureau broke its first big case, against Jack Johnson, within four years. This involved the Mann Act, also known as the White Slave Traffic Act, which made it a federal crime to transport a woman across state lines for immoral purposes. Not only was Jack Johnson the first black heavyweight boxing champion of the world, but his fiancée, with whom he had crossed the said state line, was white. Years later, Hoover told *U.S. News & World Report* publisher David Lawrence that the Mann Act had "protect[ed] the virtue of womanhood."[7]

Born the year before the Supreme Court's separate-but-equal strictures in *Plessy v. Ferguson* (1896), Hoover spent those rough and racist days growing up in Washington, D.C.[8] Jim Crow came to the nation's capital and matured at nearly the same time, within two decades visiting everything save the buses and trolleys, the libraries, the grandstands at Griffith Stadium, and once a year the White House lawn—where black and white children took part in Easter egg-rolling events. In Hoover's Seward Square neighborhood, only "colored servants" were allowed because black help constituted a visible sign of gentility and all other blacks represented a physical and moral threat. (A black maid came to help Hoover's mother, Annie, with the cooking and cleaning.) From all-white Central High, Washington D.C.'s oldest and most prestigious public school, Hoover moved on to a position with the Library of Congress while attending George Washington University law school at night. From the time he entered the Justice Department in 1917 until his death on the job fifty-five years later, Hoover carried the vision his childhood fostered—a vision of a white Christian America where all knew their place. Black men were "boys" and black women "Negresses," and they were there to serve him as he served his nation.

World War I first brought black America to the FBI's attention. Special agents flooded "colored areas" in the nation's great cities to assess attitudes toward the draft and investigate rumors of subversion. Surveillance escalated again when race riots shook some two dozen cities in 1917 and the "Red Summer" of 1919. At the time, the twenty-four-year-old Hoover headed the Justice Department's General Intelligence Division (GID), and his domain stretched across "the entire field of all so-called 'Liberalism.' " This included racial organizations ranging from Negro Elks and Shriners to the extremist African Blood Brotherhood. Inevitably, the dossiers in Hoover's collection confirmed what he had been brought up to believe. When rioting broke out in his native Washington, the root cause surfaced, if only in his mind, in what he called "the numerous assaults committed by Negroes upon white women."[9]

FBI surveillance activities declined precipitously during the New Era presidencies of Warren Harding, Calvin Coolidge, and Herbert Hoover—in large part because bureau agents had been implicated in the Teapot Dome scandals. (Among other things, the bureau broke into the offices and tapped the telephones of congressmen investigating the Justice Department's role in the Harding administration mess.) The reformers somehow overlooked Hoover's role as GID chief and even his involvement in the infamous Palmer raids, instead focusing on the thoroughly corrupt Attorney General Harry M. Daugherty and FBI Director William J. Burns. In 1924 the new attorney general, Harlan Fiske Stone, fired Burns, dissolved the Red-hunting GID, and ordered the bureau to confine its investigations to violations of federal law. At the recommendation of then Secretary of Commerce Herbert Hoover, Stone also appointed J. Edgar Hoover acting director. At year's end, Stone made the appointment permanent.

With the rise ten years later of Dillinger, Bonnie Parker and Clyde Barrow, Kate "Ma" Barker, and a score of other flamboyant Tommy-gun gangsters, President Franklin D. Roosevelt brought his New Deal to the FBI.[10] When Congress passed the administration's crime-control legislation, Hoover's men received full arrest power, authority to carry any kind of firearm, and a radically expanded jurisdiction that now included bank robbery, racketeering, and kidnapping. (This last was in response to the Lindbergh tragedy.) If the era also witnessed a wave of lynching in the deep South, including several for which newspapers announced the murders beforehand and gave weather reports for people wishing to attend, President Roosevelt had no wish to alienate white southern voters or otherwise complicate the war on crime. Because he kept antilynching legislation out of the package, the FBI's civil rights jurisdiction remained what it had been under the previous Roosevelt: little more than a few odd peonage cases.

This did not change until 1939 with the coming of World War II—

and the spectacle of home-front fascists and Hitler's Nazi propagandists drawing parallels between Third Reich policy toward Jews and United States policy toward African Americans. Attorney General Frank Murphy, a former NAACP board member, responded by creating a special Civil Liberties Unit (renamed the Civil Rights Section two years later) in the Justice Department's Criminal Division.[11] Convinced that race relations ought to remain the prerogative of the states, Hoover also objected to this latest bureaucracy because it threatened his bureau's relationship with state and local police.

Civil Rights Section attorneys based their authority to conduct investigations on Sections 51 and 52 of Title 18 of the Federal Criminal Code. These remnants of two Reconstruction Era statutes (the Enforcement Act of 1870 and the Civil Rights Act of 1866), were intended to guarantee equality of rights and to control Ku Klux Klan terrorism. Section 51, a felony statute, provided specific criminal sanctions of up to ten years in jail and a $5,000 fine against two or more persons who conspired to deprive "any citizen" of their constitutional rights. Section 52, a misdemeanor statute commonly known as the "color-of-law statute," brought local government officials, including police officers, under the umbrella of federal jurisdiction if they abused the powers of their offices to deny citizens their civil rights. Requiring proof of conspiracy and specific intent, the statutes raised hard questions about enforcement strategies and sparked a legal debate that dragged on for decades. They also provided what little authority existed for the FBI's civil rights investigations from 1939 until the Civil Rights Act of 1964.[12]

With President Roosevelt's approval, the Depression decade's march toward world war also led Hoover to reconstitute his old surveillance apparatus. FBI intelligence on communist and native-fascist infiltration included a specific "Negroes" category, and after Pearl Harbor such "Negro Question" investigations were lumped generically with "German, Italian, and Japanese" fifth columnists. Doubts about the wartime loyalties of minorities even led to the filing of weekly reports with government policy makers on "Negro Trends." And in summer 1942 the bureau launched a nationwide survey of "foreign inspired agitation" in "colored areas and colored neighborhoods." Hoover wanted to know "why particular Negroes or groups of Negroes . . . have evidenced sentiments for other 'dark races' (mainly Japanese) or by what forces they . . . adopted in certain instances un-American ideologies." (The Justice Department filed sedition charges that same year against eighty blacks, including Elijah Muhammad, chiefly on the grounds that they had a "pan-colored" identification with the Japanese.)

FBI informants, wiretaps, and mail covers provided data on thousands of subjects, including Olympic track-and-field champion Jesse Owens. With a good Christian eye to possible counterintelligence action, the bureau compared the date of Owens's marriage with the birthday of his first child—hoping to prove that the black man who beat Hitler's Aryan champions was somehow immoral, in some way an oversexed animal like the freedmen portrayed in D. W. Griffith's epic film elegy to the Klan, *Birth of a Nation*.[13]

These investigations extended to the White House following rumors about black domestics in Alabama causing trouble for their white employers as the result of "encouragement given Negroes by Mrs. Roosevelt." Eleanor Roosevelt had visited Tuskegee Institute in 1941, the bureau noted, and "was entertained throughout her visit by Negroes." The most troubling rumor on this front had black domestics joining Eleanor Clubs at the urging of "a strange white man and a large Negro organizer traveling in an automobile." Always sympathetic to those "white people who found difficulty in retaining their servants as a result of better opportunities offered by various Defense jobs," Hoover ordered his agents to determine whether female black domestics were really "demanding their own terms for working" and using the slogan, "A White Woman in the Kitchen by Christmas."[14] With servants of his own, the director no doubt took a personal interest.

Peace brought no rest. Hoover kept up such surveillance even after Germany and Japan surrendered, finding opportunity to expand them once more in the embryonic cold-war conflict with the Soviet Union. Almost every dossier sent to the Harry S. Truman White House, for example, credited the Communist party (and often only the Communist party) with "agitating" civil rights "pressure campaigns."[15] Among others, the director smeared Mary McLeod Bethune, former director of Negro Affairs for the National Youth Administration, as a Stalinist. He had bureau researchers compare the communist line on lynching with Bethune's utterances, as if only a subversive would take the party line on that horrible crime. This allowed Hoover to link a consensus opinion (that communists posed a serious threat to American institutions and values) with a more problematic one (that civil rights advocates posed an equally serious threat to those same institutions and values).

Hoover's definition of "communist dupe" stretched beyond black icons such as Mary Bethune or white liberal icons such as Eleanor Roosevelt to include such hard-liners as Chicago Mayor Richard Daley. The occasion was a March 1956 invitation to address the Dwight D. Eisenhower cabinet on the general subject of "Racial Tension and Civil

Rights." Arriving with a ton of charts and graphs (including one depicting a tug of war between a team made up of NAACP folks and communists versus a Klan-led team), Hoover began by condemning "extremists on both sides." From there, he spoke of black activists spreading across the South to preach "racial hatred" and otherwise exacerbate white fears of "racial intermarriages" and "mixed education." The Ku Klux Klan itself, he said, was "pretty much defunct," while the white-collar Klans, the Citizens Councils, were composed of "leading citizens" (that is, "bankers, lawyers, doctors, state legislators and industrialists"). These readin'-and-writin' Klans, an aide noted, posed less of a problem than the "Negro publications" that ran "inflammatory articles concerning the[m]."

Mayor Daley's name surfaced during Hoover's discussion of "the alleged lynching" of a fourteen-year-old Chicago boy, Emmett Till, and a subsequent "communist pressure campaign on government officials." Till was killed while visiting relatives in Money, Mississippi, having made the mistake of whistling when a white woman passed. The woman's husband and half brother kidnapped Emmett, murdered him, and dumped his body in the Tallahatchie River, where it was found seven days later with a .45-caliber bullet hole in the crushed skull and a seventy-four-pound cotton-gin fan tied around the neck. A local jury acquitted both suspects of murder charges, and a federal grand jury refused to indict on civil rights charges. After thousands of people (including communists) in Emmett Till's home state demanded that President Eisenhower do something, the Chicago mayor wired the White House urging federal intervention. "Daley [was] not a communist," the director reminded the cabinet. He was merely a dupe for supposedly surrendering to "pressures engineered by the communists."[16]

Such comments make it tempting to generalize about the FBI. After all, Hoover also found communist influence in the Supreme Court, particularly its decision in *Brown v. Board of Education* (1954) declaring an end to separate-but-equal doctrine in the public schools; the Montgomery bus boycott that Mrs. Parks began a year later; and the sit-in movement that North Carolina A & T students launched in President Eisenhower's last year. By the standards of the 1960s, however, the FBI response to the struggle for racial justice remained relatively moderate from Harding to Eisenhower. Again and again, the director proved to be something more than a predictable bigot. Any generalizations must be made carefully and with recognition of the paradoxes, contradictions, and ironies that were as common in Hoover's bureau as any of the civil rights groups tapped for surveillance or counterintelligence.

The NAACP File: A Case Study in Friendly Racism

Of all the dossiers Hoover had gathered on various groups, the FBI file on the NAACP most clearly demonstrates these paradoxes, contradictions, and ironies without obscuring the larger themes. The file was opened on August 21, 1923, when Walter White and Arthur Spingarn met in New York with bureau agent James E. Amos to discuss "the great Negro unrest in this country." With the NAACP men particularly interested in "the lynching and burning of Negroes," Amos summarized their position in a report to his superiors in Washington, D.C. "They are doing all in their power to prevent radicalism among the Negroes, but they intend to do all in their power at the very next election to keep men out of power who have ... refused to support the DYER [antilynching] bill."[17] Not surprisingly, the bureau and its man in New York had a different agenda. Formerly Theodore Roosevelt's valet and a Burns Detective Agency operative, Amos, a black man, had joined the bureau in 1921 to work on the Marcus Garvey case and other "Negro Radical Activities" cases, receiving his shield from Hoover himself. Both men defined "Negro Radical Activities" in broad enough terms to encompass the strategies and tactics of the moderate NAACP.

Amos's meeting with White and Spingarn marked the beginning of a strange half-century relationship between the FBI and the NAACP that seemingly confirms the popular view of Hoover and his bureaucracy as nothing more than a crude collection of inflexible and reactionary anticommunists and racists. For all that we have learned since 1974 when amendments to the Freedom of Information Act of 1966 finally opened the bureau archive, this view is perhaps now more entrenched than ever—persisting in the face of serious scholarly attempts to tear it down. If the general thrust of the reviews in the popular press and journals provide a good indication of such things, virtually all of the new scholarship has actually reinforced the very cartoon history of the FBI targeted for destruction.

Of the hundred odd reviewers of my book, *"Racial Matters,"* for example, nearly every one emphasized Hoover's obsessive anticommunism while only a handful acknowledged the actual argument made— namely, that all the rhetoric about "communism" was mostly a cover and further that in the long run anticommunist assumptions would prove relatively unimportant in shaping FBI attitudes toward the civil rights movement and the black liberation movement. Only one or two reviewers noted an FBI Executives' Conference recommendation during the

1960s to suspend "investigations, and particularly report writing, in routine Security Matter-Communist cases." Hoover approved the recommendation because such cases simply were not worth the time.[18]

Most of what has been written in the past decade about Hoover's FBI and the civil rights movement has focused on federal surveillance policy in general or the ruthless pursuit of Martin Luther King in particular, and has largely ignored the myriad of other ways in which the history of the movement and the history of the FBI overlap. Prior to the 1960s, as recently declassified files on the NAACP and its two prominent executive secretaries, Walter White and Roy Wilkins, make clear, the FBI often acted in the predictably hostile manner by disrupting the lives of "irresponsible and unreliable" civil rights leaders; exploiting the tensions and rivalries among the various civil rights groups; and otherwise interjecting itself into the politics of civil rights in the United States on the wrong side. Paradoxically, Hoover less frequently overcame his own convictions on matters of race and acted in a most unpredictable manner by moving the FBI, however belatedly, well beyond peonage to investigate police brutality, voting rights and employment discrimination, and all other bona fide civil rights cases. Even more surprising, he established liaison with White, Wilkins, and other civil rights leaders deemed "responsible" and "reliable."[19]

The pursuit of these and other seemingly contradictory tasks had an underlying consistency. On one day, Hoover might exaggerate the threat posed by his traditional subversive bogey and declare war on a particular NAACP member or chapter; on the next day, he might minimize the communist menace and actually announce (however cautiously) his support for the NAACP's work. There is no doubt that Hoover was a racist, an anticommunist of the highest order, and a determined foe of the civil rights movement; but he (usually) lead with his bureaucratic and above all political instincts—in other words more as a pragmatist than an anticommunist ideologue or visceral racist. He had complex goals and motivations in the basic areas (personal, bureaucratic, and political), and never let any one of the three get too far out in front. If he had sound bureaucratic or political reasons for doing so, he could put aside his own racism and act accordingly in particular instances.

Early on, ambivalence characterized Hoover's attitude toward the NAACP. For much of the 1920s and 1930s, FBI officials and NAACP activists showed little interest in one another. (An exception occurred a year after James Amos's 1923 meeting with Walter White and Arthur Spingarn when Hoover sat down with White to discuss the Ku Klux Klan.) With surveillance of communists and other left-wing dissidents largely dormant in the wake of Harlan Stone's Teapot Dome reformation, Hoover paid attention to the NAACP only in 1930 when the Herbert Hoover White House requested a file check. He responded by sending a "summary" of dated information about NAACP "propaganda" on such subjects as the Dyer antilynching bill and a resolution calling for withdrawal of United States troops from Haiti.[20] Though Hoover offered to obtain "additional information," he was not unduly upset by the politics of the NAACP or the specter of communist infiltration. One of his agents even cited the communist party's own exaggerated complaint that total black membership could be counted "on the fingers of one's hand."[21]

Hoover seemed generally tolerant if never quite pleased with the NAACP. He put Walter White's address in his correspondence book and commended White's group, in the language of his cold-war era bestseller *Masters of Deceit,* for its decision to withdraw from the Scottsboro case, "recognizing that the Communist party was interested only in promoting 'Red Fascism' in America."[22] (The party was heavily involved in the legal defense of the so-called Scottsboro boys—nine black Alabama teenagers sentenced to death for the alleged rape of two white women.)[23] As much as anything else, the faint, qualified praise in his book reflected the director's official attitude until 1941, when he opened a COMINFIL (communist infiltration) case in response to a request from the Navy to investigate protests of discrimination filed by fifteen African-American mess attendants.

By the time World War II ended, the COMINFIL investigation had both benign and less wholesome aspects. Hoover entered ("in the usual manner") a subscription to the NAACP magazine, *The Crisis* (strictly for data-gathering purposes). He acted more aggressively by leaking derogatory information on the group (and the National Urban League as well) to a source in New York.[24] With Attorney General Francis Biddle's approval, the FBI also wiretapped the NAACP's Philadelphia office on the assumption that it was "rapidly becoming a tool for the [Communist] party."[25]

FBI surveillance of the NAACP was part of a broader, usually color-blind COMINFIL sweep that ranged from the Catholic Youth Organization to such truly odd categories as radio comedians. (Bureau agents recorded at least a few of the Red Skelton, Bob Hope, and Gracie Allen broadcasts in search of communist and/or Axis propaganda.)[26] At the same time, the FBI continued to cooperate with those NAACP members deemed responsible. In Philadelphia, during the weeks after the tap was placed, the local FBI man, J. F. Sears, twice received an NAACP delegation in search of "advice in dealing with a communist element." They were determined "to go on record," Sears told Hoover, "as opposing such infiltration."[27]

FBI executives in Washington had already opened a channel to the NAACP. Hoover met with Walter White in November 1941 at Biddle's suggestion for "a long talk" about two civil rights cases in Texas and, more generally, "Nazi, Communist, and Fascist agitators." White came out of the meeting convinced that he had the director's pledge to act "more determinedly on the violation of civil liberties of Negroes." Hoover came out convinced that he had White's pledge to pass on information regarding "subversive activities." Since White had already done this "relative to Nazi agents . . . [working] among Negro servants employed in [the] homes of wealthy white people," the director gave the NAACP leader the home telephone number of every FBI special agent in charge and asked him to "have his various branches report any [subversive] activities to our offices." "I told Mr. White," Hoover said, "that I feel it is important that reputable Negro organizations be diligently alert to keep Nazism, Communism, and Fascism from attaching themselves to Negro movements."[28] Ultimately, Hoover would be more successful in soliciting NAACP support for this agenda than White would be in convincing the FBI to sign on for the civil rights fight.

Walter White kept trying nonetheless. He pestered the director throughout 1941 and intermittently for the next seven years about the paucity of black FBI agents.[29] Rather than review his personnel policies, Hoover prepared a testimonial for White on the occasion of his twenty-fifth anniversary with the NAACP. "A very guarded and cautious statement" would do "no harm," bureau officials reasoned when considering whether to write the testimonial or not, "but would on the other hand certainly aid us in our relations with the Negro race." That same year, when White left for a tour of Great Britain, Hoover suggested that the American Embassy extend every possible courtesy. Responding in kind, White sent Hoover a reprint of his December 1931 *Harper's* article, "The Negro and the Communists," together with Clarence Darrow's statement explaining why the NAACP had withdrawn from the Scottsboro case. When White traveled to the Midwest and the West Coast, he asked Hoover (according to the bureau's account), "Are there any services I can render while there?," and promised to "furnish" the FBI "any information" obtained.[30] All the while, the bureau kept its COMINFIL investigation in high gear, and the NAACP kept pressuring the bureau to enforce federal civil rights law more aggressively.

Three developments strained this superficial mutual ingratiation during Truman's presidency. The first occurred in November 1945 when the NAACP discovered a microphone surveillance at a dinner held at New York's McAlpin Hotel for Norman Manley of the Jamaican Peoples' National party. E. E. Conroy, the New York special agent in charge, smoothed over that glitch by somehow convincing White that there was no bug.[31] The second development that strained FBI/NAACP relations involved White's continuing criticism of the bureau's all-white agent corps. (Hoover had purged the handful of black agents hired in the late 1910s and early 1920s, or, as in Amos's case, "domesticated" them so that they functioned as office boys or chauffeurs.) The third development that strained FBI/NAACP relations involved Thurgood Marshall's charge of bias within the agent corps. Hoover contained these last two issues only with great difficulty—and with timely assistance from an odd source: the black press.

Walter White returned to the question of black agents in 1946 after lynchings in Walton, Georgia, asking Hoover again "if there are any Negro FBI operators."[32] A year later, White followed the lead of Leslie S. Perry of the NAACP's Washington branch, who scored the FBI's " 'lily-white' personnel recruiting record." Back in the late 1930s Perry himself had applied for an agent position but "was politely . . . told that the FBI did not hire 'colored agents.' My interviewer," he recalled, "explained that the agency had only one Negro agent who had gotten in because he had been a valet or something to the late President Theodore Roosevelt." Now, newspaper publicity about the large number of investigative and clerical job openings in connection with the Federal Employee Loyalty-Security Program, Perry said, had resulted in dozens of black applicants being given a similar "brush-off."[33]

This "delicate problem" led Hoover to run Perry's name through the files and advise the field to be on guard against "racial discrimination . . . 'guinea pigs' . . . sent to your office for the express purpose of testing the reception they will receive." Hoover also worked with publisher John H. Johnson, soliciting an *Ebony* article in October 1947 on black agents James Amos and Sam Noisette. But Amos was long past mandatory retirement age and in all probability had not received a regular case assignment since 1924 when Hoover took over; Noisette was a combination messenger and elevator operator. When visitors went in to see the director, Noisette took their hats. Roy Garvin of the *Washington Afro-American* criticized Johnson for "palming Noisette off," explaining that "there are no Negro FBI agents," only "special agents"—in effect, "stools" who, in Perry's words, "[may] live next door to a colored family, get himself in their good graces and then report the information he has secured to an agent who makes the arrest, and so forth." White told Perry and Clarence Mitchell, also of the NAACP Washington office, "to arm themselves with as much information as possible and ... see Hoover." With Mitchell citing a lack of hard evidence, however, the opportunity passed. The FBI remained lily white, although, thanks to the skewed *Ebony* article, some NAACP members took pains to commend Hoover on his "fairness in the hiring of Negroes."[34]

Simultaneous to the Perry flap, Thurgood Marshall wrote Hoover and Attorney General Tom Clark charging white agents with racism. Convinced that bigoted FBI agents were in fact "messing up ... cases," Walter White picked up the charge in a private letter to Hoover that itemized three instances of prejudice. When the director rebutted each charge point by point (and "in accordance with our understanding"), White backed off. But Marshall persisted. This time, he wrote Clark (with a copy to Eleanor Roosevelt) demanding "a complete investigation" of the FBI. Hoover ended up drafting Clark's response and complaining to White about how "Mr. Marshall and some of his legal associates" failed to "measure up to the standards of cooperation ... set by you." Marshall gave up for the time being, advising White of his lack of "faith in either Mr. Hoover or his investigators."[35] Eventually, he asked for a face to face meeting, finally receiving an audience in October 1947.[36]

Hoover responded to these difficulties, on the one hand, by collecting the most scurrilous rumors and sending the Truman White House reports on communist attempts to infiltrate the NAACP. One especially absurd item had the NAACP rooting for lynch mobs because lynchings boosted fund raising.[37] On the other hand, the director continued his policy of limited cooperation, giving Walter White an updated list of the names and home telephone numbers of all special agents in charge of bureau field offices and recommending White to Tom Clark for an advisory panel on juvenile delinquency.[38] Though he complained in the midst of the Marshall flap about the earlier "blunder made in committing me to this outfit," Hoover also wrote another testimonial for the NAACP, in the process recommending that Clark write one too. At the same time, the FBI asked an occasional favor of the NAACP. White obliged more than once by destroying letters and other documents in his files at the bureau's request.[39]

What one FBI official described as "the overall picture of our relationship with the NAACP" often involved the communist issue, with

Walter White approaching Hoover for help in countering charges of
infiltration. The problem began in a most unlikely manner with historian
Arthur M. Schlesinger, Jr., and his July 29, 1946, *Life* magazine article
on the Red menace. The Communist party, Schlesinger wrote, "[was]
sinking tentacles into the National Association for the Advancement of
Colored People." Remembering its problems with the colored mess
attendants, the Navy also distributed a pamphlet (*Communism in Action*)
that implied widespread infiltration. In both cases, White responded
quietly, with letters to Time, Inc., owner Henry Luce and Secretary of
Defense James Forrestal. Forrestal did not bother to reply; Luce referred
the matter to editorial director John Shaw Billings, who told White that
Schlesinger got his information "in Washington where it was given to
him in confidence."[40]

In contrast, when the blacklisting magazine *Counterattack* warned of
communist plans to "capture" the NAACP, White went straight to the
FBI, asking New York special agent in charge Edward Scheidt what
the bureau knew about that rag. "He [also] indicated," Scheidt reported
to his superiors, that "he would be glad to receive from the FBI at any
time information which the bureau might receive regarding communist
activities directed at the NAACP."[41] Even while raging at *Counterattack,* White accepted the magazine's premise. Convinced that the
Communist party had launched "a determined campaign . . . to capture
the Association," White and his closest aides decided on a full-blown
purge. To beat the real blacklisters to the punch, they would clean their
own house. No more "wrangling over what is liberal" or "hesitating
to identify ourselves with a kind of McCarthyism," as Roy Wilkins put
it. "We do not want a witch hunt," he told White, "but we want to
clean out our organization."[42] In the public arena, this decision led
White to support such groups as the All-American Conference to Combat Communism; privately, it led him to embrace the anticommunist
consensus of the Truman years largely on Hoover's terms.

In New York, Scheidt briefed White on an alleged plot by the left-
wing Civil Rights Congress to undermine his leadership, with White
sending Scheidt a "Dear Ed" thank-you letter with attachments, including (again) his 1931 *Harper's* article and copies of three blasts from
Thurgood Marshall to communist functionary William Patterson.[43] In
Washington, White and Clarence Mitchell solicited additional information from FBI Assistant Director Louis B. Nichols, Hoover's contact
with Senator Joseph McCarthy and the House Committee on Un-American Activities. They were particularly interested in Communist and/or
"Talmadgite" attempts to infiltrate the upcoming NAACP convention

in Atlanta, volunteering in return to report to the bureau "any matters that might be of interest."

Upon arriving in Atlanta, White toured the local FBI office, finding special agent in charge John Bills "cordial even to the extent of offering to lend me the air conditioning equipment . . . provided I carted it off on my back." Afterward, White told Nichols that the only problem at the NAACP convention involved a man who distributed stickers reading "WHY NOT RACIAL AND SOCIAL EQUALITY NOW?" But city police promptly arrested this fellow and warned him "so effectively," White said, "that we had no more trouble on that score."[44]

This harmonious FBI/NAACP relationship continued into the first of the Eisenhower years. Hoover again gave Walter White the addresses and phone numbers of FBI field offices (no names of special agents in charge or home phone numbers, this time); and Nichols briefed White and Wilkins on such subjects as the National Lawyers Guild and rumors of NAACP involvement in the Rosenbergs' defense.[45] And for the third time in ten years, Hoover wrote a testimonial for the NAACP. Bumping into each other at Harvey's, a Washington restaurant, the director told White that local radio no longer carried his civil rights program. After a joke about the public preferring Milton Berle, White asked for a plug to help his show get back on the air. Hoover did so, sending off a brief statement about how "Mr. Walter White's radio program makes a valuable contribution to intelligent enlightenment."[46]

Two events, one minor and one major, quickly made the director regret this latest testimonial and complain about the "turn White has taken."[47] The minor problem involved Ralph Clayton Clontz, a black North Carolina attorney and $450-a-month FBI informant who testified before the Subversive Activities Control Board and at the Smith Act trial of Junius Scales. When Clontz said he reported on NAACP affairs, White criticized the bureau in his newspaper column.[48] The major problem involved the pending Supreme Court decision in the school desegregation case brought by Thurgood Marshall and his legal division associates. In response, the FBI revived its largely dormant COMINFIL investigation, pushing the field in the weeks before *Brown* came down in May 1954 to investigate every NAACP chapter from Miami, Florida, to Anchorage, Alaska. Thereafter, as the director's secretary, Helen Gandy, put it, there would be no more public testimonials "in view of the controversial nature of the subject of integration."[49]

FBI policy appeared to shift dramatically after Walter White's death in 1955. When the NAACP named Roy Wilkins to succeed White, Hoover asked his staff, "What do we know of him?" The subsequent file check cited the *Counterattack* charge that "Wilkins sided with Paul Robeson regarding the Peekskill riot."[50] Hoover also asked for "a general memo on NAACP" later in the year. This was in response to NAACP public relations director Henry Lee Moon's release of the director's 1947 testimonial to counter Georgia Attorney General Eugene Cook's well-publicized attack on the group as a communist front. Hoover received the files and then complained, privately, that "my letter was written nearly nine years ago ... when NAACP under Walter White was a well-disciplined group."[51]

When briefing the Eisenhower cabinet in 1956 on the gathering racial storm in the South, Hoover not only lumped "ill-advised leaders of the NAACP ... [with] the Communist party" but told the president that the NAACP had "seized upon" the Emmett Till lynching "for exploitation purposes" (apparently an even greater sin than Mayor Daley's).[52] It came as no surprise, then, that in 1957, the year that saw the first federal civil rights legislation enacted since Reconstruction, the FBI's New York office compiled a 157-page report on the NAACP based on information obtained by "bag squads" (bureau burglars), wiretaps, and some 150 other "confidential informants." The report was destined for various opinion molders within the government, with portions leaked to "reliable and cooperative" newspaper reporters.[53]

FBI policy remained contradictory nonetheless. With bureau agents counting no more than "467 members or past members of the CP" out of a total active NAACP membership of more than 300,000, Hoover knew that infiltration was not much of a problem. Internal COMINFIL and COINTELPRO reports also singled out Roy Wilkins for doing "everything possible to keep the NAACP clear of communist infiltration." In a sense, Hoover wrote yet another public testimonial by praising the group's anticommunism in *Masters of Deceit.* (This prompted NAACP headquarters to suggest that each branch purchase a copy as a reference volume.)[54]

The FBI continued briefing NAACP officials on matters of communist infiltration, including a tip to Thurgood Marshall about party interest in the Prayer Pilgrimage for Freedom. Hoover's attitude toward Marshall gradually improved throughout the 1950s, with the NAACP general counsel occasionally calling for assistance on such things as his difficulties in securing a passport. If the FBI never stopped digging through its own files or HUAC files to document his left-wing "associations," by the mid-1950s Marshall would drop in to see Louis Nichols from time to time. The director himself would sometimes complain to Marshall about other NAACP activists' criticisms of the FBI.[56]

With Hoover "deeply" appreciative of a "very favorable resolution passed by the NAACP at its last convention," the FBI also moved to establish liaison with Roy Wilkins. Cartha DeLoach, Nichols's successor as head of the bureau's public relations division, met with Wilkins in February 1960 "to express his appreciation for the continuing good cooperation between the bureau and the National Association for the Advancement of Colored People." According to DeLoach, Wilkins conceded that "there were a number of communists in the NAACP" and promised "to keep in close touch with us" but didn't offer to name any names. When DeLoach complained about criticism of the FBI role in the Mack Charles Parker lynching, "Wilkins ... stated he would take every step to remedy this situation and intended seeing to it that the FBI got the credit it deserved." Before leaving, Wilkins told De-Loach that "he and Irving Ferman had engineered" the convention resolution that had so pleased Hoover. (Ferman, director of the American Civil Liberties Union's Washington, D.C., branch, functioned as an FBI informant.) Wilkins, like Walter White before him, could sometimes see his time only through the lens of anticommunism.[57]

The larger truth remains nonetheless. Hoover's FBI was a formidable enemy of the civil rights movement if not the rigid, single-minded enemy so often portrayed. The nature of the bureau's opposition, in the case of White, Wilkins, and their organization, and in most other cases as well, was complex and reflective of the director's assessment of his institutional and political interests as well as his personal and ideological preferences. In other words, Hoover was first and foremost an ambitious politician/bureaucrat who dreamed of an ever-expanding national constituency and had no objection to including black America within that constituency if it could be done on his own terms. The FBI-NAACP relationship prior to 1960 demonstrates how the director tried and failed to accommodate "the colored race." Hereafter, the bureau's relationship with that organization and most every other civil rights and black nationalist group would be more straightforward. By the next decade's third year, Hoover would fall back on a divisive, segmented politics intended to pit white against black and black against black.

Movement Days: From the Freedom Rides
to Selma, 1961–1965

These were miserable times for the sixty-six-year-old Hoover. Having spent forty-four years in the Justice Department and now entering his thirty-seventh year as FBI chief, he found himself taking (if rarely following) orders from a man thirty years his junior who wanted to change how the bureau operated. Attorney General Robert F. Kennedy ordered the director to hire black agents as part of the new administration's affirmative action push for all federal agencies and departments. He also tried to get the director to act more aggressively in civil rights cases, particularly the voting rights lawsuits that the Justice Department had decided to pursue in the deep South. Hoover resisted bitterly, never hiring more than a token number of black agents and launching a sustained campaign of bureaucratic obfuscation to slow down or otherwise impede the voting litigation campaign.[58] Still, Kennedy had raised an unprecedented challenge to his fiefdom, and things would continue to worsen. The most serious threat to the director's autonomy, however, came not from the president's brother but from the civil rights movement itself.

This threat arrived in endless waves, with the first wave taking the form of Freedom Riders traveling from Washington, D.C., south on Greyhound and Trailways buses. James Farmer of the Congress of Racial Equality came up with the idea, having done it once before through the upper South (the Journey of Reconciliation in 1947). This time, the Freedom Riders would venture into the deep South, into Alabama and then Mississippi. Farmer hoped to provoke "an international crisis" that would bring the fundamental contradiction of cold war America to the world's attention. "We were counting on the bigots of the South to do our work for us," he said. The riders would "fill up the jails, as Gandhi did in India," with a jail-no-bail strategy designed to move the struggle for racial justice onto the high moral ground of global politics.[59]

Hoover's orders as the Freedom Riders headed south ensured that Farmer would get more than he bargained for. When the Greyhound arrived in Anniston, Alabama, on Mother's Day 1961, sixty miles from Birmingham, an angry mob quickly surrounded the bus—smashing windows and pounding away until police arrived. When the bus pulled out, dozens of rioters pursued in cars, overtaking it and forcing it off the road with the help of shotguns and a homemade bomb tossed through a window. The second bus, the Trailways, pulled into Anniston within an hour. Eight rioters boarded and brutalized two white Freedom Riders. When that bus made it to the Birmingham terminal fifty minutes later, a wave of Ku Klux Klansmen appeared carrying baseball bats, chains, and lead pipes.

FBI agents and officials had known about Klan plans for the Freedom Riders weeks in advance and had actually facilitated the violence by passing details of the riders' itinerary to Police Commissioner Bull

Connor and Sergeant Thomas H. Cook. The bureau did so knowing full well that Cook relayed everything to his fellow Klansmen, and further that Connor had promised the Klan twenty minutes to break heads before sending in city police officers. An informant within the Birmingham Klan, Gary Thomas Rowe, gave the bureau this tidbit. To keep his cover, Rowe swung his ball bat at the terminal as hard or harder than any of the other thugs.[60]

Hoover responded to the Alabama violence by running name checks on the Freedom Riders to see if any of them had criminal or communist associations. Meanwhile, Diane Nash and ten other sit-in veterans from the Student Nonviolent Coordinating Committee pledged to come down from Nashville and board the Montgomery bus. (Most of the original riders were in no shape to continue.) When Greyhound had trouble locating a driver for that dangerous assignment, Robert Kennedy suggested that Hoover assign the task to an agent. The director said his men were investigators, not chauffeurs—an ironic comment because the only black "special agents" at the time were in fact chauffeurs or servants whose duties included driving for prominent Americans. Kennedy knew that Eisenhower received such bureau services. He also knew that the bureau chauffeured his own father during his travels outside the Boston area. Still, when Hoover threatened to quit, RFK dropped the idea of having a special agent drive the bus.[61]

The attorney general now pressured Greyhound on the matter of a driver and finally succeeded, allowing the Freedom Riders to move on to Montgomery. This time, an even bigger Klan mob awaited, and Robert Kennedy's own emissary, former Nashville newspaperman John Seigenthaler, ended up in the hospital along with several riders. "They had agents all over the place," Seigenthaler complained. "It galls me to think that the FBI stood there and watched me get clubbed." Remembering Seigenthaler as someone who had thus embarrassed their bureaucracy, FBI officials eventually opened a file on him—a file that included utterly ridiculous allegations about "relations with young girls." (At the time he went down under the Klan's blows, Seigenthaler was trying to help two young white female riders.)[62]

For the next two years, the FBI remained on the periphery—opening dossiers and otherwise observing the movement's seminal events at Ole Miss and elsewhere (and continuing to observe as well the brutalization of peaceful protestors). By mid-1963, however, the movement had muscled its way onto the nation's main political stage in the wake of the Birmingham demonstrations and Martin Luther King's "I Have a Dream" speech at the March on Washington. This forced the Kennedy administration to reverse its no-legislation strategy and introduce a civil rights bill; it also forced the bureau, in effect, to announce a formal declaration of war on the black struggle. Hoover's anti-civil rights agenda and the Kennedys' pro-civil rights agenda, nonetheless, were not as diametrically opposed as one might suppose. They found common ground on occasion—most notably, in the decision to wiretap King.

Acting on FBI reports suggesting that two of Martin Luther King's advisers were secret communists (Jack O'Dell and Stanley Levison), Robert Kennedy authorized taps on King's home and office telephones.[63] He also sent John Seigenthaler and Civil Rights Division chief Burke Marshall to convince King to break all ties with O'Dell and Levison. When that failed, President Kennedy himself met King at the White House and took him outside for a private walk in the rose garden. ("I guess Hoover must be bugging him too," King later speculated.) "They're communists," JFK said. "You've got to get rid of them."[64]

"Hoover can kiss my ass!" O'Dell exploded, after he found out about the FBI/White House alliance. "I am not the issue!" The real issue, as O'Dell told the movement's epic chronicler, Taylor Branch, was "control of the movement . . . and whatever Dr. King decided, he should not kid himself into believing that Hoover and the Kennedys would be satisfied with this one execution." Branch agreed that it was more "a classic purge . . . beginning with two of King's most indispensable people—O'Dell, the heart of both direct-mail fund-raising and voter registration records, and Levison, King's closest confessor and sounding board into the white world. What would keep the government from coming after any of them, including King, once he accepted their terms with a tacit admission that he had subversive ties? . . . You could not allow a witch-hunt into the movement—that's how you self-destructed."[65]

To explain the wiretap and interference in Southern Christian Leadership Conference personnel matters, Burke Marshall said JFK could leave nothing to chance since the president's "whole stake, politically and historically in a way, rode on that [civil rights] bill." Arthur Schlesinger, then a White House adviser, was equally adamant that the communist issue had to be resolved. "The Kennedys went bail for the movement," he argued, and if the FBI's reports turned out to be true the movement's ship and the administration's ship would sink together. Robert Kennedy told his press secretary that he approved the tap because "he felt that if he did not do it, Mr. Hoover would move to impede or block the passage of the Civil Rights Bill . . . and that he felt that he might as well settle the matter as to whether [Levison] did have the influence . . . that the FBI contended.''[66]

"We never wanted to get very close to [Martin Luther King]," Robert Kennedy later explained to Anthony Lewis of the *New York Times* (in an interview not intended for immediate publication). "Just because of these contacts and connections that he had, which we felt were damaging to the civil rights movement. And because we were so intimately involved in the struggle for civil rights, it also damaged us." Of Stanley Levison's sinister nature, Kennedy and Burke Marshall were absolutely convinced.

Marshall: A secret member of the Communist party.
RFK: A high official.
Marshall: Well, at that time, all that I knew was that he was a secret member.
RFK: Later on, he became a member of the Executive Board.
Marshall: Made a member of the Executive Committee, secretly, of the Communist party.
RFK: So he was quite a big figure.
Marshall: He was a very important figure in the Communist party. . . .
RFK: It's very unhealthy to have an association with a person who is elected to the Executive Board of the Communist party. . . .
Marshall: And to continue it after warning.
RFK: Continuing it. That in itself was bad.[67]

Neither Kennedy nor Marshall could make sense of King's response to their repeated warnings. "He's just got some other side to him," the attorney general concluded. "He sort of laughs about a lot of these things, makes fun of it." Marshall thought King refused to cut off Levison because "he was just probably weak about it." In fact, King revealed his "funny side" most clearly when asking to see the proof—something that the administration had never bothered to ask of Hoover for the simple reason that they had little interest in such things. The Kennedys were principally interested in wiretapping the civil rights movement's most visible leader, and "communism" provided the most convenient excuse to do so. Actually asking to see hard evidence? Now that, as they say, was funny.[68]

A year before introducing the civil rights bill of 1963, Robert Kennedy offered advice for "those of both extremes of this [communist] question." "Leave the job to the expert," he said, adding that "Mr. Hoover is my expert." The director, in other words, had his uses. His bureau could be mobilized to carry out night raids on behalf of the administration, to report back on virtually anything (including, in RFK's words, such things as which "Senators had Negro girlfriends"). The bureau also could be blamed when things got ugly (as they did years later when the King taps surfaced during Muhammad Ali's draft-evasion trial), and quickly disciplined at the first hint of unilateralism.

To prove that things were under control, Kennedy cited Hoover's dissemination of a derogatory report on King to the Army. "The Army hated Negroes," noted Nicholas deB. Katzenbach, who would succeed RFK as attorney general. "It's practically like sending it to the *Washington Post.* "[So] I called up Hoover," Kennedy said. "I said that, of course, we had the legislation up. I said that I was as concerned about this matter as he was or anybody was, but that we wanted to obtain the passage of legislation. And we didn't want to lose, to fail in the passage of legislation by a document that gave only one side. He said, 'I think it should be recalled.' So I said, 'Fine.' " The report was recalled, but the wiretaps remained (loyally) in place—as did Hoover himself, in Kennedy's blissful and wildly inaccurate view.[69]

"Hoover served our interests," said Robert Kennedy. "It was a danger that we could control, that we were on top of, that we could deal with at the appropriate time. That's the way we looked at it. In the interests of the administration and in the interests of the country, it was well that we had control over it. And there wasn't anybody he could go to or anything he could do with the information or the material. So it was fine. He served our interests."[70] Kennedy approved the King taps, in other words, because they served the administration's interests.

Hoover wanted to destroy King; the White House merely wanted to plug into the movement's center. It had to do with politics, not communism or the director's thinly veiled blackmail threats centered on the president's extramarital athleticism with, among others, the girlfriend of a Mafia boss. Hoover hoped to define how and with what information the civil rights movement would be understood by a national audience. The administration shared that goal and formed an alliance, with the Kennedy tough-guy image creating the delusion that things were under control. Hoover had an additional goal that neither John nor Robert Kennedy fully appreciated—to define how and with what information the movement would be understood by the presidency and other particular constituencies in the Department of Justice and Congress and even the Army. The wonder in all this, as historian Garry Wills noted, "is that King retained his faith in a country whose best leaders thwarted and plotted against him, while lower officials like Bull Connor threatened his life."[71]

On September 15, Hoover and the Kennedys turned their attention to the dynamite bomb that signaled the last great civil rights event of the Kennedy years. The explosion rocked Birmingham's Sixteenth Street Baptist Church, killing four African-American girls, aged eleven to fourteen. The administration's response was tepid. Beyond statements expressing moral outrage, the president's only substantive act was to call on a coach, West Point's Earl Blaik, and send him to Birmingham as a peacemaker. "When he reported back to the White House," Wills also noted, "JFK talked football with him."[72]

Otherwise, the administration relied on the FBI to bring the guilty parties to justice. With little success, the bureau looked into "all angles," including Georgia Senator Richard Russell's suggestion "that Negroes might have perpetrated this incident in order to keep emotions at a fever pitch." Failing to break the case, Hoover had Courtney Evans, his liaison with Robert Kennedy, explain that "the integration groups" were frustrating the bureau's investigation. "I had the attorney general's complete attention, and there is no question he heard what I said," Evans reported back. "Nevertheless, he only remarked 'Yeah' and immediately followed by saying, 'I think Senator McClellan is interrupting Valachi too much in his testimony.' " Still, Hoover's men kept investigating the Sixteenth Street bombing, and when John Kennedy died in Dallas two months later their taps and bugs picked up the celebrations of Birmingham's hard-core Klansmen and neo-Nazis.[73]

Hoover was not pleased when Lyndon Johnson expanded the Kennedys' civil rights bill and pushed it through Congress. Nor was he pleased when President Johnson ordered him to Mississippi to open a new field office in Jackson and otherwise assure the nation that the FBI would do everything possible to find civil rights workers Michael Schwerner, Andrew Goodman, and James Chaney. The three young men were part of the Freedom Summer force organized by SNCC, CORE, and a coalition of various other groups, and they had disappeared in Neshoba County on June 21, twelve days before Johnson signed the Civil Rights Act of 1964. Hoover's agents solved the case, though not in the manner portrayed recently by Gene Hackman in the film *Mississippi Burning*. Rather, they held out a $30,000 reward until a Klan member led them to a dam construction project on the Ollen Burrage farm. Schwerner, Chaney, and Goodman (two New York Jews and a black native son of the Magnolia state) were under thirty feet of Mississippi mud. During the course of the Klan investigation that followed, the bureau seemed equally interested in the Freedom Summer crew and any possible communist associations. This interest even led to a wiretap on the telephone of Michael Schwerner's father.[74]

Hoover, and to a lesser extent Lyndon Johnson, held to this course all the way through. At the end of Freedom Summer, SNCC helped organize the Mississippi Freedom Democratic party (MFDP) challenge to the credentials of the state's regular all-white delegation at the Democratic National Convention in Atlantic City. The bureau was there too, having been sent in by Johnson to help ensure a harmonious convention. A squad of some twenty-seven agents, including wiretap specialists, provided a steady stream of information to Bill Moyers and other White House aides. The MFDP failed in 1964, but would succeed four years later in Chicago as part of a coalition called the Loyal Democrats of Mississippi. Five bureau informers had infiltrated that coalition, and when its integrated delegation sat on the convention floor three of those informants voted as delegates or alternate delegates. All five operated out of the Jackson office, the office that Johnson had sent Hoover to open personally during Freedom Summer.[75]

President Johnson called on Hoover again in winter 1965 during the Selma demonstrations. Beginning February 1, Alabama lawmen arrested three thousand demonstrators, including Martin Luther King, in a four-day period. Events unfolded quickly in Selma during the next month. This former slave-market town reached its second climax on March 7, when mounted police beat back marchers on the Edmund Pettus Bridge—"Bloody Sunday," the single most brutal repression of any civil rights demonstration. Two days later, segregationist toughs assaulted Rev. James Reeb, a Boston Unitarian, who died on March 11. (That tragedy attracted national attention, in contrast to the earlier killing of a young black man, Jimmy Lee Jackson, by a state trooper.) Four days later, Johnson announced his voting rights bill to a joint session of Congress, placing Selma alongside Lexington and Concord as the site of a turning point in American history. Ten days later, the movement had another martyr—Viola Liuzzo, a red-haired Detroit housewife and mother of five who had come to Selma to help the movement and been shot to death by Klansmen.

The FBI solved that murder immediately for the simple reason that an informant, Gary Thomas Rowe, was among the killers. Liuzzo had spent her last day shuttling Selma-Montgomery marchers back to their homes in her car on Highway 80 near Big Bear Swamp in Lowndes County, twenty-five miles from the Edmund Pettus Bridge. On the day's last trip, Rowe and three other armed Klansmen sped past in another car and opened fire. With blood spurting from her temple, Liuzzo died instantly, crashing her car into the ditch. The only passenger, Leroy Moton, a nineteen-year-old black barber, hitchhiked into Selma for help.

Hoover took the opportunity to smear everyone involved in the demonstrations, including Liuzzo. "On the woman's body," he told the president, without any evidence whatsoever, "we found numerous needle marks indicating that she had been taking dope." He told Attorney General Katzenbach that Liuzzo "was sitting very, very close to the Negro in the car ... [and] that it had the appearance of a necking party." He told a group of newspaper editors from Liuzzo's home state that "white citizens are primarily decent, but frightened for their lives" because "the colored people are quite ignorant, mostly uneducated, and I doubt if they would seek an education if they had an opportunity. Many who have the right to register [to vote] seldom do register." For Hoover, this is what Selma and the Voting Rights Act of 1965 came down to.[76]

A Surveillance Consensus

One cannot fully understand the centrality of surveillance to the 1960s without looking at the inherent tensions in the FBI's internal security responsibilities on one plane and civil rights enforcement responsibilities on another. This dual mandate, in effect, required the bureau to spend part of its time protecting the civil rights and civil liberties of black citizens and the rest of its time violating those same rights and liberties. Outside the movement and to a degree within the movement itself, few people challenged the legitimacy of these contradictory missions because few people entirely escaped the pollution of an earlier time—the era of Senator Joseph R. McCarthy and the Great Fear. To put it another way, there was a surveillance consensus that not only touched the dossier collectors in Hoover's bureaucracy and responsible officials in the White House, but the civil rights movement itself.

Throughout the 1960s, movement people pressured the FBI to investigate complaints of police brutality and Klan violence more aggressively. A few settled for what Hoover offered instead—federal surveillance. Some of the movement's friends in the Kennedy and Johnson administrations proved willing to make the same trade-off and accept the civil rights G-man as spy rather than law enforcement officer. If the choice was an easy one for the FBI, it was also surprisingly easy for many of the New Frontier and Great Society reformers and even a few of the most prominent civil rights leaders.

The FBI slid back and forth from civil rights enforcement investigations to domestic intelligence investigations—from limited investigations of alleged violations of civil rights law to sweeping investigations of the people and groups involved in the struggle for racial justice. The FBI did so not only because that was Hoover's agenda, which even "the maximum attorney general," Robert Kennedy went along with. An equally surprising reason was the emerging consensus within the government as a whole on the need to collect intelligence about civil rights demonstrations or voting rights activity or the political associations of the people who organized the demonstrations and voter registration drives. It all fit together. If the civil rights movement was active in a particular southern county, police brutality and other violations could be expected to occur with increasing regularity. The Civil Rights Division attorneys in Robert Kennedy's Justice Department wanted to know what to expect and they asked the FBI to provide the answers.

The Kennedy administration exerted some pressure on the FBI to expand its racial investigations beyond the world of intelligence. Statistics compiled by bureau agents during the Justice Department's voting litigation campaign of 1961 through 1964 and Freedom Ride survey of segregation in interstate transportation provide examples. On the other hand, the administration put even more pressure on the FBI to expand its intelligence functions. When those sanctioned Klan mobs attacked the Freedom Riders, the Kennedy brothers thought they saw an intelligence gap. Burke Marshall summed up the feeling in the White House and the Justice Department. "When the bus arrived in Montgomery and the local police . . . [did] not meet it," he said, "I realized for the first time that we didn't have any spy system, we didn't have any information." By the end of the year, the bureau had closed one side of this gap so effectively that Marshall expressed his "deep appreciation" to the bureau "for having kept him so fully informed in connection with the current racial disturbances."[77]

On occasion, Burke Marshall's Civil Rights Division filed specific requests for such things as "photographic coverage" of activities planned for the 100th anniversary celebration of the Emancipation Proclamation. More often, the FBI reported by telephone to Marshall's office under standing instructions. Division attorneys, for their part, found it difficult to keep pace with either the sheer number of civil rights demonstrations (1,580 in 38 states plus the District of Columbia in summer 1963 alone) or the volume of intelligence on these demonstrations. In addition to the telephone calls regarding racial matters, bureau field offices forwarded, 8,114 letterhead memoranda.[78]

This escalation of FBI surveillance following Marshall's complaints during the Freedom Rides was in part a response to the pressure of events—notably, the Birmingham demonstrations, the integration crises at the University of Mississippi and the University of Alabama, the Medgar Evers murder, and the March on Washington. It was also a response to Robert Kennedy's request that all United States attorneys survey places where racial demonstrations were expected. The attorney general specifically asked the bureau to "cooperate" in this effort.[79]

Robert Kennedy issued his directive on May 27, 1963, three days after his "what do you want me to do?" meeting at his father's New York apartment with Jerome Smith, a CORE field worker who had been beaten up and jailed repeatedly, and a number of friends of novelist James Baldwin, which included Lorraine Hansberry, Kenneth Clark, Harry Belafonte, Lena Horne, Rip Torn, and others. Smith said that being in the same room with the attorney general, the man who had said the government of the United States had no authority to protect civil rights workers in the South from racist terror, made him feel like throwing up. "Bobby," as Baldwin remembered, "took it personally." The group then criticized the FBI for its habit of merely observing the brutalization of civil rights workers and refusing to make arrests or otherwise intervene. Kennedy passed this to Marshall, who said the Justice Department sent in "special men" whenever necessary. That reply produced hysterical laughter. After accounts of the meeting appeared in the press, Hoover sent the attorney general dossiers on all those present.[80]

Kennedy read the dossiers. So did Marshall and the "special men" of the Civil Rights Division. Marshall's number-two man, St. John Barrett, said Hoover provided this sort of service all the time. "Telling us between the lines that we were accepting uncritically the assertions of people who really weren't as credible as we thought." The division even received "scuttlebut" memoranda "on congressmen, on officials in the executive branch." "They'd come over dozens at a time," Barrett remembered.[81]

Burke Marshall and the Civil Rights Division never fully considered the contradiction—the FBI's strict-constructionist posture on the matter of civil rights law enforcement and its extra-constitutional activities on the surveillance front. "I took the world as I found it," Marshall explained. "We got a lot of what you might call letterhead memos," John Doar, Marshall's number-one man, said. "To tell you the truth, I didn't react much one way or the other. . . . I didn't say to myself, 'Hey, we shouldn't be doing this.' " "We didn't get into any intellectual debate,"

Barrett added. "You kind of shrug and say, 'What are these guys spending their time on this for?' But you never ask them or raise it with them. We just took whatever information was fed us. . . . [If] there was something useful we might use it."[82]

The Kennedy administration took FBI surveillance as a given. President Kennedy himself, as Arthur Schlesinger wrote, accepted the bureau as a permanent "element in the panoply of national power."[83] As a young man in the 1950s, Robert Kennedy learned how the surveillance consensus worked—first with the Justice Department's Internal Security Division and then with the McCarthy Committee. On the latter, he worked under an ex-FBI agent, Francis Flanagan, before quitting when Roy Cohn came on board as staff director. Eventually, Robert Kennedy came back as minority counsel to the Democrats on that committee. And when Senator John McClellan (D., Ark.) named the twenty-nine-year-old Kennedy chief counsel to the Rackets Committee, he worked with a bona fide bureau agent, Courtney Evans, and received dozens of "blind" memoranda on union organizers and mobsters. (To disguise bureau authorship, "blind" memoranda contained no letterhead and were typed on plain white paper without identifying watermarks.)

John and Robert Kennedy were hardly naive. They knew how Hoover operated. They were aware of the reams of information the director had accumulated on JFK's adventures with a string of girlfriends. The FBI even went to Robert Kennedy once to alert him to a rumor concerning an alleged affair he was having with a woman in El Paso, Texas. (He said he had never been to El Paso.) While it is not likely that the Kennedy brothers were aware of the name check that the bureau ran on John back in July 1960, on the eve of the Democratic National Convention, it would be hard to imagine them questioning such an exercise had they known.[84]

Under both the Kennedys and the Great Society reformers who followed, pressure on the FBI to increase its intelligence coverage of the movement sometimes came from the most unlikely directions. A number of civil rights activists pressured the bureau to increase its coverage and sometimes received briefings from bureau executives. At a July 1, 1965, press conference in Atlanta, when Ralph Abernathy was asked about allegations of communist infiltration of the Southern Christian Leadership Conference and the methods (if any) that his group used to screen people, he made a rather startling claim. "If we have a person coming to our staff and we are not sure of his background," he said, "we will check with FBI men and they will tell us if they have a communist background. We don't want anything that is pink much less anything that is 'red.' " Hoover responded by labeling Abernathy "as big a liar as King." Privately, however, he quickly qualified this. "I think he is a liar but if I find anyone furnishing information to SCLC he will be dismissed." "The same instructions," the director added, applied to the NAACP and CORE. "No information is to be given them either."[85]

At first glance, the evidence suggests that Abernathy was hallucinating. When Abernathy and Andrew Young met with Cartha DeLoach earlier that year to ask who the communists in the civil rights movement were, the FBI assistant director referred them to HUAC and the American Legion, "the very racists we've been fighting," said Young. That referral was no doubt the typical bureau response to such requests.[86] Still, Hoover's mixed reaction indicates that the possibility of free-lancing field agents providing name-check services to the Southern Christian Leadership Conference was real enough.

More to the point, formal FBI policy *required* field agents to consider such assistance and get headquarters' approval before proceeding. This was part of the COMINFIL and COINTELPRO efforts to disrupt dissident activities by "taking steps to have communists ousted" from civil rights groups and other "legitimate mass organizations." The recommended method began with the compilation of "material identifying . . . [the targeted] individual with the communist movement," followed by a discreet effort to "ascertain the most logical officer or prominent person in the organization on whom there is no derogatory information." If this person "could be expected to take . . . action to remove the communist from the organization," he would receive an anonymous letter or phone call or perhaps a blind memorandum delivered in person by a bureau agent. This purge program, a routine part of the bureau's workload during the 1960s, was not terminated when the director issued the order regarding SCLC, the NAACP, and CORE.[87]

In practice, this FBI operation meant anonymous letters regarding suspected Reds to A. Philip Randolph, then president of the Negro American Labor Council. In the case of the NAACP, it meant occasional briefings for Roy Wilkins and Thurgood Marshall and the delivery of blind memoranda to other "anticommunist officers" in New York. In the case of the Southern Regional Council, it meant regular visits from special agents. "They tried to use us," former SRC executive director Leslie Dunbar remembered. "Field men would come in to talk to us. 'What do you know about him?' 'What do you know about her?' " In the case of CORE, it meant letters to "reliable" members who had "expressed concern over possible 'radical' influences."[88]

FBI officials did not always act quietly through anonymous letters or off-the-record contacts with "reliable Negroes." In September 1961, following a wiretap revelation that two reputed communists planned to form a CORE chapter in San Francisco, the bureau mailed a bogus letter alerting CORE's national office in New York. DeLoach then went to several media "sources so that the efforts of the CP to infiltrate CORE can be given publicity." With Hoover and Associate Director Clyde Tolson both requesting to be kept apprised of developments, DeLoach continued on this track. He tipped off Strom Thurmond of South Carolina, who "exposed" the supposed communist-infiltration scheme "on the floor of the United States Senate." Thurmond also put out a press release, DeLoach told the director, and it was picked up by UPI.[89]

DeLoach went to Thurmond because he was a rabid segregationist senator who could be counted on to act. "Strom Thurmond was probably one of the strongest bulwarks in the Congress on law-enforcement problems," according to one of the agents in DeLoach's Crime Records Division. "We wanted somebody to know that CORE was being infiltrated. And if you would give it to Joe Blow down the street it wouldn't do any good. . . . [CORE] should have done something about getting those people out of there," the agent explained. "You can't have everything. You can't have it both ways."

Several of the preceding examples suggest that the FBI could also "go to its left." Information on communist infiltration efforts was leaked not only to segregationists like Strom Thurmond but "responsible leaders of organizations . . . active in the integration movement." It was all part of what the bureau described as a "liaison program." Hoover's agents were not merely interested in identifying people who could be expected to move against Reds. They also solicited "a constant flow of intelligence-type information" from their liaison sources on "the planned activities of . . . the most active groups . . . staging racial demonstrations." "Our liaison program," Hoover told Robert Kennedy, "[has] enabled us to alert local law enforcement agencies in advance in order that these . . . agencies may take appropriate action." (This included, as we have seen and as Robert Kennedy knew beforehand, Bull Connor's Birmingham police department.) Kennedy's aide, John Seigenthaler, said the bureau had excellent sources "within the civil rights movement." Hoover's aide, Alex Rosen, cited Julius Hobson, president of CORE's Washington, D.C., chapter, as one of the more effective contacts.[90]

Cartha DeLoach met in September 1963 with another CORE activist,

James Farmer, to discuss "the possibilities of the FBI advising him on a confidential basis whenever members of the Communist party sought to ... take advantage of CORE." According to DeLoach, the FBI had an "agreement" with Farmer on this issue and as well the separate question of CORE issuing statements regarding the bureau's civil rights work. If DeLoach exaggerated here, he was quite correct on the first issue. Farmer confirmed the existence of a liaison arrangement nearly ten years later when he noted one occasion where a bureau agent briefed him on a "card-carrying" part-time CORE staff member.[91]

Within the NAACP, the FBI was always trying to recruit people from state affiliates to provide information about movement strategies. On the national level, executive director Roy Wilkins remained a favorite for most of this time period. One of DeLoach's Crime Records agents described the bureau's relationship with Wilkins as excellent, and the NAACP leader even met with DeLoach once, in August 1964, to discuss how the bureau might brighten its image. (Wilkins proposed an article for *Reader's Digest.*)

Eventually, in February 1965, Hoover ordered all contact with Wilkins (and Farmer, too) terminated "in view of their visit to the president demanding my dismissal because of what I had to say re [Martin Luther King]." This was a reference, of course, to the director's November 1964 statement labeling Dr. King "the most notorious liar in the country." Although he scribbled the termination order on an action memorandum that had recommended a leak to Wilkins, this particular operation was nonetheless carried out three weeks later in slightly altered form. The bureau delivered a blind memorandum not to Wilkins but to another NAACP official in New York who had "been contacted many times in the past and [had] always been found to be discreet."[92]

Such twists and turns suggest that the FBI's relationship with the NAACP continued in the pre-1960 manner. The COMINFIL examination of the organization itself also continued, focusing now on "a discreet investigation" of forty-two national officers. On occasion, DeLoach acted much like he had with Strom Thurmond and CORE. He alerted the NAACP to communist functionary Ben Davis's attendance at the group's Chicago convention, for example, by leaking that fact to the press.[93] The passing of information from the NAACP to the FBI, in contrast, was more often, though not always, benign. E. D. Hamilton cooperated with the FBI and the local police during the Albany Movement, and Vernon Jordan, the NAACP's Georgia field secretary during the height of the Albany demonstrations, tried to explain why: "It was naïveté; it was the omnipresence of the hand of the law; it was fear; it was a kind of modus operandi."[94]

Following Medgar Evers's June 1963 assassination, Hoover and the FBI employed this modus operandi at the highest level. Roy Wilkins's rivalry with Martin Luther King provided the impetus and offered a golden opportunity to act. Taylor Branch called that rivalry a "ghoulish turf war" over memberships and contributions that began with the Montgomery bus boycott and threatened to boil over when King's people set up a bail fund in Evers's name. "Can you imagine it?," Wilkins asked his nephew. "Medgar was an NAACP man all the way, and King comes in and tries to take the money." "He hadn't been an extraordinarily passionate man," Roger Wilkins remembered, "and since he and I had never been particularly close, I was a little stunned at his opening up this way to me about King. It must mean that he's really pissed, I thought."

"To Roy Wilkins, King might as well have stolen Evers' body," said Taylor Branch. Robert Kennedy put it best when he said, simply, "Roy Wilkins hates Martin Luther King."[95] Hoover used Wilkins's hatred of King to damage both men and the larger movement of which they were a part. A decade later, when FBI documents surfaced to suggest that he participated in the campaign to destroy King, Wilkins dismissed the charge as "a damn lie."[96]

Although he was no innocent (as suggested by the denial and avoidance of any substantive discussion of the FBI in his autobiography), Wilkins remained largely oblivious to several of the FBI's strategies.[97] He was certainly unaware of the bureau's long-range plan to "remove King from the national picture" and replace him with a more malleable black leader. In what *Nation* editor Victor Navasky called "the FBI's wildest dream," Domestic Intelligence Division chief William Sullivan chose Samuel R. Pierce as the bureau's "messiah designate." (Pierce would go on to serve in the Ronald Reagan cabinet as secretary of housing and urban development.) Sullivan, however, had acted unilaterally, overruling New York special agent in charge John Malone and an apparent majority of his own Domestic Intelligence agents who favored Wilkins as the bureau's messiah designate.[98] If Wilkins cannot be faulted for the birth of that nutty scheme, his derogatory comments to the FBI about King regularly found their way into Hoover's letters to the Lyndon Johnson White House.[99] The pattern of Wilkins's behavior during this period suggests, at the least, a close relationship with the FBI that is more accurately recorded in bureau files than Wilkins's memoir.

Wilkins criticized a range of civil rights activists beyond King in his numerous meetings with Cartha DeLoach. In August 1964 DeLoach reported the NAACP leader's general ramblings about "his fight against the communists over the past 30 years" and more specific comments about "James Forman, whom other Negroes refer to as 'the Commissar.'" Wilkins complained that Forman "was actually the man . . . in control of SNCC[,] that John Lewis was merely a front man . . . that Forman had brought Lewis instructions from the CP." Dismissing Lewis as "a poor or inarticulate Negro who does not control his own organization," Wilkins went beyond SNCC to the Congress of Racial Equality, concluding that both groups "consist of immature young whites and Negroes who are obviously frustrated in their own lives and turn to irrational activities for self-satisfaction."

From there, Wilkins offered the FBI advice on the public relations front, explaining "that there are two groups in the Negro movement responsible for criticism of the FBI. One group would not change its tactics no matter what miracle the FBI might bring about. . . . These individuals [King, Lewis, Forman] deliberately foment trouble in order to add to their own stature . . . The second element [consisted of] the great majority of the Negro race who do not have good educations and intelligence, resulting in their misunderstanding of the FBI's jurisdiction." To set the record straight, Wilkins suggested that DeLoach or Hoover himself appear before the next NAACP regional conference in Denver and meet with the Negro Publisher's Association.[100]

Though Hoover approved Wilkins's recommendations, he failed to follow through. Instead he attacked Dr. King for criticizing the FBI's lethargic enforcement of federal civil rights law—calling him "the most notorious liar in the country." Placed in an awkward position by the director's public charge, Wilkins told President Johnson that the black community agreed with King's characterization of the FBI and objected to the FBI director's characterization of King. (This is what so enraged Hoover that he ordered Wilkins cut off.) Then, on the CBS program *Face the Nation,* Wilkins described Hoover as "a good public servant" with "a long and distinguished career" who was "simply wrong on this."[101]

DeLoach met with Wilkins on November 27, 1964, to ask "How in the hell could he expect the FBI to believe his offers of friendship and request for peace when King . . . was attempting to ruin us"? He told Wilkins "that the director, of course, did not have in mind the destruction of the civil rights movement as a whole . . . [but] we deeply and bitterly resented the lies and falsehoods told by King and that if King wanted war, we certainly would give it to him." Wilkins briefly "diverted from the subject of the conversation to spend some time in explaining that he had also noted "communist influence in the civil rights movement in Mississippi," claiming that the (nonsensical) cry of " 'Down with the Proletariat' was getting to be the battle cry of the militant Negroes." DeLoach remained focused. "I told him that the monkey was on his back and that of the other Negro leaders. He stated he realized this, we shook hands and he returned to New York."[102] Three days later, Hoover told President Johnson that Wilkins admitted "he had criticized me unjustly." "He said he has a difficult time controlling his board of directors," Hoover continued, "since King is a member of the board. He stated 'we're hurting' and that something must be done."[103]

A few months later, in March 1965, Hoover found himself assigned to sit between the blackballed Wilkins and General Wallace Martin Greene, Jr., commandant of the Marine Corps, at a Gridiron Club dinner. He ordered the Domestic Intelligence Division to run a file check on both men, with the Division digging out the following inanity from an earlier decade: "[A confidential informant] stated that a fight was shaping up in the NAACP between the Walter White forces and the Roy Wilkins forces. It was stated that Wilkins actually represented the Trotskyite element in the NAACP."[104] At that point the Roy Wilkins/FBI relationship was, for all practical purposes, dead. For the last seven years of Hoover's life (1965–1972), the bureau cultivated other sources in the NAACP national office (as part of a general expansion of a "liaison program" aimed at "legitimate civil rights groups"); and the development of informants in local chapters (including three "extremist informants" in Memphis by the time Martin Luther King arrived to help with the garbage collectors' strike). Finally, as part of the counterintelligence program, the FBI continued to distribute clippings from *The Crisis* that were critical of black power militants.[105]

Wilkins's own view of the new militants suggests that he was a logical if not perfect collaborator for Hoover and other FBI practitioners of a segmented politics; it also suggests that FBI files recording Wilkins's attitudes toward his fellow activists are reasonably accurate. In his memoir, Wilkins wrote bitterly of one "of the more fashionable arguments advanced at the time," the notion "that the misery of Negroes had made them part of the Third World, that their future depended on an alliance between the Third World and Black America. Marcus Garvey, Malcolm X, and Franz Fanon were to be resurrected. . . . What we got [instead] was an ersatz, dashiki-built instant culture that collapsed when everyone finally got bored with it." Wilkins wanted to know what "the Hollywood Africans of the black-power school" had accomplished with their "blacker-than-thou posing" besides "a reverse Mississippi . . . a reverse Hitler . . . a reverse Ku Klux Klan." In 1969, the same year that even Hoover recognized the absurdity of routine "Security Matter-Communist" investigations and suspended such things, Wilkins compared the new militants to the Reds of his formative years (the 1930s): Both had "precisely" the same "tactic"—"to attack the NAACP and its secretary . . . as bourgeois, as misleaders, as deceivers of the Negro people, as . . . pied pipers leading us down the wrong road to freedom and so forth and so on." Apparently, at this late date anticommunism dictated Wilkins's bend more than Hoover's.[106]

During the Kennedy and Johnson years, various administration officials referred to black leaders in terms that were scarcely indistinguishable from the FBI's descriptions. Eric F. Goldman, the Princeton historian and LBJ's intellectual in residence, pondered "the breakaway from the established organizations of the more irresponsible Negroes." The White House, Goldman maintained, needed to "help" Wilkins and the "established Negro leaders . . . reestablish control and keep the movement going in its legitimate direction." Attorney General Nicholas Katzenbach made a vaguely similar point in 1966 when he called for the creation of "a militant but peaceful organization of young people which could successfully compete with SNCC."[107] Goldman and Katzenbach, nonetheless, had a more rational view than most of Hoover's executives regarding the prospects of manipulating "responsible black leadership." As often as not, bureau notions in this area were, for lack of a better word, fantastic.

One of the wildest ideas, conceived by FBI Assistant Director William Sullivan, concerned the convening of a group of prominent black leaders—Wilkins and two or three other civil rights people and what the bureau called "top Negro judges," "top reputable ministers," and "other selected Negro officials from public life such as the Negro Attorney General from one of the New England states." Sullivan intended to enlist these men in the campaign to topple Martin Luther King by explaining "the facts" about the bureau's many civil rights accomplishments and "the truth" about King's alleged sexual and political transgressions. Certain black government officials, including Carl Rowan and Ralph Bunche, were not to be invited under any circumstances, Sullivan reasoned, "as they might feel a duty to advise the White House." Rowan and Bunche, nonetheless, did receive an occasional FBI report containing derogatory information on King.[108]

Although this meeting with "reputable Negroes" remained a dream,

Sullivan's Division Five and DeLoach's Crime Records Division were active nonetheless on other fronts. To ensure that King's rivals had the facts, DeLoach took the microphone recordings that Sullivan's men had compiled to various civil rights leaders. Chuck Stone, formerly with the *Chicago Defender* and by that time a special assistant to New York Congressman Adam Clayton Powell, Jr., said a fair number of movement people "claimed to have heard the tapes. Whitney Young heard them. Roy Wilkins heard them."

The FBI's often unbelievable plans and acts should not obscure the fact that a few prominent black leaders, like Wilkins, before he was cut off, cooperated with the bureau in limited ways. There were two basic reasons why this was so. The first had to do with the lingering effects of the domestic communist issue. For many of the older activists, especially, the anticommunist obsessions of the past remained very much alive. There was little inclination to refight the battles of the Popular Front, Nazi-Soviet Pact, and McCarthy eras. Still, some civil rights groups, like the NAACP, embraced a more conservative politics and McCarthyite rituals. For Wilkins, as we have seen, the decisions of that earlier period were still binding. Even among the younger activists, cold war values ruled as often as not. When arguing for equal educational opportunity in the Jim Crow South, SNCC's Diane Nash said a Negro child well educated today might make a contribution to the global struggle against communism tomorrow. "Maybe someday," she mused, "a Negro will invent one of our missiles."[110]

On the other hand, few movement people considered their cooperation with the FBI in a pejorative sense. If the bureau identified the Farmers and Hobsons and Wilkinses as "sources," they were not "scabs to the movement"—to use the words of the black mayor of Pritchard, Alabama, A. J. Cooper.[111] People like Julia Brown, a black woman from Cleveland and a long-time FBI informant who surfaced to testify before HUAC and the Subversive Activities Control Board, represented the real thing.[112] James Farmer, Roy Wilkins, and Julius Hobson did not. Hobson's case is particularly instructive. According to the bureau, he was paid for reporting on civil rights demonstration plans at the Democratic National Convention in Atlantic City. But Hobson's widow claimed he used the money to bus in more demonstrators.

Even when sharing information with the FBI, most movement people believed they were, in effect, informing on themselves ("us") and not their enemies or rivals ("them"). In contrast to Julia Brown, once again, the bureau's liaison sources did not, as a general rule, "name names." Former agent Arthur Murtagh made the point about "us" and "them" indirectly. While Murtagh operated a number of paid black informants who gathered information on the Southern Christian Leadership Conference in Atlanta, he claimed nearly all of the information provided could have been acquired simply by telephoning SCLC.

Murtagh was right. John Lewis said the FBI often called Julian Bond at SNCC's Atlanta office "to find out what was going on." "When you were down South and something happened, you'd call the FBI," Rap Brown confirmed. This was SNCC policy, plain and simple. Similarly, Andrew Young, James Farmer, and A. Philip Randolph kept the bureau posted on their itineraries. "I agreed to keep in touch with DeLoach," Young said, "when we were moving anywhere." John Malone, the bureau executive who ran the New York field office, asked Farmer to have his "secretary give me a call whenever you're going south." Medgar Evers kept the bureau posted on the Jackson demonstrations. And Carl Rachlin, CORE's chief counsel, sent DeLoach a list of lawyers who had volunteered to work in Mississippi.[113]

The "protection" issue (that is, the movement strategy to convince or force the FBI to protect civil rights workers in the South), perhaps even more than the communist-infiltration issue, was the key element in this willingness to cooperate with Hoover's agency. Take the case of the *Ebony* reporter who called DeLoach in the middle of the night on May 3, 1961, "to tip [the bureau] off" regarding CORE strategy during the Freedom Rides.[114] DeLoach often worked with Johnson Publishing Company, the reporter's employer. "*Ebony,* Johnson," a Crime Records Division agent told me. "Yeah, Johnson publishing . . . we had a great, we had a good relationship with *Ebony, Jet.* . . . We used the black publications for stories . . . We put Aubrey Lewis [the first black to make it through the bureau training academy on the unsegregated course] on the cover [of *Ebony*]." The agent said the reporter "was in with Lou Nichols" and then "Mr. DeLoach." But the reporter did not remember it that way, claiming that he was not in that deep with either FBI man.

Who was using whom? Johnson Publishing did not play hardball with the FBI on the protection issue and neither did black America in general. But there was a game going on. The *Ebony* reporter foresaw the Freedom Ride into the deep South as a gamble. He was close to Robert Kennedy, since the attorney general's press secretary, Ed Guthman, had been in his Nieman class at Harvard, but claimed that he did not even tell those men about his plans to accompany the Freedom Riders. But he called DeLoach. Why? Again, the protection issue can explain the anomaly. The *Ebony* reporter hoped to use the FBI. By alerting Hoover's man to the Freedom Riders' itinerary, the chances of having a federal presence when things got tense were that much greater and thus (theoretically) the chances of racist violence that much less.

A good number of movement people, along with their supporters in the black press, viewed the FBI's agents as allies or at least potential allies. "We basically looked upon them as friends," Andrew Young recalled. "They were a problem almost from the beginning as they sat around taking notes while movement people were getting beat up. But we always felt their presence was welcome and that they did serve as a restraint on southern law enforcement. . . . So in spite of the fact that we knew they were somewhat antagonistic to our goals, we always cooperated with them—all the way through, even after the harassment started."

Most civil rights activists knew they were being "tapped and bugged" and often moved, as Bayard Rustin noted, from one hotel room to the next, hoping to stay a step ahead of the inevitable FBI wireman. The parking lot of virtually every hotel used by King's group had one or two of "these little plain green Plymouths with two-way radios in them."[115] The surveillance may have made movement leaders "compulsive about freedom," maybe even a bit paranoid, Young admitted. "We used to say if you weren't paranoia [sic] living under those conditions, you were really sick." But those effects did not stop the movement, in a limited sense, from cooperating in its own surveillance. King himself told Hoover that "it was vitally necessary to keep a working relationship with the FBI." "It's hard to remember back then," Young explained, "but when you were anxious about your life, civil liberties seemed a tertiary consideration."

The movement believed "you could be completely open," Young continued, "because you were doing the right thing." "For instance, when we were going into Birmingham for a demonstration, we would call the FBI, call the Justice Department . . . just to make sure that everybody understood exactly what we were there for." "In that context," he added, "being bugged by the FBI didn't seem like any big thing." Many activists agreed with Rustin that the surveillance of SCLC had no "consequences whatever, because Dr. King never tried to hide."[116]

Not all movement people shared this perspective all the way through. SNCC's James Forman was also interested in forcing the protection issue, but he concluded that it was an impossible task. The FBI, being "part of the governmental structure," functioned as a barrier between power and "the people," Forman said. The bureau, in practice, was "the enemy of black people. [If] we did not say it that way in 1963 ... we did know that the FBI was a farce."[117] But even as late as 1968 bureau officials had enough confidence in the "good will existing between the FBI and responsible Negro leaders" to launch a major expansion of the liaison program. And Hoover's men never stopped spying on the entire movement, including those black leaders who signed up for liaison duty. Julius Hobson was targeted under COINTELPRO. Whitney Young, the National Urban League chief described by the New York field office as "a liaison source and very friendly," was the subject of a brief investigation in fall 1968 after he submitted a $600,000 grant proposal to the Mellon Foundation.[118] In Roy Wilkins's case, the bureau was constantly running his name through the files from the mid-1950s until 1969, when John Ehrlichman submitted the names of Wilkins and his wife. For that matter, Wilkins was in good company. The Nixon White House also had the FBI run a check on the extremely white Pat Boone and his wife.[119]

FBI motives were hardly benevolent. At best (Andrew Young's view), bureau agents were "friends" who were "somewhat antagonistic to our goals." At worst (Jim Forman's view), the bureau was "the enemy of black people." In either case, it would be difficult to criticize without qualification the motives of those movement people who cooperated with the FBI. Complicity in COINTELPRO and COMINFIL programs raises a number of troubling questions, but those questions can hardly be compared to the complex moral issues raised during the McCarthy era by the men and women who named names. Mostly, the movement people who cooperated with the bureau were interested in manipulating the bureau. They let Hoover know exactly what they were doing in order to shame him into providing civil rights workers protection from segregationist terror. Needless to say, this did not work. Hoover knew no shame here.

It also would be difficult to criticize without qualification the motives of the Kennedy and Johnson administration officials who encouraged the FBI to escalate its surveillance activities. Their interest in all the intelligence reports reflected, in most cases, a mixture of political calculation *and* a sincere desire to do the right thing. Early in his tenure, according to Arthur Schlesinger, Robert Kennedy "saw civil rights ... as an issue in the middle distance, morally invincible but filled for the moment with operational difficulty."[120] Perhaps. But Kennedy's people and the Johnson men who followed them swept this operational difficulty aside by turning to the bureau, by selecting the bureau's intelligence services as the best available means (that is, the only acceptable means) of protecting civil rights workers. This decision posed no threat to the bureau and had the unintended result of placing Hoover and his men in a better position to accomplish their own political goals.

Robert Kennedy and the people who worked in his Justice Department, from John Doar to Burke Marshall, were in agreement with Hoover on one point—namely, that it was necessary to limit or direct the struggle for black equality. FBI officials tried to manage the civil rights movement, and so did the attorney general and the Civil Rights Division's executives. "When you say John and Burke did it for the noblest of reasons, I don't agree with that," said Roy Wilkins's nephew, Roger, who headed the department's Community Relations Service. "They wanted to know ahead of time so they could do the things the government wanted to do.... Burke and Bobby and those guys didn't want the movement to be as aggressive as it was in the early days. John and those guys, Burke and those guys, they were for civil rights ... but they wanted it on their terms, on their timetable, to their end, their agenda."[121]

Government officials sanctioned Hoover's notion of federalism (the idea that the FBI lacked the necessary authority to protect civil rights workers) while pressuring the director to do more of the thing (spying) that he wanted to do all along. The New Frontier and Great Society reformers who debated the constitutionality of federal protection never even considered the constitutionality of federal surveillance. In retrospect, it seems surprising that more movement people did not challenge these assumptions and priorities at the time. The whole idea of civil liberties, to quote Andrew Young once more, "seemed a tertiary consideration." Even before the movement turned left and the government right in the wake of major urban rioting in Watts, Newark, and Detroit and demonstrations everywhere against the Vietnam war, a surveillance consensus had hardened.

COINTELPRO Days and Last Days, 1967–1972

On August 25, 1967, the FBI launched a formal counterintelligence program against what it called "black hate groups." Twenty-three field offices participated initially, with the various special agents in charge required to assign "experienced and imaginative" agents as "counterintelligence coordinators" and give them free reign "to expose, disrupt, misdirect, or otherwise neutralize the activities of black nationalist, hate-type organizations and groupings, their leadership, spokesmen, membership, and supporters." Initial "targets" included Martin Luther King of the Southern Christian Leadership Conference, Stokely Carmichael and Rap Brown of the Student Nonviolent Coordinating Committee, Maxwell Stanford of the Revolutionary Action Movement, and Elijah Muhammad of the Nation of Islam. A Rabble Rouser Index and a Black Nationalist Photograph Album facilitated target selection for lesser-known activists.[122]

COINTELPRO grew quickly both in size and sophistication. In March 1968 representatives from the forty-one FBI field offices then participating decided to expand the original goals—a decision made at a "racial conference" held at "the seat of government" (bureau headquarters). When seeking "to prevent the ... *growth* of militant black nationalist organizations," Hoover's men wanted "specific tactics to prevent these groups from converting young people." This goal was closely related to another basic mission—"to prevent violence by pin-point[ing] potential troublemakers and neutraliz[ing] them before they exercise their potential for violence." "Obviously," one COINTELPRO supervisor reasoned, "you are going to prevent violence or a greater amount of violence if you have smaller groups." In other words, "the programs were to prevent violence indirectly, rather than directly, by preventing possibly violent citizens from joining or continuing to associate with possibly violent groups."[123]

Other expanded COINTELPRO goals included a sustained effort to "prevent the *coalition* of militant black nationalist groups." "An effective coalition," the FBI noted, "might be the first step toward a real 'Mau mau' in America, the beginning of a true black revolution." The bureau also worked to "prevent the *rise of a 'messiah'* " (someone "who could unify, and electrify, the militant black nationalist movement"); and to discredit all black liberation movement figures in the eyes of "three separate segments of the community." These segments included "the responsible Negro community," the "white community," and the black "followers of the movement." (The bureau also broke down white America into responsible and irresponsible elements, with the latter consisting of " 'liberals' who have vestiges of sympathy for militant black nationalist[s] simply because they are Negroes.") Most bureau field agents immediately gleaned the overriding purpose of such campaigns ("to eliminate the facade of civil rights") and submitted appropriate plans of action to headquarters for approval. Some of the more tame proposals merely suggested "counterfeiting literature damaging to the [movement]."[124]

What all this meant in practice can be seen best in FBI attempts to exacerbate the bloody West Coast rivalry between the Black Panther party and Maulana Karenga's US (as opposed to "them"), a group that challenged the Panthers' revolutionary political nationalism with its own cultural nationalism. With both groups recruiting heavily among the gang kids of Southern California's major cities, the bureau realized that violence would be relatively easy to spark and maintain. The violence began in January 1969 at Campbell Hall on UCLA's Westwood campus, where the Panthers and US were competing for the right to advise administrators regarding the selection of a director for a proposed Afro-American studies program. Four or five US members gunned down two Panthers then attending UCLA, Alprentice ("Bunchy") Carter, on parole from an armed-robbery sentence, and John Huggins. One US member, Larry Stiner, was wounded in the thirteen-shot, mostly one-sided firefight.

Over the next sixteen months, Hoover's FBI agents devoted themselves to ensuring that gun play would continue. They were especially active in San Diego, using the bureau's high-tech crime laboratory to create cartoons and flyers that showed US members gloating over the fallen Carter and Huggins, and mailing their creations to the homes of Panther activists and the offices of two underground newspapers. US members also received FBI cartoons and flyers that showed Panthers calling them, among other things, "pork chop niggers." Bureau agents and informants tacked up extra copies of the art work and literature on walls and telephone poles all over the city's black neighborhoods. Simultaneously, the San Diego field office placed anonymous telephone calls to Panther leaders falsely identifying other Panthers as police informants. The campaign began in early March, and within two weeks the bureau got what it wanted. After a Panther drive-by shooting into an US home, one of Karenga's heavily armed Simba Wachuka (Young Lions) wounded another Panther.

Troubled by the specter of reconciliation in the aftermath (one agent complained that the two groups were actually trying "to talk out their differences"), the San Diego FBI office mailed a follow-up set of cartoons and flyers. In May, the bureau repeated the whole routine once again after an US activist named Tambuzio shot and killed Panther John Savage. Things kept on the same track during the summer. When an US gunman shot three Panthers, including Sylvester Bell, who died, the Panthers responded by bombing US offices. Bureau agents kept up their barrage of telephone calls, cartoons, and flyers for another year, hoping, in their own words, to keep this "internecine struggle" going strong. And with merit incentives (cash) hanging in the balance, San Diego special agent in charge Robert Evans noted the violence "in the

ghetto area'' and tried to take the credit for it when describing the
"tangible results" of this sustained COINTELPRO operation. Other
bureau field offices helped out as best they could, with even the far-
away Newark office hyping the conflict with a fraudulent letter to the
local Panther office that went on about black racists and a "hankerchief
[sic] head mama" before concluding with a warning ("watch out:
Karenga's coming") and a scoreboard (that is, bodycount):

US—6

Panthers—0.[125]

Hoover's FBI supplemented COINTELPRO with dozens of "community surveillance" programs that targeted African Americans as a class.
One of the most pervasive was the "Ghetto Informant Program"
launched in October 1967. Potential recruits included "any individual
who resides in a ghetto-type area" or "who frequent[s] ghetto areas
on a regular basis." In other words, employees and owners of taverns
and liquor stores, drugstores and pawnshops, candy stores and barber-
shops, and other ghetto businesses; honorably discharged veterans and
especially members of veterans organizations; janitors of apartment
buildings; newspaper and food and beverage distributors; taxi drivers;
salesmen; and bill collectors. The FBI steered these sources toward
"Afro-American type book stores" and asked them to identify their
"owners, operators, and clientele." The informants also reported on
persons with criminal records or teenage gang members "operating in
the ghetto," "changes in the attitude of the Negro community towards
the white community," and the "feelings of individuals who reside in
black neighborhoods." The bureau even had "a kind of quota system"
that required all field agents to develop black informants, and by the
end of President Nixon's first term operated an army of some 7,500.
Policy required every field office "to thoroughly saturate every level
of activity in the ghetto."[126]

Community surveillance outlived counterintelligence and the FBI director himself. For "security reasons," J. Edgar Hoover terminated all
formal COINTELPROs following the burglary of an FBI resident
agency in Media, Pennsylvania, by an antiwar group on March 8, 1971,
the night of the first Ali-Frazier fight.[127] (The antiwar activists liberated
approximately 1,000 pieces of bureau paper, including several counterintelligence documents, sending a steady stream of samples to the press
and members of Congress through the months of March and April.) A
year later, on May 2, the seventy-seven-year-old Hoover died alone in

his bedroom. His three black servants, James Crawford, Tom Moton, and Annie Fields, found the body.

Today, one does not have to be a war protestor cum burglar to gain access to FBI files. When the cold war's fashionable deference to the presidency broke with Vietnam and the unraveling of the Watergate scandals, Congress no longer proved willing to accept blanket claims of executive privilege based on a national-security rationale to justify a monopolization on secrets. Amendments in 1974 put teeth into the Freedom of Information Act (FOIA) of 1966, and a year later the House and Senate launched the first and only systematic investigation of the entire United States intelligence community. A wealth of FBI files have since poured out under FOIA. Many of those harassed by Hoover's men filed lawsuits (producing through the discovery process millions of more pages). The sampling of such files noted in this volume is the tip of the proverbial iceberg. It is probably accurate to say that a full accounting of bureau documents compiled under the "Racial Matters" heading and similar headings would fill a million such volumes.

It is also no exaggeration to say that Hoover's FBI waged war on black America. But any research into the depths and nature of that war ought to be tempered by the realization that the bureau was located within the government. Hoover fought his war because he hated the rising black demand for justice and because he had the power to act on that hate (that is, the material gathered in his secret files gave him the power to act autonomously as often as not). Still, one cannot escape the reality of the FBI as part of the government structure or the reality of the White House and the Justice Department egging on the director in his pitiless work much as his men egged on that bloody Panther-US feud in California. Black America's FBI story is more than the story of one brutal man's horrors or a single bureaucracy's misdeeds in seven different decades. It is really the story of a government at war with its own people.

NOTES: Hoover's FBI and Black America

1. J. Edgar Hoover to Clyde Tolson, Cartha DeLoach, and Robert E. Wick, July 6, 1966, no. not recorded, Clyde Tolson Personal FBI File, J. Edgar Hoover FBI Building, Washington, D.C.; *Miranda v. Arizona*, 377 U.S. 201 (1966).
2. Kenneth O'Reilly, *"Racial Matters:" The FBI's Secret File on Black America, 1960–1972* (New York: Free Press, 1989).

3. Harris Wofford, *Of Kennedys and Kings* (New York: Farrar Straus and Giroux, 1980), 206.

4. Karl Evanzz, *The Judas Factor: The Plot to Kill Malcolm X* (New York: Thunder's Mouth Press, 1992).

5. Director to SAC Chicago, Dec. 17, 1969, no. illegible, Fred Hampton FBI File; SAC Chicago to Director, Feb. 11, 1970, no. illegible, ibid.

6. George Sinkler, *The Racial Attitudes of American Presidents: From Abraham Lincoln to Theodore Roosevelt* (Garden City, N.Y.: Doubleday, 1971), 343–44; Stephen R. Fox, *The Guardian of Boston: William Monroe Trotter* (New York: Atheneum, 1970), 150. For peonage generally, *see* Pete Daniel, *The Shadow of Slavery: Peonage in the South, 1901–1969* (Urbana: University of Illinois Press, 1972).

7. Hoover to Tolson, John P. Mohr, and DeLoach, Dec. 8, 1964, no. 94-4-3169-127, David Lawrence FBI File; Randy Roberts, *Papa Jack: Jack Johnson and the Era of White Hopes* (New York: Free Press, 1983), 144–84.

8. Of the recent biographies, see especially Anthony Summers, *Official and Confidential: The Secret Life of J. Edgar Hoover* (New York: G. P. Putnam's Sons, 1993); Curt Gentry, *J. Edgar Hoover: The Man and the Secrets* (New York: Norton, 1991); Athan G. Theoharis and John Stuart Cox, *The Boss: J. Edgar Hoover and the Great American Inquisition* (Philadelphia: Temple University Press, 1988); Richard Gid Powers, *Secrecy and Power: The Life of J. Edgar Hoover* (New York: Free Press, 1987).

9. Hoover, Memo upon the work of the Radical Division, Oct. 18, 1919, no. OG 374217, Record Group 65, Bureau of Investigation Files, 1908–1922, National Archives, Washington, D.C.; O'Reilly, *"Racial Matters,"* 12–13.

10. Kenneth O'Reilly, "A New Deal for the FBI: The Roosevelt Administration, Crime Control, and National Security," *Journal of American History* 69 (Dec. 1982): 638–58.

11. Robert K. Carr, *Federal Protection of Civil Rights: Quest for a Sword* (Ithaca, N.Y.: Cornell University Press, 1947).

12. John T. Elliff, "Aspects of Federal Civil Rights Enforcement: The Justice Department and the FBI, 1939–1964," *Perspectives in American History* 5 (1971): 605–73.

13. "Survey of Racial Conditions in the United States," n.d. [ca. Sept. 1943], in CF, Justice Dept. (5–6), Harry S. Truman Papers, Harry

S. Truman Library, Independence, Mo.; O'Reilly, *"Racial Matters,"* 18–19.

14. D. Milton Ladd to Hoover, Sept. 11, 1942, FBI File no. 62-116758; Ladd to Edward Tamm, Oct. 21, 1942, ibid.; Richmond Field Office Rept., Jan. 26, 1943, no. 62-25889-9, Moorish Science Temple FBI File; Director to SAC Louisville, Aug. 5, 1943, no. 66-6200-44, FBI Civil Rights Policy File.

15. Memo, re Mary McLeod Bethune, Dec. 20, 1946, PSF, FBI-B, Truman Papers.

16. Memo, re Racial Tensions and Civil Rights, March 1, 1956, Whitman File, Cabinet Series, Dwight D. Eisenhower Papers, Dwight D. Eisenhower Library, Abilene, Ka. *See also* Alan H. Belmont to Leland V. Boardman, Oct. 27, 1955, no. 61-3176-not recorded, NAACP FBI File; Hoover to Herbert Brownell, Jan. 3, 1956, no. 61-3176-not recorded, ibid; Hoover to Dillon Anderson, Jan. 3, 1956, no. 61-3176-not recorded, ibid.

17. James E. Amos, New York Field Office Rept., Aug. 22, 1923, no. 61-3176-1, NAACP FBI File. For the Dyer Bill and other strategies, *see* Robert L. Zangrando, *The NAACP Crusade Against Lynching, 1909–1950* (Philadelphia: Temple University Press, 1980).

18. O'Reilly, *"Racial Matters,"* 275.

19. Ibid., 105–09; Alex Rosen to Belmont, May 22, 1963, no. 44-00-illegible, FBI Civil Rights Policy File; Hoover to Robert F. Kennedy, May 23, 1963, no. 157-00-54, FBI Racial Matters Policy File.

20. Hoover to Charles P. Sisson, April 19, 1930, Subject File—Colored Question, Herbert Hoover Papers, Herbert Hoover Library, West Branch, Iowa; memo, re NAACP, April 19, 1930, ibid.; Hoover to Walter Newton, Sept. 5, 1930, no. 61-3176-7, NAACP FBI File. Hoover's meeting with White in 1924 (or perhaps 1925) is referred to in Louis B. Nichols to Tolson, June 21, 1951, no. 61-3176-596, ibid.

21. Monograph, "The Communist Party and the Negro" (1953), 79–83, Hoover FBI Building. For a similar estimate ("[in] the 1920s, then, the black community was a vast wasteland for communists"), see Harvey Klehr, *Communist Cadre: The Social Background of the American Communist Party Elite* (Stanford, Cal.: Hoover Institution Press, 1978), 57. Though estimating a growing black membership during the depression years (2,227 by 1935), the FBI remained unworried.

22. J. Edgar Hoover, *Masters of Deceit* (New York: Pocket Books ed., 1959), 235; Hoover to File, April 28, 1930, no. 61-3176-6, NAACP FBI File.

23. The best study of Scottsboro remains Dan T. Carter, *Scottsboro: A Tragedy of the American South* (Baton Rouge: Louisiana State University Press, 1969).

24. Hoover to Tolson, Tamm, and Ladd, Sept. 30, 1942, no. 61-3176-56, NAACP FBI File; E. E. Conroy to Hoover, Oct. 10, 1944, no. 61-3176-256, ibid. For the COMINFIL opening, *see* Guy Hotel, Washington, D.C., Field Office Rept., March 11, 1941, no. 61-3176-15, ibid.; U.S., Congress, Senate, Select Committee to Study Governmental Operations with Respect to Intelligence Activities, *Final Report,* Book III, *Supplementary Detailed Staff Reports on Intelligence Activities and the Rights of Americans,* 94th Cong., 2 sess., 1976, p. 416.

25. Ladd to Tamm, Dec. 8, 1943, no. 61-3176-176, NAACP FBI File; Hoover to SAC Philadelphia, n.d. [ca. Dec. 18, 1943], no. 61-3176-178, ibid.; Hoover to Francis Biddle, Dec. 17, 1943, no. 61-3176-178, ibid.; SAC Philadelphia to Hoover, Dec. 23, 1943, no. 61-3176-181, ibid.

26. R. F. Pfafman to Coffey, Nov. 19, 1943, no. 61-31613-89, and Dec. 16, 1942, no. 62-31613-388, Walter Winchell FBI File.

27. J. F. Sears to Hoover, Jan. 15, 1944, no. 61-3176-186, and Jan. 29, 1944, no. 61-3176-194, NAACP FBI File.

28. Hoover to Walter White, Nov. 12, 1941, no. 61-3176-18X9, ibid.; Hoover to Tolson and Tamm, Nov. 14, 1941, no. 61-3176-18X11, ibid.; White to C. Herbert Marshall, Dec. 17, 1941, FBI, Box A267, Group II, NAACP Papers, Library of Congress, Washington, D.C.

29. White to Hoover, June 17, 1941, FBI, Box A268, Group II, NAACP Papers; Hoover to White, July 14, 1941, ibid.; White to Herbert Marshall, Dec. 13 and 17, 1941, ibid. Edgar G. Brown, representing a Negro employers' association, had first raised the issue in testimony before the House and Senate Appropriations Committees. Max Lowenthal, *The Federal Bureau of Investigation* (New York: William Sloane, 1950), 346–47.

30. White to Hoover, Jan. 20, 1942, FBI, Box A267, Group II, NAACP Papers; Hoover to White, Jan. 28, 1942, ibid.; White to Hoover, Feb. 6, 1942, no. 61-3176-18X15, Jan. 20, 1942, no. 61-3176-18X14, and June 18, 1942, no. 61-3176-34, NAACP FBI File; Nichols to Tolson, June 25, 1942, no. 61-3176-50, ibid. For

the testimonial, *see* Arthur B. Spingarn to Hoover, Sept. 15, 1943, no. 61-3176-150, ibid.; White to Hoover, June 19, 1944, no. 61-3176-221, ibid; J. J. Starke to Nichols, Sept. 23, 1943, no. 100-328241-X1, Walter White FBI File. For the American Embassy, *see* Hoover to Arthur M. Thurston, Sept. 23, 1943, no. 100-328241-X, ibid.

31. White to Hoover, Oct. 24, 1945, no. 61-3176-317, and Nov. 16, 1945, no. 61-3176-318, NAACP FBI File; Executives' Conference to Director, Nov. 1, 1945, no. 61-3176-317X1, ibid. The microphone surveillance was placed either by the FBI or British Intelligence.

32. White to Hoover, Aug. 21, 1946, no. 61-3176-349, ibid.; Ladd to White, Aug. 26, 1946, Box A268, Group II, NAACP Papers.

33. The Perry affair can be traced in W. R. Glavin to Hoover, Aug. 8, 1947, no. 61-3176-395, NAACP FBI File; SAC New York to Director, Aug, 13, 1947, no. 61-3176-393, ibid.; newspaper clipping, Aug. 16, 1947, no. 61-3176-393, ibid.; Leslie S. Perry to Hoover, Aug. 6, 1947, no. 61-3176-394, ibid.; Hoover to White, Aug. 9, 1947, no. 61-3176-394, and Sept. 25, 1947, no. 61-3176-402, ibid.; SAC Letter, Aug. 26, 1947, no. 61-3176-not recorded, ibid.; Perry to White, Sept. 17 and 18, 1947, FBI, Box A268, Group II, NAACP Papers; White to Roy Wilkins, Sept. 6, 1947, FBI, Box A268, Group II, ibid.; Wilkins to White, Sept. 4, 1947, FBI, Box A268, Group II, ibid; Roy Garvin to John H. Johnson, Sept. 19, 1947, FBI, Box H2, Group II, ibid.

34. For example, *see* G. Paul Lockwood to Hoover, March 13, 1950, no. 61-3176-542, NAACP FBI File.

35. Thurgood Marshall to White, Jan. 23, 1947, FBI, Box A268, Group II, NAACP Papers. *See also* White to Robert Carter, Aug. 21 and 27, 1946, ibid.; Carter to White, Aug. 26 and Oct. 14, 1946, ibid.; Hoover to White, Sept. 27, 1946, ibid.; Franklin H. Williams to White, Sept. 14, 1946, ibid.; Tom Clark to Eleanor Roosevelt, Nov. 26, 1946, ibid.; Marshall to Hoover, May 10, 1946, no. 44-1366-128, and Sept. 24, 1947, no. 44-359-33, NAACP Inc. Fund FBI File; Hoover to Marshall, May 14, 1946, no. 44-1366-128, ibid.; Marshall to Clark, Dec. 27, 1946, Civil Rights & Domestic Violence Folder, J. Edgar Hoover Official and Confidential FBI File; Clark to Marshall, Jan. 13, 1947, ibid.; note, Hoover, May 17, 1946, no. 61-3176-336, NAACP FBI File; Marshall to Clark, May 10, 1946, no. 61-3176-336, ibid.; Hoover to Clark, May 17, 1946, no. 61-3176-not recorded, ibid.; Hoover

to White, Jan. 13, 1947, no. 61-3176-367, Jan. 24, 1947, no. 61-3176-372, Jan. 28, 1947, no. 61-3176-372, and Sept. 13, 1947, no. 61-3176-404, ibid.; Hoover to Clark, Jan. 10, 1947, no. 61-3176-364; ibid.; Tamm to Hoover, Jan. 8, 1947, no. 61-3176-366, ibid.; White to Hoover, Jan. 24, 1947, no. 61-3176-372, and Feb. 3, 1947, no. 61-3176-372X, ibid.; Hoover to Tolson, Tamm, and Ladd, no. 44-1366-110, Walter White FBI File; J. K. Mumford to Ladd, May 26, 1947, no. 44-1601-1, ibid.

36. Marshall to Hoover, Oct. 9, 1947, no. 61-3176-410, and Oct. 21, 1947, no. 61-3176-411, NAACP FBI File; Hoover to Marshall, Oct. 16, 1947, no. 61-3176-410, ibid.

37. Memo for File, Nov. 1, 1946, no. 44-1421-351, Walter White FBI File. For examples of information on the NAACP sent to the White House, *see* Hoover to Harry Vaughan, Jan. 17, 1946, and Jan. 12, 1950, PSF, Communist Data, Truman Papers; Hoover to George Allen, Sept. 25, 1946.

38. SAC Letter, Aug. 26, 1946, FBI Special Agent in Charge Letter File; White to Hoover, Aug. 2, 1946, no. 61-3176-339X, NAACP FBI File; note, Hoover, n.d. [ca. Aug. 26, 1946], no. 61-3176-339X, ibid.; Hoover to Clark, Jan. 15, 1946, no. 62-26225-45, Walter White FBI File.

39. Tamm to Hoover, Sept. 26, 1946, no. 61-3176-351, NAACP FBI File. For the testimonials, *see* note, Hoover, n.d. [ca. April 20, 1947], no. 61-3176-380, ibid.; Theron L. Caudle to Leo Cadison, April 10, 1947, no. 61-3176-not recorded, ibid.; Clark to White, date ill. [ca. April 24, 1947], no 61-3176-not recorded, ibid.; White to Clark, April 8, 1947, no. 61-3176-not recorded, ibid.; Hoover to Clark, April 23, 1947, no. 61-3176-380, ibid.; White to Hoover, April 8, 1947, no. 61-3176-378X, ibid.; Hoover to White, April 14, 1947, no. 61-3176-378X, ibid.

40. Tamm to Hoover, Sept. 26, 1946, no. 61-3176-351, ibid.; Arthur M. Schlesinger, Jr., "The U.S. Communist Party," *Life,* July 29, 1946, pp. 84–96; White to Henry Luce, July 29, 1946, Communism/General, Box A201, Group II, NAACP Papers; John Shaw Billings to White, Aug. 7, 1946, ibid.; White to James Forrestal, Sept. 3, 1947, ibid.

41. Ladd to Hoover, Dec. 31, 1947, no. 61-3176-447, NAACP FBI File.

42. Roy Wilkins to White, July 21, 1950, Communism, Box 22, Roy Wilkins Papers, Library of Congress; memo, re Communist Infil-

tration, n.d. [ca. June 22, 1950], ibid.; memo, to Executive Board, June 22, 1950, ibid.

43. Nichols to Tolson, Dec. 11, 1950, no. 100-3-81-5095, Walter White FBI File; White to "Ed" [Scheidt], Dec. 15, 1950, FBI, Box A267, Group II, NAACP Papers.

44. Nichols to Tolson, June 21, 1951, no. 61-3176-596, and July 10, 1951, no. 61-3176-592, NAACP FBI File; Belmont to Ladd, July 6, 1951, no. 61-3176-597, and July 16, 1951, no. 61-3176-592, ibid.; SAC Atlanta to Hoover, June 26, 1951, no. 61-3176-588, ibid.; White to Nichols, July 11, 1951, no. 61-3176-590, ibid.; White to Hoover, June 13, 1951, no. 61-3176-594, ibid.

45. Hoover to White, March 10, 1953, no. 61-3176-639, ibid.; Nichols to Tolson, Feb. 26, 1954, no. 61-3176-not recorded, ibid.; Gerald Horne, *Communist Front? The Civil Rights Congress, 1946–1956* (Rutherford, N.J.: Fairleigh Dickinson University Press, 1988), 140, 246.

46. White to Hoover, Dec. 21, 1953, no. 100-328241-9, Walter White FBI File; Nichols to Tolson, March 4, 1954, no. not recorded, ibid.; Hoover to White, Dec. 28, 1953, no. 100-328241-9, ibid.

47. Quoted in Helen W. Gandy to [deleted], May 21, 1957, no. 100-328241-not recorded, ibid.

48. Ladd to Hoover, Feb. 19, 1954, no. 61-3176-not recorded, NAACP FBI File; Nichols to Tolson, Feb. 26, 1954, no. 61-3176-not recorded, ibid. "With the telephones being what they are and as close as we have been to [Walter White]," Nichols told Hoover and Tolson, "we could not understand why he did not pick up the phone and check with us on matters like this; that we had always tried to help whenever we could."

49. *See* the note on Gandy to E. J. Stringer, Nov. 3, 1954, no. 61-3176-837, NAACP FBI File. For the new phase of the COMINFIL investigation, *see* Director to SACs New York et al., Feb. 10, 1954, no. 61-3176-669, ibid.; Director to SAC Anchorage, April 30, 1954, no. 61-3176-725, ibid.

50. [Name deleted] to Nichols, April 13, 1955, no. 61-3176-914, ibid.; Milton A. Jones to Nichols, April 13, 1955, no. 61-3176-not recorded, ibid.

51. Nichols to Tolson, Oct. 19, 1955, no. 61-3176-1076, and Oct. 19, 1955, no. 61-3176-not recorded, ibid.; Henry Lee Moon to Editors, Oct. 17, 1955, no. 61-3176-not recorded, ibid.

52. Hoover to Dillon Anderson, Jan. 3, 1956, no. 61-3176-not recorded, ibid; Hoover to Herbert Brownell, Jan. 3, 1956, no. 61-

3176-not recorded, ibid.; memo, re Racial Tensions and Civil Rights, March 1, 1956, Whitman File, Cabinet Series, Eisenhower Papers.

53. Senate Select Committee, *Book III,* 450.
54. Memo, n.d. [ca. March 25, 1958], in Communism/Attacks on NAACP, Box A76, Group III, NAACP Papers; Wilkins to Hoover, March 25, 1958, Dept. of Justice, Box A145, ibid.; Hoover, *Masters of Deceit,* 230–31; "Communist Party and the Negro" (1953 and 1956), passim; "Current Weaknesses of the Communist Party," Oct. 1956, no. 100-3-104-47, FBI COINTELPRO (CPUSA) File.
55. Correlation summary memo, Feb. 28, 1958, no. 62-78270-2, Roy Wilkins FBI File.
56. V. P. Keay to Belmont, Dec. 11, 1950, no. 61-3176-573, NAACP FBI File; Nichols to Tolson, Jan. 18, 1952, no. 61-3176-615, ibid.; Hoover to Marshall, Sept. 30, 1955, no. 61-3176-1018, Jan. 16, 1956, no. 61-3176-1160, and Feb. 2, 1956, no. 61-3176-1202, ibid.; Marshall to Hoover, Jan. 24, 1956, no. 61-3176-1202, ibid.; Fred J. Baumgardner to Belmont, Oct. 21, 1955, no. 61-3176-1077, and Feb. 8, 1956, no. 61-3176-1224, ibid.
57. DeLoach to Mohr, Feb. 25, 1960, no. 62-78270-6, FBI Wilkins File; Kenneth O'Reilly, *Hoover and the Un-Americans* (Philadelphia: Temple University Press, 1983), 184–94 (for Ferman). For the Packer lynching, *see* Howard Smead, *Blood Justice* (New York: Oxford University Press, 1986).
58. O'Reilly, *"Racial Matters,"* 49–72.
59. Quoted in Howell Raines, *My Soul Is Rested* (New York: G. P. Putnam's Sons, 1977), 109–10. *See also* August Meier and Elliott Rudwick, "The First Freedom Ride," *Phylon* 30 (Fall 1969): 213-22.
60. For Rowe's own account, *see My Undercover Years with the Ku Klux Klan* (New York: Bantam, 1976).
61. For Hoover's account of the conversation, *see* Jones to DeLoach, Dec. 2, 1964, no. 77-68662-126, Don Whitehead FBI File; Hoover to Tolson, Mohr, and DeLoach, Dec. 8, 1964, no. 94-4-3169-127, David Lawrence FBI File.
62. Seigenthaler interview. He learned about the FBI file from his desk at the *Nashville Tennessean,* after firing a copy editor, Jacqe Srouji, who also happened to be a bureau informant and a minor figure in the Karen Silkwood case.
63. See the documents in the June Mail Folder, Hoover Official and Confidential FBI File.

64. Arthur M. Schlesinger, Jr., *Robert Kennedy and His Times* (book club ed.; Boston: Houghton Mifflin, 1978), 372.
65. Taylor Branch, *Parting the Waters* (New York: Simon and Schuster, 1988), 845.
66. Ibid., 373; Burke Marshall Oral History, Jan. 19–20, 1970, p. 22, John F. Kennedy Library, Boston, Mass. For Guthman, *see* Senate Select Committee, *Book III,* 92.
67. Edwin O. Guthman and Jeffrey Shulman, eds., *Robert Kennedy: In His Own Words* (New York: Bantam, 1988), 141–43, 46.
68. Ibid., 143.
69. Ibid., 130, 146; *Time,* Aug. 17, 1962, pp. 118–19 (for Hoover as "my expert"); Nicholas deB. Katzenbach Oral History, Nov. 16, 1964, p. 61, Kennedy Library.
70. Guthman, ed., *Robert Kennedy,* 134.
71. Garry Wills, "The Kennedys in the King Years," *New York Review of Books,* Nov. 10, 1988, p. 116.
72. Ibid., 14–15.
73. DeLoach to Mohr, Sept. 20, 1963, no. 157-1025-144, FBI BAP-BOMB File; Courtney Evans to Belmont, Sept. 30, 1963, no. 157-1025-337, ibid.; Birmingham Field Office Rept., Dec. 1, 1963, no. 157-1025-725, ibid.
74. SAC New York to Director, Aug. 10, 1964, no. not recorded, FBI Communist Influence Racial Matters File. For Freedom Summer, *see* O'Reilly, *"Racial Matters,"* 157–93; Seth Cagin and Philip Dray, *We Are Not Afraid* (New York: Macmillan, 1988).
75. SAC Jackson to Director and SAC Chicago, Sept. 5, 1968, no. 100-449498-54-5, FBI COINTELPRO (New Left) File.
76. Hoover to Tolson, Belmont, Rosen, and DeLoach, March 26, 1965, no. 44-28601-15 and -16, Viola Liuzzo FBI File; Hoover, "Off the Record Remarks . . . for Editors of Georgia and Michigan Newspapers," April 15, 1965, Hoover FBI Building.
77. Rosen to Belmont, Dec. 22, 1961, no. 44-00-illegible, FBI Civil Rights Policy File; Burke Marshall to Hoover, June 18, 1961, no. 44-00-illegible, ibid.; Victor Navasky, *Kennedy Justice* (New York: Atheneum, 1971), 23.
78. Employee suggestion, March 9, 1964, no. 157-00-67, FBI Racial Matters Policy File; Edwin Guthman to Robert Kennedy, Oct. 2, 1963, Demonstrations, Chronology, Burke Marshall Papers, Kennedy Library; David Marlin to Marshall, Aug. 22, 1963, July and Aug. 1963 Demonstrations, ibid.
79. Hoover to SACs Atlanta et al., May 27, 1963, no. 157-00-not

recorded, FBI Racial Matters Policy File; U.S., Congress, Senate, Select Committee to Study Governmental Operations with Respect to Intelligence Activities, *Final Report,* Book II, *Intelligence Activities and the Rights of Americans,* 94th Cong., 2d sess., 1976, p. 83.

80. Navasky, *Kennedy Justice,* 112–15; Schlesinger, *Robert Kennedy,* 344–48; Wofford, *Of Kennedys and Kings,* 224.

81. Barrett interview.

82. Barrett, Marshall, and Doar interviews.

83. Arthur M. Schlesinger, Jr., *A Thousand Days* (Boston: Houghton Mifflin, 1965), 697.

84. Jones to DeLoach, July 13, 1960, no. 16, Folder 96, Hoover Official and Confidential FBI File; Evans to Belmont, Aug. 20, 1962, Folder 9, ibid.

85. DeLoach to Mohr, July 11, 1965, no. 100-438794-391, SCLC FBI File; Baumgardner to William C. Sullivan, July 1, 1965, no. 100-438794-392, July 1, 1965, no. 100-438794-408, and July 6, 1965, no. 100-438794-521, ibid.

86. Andrew Young Oral History, June 18, 1970, p. 26, Lyndon B. Johnson Library, Austin, Tex.

87. Baumgardner to Sullivan, Oct. 27, 1965, no. 100-3-104-illegible, FBI COINTELPRO (CPUSA) File; Director to SACs New York et al., March 31, 1960, no. 100-3-104-1577, ibid.

88. Dunbar interview. For CORE, see SAC St. Louis to Director, Oct. 11, 1963, no. 100-3-104-42-43, FBI COINTELPRO (CPUSA) File; Director to SAC St. Louis, Oct. 24, 1963, no. 100-3-104-42-43, ibid. For Randolph, see Baumgardner to Belmont, Nov. 30, 1960, no. 100-3-104-2109, and Dec. 27, 1960, no. 100-3-104-2170, ibid.; Director to SAC Pittsburgh, Dec. 7, 1962, no. 100-3-104-39-32, ibid. For the NAACP, *see* Director to SAC New York, Dec. 4, 1959, no. 100-3-104-illegible, March 5, 1965, no. 100-3-104-31-320, and March 17, 1965, no. 100-3-104-31-illegible, ibid.; Director to SAC Newark, May 6, 1965, no. 100-3-104-illegible, ibid.; Baumgardner to Belmont, June 7, 1960, no. 100-3-104-1729, ibid.; Baumgardner to Sullivan, Feb. 15, 1965, no. 100-3-104-31-312, and March 5, 1965, no. 100-3-104-31-319, ibid.; Director to SAC Detroit, Feb. 19, 1965, no. 100-3-104-15-153, ibid.; Hoover to Brownell, May 10, 1957, cited in correlation summary memo, Feb. 28, 1958, no. 62-78270-2, Wilkins FBI File.

89. Director to SAC San Francisco, Sept. 19, 1961, no. 100-3-104-2904, FBI COINTELPRO (CPUSA) File; SAC San Francisco to

Director, Sept. 12, 1961, no. 100-3-104-2904, and Sept. 22, 1961, no. 100-3-104-2903, ibid.; Baumgardner to Sullivan, Sept. 18, 1961, no. 100-3-104-2905, and Oct. 3, 1961, no. 100-3-104-2964, ibid.; press release, Sept. 22, 1961, no. 100-3-104-2964, ibid.; U.S., Congress, *Congressional Record*, 87th Cong., 1st sess., Sept. 26, 1961, p. 21329.

90. Rosen to Belmont, May 22, 1963, no. 44-00-illegible, FBI Civil Rights Policy File; Hoover to Robert Kennedy, May 23, 1963, no. 157-00-54, FBI Racial Matters Policy File; John Seigenthaler Oral History, July 10, 1968, p. 19, Ralph J. Bunche Oral History Collection, Moorland-Spingarn Research Center, Howard University, Washington, D.C.

91. James Farmer Oral History, July 20, 1971, p. 30, Johnson Library; James Farmer, *Lay Bare the Heart* (New York: Arbor House, 1985), 270–71; DeLoach to Mohr, Nov. 20, 1963, no. 100-3-104-3882, and Nov. 27, 1963, no. 100-3-104-3882, FBI COINTELPRO (CPUSA) File.

92. Baumgardner to Sullivan, Feb. 15, 1965, no. 100-3-104-31-312, March 5, 1965, no. 100-3-104-31-319, and March 16, 1965, no. 100-3-104-15-163, FBI COINTELPRO (CPUSA) File; Director to SAC New York, March 5, 1965, no. 100-3-104-31-320, and March 17, 1965, no. 100-3-104-15-illegible, ibid.; Jones to DeLoach, March 16, 1965, no. 62-78720-not recorded, Wilkins FBI File.

93. Baumgardner to Sullivan, July 1, 1963, no. 100-3-104-9-192, FBI COINTELPRO (CPUSA) File. For the new phase of the COMIN-FIL investigation, see Director to SAC New York, Jan. 22, 1963, no. 61-3176-illegible, FBI NAACP File.

94. David J. Garrow, "FBI Political Harrassment and FBI Historiography: Analyzing Informants and Measuring their Effects," *Public Historian* 10 (Fall 1988): 11.

95. David J. Garrow, *Bearing the Cross: Martin Luther King, Jr., and the Southern Christian Leadership Conference* (New York: Morrow, 1986), 674 n43 (RFK quotation); Taylor Branch, *Parting the Waters: America in the King Years, 1954–1963* (New York: Simon and Schuster, 1988), 829, 831; Roger Wilkins, *A Man's Life* (New York: Simon and Schuster, 1982), 123.

96. *Washington Post,* May 29 and May 30, 1978.

97. In the manner of Walter White's two memoirs, Wilkins only mentions the FBI in passing. Roy Wilkins with Tom Mathews, *Standing Fast* (New York: Penguin Books ed., 1984); Walter White, *A*

Man Called White (New York: Viking, 1948), and *How Far the Promised Land* (New York: Viking, 1955).

98. Sizoo to Sullivan, Dec. 1, 1964, no. 3, Martin Luther King, Jr., Folder, Hoover Official and Confidential FBI File; SAC New York to Director, Oct. 14, 1963, no. 100-3-104-31-502, FBI COINTEL-PRO (CPUSA) File; Victor S. Navasky, "The FBI's Wildest Dream," *The Nation*, June 17, 1978, pp. 716–18.

99. David J. Garrow, *The FBI and Martin Luther King, Jr.: From "SOLO" to Memphis* (New York: Norton, 1981), 148.

100. Jones to DeLoach, March 16, 1965, no. 62-78270-not recorded, Wilkins FBI File; Jones to DeLoach, March 22, 1965, no. 100-443566-X16, James Forman FBI File.

101. Quoted in Jones to DeLoach, March 16, 1965, no. 62-78270-not recorded, Wilkins FBI File. *See also* Garrow, *FBI and Martin Luther King*, 124.

102. DeLoach to Mohr, Nov. 27, 1964, no. 62-78270-illegible, Wilkins FBI File.

103. Hoover to Lyndon B. Johnson, Nov. 30, 1964, no. 62-78270-15, ibid.

104. Jones to DeLoach, March 16, 1965, no. 62-78270-not recorded, ibid.

105. Director to SACs Albany et al., Jan. 7, 1969, no. 100-448006-580, FBI COINTELPRO (Black Hate Group) File; George C. Moore to Sullivan, June 4, 1968, no. 157-00-not recorded, FBI Racial Matters Policy File; Garrow, *FBI and Martin Luther King*, 189-90.

106. Wilkins, *Standing Fast*, 317, 319, 330; Wilkins Oral History, April 1, 1969, n.p., Johnson Library.

107. Nicholas deB. Katzenbach to Harry McPherson, Sept. 17, 1966, Civil Rights (2), White House Aides' Files—McPherson, Lyndon B. Johnson Papers, Johnson Library; Eric F. Goldman to Johnson, May 4, 1964, WHCF, Ex LE/HU2, ibid.

108. Sizzo to Sullivan, Dec. 1, 1964, no. 3, King Folder, Hoover Official and Confidential FBI File.

109. Stone interview.

110. Clayborne Carson, *In Struggle: SNCC and the Black Awakening of the 1960s* (Cambridge, Mass.: Harvard University Press, 1981), 13.

111. *Atlanta Daily World*, June 20,1978.

112. Brown testified once again, nearly twenty years later, before congressional committees holding hearings to declare King's birthday a national holiday. "If this measure is passed," she said, "we

may as well take down the Stars and Stripes that fly over this building and replace it with a Red flag.'' U.S., Congress, Senate Committee on the Judiciary and House Committee on Post Office and Civil Service, *Joint Hearings on Martin Luther King, Jr., National Holiday,* 94th Cong., 1st sess., 1979, p. 43.

113. H. Rap Brown, *Die, Nigger, Die* (New York: Dial Press, 1969), 61; *Washington Post,* May 22, 1981; U.S., House, Select Committee on Assassinations, *Hearings on Investigation of the Assassination of Martin Luther King, Jr.,* 95th Cong., 2d sess., 1978, vol. 6, p. 98; John Lewis Oral History, Aug. 22, 1967, p. 172, Moorland-Spingarn Center; Young Oral History, p. 25; Farmer, *Lay Bare the Heart,* 285; A. Philip Randolph to Hoover, Aug. 7, 1964, J. Edgar Hoover Folder, Brotherhood of Sleeping Car Porters Records, Library of Congress, Washington, D.C.; Hoover to Robert Kennedy, June 6, 1961, no. 144-1-554, Bergman Freedom Rider FBI Files; DeLoach to Mohr, June 10, 1964, no. 100-7321-not recorded, National Lawyers Guild FBI Files.

114. DeLoach to Mohr, May 4, 1961, no. illegible, Bergman Freedom Rider FBI Files.

115. Bayard Rustin Oral History, June 20, 1969, p. 4, Johnson Library.

116. Leon Howell, ''An Interview with Andrew Young,'' *Christianity and Crisis,* Feb. 16, 1976, pp. 14–16, 19–20; Young Oral History, 23; House Select Committee on Assassinations, *Hearings,* vol. 6, p. 4; Howell Raines, *My Soul Is Rested,* 430; DeLoach to Mohr, Dec. 2, 1964, no. 100-106670-634, King FBI File.

117. James Forman, *The Making of Black Revolutionaries* (New York: Macmillan, 1972), 353; Forman interview.

118. SAC Pittsburgh to Director, June 17, 1968, no. 100-448006-171, Sept. 24, 1968, no. 100-448006-not recorded, Oct. 9, 1968, no. 100-448006-not recorded, and Dec. 18, 1968, no. 100-448006-540, FBI COINTELPRO (Black Hate Group) File; Director to SAC Pittsburgh, June 28, 1968, no. 100-448006-171, and Oct. 24, 1968, no. 100-448006-339, ibid.; Moore to Sullivan, Sept. 17, 1968, no. 100-448006-illegible, and Oct. 23, 1968, no. 100-448006-338, ibid. For the liaison program's expansion, see Moore to Sullivan, June 4, 1968, no. 157-00-not recorded, FBI Racial Matters Policy File.

119. Jones to Nichols, April 13, 1955, no. 62-78270-not recorded, Wilkins FBI File; Hoover to John Ehrlichman, July 2, 1969, no. 62-78270-42, ibid.

120. Schlesinger, *Robert Kennedy,* 298.

121. Roger Wilkins interview.

122. Director to SACs Albany et al., March 4, 1968, no. 100-448006-19, FBI COINTELPRO (Black Hate Group) File; Senate Select Committee, *Book III,* 491–92; O'Reilly, *"Racial Matters,"* 275–76.

123. Moore to Sullivan, Feb. 29, 1968, no. 100-448006-19, FBI COINTELPRO (Black Hate Group) File; Senate Select Committee, *Book III,* 6.

124. O'Reilly, *"Racial Matters,"* 281–83.

125. Ibid., 305–09.

126. Ibid., 266–69, 334.

127. Charles D. Brennan to Sullivan, March 15, 1971, no. 52-94527-215, FBI MEDBURG File.

JAMES BALDWIN

(1924–1987)

Novelist, essayist, and playwright James Baldwin signaled his arrival as an intellectual force in the struggle for racial justice with the November 1962 publication of "Letter from a Region in My Mind." Originally appearing in *The New Yorker* and subsequently incorporated into the best-selling *The Fire Next Time* (1963), the essay's powerful and often frightening description of what it was like to be black in a white society briefly marked Baldwin as the nation's clearest and angriest voice on the racial problem—attracting the attention of the lowliest radio, television, and newspaper commentators all the way up to the Kennedy brothers. Attorney General Robert F. Kennedy invited Baldwin to breakfast at his Hickory Hills, Virginia, home, and during the spring 1963 demonstrations in Birmingham, Alabama, Kennedy turned to Baldwin for advice. When the attorney general did not like what Baldwin had to say, he turned to J. Edgar Hoover with a request for a dossier. If Baldwin was America's "Negro Question" expert, Hoover performed the same role for the Kennedys.

Born in Harlem on August 2, 1924, where he attended Frederick Douglass Junior High School and DeWitt Clinton High School, Baldwin had a rough and uneven early life. A Holy Roller preacher in storefront churches by age fourteen, he earned a living after high school in a succession of jobs—handyman, office boy, factory worker, dishwasher, waiter. His writing career began with reviews and essays, and by the mid-1940s he was publishing in the best New York journals and socializing on the fringes of the so-called New York intellectuals. Among others, this group included Dwight Macdonald, Lionel Trilling, Mary McCarthy, Delmore Schwartz, and Irving Howe. Baldwin won a Rosenwald fellowship in 1948 and thereafter spent his life as an expatriate (he preferred the term "commuter") with a permanent residence in Paris.

France proved productive in the 1950s. Baldwin published three novels during his first eight years abroad: the semiautobiographical *Go Tell It On the Mountain* (1952); *Notes of a Native Son* (1955); and *Giovanni's Room* (1956). A collection of essays, *Nobody Knows My Name* (1961), and another novel, *Another Country* (1961), followed. In 1964, his most successful play, *Blues for Mister Charlie,* ran for five months on Broadway. For the remainder of the 1960s, however, Baldwin's voice seemed rather tame (as did the civil rights movement itself) compared to the rhetoric of the new nationalists in the Black Panther party. In the 1970s, moreover, many literary critics in the academy and elsewhere argued that Baldwin's reputation as a novelist had been greatly inflated. Still, Baldwin remained unrepentant to the end. He criticized American military involvement in Vietnam, advocated gay rights, and accused the Richard M. Nixon administration, with help from J. Edgar Hoover, of plotting the genocide of all people of color at home and abroad. He remained a commuter to the end. When he died of cancer on November 30, 1987, at the age of sixty-three, it was at his home in southern France.

In addition to his novels and essays, Baldwin's *The Price of the Ticket* (1985) should be consulted by interested readers. Criticism and biographies include James Campbell, *Talking at the Gates: A Life of James Baldwin* (1991); A. Robert Lee, *James Baldwin: Climbing to the Light* (1991); Horace A. Porter, *Stealing the Fire: The Art and Protest of James Baldwin* (1989); W. J. Weatherby, *James Baldwin: Artist on Fire* (1989); and Quincy Troupe, ed., *James Baldwin: The Legacy* (1989).

Memorandum

TO: Mr. A. Rosen   DATE: May 29, 1963

FROM: Mr. [Bureau Deletion]

SUBJECT: JAMES ARTHUR BALDWIN
           INFORMATION CONCERNING

SYNOPSIS:

On the attached clipping from the New York *Journal American* of 5-28-63, Mr. Tolson inquired as to information in our files concerning James Baldwin who recently met with the attorney general.

Bureau files reveal that Baldwin, a Negro author, was born 8-2-24 in New York City and has lived and traveled in Europe. He has become rather well-known due to his writings dealing with the relationship of whites and Negroes. In 1960 he sponsored an advertisement of the Fair Play for Cuba Committee and was identified as one of its prominent members. This group is a pro-Castro propaganda organization in the United States. In 1961 he sponsored a news release from the Carl Braden Clemency Appeal Committee distributed by the Southern Conference Educational Fund, the successor to Southern Conference for Human Welfare cited as a communist front by the House Committee on Un-American Activities (HCUA). Braden was a communist convinced under the Smith Act. In April, 1961, he sponsored a rally to abolish the HCUA.

Baldwin has supported organizations supporting integrating and in 1961 reportedly stated [that] a period of revolution confronted the world and only in revolution could the problems of the United States be solved. He has advocated the abolishment of capital punishment and criticized the Director, stating that Mr. Hoover "is not a lawgiver, nor is there any reason to suppose him to be a particularly profound student of human nature. He is a law-enforcement officer. It is appalling that in this capacity he not only opposes the trend of history among civilized nations but uses his enormous power and prestige to corroborate the blindest and basest instincts of the retaliatory mob." He has also indicated he feels the attorney general and the President have been ineffective in dealing with discrimination and in this connection has urged the removal of the Director.

ACTION:

For information. Information concerning Baldwin and the other individuals who participated in the recent conference with the attorney general is being incorporated into informative memoranda for dissemination to the attorney general.

DETAILS:

Baldwin was born on August 2, 1924, in New York City to David Baldwin, a part-time clergyman, and Berdis Emma Baldwin, nee Jones. The eldest of nine children, James Baldwin was reared entirely in New York and in 1942 graduated from DeWitt Clinton High School where he served as a student judge and magazine editor. Baldwin has received many fellowships and awards, which enabled him to live and write in Europe for approximately eight years during the 1950s. He has traveled to many other parts of the world including Palestine, Africa, and many of the Asiatic countries.

The April 6, 1960, edition of the *New York Times* contained an advertisement by the Fair Play for Cuba Committee, and Baldwin was one of the sponsors of the committee. The April 16, 1960, edition of the *Crusader* identified Baldwin as one of the prominent members of the committee. This committee is a pro-Castro propaganda organization in the United States.

Baldwin spoke before a mass rally of the Washington, D.C., chapter of the Congress of Racial Equality for the "Original Freedom Riders" on 6-11-61 and stated in substance that the white race had better realize the emerging strength of the Negro and that he would not care to be in the shoes of the white man when the African nations become stronger.

The 10-2-61 issue of the *National Guardian* carried an advertisement of the Monroe Defense Committee listing Baldwin as one of the sponsors thereof. This committee was formed to tell the story of the racial violence [that] occurred in Monroe, North Carolina, on 8-27-61.

Baldwin's name appeared as a sponsor on a news release in August, 1961, from the Carl Braden clemency appeal committee which was being distributed by the Southern Conference Educational Fund. This organization is the successor to the Southern Conference for Human Welfare cited by the House Committee on Un-American Activities (HCUA) as a communist front. Braden was sentenced to prison for contempt of the HCUA.

The 1-10-63 issue of the *National Guardian* revealed that Baldwin was among the signers of a statement urging the Anti-Defamation League to withdraw its award, "democratic legacy," to President Kennedy unless the Department of Justice drops its "harassment" of William Worthy, Jr. Worthy is a Negro journalist who has been in trouble with United States officials as he traveled without a passport both through Red China and to Cuba.

The 4-17-61 issue of the *National Guardian* announced a rally to abolish the HCUA, and Baldwin was listed as a sponsor of the rally. In April, 1962, Baldwin was among the 550 signers of a clemency petition for convicted communist Junius Scales who was convicted for violating the Smith Act.

The 5-17-63 issue of *Time* magazine devotes its cover to Baldwin and the magazine describes some of his recent efforts in behalf of integration. He is described as a "nervous, slight, almost fragile figure, filled with frets and fears. He is effeminate in manner, drinks considerably, smokes cigarettes in chains and he often loses his audience with overblown arguments.'' The May, 1963, issue of *Mademoiselle* contains an interview-type article with James Baldwin in which he gibes to both whites and Negroes concerning the Negro situation in the United States. During this article he indicated that he was illegitimate. On the subject of homosexuality, Baldwin states ''American males are the only people I've ever encountered in the world who are willing to go on the needle before they'll go to bed with each other. Because they're afraid of this, they don't know how to go to bed with women either. I've known people who literally died out of this panic. I don't know what homosexual means any more, and Americans don't either . . . If you fall in love with a boy, you fall in love with a boy. The fact that Americans consider it a disease says more about them than it says about homosexuality.''

In connection with a discussion of why he feels both Robert Kennedy, the attorney general, the Justice Department and President Kennedy are ineffective in dealing with discrimination with the Negroes in the South, Baldwin makes the statement that he is weary of being told that desegregation is legal. He then states ''. . . because first of all you have to get Eastland out of Congress and get rid of the power that he wields there. You've got to get rid of J. Edgar Hoover and the power that he wields. If one could get rid of just those two men, or modify their power, there would be a great deal more hope. . . .''

A United Press International release dated April 29, 1963, revealed that David Susskind was fired on that day by the Metropolitan Broadcasting Company and his television program *Open End* was being removed from the air. According to the news release a dispute between Susskind and the television broadcasting company started when Susskind announced plans to present author James Baldwin and singer Harry Belafonte on a program called *The American Negro Speaks His Mind*. Officials of the television company objected to the program by Susskind on the basis that the combination of Baldwin and Belafonte ''would not offer a broad enough basis of enlightened opinion.''

Memorandum

TO: SAC, NY (100-16553)   DATE: May 29, 1963

FROM: [Bureau Deletion] SUPERVISOR, #12

SUBJECT: JAMES ARTHUR BALDWIN
           INFORMATION CONCERNING

[Bureau Deletion] on 5/21/63 requested a check of the NYO indices
and also established sources for any information, particularly of a derogatory nature, concerning captioned. Information had been developed by
the Bureau that Baldwin is a homosexual, and on a recent occasion
made derogatory remarks in reference to the Bureau.

The indices of the NYO disclose two pertinent files identical to the
captioned: 100-16553 and [Bureau Deletion]

[Bureau Deletion] James Baldwin was arrested on 9/3/54 for Disorderly Conduct, was arraigned before Judge Balsam and received a suspended sentence. The Disorderly Conduct charge was for refusal to
move on order of a policeman. At that time James Baldwin was described as Negro, age 30, novelist, residence 63 West 97th Street. . . .

AIRTEL

TO: Director, FBI   DATE: May 30, 1963

FROM: SAC, New York (100-79303)

SUBJECT: RALLY SPONSORED BY CONGRESS OF RACIAL
           EQUALITY,
           STATEN ISLAND, 5/28/63
           INFORMATION CONCERNING

[Bureau Deletion] a rally sponsored by the Staten Island group of
Congress of Racial Equality (CORE), was held at Wagner college,
Grimes Mill, Staten Island, New York, at 8:00 P.M., on Tuesday, May
28, 1963. Admission was $1.00 and a collection was taken up during
the rally. [Bureau Deletion] Between 850 and 900 people attended.

The guest speaker was James Baldwin, a Negro writer; and folk
singer, Leon Bibb provided entertainment. The affair lasted about
three hours.

Proceeds from the sale of tickets was to be given to CORE in Birmingham for help in paying attorney's fees, and aiding the integration movement.

Baldwin spoke for about 20 minutes and said he was speaking as an individual Negro rather than as a spokesman for the Negro. Baldwin gave a brief outline of his boyhood in the South. The theme of his talk was that integration in the South is the white man's problem and not the Negro's. He said it was not a southern problem, but a national problem. He was not interested in compromises for the Negro, stating compromising was a way of evading responsibility. . . .

During a question-and-answer period, Baldwin was asked about his recent meeting with Attorney General Robert Kennedy. In answer to which he more or less passed over this meeting and stated merely that he had spoken with the attorney general and he thought the attorney general "was beginning to listen."

There was no picketing or demonstrations at the rally. [Bureau Deletion]

AIRTEL

TO: Director, FBI (157-6-34)   DATE: Sept. 23, 1963

FROM: SAC, New York (157-892)

SUBJECT: RACIAL SITUATION
                  NEW YORK DIVISION
                  RACIAL MATTERS

[Bureau Deletion] They discussed the stand taken by James Baldwin and his group [Bureau Deletion].

[Bureau Deletion] . . . that this group of Baldwin was not "too deep intellectually."

[Bureau Deletion] position was with Baldwin and [Bureau Deletion] the two were better qualified to lead a homosexual movement than a civil rights movement.

. . . According to the *New York Herald Tribune*, September 19, 1963, Baldwin is quoted as bitterly criticizing the Kennedy administration and the FBI for their "lack of action" following the Birmingham bombing, September 15, 1963. The *New York Times* of September 19, 1963, quotes Baldwin as saying "I blame J. Edgar Hoover in part for events in Alabama. Negroes have no cause to have faith in the FBI.'' [Bureau Deletion]

Baldwin stated that he felt that Kennedy should go to Alabama and [Bureau Deletion]. Baldwin agreed that the feeling existed not only in Birmingham but elsewhere. Baldwin then spoke of something his sister had said to his mother, ''Negroes are thinking seriously of assassinating Martin Luther King.''

Statements attributed to James Baldwin

In an interview appearing in the June 3, 1963 issue of the *New York Times,* by reporter M. S. Handler, Baldwin made the following statements:

''No man can claim to speak for the Negro people today. There is no one with whom the white power structure can negotiate a deal that will bind the Negro people. There is, therefore, no possibility of a bargain whatsoever.''

''I was raised in the church but have abandoned Christianity as an organized religion. The church is the worst place to learn about Christianity. I have rejected it because the Christians have rejected Christianity. It is too pious, too hypocritical.''

In his interview with Handler, Baldwin also stated that he could not accept the black Muslim political ideology based on black supremacy, but thought that the Muslims were the only grass roots Negro movement in the United States.

The June 3, 1963 issue of the *New York Times* contained another article on the subject in which he stated:

''I left the country and abandoned everything in 1948, never intending to return. I couldn't bear it any longer. I knew that I would kill somebody or someone would kill me. I lived in Paris and elsewhere in Europe long enough to vomit up most of my hatred and to place America in perspective.

''It was in Paris that I realized what my problem was. I was ashamed of being a Negro. I finally realized that I would remain what I was to the end of my time and lost my shame. I awoke from my nightmare.''

[Bureau Deletion] on May 28, 1963, James Baldwin addressed a rally sponsored by the Staten Island Chapter of the Congress of Racial Equality (CORE), which was held at Wagner College, Grimes Hill, Staten Island, New York.

The June 21, 1963, issue of the *New York Post* carried an article reporting that the subject on June 20, 1963, had received the Alumnus of the Year Award from the Frederick Douglass Junior High School in

Harlem, New York City, from which he graduated in 1938. In addressing the graduating class on June 20, 1963, Baldwin stated, "This is the first time in the history of the country that it is confronted with 22,000,000 black people who can't be negotiated with anymore."

... Beginning with its issue of January 13, 1964, and ending with its issue of January 19, 1964, the *New York Post,* a New York daily newspaper, carried a six-part series of articles on James Baldwin.

In part, these articles contain the following quotes of Baldwin:

"I do not hate white people. I can't afford to. Just because I want to live. And I haven't got enough emotional energy. There's some people I hate—but some of them are black."

"I was born in Harlem, I was raised in Harlem and, indeed, as long as I live, I'll never be able to leave Harlem."

[Bureau Deletion] the subject was the last speaker at the 10th Annual Bill of Rights Dinner, held December 13, 1963, at the American Hotel, New York City, under the sponsorship of the Emergency Civil Liberties Committee (ECLC).

In his speech, Baldwin stated [that] he was not very interested in the recommendation of Mr. J. Edgar Hoover that the Negro in his quest for equality should not fight—. Baldwin contended that these established institutions have offered the Negro no real help and have, in fact, tended to maintain the Negro's lowly state.

Baldwin further stated that the ban on travel to Cuba was incomprehensible to him since he, as a Negro, was better off vacationing in Havana than in Miami Beach no matter what type of system was in effect in Cuba. He advocated unlimited issuance of passports to everyone to go anywhere.

Baldwin stated he and many other Negro leaders were well aware that the communists offered no solution to the Negro problem and that this was quite obvious since they, the communists, promised much but all Negroes knew that it was impossible to fulfill these promises.

[Bureau Deletion] in his speech at the ECLC Dinner at the Hotel American, New York City, on December 13, 1963, Baldwin stated "I have never been afraid of Russia, China, or Cuba, but I am terrified of this country." He went on to state that apathy allows thousands of people, not only Negro but also white, in the South to perish. He said the white person in the South does these things because he was told to do so generations ago and could never allow himself to fall below the level of the Negro....

Memorandum

TO: Mr. W. C. Sullivan   DATE: October 3, 1963

FROM: Mr. F. J. Baumgardner

SUBJECT: "THE FIRE THE [sic] NEXT TIME"
           BY JAMES BALDWIN

Subject book, published in 1963 by the Dial Press, Inc., New York
City, consists of two articles by Baldwin [that] were previously published in magazines. Both articles strongly advocate integration.

I. "My Dungeon Shook"
    In this brief article, Baldwin compares Harlem living conditions
    where he was reared to those described by Charles Dickens ex-
    isting in London over 100 years ago. Today, with integration,
    Baldwin says the Negroes must force the whites to stop fleeing
    from reality and begin to change those conditions.

II. "Down at the Cross" (originally published under the title "Letter
    from a Region in My Mind")
    This lengthy article again mentions Baldwin's past life in Harlem.
    He had been a preacher on occasion (no mention of being or-
    dained) until he became disillusioned with Christianity. He refers
    to Christ as a "Disreputable sunbaked Hebrew." Baldwin contin-
    ues: "If the concept of God has any validity or any use, it can
    only be to make us larger, freer, and more loving. If God cannot
    do this, then it is time we got rid of Him." Baldwin does not
    say how. Baldwin does not regard the Negro as inferior to the
    whites and says the only thing the white man has that the Negro
    needs is power. He contends that blacks and whites need each
    other if we are to become a nation and if integration is to be
    achieved. If the relatively conscious whites and blacks do not
    falter in their duty to work toward integration, he says, it may be
    possible to end the racial nightmare. If, on the other hand, they
    do not try everything to achieve that goal, then "the fulfillment
    of that prophesy, recreated from the Bible in song by a slave, is
    upon us: God gave Noah the rainbow sign, no more water, the
    fire next time!" The Director and the Bureau are not mentioned
    in the book.

Bureau files indicate Baldwin, who was born in 1924 in New York
City, has been very active and vocal in the integration movement and

his writings deal primarily with that situation. He has lent his name to subversive causes and has been critical of the Director. He has not been investigated.

ACTION:
  None. File.

New York, New York
May 8, 1964
Bufile 62-108763
NY file 100-146553
RE: James Arthur Baldwin

James Arthur Baldwin is a Negro author who resides in Apartment 6A, 470 West End Avenue, Manhattan, New York.

James A. Baldwin was born August 2, 1924, in New York, New York. He is about five feet six inches, 130 pounds, brown eyes, black hair, dark complexion, and has never married. Baldwin has written the following books: *Another Country, Go Tell It on the Mountain, Notes of a Native Son, Giovanni's Room,* and *Nobody Knows My Name.*

James Arthur Baldwin has made veiled threats as follows: the June 3, 1963 issue of *Newsweek* magazine reported an informal discussion between Attorney General Robert F. Kennedy, James Baldwin, and others. Baldwin told the attorney general that he would not think of fighting for the United States if the United States got into a war but that he was thinking of getting guns and starting to shoot white people.

The November 6, 1963, issue of the *Washington Daily News* quoted Baldwin as saying "I wonder how long we can endure . . . Stand and not fight back." "Many . . . even members of my own family . . . would think nothing of picking up arms tomorrow."

On June 30, 1963, the *Miami News* reported that Baldwin warned that there are a lot of angry young people among his race and their tempers are wearing thin and that their self-control, which Negro integrationists use in their nonviolence campaign for equality, is reaching the breaking point.

The *Washington Post* and the *Times Herald* dated September 27, 1963, quoted Baldwin as saying "We must make the establishment afraid of us."

Memorandum

TO: Mr. DeLoach   DATE: July 20, 1964

FROM: [Bureau Deletion]

SUBJECT: JAMES ARTHUR BALDWIN
                INFORMATION CONCERNING

My memorandum dated 7-17-64, which concerned the captioned individual's plans for a future book about the FBI, has been returned by the Director with this question: "Isn't Baldwin a well-known pervert?" It is not a matter of official record that he is a pervert; however, the theme of homosexuality has figured prominently in two of his three published novels. Baldwin has stated that it is also "implicit" in his first novel, *Go Tell It on the Mountain.* In the past, he has not disputed the description of "autobiographical" being attached to this first book.

The *New York Post* published a series of six articles about Baldwin in January, 1964. Written by Fern Marja Eckman, they were the result of a series of interviews by Mrs. Eckman with the novelist. She asked him why he used homosexuality in two of his novels and he corrected her by pointing out that all three novels contained this theme in one degree or another, using the term "implicit" in connection with the first book.

According to Mrs. Eckman, Baldwin explained the motivation for this recurrent theme in his fiction. He said there are two reasons for it, both of which are similar. He then launched into a diatribe about sex in America and actually never did state these so-called two reasons in any clarity. He says the situation he described in *Another Country* is true, only much worse than he depicted it. (Most of his novel dealt with the carnality of a group of whites and Negroes in Greenwich Village and Harlem. Included in it was a description of the homosexual deeds of a bisexual character in Paris.) Baldwin said he was exposed to all of this when he arrived in Greenwich Village as a Negro adolescent. He criticized American heterosexuality, saying it isn't sex at all but "pure desperation." He claims American homosexuality is primarily a waste which would cease to exist in effect if Americans were not so "frightened of it." He goes on to claim that Americans, Englishmen and Germans—the "Anglo-Saxons"—are the only people who talk about it. It should be noted, however, that he makes a point that it is these people, whom he calls the "Puritans" who speak of homosexuality in a "terrible way."

He then contrasts their approach with that of the Italians, stating, "In Italy, you know, men kiss each other and boys go to bed with each other. And no one is marked for life. No one imagines that—and they grow up, you know, and they have children and raise them. And no one ends up going to a psychiatrist or turning into a junkie because he's afraid of being touched."

He continues by saying that is the root of the "American" thing— "it's not fear of men going to bed with men. It's fear of anybody touching anybody." Baldwin concluded this particular discussion with Mrs. Eckman by saying that Negroes were frequent targets of homosexual approaches on the part of whites because they were always looking for somebody to act out their fantasies on, and they seem to believe that Negroes know how to do "dirty things."

During this particular interview, Baldwin intimates that he has had experience in this type of activity, saying, "You wouldn't believe the holocaust that opens over your head ... if you are 16 years old. . . ." He ends by stating that they understand in Italy that people "were born to touch each other."

These remarks are similar to others Baldwin has gone on record with regarding homosexuality. While it is not possible to state that he is a pervert, he has expressed a sympathetic viewpoint about homosexuality on several occasions and a very definite hostility toward the revulsion of the American public regarding it.

RECOMMENDATION:
None. For Information.

Memorandum

TO: Mr. W. C. Sullivan   DATE: July 30, 1964

FROM: F. J. Baumgardner

SUBJECT: JAMES ARTHUR BALDWIN
           SECURITY MATTER-C

[Bureau Deletion]
James Arthur Baldwin is the well-known Negro novelist and writer who has become increasingly active in recent months in the Negro civil rights movement. He has been associated with several Communist party

front organizations and has had considerable contact with members of the Communist party, USA. Baldwin is on the Security Index.

OBSERVATIONS

The fact that James Arthur Baldwin is writing a book about the FBI in the South has been known to the Bureau, as well as the fact that the book would be featured in *The New Yorker* prior to its publication in book form. The book will be published by Daily Press.

The New Yorker has over the years been irresponsible and unreliable with respect to references concerning the Director and the FBI. New York has previously been instructed to follow the publication of this book and to remain alert to any possibility of securing galley proofs for the Bureau.

ACTION:

The matter of Baldwin's contemplated book about the FBI in the South is being closely followed and you will be kept advised of pertinent developments.

UNITED STATES DEPARTMENT OF JUSTICE

FEDERAL BUREAU OF INVESTIGATION

New York, New York
February 26, 1968

Malcolm X Memorials
February 21, 1968
New York City
Racial Matters

[Bureau Deletion] who has furnished reliable information in the past, advised that there was a gathering at the auditorium of Intermediate School 201 (I.S. 201), 127th Street and Madison Avenue, New York City (NYC), at about 9:00 A.M. on February 21, 1968. This was a memorial to the late Malcolm X and was reportedly sponsored by the Afro-American Students Association.

[Bureau Deletion] the auditorium was full to capacity, with approximately 700 persons in attendance and the audience was composed of a few school teachers, some small school children; however, most of those present were adult Negroes.

[Bureau Deletion] speakers at this memorial as Conrad Lynn, attorney, James Baldwin, Negro author, Leroi Jones, Negro playwright, Betty Shabazz, widow of Malcolm X, an unknown female from Chicago who was reportedly a friend of Shabazz, and Herman Ferguson.

[Bureau Deletion] Conrad Lynn spoke generally about the need for defeating the present governmental power structure. Leroi Jones talked about the need for getting guns and that everyone should know how to use guns. Betty Shabazz talked about her husband, Malcolm X, and their children. James Baldwin also spoke and furnished a general tribute to Malcolm X.

SUMMARY FROM FRENCH

The article, "L'Express Continues with James Baldwin," is taken from the August 21–27, 1972, issue of *L'Express.*

Question: You believe in the possible victory of the black minority?

Answer: We represent around 10 percent of the American population. Without talking about starting revolution, it is certainly enough to destroy society.

Q: In what way?

A: It is easy for us, for example, to make the cities uninhabitable. It is the blacks who form the bulk of the urban services. In real estate, we are in the basement and the basement directs the life of the rest of the floors. It is very simple. In order to organize this type of resistance, it is not necessary to have a lot of people. And the war in Vietnam, in this regard, is very significant. That the most powerful country in the world, in twelve years, cannot manage to get the better of one of the poorest and most underdeveloped countries in the world, makes many blacks wonder.

Q: In your opinion, is violence necessary or only inevitable?

A: You cannot speak of violence as if it could take place tomorrow. It is already there. But violence where, against whom? When President Nixon said: "We will not tolerate violence any longer," I still wonder to whom he was speaking. Who must no longer tolerate it? He? Or us? Because the main victims of American violence are the blacks. I would certainly prefer to be able to avoid violent confrontations. But it does not depend on the blacks. The choice is not in their hands.

Q: You returned to the U.S. in 1957 because you felt that some-
        thing was stirring. Fifteen years later, you decided to live in
        France. Why?

A: I decided to return to France and then to stay there after
        Martin Luther King's assassination in April of 1968. I hesi-
        tated for two years. And then I felt that it was necessary to
        go away to begin again: as a writer, as a political militant,
        as a man. The death of Martin Luther King was the end of
        a certain period of time in American politics in which I was
        closely involved. It was also the end of a certain hope.

Q: The way chosen by Martin Luther King, was it feasible?

A: I do not know. That is very difficult to say today. Perhaps
        the methods used by Martin were not the most effective but
        they were, at that time, the strongest. Anyhow, I could not
        stand the idea of remaining in France, because they were
        trying to change me. I returned to work at Martin's and
        Malcolm's side.

Q: Was this the hope that was broken when Martin Luther
        King died?

A: Yes. Hope in American morality.

Q: And you returned to France?

A: Yes, to breathe. And, to withdraw once again. To try and
        see clearly. I was very strongly connected with the Black
        Panther movement and I was afraid, then, of being useless
        to them. What they do is done by youths in a world which
        is already different from mine. The only way to help them
        is to contribute my support. To listen to them, to respect
        them, hoping sometimes to be heard. I am, after all, first a
        writer. If I do not find the time to reflect, to write, I will
        not be of any use to anyone. I would not have any reason
        for being.

Q: What do you think about Angela Davis?

A: I do not know her personally. She is much younger than I.
        She belongs to another generation. All I can do is listen and
        try to help while there. I know that her trial is absurd. The
        only fault she has is being a bad example for the other slaves.
        Angela Davis and Paul Robeson are, in the eyes of the
        whites, bad "niggers."

Q: What do you mean?

A: Paul Robeson went through the world as if the world be-
        longed to him. Whites cannot stand to be surrounded by

black people. It is necessary to quickly give an example. Angela Davis answered Ronald Reagan that she was a communist. The problem was not what she was accused of. What does the answer matter when you have no right to ask the question anyway? Whether I do or do not agree with her ideas means nothing. As I am 20 years older than she is, I necessarily have another viewpoint. Anyhow, she is a victim. Therefore, she is my sister.

Translator's Note: James Arthur Baldwin's interview with Margaret Mead is called *Racism in Question,* a Calmann-Levy publication.

Q: You have written that "If catastrophe comes one day, the rebirth will only be able to come from the South." What do you mean?

A: Because the people live in such a nightmare, that unconsciously they will be looking to free themselves. In order to leave this hell, the southerner will have an enormous price to pay. But perhaps he will finish by saying to himself: "Anything but this hell." While the northerner does not live surrounded by blacks, the black is not a daily element, permanent in his life. He passes by him in the elevator, on the sidewalks. He is not a part of the view all the time. The journey will take much longer for him.

Q: Do you believe that the cultural contributions of the black civilizations can influence society?

A: Yes, I believe that it is in this way, through cultural contributions, that you can manage to profoundly change society. Our way of listening, seeing, feeling, thinking can contribute to these changes. It is for this reason that I find the word "revolution," in this day and age, to be a bit romantic. It is, in reality, the hidden fountain of humanity that one must exploit, in order to disconcert, to establish communications. To be born, to learn to walk, to grow up, to grow old, all this is difficult for everyone. No one has the right to add another problem, that of the color of one's skin.

W. E. B. Du BOIS

(1868–1963)

By the time William Edward Burghardt Du Bois joined the Communist party in 1961 at the age of ninety-three, the FBI had been tracking him for more than forty years. The old Bureau of Investigation opened a dossier during World War I and J. Edgar Hoover's bureau opened a new file during the next great war. "Subject favors equality between the white and colored races," the first document in that latter file reads, and that was all the reason Hoover's men needed to place Du Bois on a Custodial Detention list of persons to be detained in the event of a national emergency and to solicit the assistance of the CIA, State Department, U.S. Information Agency, and virtually every other intelligence community branch to keep pace as Du Bois traveled the world. To much of the world, Du Bois was a teacher, author, editor, poet, scholar, and Pan-Africanist. To Hoover, he was exactly what he had always been—just another Negro subversive who happened to speak with a "precise and cultured" accent.

Born on February 23, 1868, in Great Barrington, Massachusetts, Du Bois attended Fisk University in Nashville and then became the first black man to receive a Ph.D. from Harvard, the nation's most distinguished university. One of only five students selected to speak at commencement, his choice of subject (Jefferson Davis and slavery) demonstrated the audacity that characterized his entire life with two notable exceptions: his position during World War I and his part in the hounding of Marcus Garvey.

From 1895 to 1910 Du Bois taught at Wilberforce University and Atlanta University, finding time to publish prolifically; start and edit a magazine (*Moon*) and a newspaper (*Horizon*); and found the Niagara Movement as a vehicle to oppose Booker T. Washington's accommodationist policies. In 1910–1911 he was among the original founders of the National Association for the Advancement of Colored People and subsequently worked as director of publicity and research, sat on the board of directors, and edited its publication (*The Crisis*).

Du Bois's most famous and controversial *Crisis* editorial, "Close Ranks" (in the July 1918 issue), represented the first time in his long career that he took a position in support of those in power. "Let us while this war lasts," he counseled, echoing the Woodrow Wilson administration's position on World War I, "forget our special grievances and close our ranks shoulder to shoulder with our white fellow citizens and the allied nations that are fighting for democracy." While other blacks screamed "sell out," the *Crisis* editor, already fifty-eight years old, sought a commission in Military Intelligence.

That commission never came. Instead, Du Bois led an NAACP investigation in 1919 of discriminatory treatment of black troops in Europe. In the 1920s, he organized the First Pan-African Congress held in Paris and subsequent congresses held in London, Brussels, Lisbon, and New York. He also engaged in a feud with Marcus Garvey, calling "the Negro Moses" a "lunatic" and "traitor"—and Garvey responded in kind, calling Du Bois a "white man's nigger." At that point, Du Bois acted for the second and last time in furtherance of an incumbent government. He helped, in a fashion, Hoover's Bureau make a case against Garvey and was among those cheering Garvey's eventual imprisonment for mail fraud and deportation. Another feud, with NAACP executive secretary Walter White, crested in 1934 and led to Du Bois's ten-year break with the group. Returning to Atlanta University, he came back to the NAACP in 1944 to serve as director of special research. Among other duties, he attended the United Nations founding conference in San Francisco. But his criticism of the Harry S. Truman administration's position on the cold war and kind words for Henry Wallace, the Progressive party nominee for the presidency, led in 1948 to a permanent severance.

In the late 1940s and early 1950s Du Bois co-chaired the Council on African Affairs, chaired the Peace Information Center, helped organize the Cultural and Scientific Conference for World Peace, and ran for United States senator on the Progressive ticket. In 1961 he not only joined the Communist party but took up residence in Ghana at Kwame Nkrumah's invitation. He died there two years later on August 27, 1963—the same year that he became a citizen of Ghana and the day before Martin Luther King, Jr., told the March on Washington throng of his dream. If he died a bitter old man and a Stalinist, that is not how he should be remembered.

Du Bois's most important works include *The Souls of Black Folk* (1903) and *Black Reconstruction* (1935). For his musings on his life and times, see *A Pageant in Seven Decades, 1868–1938* (1938); *Dusk of Dawn* (1940); *In Battle for Peace* (1952); and *The Autobiography of W. E. B. Du Bois* (1968). Herbert Aptheker edited the latter, and also *The Correspondence of W. E. B. Du Bois* (3 vols.; 1973–1978). Also of value are Rayford W. Logan, ed., *W. E. B. Du Bois: A Profile* (1971), and Shirley Graham Du Bois's, *His Day Is Marching On: A Memoir of W. E. B. Du Bois* (1971). Gerald Horne, *Black and Red: W. E. B. Du Bois and the Afro-American Response to the Cold War* (1985), provides an interesting perspective, as does Arnold Rampersad in *Art and Imagination of W. E. B. Du Bois* (1990), and Manning Marable in *W. E. B. Du Bois: Black Radical Democrat* (1986). See also David L. Lewis, *W. E. B. Du Bois: Biography of a Race, 1868–1919* (1993).

FEDERAL BUREAU OF INVESTIGATION

This case originated at: Atlanta, Georgia
Report made at: New York City
Date when made: 5/1/42
Period for which made: 3/25; 4/2, 11/42
Report made by: [Bureau Deletion]
Title: WILLIAM EDWARD BURGHARDT DU BOIS (Colored)
Character of case: Internal Security—J & I

SYNOPSIS OF FACTS:
Subject [is] presently professor at Atlanta University, Atlanta, Georgia. He received his higher education at Harvard, traveled in Europe, and studied in Berlin. Subject is poet and former editor of *Crisis* magazine, a publication sponsored by the N.A.A.C.P. He now writes a column in the *Amsterdam New York Star News*. His writings indicate him to be a socialist. However, he has been called a communist and at the same time criticized by the Communist party. Subject favors equality between the white and colored races. No evidence of subversive activity in New York.

-RUC-

DETAILS:

The following investigation is predicated upon a copy of a letter sent
to the Charlotte Field Division by the Atlanta Field Office dated February 8, 1942, in which the following information was not out:

"Information was received by the Atlanta Office that subject, William
Edward Burghardt Du Bois (Colored), whose residence was given as
226 West 150 Street, New York City, business address 69 Fifth Avenue,
New York City, had stated in a speech made while in Japan that the
Japanese were to be complimented on their progress and especially
upon their military prowess. Further, that in the Japanese he saw the
liberation of the Negroes in America, and that when the time came for
them to take over the United States, they would find they would have
help from the Negroes in the United States."

In checking the sources in the New York Office, the following information regarding the subject was obtained from the 1937 issue of *Who's
Who in America,* edited by Albert Wilson Markuis:

"William E. B. Du Bois, editor and author was born in Great Barrington, Massachusetts, February 23, 1968, of Negro descent, the son
of Alfred and Mary Du Bois. He received an A.B. degree from Fisk
University, Tennessee, in 1888. Subsequently, he attended Harvard
University, where in 1890 he received his A.B. degree; in 1891 N.A.
degree; and in 1895 his Ph.D. degree. He also studied at the University of Berlin. He was married to Nina Gomer of Cedar Rapids, Iowa,
May 12, 1896. Subject was Professor of Economics and History at
Atlanta University from 1896 to 1910. He was director of publica-
tions of the National Association for the Advancement of Colored
People and was editor of the *Crisis* magazine from 1910 to 1932.
Further, he has been professor of sociology at the Atlanta University
since 1932. He was also founder of the Pan-African Congress. Sub-
ject was author of the following: *Suppression of Slave Trade*—1896;
Philadelphia Negro—1899; *The Souls of Black Folk*—1903; *John
Brown*—1909; *The Quest of the Silver Fleece*—1911; *The Negro*—
1915; *Dark Water* [sic]—1920; *The Gift of the Black Folk*—1924;
The Dark Princess—1928; *The* [sic] *Black Reconstruction*—1935.
Subject was also editor of the Atlanta University, *Studies of the
Negro Problem,* from 1897 to 1911 and his home address was given
as 210 West 105 Street, Atlanta, Georgia."

In an effort to ascertain the background of the subject before conducting an active investigation, a number of the copies of the *Crisis* maga-

zine were briefly reviewed, and it was noted that Du Bois was editor
of this magazine, which is published by the National Association for
the Advancement of Colored People, 70 Fifth Avenue, New York City,
from 1910 to 1934.

In the subject's writings in this publication, it appears that he leans
to the writings and beliefs of the socialist, also that he is impressed
with the success of Russia and of communist[s], but at the same time,
he criticized the Communist party of America. He constantly writes of
racial discrimination and how his race is oppressed, especially in the
South. He urged Negroes to migrate to the North. Further, he believes
that there should be social equality between all people, regardless of
color, and, although he does not recommend marriage between the black
and white races, he demands one's right to do so should [one] so desire.

It is noted that many of the thoughts portrayed in the writings have
become the reported issues upon which the Communist party of
America have exerted their efforts to cause agitation among the Negroes. Du Bois from time to time sneered at those persons who branded
the N.A.A.C.P. as being a communistic-enforced organization.

In an April issue of the year 1931, in a postscript on page 39, subject
spoke of his travels in Russia and Berlin and made the statement that
he had friends who were representatives from Japan.

Some of the subject's later writings display that he had a kind of
fatalistic acceptance of the basic condition as to the colored people as
being unchangeable, and he now urges a Negro nation within a nation,
economically, not politically.

In a January issue of the *Crisis,* year of 1920, on page 107, is the
following notation: "Leave the black and yellow world alone. Get out
of Asia and Africa and the Isles. Give us estate and town and section
and let us rule them undisturbed. 1. Absolutely segregate the races and
sections of the world. 2. Let the world meet as men with men; give
justice to all, extend democracy to all, and treat all men according to
their individual desert."

It was further noted that in the December issue of the above publication in the year 1920, Du Bois praised Garvey, the Negro champion of
the past who was one of the original organizers of the "Back to Africa
Movement." Subject stated that he did not believe that Garvey was
dishonest, complimented him on his leadership but criticized his business methods.

[Bureau Deletion]

It is also noted from a review of the above publication that Du Bois
resigned his position of editor of *The Crisis* magazine in June, 1934,

at which time the N.A.A.C.P. stated that the writings of its editor do
not necessarily portray the views and opinions of the N.A.A.C.P. About
this time, Du Bois wrote an article regarding segregation of the races,
which article the N.A.A.C.P. did not endorse.

In a recent investigation in this Office, the writer had occasion to
review a number of pamphlets distributed by the Communist party in
New York City and in a number of these copies, it was noted that the
subject was severely criticized.

[Bureau Deletion] on March 30, 1942, reported the following information: Subject was a member of the National Committee of the Civil
Rights Defense Committee, a group organized to aid the followers of
Trotsky tried for sedition in Minneapolis. This would indicate that [the]
subject is not a supporter of the Communist party, which opposed the
defendants.

[Bureau Deletion]. He advised at that time [that the] subject was
considered a radical, that he was editor of *The Crisis* magazine, and
that to his knowledge this paper during the latter part of the war was
denied the mail privilege. He recalled that one of the statements [the]
subject made at that time was "The American officers spend more time
fighting the Negroes than the Germans."

[Bureau Deletion] also furnished the following information in regard
to [the] subject: About the year 1892, the subject won a fellowship and
went to Europe where he spent two years. He returned in 1894, at
which time he taught at the Wilberforce University, and also about that
time he spent one year in the University of Pennsylvania, Philadelphia,
Pennsylvania. Further, he was connected with the N.A.A.C.P. from 1910
to 1934, and in 1911 he attended a race congress that was held in
London, England. He went on to say that [the] subject was one of the
permanent workers in racial problems and that after the war in 1918,
he organized the Pan-African Congress, which held one conference in
Paris, France, and in 1927 met in New York City. This Congress was
scheduled to meet again in Tunis, France, but the French stopped them,
after which they attempted to charter a boat in order to hold the conference at sea but he does not believe that this materialized. [Bureau
Deletion] further stated that in 1927 two Russian impresarios, a man
and a woman, came to Du Bois to discuss his organization among the
Negroes. A German individual also accompanied them. As a result of
this conference, [the] subject visited Russia in 1928, where he visited
such places as Leningrad, Moscow, Kiev, the Ukraine, and countries
surrounding the Mediterranean. [Bureau Deletion] further advised that

he is of the belief that Du Bois broke with the N.A.A.C.P. in 1934 due to [a] disagreement over the defense in the Scotsboro case [sic].

[Bureau Deletion] subject also went abroad again in 1936, at which time he spent five months in Germany and two months in Russia. The purpose of this trip was to write a Negro encyclopedia. About this time, [the] subject was also reported to have traveled in China, Manchuria, and Japan, [Bureau Deletion] has not heard of any subversive activities on the part of the subject, and he advised that today [the] subject is a current writer in the *Amsterdam New York Star News,* a weekly colored paper published in New York City and that [the] subject is considered to be more or less a conservatist in comparison with the younger colored writers of today. His column under date of March 14, 1942, has been clipped. A copy is being furnished to the Bureau and a copy is being furnished to the Atlanta Field Division, as enclosures with this report. A copy is also being maintained in the New York files. This column is indicative of his writing of today.

The subject's business address, [Bureau Deletion] New York City, referred to above, is the address of the building maintained by the N.A.A.C.P. in which is published *The Crisis* magazine. Inquiry was made of the [Bureau Deletion] whose identity was not ascertained, and he advised that Du Bois has not been with the N.A.A.C.P. for several years and is now teaching at some University in the South.

It was noted that [the] subject's residence was given as [Bureau Deletion] New York City, which is the [Bureau Deletion] Apartments, one of the largest apartment houses in the colored sections, comprising over five hundred apartments. An inquiry revealed that [the] subject has not resided there for over two years. When he did reside there, he occupied two apartments. Inquiry at this address and also at the office of the publication, the *Amsterdam New York Star News,* revealed that [the] subject is now located at Atlanta, Georgia, where he is professor of sociology at the Atlanta University.

[Bureau Deletion]

Enclosure for the Bureau

1 clipping of a column written by the subject under date of March 14, 1942, for the publication, the *Amsterdam New York Star News.*

Enclosure for the Atlanta Field Division

1 clipping of a column written by the subject under date of March 14, 1942, for the publication, the *Amsterdam New York Star News.*

-REFERRED UPON COMPLETION TO OFFICE OF ORIGIN-

The Amsterdam New York Star News
New York, New York
March 14, 1942

As the Crow Flies
By W. E. B. Du Bois

Listen, fellow white Americans.

Yes, yes, yes! We are going to do our bit in this war as in others; we will be neither slackers nor traitors. We are going to fight for this country, not because we think that it is always right, or always just; or even always decent. Whatever this country is it is because of our blood and our toll and our sacrifice; together with the help of some Americans and despite the hurt and hindrance of other Americans.

We fight not in joy but in sorrow with no feeling of uplift; but under the sad weight of duty and in part, as we know to our sorrow, because of the inheritance of a slave psychology which makes it easier for us to submit and obey rather than rebel. Whatever all our mixed reasons are, we are going to play the game; but listen, Fellow Americans, for Christ's sake, stop squawking about democracy and freedom. After all, we are black men and we live in America.

Programs

I wonder if it isn't possible for Negro Americans consciously and clearly to set before themselves and at once follow three programs which always appear, disappear, and re-appear among us and yet all are logical and rational and not contradictory. First, a program of immediate objectives, March, 1942: Admission into labor unions without discrimination; share of defense jobs; fighting all new appearances of racial discrimination; attacking the oldest and weakest of former discriminations as, for instance, the denial of accommodations in Pullman cars, the denial of admissions to publicly supported places of recreation; demand for equal pay in return for equal services. These and a half dozen other matters varying from place to place and from time to time are immediate demands [that] the American Negro should make. The movement to gain them ought to be put into the hands of young and energetic men and women, who are ready to sacrifice place, popularity, and money in order to advance the interests of the Negro race. It is probable that all these objectives can be reached within the next few years and all of them are worth trying for.

New Group Pressure

Second, group pressure and organization: This is a program of careful offensive and defensive organization. It should fight for effective and complete education even if that involves separate educational institutions. It fights for economic security and such a measure of economic autonomy as is necessary and possible in order to secure Negroes a decent income, so that they can support their own institutions. It would involve consumers' cooperation and, wherever feasible, producers' co-operation; racial business organization, racial institutions like churches and social settlements. It would look forward toward the organization of adequate recreational facilities, not simply for children but for youths and adults; organized social activity giving the opportunity for young people of marriageable age to meet under the proper circumstances and choose their mates by deliberation and not by sheer chance. The organization of homes and neighborhoods so as to be protected, not only from slum influences, but from race hate; and the encouragement of family life and the reproduction of an adequate number of children to maintain our present population.

All these we are doing with hesitancy and often lack of conviction. We are forced into these lines of effort by race prejudice and in our resentment against race prejudice we allow ourselves often to plan and organize poorly or not at all. This work should be carried on by the middle-aged group, liberal in education and thought, and fairly secure in their economic surroundings. It need have no quarrel with the young radicals. On the other hand, it can often furnish them sinews of war and advice, and in parts of their program it may be possible for them to share. Nevertheless, their main object is to put the Negro group today in a position of security and progress, whether or not that involves segregation and group loyalty.

FEDERAL BUREAU OF INVESTIGATION

This case originated at: New York, New York
Report made at: Charlotte, N. C.
Date when made: 7/29/42
Period for which made: 7/22/42
Report made by: [Bureau Deletion]
Title: WILLIAM EDWARD BURGHARDT DU BOIS
Character of case: Internal Security—J

DETAILS:
    Reference letter of [Bureau Deletion] Atlanta, Georgia, advised of
information furnished by [Bureau Deletion] to the effect that [the] subject had been reported as having made a speech while in Japan to the
effect that in the Japanese he saw the liberation of the Negroes in
America and that when the time came for them to take over the United
States, they would have help from the Negroes in the United States.
    ... In 1937 or 1938 she heard Du Bois make a speech at Osaka,
Japan. She stated that at that time Du Bois was making a speaking tour
of Japan and that he was widely heralded and advertised there as an
American Educator. [Bureau Deletion] advised that the address which
she heard was made to an audience which was for the most part Japanese, that Du Bois spoke in English, and that the speech was given to
the audience through an interpreter. [Bureau Deletion] stated that the
drift of Du Bois' talk was to the effect of his resentment in being a
Negro in America and that she gained some impression of a desire on
the part of Du Bois to unite the yellow and black races in opposition
to the white race.
    She recalled that Du Bois said that the Japanese should be leaders
in their part of the world and that he further said that "the Negroes in
America will extend to the Japanese in their leadership a weak but a
willing hand." [Bureau Deletion] advised that Du Bois spoke at length
of how the Negroes in America had advanced in culture and in art and
that he employed the general speaking device of flattering the Japanese
on their culture and general ability.
    [Bureau Deletion] denied that Du Bois made any such statement as
that credited to him in [the] referenced letter, namely, "that in the
Japanese he saw the liberation of the Negroes in America and that when
the time came for them to take over the United States they would have
help from the Negroes in the United States."
    [Bureau Deletion] denied that Du Bois made any such statement as

that credited to him in referenced letter, namely, "that in the Japanese he saw the liberation of the Negroes in America and that when the time came for them to take over the United States, they would have help from the Negroes in the United States."

Speaking further of Du Bois, [Bureau Deletion] stated that she understood that he was a professor probably of psychology in a Negro university in Atlanta, Georgia. She further stated that after the above discussed speech, she spoke personally to Du Bois for the purpose of greeting him and at that time he told her that he was residing in Boston or New York and was teaching in Atlanta.

[Bureau Deletion] further stated that several Americans in addition to her were present and heard instant speech, but she was unable to furnish their names. . . .

FEDERAL BUREAU OF INVESTIGATION

This case originated at: Atlanta, Georgia
Report made at: Baltimore, Maryland
Date when made: 2/13/43
Period for which made: 12/31/42; 1/29, 2/1/43
Report made by: [Bureau Deletion]
Title: WILLIAM EDWARD BURGHARDT DU BOIS
Character of case: Internal Security—J. Custodial Detention

SYNOPSIS OF FACT:
Neighborhood investigation revealed subject to be a great Negro educator, author, lecturer, and publisher; very studious and not inclined to be a social mixer. Interview with active member and officer of Harvard Club of Md. revealed nothing of subversive nature. Physical description set out.

REFERENCE:
Report of Special Agent [Bureau Deletion] dated 11/12/42 at Atlanta, Georgia.

DETAILS:
AT BALTIMORE MARYLAND:
Interview with [Bureau Deletion] colored, [Bureau Deletion] Baltimore, indicated that she has known the subject and has not seen him for many years. She stated that she has known Du Bois personally for

over fifteen years and he is a writer and was at one time connected with the International Association for Colored People [sic] in New York. She advised that the subject has always been an outstanding man, and a number of books were written by him and about him. [Bureau Deletion] further advised that Du Bois is the author of *Souls of Black Folk* and the *Quest of the Silver Fleese*. [sic]. He is a graduate of Harvard University and was class orator when he received his degree there. She believes that the subject was sent to Europe in World War No. 1 for some official capacity. [The] subject's wife and daughter were in France during World War No. 1. [Bureau Deletion] also advised that subject is a member of the Boule, which is a sort of fraternity of colored people who are outstanding professional men in their communities. They have an organization in Philadelphia, Chicago, and New York, and all the leading cities of the United States. She advised also that the subject is about 75 years old, and is a very active person mentally and physically. He might be a member of the Harvard Club of Maryland [Bureau Deletion] does not know of any church affiliations. He has never said anything against the government and is a good American citizen, whose loyalty she would not question. Du Bois is presently employed as a teacher of sociology in Atlanta University, Atlanta, Georgia. His wife and daughter are living here in Baltimore. [Bureau Deletion] stated that some people did not like Du Bois because he is not a social person and does not mix with people a great deal. He and his family are very agreeable and good neighbors. They have lived at the Montebella Terrace address for about three years [Bureau Deletion].

The following [Bureau Deletion] were interviewed and offered substantially the same information:
[Bureau Deletion]
[Bureau Deletion] a member of the Harvard Club of Maryland, stated that he does not know of the subject ever having been a member of the club [of] which he is a member, but he stated that he has heard of the work the subject has done for the Negro race. [Bureau Deletion] produced a membership list of the Harvard Club of Maryland dated November 1942 and subject's name was not on it, and no Negro has ever been a member of the Harvard Club of Maryland. [Bureau Deletion] stated further that Du Bois attended Harvard at the same time he did and he was an outstanding student. He stated that the subject does not have the appearance of being a Negro but rather the appearance of a West Indian and he stated that the subject presents a very intelligent and neat appearance. [Bureau Deletion] stated that he does not believe

that the subject has ever been engaged in any subversive activities of any kind.

The following is a description of the subject as furnished by [Bureau Deletion]:

Age	70, but appears much younger
Complexion	Medium brown
Weight	155–165 lbs.
Height	5' 8" to 5' 10"
Hair	Grey mixed with black, curly
	Wears pointed goatee
Eyes	Dark brown
Build	Stocky
Accent	Precise and cultured

[Bureau Deletion] has known the subject personally for 6 or 8 years, and states that his loyalty is unquestionable and that he is a fine neighbor. . . .

Activities of the subject as reported in news media and by FBI informants for the period of August to October 1950 follow:

[Bureau Deletion] advised on August 29, 1950, that Dr. W. E. B. Du Bois was listed as Chairman of the Peace Information Center, with offices at 23 West 26th Street, New York City.

The *Daily Worker* of September 7, 1950, page 4, column 1, carried an article [that] reflected that W. E. B. Du Bois was nominated for the United States Senate on the American Labor Party ticket.

The *Daily Worker* for September 19, 1950, page 2, column 4, carried an article [that] reflected that Dr. W. E. B. Du Bois was one of ten Negro leaders who urged Supreme Court Justice Robert Jackson to grant the petition of the ten communist leaders for continued bail pending appeal to the Supreme Court from their convictions for alleged violation of the Smith Act.

The *Daily Worker* for September 25, 1950, page 2, column 1, carried [an] article [that] reflected that Dr. W. E. B. Du Bois, Chairman of the Peace Information Center, released a statement advising that nearly 600 prominent Americans are urging a ban on atomic warfare.

The *Daily Worker* for October 11, 1950, page 5, column 1, carried a picture of Dr. W. E. B. Du Bois, a board member of the China

Welfare Appeal, reviewing the Columbus Day Friendship Cargo for China Welfare Appeal, Inc., 439 4th Avenue, New York 16, New York.

[Bureau Deletion] of known reliability, advised that there is no doubt in his mind that the China Welfare Appeal is a communist front and that it is considered a Communist party front by Chinese familiar with its activities.

[Bureau Deletion] of known reliability, advised that on October 10, 1950, the American Labor party of Queens County held a gala election rally at the Jamaica Arenas, 144th Place and Archer Avenue, Jamaica, New York. Informant stated that Dr. W. E. B. Du Bois, candidate for United States Senator on the ALP ticket, was principal speaker, and that he stated in substance: "The Soviet Union is the only country in the world which represents the interests of the people." Du Bois elaborated on the history of the present Russia and emphasized that the capitalist countries led by the United States are trying to destroy the peaceful efforts and endeavors of the Soviet Union. Du Bois claimed that pressure was the defiance of United States policy and the praising of whatever the Soviet Union is doing or has done in the past.

[Bureau Deletion] advised that he did not know whether or not Dr. Du Bois was a member of the Communist party as he has never seen him at any Communist party meetings or functions, but that he has heard from a reliable source [that] he did not divulge that Du Bois has joined the Communist party.

The Worker (Harlem), Sunday edition of the *Daily Worker,* of October 27, 1950, page 1, column 3, carried the following article in which Dr. W. E. B. Du Bois indicated his position as American Labor party candidate for the United States Senate. Du Bois issued the following statement on Korean peace:

"Another crucial moment has come in the Korean War, now that the United Nations, forced by the United States, has pushed the North Korean troops beyond the 38th parallel. There were those of us who from the first believed this war, with its heavy cost in death, maiming, and destruction was unnecessary; that it was a civil dispute for which the U.S. and especially South Korea were primarily responsible and which could have been settled with a minimum of hostilities if the UN had exhibited the restraint and wisdom in Korea which it exercised in the case of Palestine. This would surely have happened had not the United States insisted on war and started war before the UN consented to join.

"Our excuse was that Korean aggressors represented the Soviet Union. But no proof of this has ever been adduced; nor has China been proven an instigator of this war. Instead we tried to drag China in. Indeed, as the war progressed, it has become clear that neither Russia nor China desired this war nor advised it, nor added it; nor was it to their interest to have it occur. It was the U.S. alone that seemed willing to make this evil upheaval the beginning of a Third World War.

"Apparently what the U.S. now fears is that this horrible interlude will really end in peace and not in world war. Our troops are pushing the South Koreans to invade the North."

[Bureau Deletion] advised on September 22, 1950, that [at] a meeting of the Maspeth Communist party club executives on September 22, 1950, a topic for discussion was the preparing at once for the election campaign because the Communist party is going all out to see that [Bureau Deletion] is reelected and also that Du Bois gets a large vote.

[Bureau Deletion] advised on September 27, 1950, that a news letter of the Peace Information Center carried an article by Dr. W. E. B. Du Bois in which he states: "More than two million signatures to the Appeal have been collected since the beginning of hostilities in Korea despite the general 'preventive war' hysteria and Red-baiting and attacks of the Secretary of State, Department of Justice, the House Un-American Activities Committee, the press, and leaders of various organizations."

[Bureau Deletion] advised on October 10, 1950, that an American Labor party rally was held at Jamaica Arena, 144th Place and Archer Avenue, Jamaica, Long Island, New York. Dr. Du Bois was a speaker and stated that the ideas for peace and agreement with Russia should be followed on the Russian ideas.

[Bureau Deletion] advised on October 4, 1950, of a regular meeting of the Ozone Park Communist party club held the communists must fight to get Du Bois elected in the 11th Assembly District. Volunteers were asked to work each and every night until the end of the Election. [Bureau Deletion]

FEDERAL BUREAU OF INVESTIGATION

This case originated at: New York
Report made at: Los Angeles
Date when made: 12/11/51
Period for which made: 10/24; 11/13, 16; 12/6/51
Report made by: [Bureau Deletion]
Title: Dr. W. E. B. DU BOIS
Character of case: Internal Security—C

SYNOPSIS OF FACT:

Du Bois and wife, Shirley Graham, arrived in Los Angeles 6/17/51 on five-day visit. During this period they attended several meetings and receptions sponsored by Hugh Gordon Bookshop, Independent Progressive Party, and Hollywood Arts, Sciences and Professions Council, all communist-dominated organizations.

—RUC—

DETAILS:

ACTIVITIES

All informants referred to in this report are of known reliability unless otherwise stated.

Investigation in this case is predicated upon information received from [Bureau Deletion] to the effect that Dr. W. E. B. Du Bois should arrive in Los Angeles for a five-day visit and would make two public appearances. [Bureau Deletion]. . . .

[Bureau Deletion] attended a mass meeting at the Embassy Auditorium 9th and Grand Streets, Los Angeles, on June 21, 1951, sponsored by the Independent Progressive party and featuring Dr. W. E. B. Du Bois. According to the informant, Du Bois commenced his speech with the statement that the world was astonished at the United States inasmuch as the rest of the world believes that the United States wants war. The [Bureau Deletion] quote Du Bois as follows:

"We have warned and insulted Russia and prepared for war while Russia prepared for peace. We have turned Korea into a shrinking desert and are set to drop bombs on Moscow and lick the world. In order to make their investments safe our masters will lead us into total war unless we say no. This cannot happen. American business dominates the government. The small minority are so large and powerful that they own the earth. The capitalists believe that whole industries will collapse unless we have war. American investments will seek to dominate the world. We need to reform ourselves before teaching others. Free speech and opinion are throttled. Unless you hate Russia you are slandered and subjected to personal violence.''

The [Bureau Deletion] said that Du Bois in closing referred to the policies of the United States as an attack on civilization. . . .

Memorandum

TO: Director, FBI   DATE: July 23, 1951

FROM: SAC, LOS ANGELES

SUBJECT: Mrs. W. E. B. Du Bois
               SECURITY MATTER—C

On June 16, 1951, [Bureau Deletion] advised [Bureau Deletion] had given [Bureau Deletion] an invitation to a luncheon honoring Shirley Graham, also known as Mrs. W. E. B. Du Bois, at Ciro's, 8433 Sunset Boulevard, on Friday, June 22, 1951, at 12:30 P.M.

[Bureau Deletion] attended the above-mentioned luncheon and observed that approximately 150 women were in attendance. About 25 of these women were colored.

Sarajo Lord, Executive Secretary of the Southern California Council, ASP, introduced Mrs. Lou Solomon, also known as Wilma, who spoke briefly on the question of peace. She said that the subject of peace was of particular interest to the mothers, wives, and Negro women because of the persecution of the leaders for peace. She stated that Shirley Graham had been on the battle front in the fight for peace. She further identified Shirley Graham as chairman of the National Committee for the Defense of Dr. W. E. B. Du Bois, and a charter member of the ASP.

Mr. Lloyd Gough made some humorous remarks and finally asked for contributions. One Salka Viertel donated a large solid gold ring, stating that she had no money to give at this time.

Shirley Graham began her talk by stating that she felt very much at home among members of the ASP, and further that she did not intend to make a speech but that she wanted to make a frank talk as one worker for peace to another. She told of a recent dinner party given by New York attorney Martin Popper at which John Howard Lawson, Dalton Trumbo, Dr. Du Bois and herself were present. During the preliminary cocktails at this dinner, Martin Popper's son commented that everyone present at the party had either been in jail or was going to jail. In this regard, Shirley Graham commented that it was ridiculous and fantastic that America's best minds were being sent to jail. She said that with all of the great progress [that] had been made in this country, we had not advanced in the commonest of ideas. "We in this room are the protectors of the culture of America." She said that "squads" were going into bookstores and libraries taking books off the shelves. "Writers are being deprived of making a living and it is up to us to seriously face the problem—unafraid."

She described the Peace Information Center, which had been set up in April of 1950, as a point for the gathering of information regarding peace movements around the world and the dissemination of the same. She told of the peace conference [that] was started by ASP and held at the Waldorf Hotel in New York. She said that it had been started by Harlow [sic] Shapley and further that some of the best minds in the country were present. Some of the great minds of Europe were prevented from coming to the United States by our State Department.

Miss Graham said that she went to France to attend the Paris Peace Conference. She paid her expenses from money received on an advanced payment of her forthcoming book. She said that every nation, creed, color, and class came to discuss how world peace could be obtained. "We will not be driven to murder each other," they said. She mentioned (Pablo) Picasso and others who were present. She described them as "workers." Their slogan at the end of the conference, "We shall have peace." She gave a short discussion of the peace conference at Cuba and was at one held in Mexico City. She said that writers were the "core" of the peace movement. They must give out information. The Peace Information Center sent out postalgrams all over the country. She said that the Stockholm Peace Appeal had been drawn up in Stockholm by the people of the world. She mentioned that O. John Rogge from the United States had signed the appeal in Stockholm. She said that the Peace Information Center had obtained several million signatures on the peace appeal. The State Department of the United States then noticed this group, the American Peace Committee, and ordered them to register as [a] foreign agent. "We laughed," she said. They were all volunteer workers with the exception of Sylvia Soloff (ph.) who worked overtime in the office. They were not receiving money from any foreign sources, only from poor American working people who wanted peace.

Miss Graham said the government had decided to close the office of the Peace Information Center and Dr. Du Bois asked the State Department for an opportunity to explain and show the records of that organization. Soon thereafter five officers of the Peace Information Center were indicted as "foreign agents." Sylvia Soloff received a $10,000 fine and five years in jail. She said that another man of the group, a war veteran who had been on the staff of General MacArthur and who had seen Hiroshima and Nagasaki, said, "We must work against the atomic bomb." He also received five years in jail and a $10,000 fine. Miss Graham referred to General MacArthur as "that madman from Tokyo." She said that the treasurer of the group was a businessman with offices in New York, London, and Paris. He was sentenced to five years in jail. He said, "If this can happen to me it can happen to TAFT." She said that another cultured New England woman who had taught in an exclusive New England school had been in Czechoslovakia studying conditions, and upon her return to the United States, was captured at the airport on Long Island by the FBI.

Graham said that Dr. Du Bois, who speaks for all people who are oppressed, black or white, and workers everywhere, has been called a "dangerous agent." She said, "He is dangerous to tyrants who would oppress the people." She said if the Peace Information Center can be indicted, then all of us can be indicted and civilization can be crushed and annihilated. She said the bill of particulars of the indictment of the Peace Information Center says that it disseminated in the United States information about war, about peace and matters related thereto. Miss Graham said, "If this is a crime, then everyone in this room is guilty— every worker for peace."

The following activities of the subject were reported for June 1951:

. . . [Bureau Deletion] who has furnished reliable information in the past, advised on July 1, 1951, that on June 14, 1951, the Subject addressed a gathering at the Oakland Auditorium, 12th and Fallon Streets, Oakland, California. [Bureau Deletion] advised that the theme of Du Bois' speech was, "We Must Have Peace." Du Bois stated he had been called a dangerous man because he speaks for peace. Du Bois declared he was American and not a communist. . . .

In the DPW issue dated June 15, 1951, on page 1, of [the] "Our World" section, there appeared an article entitled, "Dangerous Man." This article pertained to an interview by Terry Pettus, Northwest Editor of the DPW, with the Subject. Below are comments made by the Subject to Pettus. In answer to the question as to the reason for the lack of information as to what is happening in the world today, Du Bois replied:

"It is due to nothing more nor less than the complete and planned blackout in the commercial press and radio of every shred of information, the most important of every shred of information on the most important and controversial issue of our time. I have seen nothing like it in my career. This blackout is much worse in our own country than anywhere else in the world—even in Europe. . . ."

As to Senator Johnson's Korea Peace Resolution, Du Bois stated:

"That is why it is also being suppressed by the newspapers. Senator Johnson is no great liberal but he is a shrewd politician. We must make the people aware of his resolution. . . . The fighting in Korea must be brought to a halt. Now is the time for the people to make themselves heard."

In his description of what one must do to "be sure of earning a living, avoiding slander and abuse, possibly personal violence, and even keeping out of jail," Du Bois stated:

"To accomplish these ends in our 'free' country today you must repeatedly and loudly make it abundantly clear that you hate Russia— that you oppose socialism and communism—that you support without reservation the war in Korea—that you are ready to spend any amount for more war anywhere and any place—that you are ready to fight China, the Soviet Union and any other country or all countries put together—that you favor the use of [the] atomic bomb or any other mass destruction weapon and you regard those who believe otherwise as traitors—that you not only believe in all these things but that you are willing to spy on your neighbors and denounce them."

As to the question of "Economic Serfdom" of the Negro people, Du Bois stated:

"This is a close personal question that touches the lives of all of us. It involves the very special evil of low-paid colored labor. That is what is back of the aggression in the Far East. That is what is back of the slaughter in Korea. It is the business of stripping [a] colonial country of its raw materials—or processing it in part with cheap labor.

"Capitalism uses these profits to bribe the workers and thinkers of the more powerful countries by high wages and privilege. In this way the imperialists seek to build a false and dishonest prosperity on the slavery and degradation, the low wage and disease and very lives of the colored peoples of Asia and Africa and the islands of the sea. And to pay the price for this they demand that we in the United States,

Negro and white, give up our liberties and our sons and daughters in an endless stream to be murdered and crippled in endless wars.''

The closing paragraph of the interview quotes Du Bois:

''I see in the future and the not-too-distant future a new era of power, held and exercised by the working classes the world over. It is dawning before the eyes of those who want to see, and while its eventual form is not clear its progress cannot be held back by any power of man.'' ...

FEDERAL BUREAU OF INVESTIGATION

This case originated at: New York
Report made at: Washington Field
Date when made: 5/29/58
Period for which made: 5/8, 15, 26/58
Report made by: [Bureau Deletion]
Title: Dr. W. E. B. DU BOIS
Character of case: Security Matter—C

SYNOPSIS:

Information reported regarding appearance of subject at Howard University, Washington, D.C., 3/31/58. Du Bois reportedly very critical of capitalistic system and stated socialism is coming to the U.S. Reaction of local persons set out.

DETAILS:

AT WASHINGTON, D.C.

Lecture, 3/31/58, Howard University, Washington, D.C. ...

[Bureau Deletion] furnished information on April 2, 1956, concerning the subject's lecture on March 31, 1958. [Bureau Deletion] stated an overflow audience attended and listened to Du Bois speak of the plight of this country, tracing the development of Western capitalism from the beginnings of World War II to the present. Du Bois stated that the ''allies'' oppressed the poor Russian people during the periods following World War I and World War II. Du Bois referred to the Korean War, according to [Bureau Deletion] as ''a movement that started as police action.'' He said that the United States had used germ warfare during the Korean War and at the same time was persecuting eleven communist leaders of the United States. He said that after Russia had the atom bomb, the United States executed (Julius and Ethel) Rosenberg when no evidence was available indicating that they had transmitted (atomic) secrets.

[Bureau Deletion] also furnished information on April 3, 1958, concerning the above affair. [Bureau Deletion] Du Bois made critical statements regarding the capitalist system in the United States and stated that the "New Deal" was just a form of socialism. He stated that whether America wants to believe it or not, socialism is coming to this country. Du Bois commented upon various other issues including the use of the atomic bomb by the United States on Hiroshima, Japan, (World War II), referring to it as "one of the most atrocious acts in modern civilization." [Bureau Deletion]

[Bureau Deletion] stated at the conclusion of the Du Bois lecture that "If Du Bois were a younger man he would be in jail tomorrow for what he said tonight." ...

Among the subject's activities abroad in 1958–59, as reported in the FBI files, are the following:

The *China Daily News,* issue of March 3, 1959, page 1, columns 3 through 6, contained information from Hong Kong captioned, "Ovation Accorded to American Negro Leader." According to this article, the students of the University of Peking held a big meeting to celebrate the 91st birthday of Du Bois.

In returning his thanks, the subject praised Communist China for the work done in economic reconstruction, and asked her to tell the people in Africa and the world, about the aggression brought against her by the imperialists. Du Bois warned the Africans to put themselves on guard against the West. Finally, he advised the African people to befriend Soviet Russia and her allies especially Communist China, according to this article. ...

[Bureau Deletion] furnished a summary of World Broadcasts, [Bureau Deletion] dated January 16, 1959, which was published by the [Bureau Deletion]. The summary was for the period January 11–13, 1959, and it included an interview over Radio Moscow, which was had with the subject and his wife.

During the interview, Du Bois stated, in part, to the effect that Russia's Sputnik was proof of Russia's advancement in education and science and that hereafter in the United States of America the people are going to believe what the USSR is doing in education and science and will be more disposed to live in peace and harmony with this great nation.

Du Bois, in a message to Africa, advised the people of Africa that they had to choose socialism rather than to attempt to remain neutral or to go through a preliminary trial of transient capitalism.

When asked if he thought the colonial countries in Africa would achieve the same economic and political successes as had the countries of the "East" when they obtained their independence, Du Bois replied in the affirmative and stated as follows:

"The achievements in the USSR and in China were made under unusual difficulties, difficulties that have been increased by the enmity of large numbers of people. . . ."

Du Bois further stated that if Africa started immediately to hitch her advancement in the near future to the "old communism of the African tribe" she had [to] change to make her progress much faster than otherwise would be the fact.

The *National Guardian,* issue of December 22, 1958, page 7, in an article captioned, "The Future for All of Africa Lies in Socialism," pertained to a speech [that] was to have been given in Ghana, Africa, by Du Bois, but on a doctor's advice, he did not travel to Ghana but instead his wife made the trip and read the speech for him.

According to the article, Du Bois' prepared speech referred to socialism and cited as foremost examples, "The great communist states like the Soviet Union and China."

The following is quoted, in part, from this article:

"Africa wake! Put on the beautiful robes of Pan-Africa socialism! You have nothing to lose but your chains! You have a continent to regain! You have freedom and human dignity to attain."

The Worker, issue of December 7, 1958, page 7, Columns, 1–2, contained a photograph of the subject as he was being welcomed at Prague Airport by the Czechoslovakian Vice Minister of Education and Culture. According to the article, Du Bois was later given an honorary doctorate degree at Charles University.

The *National Guardian* on November 10, 1958, page 6, columns 2 through 4, contained an article [that] indicated that Du Bois had been honored by the 600-year-old Charles University in Prague, Czechoslovakia.

In his acceptance speech, Du Bois said, in part, as follows:

"The salvation of American Negroes lies in socialism. They should support all measures and men who favor the welfare state; they should vote for government ownership of capital in industry; they should favor strict regulation of corporations or their public ownership; they should vote to prevent monopoly from controlling the press and the publishing of opinions. They should favor public ownership and control of water, electric, and atomic power; they should stand for [a] clean ballot, the encouragement of third parties and independent candidates—and the elimination of graft and gambling on television and even in churches. The question of the method by which the socialist state can be achieved must be worked out by experiment and reason and not by dogma.''

The *National Guardian,* issue of October 27, 1958, page 7, columns 1–4, contained an article, datelined Tashkent Uzbek, USSR, which revealed that in a speech concerning ''Socialist Africa,'' Du Bois made statements to the effect that a Socialist Africa was inevitable ''because this is a socialist era'' and that ''Village socialism in Africa could pass directly to modern socialism and the capitalist stage could and should be skipped.''

The *National Guardian* of March 2, 1959, page 12, column 3, contained an article [that] indicated that the subject had a two-hour meeting with Soviet Premier Khrushchev. According to the article, it stated, in part, that Du Bois said, ''We talked about peace and ways to develop closer and friendlier relations with the United States.''

The United States Department of State furnished information from its files in October, 1958, which revealed that the subject had made a speech at The Hague, Netherlands, on September 11, 1958.

According to the information furnished, Du Bois opened his speech by stating to the effect that America had no policy for peace . . . and that United States democracy was doing everything possible to prepare for war . . . while the Soviet Union does not want war.

According to the information furnished, Du Bois stated to the effect that the United States was big business, run by business, and that business was doing everything possible to start war against the Soviet Union and China.

According to the information furnished, Du Bois also stated to the effect that he hoped that Europe would ask the United States to cease its policy of fighting against communism.

Memorandum

TO: Director, FBI   DATE: May 14, 1959

FROM: [Bureau Deletion]

SUBJECT: Dr. W. E. B. Du Bois
         SECURITY MATTER-C

The following is a summary of New China News Agency releases appearing in the press on the Chinese Communist mainland as obtained from translations furnished by the American Consulate General, Hong Kong, B.C.C.:

3/27/59 Kunming: The noted American scholar and member of the World Peace Council, Dr. W. E. B. Du Bois, arrived here with his wife by plane from Chengtu yesterday. They went sightseeing and in the evening they were entertained at dinner by Liu Pi-yun, Governor of Yunnan Province.

3/30/59 Kunming: Dr. Du Bois and his wife left yesterday by plane for Canton. They were accompanied by Chu Po-shen, vice secretary-general of the Chinese People's Association for Cultural Relations with Foreign Countries. Among those seeing them off were Heu Chia-Jui, Chairman, and Ma Chung-ming, secretary-general of the Yunnan branch of the China Peace Committee.

4/5/59 Canton: Dr. Du Bois and his wife left yesterday by train for Shanghai. Before their departure, Chen Yu, Governor of [the] Kwang-tung Province, gave a dinner in their honor.

4/12/59 Shanghai: Dr. Du Bois and his wife left Shanghai for Nan-king by train yesterday. They were seen off at the station by Chang Chun-chia, Chairman of the Shanghai Branch of the Chinese People's Association for Cultural Relations with Foreign Countries; Pa Chin, Vice Chairman of the Shanghai Branch of the China Peace Committee; and Li Yun, Secretary General of the China Welfare Institute.

4/14/59 Nanking: Dr. Du Bois and his wife left Nanking for Peking last night. They were seen off at the station by Wu Yi-fang, Chairman of the Kiangsi provincial and Nanking city branches of the Chinese People's Association for Cultural Relations with Foreign Countries; Liu Shu-shun, Vice Chairman of the Kiangsu provincial and Nanking City branches of the China Peace Committee; and Chou Tsun, Vice Chair-man of the Kiangsu Federation of Literary and Art Circles. During their stay, Kuang Wen-wei, Vice Governor of Kiangsu Province, and Pong Chung, Mayor of Nanking, met the guests and gave a banquet for them.

4/20/59 Peking: Dr. Du Bois and his wife, Shirley Graham, were guests of honor at a farewell banquet given today by the Chinese People's Association for Cultural Relations with Foreign Countries.

4/21/59 Peking: Dr. Du Bois leaves China for home. They were seen off at the airport by Chu Tu-nan, President of the Chinese People's Association for Cultural Relations with Foreign Countries, and Wu Han, Vice Mayor of Peking. During their stay in China they visited Peking, Shanghai, Wuhan, Naking, and other places.

TRANSLATION FROM RUSSIAN
"DO NOT KNOW ANY OTHER COUNTRY WHERE THE NUMBER OF SELFLESS CITIZENS-PATRIOTS WOULD BE SO GREAT" By WILLIAM DU BOIS, Laureate of the International LENIN Prize/Strengthening of Peace Among the People"
(PRAVDA, May 4, 1959, page 3)

In connection with the awarding of International Lenin Prize "For Strengthening of Peace Among the People," a prominent American scientist, writer, and a public figure William Du Bois stated to "Pravda" correspondent:

"It is a great honor for me to become a laureate of the international Lenin prize.

"As an American citizen, I was greatly surprised by the awarding of this prize to me, considering what the Government of the United States is doing for a preparation of war. It was hardly to be expected under those circumstances that the highest award for the struggle in defense of peace would be conferred on me, [a] citizen of the U.S.A.

"I am boundlessly happy that my modest work received so high an evaluation.

"There is no doubt that the people of the world vigorously express themselves against war. Their feelings become a powerful weapon of the struggle against war threat. These are all reasons for believing that the peace movement will grow and expand.

"I have not been in the United States for about a year already and, naturally, it is very difficult for me to judge about the processes [that] are taking place there at present. I am deeply convinced that changes will come in the U.S.A. However, this is not the time to speak about them. The present American Government will continue to carry out the preparations for war, as before. The symptoms of depression, unemployment, and the falling-off of export distract the attention of the public of the U.S.A. from the essential problems of war and peace.

The growth of the Soviet Union literally went on under my own eyes: I visited the U.S.S.R. in 1926, 1936, 1949, and am here at present. The duration of my visits fluctuated between one week up to a month and more.

After writing this, I felt the contradiction of my statement. It is impossible to become acquainted with any one country in a month or even in a year. This is particularly applicable to a vast country such as yours, which, in addition, is constantly moving ahead and with such headlong speed, that it takes one's breath away. Of course, much depends on the knowledge about the country possessed by a visitor, upon his disposition and prejudices. I do not know the Russian language because I was born in the middle of the nineteenth century when even some Russians preferred to speak French. However, I had definite advantages because of my Negro origin. I felt deep sympathy for the Russian peasants, partially liberated from slavery simultaneously with the liberation of the American Negroes, I know perfectly well what it means to be a slave.

I came to the Soviet Union in 1926, knowing only a little of Russian history of the period of tsarism. I knew comparatively little about socialism and had no idea whatsoever of Marxism. When I was a student, I did not have an occasion to read Karl Marx. Nevertheless, I saw people in Kronshtact, Leningrad and Moscow, in Gorky, and Odessa, whom I understood. Conditions of their life were understandable for an American Negro. Destruction and poverty, results of war and suffering; homeless children, digging in rubbish heaps; ruined homes and public buildings.

"Wait a moment." I used to exclaim: "The war has ended about ten years ago."

"Perhaps, but not in Russia," they answered me.

Here I saw for the first time with my own eyes the grievous consequences of a civil war through which the Soviet Union had passed and which they tried to picture in the United States as anarchy and aimless destruction.

Against the general background of ruins, nevertheless, I saw a tendency [that] excited me, in proportion to [the] degree [that] its purpose became clear to me. I saw the beginning of bold plans of creation of a national system of public education. I saw astute methods of education of homeless orphans. A tremendous attention devoted to workers was clear to me. And it was only here that an idea came into my mind that the wages are not simply money but also the protection of health, pensions for the aged, and a system of vocations.

I thought how American Negroes could achieve a similar system of planning and felt a desire to become acquainted with the works of Karl Marx.

Ten years had passed before I had an opportunity again to visit the Soviet Union. Rumors of great variety reached us in the United States regarding the fate of Soviet experiment. We heard about famine among peasants and about the struggle against kulaks and against treason. Some sensational reports came in, many of which I believed. The true picture of what was happening then in Russia became clear to me only after I became acquainted with the book by Seyers [sic] and Kaen [sic]. [*A Secret War Against the Soviet Russia.*]

By that time I was already teaching at one of the higher institutions of learning for Negroes, the University of Atlanta, *The Communist Manifesto* by Karl Marx and Friedrich Engels. At this time I was already trying to study the Negro problem in the United States from the scientific point of view and to find a socialist solution for it.

In 1936, passing by the Trans-Siberian Railroad, I was studying the U.S.S.R. for ten days, attentively and from various points of view. The train was going very slowly and made long stops at the stations. This huge, almost boundless country, with its poverty and wealth, but above all, with its resolution to build socialism, was opening in front of us. I saw Moscow, which was going through the first period of the great reconstruction. My way was going through Kazan and Omsk, through the Ural mountains, through the great Siberian steppes and [Lake] Baykal. I saw the flares of factories working in order to transform the Soviet industry. I had an opportunity to discuss questions of socialism. The guide in our car told me how the state provided an education for him. It also provided education for his brothers and sisters and showed concern for his parents.

I returned home through China and Japan, circumnavigating in this way the entire world. Two years after my return, the world was again gripped by war. The Soviet Union defended the world from Hitlerism.

It was necessary to prevent another act of military folly from happening and I joined my voice to the 600 American leaders of art and science who gathered in New York in March 1949, at a Peace Congress. The entire world was in solidarity with this Congress and the Soviet Union in particular, which sent in (its) outstanding leaders for participating in it.

This Congress was subjected to attacks, some of the most disgusting attacks against civilization known in the modern world. It was abused and reviled. Some of the outstanding leaders became victims of insults and the majority of them had to retreat. The results were sad. However, when in the same year, 1949, the Peace Congress convened in Paris, I hastened to take part in it. This was the greatest gathering reflecting the spiritual enthusiasm of mankind. My hopes grew and, when in the end of 1949, the Soviet Union invited twenty-five Americans to come to Moscow and to take part in the work of the All-Union Conference in Defense of Peace, I accepted this offer.

Thus, I saw your country for the third time. I remember how I told the Soviet people about sincere striving for peace in America. From hopes and doubts of 1926, through the presentiments of 1936, I came in 1949 to a belief in the ultimate triumph of communism not only in Russia but throughout the world. The face of almost every man met by me in the Soviet Union radiated hope.

American authorities started legal proceedings against me for my struggle in favor of peace. After I returned home, they brought formal charges against me and only the protest of the civilized world saved me from prison. However, in the course of the next seven years, I was deprived of the right to leave the country. When, in 1958, the Supreme Court of the United States declared that our Department of State has no legal right to deprive citizens of foreign passports, I and my wife, Shirley Graham, immediately took advantage of this.

Thus, I visited the Soviet Union for the fourth time. I saw people who were sure of themselves and calm. I saw how thirty-year-old hopes are being carried out in reality.

I was particularly impressed by one small detail. I looked out of a hotel window at the Red Square after half a million people passed through it. There was not a single scrap of paper in the square. This was not simply a result of the work of municipal employees. It was a result of [the] feeling of responsibility of the socialist people, who felt that the Red Square was their property and that all were obliged to take care of its cleanliness. If half a million people would demonstrate along the streets of New York, a week will be required in order to clean the rubbish left by them.

But it is not only this. The population of the Soviet Union is delivered from cares [that] oppress an American: How will he live when he gets old? How will he get medical attention when he gets ill? How to provide education for his children, for the cost of education is growing, not by day but by hours? How can he permit himself to take a vacation when every penny is needed in the home? A Soviet citizen knows that the state protects him in all these problems.

Many Americans inquire: how does the state know that every citizen performs his duty and works as hard as though he were threatened with poverty? The government, they say, is dealing with human beings who are selfish in their nature. The answer to this question is simple: The Soviet Union achieved unprecedented successes in the field of reeducation of its citizens into disciplined servants of the people—of all people and not [just] of a handful of the chosen ones.

Such a discipline, to its considerable degree, is not forced from above and not brought in from the outside. It is organically inherent in the citizens of the U.S.S.R. It is self-discipline. Of course, in the U.S.S.R., too, there are still people who think only of themselves. Also, there are criminals. However, I do not know any other country where the number of self-sacrificing citizens—patriots—is so great.

This is, of course, my personal opinion [and] based upon official statistical data. But behind it stands the experience of my travels throughout the world. I openly admit my prejudice. It is the rarest opportunity to be in a country and not to be subjected to insults because of one's racial origin and to enjoy respect for the things [that] one [has] tried to accomplish. I am prejudiced in favor of the Soviet Union. My prejudice is based upon the things I saw and experienced. Many Soviet people belong to the white race. However, there are no racial prejudices in the Soviet Union, nor racial hatred characteristic of the Anglo-Saxon countries in their relations with the world of the colored people.

I and my wife Shirley Graham were granted the honor of talking with the Chairman of the Council of Ministers of the U.S.S.R. N. S. Khrushchev. We devoted the greater part of our two-hour talk to the discussion of the problems of the colored people. I was telling him about what has happened in America in the last forty years and N. S. Khrushchev listened to me with great attention and sympathy. I asked him about the attitude of the Soviet Union toward Africa, meaning by this not the alms or problems of defense but the field of cooperation. I proposed that the Soviet Academy of Sciences join with the African scientists in the cause of the study of Africa, particularly in culture and history. I could never achieve such cooperation in America and seldom met with interest toward it in Western Europe. However, N. S. Khrushchev quickly and with enthusiasm offered his aid in this cause.

We left the Kremlin filled with most pleasant hopes.

The Negro Problem in the U.S.A.
Moscow in Russian for Abroad 11.00 GMT 17/6/59
Broadcast text of ''Pravda'' article by William Du Bois:

Europeans, and especially the inhabitants of Eastern Europe, are somewhat anxious about the position of Negroes or persons of Negro origin in the U.S.A. They hear that Negro slaves were liberated in 1863 and later became citizens enjoying social and political equality. They also hear about widespread lynching, murder, and mob violence. The Negroes continue their struggle for equal rights with the whites. If one was to believe newspaper reports, these have been basically achieved, notably after the Supreme Court decision allowing Negroes to attend schools for white children. U.S. inhabitants of various colors of skin and of various levels of education, descendants of former black slaves, have often convinced the Europeans that at home they enjoy complete equality with white citizens; by way of confirmation they have referred to colored statesmen and even holders of the Nobel Prize. But the events in Little Rock have revealed the presence in the U.S.A. of a degree of racial hatred unprecedented in any civilized country. ''What is the truth?'' Europeans ask.

The facts correspond with reality in both cases. Negro slavery has been abolished in the U.S.A. by law. However, at least five million U.S. inhabitants of Negro origin are still outcast slaves living in poverty. The majority of U.S. Negroes can read and write, but millions of them are as yet illiterate. They are being pushed onto the path of crime and poverty by the system of private capitalism and by racial hatred of white workers [who are] competing with them. In fact, the high wages of part of the white workers are partially paid by the money underpaid to Negro workers. Class differences are developing among the Negro population itself. On the one hand, there is a group of rich Negro exploiters, on the other the masses of the exploited—white and Negro. About ten percent of the Negro population of New York are business-men and specialists earning over five thousand dollars a year. On the other hand, fifty percent of this population lives on the brink of poverty.

For a long time the leading TUs [Teamsters Unions] did not admit Negro workers. However, after the crisis in the 1930s the majority of TUs began admitting Negroes. It should be noted that these Negroes are under the influence of the reactionary leadership and essentially institute a part of capitalist organizations. Since the U.S. Government established its control over the issue of passports for traveling abroad; this control has been used for preventing those Negroes from traveling abroad who criticize the racialist system in the U.S.A. Thus, for example, Paul Robeson was deprived of his passport for seven years. I also was refused a passport, although Negroes who favorably described America or kept silent about the racial situation in the U.S.A. could get passports.

As time went on, however, big business became aware of the discrepancy between declarations of desire for trade and friendship with Asian and African countries and discrimination against the colored population at home. This led to the attempts to introduce reforms in the system of public primary schools. Independent schools for Negroes—which achieved certain successes thanks to the efforts of the Negroes themselves and to the aid of white philanthropists—were formed. But as general education embraced wider straits of Negroes and as charity worsened, the position of the Negro schools became worse. The States were unable to support the parallel system of schools for whites and Negroes. The only solution was to create a single school system embracing all races. Such an interpretation of the Constitution was supported by the Supreme Court. However, the majority of former slave-owning southern states opposed this. Their attitude has led to such incidents as [the one] in Little Rock.

This problem has still to be solved if one is to eliminate the last vestiges of slavery, at least in education. It represents only a part of more serious problems, which are not only of a racial character. The matter concerns, first of all, the problems of labor and wages. The U.S. Negroes need socialism. They need something similar to what is possessed by the national minorities in the Soviet Union: the opportunity to develop their own national culture, preserving their historic traditions, and to develop their art and culture. Only in this way will it be possible to preserve the originality of their music and dances and the rest of this cultural heritage. Furthermore, the Negroes should have employment according to their abilities and receive wages according to their needs. This is the aim of communism, but the Negroes do not know about it. The leaders of the Negro people make a serious mistake and often force them to support the ''witch-hunting'' campaigns directed against communism.

If the American Negroes and all other Americans of all colors of skin could take into consideration everything that is today happening in the world, if they could study the history of Russia and China, if they could acquaint themselves with the teachings of Marx and Lenin, they would support socialism. However, at present the U.S. primary schools do not teach this. The U.S. colleges pay little attention to these subjects. Socialism is presented as a failure, and communism as a crime.

This, however, cannot last forever. Despite various obstacles, the number of literate Negroes is increasing. Thanks to the aid rendered by their white friends, the effectiveness of Negro organizations is growing. One day the Negroes will attain complete liberation not only from slave labor, but also from wage slavery and from racial hatred.

The Negroes have already made their contribution to history. They helped the U.S.A. in the liberation from the yoke of the British Empire. Five million Negroes fought for the abolition of slavery in the U.S.A. and Abraham Lincoln emphasized that without their aid the North would have been unable to achieve victory in the Civil War in 1861–1864. American literature has been created mainly by Negroes, either by Negro writers or Negro heroes in literary works. Art is to a great extent of Negro origin. American science is irredeemably indebted to Benjamin Domicker, John Nesteliger, and Ernst Just. Had Negro children been able in the past twenty-five years to have the same education as Soviet children, all human values would have been preserved.

UNITED STATES DEPARTMENT OF JUSTICE

FEDERAL BUREAU OF INVESTIGATION

Chicago 6, Illinois
November 18, 1959

CHICAGO COUNCIL OF AMERICAN-
SOVIET FRIENDSHIP
AFRO-AMERICAN HERITAGE ASSOCIATION

On November 12, 1959, [Bureau Deletion] who has furnished reliable information in the past, advised that the Chicago Council of American-Soviet Friendship (CCASF) and the Afro-American Heritage Association (AAHA) cosponsored a function in honor of the forty-second Anniversary of the Russian Revolution and the twenty-sixth anniversary of the founding of diplomatic relations between the United States and the U.S.S.R., said function being held on November 11, 1959, at 32 West Randolph Street, Chicago, Illinois. Source advised that the featured speakers at this function were Dr. W. E. B. Du Bois and Mitrofan P. Fedorin, a Soviet official from the U.S.S.R. Embassy, Washington, D.C.

[Bureau Deletion] advised that in addition to Dr. Du Bois and Mitrofan P. Fedorin, other individuals who spoke at this function were Mandel Terman, Chairman, CCASF; Shirley Graham, the wife of Dr. W. E. B. Du Bois; LeRoy Wolins, Secretary, CCASF, and Ishmael Flory, an official of the AAHA. Source also advised that Pearl Hart, a Chicago woman attorney, acted as chairman. [Bureau Deletion]

Concerning the speeches made by the above mentioned individuals at this function, [Bureau Deletion] advised that the topic of the address by Dr. W. E. B. Du Bois was "Co-existence, Colonialism, and Peace." [Bureau Deletion] advised that Dr. W. E. B. Du Bois spoke on a recent world tour he had taken [that] had included two trips to the Soviet Union and a visit to China, where he was feted by top government leaders on the occasion of his ninety-first birthday. Du Bois in his speech, noted that his trip to China of recent date was the first trip he had taken to that country since 1936. He said that on this recent trip he was within the borders of China for nine weeks and that everything he saw in that country fills him with admiration for the Chinese people. Du Bois claimed that the Chinese people, under the Chinese People's Republic, have made tremendous strides. He claimed that the industrialization of various industries and plants in China has brought great prosperity to the Chinese people. He said that the Chinese, in addition to organizing their industry, have also tremendously organized their schools. He stated that children in China and also in Russia, come first. He noted that children in China are not permitted to become a degenerate group. He also stated that they were not permitted to become subject to a dogmatic, decadent religion. He said this pertains to children in the Soviet Union, as well as in China, from infancy on. He noted that the discipline of the children in the school, particularly since it is not hindered by religious teaching, is such that the children's actions are closely controlled and they are not permitted to do as they please, such as they are in the United States. Du Bois stated that in spite of this closely controlled discipline taught in the schools and the homes in China, the Chinese children appear to be very contented. According to Du Bois, the excellent school systems that China and Russia have developed under the socialist system are such that they outstrip both Western Europe and the United States in their current teachings.

Dr. Du Bois, [Bureau Deletion] also commented on a health program [that] had been adopted in China. He compared it to the health program [that] England had adopted and [which] the Tories tried to do away with but were prevented from doing so by the people. Du Bois also claimed that the Chinese people—because of their present form of government—are advanced in their freedom and liberties. He stated that all the Chinese people look forward with confidence to the future. Du Bois noted that the Chinese people are giving their government wonderful cooperation. During his speech, Du Bois referred to Dr. Sun Yat Son as the great liberator of China. During his comments, he stated that Dr. Yat Son once asked the United States for help in solving the Chinese people's problems; however, the United States refused to help and consequently, Dr. Sun Yat Son turned to Russia for help. Du Bois stated that the Russians sent technicians to the assistance of Dr. Sun Yat Son and that this act by Russia was the beginning of communism and socialism in China. Dr. Sun Yat Son, according to Du Bois, with the help of Russia, drove out of China the Western Colonial Masters and the Chinese War Lords. Du Bois concluded by noting that China, as a nation, is changing history. He stated that China is a miracle land and that so long as the United States ignores China, China will ignore the United States. He stated that at the present time, Soviet Russia and other socialist people are the only ones who will help China. He concluded by saying that people everywhere in the world, who are under the communist banner, including China, have no regrets and no fears. [Bureau Deletion]

In addition to the above mentioned featured speakers [Bureau Deletion] Shirley Graham, Dr. W. E. B. Du Bois's wife, made a short talk in which she commented upon the role of women in Chinese life as it is lived today. In her talk, Shirley Graham stated that she had returned from China and Russia, "a new born woman." She stated that her trip to China and Russia was one of friendship and peace. She stated that she and her husband had traveled in excess of 7,000 miles within China. She said that her eyes were opened by this trip and that she and her husband found Chinese people to be the most friendly people in the world. She also stated that [the] Chinese people they had met could not do enough for them. She noted that her husband had been received by the heads of the Chinese government at a reception held for him in Peking, China, in honor of his ninety-first birthday. She stated that at this reception, both she and her husband received a tremendous ovation. Concerning the role of women in China, Shirley Graham stated that Chinese women have a very important role in China. She stated as an example of their importance that the Minister of Health in China is a woman as is the Minister of Justice. Shirley Graham stated to the audience that American women, in order to compete with their Chinese equivalent, must get together and work for peace and friendship and freedom and liberty. She said that women in the United States must also get into politics and start a real political program for women. She stated that in order to do this, women will have to start in the home. According to source, Shirley Graham received the greatest ovation when she spoke of the organization of women in the United States for political purposes.

[Bureau Deletion]

Following are excerpts from reports on the subject's activities in New York City in 1960.

On February 19, 1960, [Bureau Deletion] furnished the following information, which was stated by Du Bois, in part, on that date at Carnegie Hall, New York City, during the celebration of the thirty-sixth anniversary of "The Worker" and Negro History Week:

". . . but it becomes clearer and clearer today that communist lands are doing the job of public welfare, full employment, education and care of the needy best. They are not doing it perfectly, but infinitely better than we are. . . .

". . . After being imprisoned in the United States for ten years, I made recently a year's journey around the world. I did not see everything. I may have been in part deceived. But I saw enough in this and previous trips to be convinced that the Soviet Union and China; Czechoslovakia, Poland and East Germany; Hungary and the Balkans have become nations where in the last quarter century the mass of people have arisen from the dust and dirt and today stand on the threshold of a rapidly rising civilization. There is no use of suppressing the truth. The world is amazingly moving toward communism.

". . . For eleven months while abroad, I was treated as a normal human being despite my brown skin. I met a sympathy and respect [that] never before in my life have I known. This influenced me, and prejudiced me. Of course it did. But it did more than that. I saw millions of people content, with happy, clean, healthy children, full of hope in the future and of faith in each other; working, sweating, and singing; and with them I believe again in this world. . . .

". . . Lying about China won't build a decent capitalism in America and frightening children about the Soviet Union won't beat the Russians to the back of the moon. . . .

". . . Today the rich and powerful rulers of America divide themselves into Republicans and Democrats in order to raise ten million dollars to buy the next election and prevent you from having a third party to vote for, or to stop war, theft, and murder by your votes.

"You have here tonight the newspaper of a third party, *The Worker,* organ of the Communist party. . . .

". . . If you want to know about communism read this paper. If you know a better party than the Communist, vote for it. . . .

". . . The communists read your papers and know you. That is the reason they are communists. But you should realize why communism exists. Realize the disgraceful trial [that] imprisoned communists as criminals was the lowest depth of justice in America, save two: the crucifixion of the Rosenbergs and germ warfare in China. If you believe in communism, build without apology a party on a platform of peace, national ownership of capital and the welfare of the state. If you want to be a socialist, stop quibbling over trifles. Decide what socialism is and dare to follow it. But do something. Act! Speak! Let us have freedom again in America, but freedom to serve and not to divide. Freedom to build and plan and not to destroy and imprison.

"Shall you complain who feeds the world, who clothes the world, who houses the world. Shall you complain who are the world or what the world may do. As from this hour if you use your power the world must follow you. Then rise as you never rose before, dare as you have never dared before, and show as you have never shown before justice done, believe and dare do." . . .

The Worker, April 24, 1960, page 15, column 1, contained an announcement [that] indicated that Dr. W. E. B. Du Bois was to speak at a memorial meeting for Louis E. Burnham on April 28, 1960. Page 5, column 4, revealed that Du Bois was listed as a speaker at the above meeting on April 28, 1960.

[Bureau Deletion]

The *National Guardian,* issue of June 20, 1960, page 5, columns 1–5, contained an article with a preface [that] revealed that the article was printed from the address given by Du Bois at the memorial meeting for the late Louis E. Burnham of the *Guardian* staff and advocated Du Bois's advice to younger people was "especially appropriate."

In advocating better health care and preventive medical care in the United States, Du Bois said in part:

". . . The provisions for vacation, treatment, operations, and hospitalization in the socialist and communist land of the world go beyond that of social medicine in Britain. It is here in America—one of the wealthiest nations in the world—that health is grievously neglected, that there are far too few nurses and physicians, and that the loss of life because of neglect and poverty is far greater than is necessary. . . . Then we can take a further step, which is so needed today, and try to build up in the United States health services paid for by the states from our taxes and servants of health trained and paid by the state which will bring social medicine to the United States; . . . We should try to bring to this nation something of the health services [that] can be found in the Soviet Union, in China, and in all socialist and communist states. . . .

" 'And by contagion of the sun we may catch at a spark from that primeval fire,

" 'And learn that we are better than our clay and equal to the peaks of our desire!'

The *National Guardian,* issue of May 23, 1960, page 3, contained an article attributed to the subject, in which the following was quoted in part:

"Daily lately, as I read the morning news I find myself asking if age is driving me a bit crazy or if I am living in a crazy nation. . . . Governments and rulers have always lied, but never with the quick, bland, easy assurance such as our transformation of a spying trip [that] failed into a weather exploration and then blaming the Soviet Union for 'propaganda'. . . . Today we learn that Turkey is not our spy base, but a 'bastion of freedom' where the NATO of the 'free world' dares not stay long enough to hear the President's welcome because Prime Minister Menderes is trying to outrun angry students threatening his life. . . .

". . . We are deliberately destroying history . . . but especially to twist and distort the world wars and the triumph of socialism. . . .

". . . The nation was led to believe that communism was a conspiracy of crime, and socialism its handmaid. We were told that the communist states were failures, their citizens serfs and prisoners seething with revolt; their women prostitutes and their education only 'brainwashing propaganda.' Many wanted to use our atom bomb immediately on Moscow but when we found the Soviets already had it we accused them of stealing it from us, as they were certainly too dumb to have invented it. . . .

". . . We continue to sneer at education and progress in the Soviet Union. . . . A few years later came Sputnik and the photographing of the back of the moon. We had to acknowledge the superiority of Soviet education, the progress of her science and the fact that her industrial development might soon equal or even outstrip ours. . . .

". . . Whether a Democrat or a Republican wins, it will be the same

gang. You will have no chance to vote for a meaningful third party. . . .
We must first demand the right to have a third party on the ballot. . . ."

Du Bois advocated a program to ". . . Forget the presidency. . . .
Concentrate on Senators and Congressmen, legislators and city coun-
cilmen and ward healers.

"Insist on a chance to vote for peace . . . for no family income above
$25,000 or below $5,000; for free education from kindergarten through
college; for housing on a nationwide scale; for training of all for the
work they can do insofar as such work is needed for the best interests
of all. Insist on discipline for this work. Allow no laborer to be paid
less than his product is worth; and let no employer take what he does
not make. Curb corporations by putting most of them under government ownership."

"Heal the sick as a privilege, not as a charity. Make private ownership of natural resources a crime . . . Calling this socialism, communism,
reformed capitalism, or holly rolly . . . Call it anything—but get it
done."
[Bureau Deletion]

The *National Guardian* issue of June 13, 1960, page 8, contained an
advertisement stating that a dramatic production of the highlights of
the first ninety-two years of Dr. William Edward Burghardt Du Bois's
"dauntless leadership," was to be produced by the Emergency Civil
Liberties Committee, 421 7th Avenue, New York City, at the Hotel
New Yorker, on June 15, 1960. . . .

*Following are excerpts from reports on the subject's activities re.
Ghana in 1960:*

The United States Department of State furnished the text of a speech
delivered by Du Bois in Accra, Ghana, on July 5, 1960, at a dinner
given in his honor by the Ghana Academy of Learning.

Du Bois purported to assay three thousand years of African history
in fifteen minutes, and in so doing, gave his impression of world history
and the beginning of capitalism in which he stated in part, ". . . But in
Europe after the industrial revolution capital goods were owned by
private persons who seized the land and with a stock of consumer goods
hired labor to use the tools and machines and make more goods. Thus
arose the private capitalist system contradicting and replacing primitive
communism. . . ."

In advocating freedom, independence, and unity for Africa, Du Bois said to the effect, freedom and independence in the modern world mean industry, the use and control of capital and it must be built upon this basis. Du Bois stated in part:

"... Here again Africa faces serious difficulties. The modern world has become divided into two parts, one part following the principles laid down by Karl Marx who saw that capital in private hands was doing infinite harm and proposed a socialism [that] in time would lead to communism—that is, the ownership of capital by the state, individual work distributed according to ability and income according to need. Opposing this was North America and Western Europe who had developed private capital to a tremendous degree and through it was dominating Eastern Europe, all of Asia, all of Africa, the Western Indies, Central and South America. ..."

NY 100-20789

Du Bois pointed out the need for Africa to obtain capital and stated in part:

"... On what terms can African states borrow this capital? There is a tendency for them to assume that the loan of this capital by Europe and North America is a matter of favor or of charity. This is not true. Western Europe and North America must sell the capital [that] they are accumulating or their whole economy will collapse. Moreover, they cannot continue to produce this capital under present conditions because that involves slavery and political control of colonies. It threatens world war!

"Borrowing capital is then, a matter of bargain. ..."

"... I am not arguing as to whether the leaders of independence and freedom on Africa be communists or capitalists, favoring Britain, France, or the United States on the one hand or the Soviet Union, Czechoslovakia, and China on the other. But I am interested in the question as to whether you are going to own your lands and materials, and control your own labor and be masters in your own house or whether the power is going to be exercised by foreigners; and that depends on how and from whom you borrow money. ..."

"... The capital which you borrow must have no strings. It must be loaned at low interest, it must include no domination of foreigners, it must involve no promise on your part to fight anybody; and the technical aid [that] is furnished must be furnished freely with democratic association of the workers sent here teaching Negro apprentices, and without building a separate social class of white skilled workers who will sit here in your own country in favored positions and tax and rule you as is the case in Rhodesia and other South African states and, until yesterday, in the Congo.

"If you can get machines and techniques from the Soviet Union at two percent and no strings attached, it would be crazy of you to borrow from the United States and Britain at four, five, or six percent with the resultant industry under their control and with them strutting as masters in your midst. You must remember that in the history of your own industry, right here in Ghana, you began with a communist state. You began with the chief and tribe owning accumulated capital and spending it for the interests of the whole tribe and not for a select few. That is the reason why your main industry, the raising of cocoa, is today dominated by the state in a system [that] is almost completely socialistic. Such other industry as you organize should also be under social control, medicine and insurance should be socialized. This is the future of the modern world; it is the modern world that you are trying to join, cooperate with, and eventually help lead.

"Thus may Africa live again as in the mighty past, through peace without force and violence."

The United States Department of State also furnished information [that] revealed that on July 8, 1960, Du Bois spoke at the West End Palladium, Accra, Ghana, in which he stated in part:

". . . You and the world must admit that in the exact science today, the Soviet Union leads mankind . . . In peace and plenty let Ghana join the Soviet Union and China and usher in the new world."

The *National Guardian,* issue of September 19, 1960, page 7, contained an article attributed to Du Bois from Accra, Ghana.

In speaking of his impression of the political and economic history and conditions in Ghana, Du Bois said in part:

". . . Ghana knows this foe is the threat of international investment, knows the best international monopolies, the trusts which seek to rule the world. It treats them with courtesy and yet begins to invite Soviet investment, recognizes the People's Republic of China and announces its aim to Pan-African socialism. . . ."

The *National Guardian,* issue of September 26, 1960, page 5, columns 2–4, contained an article attributed to Du Bois from Florence, Italy. In the article Du Bois stated in part:

"In 1960 the bubble burst and black Congo demanded not only a share in government but independence. . . .

"Ghana, the Soviet Union, and China must furnish capital and technical skill to keep the great wheels of Congo enterprise running; but running not for profit of white skilled labor and the idle rich, but for the starving, sick, and ignorant Africans. . . .''

"But the truth is winning; socialism is spreading, communism is becoming more and more possible to increasing millions: 'Fear not, O little flock, the foe, that madly seeks thine overthrow, fear not its rage and power!'

"Finally down toward Lands End, on the Cape of Evil Omen, are some three million whites in the Union of South Africa, the Rhodesians and Southwest Africa, who are determined to rule twenty or more million blacks as slaves and servants. They say this brazenly and openly in the face of the world and none do anything, save black Africa. And here the next world war will begin unless the world wakes up and wakes soon.''

The following writings by the subject were cited by the Bureau as "Evidence of Pro-Communist Sympathy" in 1961.

The *Evening News,* October 11, 1961, at Accra, Ghana, Africa, carried an article by W. E. B. Du Bois entitled "Ghana [sic] Need Discipline and Faith in Their Future." The following is excerpted from this article:

"Science is a stern unyielding master. It brooks no rival neither [sic] in church nor state, neither in wish nor dream. It seeks eternal and immutable truth attained slowly and painfully with infinite toil and endless sacrifice. Either it guides civilization or civilization dies. You must master science. You must obey its laws. You and the world must admit that in exact science today, the Soviet Union leads mankind: not in war but in [the] search for truth.

"Year before last, in 1958, I took a marvelous journey. Already before that I had traveled widely. Beginning as a young man I had traversed the United States, North, East, West, and South. I had seen Canada and Mexico. Then I made in the next sixty-six years fifteen trips to Europe.

"I also saw something of China and Japan and a bit of Africa. In these years I saw mostly what I already knew by reading and listening. I was European-cultured. I believed in the unfortunate necessity of wealth and poverty, in the inevitability of disease, in the natural backwardness of Asia and Africa. Of course, this belief was not complete. My faith in Europe was not absolute. But on the whole I thought I was living in a world about as good as humanly possible.

"Then I spent a sudden year abroad mostly in a new world of socialism: in the Soviet Union, in China, in Czechoslovakia and East Germany, in Sweden. And then back to a new view of France, Holland,
and England. I returned to America a man renewed in faith and spirit
reborn in vision, revived in strength.

"What struck me in these socialist and communist countries was the
discipline under which the people were working. It was not slavery. It
was discipline born out of the conception of right and wrong, of respect
for the manners of former days of obedience to law, willingness to
sacrifice, and a belief in justice for all.

"There is a widely held belief that citizens of socialist and communist lands are prisoners and that prisoners of the state are slaves. On
the contrary, I have nowhere in the world seen such satisfied workers
as in the Soviet Union or such happy workers and healthy children as
in China. While the prisons of the United States are filled with discontent and despair, the prisons of Russia are schools [that] lead criminals
to citizenship and train them in trades with happiness in family life.

"I do not say that all the world will follow Russia or China, Czechoslovakia and East Germany, Hungary, Romania, Bulgaria; but I am
absolutely certain that the overwhelming trend of humanity today, is
towards socialism. India is a socialist country. In Scandinavia are socialist states; Britain resists socialism in vain. West Germany has intended
socialist institutions. Italy and France are owning and controlling capital. Even the United States is continually taking steps towards state
control of capital and ownership of natural resources; and all socialist
countries are gradually envisioning a complete communism of equal
men, each doing what he can do best, and receiving what he needs for
health and comfort and as free as the welfare of all men allows men
to be free. To this great end I want Africa to march."

The article concludes with the sentence "In peace and plenty let
Ghana join the Soviet Union and China and usher in the new world."
[Bureau Deletion] . . .

The Worker, November 26, 1961, on page 6, quoted the text of Du
Bois's letter of application for membership in the CP, USA. This letter
is quoted as follows:

TO GUS HALL,
Communist Party of the U.S.A.
New York, New York

On this first day of October, 1961, I am applying for admission to membership in the Communist party of the United States. I have been long and slow in coming to this conclusion, but at last my mind is settled.

In college I heard the name of Karl Marx, but read none of his works, nor heard them explained. At the University of Berlin, I heard much of those thinkers who had definitely answered the theories of Marx, but again we did not study what Marx himself had said. Nevertheless, I attended meetings of the Socialist party and considered myself a socialist.

On my return to America, I taught and studied for sixteen years. I explored the theory of socialism and studied the organized social life of American Negroes; but still I neither read nor heard much of Marxism. Then I came to New York as an official of the new N.A.A.C.P. and editor of *The Crisis* magazine. The N.A.A.C.P. was capitalist oriented [sic] and expected support from rich philanthropists.

But it had a strong socialist element in its leadership in persons like Mary Ovington, William English Walling, and Charles Edward Russell. Following their advice, I joined the Socialist party in 1911. I knew then nothing of practical socialist politics and in the campaign of 1912, I found myself unwilling to vote the socialist ticket, but advised Negroes to vote for Wilson. This was contrary to Socialist party rules and consequently I resigned from the Socialist party.

For the next twenty years I tried to develop a political way of life for myself and my people. I attacked the Democrats and Republicans for monopoly and disenfranchisement of Negroes; I attacked the socialists for trying to segregate Southern Negro members; I praised the racial attitudes of the communists, but opposed their tactics in the case of the Scottsboro boys and their advocacy of a Negro state. At the same time I began to study Karl Marx and the communists; I read *Das Kapital* and other communist literature; I hailed the Russian Revolution of 1917, but was puzzled at the contradictory news from Russia.

Finally in 1926, I began a new effort: I visited communist lands. I went to the Soviet Union in 1926, 1936, 1949, and 1959; I saw the nation develop. I visited East Germany, Czechoslovakia, and Poland. I spent ten weeks in China, traveling all over the land. Then, this summer, I rested a month in Romania.

I was early convinced that socialism was an excellent way of life, but I thought it might be reached by various methods. For Russia I was convinced she had chosen the only way open to her at the time. I saw Scandinavia choosing a different method, halfway between socialism and capitalism. In the United States I saw consumer cooperation as a path from capitalism to socialism, while England, France, and Germany developed in the same direction in their own way. After the depression and the World War I, I was disillusioned. The progressive movement in the United States failed. The cold war started. Capitalism called communism a crime.

Today I have reached a firm conclusion:

Capitalism cannot reform itself; it is doomed to self-destruction. No universal selfishness can bring social good to all.

Communism—the effort to give all men what they need and to ask of each the best they can contribute—this is the only way of human life. It is a difficult and hard end to reach—it has and will make mistakes, but today it marches triumphantly on in education and science, in home and food, with increased freedom of thought and deliverance from dogma. In the end communism will triumph. I want to help to bring that day.

The path of the American Communist party is clear: It will provide the United States with a real third party and thus restore democracy to this land. It will call for:

1. Public ownership of natural resources and of all capital
2. Public control of transportation and communication
3. Abolition of poverty and limitation of personal income
4. No exploitation of labor
5. Social medicine, with hospitalization and care of the old
6. Free education for all
7. Training for jobs and jobs for all
8. Discipline for growth and reform
9. Freedom under law
10. No dogmatic religion

These aims are not crimes. They are practiced increasingly over the world. No nation can call itself free [that] does not allow its citizens to work for these ends.

W. E. B. Du Bois

Memorandum

TO: [Bureau Deletion]   DATE: November 17, 1961

FROM: [Bureau Deletion]

SUBJECT: WILLIAM E. B. DU BOIS
           SECURITY MATTER-C

Subject is a ninety-three-year-old Negro anthropologist, author and educator whose name is included in the Security Index. Du Bois, who has had a long history of association with communist front groups [Bureau Deletion]

BACKGROUND:

Du Bois was born February 23, 1868, age ninety-three in Massachusetts, was educated at Fisk and Harvard Universities, receiving a Doctor of Philosophy degree from Harvard in 1895. He was co-founder in 1909 of the National Association for the Advancement of Colored People (NAACP) and was also founder of the Pan-African Congress. In 1934 he resigned his position as editor of the NAACP publication *Crisis* [sic] and ceased his activities with that organization. In his later years he associated with many communist front groups; he has testified that he has been associated with the Council on African Affairs, the American Peace Crusade, the National Council of American-Soviet Friendship, and American Committee for Protection of Foreign Born, all of which have been designated pursuant to Executive Order 10450. He was awarded in 1959 an International Lenin Peace Prize for 1958 by the Soviet Union at which time he was quoted in an article in the May 4, 1959, issue of the *New York Times* as stating "I have never been a member of the Communist party . . . but I think communism is the best system for all countries after this trip. . . ."

Du Bois is considered by many as the father of "Pan-Africanism" and is held in high regard by many Africans. He attended the inauguration of the new government of Ghana in 1960 as an official guest of President Kwame Nkrumah. Also during 1960 he was invited to attend the inauguration of the first government of Nigeria as a guest of the

Nigerian Government. He is presently visiting Ghana, having arrived October 11, 1961, where he is engaged in the preparation and publication of an Encyclopedia Africans, a study of Africa's peoples and history and culture, the plan of which was originally conceived by him in 1909.
[Bureau Deletion]

MEDGAR EVERS

(1925–1963)

Born the third of four children on a small farm in Decatur, Mississippi, Medgar Evers learned the value of education early on. He walked twelve miles each way to attend a one-room school in Newton, and after military service in World War II enrolled at Alcorn Agricultural and Mechanical College. With his brother, Charles, he attempted to register to vote and saw his family receive death threats in response. He joined the National Association for the Advancement of Colored People in 1952 and within two years earned a position as Mississippi field secretary, spending the remaining nineteen years of his life working tirelessly for civil rights.

Evers's courage and willingness to speak his mind made him one of Mississippi's most controversial figures. He called for the immediate implementation of the Supreme Court's ruling in *Brown v. Board of Education* (1954) and endorsed the Montgomery, Alabama, bus boycott that began in December of the following year. In the early 1960s, he counseled James Meredith as he prepared to challenge segregation at the University of Mississippi and worked closely with Justice Department attorneys John Doar and Robert Owen as they prepared voting rights lawsuits against various county registrars. Having marched with SNCC in Greenwood and observed the Birmingham demonstrations, Evers was somewhat torn between the NAACP strategies of legal action and low-key boycotts against selected companies and the new direct action protests. In spring 1963 he found himself leading the latter after Jackson Mayor Allen Thompson backed out of an agreement to desegregate downtown Jackson restaurants, department stores, and other businesses.

The Jackson movement began not with Evers but four students and a white professor at Tougaloo College who staged a sit-in at the Woolworth's lunch counter. With Birmingham as the students' model, mass demonstrations and marches quickly followed and by June 1 nearly seven hundred protesters had been arrested—including Evers and NAACP executive secretary Roy Wilkins, who had flown in from New York for that exact purpose. They were pulled off a picket line outside Woolworth's and stuffed into a police wagon. For Wilkins, it was his first arrest in some thirty years.

There would be no children's miracle or any other kind of miracle in Jackson as there was in Birmingham. By June 11 all but nine of the demonstrators were out of jail and the movement had lost much of its momentum. Evers watched President John F. Kennedy's historic civil rights address that evening during a dispirited strategy session and drove home shortly after midnight. His wife and three children were watching television when the Oldsmobile pulled into the driveway of the family home. Mrs. Evers had promised the two oldest that they could discuss the president's speech with their father, but a single rifle shot ended that hope. Evers was shot to death in his own driveway. "[He] went to a lonely death, as he had feared he would," James Wechsler of the *New York Post* wrote, "while the G-men slept."

FBI agents had in fact been active in Jackson for some time, covering the picketing of Capital Street stores and shops and now sending note takers out to the funeral home. Everyone expected a riot and one nearly broke out—averted not by the bureau but by John Doar. Stepping between a line of angry blacks hurling rocks and bottles and a line of city police and state troopers armed with shotguns, carbines, and tear gas (and with a corps of German shepherds and their handlers nearby), Doar spoke calmly and the tension broke.

Meanwhile, the FBI investigated the killing on the grounds that the murderer or murderers had conspired to deprive Evers of his civil rights. Ballistic and fingerprint evidence helped identify a new Golden Hawk telescopic site found in a vacant lot near the thicket where the sniper and his 30.06 had waited. Special agents traced the scope to a Greenwood fertilizer salesman, Byron De La Beckwith, who wondered "why the world was in the hands of the communists." Arrested by the FBI and turned over to the Jackson police on June 22, eleven days after Evers was buried with full military honors at Arlington Cemetery, he faced two murder trials. Both ended in mistrials. Maryanne Volters's thoughtful article, "The Haunting of the New South," for *Esquire* (July 1991), revolves around a third attempt to prosecute Byron De La Beckwith for the murder. She is also working on a book.

Evers's widow and brother both wrote memoirs. Myrlie Evers, with

William Peters, wrote *For Us, The Living* (1967); and Charles Evers wrote *Evers* (1971). (Charles succeeded Medgar as NAACP field secretary in Mississippi and went on to be elected mayor of Fayette.) John R. Salter, Jr., wrote *Jackson, Mississippi: An American Chronicle of Struggle and Schism* (1979), which provides a firsthand account of the Jackson movement.

FEDERAL BUREAU OF INVESTIGATION

Reporting Office: New Orleans
Office of Origin: New Orleans
Date: 3/31/61
Investigative Period: 3/29–3/31/61
Report Made By: SA [Bureau Deletion]
Title of Case: "CHANGED", UNKNOWN SUBJECTS, Officers, Jackson, Miss. Police Department; [Bureau Deletion]—VICTIM; [Bureau Deletion] VICTIM; MEDGAR WILEY EVERS—VICTIM; [Bureau Deletion]—VICTIM; [Bureau Deletion]—VICTIM
Character of Case: Civil Rights

The title of this case is being changed to include Medgar Wiley Evers as a victim and to add the correct name of [Bureau Deletion]

REFERENCES:
Bureau telephone call to new Orleans, 3/29/61.
New Orleans teletype to Bureau, 3/30/61, entitled, "NEGRO STUDENT SIT-IN ATTEMPT, JACKSON MUNICIPAL LIBRARY, WHITE BRANCH, JACKSON, MISS., 3/27/61; RACIAL MATTERS"
New Orleans teletype to Bureau dated 3/30/61.

DETAILS:
This limited investigation was instituted on the basis of a request made of the Federal Bureau of Investigation by Mr. John Doar, Acting Assistant Attorney General, Civil Rights Division, United States Department of Justice.

Medgar Evers, [of] Jackson, Mississippi, a representative of the National Association for the Advancement of Colored People (NAACP), informed the Department on March 29, 1961, that fifty persons had been demonstrating in Jackson that day in connection with the arrest of nine students for a sit-in at the public library in Jackson and that they had been beaten by the police.

Mr. Medgar Wiley Evers, Field Secretary, National Association for the Advancement of Colored People, 2332 Guynes Street, was interviewed on March 29, 1961, and furnished the following signed statement:

"Jackson, Miss.

"March 29, 1961

"I, Medgar W. Evers, make the following free and voluntary statement to [Bureau Deletion] and [Bureau Deletion] who have identified themselves to me as Special Agents of the Federal Bureau of Investigation. No threats or promises of any kind were made me to induce me to make this statement and I have been advised that it may be used in a court of law.

"I am Field Secretary for the National Association for the Advancement of Colored People for the State of Mississippi and live in Jackson, Mississippi.

"At about 3:25 P.M. March 29, 1961, I parked my car on a commercial parking lot just west of the Jackson Mississippi Municipal Court Building and Police Station. I was accompanied by [Bureau Deletion] for the southwest United States who lives in [Bureau Deletion] and who was in Jackson on business. A [Bureau Deletion] who works for [Bureau Deletion] was also with me. We had come to observe the trial of the nine students of Tougaloo Southern Christian College who were being tried in the Jackson Municipal Court in connection with a sit-in at the Jackson Municipal Library on N. State Street on March 27, 1961.

"Prior to parking the car I had let [Bureau Deletion] and [Bureau Deletion] out at the entrance to the parking lot and parked my car alone.

"After parking I walked toward the Pascagoula Street entrance of the lot and passed in view of the Jackson Police Station, which is in the same building as the Municipal Court.

"As I was walking I saw three uniformed officers of the Jackson police department, whom I cannot identify or describe, looking out a window at me and one of them remarked "There he is, we ought to kill him." I smiled, did not reply, and joined my friends at the parking lot entrance.

"We were told by a police officer, uniformed, of the Jackson police department, that we could not get in to the trial because the court room was filled and that we would have to go across the street to stand. This street is Pascagoula Street. We crossed the street and were told by the same officer, whom I would recognize if I saw him again, that we must stand behind the sidewalk on the North side of the street, which borders a parking lot.

"We obeyed these instructions and stood there for about ten minutes when two of the defendants crossed the street at S. West and Pascagoula. At this time there were about 100 or more Negroes in this area together and a larger number of whites were in other areas of the parking lot near Justice of the Peace Bell's office.

"At this time I would like to state that I parked my car in one parking lot as described and across the street there is another parking lot in the rear of the Mississippi Publishing Company building. The latter lot is where we were standing at this time.

"As the students crossed the street and walked toward the Municipal Court Building many of the Negroes applauded in a spontaneous recognition.

"At this point, which was at about 3:45 P.M. I heard an officer yell 'disperse them' and at this time two police dogs were used to disperse the Negroes while at the same time 'billy' clubs were being used. Three dogs were on long leashes held by officers who were wearing white shirts.

"At this time [Bureau Deletion] left us and I did not see him again during the day. [Bureau Deletion] and I were crossing S. West going toward Pearl Street when we became separated and I did not see her until about 35 minutes later at my office on Lynch St. As I was going towards Pearl Street I was struck once on the left rear part of my head with an object I assume was a revolver, by a white man in plain clothes. I do not know if he *were* [sic] an officer or not. I believe the object that struck me was a revolver because immediately after being struck I saw a snub-nose revolver, blue steel, approximately .38 caliber in his hand. He did not say anything to me. This blow did not knock me down and must have been a glancing blow. I did not say anything to him but kept on going as uniformed officers were hurrying the Negroes along away from the parking lot.

"I reached the corner of Pearl and S. West Street and as I turned west on the south side of Pearl Street I saw two uniformed officers chasing and striking Negroes indiscriminately with 'billy' clubs. I believe I recognized one of the men being struck as a Tougaloo student, but I cannot recall his name at this time. I do not know the officers.

"After the officers stopped chasing the young men they turned and headed back toward the Municipal Court Building, going east. As they approached me, one of them who was ahead of the others said, 'Get going, boy' and I replied that I was going. As I passed him he struck me across the back just above the waist with his 'billy' club. The other officer also struck me with his 'billy' club in the same general part of the back.

"As I was going west on Pearl Street, I met a [Bureau Deletion] who had been bitten by a police dog and whose coat I observed torn on the forearm of the left sleeve. He told me he had been bitten by a dog.

"At this point I was picked up by two friends, [Bureau Deletion] and a lady with them, whom I know, but whose name I cannot recall who took me to my office. [Bureau Deletion]

"Shortly after arriving at my office I was asked to come to [Bureau Deletion] Office on [Bureau Deletion]. Upon arriving there I was shown [Bureau Deletion] who was being treated by [Bureau Deletion] for lacerations of the head and bruises of the right shoulder and right arm. [Bureau Deletion] told me that he had been beaten on the arm and shoulder by the police, but he recalled he was struck on the head by a white man not in uniform. He said he had been beaten as the crowd was being dispersed. He told me he was refused entrance to the Municipal Court Building where he intended to attend the trial.

"While at [Bureau Deletion] office I asked him to examine me, which he did, and he said I was not seriously hurt. No cuts, bruises, or swellings were visible but the places where I was struck give me pain now.

"I have read this statement consisting of this page and two preceding pages and state that it is true to the best of my knowledge.

"/s/ Medgar W. Evers

"Witness:
"/s/ [Bureau Deletion] Special Agent, FBI, New Orleans, La., 3/29/61.
"/s/ [Bureau Deletion] Special Agent, FBI, New Orleans, La., 3/29/61."

In addition to the above information, Mr. Evers stated that he could offer no further identification of the parties referred to in his statement.

Mr. Evers stated that also he did not have any witnesses that he could name as having seen the attacks upon his person unless possibly [Bureau Deletion] had seen him. He said that [Bureau Deletion] was alongside him momentarily while he, Evers, was leaving the scene and [Bureau Deletion] was taking moving pictures of the action.

Evers said that while he did not know the names of the two officers who struck him with "billy" clubs, he felt that he would be able to recognize them if he saw them in uniform.

Mr. Evers, while [the] interview was in progress, rubbed the back of his head and commented that it was sore. He turned his head to demonstrate where he was struck; however, Agents observed no visible marks or swelling.

Evers also stated that all Negroes present in the area of the trial were dispersed by many police officers using "billy" clubs and two dogs, while whites in the same area were not molested. Mr. Evers said that while he could not furnish the names of witnesses to the above other than as named, he would be able to obtain names of other persons at the scene. He said neither [Bureau Deletion] nor [Bureau Deletion] reported injuries to themselves.

AIRTEL

TO: Director, FBI   DATE: June 11, 1963

FROM: SAC, New Orleans (44-new)

RE: UNKNOWN SUBJECTS;
           JACKSON, MISSISSIPPI POLICE
           OFFICERS, LICENSE [Bureau Deletion];
           MEDGAR EVERS—VICTIM
           CR

At 3:35 P.M., 6/11/63, Medgar Evers, Field Secretary, NAACP, telephonically advised that some time between 4:00 and 5:00 P.M., 6/8/63, he was almost hit by a Jackson, Mississippi, police car.

Evers said he was walking east on Lynch Street and started to cross Franklin Street. At the time, a Jackson, Mississippi, police car containing two officers was headed east on Lynch Street. This car had slowed down, stopped and was starting to back into Franklin Street, apparently to turn around. Evers said that when officers saw him across Franklin Street, the driver of the police car accelerated causing the speed of the car to increase and Evers had to jump back on the curb of Franklin Street to keep from being struck by the police vehicle. Evers said the officers laughed about this. According to Evers this police car bore license [Bureau Deletion]

Evers also advised that on 6/11/63 he was followed by police vehicles wherever he happened to go in Jackson, Miss.

Evers was informed the above information would be furnished to the Civil Rights Division of the U.S. Department of Justice.

No investigation being conducted. Closing report being submitted.

UNITED PRESS INTERNATIONAL
June 17, 1963

Washington, D.C. The body of slain integration leader Medgar Evers was met today by some 1,000 persons who gathered at Union Station today to escort the hearse through the streets of the capital to a funeral home.

The flag-draped coffin was loaded on a baggage cart at the train station and wheeled to the waiting hearse. Bystanders watched silently.

Later, they fell in behind the hearse to follow it on a 25-block procession to a funeral home in northwest Washington, D.C.

One woman made the sign of the cross as the baggage cart went by, but most of the onlookers just stared.

Clarence Mitchell, director of the Washington Bureau of the NAACP, said that Evers's wife would arrive in Washington tomorrow with her two children, Darryl and Denise.

Approximately 115 police flanked the crowd as it gathered for the procession. But the group was orderly and quiet.

On Wednesday, Evers, a veteran of World War II, will be buried in Arlington National Cemetery with full military honors.

TELETYPE

TO: DIRECTOR, FBI   DATE: APRIL 17, 1964

FROM: NEW ORLEANS

BYRON DE LA BECKWITH, AKA., MEDGAR EVERS/VICTIM, CR, RM.

RE NEW ORLEANS TEL CALLS TO BUREAU TODAY

AT ELEVEN FORTY AM TODAY BECKWITH JURY ADVISED HINDS COUNTY CIRCUIT JUDGE LEON HENDRICK THEY WERE HOPELESSLY DEADLOCKED AND UNABLE TO REACH A VERDICT. JUDGE HENDRICK DECLARED A MISTRIAL AND DISCHARGED THE JURY. CASE CONTINUED UNTIL MAY NEXT TERM OF HINDS COUNTY CIRCUIT COURT.

[BD]

UNITED PRESS INTERNATIONAL
April 17, 1964

Jackson, Miss.—A second mistrial was declared today in the case of Byron De La Beckwith, a white segregationist charged with the sniper slaying of Negro leader Medgar Evers.

The twelve-man all-white jury reported after ten hours deliberation [that] it was deadlocked and Circuit Judge Leon Hendrick declared a mistrial at 11:35 A.M CST (12:35 P.M. EST).

It was not immediately known whether Beckwith would be set free or ordered to stand trial for a third time.

There is nothing in Mississippi law to prevent Beckwith from being tried again. But there was speculation prior to the verdict that if another mistrial was declared in the case, the entire matter would be put in an inactive file.

UNITED PRESS INTERNATIONAL
April 17, 1964

Jackson, Miss.—Circuit Judge Leon Hendrick said today Byron De La Beckwith's case was being continued until the May term of court and a decision on a third murder trial for Beckwith would be determined later.

MARCUS GARVEY

(1887–1940)

A powerful, often spellbinding speaker, Marcus Garvey created the first mass movement of black Americans. Born on August 17, 1887, of unmixed African descent in St. Ann's Bay on Jamaica's northern coast, Garvey worked as a printer in Kingston and on newspapers in Port Limon and Colon, Panama, before leaving the Caribbean for London at the age of twenty-five. Influenced by the Egyptian nationalist Duse Mohammed Ali and Booker T. Washington's autobiographical *Up From Slavery* (1901), he returned to Jamaica in 1914 to organize the Universal Negro Improvement Association (UNIA). Arriving in New York on March 23, 1916, to open a Harlem branch of that organization, within two years he began publishing the *Negro World* as a vehicle for a nationalist philosophy of racial pride and unity. Thereafter, his movement achieved explosive growth with tens of thousands of members and dozens of branches chartered in the Americas and even Africa. In 1919, he launched the Black Star Steamship Line to demonstrate that black people could create their own economic opportunities. By late 1920, the Black Star Line had emerged as the focus of a back-to-Africa campaign.

Given the pressures of World War I and the race riots of the "Red Summer" of 1919, Garvey and his UNIA attracted the attention of the Justice Department's Bureau of Investigation and General Intelligence Division (GID) early on. J. Edgar Hoover, eight years Garvey's junior but already GID chief by 1919, led the government's charge. Having first decided that Garvey ought to be jailed, the future FBI director then searched for an appropriate crime. He hired four black men to work the case and sent one of them to infiltrate the UNIA and otherwise shadow "the Negro Moses" in Harlem. Among other strategies, Hoover

139

tried to prove Garvey an operative of the British and/or Canadian governments. He even looked into the possibility of a White Slave Traffic Act conviction. Finally, in 1922, Hoover's efforts paid off. The government secured an indictment on a charge of using the mails to defraud in raising money for the Black Star Steamship Line.

Garvey, serving as his own attorney, used the summer 1923 trial as a forum for his nationalist ideas. Neither judge nor jury were much impressed. Found guilty and sentenced to a five-year prison term, he served two of those years in the Atlanta Penitentiary before President Calvin Coolidge ordered his deportation in 1927 as an undesirable alien. Coolidge acted to rid the land of "a race martyr" and avoid a possible exposé of what even Attorney General John Sargent considered prosecutorial misconduct. By that time, Hoover had been FBI director for nearly three years. Outside of the infamous Palmer raids (for which he wished no credit), the Garvey case was Hoover's first big case and probably as important or more so than any other in the Coolidge administration's decision to give him the directorship.

Garvey spent the next eight years in Jamaica where he tried to build up the UNIA once more and recapture its glory days. He also formed the Jamaican People's party. In 1935, he moved to London where he kept writing, teaching, and organizing. But few attended his UNIA conventions and fewer still enrolled in the correspondence courses offered by his School of African Philosophy. Weakened by pneumonia, chronic asthma, and a stroke that left him badly paralyzed on the right side, he died in obscurity in London on June 10, 1940, following a second stroke.

Garvey's widow, Amy Jacques Garvey, compiled two volumes of his early writings, *Philosophy and Opinions of Marcus Garvey* (1923 and 1926); and Robert A. Hill has edited *The Marcus Garvey and Universal Negro Improvement Association Papers* (7 vols., 1983–1991). The best biography remains E. David Cronon's, *Black Moses* (1955), but Judith Stein's, *The World of Marcus Garvey: Race and Class in Modern Society* (1986) is also of great value.

Unidentified Newspaper
Undated Clipping

Marcus Garvey Indicted on Stock Fraud Charge
Head of Negro Ship Line and Three Associates Accused of Using Mails
in Swindle

Marcus Garvey, president of the Association for the Advancement of the Colored Race [sic], was indicted by the federal grand jury yesterday as head of the Black Star Line, Inc., together with Elie Garcia, George Tobias, and Orlando M. Thompson. The charge against them is similar to that on which Garvey was arrested several days ago—using the mail to defraud.

It is alleged that in a campaign to sell 200.00 shares of stock of $5 par value, prospective investors were informed in circulars sent by mail that the concern intended to buy one more steamship, in addition to an excursion boat, to be operated at a profit. This information is asserted to have been part of the scheme to defraud.

"It was represented," it is said in the indictment, "that a steamship larger than any which they had theretofore intended to secure and to be known as the *Phyllis* . . . to be taken over after inspection and used for passenger . . . between the United States and Africa, when in truth and in fact, no such steamship existed."

Mention is made also in the indictment of a scheme to raise money by a "dollar drive" for the purchase of a larger vessel in which workmen and materials were to be taken to Africa to build up the "great republic of Liberia" for Negroes.

FEDERAL BUREAU OF INVESTIGATION

Report made at: New York City
Date when made: 1/21/22
Period for which made: 1/18/22
Report made by: Mortimer J. Davis
Title: In re: Black Star Line, Inc., Marcus Garvey, et al.,
        Vio. Sec. 215, U.S.C.C., Using the Mails to Defraud.

FACTS DEVELOPED:

On this date Hubert H. Harrison brought Cyril Crichlow, #92 Ege Avenue, Jersey City, N.J., also #28 W. 44 St., New York City, to the Bureau office. Crichlow advises me that he is willing to testify to:

1. Conditions in Africa
2. Speeches delivered by Garvey in the U.S.
3. The purpose of Garvey's trip to the West Indies during 1921

Crichlow was for a long period Official Reporter of the U.N.I.A. In this capacity he traveled throughout the United States with Marcus Garvey, reporting stenographically his various speeches, many of which subsequently appeared in the *Negro World* verbatim. He is willing to testify to any of the speeches so reported, and believes he can produce the original notes of many.

During 1920, I believe, Crichlow was selected by the U.N.I.A. to head a delegation of its members, which made a trip to Liberia, Africa. Crichlow's findings there are embodied in several letters, photostats of which are in possession of this office. He is willing to testify as to the African situation. In general, he found that neither Garvey nor the U.N.I.A. had any standing or holdings in Liberia; that the Liberian government was antagonistic to Garvey's proposed colonization scheme; that climatic and economic conditions were such that this scheme would be impractical, and that he notified Garvey in writing and in person of these facts. It is of course well known that not only did Garvey suppress Crichlow's report, but in addition, continued to publicly misrepresent the facts after receiving it. Crichlow is now suing Garvey for $1300 back pay, which he claims is due him from the African trip.

Regarding Garvey's trip to the West Indies during 1921, Crichlow states that the former freely discussed it with him prior to leaving the country, and while they were both traveling around the U.S. visiting different divisions of the U.N.I.A. Garvey, states Crichlow, told him that things looked very bad financially for the Black Star Line at the time and that a crash was imminent. Therefore, Garvey is alleged to have said, he intended leaving the country so that should anything happen he could claim ignorance because of his absence. This is probably true, for I have received information from several sources during the past week that Garvey's defense in this case, so far as it refers to the phantom *Phyllis Wheatley* will be that all transactions regarding it took place during his absence from the country.

—O—

Harrison today submitted voluntarily the following memoranda:

"Mrs.—Parris, 117–119 West 142 St., one flight up, front, east side. Bought passage for Africa (for herself and family). Sold land in Yonkers and in St. Croix, V.I. Also sold household furniture in preparation for trip. Constant attendant at Liberty Hall. Sick of Garvey's lies and crookedness, but has pathetic regard for "welfare of movement" for which reason she is slightly inclined to rally round him until [those] on the inside can deal with him themselves. Rich in witness stand possibilities. I could coach you somewhat on line of questioning her.

"Capt. Joshua Cockburn, 201 W. 128 St. Very valuable person, from whom could be had the addresses of Edward Smith Green, former Secretary of Black Star Line, and Mr. Johnson, former passenger and traffic agent. All three 'have it in' for Garvey. Perhaps they would be more valuable for Dept. of Justice than for restricted limits of P.O. case. Their names might be passed on.

"Capt. Jones, of *Negro World*. If *privately examined*, could give name and address of man to whom passage to Africa on the phantom *Phyllis Wheatley* was sold as late as Dec. 6th, 1921, for $250. At any rate, he talked in office with many to whom such passageways sold in summer of 1921. He too, could be benevolently 'forced.'

"Cyril A. Crichlow, 92 Ege Ave. Jersey City. Eager to testify. Went to Liberia for Garvey in 1921. Can expose the whole swindle and prove that Garvey has no U.N.I.A. lands or concessions in Liberia and never had.

"In re: *Negro World* of Jan. 21, 1922, Garvey seeks to shift responsibility by pretending that he was not here when certain things were planned. But the series of 'book your passage' ads (now in the hands of Mr. Spewak of *New York World*) began as early as Jan. 1921 when Garvey was here, and ran uninterruptedly to Dec. 17th of the same year.

"If you look up *Negro World* for April and October 1921 you will find statements of ownership of paper (African Communities League). This was sworn to, and proves that there has been no transfer of ownership as alleged by Garvey, and Garcia, in print, to explain speculations and wastage [sic] of funds of Liberation Construction Loan (about $46,000) as payment for the *Negro World*.

"Harrison bought a bond of this loan [that] was advertised for months as a 'Liberation Loan.' In speeches printed in the *Negro World*, Garvey first conveys [the] impression that it was a loan *to* Liberia. Harrison paid in weekly installments of a dollar each, missing many weeks, and taking about twenty weeks to pay. So that during all that time he was under [the] impression first created by Garvey. Then, when he had paid, he received bond and noted that Liberia's name never occurred once on it, and the word 'Africa' only once, near the end. It had been transformed into a loan to the 'Parent Body of the U.N.I.A.' All the office employees were *forced* to buy bonds, even the poor typists [earning]

$12 and $15 a week. The money was simply taken from their pay envelope without any precedent explanation. So also in Harrison's case.

"Re African Construction Loan 'Bonds': Garcia's report made to Garvey on his return from Liberia in 1920 before first convention shows that Garvey knew the U.N.I.A. had no lands or concessions of any sort when he launched this swindle. Harrison was head of a delegation to go to Liberia and could be 'forced' to show in his testimony that Garvey had no plans whatever for getting concessions up to time set for sailing.

"In *New York World* of Sat. Jan. 14, 1921, Garvey said to Spewak that the figures showing that only about $6,000 out of $144,000 went to Liberia, were the lying [sic] work of an enemy. One of the *Negro World* issues for August shows Garvey's own official figures given by Chancellor Stewart and 'explained' in a two-column article by Garcia as Auditor Genl. The printing was forced by Noah D. Thompson, delegate from Los Angeles, Calif."

—O—

Copy of this report is being furnished to P.O. Inspector Williamson for his information.

FEDERAL BUREAU OF INVESTIGATION

Report made at: Baltimore, Md.
Date when made: Feb. 8, 1922
Period for which made: Feb. 1–3, 1922
Report made by: Harold Nathan
Title: MARCUS GARVEY—Universal Negro Improvement Association

FACTS DEVELOPED:
Upon instructions from agent in charge McKean, based upon telephonic advices received from the Bureau to the effect that the above mentioned subject contemplated making an address in this city on the evening of February 1, arrangements were made to secure the services of a competent and reliable Negro informant to cover any meeting or meetings at which subject might appear.

On the night of February 1, 1922, subject spoke at the Trinity Baptist Church (colored), this city, to an audience of approximately 200 persons. The pastor of this church, one Joseph Diggs, who is the head of the local branch of the Universal Negro Improvement Association, made a few introductory remarks, referring to the distinguished honor that was to be conferred upon the audience by the universally known and loved speaker of the evening in addressing them. . . .

Garvey was introduced as the president-general of the Universal Negro Improvement Association. His remarks, which consumed about an hour's time . . . made no attempt to secure members for any other organization or to sell stock or solicit subscriptions or contributions in any of his other enterprises. He did, however, appeal to his hearers to join the Universal Negro Improvement Association for their own benefit and for the benefit of Negroes in general throughout the world. He made a single reference to the Black Star Line, stating that the pride of the Black Star Line fleet was now at Hampton Roads, where she might be seen by all those who scoffed at the efforts of the Negro in this or any other enterprise. He referred to his recent arrest in New York, stating that he must return to New York on the night of the first, so as to appear in court on the morning of the following day, but that he would again conquer his enemies and reappear in Baltimore for a further address on the night of the second, as well as on the night of the third. He stated that the Negro race must win back Africa from the hands of the alien races who had stolen it from them; that the Negro race would predominate in Africa, ruling the entire continent, under a Negro president; that in order to conquer Africa, it will be necessary to "spill rivers of blood," but that he was ready and hoped that all his hearers possessed the same feeling—to serve their race as true patriots. He stated that one could die but once, and that he was ready to die on behalf of his race. . . . He spoke of the suffering of the Negroes throughout the world, stating that when a white child is born the world is ready and willing to receive it, but that the Negro child must struggle against all adverse conditions—prejudice, hate, malice, and envy; that a white child might someday become President of the United States, but not a Negro child; that, therefore, the true home of the Negro is in Africa, where a black child might be born, grow up, and go through life with every possible advantage, even that of becoming President of the African Continent; that there must be a greater spirit of self-sacrifice manifested on the part of all loyal Negroes; that he had always adopted the policy of going "fifty-fifty" with all of his race—if he had a dollar his hearers could have half of it—and that this is the spirit that must animate them all—they must be ready to share all they have with their brethren. He stated that not only the whites, who hated him for his efforts on behalf of the Negroes, but hypocritical and self-seeking Negroes as well had been combatting his efforts and ridiculing him; that the government had spent thousands of dollars in opposing him; that when he was arrested recently, there were Negro papers, as well as white, that could not find headlines big enough to announce to the world that Marcus Garvey had been arrested, but that he would conquer them all and live to lead the Negro race to victory. He stated that he had been arrested three times before, but that they could not conquer him, and he assured his hearers that he would be back from New York a free man the following evening to address them again. He spoke of the small cost of joining the Universal Negro Improvement Association, stating that the initiation fee was only 35 cents, and that all extras only amounted to one dollar. . . .

On the night of February 2, 1922, Garvey again spoke at the same place. . . . He stated that it was only a matter of time before the whites could drive the Negro out of this country . . . that white immigrants of all races were being received for the sole purpose of taking the place of the Negroes; that the Negro is not welcome anywhere. . . . He further stated that he did not blame England or the United States for not having colored representatives, colored Congressmen and colored Senators, but that he blamed the Negroes themselves; that they were not willing to stand up for their rights, consequently suffering all the indignities that were heaped upon them at all times and all places. . . . He repeated that the true home of the colored race is in Africa, and that in order to regain the Colored Fatherland, it would be necessary to "wade through blood." He spoke of the Negro whose only desire it was to secure from their race political power, adding that these were the Negroes who had always opposed him and the Universal Negro Improvement Association, because they knew that the latter organization aimed solely to benefit its members, and not to secure political power of any kind. He stated that four years ago the U.N.I.A. started with 13 members, and that they now have four million and over; that there are over four billion members of the black race throughout the world; that this great race of colored humanity is now going to demand fair treatment of this country and of all other countries, and they are going to get it. He referred to the rapid advancement of Japan in the last decade, stating that what the yellow race did the black race could also do; that the black race would soon join hands with the yellow race, possess warships and all the paraphernalia of war and make itself a real power in the world. He again appealed for increased membership in the U.N.I.A. A collection was taken up, netting twenty-eight dollars and some cents. . . .

The third and last address of subject was held at the same place on the night of February 3. There were some 300 present. There was the usual "theatrical" opening of the proceedings, the singing of "Onward Christian Soldiers," the grouping of the American and the supposed African flag, etc. Henrietta Winston Davis delivered a short, but fervent address along the lines of her address on the occasion of the first meeting on February 1. She spoke of the so-called Tulsa atrocities, stating that she had been there shortly afterwards and was greatly surprised to see the male members of her audience gradually disappearing. She inquired [as to] the reason for this withdrawal, and was informed that the Klu Klux Klan [sic] was holding a meeting that evening and that it was not safe for any Negro to be seen either in the hall or on the streets. She drew from the alleged incident that the Negro race was everywhere oppressed and subject to the ill-treatment and abuse of the white race in all parts of the country, and attributed these conditions to the fact that the Negroes had not asserted themselves racially and had no country or home that they could call their own. She appealed to her hearers to continue the struggle for better conditions here, but not to forget that their true home was in Africa and to uphold the great president-general of the U.N.I.A. in his efforts to advance the interests of this race, stating that he was a true leader of the race—a modern Toussaint L'Overture.... A coronet solo also followed. Marcus Garvey then spoke.

At the beginning, Garvey stated that his topic would be the "Laziness of the Negro," by which he meant to imply that the only thing that prevented the Negro race from attaining real leadership was their apparent inertia and lack of desire to free themselves from the disappointments by which they were enslaved. He stated that the Negroes of America were asleep and ... that he had been endeavoring to wake them up for some years, and in his efforts has encountered opposition not only from individuals, but from the Government of the United States; that the United States Department of Justice has a room in Washington loaded down with Marcus Garvey's speeches and literature; that they had been following him everywhere he went; that white men had occupied seats in the rear of churches and halls where he spoke in order to hear what he might say, and that Negroes had also been employed for this purpose; that everything that he has said had been collected by the Department of Justice, and ... that if they continue to do so they will not only need one room but that they will need a whole building in order to keep his speeches and addresses. He appealed to those present to redeem Africa, stating that they could never find a real home in this country. He stated that the Ku Klux Klan had been organized ostensibly to oppose the Jews, the Catholics and the Negroes, but that, in reality, they are not opposing the Catholics or the Jews—their real object is to crush the Negro. He stated that Africa, the home of the race, had been conquered by the whites for three hundred years, but that it would not take the Negro race that time to win it back;

that sooner or later the flag of the African Republic will wave from Cairo to Capetown. He attacked those of the Negro race who had opposed him, stating that they were but self-seeking politicians and jealous because he served the true interest of his race. He stated that . . . they are only the white man's lackey and the white man's slave, and would sell their race for a few dollars; that his intention is to have the race free not only from political oppression, but free from adverse economic conditions; that he wants the Negroes here to own and operate factories, banks, stores, steamship lines, railroad lines, and public utilities of all kinds, but that they must never forget that Africa is their real home and that the time was soon coming when they would have a country of their own, their own military forces and their own navy, and should any other nation ever oppose them, it would do so at its peril; they would then be respected throughout the world. . . . In less than one hundred years the world would know that he was right; that unless the Negroes of this country unite, they will be herded together like sheep and driven out; that every nation has its own flag, and the African Republic must have its flag, which will wave in the capital of Africa. . . .

FEDERAL BUREAU OF INVESTIGATION

Report made at: Buffalo, N.Y.
Date when made: 2/24/22
Period for which made: 2/19–24/22
Report made by: W. L. Buchanan
Title: MARCUS GARVEY, LADY HENRIETTA VINTON DAVIS/ UNIVERSAL NEGRO IMPROVEMENT ASSOCIATION

FACTS DEVELOPED:
   At Buffalo, N.Y.
   Information having been received that Marcus Garvey was to speak in Miller's Hall, 264 East Genesee Street, Buffalo, N.Y., on Sunday night, February 19th, pursuant to instructions Agent proceeded to this hall at 7:30 P.M. to cover same. There were about 750 Negroes present, and they seemed to be of the better class of Buffalo's colored people. An admission of 35 cents was charged. After being in the hall a short time, Agent heard voices from an adjoining hall, where the doors were closed, and the voices sounded as if military orders were being given. Agent opened the door and went into the next room, which was a large banquet hall, and there were a number of colored men and women drilling. They were all lined up; about twenty men were not in uniform; about fifteen women were

dressed in motor corps uniforms of dark color, and about thirty women were dressed in white representing the African Black Cross. Agent learned that the men are to receive uniforms later and will be known as the African Legion. At promptly 8 o'clock they marched into the large hall and formed a double line down through the center aisle to the stage, through which Marcus Garvey and Lady Henrietta Vinton Davis, clothed in flowing robes, with several attendants in uniform, marched to the stage.

In substance, [Garvey] spoke as follows:

He stated . . . that there were three types of people: white, yellow, and black; that recently the white race had become power crazy and almost challenged the power of God; that the yellow race was nearly the same, and both these races exchanged compliments; that the black race had been three hundred years in doubt and struggled along doing the bidding of the Caucasian race; that there were four hundred million colored people in the world, and what any white or yellow race had been able to accomplish the black race could also do . . . that while the colored people had been slaves in the past, the Negro himself was responsible for his present inferior position, and if they wished to go on being called apes, monkeys, missing links, and niggers, it was up to them, but the time had come when they should rise from slavery, both economic and industrial . . . powers; that the new Negro has discovered that he is a man, a lord of creation, recognizing no master except God; that the white race should not be blamed as long as the Negro submitted to his present treatment. . . . He stated [that] it was up to the Negro to improve his position socially and politically, because a race with nothing could expect nothing. . . . [He stated] further . . . that the world would only recognize the colored people when they had an African Commonwealth of their own . . . that Africa was the motherland of the Negro and they should take possession of it, and build the greatest empire on the face of the earth.

In connection with these remarks, Garvey referred to the return of the Jews to Palestine, of the nationalistic movement in India and Egypt, the Irish free state, and said if it was right for the Caucasians to rule and govern Europe, for the yellow races to rule and govern Asia, that it then was equally right and proper for the black race to rule and govern Africa. . . .

Lady Henrietta Vinton Davis addressed the meeting on Tuesday night, and after eulogizing Garvey talked along lines similar to Garvey's the night previous. She stated that Garvey was thirty-four years old; that he was born in St. Ann's parish, Jamaica, West Indies; that he came to New York about four and a half years ago, and after speaking on the streets of New York, where he commanded much attention, he organized the U.N.I.A., and African Communities League, in Lafayette Hall, in New

York City, beginning with thirteen members, and that the organization had extended around the world, and now had four million members. She is the National Organizer for the association, and is a very eloquent speaker. She also stated that there was an Egyptian in New York City at the present time whom Garvey met in Europe, and he was now working with the Universal Negro Improvement Association for the freedom of India.

FEDERAL BUREAU OF INVESTIGATION

Report made at: New York City
Date when made: 8/1/22
Period for which made: 7/22 to 29/22 incl.
Report made by: Andrew M. Battle
Title: IN RE: U.S. vs MARCUS GARVEY, et al.—VIOLATION SECTION 215, U.S.C.C.—USING MAILS TO DEFRAUD.

FACTS DEVELOPED AT NEW YORK:

July 22nd: Today I interviewed Mr. J. H. Morris, founder of the Merchant Tailor's Amusement and Industrial Association, who informed me that the Ku Klux Klan had sent for Garvey for the purpose of securing all information possible concerning the U.N.I.A., and that Garvey was informed by an official of the aforementioned secret organization that they have no intention whatsoever of harming the Negroes, but, to the contrary, they were trying to help them. Morris further stated that he was in sympathy with the Garvey movement and that he attends every meeting that Garvey addresses.

I next conversed with Rev. Garvey E. Stewart, Treasurer of the Black Star Line and of the U.N.I.A., who informed me that he expected to have a conference with McLenard on Monday night when he would be in a position to state whether it would be safe for him to remain in the United States after he resigned his office during the coming convention and that he intended to consult a lawyer on the matter. I also interviewed Mrs. M. W. Johnson of 100 West 136th St. [whom] I found was not at all in sympathy with Garvey's action in interviewing the officials of the Ku Klux Klan.

July 23rd: Today I attended a radical meeting held at 196 W. 131st St., which meeting was addressed by D. T. Tobias, Mrs. A. K. Lewis and Miss Grace Cambell. The first named in this address, stated that he supported Garvey in his controversy with Harris: that the latter was endeavoring to break up the Garvey movement so that he, Harris, could obtain more financial support, but that neither of the men showed good sense in referring to the matter of the history of the Negro in the newspapers. . . .

July 24th: Today I interviewed Mr. W. D. Lee, of 17 West 134th Street, who brought up the subject of the controversy between Harris and Garvey, saying that both of them were trying to swindle the Negroes, but that Garvey seemed to have the upper hand. . . .

July 25th: Today I again interviewed Mr. J. H. Morris of 139 W. 134th St. I joined the association [that] he is conducting in order that I might be able to meet with the younger element of the colored race in this city who are said to congregate in his place.

Dr. G. E. Stewart, Treasurer of the U.N.I.A., called on me today and stated that F. A. Toot, Secretary of the organization, was going to try to put a stop to Garvey in the coming convention and that he heard that Garvey would marry Amy Jacques sometime this week. . . .

July 27th: Today I interviewed F. A. Toot, Secretary of the U.N.I.A. and Black Star Line, who informed me that he was going to resign his office as Secretary, as was Gasher and Stewart; that as soon as he, Toot, leaves the organization he is going to England. He made mention of the fact that he knew more about the business of the concern than any other person and that he could not afford to remain in office after the Rev. Stewart resigned, as there would be danger for him to do so. He remarked that Garvey was not a clean man, nor is he honest; therefore, he, Toot, must get away.

FEDERAL BUREAU OF INVESTIGATION

Report made at: New York City
Date when made: 8/10/22
Period for which made: 8/6–7–8/22
Report made by: Andrew M. Battle
Title and character of case: IN RE: U.S. vs. MARCUS GARVEY— VIOLATION SEC. 215, U.S.C.C.—USING MAILS IN FURTHERANCE OR SCHEME TO DEFRAUD

FACTS DEVELOPED AT NEW YORK:

August 6th: Today I attended the meeting of the Friends of Negro Freedom in the hall at the corner of 131st St. and 7th Avenue where William Pickens was the chief speaker. He criticized Marcus Garvey and his movement very sharply and stated that no man who had good sense would listen to Garvey's advice to renounce his citizenship and leave the United States to go to Africa. He said that Garvey was a liar and a traitor and that Garvey would never go to Africa and if he could they would not let him land as Garvey had caused more trouble amongst other nations by his fool dreams than any other man of today. There were about 2500 people in the hall of which about half were Garvey followers and as a result there were constant interruptions, but no real trouble. At 8:00 P.M. I attended a meeting at Liberty Hall where William Ferris spoke and advised all those present to follow the leader Marcus Garvey. Marcus Garvey also spoke and predicted that there would be another war and that he was not prepared to say what side the Negro would be on, but that when the time came the Negro would be ready to strike the blow and get what they want. He also issued a warning to all those who are against the U.N.I.A. and stated that harm might come to them if they did not stop their criticism.

The attendance at the meetings seems to have fallen off and from all I have been able to gather through conversations with the various delegates, there seems to be considerable dissension amongst them and some feeling against Garvey because of the high-handed methods he has used in running the convention.

FEDERAL BUREAU OF INVESTIGATION

Report made at: New York City
Date when made: 8/18/22
Period for which made: 8/13–14–15–16/22
Report made by: Andrew M. Battle
Title and character of case: IN RE: U.S. vs. MARCUS GARVEY, VIOLATION SEC. 215—USING MAILS IN FURTHERANCE OF SCHEME TO DEFRAUD

FACTS DEVELOPED AT NEW YORK:

August 18th: Today I attended the convention at Liberty Hall where more than five thousand people were in attendance. Barrell of Cuba was one of the speakers who, among other things, stated that Marcus Garvey was referred to all over Cuba as "the [black] Moses." Garvey also spoke and in the course of his remarks said that if anyone ever saw a white man patting a Negro on the shoulder, he could be sure that the Negro was a traitor to his race and that that is what Professor William Pickens was having done to him. . . . G. E. Stewart called to see me and told me he would be out of the U.N.I.A. on Wednesday next.

A. F. Toot also said he would resign as soon as he read his report.

August 14th: ... At the evening session the subject for discussion was "Ways and Means to Restore the Black Star Line." One delegate said that nothing could be done until the report had been received and asked why a committee [that] had been sent out had not reported. Garvey, in discussing the Black Star Line, said, "What is two or three million dollars?; that will only shape the Negro race to guard against mistakes next time."

FEDERAL BUREAU OF INVESTIGATION

Instructions received from Special Agent in Charge, Edw. J. Brenna
Report made at: New York, N. Y.
Date when made: 3/1/1923
Period for which made: 2/11/1923
Report made by: Andrew M. Battle
Title and character of case: RE: U.S. vs. MARCUS GARVEY, ET AL: Violation Section #215 U.S.C.C. (Using the Mails to defraud.)

FACTS DEVELOPED AT NEW YORK, N.Y.

Continuing the above matter, tonight the writer attended a meeting of the U.N.I.A. at Liberty Hall. The attendance was about 2500, two thirds male and one third female. The speakers for the evening were Wm. Sherrill, R. L. Postum, and Marcus Garvey.

In Mr. Sherrill's address he pointed out facts to substantiate his suspicion that Wm. Pickens, Harry H. Pace, Robert S. Abbot, John H. Neil, Julian P. Coleman, Chandler Owens, Robert W. Bagnail, and George Harris were all traitors to the Negro race and that they were telling the white race that Garvey's teaching to the Negro was to hate the white race. The speaker further stated that if the Negroes did hate the white race, the white man had no one to blame but himself for his mistreatment of the Negro and that after the world war and even up to the present time, Garvey was showing the Negro the real facts as to the Negro's rights and that the above mentioned men were betraying this great man, Garvey, into the hands of his enemies.

The next speaker, was R. L. Postum, an officer of the U.N.I.A., but his talk was simply to corroborate the things pointed out by Mr. Sherrill.

Garvey then spoke and the first words he uttered were a request for $500, stating that he wanted this sum for real work in Liberia and saying that he could not tell the audience just what the work was because Pickens would go immediately and tell the white people.

Immediately after Garvey's talk a collection was taken up at the conclusion of which Garvey again spoke, and among other things, said that if the Negro intended to command respect he must first establish power and to have power he must get guns and plenty of ammunition, gas, submarines, and every other thing that is used to command respect by the white people and that after they got them, they must be used properly, as there is no other method whereby respect for the colored race can be more quickly enforced. He then asked a question, addressing the audience, "Why did those eight men write to the Government and complain to the Government about the Ku Klux Klan in the South, as it is common gossip that they got together and sent a complaint to Washington about me (Garvey) warning this race of mine what they might expect if they did not get together and do something for themselves, and I want everybody in this [room to attend] the meeting to be held at Carnegie Hall (on the 23rd of February this month) at which time we will tell the white people the aim and object of the U.N.I.A., and then, after my case is over, I will start on my tour of the world."

The writer observed that practically the entire audience was West Indian and everything said by the speakers caused an outburst of applause. There will be nightly meetings at Liberty Hall until the big meeting of February 23rd, at Carnegie Hall.

FEDERAL BUREAU OF INVESTIGATION

Report made at: New York, N.Y.
Date when made: 2/28/1923
Period for which made: 2/14/1923
Report made by: Andrew M. Battle
Title and character of case: RE: U.S. vs. MARCUS GARVEY, ET AL.: Violation Section #215 U.S.C.C. (Using the mail to defraud.)

FACTS DEVELOPED AT NEW YORK, N.Y.

The writer attended a meeting of the U.N.I.A. at Liberty Hall, 138th Street & Lenox Avenue, at 8:00 P.M. . . .

During Garvey's address he stated that the greatest enemy of the U.N.I.A. is the disloyal member who will tell outsiders of the inside workings, and the only thing that will enable the U.N.I.A. to get even with said members after they had once taken the oath is for the U.N.I.A.

to treat them like the Russians treated their soldiers, that is, to pull them up to a post and cut off their heads, and that any man once taking the oath of the U.N.I.A. and betraying same deserves just such punishment, and that all of those eight men who put their names to that letter could be made to look very foolish if the members of the U.N.I.A. would only stand together. Garvey further stated, ''And after I am finished with my case, I will start my promised trip around the world. I will go to Germany, Japan, and China and will arrange certain matters with them [that] will help us in the program to be adopted at the convention [that] will be held in Liberia in 1934. I will attend the League of Nations while I am on my trip. In fact, my trip around the world will be made for the purpose of making known our plans throughout the world, but before I start I will close down all business of the U.N.I.A., because I cannot trust some of the officers; as a matter of fact I would not trust one of them with a five cent piece as far as I could see them. . . .

FEDERAL BUREAU OF INVESTIGATION

Report made at: New York, N.Y.
Date when made: 3/1/23
Period for which made: 2/17/23
Report made by: Andrew M. Battle
Title and character of case: RE: U.S. vs MARCUS GARVEY, ET. AL.
Violation Section #215, U.S.C.C. (Using the mail to defraud)

FACTS DEVELOPED AT NEW YORK, N.Y.

Continuing in this matter, the writer interviewed Wm. Ferris, the editor of the *Negro World*. During the conversation, Ferris stated that he had been informed that Garvey stood a very good chance of winning his case until he had Dr. Eason killed, and that Virgil Williams, Counselor for the U.N.I.A., and for Garvey, was very much downhearted now that he knew Garvey was mixed up in this matter.

Ferris also stated that Garvey stood in well with a man close to the prosecuting attorney and that they had agreed to favor Garvey and let him go free, but since the killing of Dr. Eason the Government was using all its resources toward the conviction of Garvey, so Garvey did the wrong thing to pull that trick and since Dr. Eason's death, the U.N.I.A. has had to take all of the reserve money out of the treasury to pay up all the Liberty Loans, which amounted to $40,000. . . .

The writer then asked Ferris if he were sure that Garvey had had an agreement with an inside man close to the prosecuting attorney and if it were true that they were in favor of letting Garvey go free. Ferris answered, "Oh, yes, I am sure of that, but I do not know how Garvey will make out now; he may have some other strings he intends to pull."

FEDERAL BUREAU OF INVESTIGATION

Report made at: New York, N.Y.
Date when made: 2/28/23
Period for which made: 2/18/1923
Report made by: Andrew M. Battle
Title and character of case: RE: U. S. vs. MARCUS GARVEY, ET AL. Violation Section #215 U.S.C.C. (Using the mails to defraud.)

FACTS DEVELOPED AT NEW YORK, N.Y.

Continuing the above matter, Wm. Ferris, editor of the *Negro World* called on the writer and stated that Garvey had sent out 300 invitations to white people to attend the meeting of the U.N.I.A. to be held at Carnegie Hall on February 23rd, but did not invite any of the leading colored men or women because they were never in favor of the U.N.I.A.

Ferris also said that Garvey was foolish to become mixed up in the killing of Dr. Eason, especially at this time, because the colored people of this country did not lean any too strongly toward the U.N.I.A. movement and it was generally believed by them that the U.N.I.A. was mostly composed of West Indian non-citizens and without vote, and the Government was familiar with this condition, which opened a route for the reported acquaintance between Garvey and men high up in the prosecuting attorney's office and also permitted Garvey to arrange for the setting aside of his case, and by the spending of a little money they are able to get things pretty well fixed up in Garvey's favor, but after Garvey became foolish and had Dr. Eason killed, the colored people of America were only too willing to assist the prosecuting attorney in fulfilling his duty against the man (Garvey) responsible for Eason's death and the different statements made by Garvey before and after the death of Dr. Eason were sufficient to indict him before a grand jury and in the event they should get the third man hired to kill Eason, it would be "goodbye" to Garvey, as that third party would tell all he knew. . . .

Instructions received from Special Agent in Charge Edw. J. Brennan

FEDERAL BUREAU OF INVESTIGATION

Report made at: New York, N.Y.
Date when made: 3/1/1923
Period for which made: 2/19/1923
Report made by: Andrew M. Battle
Title and character of case: RE: U.S. vs. MARCUS GARVEY, ET AL. VIOLATION SEC. #215 U.S.C.C. (USING THE MAILS TO DEFRAUD)

FACTS DEVELOPED AT NEW YORK, N.Y.

Continuing the above matter, the writer again had a talk with the Rev. C. R. Duvalle, #12 West 130th Street, who was once an officer in the U.N.I.A., and who resigned because he found that Garvey was not playing fair with the people's money.

The writer urged Dr. Duvalle to go down to the prosecuting attorney as he was called to do and tell all about his (Duvalle) selling stock for the Black Star Line when he knew the stock was worth nothing. Dr. Duvalle said he would do so.

FEDERAL BUREAU OF INVESTIGATION

Report made at: New York, N.Y.
Date when made: 2-28-23
Period for which made: 2-23-23
Report made by: Andrew M. Battle
Title and character of case: RE: U. S. vs. MARCUS GARVEY, ET AL. Violation Section #215 U.S.C.C. (Using the mails to defraud.)

FACTS DEVELOPED AT NEW YORK, N.Y.

The writer attended a meeting held at Carnegie Hall, 154 West 57th Street, at 8:00 P.M. The speakers for the evening were William Ferris, editor of the *Negro World,* R. L. Postum, an officer of the U.N.I.A., Fred A. Toot, organizer for the U.N.I.A., William Sherrill titular leader and Assist. Third Pres. Gen., and Marcus Garvey, President General of the U.N.I.A.

Among other things, William Ferris said that Marcus Garvey is the greatest leader the world has ever seen.

William Sherrill in his address said that the only way for the black race to become a great nation is to have a Government of our own and to do that there must be sacrifice, blood must be shed, and the U.N.I.A. was prepared to go all the way. He said the U.N.I.A. is not a church that rises up over night, going out of existence the next day—the U.N.I.A. will never be blotted out. He said, "You may kill its leader, but that will not stop the U.N.I.A.—you may jail the head, but that will not stop the U.N.I.A., nothing will stop the U.N.I.A."

In Fred A. Toot's address he said that the U.N.I.A. will never stop its march, and that if every man would subscribe for [sic] the *Daily Times* and stand by the U.N.I.A., there would be no defeat for the U.N.I.A.

In Marcus Garvey's address, he said among other things, that he was prepared to go to jail, if necessary, and if he was sent to the chair and killed, he was prepared for that. He said, "No matter what they do to me, I am prepared to take it. The job I have undertaken is a man's job, and I am a man. Those scoundrels who [wrote] that letter to the Attorney General against me and the U.N.I.A. are salaried men. The U.N.I.A. men have worked six months without pay, but didn't give up, but let those knockers of the U.N.I.A. rail to get their check for two months and they will be looking for a new job. This country is not big enough for two Presidents, so we will have to get a place where we can have a President of our own. We are not against the white men—we have no ill will against the white man, the only thing we want is to have a fair chance the same that other men have, and if we have to die to get it, we will do that."

FEDERAL BUREAU OF INVESTIGATION

Report made at: New York, N.Y.
Date when made: 3/1/1923
Period for which made: 2/25/1923
Report made by: Andrew M. Battle
Title and character of case: RE: U. S. vs. MARCUS GARVEY, ET AL. Violation Section #215 U.S.C.C. (Using the mails to defraud.)

FACTS DEVELOPED AT NEW YORK, N.Y.

Continuing the above matter, this morning Sidney DeBourg called to see the writer, and during the conversation the writer asked why Garvey was so much against Dr. Eason. DeBourg said the prize had been offered on the first of last year to the individual who sold the most Black Star Line stock, and finally the contest was between Garvey and Eason.

Dr. Eason was awarded the prize and Garvey felt that that was too much of a hit for Eason and from that night on began to plan to get Dr. Eason out of the U.N.I.A.

This evening Agent attended a meeting held at Liberty Hall. . . .

Among other things Marcus Garvey said that he had learned to love William Jennings Bryan [sic] and the Klu Klux Klan, [sic] for he said Mr. Bryan [sic] was honest enough to come out and tell the world that this country was a white man's country and ever will be, and that the white man will ever rule supreme. Garvey further said that every white man in this country has the spirit of the Klu Klux Klan, [sic] and if they deny it, they are lying. He said, "The Negro will not be safe in America as long as there are two white men here. The white men can't follow me, and if you will follow Marcus Garvey, he will lead the black and the green to a country of our own. The U.N.I.A. must be ready for the unexpected to happen, and when it does happen, we will be ready to grasp the opportunity and hold fast to it. I want you all to know that I respect the Klu Klux Klan [sic] and their spirit, for they have warned the Negro that they will never let him hold a high office in this Government. It makes no difference what the white men say, I do not believe them."

R. L. Postum asked every member to do all they could in the collection as the U.N.I.A. had to get a new bond for Garvey on Monday morning.

FEDERAL BUREAU OF INVESTIGATION

Report made at: New York, N.Y.
Date when made: 2/28/1923
Period for which made: 2/24/1923
Report made by: Andrew M. Battle
Title and character of case: RE: U. S. vs. MARCUS GARVEY, ET AL. Violation Section #215 U.S.C.C. (Using the mails to defraud.)

FACTS DEVELOPED AT NEW YORK, N.Y.

The writer interviewed Arnold J. Ford, Music Director of the U.N.I.A., #38 W. 131st Street. The writer asked Ford what he thought about the statement made by Garvey at Carnegie Hall, to the effect that he was prepared to go to jail and to be killed if necessary. Ford said the statement was a dead giveaway for Garvey, as it only goes to show that Garvey has done enough to go to jail or be killed, the climax of his activities being the death of Dr. Eason. Ford said, "I will warn Mr. Garvey not to make such a statement again, as it plainly shows that Garvey has violated the law of this state and Government, as he knows that the arrest of Ramus will cause Garvey's imprisonment and death. They have told at New Orleans that Ramus did the killing, and Ramus came right back to Garvey after he shot Eason, then Garvey gave him the money to get away, which is all very bad for Garvey."

At 8:00 P.M. William Ferris, editor of the *Negro World* called #72 W. 131st Street to see me. Among other things he said that Ramus, the man who shot Dr. Eason in New Orleans, left New Orleans the day after the crime, came to New York, saw Mr. Garvey and Garvey gave him more money and told him to keep out of the way. Ramus then went to Philadelphia, saw counselor Norris about handling his case and then proceeded to Detroit, Mich. Ferris also said that . . . [Garvey] can't get out of being implicated in the death of Dr. Eason, because Garvey gave Ramus the money and a letter to go to New Orleans, instructing him to stay there until Eason was killed [and] . . . Ramus sent a telegram to Garvey stating that he had killed Eason." The writer then said to Ferris, "Is it not true that G. Amos Carter received the telegram." Ferris said that one or the other got the telegram, but anyway Garvey received the message. "From what I know there is no way for Garvey to get out of this charge of helping to kill Dr. Eason." "Ramus had sent Dr. Eason a letter warning him not to go to New Orleans, because Dr. Eason had blocked Garvey from ever speaking in New Orleans again. Eason told Garvey on the steps of the *Negro World* office that he had blocked him from ever doing business in New Orleans again."

FEDERAL BUREAU OF INVESTIGATION

Report made at: New York, N.Y.
Date when made: 3/1/1923
Period for which made: 2/28/1923
Report made by: Andrew M. Battle
Title and character of case: RE: U.S. vs. MARCUS GARVEY, ET AL. [sic] Violation Section #215, U.S.C.C. (Using the mails to defraud)

FACTS DEVELOPED AT NEW YORK, N.Y.

Continuing the above matter, the writer interviewed Arnold J. Ford, Music Director for the U.N.I.A.

Among other things Ford said that he had warned Garvey not to say in public again that he was ready to die or go to jail, as it was too much of a giveaway and in time would lead up to the death of Dr. Eason. Ford said that Garvey at one time planned to have him (Ford) killed, but one of Ford's friends told him of the plot. He said that Garvey would plot against anybody and really have them killed if he should become the least bit angry with them. The other two talked along the same lines.

The writer attended a meeting in Liberty Hall, 138th Street & Lenox Ave.

Marcus Garvey stated, among other things, that Abraham Lincoln set the Negroes free so they could die from starvation, but since they didn't die, the Socialist party found that the Negro could be used to great advantage for cheap labor and so keep the other class of white folks afraid to make strikes for higher wages, for fear the Negroes would be given their jobs. So the white man looked around and found Owens and Randolph and had them teach socialism, and the very moment when the Negroes rise up to the point of demanding social equality, the white man will pull himself away from the Negro entirely, then the Negro will be left alone to die in this country for the want of employment. So Owens and Randolph are digging a ditch for the Negro to fall in and die. He further said, ''I will advise all Negroes to stay out of all white men's unions and Socialist parties, for even Abraham Lincoln and his bunch didn't mean the Negro any good when he set the four million Negroes free, for the Government is made up of white men, and they want to keep the Negro down and will do that at any cost. The only thing for the Negro to do is get a country of his own— Liberia—where the red, black, and green can practice socialism itself.''

. . . The writer had another interview with Sidney DeBourg, and he said that Clifford S. Baum, A. Yearwood, Fred A. Toote [sic] and Mrs. V. H. Davis of the U.N.I.A. are all waiting for the Government to call them so they can [give] such evidence as will convict Marcus Garvey. The reason they do not come out in the open is that they are afraid that if they come out to [sic] soon, Garvey will put them all out of office before he is convicted, in which event they will not be reelected, because after the death of Garvey they expect to carry on the U.N.I.A.

Clifford S. Baum has the checks that Garvey drew for Ramus when he went to New Orleans for the purpose of killing Dr. Eason and Baum also has the check that Garvey gave to Ramus when he went to Detroit, (Amount, $60.00). Baum is ready to turn all information over to the Government, and Yearwood, if called on, will tell all about Garvey trying to go to Mexico, which he did not succeed in doing, as he was

watched to [sic] closely. De Bourg said that Yearwood was afraid to
tell what he knew as most of the Garveyites would not believe it and
they might try to put Yearwood out of the way.

FEDERAL BUREAU OF INVESTIGATION

Report made at: Washington, D.C.
Date when made: 4/21/23
Period for which made: 4/18/23
Report made by: A. L. Brent
Title and character of case: Re: Marcus Garvey, Mass Meeting

FACTS DEVELOPED AT WASHINGTON, D.C.

A Mass Meeting under the auspices of the Washington Chapter No.
153, National [sic] Negro Improvement Association was held at the
Lincoln Temple Church, 11th & R Streets, N. W., Wednesday evening,
April 18, 1923, at which Marcus Garvey, President General of the
U.N.I.A. and first Provisional President of Africa was the principal
speaker.

. . . Mr. Garvey at once took up the question of the redeeming of
Africa for the Negroes of the world, declaring that this is the only way
whereby Negroes will ever enjoy freedom in its real sense, as the restrictions placed on them in this country not only prevent them [from]
reaching the highest endeavor, but crush his spirit to such an extent
that future generations will suffer from the obstacles placed in the way
of the Negro of today.

Mr. Garvey then took up the matter of the European nations now
holding vast concessions in Africa, and claims that all of these nations
are now trying to increase their power and territory on the dark continent. He was particularly bitter against Belgium, and referred to the
alleged atrocities committed on the Congo during the reign of King
Leopold, the father of the present ruler of Belgium; he said that enough
Negroes could be recruited right here in Washington to throw the Bel-
gians out of Africa, and that the four hundred millions of Negroes
represented by the U.N.I.A. could free Africa entirely of the white
race. . . .

Mr. Garvey does not advocate an exodus of Negroes from the continent to Africa, as generally supposed—in fact he claims that he would
oppose such an idea, he is simply working to bring the Negro people
of the world together; cohesion and cooperation is the watchword for

the present. He said he would be glad to see professional men and women going to Africa as they could be training the natives while the work of cooperation is being carried on throughout the world. He also said that he hoped to be able to get the financial support of all Negroes at this time as the work to be carried on cannot be done without capital. . . .

FEDERAL BUREAU OF INVESTIGATION

Report made at: Cleveland, Ohio
Date when made: 5/2/23
Period for which made: 4/30/23
Report made by: R. C. NOVARIO
Title and character of case: MARCUS GARVEY, Alleged Negro Propagandist and Agitator

FACTS DEVELOPED AT CLEVELAND, OHIO
    Acting under instructions from Agent in Charge J. V. Ryan, this Agent attended the meeting at 2226 East 55th St., Eagles Hall, and about 800 Negro men and women were present.
    Subject entered the hall about 8:30 P.M. escorted by a uniformed body of about twenty-five men, headed by an American flag and a red, black and green flag, followed by about twenty women dressed as nurses with green cross [sic] on white caps and about twenty women, in white, composing a choir singing a church hymn.
    . . . Subject was next introduced as Provisional President of Africa and widely cheered and stated as follows: . . . that it was his purpose to organize all the Negroes in the world and reclaim Africa as . . . their own, where England owns the Kimberly Diamond mines and Belgium controls the rubber trees in Congo, and to build an empire for the Negroes in Africa, and that he teaches to love everybody who loves us, and to hate everybody who hates us, and that the white man assumed control of the world by using his head and the Negroes used their hands and feet—that is why they are down, and it is time that the Negro used his head and organized to get control of Africa, which is 100 times richer in resources than America. . . .
    Subject . . . blamed the Negroes for not using their brains; that 60 years ago a black man thought that all he had to do was obey the white man, but now the Negro represents a new school of thought, and history tells us that in the early ages the black man ruled the world, for in

Egypt, Ethiopia and Timbucktoo [sic], the black man was a master of arts and science and the white man lived as cannibals in caves, and that is when the black man had white slaves, and only a few months ago a tomb was resurrected in Egypt that has been buried for three thousand years and when they found King Tutankamen's body—what did they find? That King Tut's head looked like Marcus Garvey; that King Tut's nose looked like Marcus Garvey, [sic] and King Tut's lips looked like Marcus Garvey, [sic] which proves that the black man ruled Africa three thousand years ago. . . .

JOSEPH G. TUCKER   SPECIAL REPORT   JAN. 12, 1924

UNIVERSAL NEGRO IMPROVEMENT ASSOCIATION

At the Sunday meeting of the Universal Negro Improvement Association held at Liberty Hall on the 6th instant, the principal speaker, as usual, was Marcus Garvey. Garvey took as his subject, "The Struggle for Power," and aside from his customary attack on Du Bois of the National Association for the Advancement of Colored People, he sharply criticized Congressman Dyer, the father of the Dyer Anti-Lynching Bill, whom he charged with bad faith in that he, Mr. Dyer, knew that his Anti-Lynching Bill would never become a law and that he was merely playing politics in introducing it into Congress because a large percentage of his constituents in Missouri are Negroes.

Garvey followed his usual method in stirring up race hatred. In part of his speech he said:

"... I understand that Congressman Dyer was around his neighborhood in New York today, talking about his Dyer Anti-Lynching Bill, under the auspices of the National Association for the Advancement of Colored People. I want to say this frankly and openly, that any measure that would render assistance and protection to the Negro is heartily endorsed by the sacred world-wide membership of the U.N.I.A. We are for every measure that seeks to bestow benefit or advantage upon this race of ours, but we are against hypocrisy whether it comes from the public or any liar moving around trying to deceive the Negro race. Mr. Dyer knows that he does not mean it any more than the devil means to make it comfortable for a sinner when they come to their region. Mr. Dyer knows that he is but playing the trick his race has played for centuries—trying to introduce the same camouflage, the same hypocrisy, the same subterfuge as Livingston conveyed to Africa—and as the missionaries took to Africa, India, and to Asia. . . .

"In the very congressional district that he comes from—and that is not the heart of the South now, that is just St. Louis—a Negro cannot drink a soda in a white drug store, a Negro cannot eat a meal in a white restaurant. Mr. Dyer has come all the way to New York to tell us about the Dyer Anti-Lynching Bill and to prove how much he loves the colored folks. Brother, love commences at home. Charity begins at home. If he had no love for the Negroes of St. Louis, by God, he could have no love for the Negroes in Mississippi."

JOSEPH G. TUCKER   SPECIAL REPORT   JUNE 21, 1924

The Universal Negro Improvement Association, which is attempting to raise a fund of $2,000,000 for building its first colony in Liberia has so far received $3,402.62.

The Convention and General Fund of the Association for the 1924 Convention now totals $831.49. . . .

JOSEPH G. TUCKER   SPECIAL REPORT   JUNE 28, 1924

. . . The universal Negro Improvement Association and General Fund has reached the sum of $1,101.85. . . .

JOSEPH G. TUCKER   SPECIAL REPORT   JULY 26, 1924

UNIVERSAL NEGRO IMPROVEMENT ASSOCIATION

Marcus Garvey seems to have [been] very much disturbed by an article [that] appeared recently in [the] *Pittsburgh Carrier,* [sic] which stated that no arrangement had been made with the Liberian Government for the reception of members of the Universal Negro Improvement Association who proposed to colonize in that country. Touching upon the matter, Garvey, in the *Negro World,* issue of July 26th, says in part:
"SCATTERING 'DOCTORED' NEWS
"The latest effort of these spineless, cringing, dog-like, characterless, soulless, unscrupulous and raceless curs is to be circulating through the usual agency of currupt and policyless 'nigger newspapers' (that can

be bought for 50 cents, and if you refuse to make an offer to be blackmailed with malicious articles published therein from week to week) the 'cooked up', 'paid for', 'arranged', 'timed' and 'doctored' statement made by Ernest Lyons, Liberian Consul-General of Baltimore (where the Afro-American newspaper of [the] Murphy Brothers is published, against which the Universal Negro Improvement Association instituted a libel suit three weeks ago to the extent of one-half million dollars for their falsely publishing that the organization was to invade Liberia Government against the organization) not to vise [sic] the passports of Garveyites or members of the 'Garvey movement.' The wretches know well that there is no Garvey movement or Garveyites, but for the purpose of confusing the minds of people, and at the same time to escape libel damages, they mention the Garvey movement when they really mean the Universal Negro Improvement Association. The idiots do not seem to realize that the Universal Negro Improvement Association has more to lose than to gain in spending its money in helping to develop Liberia, which, no doubt, some of these scoundrels would like to exploit and rob."

"AN OFFER NOT REFUSED.

"Liberia has not refused the offer of the Universal Negro Improvement Association as yet to help in her industrial, cultural, and commercial development. On the contrary, the Universal Negro Improvement Association is chartered in the Republic of Liberia with a capital of one million dollars, and when the Liberian people state their opposition to the Universal Negro Improvement Association, then it will be time enough for us to pay any attention to the ravings of a few wicked, purchasable Negroes who would sell their race into hell for a few dollars. If the time should ever [come] when Liberia does not need the help of the Universal Negro Improvement Association, then we can find many more outlets for our energy and money to help our race, and the outlets are many and pressing."

JOSEPH G. TUCKER   SPECIAL REPORT   AUGUST 9, 1924

Marcus Garvey in the course of a speech made at a session of the Convention of the Universal Negro Improvement Association, touched upon his trial and had the following to say:

"I am here tonight not to blame the white man for what happened to me or the Universal Negro Improvement Association. It was the white man's duty to put Marcus Garvey in jail. It was the white man's duty to send Marcus Garvey to hell as quickly as he could get him there because it was a fight for existence between peoples. But the individual I cannot forget, the individual I cannot forgive, the individual I cannot understand—the Negro himself who constituted himself of [sic] a stumbling block in his own progress. It is natural that the white man would want to send Marcus Garvey to jail for five years to prevent Marcus Garvey leading four hundred million Negroes to a free redeemed Africa, because white men have their eyes on the goldfields, on the diamond fields, on the radium deposits, the iron deposits of Africa. A white jury and a white judge and a white prosecutor would not only send Marcus Garvey to Leavenworth, but to hell. And I don't blame them for doing it. I am reasonable to say that and feel it.

"If I were a white man, I would send everything to hell that did not look like me, that stood in the path of my progress, and since I am not Chinese, since I am not Japanese, since I am not Turk, I am going to send everything to hell that stands in the way of four hundred million Negroes. (Applause).

"I was in jail last August. I am ready to go back to jail or hell for the principles of the Universal Negro Improvement Association. (Applause). Some men make a big noise about jail. Every time they write about the Universal Negro Improvement Association they say Marcus Garvey was sentenced to jail, and so on. Now, Mr. Newspaperman, let jail go to hell. Now you tell the whole world that Marcus Garvey does not give a damn about jail, when it comes to the emancipation of four hundred million Negroes."

FANNY LOU HAMER

(1917–1977)

Fanny Lou Hamer was the product of her own courage and the Student Nonviolent Coordinating Committee (SNCC) push to develop grass-roots leadership in the Mississippi Delta. Born the youngest of Jim and Lou Ella Townsend's twenty children on October 6, 1917, she moved with her family at the age of two from Montgomery County to Sunflower County, and in 1944 married Perry Hamer, a tractor driver on the W.D. Marlow plantation. By then, she had been chopping and picking cotton for twenty-one years. For the next eighteen, she kept time and records for Marlow—until three SNCC voter-registration workers arrived in Sunflower County in 1962 and convinced her that she had as much of a right to vote as any white man or woman. When she went to the county courthouse in Indianola and tried to put her name on the voter rolls, however, punishment was immediate and nearly fatal. Arrested and evicted from the shack that had been her home since World War II, Hamer fled Mississippi after gunmen fired shots into the Ruleville house of the friend who had put her up. She came home after a few weeks to work as a SNCC field secretary and emerged as perhaps the most beloved movement activist in the state. Deeply religious and with a rousing, gospel-style singing voice, she opened countless voter-registration meetings with "This Little Light of Mine."

Hamer had no confidence in J. Edgar Hoover's FBI. When the SNCC pressed for an investigation of the arrest, eviction, and shooting, bureau agents said nothing could be done. When another arrest followed on June 9, 1963, in Winona, Mississippi, the FBI pursued this violation of Hamer's civil rights more aggressively (if only in response to extenuating circumstances and pressure from Attorney General Robert F. Kennedy). But no matter how proper the investigative reports looked, Hamer's firsthand ob-

168

servations indicated where the bureau's heart lay. "I just don't *trust* 'em," she said after her jailhouse interview with an FBI agent. "He said, 'Well we would like to talk to you,' and I said, 'Well, I just can't do it.' You see, I didn't know whether if I said what had happened to me then he could tell the jailer, and I just couldn't do it—I just *couldn't*! But we [sure] wanted—if we could have just seen anybody.... I reckon now God is the only refuge we have because there wasn't nobody there from the Justice Department, nobody there to say *nuthin'*—just the Negro out by theirself."

That Winona incident began when Hamer and five companions were returning from a workshop in South Carolina and their bus pulled in for a rest stop. While Hamer remained on the bus, June Johnson, James West, and Annell Ponder went into the restaurant and sat at the whites-only lunch counter. Euvester Simpson and Rosie Mary Freeman visited the whites-only restroom. Within minutes, the Winona police chief arrived and ordered all five outside. While arrests were made in the parking lot, Hamer got off the bus to see if she could do something. "Get that one, too," the chief said. At the Montgomery County jail, the police brutalized Hamer and three others. They botched the first beating. June Johnson, a fourteen-year-old girl in a pink dress, bled profusely. So they used blackjacks on the others, forcing two black male prisoners to pound Hamer. With a limp in her walk since a childhood bout with polio, she now had a permanently damaged kidney and eye. When SNCC's Lawrence Guyot showed up to see about charges and bail, the police assaulted him with fists and gun barrels, then turned him over to the Klan for a terror-filled automobile ride and another beating in the hills surrounding the town. Hamer and everyone else thought Guyot would be lynched.

Robert Kennedy's interest in pushing an FBI investigation of the Winona incident was largely the result of timing. The spectacle of Bull Connor's police dogs and firehoses in Birmingham had brought the struggle for racial justice to the top of the nation's political agenda. Then, on June 11, two days after Hamer's arrest and the same day as the administration's showdown with Governor George Wallace over integration of the University of Alabama, President John F. Kennedy announced his support for civil rights legislation in a nationally televised address. Later that evening, a racist gunman murdered Medgar Evers, the NAACP's field secretary in Jackson.

Hamer brought her story to much of the nation a year later during her televised appearance before the credentials committee at the Democratic National Convention in Atlantic City, New Jersey. By any standard, her testimony was riveting and emotional, so much so that President Lyndon B. Johnson saw it as a threat to his dream of a harmonious convention.

(To get the cameras off Hamer, he called an immediate press conference.) Among the founders of the Mississippi Freedom Democratic party (MFDP), which led the effort to unseat the state's regular all-white delegation, Hamer also ran as that party's candidate for Congress on a "Freedom Ballot" that included the names of all candidates, black and white. The regular Democratic party, in contrast, disallowed her name and the names of all other MFDP candidates on the official ballot. For their troubles, the Freedom Democrats saw their party wiretapped by the FBI at President Johnson's direction.

Thereafter, Hamer remained active in national politics and community organizing and continued to attract the FBI's episodic attention. She served as a delegate in 1968 to the Democratic National Convention in Chicago, and a year later founded the Freedom Farms Corporation to help Mississippi's poor with crops and livestock. She also was a vocal critic of American military involvement in Vietnam. Her own war with cancer dominated her last years and she died on March 14, 1977, at Mound Bayou Community Hospital, leaving behind a legacy of courage and the memory of that wonderful voice telling the world how tired she was of being sick and tired. Kay Mills tells Hamer's story in *This Little Light of Mine* (1993).

TELETYPE

TO: DIRECTOR, FBI AND SAC, MEMPHIS/44-1063/

DATE: JUNE 11, 1963

FROM: SAC, ATLANTA /44-1452/

CHANGED. USNUBS, FANNY LOU HAMER, ET AL. DASH VICTIMS. CR.

TITLE MARKED CHANGED TO SHOW THE CORRECT NAME OF HAMER AS FURNISHED BY HER. TITLE FORMERLY CARRIED AS FANNY HAMER.

RE ATLANTA TELEPHONE CALL TO MEMPHIS JUNE THIRTEEN, LAST.

VICTIM HAMER ARRESTED BY UNSUB BELIEVED TO BE A SHERIFF OR DEPUTY ON JUNE NINE, LAST, WINONA, MISSISSIPPI. BUS STATION. VICTIM DID NOT USE FACILITIES AT TERMINAL BUT WAS ARRESTED WHEN SHE INQUIRED ABOUT OTHER VICTIMS BEING ARRESTED. SHE WAS NOT FURNISHED THE NATURE OF THE CHARGES UNTIL HER APPEARANCE IN COURT

JUNE ELEVEN, LAST, WHEN SHE WAS CHARGED WITH IM-
MORAL CONDUCT AND RESISTING ARREST. SHE WAS RE-
LEASED ON TWO HUNDRED DOLLARS BOND, JUNE TWELVE,
LAST. VICTIM CLAIMS SHE DID NOT RESIST ARREST AT ANY
TIME AND SHE WAS KICKED BY UNSUB SHERIFF OR DEPUTY
WHEN ENTERING HIS CAR TO GO TO JAIL. AFTER BEING
PLACED IN JAIL VICTIM WAS BEATEN BY TWO NEGRO MALE
PRISONERS WITH BLACKJACK ON INSTRUCTION FROM UNSUB,
MISSISSIPPI HIGHWAY PATROLMAN IN THE PRESENCE OF TWO
OTHER WHITE MALES, ONE OF WHOM WAS SEEN LATER IN
THE UNIFORM OF WINONA, MISSISSIPPI POLICE OFFICER. THE
THIRD WHITE MALE IN THE CELL STRUCK VICTIM WITH HIS
HAND IN ATTEMPT TO QUIET HER SCREAMING WHEN BEATEN
BY THE PRISONERS. NO MEDICAL TREATMENT AFFORDED HER.
   VICTIM HAMER SAID FBI PHOTOGRAPHED HER IN GREEN-
WOOD, MISS., AND MADE APPOINTMENT TO INTERVIEW HER AT
TEN A.M. JUNE THIRTEEN, LAST BUT SHE HAD TO LEAVE TOWN
TO GO TO ATLANTA. VICTIM LEAVING ATLANTA TO GO TO
WASHINGTON, D.C. TO SEE JUSTICE DEPARTMENT OFFICIALS AC-
CORDING TO WYATT T. WALKER, EXECUTIVE DIRECTOR OF THE
SOUTHERN CALIFORNIA LEADERSHIP CONFERENCE.

FEDERAL BUREAU OF INVESTIGATION

Reporting Office: Atlanta
Office of Origin: Memphis
Date: 6/14/63
Investigative Period: 6/13/63
Report Made By: SA [Bureau Deletion]
Title of Case: UNKNOWN SUBJECTS; FANNY LOU HAMER; ET
AL-VICTIMS
Character of Case: Civil Rights

REFERENCES:
   Atlanta telephone call to Memphis 6/13/63.
   Atlanta teletype to Bureau and Memphis dated 6/14/63.

ADMINISTRATIVE:
   Victim Hamer advised that FBI had taken her photograph in Greenwood, Mississippi, and had made an appointment to interview her at

10:00 A.M. 6/13/63 but she had to break the appointment and come to Atlanta, Ga. Victim Hamer was not located until 8:30 P.M. on 6/13/63. The interview was arranged and completed at 11:30 P.M. since she advised that she was catching a late plane out of Atlanta that night. Victim Hamer would not advise of her destination; however, Wyatt T. Walker, Executive Director of the Southern Christian Leadership Conference, said Hamer was going to Washington, D.C., to see some Justice Department officials. At the conclusion of the interview victim Hamer advised that she did not have time for a written statement to be prepared for her to sign regarding her account of the events that happened in Winona, Mississippi. The reason for not having time for the written statement to be prepared was that she had to catch her plane.

During referenced telephone call Memphis advised that victim Hamer had been examined by a physician in Greenwood, Mississippi, and that the doctor diagnosed injuries. In view of this, Atlanta is not submitting an FD 302 to set forth results of observations of injuries.

FEDERAL BUREAU OF INVESTIGATION

Fanny Lou Hamer, Ruleville, Mississippi, housewife and voter registration worker for Southern Christian Leadership Conference, was interviewed at 1389 Lansing Street, S.E., Atlanta, Georgia.

She furnished the following information:

She was traveling with a group of ten individuals on June 9, 1963, by Continental Trailways Bus en route from Charleston, South Carolina, to Greenwood, Mississippi. The group had attended a Citizenship Training Class in Charleston and was returning home. The bus stopped at the terminal in Winona, Mississippi, about 11:15 A.M. on June 9, 1963. Several of the group got off the bus to get something to eat but Mrs. Hamer remained on board. About fifteen minutes after arriving Mrs. Hamer saw one of the group, Annelle Ponder, and two or three of the other girls come out of the bus station restaurant quickly with Winona Police and Mississippi Highway Patrolmen. She saw the officers put Annelle and several others in police cars. Mrs. Hamer got off the bus and asked Annelle what was wrong. At this time Mrs. Hamer was ordered by (Unknown Subject Number One), a Sheriff or Deputy Sheriff, who was wearing civilian clothes and a badge to get into his car, that she was under arrest. There was another white male (Unknown Subject Number Two) who rode in the car to the Winona County Jail with Mrs. Hamer and Unknown Subject One.

When entering the car Mrs. Hamer said that Unknown Subject Number One kicked her and she asked him why he had done this. His only answer was curses. Mrs. Hamer said she did not resist arrest but only asked what the charge was against her but neither Unknown Subject One or Two would tell her the nature of the charges.

There were six of the group of ten who were arrested including Mrs. Hamer, and Mrs. Hamer believes the cause of the trouble was the group attempting to eat at the bus terminal restaurant; however, she never heard any of the officers actually state that this was the reason for the arrest being made. Included in the group of six were Annelle Ponder, June Johnson, Euvester Simpson, James West and Mrs. Hamer.

After arriving at the county jail in Winona, Mrs. Hamer was placed in a cell with Euvester Simpson and she heard one of the policemen say something to the effect [that] they had been disturbing the peace but no formal charges were brought at this time. Soon after being placed in the cell Mrs. Hamer said that June Johnson was beaten in her cell. She said she did not see this but she could hear June screaming. A little later, Mrs. Hamer observed that Annelle Ponder was taken from her cell to another cell where she was beaten. She did not see anything but could hear Annelle screaming. After the beating she saw Annelle with her mouth bloody staggering back to the cell she had been placed in originally.

A short time later Mrs. Hamer was taken from her cell to another cell where there was a State Highway Patrolman (Unknown Subject Number Three). Also in this cell were two other white men, Unknown Subject Number Two and Number Four. Unknown Subject Number Four was recognized a day or two later by Mrs. Hamer wearing a Winona, Mississippi, Police Officer's Uniform; however, while he was in the cell on June 9, 1963, he was wearing a light blue shirt and navy pants with nothing to identify him as an officer.

A Mississippi State Highway Patrolman questioned Mrs. Hamer about where she had been and why she had been in Charleston, South Carolina. She told him she had gone to a Citizenship Training School and he contradicted her saying "you went to march," and "you went to see Martin Luther King," and "we are not going to have it." The Highway Patrolman then gave a blackjack to one of the Negro prisoners and told Mrs. Hamer to lay on the bed in the cell. The other prisoner then sat on Mrs. Hamer's feet and the first prisoner was ordered by the Patrolman to beat her. The Highway Patrolman said they were not going to kill her but she would wish she were dead before it was over. Unknown Subject Number Two who was wearing dark trousers and white shirt and nothing that would identify him as an officer, hit Mrs. Hamer in the face and on the head a couple of times with his hand when she was screaming from the blows of the blackjack and told her to shut up. After the first prisoner finished beating her the second prisoner was ordered by the Highway Patrolman to take his turn and then Unknown Subjects Two, Three, and Four left the cell during the second beating. At an unrecalled later time the Highway Patrolman came back to the cell and told the prisoner to stop the beating. The Patrolman then led Mrs. Hamer back to her cell where she had originally been placed with Simpson. No medical treatment was afforded although she had been beaten severely with the blackjack over her entire body including her arms, legs, and head.

On the night of June 10, 1963, all the group was taken out of the cells for a short time and the Highway Patrolman made photographs.

On the morning of June 11, 1963, the group was taken out of jail to appear in court. Mrs. Hamer rode with a police officer (Unknown Subject Number Four) who was driving a marked police car. She did not recognize any number or identifying mark on this car.

When Mrs. Hamer appeared in court she was charged with immoral conduct and resisting arrest and the only testimony against her was given by Unknown Subject Number Three, the Highway Patrolman, and Mrs. Hamer pleaded not guilty. She was given a choice of paying a $100 fine or posting $200 bond. Mrs. Hamer was taken back to her cell immediately after this session in court. On the afternoon of June 12, 1963, she posted bond and when she left to go to Greenwood, Mississippi, James West was the only one of the group still in jail. She said that West wanted to stay there at this time with his friend (First Name Unknown) Guyot who had come over to Winona from Greenwood, while they were in jail in order to try to help him. Guyot became involved in some trouble with police and he was put in jail.

Mrs. Hamer said that since she was about ready to catch a plane out of Atlanta she would not have time for a written statement to be prepared although she had no objection to signing one. She stated that the FBI had taken her picture in Greenwood, Mississippi, after her release from Winona Jail.

Unknown Subject Number One was described by Mrs. Hamer as follows: White male, age late 50's or 60's, height 5'10", weight 160, build medium, complexion, hair, and eyes unknown. Wearing a white shirt, beige Panama hat with a darker brown band, wearing glasses, badge number not noted. Car Number or license not observed. Scars, marks, and tattoos—none observed.

Unknown Subject Number Two white male, age about 30, height 5'9", weight 170 pounds, medium build, dark almost black hair, wearing dark pants, white shirt, and no hat. No identifying marks, scars, or peculiarities.

Unknown Subject Number Three, white male, age early 30's height 5'9", weight possibly 200 pounds, build stocky, hair light brown, sun-tanned complexion, wearing State Highway Patrol uniform, no identifying rank or badge number noted.

Unknown Subject Number Four, white male age 30-35, height 6'-6'1", weight 170-175, build slender, hair brown, complexion fair. Wearing Winona, Mississippi, Police Officer's Uniform, on June 11, 1963. Wearing on June 9, 1963, light blue shirt and navy blue pants. No identifying badge number or rank or police car number noted.

Memorandum

TO: The Director, FBI   DATE: June 15, 1963

FROM: Burke Marshall, Assistant Attorney General, Civil Rights
             Division

SUBJECT: Police Brutality,
             Thomas Herrod, Chief of Police, Winona, et al;
             Fanny Hamer, et al-Victims
             Civil Rights

With respect to the allegations already being investigated by your Bureau of the beating of Fanny Hamer, Annell Ponder, Rosemary Freeman, Euvester Simpson, James West, and Lawrence Guyot in the Montgomery County Jail in Winona, Mississippi, on June 9, 1963, the following investigation is desired:

1. Interview all persons who were in the jail on June 9, 10, 11, or 12, 1963, who may have any knowledge of the beatings or of injuries sustained by the victims.

2. Interview all jail personnel.

3. Interview any visitors at the jail during the period June 9 through 12, 1963. The victim Fanny Hamer relates that a man who appeared to be a white clergyman visited the jail one occasion. The wife and daughter of the [Bureau Deletion] also saw and spoke to the victims during their incarceration.

4. Identify and interview all persons who were present at the trials of the victims in police court on June 11. According to the victims the trial was held in a small room with few persons present. Victims Hamer, [Bureau Deletion] state that most of the men present at their beatings were also present at their trial.

5. Identify and interview all persons present at the Trailways Terminal when the victims were arrested and transported to the county jail. In particular, identify and interview "a young man" with a "crew cut" who is reported by Mrs. Hamer as riding in the front seat with [Bureau Deletion] when she was driven to the county jail. Also identify and interview the city patrolmen as well as any other law-enforcement officers. Also seek to identify the white man reported by the victims Hamer [Bureau Deletion] to have boarded the bus for a few minutes outside of Winona and then to have boarded the bus again for a few minutes after it had arrived in Winona.

6. Inspect the radio log of the Winona Police Department, which may have information bearing upon the arrest and incarceration of the victims. In this connection interview the [Bureau Deletion] of Winona who is stated by [Bureau Deletion] as having made the initial complaint of a disturbance at the terminal.

7. Make a floor plan of the county jail showing the location of the cells in which the victims were held, interview rooms, etc.

8. Obtain and preserve all pertinent physical evidence in possession of victims, such as bloodstained, torn clothing, broken jewelry, etc.

9. Identify and interview the driver and other passengers aboard the Trailways bus on which the victims arrived in Winona. They should be questioned regarding the demeanor and conduct of the victims en route to Winona as well as any knowledge they may have of the events at the terminal.

John Rosenberg, an attorney of this division, will be interviewing the victims in Mississippi with a view to obtaining affidavits within the next day or two. He will contact your resident agent in Greenwood upon his arrival to review any reports on the case [that] are available. He will also furnish your Greenwood office any additional specific leads [that] he may have.

This investigation should be conducted as expeditiously as possible.

DEPARTMENT OF JUSTICE
FOR IMMEDIATE RELEASE
MONDAY, JUNE 17, 1963

The Department of Justice today brought suit to secure an immediate halt to further prosecution of six Negro voting registration workers arrested June 9 on baseless charges outside the bus terminal in Winona, Mississippi.

Attorney General Robert F. Kennedy said a civil complaint filed today in Oxford, Mississippi, asserted that the purpose of the arrests—for disorderly conduct and resisting arrest—was to discourage the six and other Negro passengers from attempting to use the terminal facility freely.

The prosecution of the six constitutes an unlawful and unconstitutional interference with interstate commerce and with Interstate Commerce Commission regulations forbidding racial discrimination, Mr. Kennedy said.

Named as defendants were the City of Winona, located in Montgomery County, in north central Mississippi; Martin C. Billingsley, its mayor; Thomas Herrod, its police chief; and Earl W. Patridge, the county sheriff.

The complaint asked the United States District Court for the Northern District of Mississippi for temporary and permanent injunctions forbidding the defendants to interfere in any way with Negroes' use of bus terminal facilities in Winona.

The suit also asked that they be required to drop any further prosecution of the six Negroes arrested. The six were convicted June 11 and subsequently released on $100 appeal bond. Their appeals to Mississippi Circuit Court would require new trials.

Mr. Kennedy said filing of the suit followed unsuccessful efforts by the Department to secure voluntary action by Winona officials.

The six Negroes, all from Mississippi, included one man, James West, and five women, Mrs. Fanny Hamer, Annell Ponder, June Johnson, Rosemary Freeman, and Euvester Simpson.

The six were in Winona June 9 on a brief rest stop during a bus trip from Charleston, S.C. to Greenwood, Mississippi. Five of them entered the terminal restaurant, but were ordered out by Herrod.

They left and were standing peaceably outside the terminal. Herrod arrested them, nonetheless. Immediately afterwards, Patridge arrested Mrs. Hamer, who had not gone into the restaurant but who also was standing outside.

There was no lawful reason or justification for any of the arrests, the complaint said.

They were convicted June 11 in the Winona Police Court with Mayor Billingsley sitting as Police Justice.

According to the complaint, Mayor Billingsley gave assurances to the Department in early 1962 that the city of Winona would not interfere with ICC regulations forbidding racial discrimination in interstate commerce. The regulations went into effect November 1, 1961.

FANNY LOU HAMER

August 18, 1967

Fanny Lou Hamer, who was born on October 6, 1917, in Montgomery County, Mississippi, has not been the subject of an FBI investigation. The central files of the FBI indicate that Mrs. Hamer is a leader of the Mississippi Freedom Democratic Party, which has worked for registration of Negro voters in Mississippi. As an active member of the civil rights movement, she has participated in anti-Vietnam demonstrations sponsored by various groups. In March, 1966, she spoke at an anti-Vietnam meeting where a resolution was adopted which deplored the attacks on the W. E. B. Du Bois Clubs of America, a communist-inspired, Marxist-oriented youth group.

. . . On August 20, 1966, SAs observed a rally held at the Washington Monument, Washington, D.C. Charles Fishman of the National Committee to Defend Civil Liberties of the Anti-War movement acted as Master of Ceremonies and introduced all the speakers, including Fanny Lou Hamer. Hamer stated that the deaths in Vietnam were murders just as much as the murders taking place in Mississippi in the civil rights movement. She compared what was being done in Vietnam as being just as wrong as the denial of civil rights in the South.

MARTIN LUTHER KING, JR.

(1929–1968)

Early on, Martin Luther King, Jr., was a most unlikely candidate to find himself at the heart of what became one of the FBI's most brutal and relentless pursuits. Born on January 15, 1929, the second of three children of Rev. Martin Luther King, Sr., and Alberta (Williams) King, young Martin participated in the Atlanta celebrations marking the premier of the film *Gone With the Wind* by dressing up as a pickaninny. Two decades later, he would lead the first great direct-action protest of the modern civil rights movement, the Montgomery, Alabama, bus boycott, and through the Birmingham demonstrations and March on Washington during spring and summer 1963 he would emerge as the movement's most charismatic and visible leader. Of the enemies made along the way, only the assassin who ended his life would prove more harmful than J. Edgar Hoover and the agents assigned to the FBI's Domestic Intelligence Division.

King prepared for his father's world, the world of the Baptist preacher. Having studied at Morehouse College and Crozer Theological Seminary, he entered Boston University and pursued a Ph.D. in systematic theology with a dissertation on Paul Tillich and Henry Nelson Wieman. (In its endless search for dirt during the 1960s, the FBI somehow failed to realize that much of the dissertation was plagiarized.) On September 1, 1954, King took his first pastorate at the Dexter Avenue Baptist Church in Montgomery, and a year later, on December 1, 1955, the bus boycott began with Rosa Parks's refusal to surrender her seat to a white man in defiance of a municipal ordinance. Encouraged by Jo Ann Robinson, E. D. Nixon, Ralph Abernathy, and other boycott organizers and supporters, King accepted the position as spokesman for the Montgomery movement and quickly catapulted into national prominence with a doctrine of nonviolent protest based on Gandhian principles.

Thereafter, King's life was a whirlwind. He traveled widely in the United States, Africa, and India; helped organize a Prayer Pilgrimage at the Lincoln Memorial in Washington, D.C.; met with Vice President Richard M. Nixon and President Dwight D. Eisenhower; survived a stabbing by a deranged black woman in a Harlem department store; formed the Southern Christian Leadership Conference (SCLC); and demonstrated a willingness to accept incarceration for the benefit of the cause. While he sat in Georgia's Reidsville State Prison on the eve of the 1960 elections, the Democratic party candidate, John F. Kennedy, telephoned a pregnant Coretta Scott King to express his concern for her husband's safety. Campaign manager Robert F. Kennedy made his own call to the Georgia judge who had ordered King locked up. Republican candidate Richard M. Nixon, in contrast, chose not to intervene; which probably influenced the razor-thin outcome of the election. King was already a sufficient force to affect national politics.

For the next three years, King followed as often as he lead. This was particularly true during the Freedom Rides in Alabama and Mississippi and the Albany, Georgia, desegregation movement, where CORE and especially Student Nonviolent Coordinating Committee activists showed the way. (Albany, it should be noted, represented King's first major civil rights defeat.) But of all the demonstrations that made the movement, the most important took place in Birmingham, where King and SCLC were in the forefront. The words he wrote and spoke, especially "Letter from Birmingham Jail" and the "I Have a Dream" speech at the March on Washington, marked him as one of the greatest Americans of any century. In January 1964 *Time* magazine named King its "Man of the Year," the first black to be so honored. In December 1964, he became the fourteenth American (and the second African American, after Ralph Bunche) to win the Nobel Peace Prize.

Just as the momentum created by the Birmingham demonstrations led to the Kennedy administration's support for civil rights legislation and eventual passage of the Civil Rights Act of 1964, King's next major direct-action protest, the Selma, Alabama, demonstrations and bloody Selma-Montgomery March of early 1965, led to the Voting Rights Act of 1965. Frustrations and defeats followed that high point. In summer 1965, King went to Watts, the scene of terrible rioting, and learned that his message had little or no appeal in the ghettos of Los Angeles or in the urban North. In 1966, nonetheless, he brought the civil rights movement north by launching a frontal if largely ineffectual assault in Chicago on segregated housing and other racial problems. Then, when returning south for a Freedom March in the wake of the James Meredith shooting, he was upstaged by Stokely Carmichael and the call for black power.

King seemed to pause for a moment, as if stuck between the movement's glory days from Montgomery to Selma and its uncertain future, and then moved left. On April 4, 1967, at New York's Riverside Church, he attacked President Lyndon B. Johnson for waging war in Vietnam while poor people suffered at home. He died exactly a year later, on April 4, 1968, in Memphis, Tennessee, where he had gone to assist striking municipal sanitation workers. His dream of black and white boys and girls holding hands and singing songs on hillsides never died, but by the time King himself died he had added a caveat that many found uncomfortable. "We are not interested," he said, "in being integrated into *this* value structure." To use a single-word cliche from those times, he did not want to enter the "system." He wanted to change it. Thus by any definition he was a radical and not a harmless black icon.

Hoover's FBI tried to destroy King on both a political level (by arguing that his association with Stanley Levison and other alleged communists and his opposition to the Vietnam War marked him as a Soviet dupe at best and a traitor at worst); and a personal level (by arguing that his alleged affairs with a string of white women demonstrated the absurdity of this man wearing God's cloth and claiming to lead a moral crusade). The most disturbing aspect of this dual campaign, however, has less to do with the things Hoover and his men did but the implicit sanction they had from the Kennedy and Johnson administrations. Elected officials expected the FBI to provide answers and to help with the complex task of managing the civil rights movement and slowing it down. They signed off on the wiretaps and read the dossiers not because the bureau was out of control or because the director blackmailed them with dirt from his secret files. They allowed Hoover a free run because his FBI was part of the governing process, a resource to be used for the benefit of the current occupant of the oval office.

The literature is, of course, extensive. King's own published writings include *Stride Toward Freedom* (1958); *Why We Can't Wait* (1964); *Strength to Love* (1964); and *Where Do We Go From Here? Chaos or Community* (1967). Clayborne Carson has also edited the first volume of *The Papers of Martin Luther King, Jr.* (1992), covering the years 1929 through 1951. Also valuable is Keith D. Miller's, *Voice of Deliverance: The Language of Martin Luther King, Jr., and Its Sources*

(1992). The major biographies (in some cases semibiographies) are Taylor Branch, *Parting the Waters: America in the King Years, 1954–1963* (1989), the first volume of a projected two-volume study; Adam Fairclough, *To Redeem the Soul of America* (1987); and David L. Lewis, *King: A Critical Biography* (1970). James A. Cone's, *Martin and Malcolm and America* (1991), is also a valuable resource. David J. Garrow, author of *Bearing the Cross: Martin Luther King, Jr., and the Southern Christian Leadership Conference, 1955–1968* (1986), has also written the only book on the specific topic, *The FBI and Martin Luther King, Jr.: From "SOLO" to Memphis* (1981). In contrast to my view, he argues that the FBI's investigation included three phases fueled by three distinct forces: a legitimate fear that communists had King's ear; a voyeuristic interest in King's sex life once all the taps and bugs were set and began to pick up data; and a political interest in King's later opposition to the Vietnam War.

The biographical details that follow are attached to a report dated April 25, 1962, in Section 1 of the FBI file on Martin Luther King, Jr.

The 1961 edition of *Who's Who in America* furnishes the following background information concerning subject:

MARTIN LUTHER KING, JR., clergyman, born Atlanta on January 15, 1929, to MARTIN KING and ALBERTA WILLIAMS. Received A.B. Morehouse College, 1948 LHD, 1957; B.D. Crozer Theological Seminary, 1951; Ph.D. J. Louis Crozer Fellow Boston University, 1955, D.D. 1959; D.D. Chicago Theological Seminary, 1957; LL.D. Howard University, 1957; Morgan State College, 1958; L.H.D. Central State College, 1958; Special Student, University of Pennsylvania, Department of Philosophy, Harvard. Married CORETTA SCOTT, June 17, 1953; children—YOLANDA DENISE, and MARTIN LUTHER III. Pastor of Dexter Avenue Baptist Church, Montgomery, Alabama; President of Southern Christian Leadership Conference (SCLC); Vice President of National Sunday School and Baptist Training Union, Congress of National Baptist Convention, Inc.; President of Montgomery Improvement Association; recipient of Pearl Plafkner Award for Scholastics, Crozer Theological Seminary, Chester, Pennsylvania, 1951; selected one of ten outstanding personalities of 1956 by *Time* magazine, 1957. Member of National Association for the Advancement of Colored People (NAACP), Alpha Pi Alpha, Sigma Pi Phi, Elk, Author of *Stride Toward Freedom*,

1958, and contributor of articles to popular and religious periodicals. Home—309 South Jackson Street; Office—454 Dexter Avenue, Montgomery, Alabama.

The *Atlanta Daily World* newspaper on December 1, 1959, carried an article entitled "Dr. King Resigns to Take Post in Atlanta." This article stated that subject had resigned as Pastor of the Dexter Avenue Baptist Church in Montgomery, Alabama, and had accepted the post of co-pastor of the Ebenezer Baptist Church in Atlanta, Georgia, with his father. The article stated that he had been pastor of the Dexter Avenue Church since 1954 and that he would come to Atlanta on February 1, 1960. The article reported that he had founded and headed the Montgomery Improvement Association, which organized the successful protest that ended bus segregation in Montgomery, Alabama. The subject was also described as President of the SCLC.

The May 23, 1961, issue of the *New York Herald Tribune* carried an article entitled, "Dr. King Maps Alabama Strategy." This article stated that the SCLC was an outgrowth of the Montgomery bus boycott of 1955 to 1956 in which the subject, then pastor of the Dexter Avenue Baptist Church in Montgomery, sprung into national prominence as a leader of Negroes seeking to end segregation by using such tactics as sit-in movements and freedom rides.

Selected references to the activities of the subject as reported in the news media and by FBI informants for the period from November 1958 to February 1961 follow.

. . . claimed he learned that Rev. Martin Luther King, Jr., would leave Montgomery at 8:15 P.M. on **11/3/58** for Mobile. Also that King would travel alone in his automobile. . . . implied that this would have been a good chance to kill or at least to do bodily harm to King. . . . said he would try to find out when King planned to return to Montgomery.

. . . a Temple meeting held at MTI [Muslim Temple of Islam] No. 2, 5335 South Greenwood Ave., Chicago, Ill. Elijah Muhammad, national leader of MTI, spoke on civil rights, stating that Rev. Martin Luther King's intentions were good but that he, King, should be fighting for independence in the form of a separate state.

. . . a Temple meeting . . . stated that King was seeking to become more closely associated with the white man instead of trying to improve his black brother. . . . said King's ways were wrong and if 10,000 of the so-called Negroes got together, they would be able to demand more from this Government and become more economically independent.

... furnished the Birmingham Office an unsigned copy of a statement made on **12/8/58** ... by the unidentified informant ... This statement, which was quoted verbatim in reference, contained information regarding the collection of money to have some Negroes killed and noted that a list of ten names picked out of the air included Martin Luther King of Ala. It was also noted that the news that King was going to be killed had gotten out all over the country and the plans were stopped.

... reported that judging from remarks made by members ... the Ku Klux Klan, ... they were constantly looking for an opportunity to harm Rev. Martin Luther King, Jr.

The **March 1960** issue of *The Packinghouse Worker*, the official publication of the United Packinghouse Workers of America (UPWA) (100–35658) published an article entitled "Alabama Hits Rev. M. L. King: Lasley Joins Defense Group." This article revealed that UPWA Vice President Russell R. Lasley had joined a committee to defend Rev. Martin Luther King against perjury charges brought against him by Ala. authorities.

The state of Ala. had accused King, who addressed UPWA's 1957 National Wage Policy conference, of failing to declare $45,000 income in 1958. The committee stated that the state created the $45,000 figure by adding King's personal income to expenses incurred in his leadership in the civil rights movement. The committee planned to raise $200,000 to defend King and to aid the SCLC in a drive to register Negro voters.

King headed the SCLC and was the leader of the successful Montgomery, Ala., bus boycott.

In a public statement the committee declared "the Dixiecrats have unleashed this evil and groundless attack on his honesty, hoping to remove Dr. King from the scene and to restore themselves as the unchallenged, tyrannical masters of the life and destiny of the Negro in the South."

The **3/10/60** issue of the *Evening Star* published an article entitled "Halt Reign of Terror! King Asks President," which concerned a telegram sent to President Eisenhower by Martin Luther King, Jr., president of the SCLC, at Atlanta. King requested the President to end a reign of terror on Montgomery, Ala., by instructing the AG "to take immediate action in your name" to restore law and order. King declared that Gestapo-like methods were being used to intimidate Negroes in Montgomery.

This article also revealed that King led a successful boycott to integrate Montgomery's city buses before he moved to Atlanta.

The *Atlanta Daily World* newspaper on **October 16, 1960,** carried an article entitled "Sit-inners Meet at Morehouse College and Clark in 3-Day Conference." The article reported that the subject, who was one of the speakers, urged the students to accept the philosophy of nonviolence not only "as a technique but as a way of life." King also stated that nonviolence rejects the method of communism.

A press release dated **11/6/60** from the "Washington Capital News Service" revealed that Dr. Martin Luther King, Jr., praised senator John F. Kennedy for his stand on the civil rights issue. King's statement was the closest he had come to an outright endorsement of Kennedy for President.

The *Atlanta Journal* of **February 23, 1961**, carried an article entitled "Highlanders and Dr. King Join Forces." This article stated that the Atlanta SCLC, headed by the Rev. Martin Luther King, Jr., and Tennessee controversial Highlander Folk School have joined forces to train Negro leaders for the southern civil rights struggle. The article said that the Highlander Folk School located in the Tennessee Cumberland Mountains had been involved in the past in several political controversies. It had been staunchly defended by Mr. Franklin D. Roosevelt, among others, but in 1960, a Tennessee State Court revoked its charter after a legislative investigation charged that communists had lectured there.

May 22, 1961

MARTIN LUTHER KING, JR.

Martin Luther King, Jr., clergyman and integrationist, was born on January 15, 1929, at Atlanta, Georgia. King has not been investigated by the FBI.

King has been widely publicized since he led a bus boycott by Negroes in Montgomery, Alabama, as President of the Montgomery Improvement Association, Montgomery, Alabama. He has remained nationally prominent in integration efforts particularly with regard to the so-called "sit-in demonstrations" and his association with the National Association for the Advancement of Colored People and the Congress of Racial Equality.

In 1960 he left Montgomery, Alabama, to become joint pastor with his father of the Ebenezer Baptist Church, Atlanta, Georgia. As a result of his above activities, King has been arrested on numerous occasions charged with misdemeanors and has claimed he was the victim of police brutality. Many of King's speeches have stressed nonviolent action in integration efforts.

Bureau files reveal the following information concerning King.

In January 1957, it was reported that King was honorary chairman of the ''Enroll for Freedom'' campaign to provide economic relief for victims of racist terror in the South sponsored by the Young Socialist League.

In 1957 and 1958 the Bureau was advised that efforts were being made to obtain funds for the purpose of assassinating leaders in integration efforts in the South, including King.

In September 1958, King was stabbed by a female in Harlem, New York, and subsequent thereto directed a letter to Benjamin Davis, Jr., Communist party official, thanking Davis for the donation of blood made when King was a patient in a New York hospital recuperating from the attack.

In August 1960, it was reported that King's secretary advised the Committee to Secure Justice for Morton Sobell (cited by the House Committee on Un-American Activities as a communist front succeeding the National Committee to Secure Justice in the Rosenberg Case) that King would be happy to lend his support for obtaining freedom for Morton Sobell.

The February 4, 1961, issue of *The Nation* magazine published an article by King making a plea for faster integration of the races by indicating much could be done by the present administration through Executive Order. In this regard, King stated, ''if, for instance, the law enforcement personnel in the FBI were integrated, many persons who now defy federal law might come under restraints from which they are presently free. . . .''

The Bureau has been advised that on May 21, 1961, Martin Luther King was in attendance at the church of Reverend Ralph D. Abernathy in Montgomery, Alabama, along with other integration leaders. Reportedly, a large mob had gathered outside the church.

A Bureau memorandum dated **July 14, 1961**, revealed that a national meeting of the Knights of the Ku Klux Klan (KKKK) was held jointly with the Dixie Klans in Anniston, Alabama, on July 8, 1961. At this meeting Earl George and James Venable, both of Atlanta, Georgia, and the leaders of the US/KKKK, were speakers. Venable during his speech advocated the killing of Martin Luther King. George stated "King has to go and we might as well make up our minds to get him killed even if someone has to go to prison."

April 20, 1962

Honorable P. Kenneth O'Donnell
Special Assistant to the President
The White House
Washington, D.C.

My dear Mr. O'Donnell:

On February 14, 1962, I furnished you information concerning Martin Luther King, Jr. I thought you would be interested in additional information concerning the influence of Stanley David Levison, a secret member of the Communist party, on King.

A confidential source who has furnished reliable information in the past advised on April 16, 1962, that he had learned that Levison is forming in King's name an organization to be known as the Gandhi Society for Human Rights. Levison contemplates sending invitations signed by King to approximately twenty prominent people to attend a luncheon on May 17, 1962, in Washington, D.C. A public announcement will be made at that time of the formation of the organization. The President and the attorney general are among those being considered to be invited to the luncheon. Senator Clifford Case, Senator Eugene McCarthy and former Attorney General William P. Rogers may also be invited to the luncheon.

The informant said that he is under the impression that Theodore Kheel, arbitrator for the New York City Transit Authority; Harry Belafonte, well-known singer; and A. Philip Randolph, prominent labor leader, are involved in the formation of the organization.

This information is being furnished to the attorney general.

This information has been classified "Secret" because of the sensitive nature of our sources.

Sincerely yours,
J. EDGAR HOOVER

UNITED STATES DEPARTMENT OF JUSTICE

FEDERAL BUREAU OF INVESTIGATION

New York, New York
August 6, 1962

Re: Martin Luther King
Security Matter-C

A confidential source, who has furnished reliable information in the past, advised on August 3, 1962, that on that date Stanley Levison had a conversation with an unidentified male in Levison's office located at 6 East 39th Street, New York City.

Levison told the unidentified male that Clarence (believed to be Clarence Jones, who is associated with the fund-raising projects on behalf of Martin Luther King and the Southern Christian Leadership Conference) had informed him of a telephone conversation that had taken place between "Bobby" Kennedy and Martin Luther King.

Clarence told Levison that when King was considering violating the Federal Injunction (apparently at Albany, Georgia), he informed Kennedy of this decision and according to Clarence "He could hear Bobby Kennedy fall at the other end of the phone. That's how absolutely shocked he was."

Clarence also informed Levison that Kennedy attempted to talk King out of violating the Injunction and King "began telling him off in real tough terms."

Levison then told the unidentified male that yesterday (August 2, 1962), he had received a copy of a letter from King, from jail, in which King called on Kennedy to arrest the City Council in Albany, Georgia.

The Attorney General   August 11, 1962

Director, FBI

RACIAL SITUATION
ALBANY, GEORGIA
RACIAL MATTERS

Reverend Martin Luther King, Jr., Dr. W. G. Anderson, Reverend Ralph Abernathy, and Slater King were all found guilty in Albany City

Recorders Court on August 10, 1962. Each was sentenced to sixty days and a $200 fine with both suspended.

According to ... Albany, Georgia, Police Department, all Negro demonstrators previously arrested have been released on a blanket bond and have been given summons. He estimated sixty persons were released on the night of August 10, 1962, including those in out-of-town jails.

Mr. William M. Kunstler, attorney for the American Civil Liberties Union, New York, New York, on August 10, 1962, presented a petition for a writ of habeus corpus to the Clerk, United States District Court, Albany, asking the release of Elizabeth Porter Wyckkolf, white, of New York City, who was arrested in Albany on July 30, 1962, in a kneel-in at the City Hall along with fifteen Negroes. Wyckkolf is the only one still in custody and is eligible for bond; however, she does not desire to make bond. To date, the court has taken no action on this position.

A mass meeting was held on the night of August 10, 1962, at the Mt. Zion Church with a capacity crowd attending. No incidents were reported.

Officials of the Albany Movement on this afternoon of August 10, 1962, sent a telegram to the Albany City Commission requesting an audience and announced they were withholding further demonstrations pending an audience. The City Commission was to meet at 9:00 A.M. on August 11, 1962.

UNITED STATES GOVERNMENT
Memorandum

TO: MR. MOHR   DATE: January 15, 1963

FROM: C. D. DELOACH

SUBJECT: RACIAL SITUATION, Albany, Ga.
          RACIAL MATTERS (Article by Martin Luther King, Jr.,
          critical of FBI)

Mr. Belmont's memorandum of November 26, 1962, reflected the alternatives in interviewing Rev. Martin Luther King, Jr., who had criticized the work of the FBI in relation to the Albany situation. The Director approved the suggestion that Mr. Sullivan and I handle the interview with Rev. King.

Following approval, I immediately tried to contact Rev. King telephonically on November 27, 1962.

Rev. King does not have a phone at his residence. We then attempted to contact him at his church in Atlanta. His secretary advised, upon being told who was trying to contact him, that Rev. King was "off in another building writing a book." She further stated that Rev. King preferred not to be disturbed and that it would be impossible to talk to him. That same day I called the SAC at Atlanta and instructed him to attempt to contact Rev. King and set up an interview for Mr. Sullivan and me. SAC Atlanta advised the following day, November 28, 1962, that Rev. King had left instructions with his secretary that he did not have time for an interview, that he was moving around the country. The secretary further advised the SAC that Rev. King would call us when he was willing to sit down for an interview. Rev. King has not called since that date.

It would appear obvious that Rev. King does not desire to be told the true facts. He obviously uses deceit, lies and treachery as propaganda to further his own causes. . . .

UNITED STATES DEPARTMENT OF JUSTICE

FEDERAL BUREAU OF INVESTIGATION

New York, New York
June 12, 1963

Re: Martin Luther King
Racial Matters

On June 12, 1963, a confidential source, who has furnished reliable information in the past, advised that Stanley Levison, a New York attorney, had a discussion with Martin Luther King, leader of the Southern Christian Leadership Conference (SCLC) on June 12, 1963.

Stanley Levison informed Martin Luther King that, after he had read President Kennedy's speech of June 11, 1963, his feelings are stronger than ever that the focus of any Washington action should not be directed against the President. King agreed and asked Levison if he had heard the President's speech. King said it was the strongest statement the President has made and "he was really great."

Levison commented that he had not heard the President's speech, but this is what King has been asking the President to do and, therefore, King has to take a positive approach to it, otherwise it would sound as if King was not dealing with changing realities of himself.

They then discussed the proposal that had been made by the National Council of Churches that a commission of 25 persons be set up . . . for the purpose of assisting King in his fight for racial equality. They agreed that the assistance from the National Council of Churches on the proposed march on Washington would be invaluable, particularly if a white churchman was to lead a demonstration to the Capital in protest of the anticipated filibuster of the Civil Rights legislation, which is to be presented to Congress.

The source further advised on June 10, 1963, that Levison took part in a conference with the Reverend Martin Luther King, Clarence Jones, the Reverend Wyatt Tee Walker, and the Reverend Ralph Abernathy, among others. According to the source, the purpose of this conference was to obtain ideas as to how to dramatize the proposed march on Washington. Reverend King stated that the basic purpose of the march on Washington would be to put the pressure on Congress so that the civil rights legislation would be passed. King said that President Kennedy would be able to get off the hook if the legislation was not passed by saying that he attempted to get it through.

It was felt that the National Council of Churches can be utilized in this demonstration and also in the similar demonstrations that will be held simultaneously throughout the rest of the country. Reverend King stated that he had mixed emotions about President Kennedy in that the President should be made to know that "we" are not satisfied with him and what he has done in the field of civil rights. On the other hand, according to King, there are some Negro people that think Kennedy has done a good job in this field.

Those participating in the conference were in agreement that the Washington demonstration should be focused on the Congress rather than the White House. It was felt that the timing of the demonstration should coincide with the anticipated filibuster of the civil rights legislation. However, Clarence Jones did not agree with this because he felt it would be impossible to properly prepare a demonstration in advance if the demonstration has to wait for the filibustering to begin before it can be put into effect. It was felt that possibly 100,000 people, including children, would be utilized in the Washington demonstration in order for it to be politically impressive and that the demonstrations can possibly start in the balcony of Congress. It was felt that, more than likely, some time in August 1963 would be when the demonstration and the march on Washington would take place.

UNITED STATES DEPARTMENT OF JUSTICE

FEDERAL BUREAU OF INVESTIGATION

New York, New York
August 29, 1963

Re: Martin Luther King
Security Matter-C

A confidential source advised on August 28, 1963, that Stanley Levison in commenting on the March on Washington that day, singled out Martin Luther King as the "man of the hour" for everybody. Levison stated it was marvelous the way King handled the white and Negro question in his speech, completely repudiating "the nonsense" of Adam (Clayton) Powell and the "Muslims" (Nation of Islam). Levison also said King measures up to his introduction "the moral leader of America." Levison described this as the "mark of a man." Levison characterized King as a "pure guy."

Re: Communist Party,
    United States of America—
    Negro Question
    Communist Influence in
    Racial Matters
    Internal Security-C

The *New York Herald Tribune* of Sunday **November 24, 1963** on page 13, column three, contains an article captioned, "An Appreciation of Kennedy: Dr. King and Wilkins on Rights." This article was written in two parts; one written by Martin Luther King and the other by Roy Wilkins, of the National Association for the Advancement of Colored People (NAACP). The article written by King indicated that in a period of change, the nation has lost a leader who was unafraid of change. It said that he (President Kennedy) had the courage to be a friend of civil rights and a stalwart. King said that it is a sad commentary on our time that it took a brave man to be a leader for those human necessities. King stated in the article, "The murder of the President, regardless of the precise identity of the assassin, occurred in a context of violence and hatred that has been building up in our nation for the past several years." King mentioned "We have seen children murdered in church, men shot down in ambush in a manner so similar to the assassination of President Kennedy that we must face the fact that we are dealing with a social disease that can be neglected or avoided, as we have done, only to our deadly peril.'' King said the tragic fact must be faced that President Kennedy was the victim of developments that have made violence and hatred a popular pastime in all too many quarters of our nation. It was indicated that many people will ask the question of whether the assassination of President Kennedy will mean an inevitable setback for the cause of civil rights. In answer to this question, King said, "When Abraham Lincoln was assassinated, he was succeeded by a Vice President of southern origin" and "his successor had neither the experience nor the passion of Lincoln." King stated in the article that "the reconstruction movement ended and the release from physical slavery was carried through because the forces [that] had generated that change were too powerful to be turned back." He stated that "later Negroes suffered a setback in being denied full freedom and equality, but different elements were responsible." It was also indicated in the statement that the Negroes will continue their movement for civil rights, and it was stated, "It will not dissolve, because it was not a protest of one man, or one leader, but a genuine movement of millions whose long patience had run out." King stated, "I had several meetings with President Johnson when he served as Vice President," and King said, "I felt he had a statesman-like grasp of the problem and great political sagacity. I think he will realize that civil rights is not one of several issues, but is the dominant domestic issue."

In closing, King quoted from President Lincoln's Gettysburg Address and used President Kennedy's words that "those who do nothing are inviting shame as well as violence. Those who act boldly are recognizing right as well as reality."

Memorandum

TO: Mr. W. C. Sullivan   DATE: March 4, 1964

FROM: Mr. F. J. Baumgardner

SUBJECT: MARTIN LUTHER KING, JR.
               SECURITY MATTER—COMMUNIST

This memorandum recommends that an extremely discreet contact be made ... Marquette University to prevent its awarding of an honorary degree to Martin Luther King, Jr.

We recently learned that Marquette University, Milwaukee, Wisconsin, is considering the awarding of an honorary degree to King. The University had proposed giving King a degree on 6/7/64 but King was unable to make that date since he had another commitment on the same day. At the present time negotiations between Marquette and King are in a state of suspense relative to the selection of a date. Marquette, however, is favorably disposed toward giving King such a degree.

Marquette is the largest Jesuit university in the country and the Director, on 6/11/50, at Milwaukee, was presented with an honorary degree on behalf of Marquette University.... can be relied upon completely if we were to make any information available on a strictly confidential basis.

OBSERVATIONS:

It is shocking indeed that the possibility exists that King may receive an honorary degree from the same institution [that] honored the Director with such a degree in 1950. We ought to take positive steps to head this off if at all possible within the framework of the security of our information and sources. By making pertinent information concerning King available . . . at this time, on a strictly confidential basis, we will be giving the university sufficient time to enable it to take positive action in a manner that might avoid embarrassment to the university.

UNITED STATES GOVERNMENT
Memorandum

TO: Mr. Mohr   DATE: April 8, 1964

FROM: C.D. DeLoach

SUBJECT: MARTIN LUTHER KING, JR.
           SECURITY MATTER—COMMUNIST

Mr. Baumgardner's memo to Mr. Sullivan 4/2/64 recommended that I orally brief . . . in accordance with an attached "Top Secret" summary indicating Reverend Martin Luther King's communist connections . . . The purpose of such action was because Reverend King had been invited to make the commencement address and receive an honorary degree from Springfield College, Springfield, Massachusetts....

I called upon . . . at 10:30 A.M., 4/7/64 in his office. At the beginning of our conversation I told . . . that my remarks should be held in the strictest of confidence. He agreed to this. I then mentioned that he had long been a supporter of the FBI's and, therefore, the Director wanted me to brief him concerning a matter of potential embarrassment to a college he obviously was very personally interested in. . . . was told that captioned individual was to receive an honorary degree and make the commmencement address at Springfield College at the end of this scholastic year, June 1964. He was advised that King for some time has been maintaining a close liaison with a number of secret members of the Communist party. I told him that King had received guidance and counsel and had relied greatly upon one of these members.

. . . told me he was shocked to receive this information. He stated it was hardly believable. He said if it were not for the integrity of the FBI he would disbelieve such facts. I told him that our information was very obviously truthful and based upon indisputable facts. He wanted to make it absolutely certain that Reverend King did not appear at Springfield College. I told him that under the circumstances then that I would see . . .

. . . After making an appointment, came by my office at 4:00 P.M., 4/8/64. He opened the conversation by stating that he fully recognized the necessity to keep the information concerning King in strict confidence. He stated he wanted us to know that he would maintain this confidence and would not advise anyone of this information. He pointed out that he had been very shocked when . . . told him of these facts and had insisted that Reverend King be prevented from making the commencement address at Springfield College. . . . who impressed me as being a very sensible, intelligent individual, stated that due to the fact that he will keep this information confidential, it would be impossible . . . to "uninvite" King to make the appearance at Springfield College. . . . I told . . . at this point that any action he took in this regard was entirely up to him but that no information was to be attributed to the FBI and that we were to be kept strictly out of this matter. He stated he fully recognized this fact and no one would ever know that the FBI had given . . . this information. . . . immediate steps to prevent Reverend King from receiving an honorary degree. He said he wanted to think about the possibility of preventing King from making the address but at this step of the game he did not see how it could be done.

. . . expressed a desire to shake hands with the Director some day. . . . the Director [was given] two invitations in the recent past to receive an honorary degree and make the commencement address at Springfield College. However, the Director's schedule had caused him to not accept these invitations. I explained the Director's heavy schedule and the fact that he was reluctant to leave Washington while Congress was in session.

Upon leaving . . . assured me that no information would be released and none would be attributed to the FBI. I told him that we would, of course, deny any such information had been furnished. At this point he advised me that, of course, his main reason for coming to the FBI was to determine if we could suggest any course of action he might take. I told him we could suggest nothing, that any action taken was entirely up to him.

ACTION:

For record purposes.

UNITED STATES GOVERNMENT
Memorandum

TO: Mr. DeLoach   DATE: 5-11-64

FROM: M. A. Jones

SUBJECT: REVEREND MARTIN LUTHER KING, JR.
          APPEARANCE ON *FACE THE NATION*
          SUNDAY, MAY 10, 1964
          12:30 P.M., CHANNEL 9, WTOP-TV

Captioned individual is president of the Southern Christian Leadership Conference and was interviewed by a panel of reporters on captioned program.

REFERENCES TO THE DIRECTOR:

King was asked about communist infiltration of the Negro civil rights movement. He said that to him infiltration implied that a large number of communists would be found in leadership positions or on a policymaking level. This is not the case in the civil rights movement.

He went on to say that communism is not freedom but rather is totalitarian in nature. Consequently, communism is incompatible with the civil rights movement. He said that if there were communists in the movement, he would like to know so he could get rid of them. He admitted that there may be one or two individuals who drift into Negro organizations but they are certainly not holding down jobs of leadership.

He was asked about the Director's recently released statement to the effect that some communists were participating in the movement. He said again that this was not true and that it was "unfortunate that such a great man as J. Edgar Hoover" would "aid rightists" by such a statement. He said he would hope rather that the FBI would come out with a statement to the effect that it was amazing that so few Negroes, in view of the treatment they have received, have turned to communism.

He said that the Justice Department had informed him concerning only one communist known to be participating in King's organization and King said that when given this information he promptly expelled this man from the organization.

FEDERAL BUREAU OF INVESTIGATION
U.S. DEPARTMENT OF JUSTICE
COMMUNICATIONS SECTION

JUNE 9, 1964

TELETYPE

FBI WASH DC
1116AM URGENT 6-9-64 LRA
TO ATLANTA JACKSONVILLE
FROM DIRECTOR 100-106670 1P
MARTIN LUTHER KING, JR. SM-C

... BLUFFTON, GEORGIA, TELEPHONICALLY CONTACTED THE BUREAU DURING THE EVENING HOURS OF SIX EIGHT SIXTY FOUR RELATIVE TO THE SUBJECT. HE ADVISED SOME- ONE HAD BETTER GET KING OUT OF ST. AUGUSTINE, FLOR- IDA, BEFORE HE GETS KILLED. HE STATED HE WAS NOT THREATENING KING OR [sic] DID HE HAVE ANY SPECIFIC IN- FORMATION AS TO WHO MIGHT KILL KING, HOWEVER, KNOWING THE TEMPERAMENT OF THE PEOPLE IN THE SOUTH, HE FELT KING'S LIFE WAS IN JEOPARDY.

IT IS NOTED ... APPEARED TO HAVE BEEN DRINKING AND DURING THE CONVERSATION USED CONSIDERABLE PROFAN- ITY ...

BUREAU FILES CONTAIN NO INFORMATION IDENTIFIABLE
WITH . . .
   ATLANTA, ABOVE IS FOR YOUR INFORMATION.
   JACKSONVILLE, ALERT LOCAL AUTHORITIES.
END

June 10, 1964

Honorable Walter W. Jenkins
Special Assistant to the President
The White House
Washington, D.C.

Dear Mr. Jenkins:
   A confidential source who has furnished reliable information in the
past furnished the following information concerning a contact had between Clarence Jones and Wyatt Walker on June 8, 1964.
   Walker voiced concern over the safety of Martin Luther King, Jr., in
view of threats [that] have been made on King's life. Walker said that
King is returning to St. Augustine, Florida, on June 10, 1964, and that
he should have protection. Walker indicated that what was needed was
to have some outside pressure brought to bear on President Johnson
and Attorney General Kennedy.
   Jones stated that a commitment must come from the Department
of Justice that all reasonable steps will be taken to protect King's
life. Jones also stated that the only pressure [that] will move Attorney
General Kennedy will be that which comes from prominent people.
Walker suggested that they contact James Baldwin and people like
him. Jones agreed with this but stated he would also like to get some
people in the city government of New York City and other civic-
minded people. Jones indicated that he would work on something
to be sent to the Justice Department in connection with the safety
of King.
   On June 9, 1964, Walker contacted our Atlanta, Georgia, Office and
advised that King and other Southern Christian Leadership Conference
officials were to depart Atlanta on the morning of June 10, 1964, en
route to St. Augustine, Florida. Walker explained his reason for making
contact with the FBI in Atlanta was that the Southern Christian Leadership Conference office in St. Augustine had received two local calls
threatening to assassinate King and that the house where Southern
Christian Leadership Conference personnel, including King, were stay-

ing in the St. Augustine area had been shot into and burned. Walker said that there apparently had been no investigation by the local police or Federal officers and he expressed regret concerning this. He claimed to have already advised the Department of Justice in Washington, D.C. He also claimed that there has been a complete breakdown of law and order.

Walker admitted that to his knowledge no complaint had been made to the St. Augustine Police, State of Florida officials, or the FBI at St. Augustine. Walker was advised that the information he had furnished did not appear to be a federal violation coming within the jurisdiction of the FBI and information concerning threats against the life of King should be furnished to local law enforcement authorities. He was also advised that if he had any information [that] he believed related to civil rights violations at St. Augustine, he should report the information to our Jacksonville, Florida, Office.

An Associated Press news release from St. Augustine dated May 29, 1964, reported that local authorities were aware of and had conducted investigation relative to the firing upon a cottage [that] King had rented in the St. Augustine area. Investigation was also conducted by local authorities concerning a fire of unknown origin in King's cottage.

Wyatt Walker is the Executive Assistant to King. James Baldwin is a well-known author. Clarence Jones has been identified as a person in a position of leadership in the Labor Youth League in late 1953 or early 1954. . . .

The information above was also sent to the Attorney General by the Director in a memorandum under the same date and caption.

UNITED STATES DEPARTMENT OF JUSTICE

FEDERAL BUREAU OF INVESTIGATION

New York, New York
June 26, 1964

Re: Communist Party, United States
of America—Negro Question
Communist Influence in Racial Matters
Internal Security-C

On June 25, 1964, a confidential source, who has furnished reliable information in the past, furnished information that Martin Luther King, Jr., contacted Clarence Jones on that date. King mentioned that "they" (the Southern Christian Leadership Conference (SCLC) and those demonstrating against segregation in St. Augustine, Florida), are having a tough time in St. Augustine. He stated that there is a complete breakdown of law and order, and King remarked that the Klan (the Ku Klux Klan) "is making a showdown down here and the federal government has not done a thing."

King told Jones that forty people were beaten that evening, and he added that this was the worst night [that] they had ever had. King remarked that the Klan (Ku Klux Klan) is very close to the police (in St. Augustine). King indicated that the demonstrators are the people being beaten and that they are also the people being placed in jail.

King remarked that the reporters (newspaper reporters covering the situation in St. Augustine) say that if federal troops are not brought in "it is going to be bloody." In this connection, King said he is going to have many telegrams poured into the White House. Jones replied that Johnson (President Johnson) is very sensitive to public opinion, and he remarked that King is the most powerful Negro leader. Jones instructed King to continue to make sharp statements to the press blaming the federal government for not doing more.

King stated that they (the Ku Klux Klan) feel that they can beat us into submission, and King added that he is afraid someone will be killed. Both men agreed that President Johnson is preoccupied with the election and Mississippi (the situation in Mississippi where three civil rights workers have been missing since June 21, 1964). King stated he will tell the press that the government is not protecting them. According to Jones, the "hard core" in the South will not respect the Civil Rights Bill, and they agree that the government will have to enforce it.

Jones stated that he will get some people to work sending telegrams. King indicated that he is considering having a march on the White House to protest actions in St. Augustine and Mississippi.

UNITED STATES DEPARTMENT OF JUSTICE

FEDERAL BUREAU OF INVESTIGATION

New York, New York
October 16, 1964

Re: Communist Influence in
Racial Matters
Internal Security-C

On October 15, 1964, a confidential source, who has furnished reliable information in the past, advised that Bayard Rustin was in contact with A. J. Muste on that date. Rustin said his purpose in contacting Muste was to discuss plans concerning Martin Luther King's trip to Europe to accept the Nobel Peace Prize. In that regard, Rustin said he had been asked by King to accompany him (to Oslo, Norway) for the purpose of handling arrangements for him. Rustin, the source said, remarked that King did not trust any of the people "around him" to be knowledgeable enough to know whom he should or should not contact when he goes over to accept the award.

Rustin, in commenting on King's request, said he thought he should go, but was faced with a problem as to where he could get the money ... for transportation, as well as other expenses incidental to the trip. In regard to his expenses, Rustin said he thought "we" should appeal to some of "our friends" (Rustin's and Muste's friends) to raise the money.

With regard to King's use of money that he will receive with the award, Rustin said Coretta King (wife of Martin Luther King) desired that Martin place in trust $5,000 for each of their children's education, but that King opposed the suggestion. As a consequence of their indecision as to what to do with the money, Rustin said King had invited him down to Atlanta on Monday, October 19, 1964, to discuss what the money should be used for.

Rustin told Muste that he was of the opinion that King should make a decision and an announcement to the effect that of the $54,000 award, he was going to set aside $30,000 for the Southern Christian Leadership Conference (SCLC) for the express purpose of teaching the doctrine of nonviolence. He said this could be accomplished through the establishment of institutes in this country for the purpose of acquainting young people with the tactics and philosophy of nonviolence. As to the remaining $24,000, Rustin said he was of the opinion that it should be placed in trust for the children of the Kings. This, Rustin said, would benefit the children because Martin was not a wealthy man. He said his only reservation about the trust for the children was whether it would appear to the public that the Kings were trying to take care of their own (alluding to King's provision for his children).

Muste said in reply to Rustin's feelings about the children of King, that he did not think King should provide for them but instead, should give all the money to the SCLC. This, Muste said, would not subject King to criticism for taking a part of the money for himself. Rustin said he was of the opinion that if King does give away part of the money, then it should go exclusively to the SCLC for the purpose of teaching nonviolence, and for nothing else. He said the SCLC could raise funds for its regular budget. Muste agreed, stating that King received the Prize for advocating nonviolence, therefore, [he] should apply the money for [sic] that purpose.

Rustin, in commenting on his forthcoming meeting with King, said King wanted him to help prepare a speech [that] he would make (apparently in regard to his decision about what to do with the money). In that regard, Rustin asked Muste to prepare a few thoughts that he could use when he meets King.

According to the source, Rustin and Muste concluded their contact with a promise by Muste that he would help Rustin raise the money with which to make the trip with King.

The April 14, 1957 issue of *The Worker*, an East Coast communist publication, page 16, column 1, described A. J. Muste as the dean of the socialist pacifists.

UNITED STATES GOVERNMENT
Memorandum

TO: Mr. W. C. Sullivan   DATE: November 2, 1964

FROM: Mr. F. J. Baumgardner

SUBJECT: MARTIN LUTHER KING, JR.
           INTERNAL SECURITY—COMMUNIST

By telephone calls from our Atlanta Office 10:45 A.M. and 11:40 A.M. today (11-2-64), we learned of the following information through a highly sensitive source. Martin Luther King, Jr., just learned this morning of a campaign [that] has been initiated to encourage people to vote for King for President as a write-in candidate [on] 11-3-64. The campaign is taking several forms, including telegrams being sent to Negroes throughout the country; efforts to gain radio time to urge people to vote for King; and the circulation of handbills in larger cities encouraging a vote for King. The handbills reveal distribution by "Committee for Negroes in Government," Louisville, Kentucky. (No record of this organization Bufiles.)

According to our source, King interpreted the actions described above as an obvious attempt to cancel out the Negro vote and to confuse Negroes in their voting. King believes that the campaign was initiated by Goldwater forces because any votes for King by Negroes would obviously diminish the number of such votes for President Johnson.

King held an immediate press conference in Atlanta, Georgia, this morning in which he told the press of the foregoing and denied having any connection with the campaign. He urged people not to pay any attention to the efforts to have people vote for him.

ACTION:

The foregoing information was immediately telephonically furnished to Mr. DeLoach's office so that he might alert the White House. This is for your immediate attention. Letters to the White House and to the acting Attorney General are being expeditiously prepared.

The following is a telegram that Martin Luther King, Jr., sent to J. Edgar Hoover on November 19, 1964.

FEDERAL BUREAU OF INVESTIGATION
U. S. DEPARTMENT OF JUSTICE
COMMUNICATIONS SECTION
NOV 19 1964
WESTERN UNION
BIA025 1053A EST NOV 19 64 AB034
A LLM73 PD FAX ATLANTA FA 19 1034A EST
J EDGAR HOOVER
FEDERAL BUREAU OF INVESTIGATION WASHDC I WAS AP-
PALLED AND SURPRISED AT YOUR REPORTED STATEMENT
MALIGNING MY INTEGRITY. WHAT MOTIVATED SUCH AN IR-
RESPONSIBLE ACCUSATION IS A MYSTERY TO ME. I HAVE
SINCERELY QUESTIONED THE EFFECTIVENESS OF THE FED-
ERAL BUREAU OF INVESTIGATION IN RACIAL INCIDENTS,
PARTICULARLY WHERE BOMBINGS AND BRUTALITIES
AGAINST NEGROES ARE AT ISSUE, BUT I HAVE NEVER AT-
TRIBUTED THIS MERELY TO THE PRESENCE OF SOUTHERN-
ERS IN THE FBI. THIS IS A PART OF THE BROADER QUESTION
OF FEDERAL INVOLVEMENT IN THE PROTECTION OF NE-
GROES IN THE SOUTH AND THE SEEMING INABILITY TO GAIN
CONVICTIONS IN EVEN THE MOST HENIOUS [sic] CRIMES PER-
PETUATED AGAINST CIVIL RIGHTS WORKERS. IT REMAINS A
FACT THAT NOT A SINGLE ARREST WAS MADE IN ALBANY,
GEORGIA, DURING THE MANY BRUTALITIES AGAINST NE-
GROES. NEITHER HAS A SINGLE ARREST BEEN MADE IN CON-
NECTION WITH THE TRAGIC MURDER OF THE FOUR
CHILDREN IN BIRMINGHAM, NOR IN THE CASE OF THE
THREE MURDERED CIVIL RIGHTS WORKERS IN MISSISSIPPI.
MOREOVER, ALL FBI AGENTS INEVITABLY WORK WITH
LOCAL LAW ENFORCEMENT OFFICERS IN CAR THEFTS, BANK
ROBBERIES, AND OTHER INTERSTATE VIOLATIONS. THIS
MAKES IT DIFFICULT FOR THEM TO FUNCTION EFFECTIVELY
IN CASES WHERE THE RIGHTS AND SAFETY OF NEGRO CITI-
ZENS ARE BEING THREATENED BY THESE SAME LAW EN-
FORCEMENT OFFICERS. I WILL BE HAPPY TO DISCUSS THIS
QUESTION WITH YOU AT LENGTH IN THE NEAR FUTURE. AL-
THOUGH YOUR STATEMENT SAID THAT YOU HAVE AT-
TEMPTED TO MEET WITH ME I HAVE SOUGHT IN VAIN FOR
ANY RECORD OF SUCH A REQUEST. I HAVE ALWAYS MADE
MYSELF AVAILABLE TO ALL FBI AGENTS OF THE ATLANTA
OFFICE AND ENCOURAGED OUR STAFF AND AFFILIATES TO

COOPERATE WITH THEM IN SPITE OF THE FACT THAT MANY
OF OUR PEOPLE HAVE SUSPICIONS AND DISTRUST OF THE
FBI AS A RESULT OF THE SLOW PACE OF JUSTICE IN THE
SOUTH.

December 1, 1964

MARTIN LUTHER KING'S CRITICISM OF THE
DIRECTOR AND FBI

CURRENT ATTACK:

On November 19, 1964, Martin Luther King, Jr., sent a telegram from Atlanta to FBI Director J. Edgar Hoover concerning Mr. Hoover's remarks to the press the previous day. Set forth below is an analysis of this telegram.

King States: He has questioned the FBI's effectiveness but has never attributed this merely to the presence of Southerners in the FBI.

Facts: In November 1962, in discussing racial disturbances in Albany, Georgia, King was widely quoted in the press as stating that one of the greatest problems regarding the FBI in the South is that the Agents are white Southerners who have been influenced by the mores of the community. This is, of course, absolutely false, and it is noted that four of the five Agents then assigned to Albany, Georgia, were Northerners.

King States: Not a single arrest was made in Albany, Georgia, during the many brutalities against Negroes.

Facts: During the summer of 1962, there was a continuing series of mass racial meetings, marches and demonstrations by Negroes in the Albany, Georgia, area. This resulted in numerous multiple arrests of Negroes for lying down in the street, blocking traffic and disorderly conduct. During this period, numerous allegations of civil rights violations were made to FBI Agents and Department of Justice officials. In every instance the Department of Justice was advised of the complaint and the results of any investigation conducted. Any additional investigation requested by the Department was immediately and thoroughly run out and the results furnished to the Department. The Department of Justice did not see fit to prosecute any of the incidents arising out of these demonstrations.

During this same period, however, prosecution was brought against Denver Edgar Short, Jr., Deputy Marshal; Sasser, Georgia, which is about 20 miles from Albany. Short allegedly intimidated voter registration workers on August 30, 1962, and FBI investigation developed that Short cursed the victims, ordered them out of town, and fired his gun in the direction of their tires. A U.S. District Court petit jury acquitted Short of civil rights charges on January 25, 1963.

It is also noted that on 9-17-62, FBI Agents arrested four white subjects in the vicinity of the I Hope Baptist church, a Negro church near Dawson, Georgia, and about 30 miles from Albany, which had been burned that day. In the absence of a Federal violation, confessions obtained by FBI Agents were made available to local authorities resulting in a seven-year sentence for each of the three adult subjects and three years probation for the fourth subject who was a juvenile.

On 1-4-62 FBI Agents arrested Jack Phelix Smith and a detainer was placed against Douglas Howard Parker, a state prisoner, on civil rights charges in connection with the burning of the Shady Grove Baptist Church near Leesburg, Georgia, on 8-15-62. This was a Negro church approximately 12 miles from Albany. Smith and Parker are white. A Federal Grand Jury failed to indict, the FBI evidence was made available to state officials who presented the case to a local grand jury which also returned no bill.

King States: Not a single arrest has been made in connection with the bombing in Birmingham or the three murdered civil rights workers in Mississippi.

Facts: The Sixteenth Street Baptist Church, Birmingham, Alabama, was bombed 9-15-63 killing four Negro children. The FBI immediately launched the most intensive type of investigation, which is still vigorously continuing. The investigation was prejudiced by premature arrests made by the Alabama Highway Patrol, and consequently, it has not yet been possible to obtain evidence or confessions that would ensure successful prosecution although the FBI has identified a small group of Klansmen believed to be responsible.

The FBI launched a massive investigation following the disappearance of the three civil rights workers in the vicinity of Philadelphia, Mississippi, on June 21, 1964. The FBI located their bodies in an earthen dam and has developed information identifying those responsible. Intensive investigation is continuing to develop the case for prosecution as quickly as possible.

It should be noted that FBI recent investigations in Mississippi have produced the following positive results: (1) Eleven arrests in McComb on state charges involving bombings and other violence. Nine of those arrested have pleaded guilty or nolo contendere and received probationary sentences; (2) Seven arrests in Natchez on state charges involving shooting incidents and a beating; (3) Two subjects arrested on state murder charges 11/6/64 in connection with the killing of Henry Hezekiah Dee and Charlie Eddie Moore; (4) Seven arrests for racial violence by the Sheriff of Pike County who stated this resulted from his success in practicing FBI methods he observed during the FBI's recent investigations; and (5) FBI Agents have arrested five present and former law enforcement officers in Neshoba County on charges of police brutality. They are presently awaiting trial.

King States: FBI Agents work with local officers on criminal cases making it difficult for them to effectively function where Negroes are threatened.

Facts: This is a shopworn canard, the falsity of which is clearly illustrated by the FBI's currently effective cooperation with local officers in Mississippi, FBI's arrest of five officers in Neshoba County, Mississippi, FBI's effective cooperation with local officers in the Georgia church burning investigations, the Penn murder case and many other cases in all parts of the country.

King States: He has no record of a request from the Director to meet with him.

Facts: In November 1962, FBI officials sought to make an appointment with King to straighten him out with regard to his public remarks concerning the FBI's performance in Albany, Georgia. King was never available on the telephone and left instructions with his secretary on 11/28/62 that he would call the FBI when he was willing to arrange an interview. He made no further response.

King States: He has always made himself available to Atlanta FBI Agents.

Facts: In July 1961, it was necessary for the FBI to contact King in connection with a special inquiry investigation for the Peace Corps. An appointment was made through King's secretary for his interview 7/22/61; however, King kept the FBI Agent waiting for one hour past the appointed time and stated he was behind in his paperwork and had completed some of it before admitting the Agent.

In June 1962, the FBI made efforts to obtain an appointment with King in connection with a case involving a Peace Corps applicant. Beginning on approximately 6/5/62, King's secretary kept stating that he was not available for interview although it was known to the FBI that he was in his office daily. On 6/8/62 Wyatt T. Walker, King's assistant, advised the Atlanta Office that he and King were proceeding to Shreveport, Louisiana, in connection with the voter registration drive and that the Little Union Baptist Church in Shreveport had received a bomb threat. At that time, Walker was informed that FBI Agents had been urgently trying to make an appointment with King and Walker stated an appointment would be made. On 6-8-62, King telephoned the Atlanta Office from Shreveport to inquire as to why the Agent wanted an appointment and to advise of the bomb threat previously furnished by Walker. King consented to interview which was conducted 6-9-62.

King was also interviewed by the Atlanta FBI office on 7-24-62 in connection with racial incidents at Albany, Georgia, involving alleged violation by King of a temporary restraining order issued by the U.S. District Court to stop demonstrations. The interview was conducted in the U.S. courtroom where King had appeared for a hearing.

On 11-30-62, when FBI Headquarters officials were attempting to arrange an interview with King, the Atlanta FBI office contacted King's secretary to make such an appointment at King's convenience. The Agent was advised that King was writing a book and could not be reached. King's secretary was requested to have King contact the Atlanta Office on an urgent matter but he never made such a contact.

On 6-25-63 the Atlanta FBI Office attempted to contact King to advise him of a threat against his life. Efforts to contact him were at first unsuccessful, but after a delay of some hours, King's secretary informed him of the Bureau's interest in talking to him and arrangements were made for an Agent to contact King by telephone.

In connection with this whole matter, it should be kept in mind that the FBI's function is purely investigative in nature. It is not empowered to offer protection to anyone, at any place, at any time.

PREVIOUS ATTACKS:

Generally, King's previous attacks against the Director and the FBI in the civil rights field have been similar to those outlined above. As an example is the criticism carried in the *New York Times* of November 19, 1962; in essence King claimed the FBI in Albany, Georgia, sides with the segregationists. He also said the FBI has not done an effective job in investigating beatings of Negroes in Georgia. His remarks were made after giving a sermon at the Riverside Baptist Church in New York City.

December 1, 1964

ORGANIZATION OF THE CURRENT
ATTACK AGAINST THE FBI
BY MARTIN LUTHER KING

On November 19, 1964, the day after the Director's press conference, Martin Luther King, Jr., contacted his secretary, Dora McDonald, at the Atlanta, Georgia, office of the Southern Leadership Conference (SCLC), according to a reliable source. She told him his telegram to Mr. Hoover regarding the Director's criticism of King was going out to the press. King stated he wanted to issue a statesmanlike "covering statement" in connection with the telegram.

King declared the nature of the follow-up statement would be that he cannot conceive of Mr. Hoover's labeling King a liar unless he (Mr. Hoover) was under extreme pressure and apparently had faltered under the tremendous burdens, complexities, and responsibilities of his office. King said he would state he cannot become involved in a public debate with Mr. Hoover and that he has nothing but sympathy for the Director who has served his country so well. King told his secretary the telegram and the statement will be the only comment he will personally issue in this matter. He told her, Mr. Hoover should retire because he is "too old and broken down."

King instructed his secretary to have Randolph T. Blackwell, Program Coordinator of SCLC, go over the press release and telegram. He stated the release should be given to those who are "for us," naming Catherine Johnson of Associated Press or United Press International, one Don McKee, and Ted Poston of the *New York Post.*

King later talked to his aide, Bernard Lee, the source advised, and told Lee to be sure all Negro news media get the release. He told Lee to call *Jet* magazine, a Negro publication, and to give a copy of the release to one John Herbert in New York. Lee told King, in answer to a question as to what was wrong with Mr. Hoover, that he thought the Director was getting old and is a "sacred cow."

King directed Lee to have Bayard Rustin in New York and Walter Fauntroy, SCLC representative in Washington, D.C., contacted and told to start criticism of the FBI in those areas. He said he already had started in Miami, Florida. He instructed that Slater King, a civil rights leader in Albany, Georgia, should be contacted since he would welcome an opportunity to make a statement against the FBI and the Director. Blackwell did this later that day. King declared people in the western states who are SCLC members must be contacted to have them begin the attack against the FBI. King told Lee that telegrams to Mr. Hoover should also be sent to the President.

King declared that Blackwell and Cordy T. Vivian, director of Affiliates of SCLC, should handle the attack on the FBI so it would not appear that King was fighting the Director over a personal matter. He said the President should censure Mr. Hoover and it would be a good idea for all telegrams to the President to request this.

On the same date, according to the source, King told Vivian this is the time to attack the whole FBI. He declared that he cannot be the one who does it, stating "we" need people in the South to make statements about the laxity of investigations and law enforcement, especially concerning civil rights. People in the North are needed to protest Mr. Hoover's charge against King. King suggested telegrams be sent to the President urging Mr. Hoover be censured and urging he be retired because "he is old and getting senile."

The source reported Vivian suggested the attack be based on Mr. Hoover's ineffectiveness in civil rights; that he is past retirement age and would have been out last year except for certain people asking that he stay on. King disagreed, asserting he wanted Mr. Hoover "Hit from all sides."

Later on November 19, 1964, the source related that Wyatt Walker, a former SCLC executive now employed by a firm in New York City, contacted Vivian. He was told by Vivian to "get things going" in New York. Vivian told Walker to handle the East Coast and said Tom Kilgore, an official of the Western Christian Leadership Conference in Los Angeles, California, was to handle the West Coast. Vivian instructed Walker to get telegrams sent to the President, Department of Justice, and the FBI, demanding that Mr. Hoover apologize to King.

Vivian told Walker that this is an opportunity to mount an attack against police brutality. He said the FBI will try to defend itself with the statement that it is an investigative agency and that people making the protests should know what to expect from the FBI. Vivian later contacted Kilgore and gave him similar instructions.

According to a highly confidential Atlanta informant, one Reverend Hodge, location unknown, contacted Vivian and wanted [to know which] methods SCLC was using against Hoover. Vivian advised SCLC files failed to indicate Hoover ever tried to contact King. Vivian gave Hodge the following points to get across concerning Hoover and the FBI:

(1) FBI has been ineffective in that no persons have been brought to trial (In Albany only Negroes went to jail.);

(2) FBI is only investigative arm, which Vivian claims is ridiculous in that investigations have not been good enough for convictions and reports are available only to FBI and Department of Justice. (For example, one of SCLC staff members was shot at Greenville along with two other people and nothing was done about it.);

(3) Hoover never tried to get in contact with King to verify statement;

(4) King did not tell people to contact FBI;

(5) FBI has jurisdiction whenever civil liberties have been violated. Vivian claimed Director had no evidence to support Director's statements against King. Vivian further claimed King does not want to debate the Director but it is their job as subordinates to handle the criticism against Hoover and the FBI. Vivian claims the Director's statement concerning pressure groups is vague and full of generalities and Hoover is more interested in the John Birch Society, Minutemen, and Ku Klux Klan but will not attack them. Vivian claimed "we" had

statements sent from all civil rights leaders to the President from James Farmer of CORE, Wilkins of NAACP and Jack Greenberg of African Union.

The source continued that Vivian claimed the main points to drive home are that the investigations and reports of the FBI can only be seen by Justice Department and he feels reports are inadequate.

Identities of Individuals Mentioned:

Randolph T. Blackwell, according to a confidential source in 1953, had been a member of the Communist Party (CP) in the District of Columbia, and another source indicated Blackwell attended a Labor Youth League (cited by the Department of Justice) Convention.

A confidential source advised in November 1947, that Cordy T. Vivian was a member of the CP in Peoria, Illinois, and had been active in CP affairs for some time.

Bayard Rustin, in July 1964, issues of the *Saturday Evening Post* was said to have gone to New York in 1938 as an organizer for the Young Communist League and as such had the job of "recruiting students for the party." He reportedly left the party in 1941.

FBI ACCOMPLISHMENTS IN THE CIVIL RIGHTS FIELD

Every civil rights complaint is given thorough, prompt, and impartial attention. Special Agents handling these cases are highly trained investigators who have completed advanced training courses which qualify them to conduct civil rights investigations. At Bureau Headquarters, a select staff of men with great experience and knowledge of this type of investigation supervise the cases.

The duty of maintaining law and order in civil rights demonstrations, preserving the peace and protecting life and property is the primary responsibility of local and state law enforcement agencies. The FBI is solely an investigative agency as distinguished from a police agency, and as such, is without authority to maintain the peace or furnish protection. It is the duty of the FBI, however, to furnish factual data to the Department of Justice so that a determination can be made as to whether there is any basis for Federal action under the civil rights statute.

Our work in the field of civil rights is increasing. In fiscal year 1960, the FBI handled 1,398 civil rights cases. In fiscal year 1963, the number of cases jumped to 2,692 and in fiscal year 1964, it increased to 3,340.

Although a substantial number of arrests and convictions have resulted from our investigations in these matters, the effectiveness of our work in this field can never be precisely assayed on the basis of such statistics. Perhaps the greatest value of our work in this field lies in the results of our intelligence and liaison programs, which can never be traced to direct prosecutive action. We continuously gather information on a day-to-day basis which indicates that some violent action is either being definitely planned or that a situation will occur which has a high potential for violence.*

The fact that we vigorously investigate civil rights violations undoubtedly serves as a deterrent to discourage violations on the part of law enforcement officers and spurs these officers to immediately and vigorously investigate civil rights situations that otherwise might be ignored.

Liaison with Governors and ranking state officials has also been effective. Also, although we may not have jurisdiction in a particular case the cooperative facilities of the FBI Laboratory and Identification Division are made available.

It is also noted that on July 10, 1964, the Director traveled to Jackson, Mississippi, to open a new FBI office in that city. With this office, we feel we can more efficiently and effectively meet our growing responsibilities.

There follows thumbnail sketches of some of the FBI's more recent specific accomplishments in the civil rights field.

Racial Discrimination and Intimidation of Voters

Under the Civil Rights Acts of 1957 and 1960, the Attorney General was empowered to institute civil actions seeking injunctive relief against racial discrimination and intimidation in voting. We have conducted investigations under these in 168 counties in six southern states. As a result, 67 suits have been filed in the States of Alabama, Florida, Georgia, Louisiana, Mississippi, and South Carolina. As a result of suits filed based on our investigations into discrimination in voting, thousands of previously disenfranchised Negro citizens have been enabled to register for voting.

Assaults Upon Voter Registration Workers in Mississippi

Rabbi Arthur Joseph Lelyveld and two other white voter registration workers were assaulted by two white men in Hattiesburg, Mississippi, on June 10, 1964. Local authorities were furnished with the results of our investigation which identified two local white men who perpetrated

---

*Such information is immediately disseminated to appropriate authorities.

the assault. The subjects were prosecuted on charges of assault and battery, fined $500 each and each was sentenced to 90 days in jail. The jail sentences were suspended pending good behavior.

Two white civil rights workers accompanied by a young Negro were assaulted in Jackson, Mississippi, on July 22, 1964. FBI investigation identified a local Klansman as having struck one of the victims with a club. Results of our investigations were furnished to local authorities. The subject pleaded guilty to local assault charges and was fined $50.

Three voter registration workers were intimidated and one was assaulted at Itta Bena, Mississippi, on June 25, 1964. FBI Agents arrested three local white men on June 26, 1964, for violation of Federal Civil Rights Statues. A Federal Grand Jury at Oxford, Mississippi, considered this case on July 17, 1964, but failed to indict although the intimidation and the identities of the subjects were clearly established.

Civil Rights Act of 1964

The Civil Rights Act of 1964 added tremendously to the work of the FBI. Approximately 1,800 reports and memoranda concerning alleged violations have been prepared by FBI Agents since the Act became effective on July 2, 1964.

Based on extensive FBI investigations, a three-judge Federal Court in Atlanta, Georgia, found the Act constitutional and enjoined the Pickrick Restaurant and the Heart of Atlanta Motel from racial discrimination. The Heart of Atlanta Motel case has been heard by the Supreme Court and a decision is expected momentarily. Another case [that] has been heard by the Supreme Court involves a restaurant in Birmingham (Ollie McClung Case) which case was heard by a three-judge Federal Court and the Act was ruled unconstitutional, regarding this specific restaurant. A decision is expected momentarily on this case also and on the decision of this case and the Heart of Atlanta Motel Case rests the fate of the effect of the Civil Rights Act. Based on FBI investigations, suits have been filed against restaurants and motels in Florida and numerous restaurants in Alabama that discriminate. Additional court actions are anticipated in South Carolina, Georgia and Alabama. A federal suit now pending seeks to restrain the Mayor of Greenwood, Mississippi, and other public officials from interfering with the right of Negroes to attend a theater and for failing to provide adequate police protection in the operation of a theater.

On July 23, 1964, three white men, Willie Amon Belk, his son, Jimmy Allen Belk, and Sam Allen Shaffer, Jr., were arrested by FBI Agents at Greenwood, Mississippi, on charges of conspiracy to violate the Civil Rights Act of 1964. The arrests followed a thorough, intensive, and immediate investigation concerning the beating of Silas McGhee, which occurred on July 16, 1964. The facts in this matter will be presented to a Federal Grand Jury in January 1965.

School Integration Matters

During August and September 1964, the FBI investigated desegregation of public schools in eighteen possible trouble spots in southern states. In connection with these investigations, we determined plans or activities of Klan and other hate groups which might have interfered with desegregation or resulted in acts of violence, and this information was disseminated to local authorities.

Three Civil Rights Workers Murdered

The FBI conducted an all-out investigation concerning the disappearance of Michael Schwerner and two other civil rights workers in the vicinity of Philadelphia, Mississippi, on June 21, 1964. The victims' burned-out automobile was located by FBI Agents on June 23, 1964, and the bodies of the three murdered victims were found in an earthen dam on August 4, 1964. Arising out of this investigation the FBI established other civil rights violations and on October 2, 1964, a special Federal Grand Jury returned indictments against Sheriff Lawrence Andrew Rainey and three other local law enforcement officers and a former sheriff of Neshoba County, Mississippi. All five subjects were arrested by FBI Agents and are awaiting trial on police brutality charges not connected with the murders. While the FBI is certain as to the identities of the subjects responsible for the murders of the three civil rights workers, intensive innvestigation is being conducted to develop suitable evidence. Today (12-1-64) representatives of our Civil Rights Section are discussing with Assistant Attorney General Marshall possibilities of prosecution of the subjects regarding the murders.

Murder of Lieutenant Colonel Lemuel A. Penn

On 7-11-64 Lieutenant Colonel Lemuel A. Penn was murdered near Colbert, Georgia. FBI investigations resulted in the arrest of four subjects by FBI Agents on 8-6-64. Complete details of FBI investigations were made available to the State for prosecution of the subjects on murder charges. Two of the subjects were acquitted in local court on 9-4-64; a third subject has not yet been tried in local court but is still under indictment for murder and the local case against the fourth subject has been dismissed.

On 10-16-64 indictments were returned by the Federal Grand Jury at Athens, Georgia, charging six men with conspiracy to injure, oppress, threaten, and intimidate Negro citizens in the free exercise and enjoyment of rights and privileges secured to them by the Constitution. These individuals were Denver Willis Phillips, George Hampton Turner, Herbert Guest, Cecil William Myers, Joseph Howard Sims and James S. Lackey. Guest, Lackey, Myers and Sims were the four men arrested by the FBI in connection with the murder of Penn. A second indictment on 10-16-64 charges Guest with possession of a shotgun having an over-all length of less than 26 inches which had not been registered by Guest with the Secretary of Treasury or his delegate. All except Lackey were 11-30-64 on a Federal indictment—pleas of not guilty rendered to the charges. Trial is set for 1-11-65.

Bombing of Home of Iona Godfrey

FBI investigation established that William Sterling Rosecrans, Jr., a 30-year-old Klansman, had participated in the home bombing of Iona Godfrey, a Negro in Jacksonville, Florida, on 2-16-64. Godfrey's six-year-old son was attending a white school under a Federal Court Order. Rosecrans pleaded guilty to obstructing a court order and was sentenced on 4-17-64 to seven years by the U.S. District Court. Five other Klansmen, who allegedly were involved in the bombing, were also arrested by FBI Agents, but one of these subjects was acquitted in U.S. District Court and the jury was unable to reach a verdict regarding the other four. Retrial of latter four began November 16, 1964, and resulted in acquittal of all four on 11-25-64.

Bombings in McComb, Mississippi

Intensive FBI investigation was conducted in connection with a series of bombings in the McComb, Mississippi, area from June to September 1964. Through the diligent efforts of the FBI and the Mississippi Highway Patrol, nine white men were tried by Circuit Court Judge W. H. Watkins at Magnolia, Mississippi, in connection with charges that they were involved in bombings of homes and churches at McComb. The nine entered pleas of guilty and nolo contendere. After a 30-minute lecture Judge Watkins suspended their sentences and placed all on probation. Judge Watkins, who was appointed by former Mississippi Governor Ross R. Barnett, cited the defendants' youth and good families in taking this action. He stated also that in committing these crimes they had been "unduly provoked and undoubtedly ill advised." It may be noted that four of the bombers were aged 44, 38, 36, and 35.

Murder of Two Negroes

Two Mississippi white men were arrested 11-6-64 in connection with the murder of Henry Hezekiah Dee and Charlie Eddie Moore, two Negroes from the Meadville, Mississippi, area. The lower portions of the bodies of these two Negroes were found in the Old River backwater of the Mississippi River on 7-12 and 13, 1964. The white men, James Ford Seale, aged 29, and Charles Marcus Edwards, aged 31, were charged under warrants issued by Meadville Justice of the Peace Willie Bedford, with willfully, unlawfully, feloniously and with malice of forethought killing the two Negroes on or about 5-2-64. Dee and Moore were last seen alive on 5-2-64. One of the subjects, Edwards, is a self-admitted Klansman.

Murder of Medgar Evers

In connection with the murder of Medgar Evers, a field secretary of the National Association for the Advancement of Colored People on 6-12-63, Byron de la Beckwith is under state indictment. Local prosecution is based upon an investigation [that] traced a rifle [that] local authorities believe could have been the murder weapon to Beckwith. The FBI traced the rifle's telescopic sight to Beckwith and, further, identified a fingerprint found on the sight with Beckwith's. He was tried twice (2-7-64 and 4-17-64) in State court, but that jury could not reach a verdict in either case. The local district attorney has indicated he will not try Beckwith again without new evidence.

Plot to Dynamite Building Occupied by Civil Rights Organization

The combined efforts of FBI Agents and the Mississippi Highway Safety Patrol resulted in the arrest of James Rutledge at Meridian, Mississippi, on 10-8-64, on State charges of feloniously possessing explosives. Rutledge was in possession of a large quantity of dynamite and literature of the Ku Klux Klan at the time of his arrest. The arrest resulted from information developed by the FBI [that] indicated the dynamite was to be used to damage a building occupied in the Neshoba County, Mississippi, area, by the Council of Federated Organizations.

The FBI immediately instituted an investigation following a recent explosion adjacent to the Bishop Dennis J. O'Connell High School in Arlington, Virginia. The FBI obtained confessions implicating three former students in the bombing and on 10-29-64, the three appeared before an Arlington County Juvenile Judge. Two of the youths who were aged 17 were found guilty of a misdemeanor and the third youth, aged 18, was found guilty of contributing to the delinquency of a minor. The three subjects are awaiting sentence. The subjects were prosecuted locally as there was no Federal violation.

On June 20, 1964, indictments were returned by the Federal Grand Jury in Nashville, Tennessee, against seven officers of the Nashville-Davidson County Sheriff's Office and the Rutherford County Sheriff's Office. The indictments charged police brutality in violation of a Federal civil rights statute and the officers are presently awaiting trial in U.S. District Court, Nashville, Tennessee.

UNITED STATES GOVERNMENT
Memorandum

TO: Mr. Mohr   DATE: December 1, 1964

FROM: C. D. DeLoach

SUBJECT: MARTIN LUTHER KING

Following is a transcript of the brief statement that Reverend Martin Luther King made to newsmen immediately after leaving the Director's Office this afternoon. While this is not a verbatim account of the statement, it is as near accurate as possible:

I am pleased I had the opportunity to meet with Mr. Hoover this afternoon and I might say the discussion was quite amicable. I sought to make it clear to Mr. Hoover that the plight of Negroes in the South is such that there must not be any misunderstanding between the FBI and civil rights leaders but must be a determination to defend the rights of all.

We talked specifically about those areas where SCLC will be working in the months ahead. We discussed areas where there will be strong resistance to the implementation of the Civil Rights Bill. We made it clear that we found our most difficult problems in Alabama and Mississippi and in these communities there are areas where we see a great deal of potential and sometimes actual terror.

I sincerely hope we can forget the confusion of the past and get on with the job the Congress, the Supreme Court, and the President have outlined as America's most crucial problem; namely, the job of giving and providing security and justice to all the people in the world.

NBC's Russ Ward and one of the NBC men equipped with a tape recorder followed King down the hall and on through the courtyard where his car was parked. According to the NBC technician, King was talking with them all the time. He said that King expressed "the usual pratter" [sic] and the only statement of any consequence was something to the effect that arrests in the Mississippi murder case could be expected within the next few days.

The Director next spoke of civil rights violations. He told the reporters he wanted to dispel a number of myths concerning FBI jurisdiction and the assignment of personnel in such cases. He stated it was a common belief in some circles that Special Agents in the South were all, without exception, southern-born Agents. As a matter of fact, 70% of the Agents currently assigned to the South were born in the North. He stated that the "notorious" Martin Luther King had attempted to capitalize on this matter by claiming that all Agents assigned to the Albany, Georgia, Resident Agency, were southern-born Agents. As a matter of fact, four out of five of the Agents assigned to the Albany, Georgia, Resident Agency were northern born. The Director stated He had instructed me to get in touch with the Reverend King and line up an appointment so that King could be given the true facts. He stated that King had refused to give me an appointment and, therefore, he considered King to be the most "notorious liar" in the country.

The Director stated he wanted to make it clear that the FBI is not a "police agency." We do not guard anyone; we are "fact finders"; the FBI cannot "wet nurse" anyone. The Director explained that the FBI has had remarkable success in civil rights cases, although, to hear Martin Luther King talk, the FBI has done nothing. The Director stated that we have been able to penetrate the Ku Klux Klan and that as a result we know what the Klan is doing currently and what they plan to do in the future. He added that in the case of the three murdered civil rights victims in Mississippi he had instructed that FBI Agents interview all members of the Ku Klux Klan to put them on notice that the FBI was going to thoroughly investigate violations of the law. He added that Governor Johnson of Mississippi had fired five or six officers who had been members of the Klan. The next question asked for Mr. Hoover to given them more details about Martin Luther King. He stated, off the record, "He is one of the lowest characters in the country." There was an immediate inquiry as to whether he could be quoted on the original statement that Martin Luther King was a liar and he stated, "Yes—that is public record."

UNITED STATES GOVERNMENT
Memorandum

TO: Mr. Mohr   DATE: December 2, 1964

FROM: C. D. DeLoach

SUBJECT: MARTIN LUTHER KING
           APPOINTMENT WITH DIRECTOR
           3:35 P.M., 12-1-64

At Reverend King's request, the Director met with King; Reverend
Ralph Abernathy, Secretary of the Southern Christian Leadership Conference (SCLC); Dr. Andrew Young, Executive Assistant to King; and
Walter Fauntroy, SCLC representative here in Washington, at 3:35 P.M.,
12-1-64, in the Director's Office.

I met King and his associates in the hallway outside the Director's
office. An attempt was made to rush directly through the reception
room, however, King slowly posed for the cameras and newsmen before proceeding.

Upon being introduced to the Director, Reverend King indicated his
appreciation for Mr. Hoover's seeing him then stated that Reverend
Abernathy would speak first. Reverend Abernathy told the Director it
was a great privilege to meet the distinguished Director of the FBI—a
man who had done so much for his country. Reverend Abernathy expressed the appreciation of the Negro race for the Director's fine work
in the field of civil rights. He stated that the Negroes had problems,
particularly in the South, and, therefore, had requested a discussion with
the Director at the very time their people were continuing to "raise up
from their bondage."

Reverend King spoke up. He stated it was vitally necessary to keep
a working relationship with the FBI. He wanted to clear up any misunderstandings [that] might have occurred. He stated that some Negroes
had told him that the FBI had been ineffective, however, he was inclined to discount such criticism. Reverend King asked that the Director
please understand that any criticism of the Director and the FBI [that]
had been attributed to King was either a misquote or an outright misrepresentation. He stated this particularly concerned Albany, Georgia. He
stated that the only time he had ever criticized the FBI was because of
instances in which Special Agents who had been given complaints in
civil rights cases regarding brutality by police officers were seen the

following day being friendly with those same police officers. King stated this, of course, promoted distrust inasmuch as the police sometimes "brutalized" Negroes.

Reverend King stated he personally appreciated the great work of the FBI which had been done in so many instances. He stated this was particularly true in Mississippi. He added that FBI developments in that state have been very significant. The FBI is a great restraining influence. Reverend King denied that he had ever stated that Negroes should not report information to the FBI. He said he had actually encouraged such reporting in many instances. He claimed there were good relationships in many communities, especially Atlanta, Georgia, between Negroes and the FBI. He stated he would continue to strongly urge all of his people to work closely with the FBI.

Reverend King stated he has never made any personal attack upon Mr. Hoover. He stated he had merely tried to articulate the feelings of the Negroes in the South in order to keep a tradition of nonviolence. He added that the Negro should never be transferred from a policy of nonviolence to one of violence and terror.

Reverend King said that the Director's report to the President this summer on rioting was a very excellent analysis.

Reverend King advised that Negroes are currently laboring under a very frustrating situation. He stated that, "We sometimes are on the verge of temporary despair." He added that it was a challenge and a duty for him to keep the Negro from coming to a boiling point. He stated that sometimes the cries coming from the Negro represent a real feeling of lonesomeness and despair. He, however, has pointed out that the path to success is nonviolence rather than violence.

Reverend King stated he has been, and still is, very concerned regarding the matter of communism in the civil rights movement. He stated he knew that the Director was very concerned because he bore the responsibility of security in the nation. Reverend King stated that from a strong philosophical point of view he could never become a communist inasmuch as he recognizes this to be a crippling totalitarian disease. He stated that as a Christian he could never accept communism. He claimed that when he learns of the identity of a communist in his midst he immediately deals with the problem by removing this man. He stated there have been one or two communists who were engaged in fundraising for the SCLC. Reverend King then corrected himself to say that these one or two men were former communists and not party members at the present time. He then identified "Jack O'Dell" as an example. He stated that he has insisted that O'Dell leave his staff because the success of his organization, the Southern Christian Leadership Conference, was far more important than friendship with O'Dell.

The Director interrupted King to state that the FBI had learned from long experience that the communists move in when trouble starts. The Director explained that communists thrive on chaos. The Director mentioned that his riot report to the President reflected the opportunistic efforts of communists. He then stated that communists have no interest in the future of the Negro race and that King, of all people, should be aware of this fact. The Director spoke briefly of communist attempts to infiltrate the labor movement.

The Director told King and his associates that the FBI shares the same despair [that] the Negroes suffer when Negro leaders refused to accept the deep responsibility they have in the civil rights movement. He stated that when Negroes are encouraged not to cooperate with the FBI this sometimes frustrates or delays successful solution of investigations. The Director told King that he had personally gone to Mississippi to meet with Governor Paul Johnson inasmuch as there had been practically no liaison between the Department of Justice, the President, and the State of Mississippi beforehand. The Director stated that upon meeting Governor Johnson the Governor explained honestly that he was a segregationist, however [*sic*] abhorred violence. The Director stated that he had told Governor Johnson they had a common meeting ground inasmuch as he was in Mississippi to put an end to violence and brutality. The Director told Governor Johnson that he would like to do this in collaboration with the State Police, however, if the FBI could not receive such cooperation we would do it on our own. The Director then made reference to water moccasins, rattlesnakes, and redneck sheriffs, in that order, who still exist in Mississippi who represent the trashy type of characters who are promoting civil rights violations. The Director told King that he had trained twenty representatives of the Mississippi State Highway Patrol and that this had represented a good move to promote better cooperation and solution of civil rights cases.

The Director told Reverend King that the FBI had put the "fear of God" in the Ku Klux Klan (KKK). He told King that we knew of the identity of the murderers of the three civil rights workers and that these murderers would soon be brought to trial. The Director then spoke of the terror in Mississippi backwoods and of the fact that sheriffs and deputy sheriffs participate in crimes of violence. He summarized by telling King that we, therefore, are under the same strain that sincere Negro leaders are under. The Director added that the KKK constantly damns the FBI and that we have currently been classified as the "Federal Bureau of Integration" in Mississippi.

The Director told King that many cases, which have been brought about as a result of FBI investigation, must be tried in State Court. He spoke of the difficulty in obtaining a verdict of guilty in instances in which white juries are impaneled in cases involving white men. The Director spoke of the KKK involvement in the Lemuel Penn case just outside of Athens, Georgia. He stated this was an outrageous miscarriage of justice in that the defendants, despite the open and shut evidence on the part of the FBI, had been acquitted.

The Director made it clear to Reverend King and his associates that the FBI could not state whether a conviction would be obtained or not in the case involving the murdered three civil rights victims. He stated, however, that the FBI has excellent evidence in this case. The Director then explained that it was most necessary for the FBI not to "jump the gun" unless we had sufficient evidence in which a case could be brought to trial.

The Director made reference to Reverend King's allegation that the FBI deals or associates with law enforcement officers who have been involved in civil rights violations. He stated emphatically that, "I'll be damned if the FBI has associated with any of these people nor will we be associated with them in the future." The Director explained that the FBI, not only because of the very nature of the law but also because of the background of our investigative employees, was in full sympathy with the sincere aspects of the civil rights movement. He stated that the FBI constantly needs cooperation and assistance in order to solve cases. He added that he made it a point, several years ago, to transfer northern Special Agents to southern offices. He stated that, for the most part, northern-born Agents are assigned civil rights cases in the South. The Director added that he feels that our Special Agents, regardless of where they are born, will investigate a case impartially and thoroughly. He mentioned, however, that it was unfair to the Agent and the FBI to "have a strike against him" in that criticism had been leveled over the fact that southern Agents would not give Negroes a "fair shake." The Director stated that such criticism was entirely unjustifiable and that no case had ever been brought to our attention proving such a fact.

The Director made reference to the recent case in McComb, Mississippi, in which nine men had been charged with burning churches and violence against Negroes. He stated this again was a miscarriage of justice. He added that the judge's decision in releasing the defendants because they had learned their lesson was entirely wrong and that it caused some people to question where youth really began. He explained that some of the defendants had been in their forties. The Director added that a deal probably, of course, had been made, however, this would certainly not represent any deterrent to future actions of violence by these men.

The Director explained that there is a great misunderstanding today among the general public and particularly the Negro race as to what the FBI can and cannot do in the way of investigations. The Director emphasized that the FBI cannot recommend prosecution or declination of prosecution. He stated that Agents cannot make "on the spot" arrests. He stated that the FBI merely investigates and then the Department of Justice determines whether prosecution be entertained or not. The Director added that the question is sometimes raised why prosecution is not scheduled sooner. He stated this, of course, was not the responsibility of the FBI in any way whatsoever. He pointed out that our civil rights investigations are conducted in a very thorough and expeditious manner once the Department has authorized such investigations.

The Director spoke of the FBI's successful penetration of the KKK. He stated that the FBI has interviewed all members of the KKK in Mississippi and has served notice to these members that if trouble occurs we plan to come to them first. He stated our penetration of the KKK has been successful as the manner in which we infiltrated the communists and the Soviet espionage services. He stated that our progress in infiltrating the KKK has been so rapid that Klan members now suspect each other and are fighting among themselves. The Director mentioned that we have two confessions in the killing of the three civil rights workers. He added that the Klan in Mississippi has failed to meet for some time because the members of this organization are apprehensive as to the identity of FBI informants in their midst. The Director stated he had personally been an enemy of the KKK for a long time.

He spoke of the FBI's case in Louisiana in the late 1920's in which FBI evidence successfully culminated in the conviction of the top Klan leader. He stated the KKK fully concentrated on Negroes, Jews, and Catholics, however, concentration now is strictly on the Negro race.

The Director explained that in Alabama the FBI cannot deal with the Highway Patrol because of psychoneurotic tendencies of the Alabama Governor. He stated that the State of Georgia has a good Governor and that the Georgia Bureau of Investigation, while not comparable to the Mississippi Highway Patrol, has cooperated with the FBI.

The Director told Reverend King and his associates that FBI representatives have held several thousand law enforcement conferences in which southern police officers have been educated as to civil rights legislation. He stated this has clearly assisted law enforcement, particularly the FBI, however, admittedly, this represents slow progress, but progress nevertheless. He added that this educational campaign will be continued and that it will eventually take hold. The Director gave the example of a Mississippi sheriff who recently broke a case as a result of FBI training.

The Director made it very clear to Reverend King and his associates that FBI Agents conduct very thorough interviews in civil rights cases. He stated he would like to know immediately if any of our Special Agents ever act in a supercilious manner or if they mishandle a complaint regarding civil rights. He stated that if the facts reflect that our Agent is in the wrong he will be called on the carpet fast. The Director asked that Reverend King or any of his representatives feel free to call the FBI at any time they have such complaints.

The Director told Reverend King he desired to give him some advice. He stated that one of the greatest things the Negro leaders could accomplish would be to encourage voting registration among their people. Another thing would be to educate their people in the skills so that they could compete in the open market. The Director mentioned several professions in which Negroes could easily learn skills. The Director also told King he wanted him to know that registrars in the South were now more careful in their actions. He stated that there were fewer attempts now to prevent Negroes from registering inasmuch as the FBI is watching such actions very carefully. The Director told Reverend King that the FBI was making progress in violations regarding discrimination in eating places. He gave as a specific example a restaurant in Atlanta, Georgia, in which surveillances have taken place to ascertain if out-of-state cars are being served at this particular restaurant. The Director stated he personally was in favor of equality in eating places and in schools. He stated emphatically, however, he was not in favor of taking Negro children 10 or 12 miles across town simply because their parents wanted them to go to a school other than those in their specific neighborhood.

The Director told Reverend King that in due time there will be a complete change in the mores of community thinking in the United States regarding the racial problem. He stated that meanwhile the FBI will continue to handle its responsibility in a thorough and impartial manner. He reiterated that the FBI cannot encourage prosecution in

Federal Court despite the fact that some local courts cannot be trusted. He added that some judges cannot be trusted.

The Director praised the Georgia papers that declared the verdict of the Penn case to be a travesty of justice. He added that the Jackson, Mississippi, papers had contained several editorials deploring violence against Negroes and participation in church burnings. The same editorials declared that this was no way to solve racial problems. The Director stated that his statements made at a press conference in Jackson, Mississippi, this summer to the effect that he was in Mississippi to see to it that an end was put to the violence of bombings and burning churches had had some effect upon backwoods terrorists.

The Director told King that he wanted to make it very clear that the question is often raised as to whether the FBI will protect civil rights workers or Negroes. He stated that he has in the past and will continue to answer such questions on the basis that the FBI does not have the authority nor the jurisdiction to protect anyone. He stated that when the Department of Justice desires that Negroes be protected this is the responsibility of U.S. Marshals. The Director reiterated that the FBI is strictly an investigative agency and cannot and will not extend itself beyond legislated jurisdiction. The Director repeated very emphtically that while our investigations are very definitely thorough and impartial he wanted to state once again that if Reverend King or any of his associates ever knew of a Special Agent showing bias or prejudice he wanted to know about this matter immediately.

The Director explained that we have civil rights cases not only in the South but also in the northern cities. He gave examples of New York and Chicago. He stated that there have been some cases in Miami, Florida.

The Director spoke once again of the necessity of the Negro educating himself in order to compete in manual and professional skills. He mentioned the examples of a shoeshine boy in Miami, Florida, who turned out to be, after questioning by the Director, a graduate of Howard University. This shoeshine boy, a Negro, explained to the Director that he could not get a job above the level of shoeshine boy because of the color of his skin. The Director stated this, of course, was wrong and that under no circumstances did he, or anyone in the FBI, share the opinion that the Negro, or any other race, should be kept down. The Director spoke of his pride in Negro Agents and particularly mentioned Special Agent Aubrey Lewis, the former Notre Dame track star who is currently assigned to the New York Division.

The Director spoke of a Miami Special Agent who was transferred to that Office from St. Louis. This Agent explained to the Director on one occasion that he was first a little upset about being transferred to Miami because he felt his race would be against him. He stated, however, much to his surprise, that the white people in Miami treated him with the greatest of courtesy while people of his own race referred to him as a "fink" simply because he was a representative of law enforcement.

Reverend King interrupted the Director at this point and asked if this same Negro Agent is still assigned to the Miami Division. The Director replied in the affirmative. The Director stated that at a recent dinner Father Hesburgh, the President of Notre Dame University, explained to the Director that his institution had difficulty getting Negroes on the football team because their grades were never high enough. The Director told Reverend King that same thing is true of Negroes who apply for the position of Special Agent. He stated in most instances they lack the qualifications, however, we were very happy to hire any Negro who was qualified for the position. The Director told Reverend King that we, of course, could not let down our qualifications simply because of the color of a person's skin.

The Director told Reverend King and his associates that the problems that he and the Negro leaders have is a mutual problem. He stated in most instances in civil rights matters we have learned that "you are damned if you do and you are damned if you don't." The Director stated nevertheless the FBI would continue to do its job. He stated that we additionally are very proud of ten or eleven Indian Special Agents and of a number of Special Agents who have Mexican blood in them. He stated the color of a man's skin makes no difference to the FBI whatsoever; however, we do merit the cooperation and assistance of all groups and it is most unfair when these groups are taught not to cooperate with the FBI.

The Director mentioned that he wanted to make it very plain that the FBI will not tolerate any of our personnel being slapped around. He gave an example of the Lombardozzi case in New York where one of our Agents was jumped by five hoodlums outside a church. He stated these hoodlums were immediately taught a lesson. The Director mentioned that in the war with hoodlums, for every man we lose we make certain, through legal means of course, that the hoodlums lose the same number or more.

The Director proudly spoke of the ability of Agents to outshoot and outfight hoodlums and other individuals who attempted to take advantage of our personnel. He stated the KKK is afraid to "mix" with our

Agents. He mentioned that the Klan was "yellow." He stated they are brave as long as they have the majority with them but afraid when they face an equal number.

The Director spoke of the Mack Charles Parker case in Poplarville, Mississippi. He stated that our evidence in this case had been turned over to Governor Coleman, the then governor of the State. He mentioned that Governor Coleman was a decent type of individual who had immediately seen to it that a State Court received evidence contributed by the FBI. The Director mentioned that our evidence in this case was excellent, however, the Grand Jury refused to indict the subjects involved in the lynching of Parker.

The Director told Reverend King that in many instances our Agents have been spit upon, then have been refused food and lodging and many things are done to thwart hard-hitting investigations by the FBI. He stated that nevertheless we continue to gather evidence in an expeditious and thorough manner.

Reverend Abernathy stated that the Negroes have a real problem in tearing down the current system of segregated voting tests in the South. He stated it was most important that there be kept alive in the Negro communities a ray of hope. He stated that the Negro people should not be allowed to fall into an atmosphere of despair.

The Director explained that this was a very important point. He stated that real progress has been made in higher wages, voting registration, and housing matters. The Director pointed out, however, that such progress has not been emphasized by the rabble-rousers who constantly attempt to stir up the Negroes against the whites. The Director gave as an example the communist, Epton, in New York City. The Director stated that Epton is sometimes pointed to as a person the Negro should emulate because of his militancy. The Director stated this was wrong and it is also wrong to "mislead" the Negroes.

Reverend Abernathy stated that the SCLC does not want Negroes like Epton in their movement. He stated that Reverend King, more than anyone else, has prevented people like Epton and the Muslims from taking over the civil rights movement. Reverend Abernathy stated that actually the Negroes are a part of the Federal Government, therefore, anything that represents the Federal Government is an encouragement to the Negro. He added that even the side [sic] of a post office building or a Federal courtroom is an encouragement to the Negro. He mentioned that when a Negro receives information that a case in which he has been brutally mistreated is going [to] Federal Court he feels encouraged over the fact that he will get a fair trial. Reverend Abernathy continued that the same problem is true when a Negro sees an FBI Agent. He stated that the Negro feels open encouragement inasmuch as the FBI will not only fairly handle his case but will serve as a great deterrent of violence.

The Director stated that the KKK today is represented by common white trash. He stated that the Klan was actually worse than the Communist party inasmuch as the Klan resorts to violence while the communists usually emulate termites in their activities.

The Director reiterated that King and his associates should feel free to call him at any time when they have knowledge of possible civil rights violations. King replied that over the past few years he has noted amazing signs of progress in the civil rights field. He stated he has been very surprised to see some communities comply with the new civil rights statutes. He stated there still are some pockets of resistance particularly in the South. He added that the SCLC is planning to stimulate voting registration activities in Selma, Alabama, in the near future. He mentioned that some members of his organization have been successful in infiltrating this white community and have learned there is a great potential for violence in Selma.

The Director interrupted King and briefly detailed five cases in which the FBI has gathered evidence in Selma, Alabama. The Director mentioned that these cases came about as a result of FBI investigation and that we were continuing our investigations in Selma, Alabama. He mentioned that one case would come to trial on December 9, 1964. The Director particularly made reference to the fact that we have three excellent cases in Selma at the present time.

Reverend King inquired as to whether his representatives should notify the FBI when they arrive in Selma, Alabama. He quickly corrected himself that he knew his representatives should contact the FBI upon arrival, however, he asked the Director what would be the possibilities of FBI Agents being in Selma, Alabama, inasmuch as there appeared to be a potential for violence. The Director specifically asked Reverend King when his activities would take place. Reverend Abernathy indicated such activity would take place around January 1, 1965. The Director clearly explained that FBI Agents would be in Selma, not for the purpose of "protecting" anyone, but for the purpose of observing and reporting to the Department of Justice any possible violations of civil rights that might occur. Reverend King expressed appreciation in this regard.

Reverend King stood up and stated he wished to express his personal thanks for a most fruitful and necessary meeting. The Director told

Reverend King that he should get in touch with us anytime he felt it was necessary.

Reverend King mentioned that there were representatives of the press in the Director's reception room. He turned to me and asked if the FBI planned to make any comment regarding the meeting. I told him that the Director had instructed that we make no comment whatsoever. Reverend King asked the Director if there would be any objections if he read a short prepared statement to the press. The Director told Reverend King this, of course, was up to him.

In proceeding to the reception room, Reverend King pulled a press release, hand-written in ink, out of his right coat pocket. This press release obviously had been prepared prior to the time Reverend King arrived at FBI Headquarters. A previous memorandum has been sent through reporting verbatim the comments by King in the Director's reception room.

ACTION:

It is suggested that the attached letter be sent to the President concerning the meeting between the Director, Reverend King, and his associates.

The General Investigative Division, Civil Rights Section, should take due note of the proposed activities in Selma, Alabama, and should instruct the appropriate office to make certain that Agents are on hand to observe activities in Selma, Alabama, on or around January 1, 1965.

December 2, 1964

The President
The White House
Washington, D.C.

My dear Mr. President:

In response to his request to see me, I conferred for about an hour with the Reverend Martin Luther King in my office yesterday afternoon. He was accompanied by the following members of the Southern Christian Leadership Conference of which he is president: Reverend Ralph D. Abernathy, Treasurer; Andrew J. Young, Program Director; and Walter E. Fauntroy, Director of the organization's Washington, D.C., office.

The meeting was most amicable and King indicated that he had requested to see me in an effort to clear up any misunderstandings that we might have. He apologized for remarks attributed to him criticizing the FBI and me with specific reference to Albany, Georgia. He stated that in this connection he had either been misquoted or there had been an outright misrepresentation.

He said that while some Negroes have complained to him that the FBI has been ineffective in investigating civil rights violations, he personally discounts such complaints and said he appreciated the fine work the FBI has been doing in this regard.

He said he had been critical of the FBI only in connection with instances where our Agents, who had been furnished complaints involving policy brutality, were, thereafter, observed being friendly toward these same officers. He said situations like this serve to breed Negro distrust for the FBI. I advised Reverend King that I was aware that allegations of this nature had been made and that I looked into the matter. It was determined that these charges were without basis.

Reverend King categorically denied ever having made a personal attack on me and also denied that he had ever instructed Negroes not to cooperate with the FBI. I told him that when Negroes are encouraged not to cooperate with the FBI, the solution of cases is delayed and sometimes frustrated. He said, to the contrary, he encouraged such cooperation. He explained that Negroes in many areas are frustrated. He said he feels it is his duty to keep them from expressing their frustrations through violence. Reverend King made reference to my report to you on the rioting that took place in some of our modern cities last summer. He indicated he considers it an excellent analysis of the situation.

Communist infiltration of the civil rights movement was discussed. Reverend King stated that as a Christian he could never accept communism and that he shared my concern with the problem. He described communism as a "crippling, totalitarian disease." He said that while there are "one or two" former communists currently engaged in the fund-raising activities for the Southern Christian Leadership Conference, he does not tolerate communists in his organization. He cited the communist background of Hunter Pitts O'Dell and noted that he considered the success of the Southern Christian Leadership Conference more important to him than his friendship with O'Dell. Consequently, he claimed, O'Dell is no longer associated with his organization.

The problems confronting the FBI in civil rights investigations were explained to the Reverend King in detail. I made it clear to him that cases developed as a result of FBI investigation must often be tried in local courts where there are difficulties involved in getting white juries to convict white defendants in connection with civil rights matters. I cited some of our experiences in this regard.

He and his associates were advised of the recent conferences held for local law enforcement officers throughout the United States for the purpose of fully acquainting them with civil rights legislation and their responsibilities in connection with same. I told him that the results of this campaign have been encouraging in the cooperation received.

I pointed out to him that there is a great misunderstanding today among the general public and particularly the Negro race as to the FBI's role in civil rights matters. I emphasized that the FBI is an investigative agency, that it cannot recommend prosecution or make-on-the-spot arrests where federal laws have not been violated. He was advised that the FBI will not protect civil rights workers or Negroes because the FBI does not have the authority or jurisdiction to do so. He was also advised that the FBI cannot and will not exceed its authority. Reverend King was told that our investigations are conducted in a thorough and impartial manner, but if he or any of his associates knew of a Special Agent who had shown bias or prejudice, I wanted to know about it immediately.

Reverend King indicated that the Southern Christian Leadership Conference is planning to engage in voter registration activities in Selma, Alabama, on or about January 1, 1965, and that he has learned that there could be violence. I told him that our Agents would be on the scene, not for the purpose of rendering protection, but to observe and report to the Department of Justice any possible violations of civil rights that may occur.

Reverend King expressed his gratitude for having the opportunity to meet me. He said he felt our meeting had been a productive one, and I told him to feel free to get in touch with me any time he thought it necessary to do so.

Respectfully submitted,
J. Edgar Hoover

February 3, 1965

Honorable Bill D. Moyers
Special Assistant to the President
The White House
Washington, D.C.

Dear Mr. Moyers:

On January 2, 1965, Reverend Martin Luther King, Jr., appeared in Selma, Alabama, where he announced the beginning of a statewide drive to enable Negroes to register for voting. Since that time, there has been a continuing series of demonstrations by Negroes seeking to register to vote in Selma, and many demonstrators have been arrested on such charges as violating the city's parade ordinance, disorderly conduct, and refusing to obey an officer.

On February 1, 1965, King led a group of approximately 264 Negroes from a church in Selma toward the county courthouse. They were confronted by J. Wilson Baker, Commissioner of Public Safety, who stated they were violating a city ordinance by parading without a permit. The group continued approximately three blocks when they were again confronted by Commissioner Baker who placed the entire group under arrest.

The group was taken to the City Hall where Commissioner Baker told King and Reverend Ralph Abernathy, an associate of King's, that they were not under arrest and advised them to leave the building. King and Reverend Abernathy then held a press conference on the steps of the City Hall, and they were instructed by a police officer to leave the premises. When they refused to do so, they were arrested and charged with violating the city's parade ordinance. All others arrested have been released on bond, however, King and Reverend Abernathy remain in jail in Selma in lieu of a $200 bond each.

On February 3, 1965, we received information from a reliable source to the effect that Andrew Young, an assistant to King in New York City, held a discussion with Clarence Jones, an attorney in New York who is an advisor to King. Young and Jones discussed a request from King that "show people" visit him in Selma, and it was indicated that this might be arranged for February 4, 1965.

Young and Jones also discussed a request of King's that Young make a personal call to the President to have him intervene in some way. Young indicated that he did not think he would be able to speak directly to the President but thought that he could discuss the matter with Mr. Lee White.

Jones advised Young that it should be made clear to the President they do not want troops in Selma but are requesting that the President set the issue straight before the nation regarding the right to vote without obstruction, chastise Alabama for obstructing the right to vote and take legislative or executive action to clear up the confusion in this area.

Jones also suggested to Young that the President dispatch a small force of United States Marshals specially deputized by the President or the Attorney General and he alleged that the United States Marshal at Selma is afraid of Sheriff James Clarke.

Clarence Jones was a member of the Labor Youth League in the mid 1950s. The Labor Youth League has been designated as subversive pursuant to Executive Order Number 10450.

It is suggested that the above information may be of interest to the President, and the attorney general is also being advised.

Sincerely yours,

J. Edgar Hoover

UNITED STATES DEPARTMENT OF JUSTICE

FEDERAL BUREAU OF INVESTIGATION

New York, New York
February 8, 1965

Re: Communist Influence in Racial Matters
Internal Security-C

A confidential source, who has furnished reliable information in the past, furnished information on February 4, 1965, indicating that Clarence Jones received information on that date [that] revealed that Harry Wachtel wanted him (Jones) to attend a meeting of the "Research Committee" (a meeting of Martin Luther King's advisors) on February 5, 1965. According to the source, the meeting was to take place at Wachtel's office, 575 Madison Avenue, New York City, between the hours 12:30 and 5:30 P.M.

Another confidential source, who has furnished reliable information in the past, advised that Harry Wachtel and Clarence Jones were in contact on February 5, 1965, regarding the scheduled "Research Committee" meeting for that date. Wachtel said in that regard that he was certain that King and Andrew Young would not attend, and that only

Bayard Rustin (Organizer of the March on Washington), Cleveland Robinson (Secretary-Treasurer of District 65, Retail, Wholesale and Department Store Workers Union; American Federation of Labor—Congress of Industrial Organizations, AFL-CIO), Walter Fauntroy, (Director of the Washington office of the SCLC), Mike Harrington (National Committee member of the Socialist party) and he (Wachtel) would attend.

Wachtel and Jones also took the opportunity to discuss a letter [that] appeared in the *New York Times* on February 5, 1965, which solicited funds on behalf of King and the SCLC. In that regard, Wachtel said he was a "little unhappy that he had not been in on the composition of the letter, and how big a bomb it would have been if King had been released from jail." Wachtel said he desired that King get out of jail, but Jones said he trusted King's timing and urged Wachtel not to worry about it.

With regard to the letter in the *New York Times*, which Wachtel and Jones discussed, it is noted that on February 5, 1965, the *New York Times*, page 15, carried an advertisement captioned, "A Letter from Martin Luther King from a Selma, Alabama, Jail." In the letter, King opens with a statement that little did the King of Norway realize when he presented him the Nobel Peace Prize that in less than sixty days he would be in jail, adding that he (the King of Norway) and the world will be shocked because they are little aware of the unfinished business in the South.

King continues: "By jailing hundreds of Negroes, the City of Selma, Alabama, has revealed the persisting ugliness of segregation to the nation and the world."

King, in answering a question as to why they were in jail, said, "have you ever been required to answer 100 questions on government, some abstruse even to a political science specialist, merely to vote? Have you ever stood in line with a hundred others and after waiting an entire day seen less than ten given the qualifying test?"

King said: "We are in jail simply because we cannot tolerate these conditions for ourselves or our nation."

A plea for funds is then made by King in behalf of the SCLC.

UNITED STATES DEPARTMENT OF JUSTICE

FEDERAL BUREAU OF INVESTIGATION

New York, New York
August 16, 1965

Re: Communist Influence in Racial Matters
Internal Security-C

On August 13, 1965, a confidential source, who has furnished reliable information in the past, advised that Dora McDonald (Secretary to Martin Luther King, President, Southern Christian Leadership Conference, SCLC) and Stanley Levison were in contact on that day concerning the rioting in Los Angeles, California. In that regard, McDonald said King had been contacted by a radio station in Los Angeles, who urged that he issue a statement appealing to the Negroes to end the rioting. She said that King, in turn, had requested that she contact him (Levison) and request that he prepare a statement dealing with the matter. According to the source, Levison prepared the following statement:

"I know that you have grievances that are hard to live with—I know that any Negro can reach the end of his patience and want to strike out and strike back. But it is not courage nor militancy to strike out blindly. Our enemies have always hoped that we would lose our heads and riot against the guilty and innocent alike. This enables them to argue that we haven't decency or good sense. I speak to you as one who had to march with other Negroes against guns, clubs, dogs, and whips and who won victories over cruel and barbarous sheriffs and klansmen. We won victories because we had a greater weapon—disciplined cool heads, and iron determination not to [be] provoked into violence. Our adversaries have always known what to do when we lost our heads—it gave them a chance to beat our heads. They have never known what to do when we refused to be sucked into the trap of violence.

"Tonight the whole world is watching you. If you want all America to respect you, if you want the world to know you are men, put down your weapons and your rocks. Get a committee together and draw up demands. If you want my help I will sit with you and plan how to improve your conditions.

"Negroes in the South were not less oppressed than you and we have run Jim Crow from thousands of places without using a rock or a bullet. We made millions of white Americans sick and ashamed of their practices and by our discipline won many to our side. You are harming yourselves, not the segregationists. Tonight in the South, the segregationist is delighted. He has made you lose your temper and for a few moments of emotional excitement and relief you are conducting yourself without reason, without a name and without a goal. You are not an army of Negro people if you fight without reason. Our people are not rioters and are not looters. Come back to our ranks where there is room for honest courage and militancy, where real and permanent victories have been won and will be won in the right way.

"The man who cools off, who puts down his weapon and stands up with only his body is the man of courage. Don't let us down here in the South. Don't discredit brave Negroes in jails in Johannesburg. Don't set yourself back. You can still win a great victory by halting the fighting because there is more honor and dignity in looking the other side squarely in the eye and demanding your rights than there is in struggling in blind fury. In the name of brave Negroes who have died in the South over the past ten years of bitter struggle, I appeal to you to end the hostilities so that together we can march forward for real gains for our people everywhere."

A confidential source, who has furnished reliable information in the past, advised on August 14, 1965, that Bayard Rustin (organizer of the March on Washington), and Martin Luther King were in contact on that date. Their contact, according to the source, dealt with the rioting in Los Angeles. King told Rustin that he was on his way to Puerto Rico to deliver a speech, and that upon arrival he would issue a press release dealing with the situation in Los Angeles; therefore, [he] wanted Rustin's suggestions on the matter. Rustin suggested to King that the following points should be contained in any statement to the press:

"That we deplore resorting to violence no matter who is engaged in the violence because it is wrong and socially destructive. That while we deplore violence, we also deplore the concentration of the ghetto life which leads, with the absence of jobs, bad education and slums, to the hopelessness and despair where the Negro youth, out of these conditions, feel that they have no stake in American society." Rustin suggested in reference to that point that King make mention of President Johnson's conference scheduled to be held in November 1965, which will deal with the whole ghetto and family life problem, by stating that he hoped new and stirring ideas would emerge from the conference.

In continuing his suggestions, Rustin said that King should point out that, "Rightly or wrongly, whether or not there was, in fact, police brutality in Los Angeles, almost every Negro in every family has, at one time or another, felt that he has been maltreated by the police; therefore, in addition to the social problems, in every city there needs to be a civilian review board. This board is to protect the policeman when he is right and to protect the citizen when the policeman is not right.''

King and Rustin both remarked that they had been asked to go to Los Angeles to help suppress the riots, but both opined that they would not be able to be of much assistance since the situation had deteriorated to such a point that it was a job for the National Guard. They ended their contact by speculating on whether or not they would be of any help subsequent to the riots.

The same confidential source furnished information on August 14, 1965, which disclosed that Rustin and Roy Wilkins (Executive Secretary of the National Association for the Advancement of Colored People, NAACP) were in contact on that date concerning, among other things, the rioting in Los Angeles, who had done nothing (to end the riots), were putting pressure on King to come to Los Angeles to aid in quelling the riots. Rustin said King was going to Puerto Rico to speak, but had airline tickets to travel to Los Angeles on his way back from Puerto Rico. Rustin said King would do nothing but create more confusion and embarrass himself if he went to Los Angeles. Wilkins concurred, adding that if King did go to Los Angeles, he would be regarded as an emissary sent to quiet the rioters.

The source advised on August 14, 1965, that Rustin and Harry Wachtel were in contact on the above date. During their contact, Wachtel spoke in regard to the rioting in Los Angeles, stating that he was not unhappy because the ''power structure acts as if they are only dealing with King and they are not dealing with guys who are easily incited, who live in stinking conditions.'' Rustin said he had dissuaded King from going to Los Angeles at this time.

UNITED STATES DEPARTMENT OF JUSTICE

FEDERAL BUREAU OF INVESTIGATION

San Francisco, California
August 10, 1965

UNKNOWN SUBJECT;
Governor EDMUND G. BROWN,
California-Victim

Information was received on August 18, 1965, from John McInerney, Governor's Office, Sacramento, California, to the effect that an anonymous postcard was received on the morning of August 18, 1965, addressed to Governor Edmund G. Brown marked ''Urgent.'' This card was postmarked at Los Angeles, California, during the afternoon hours of August 17, 1965. It stated, ''Dear Sir, King will be shot!!! even by one of his so as to create greater havoc. Remember you have been told!''

UNITED STATES DEPARTMENT OF JUSTICE

FEDERAL BUREAU OF INVESTIGATION

Los Angeles, California
August 23, 1965

MARTIN LUTHER KING, JR.
SECURITY MATTER-C

... advised on August 19, 1965, that King was scheduled to meet with Los Angeles Mayor Samuel W. Yorty and Police Chief William H. Parker around noon on August 19, 1965, for a conference.

The *Los Angeles Times,* a daily Los Angeles metropolitan newspaper, home edition, for August 20, 1965 part 1, page 1, carried an article captioned ''King Assailed by Yorty after Stormy Meeting.'' The article stated that Mayor Yorty, Police Chief Parker, and nine other persons, not identified, but described as mainly civil rights figures and aides to Yorty and Parker, held a two hour and 45 minute meeting with King in Mayor Yorty's office on August 19, 1965.

Mayor Yorty was quoted as stating after the conference that King had performed "a great disservice to the people of Los Angeles and the nation." Yorty criticized King for "talking about lawlessness, killing, looting, and burning in the same context as our police department." The Mayor staunchly defended Parker against Dr. King's suggestion that many Negroes want Parker to resign.

The article quoted Bayard Rustin, a deputy to Dr. King who attended the meeting, as stating that some of the participants used "crude" language and that the longest and most heated debate concerned King's demand for a civilian police review board. Another official present, not identified, stated that much of the argument at the conference "was over unfounded charges of police brutality."

Yorty was quoted as stating, "I don't think that it's wise for Dr. King to try and simplify all the complex issues that led to the riot and personify them in Chief Parker" and that Dr. King "shouldn't have come here."

King was quoted as stating that the rioting had an economic cause and this could be alleviated if Mayor Yorty could obtain sufficient anti-poverty funds.

King stated that Yorty and Parker would not permit him to visit arrested rioters in Lincoln Heights Jail, and he suggested that Yorty should tour the Watts area so that residents could tell him personally of their grievances. Mayor Yorty stated that he refused to let Dr. King visit the jail because he did not want to set off a prison riot.

King was quoted as stating that an independent police review board could "do a lot to ease tension by investigating specific charges of brutality." Yorty stated that a police review would tend to duplicate the present five-member police commission which, he noted, includes a Negro, a Mexican-American, and a Jew. Yorty was further quoted as stating [that] even if Parker wanted to resign he would refuse to accept the resignation.

... advised on August 19, 1965, that King had planned to visit the Watts area of Los Angeles where the rioting centered again on the afternoon of August 19, 1965, but for some reason canceled his plans. ... did not know the reason but surmised it might have been because of the prolonged conference King had with Mayor Yorty and Chief Parker that day and that time did not permit.

... advised further on August 20, 1965, that the proposed meeting between King and Los Angeles labor leaders on August 20, 1965, was not held. Bayard Rustin had hoped to arrange such a meeting but it did not materialize. Apparently time did not permit arranging such a meeting on short notice. . . . did not know the identity of the labor leaders that King had hoped to meet with.

The *Los Angeles Times*, home edition for August 21, 1965, part 1, page 4, carried an article "L.A. Lacks Leadership on Rights, King Says."

The article quoted Dr. Martin Luther King as stating at a press conference at the International Hotel, Los Angeles, on August 20, 1965, that he had failed to find any "statesmanship and creative leadership" to resolve the situation in the South Los Angeles riot-torn district.

When asked whether he was referring to Mayor Yorty and Governor Brown, King replied, "I think the governor has been moving in a forthright and committed way but I am not going to get into any name calling." He added [that] he had not seen on the city level the kind of "sensitive and determined leadership capable of solving the problem."

King stated that he had been in contact with the White House on the morning of August 20, 1965, and had an appointment to talk to President Johnson by telephone that night from Atlanta about the Los Angeles situation.

King was further quoted as stating, "There are serious doubts that the white community is in any way concerned or willing to accommodate their needs. There is a growing disillusionment and resentment (by Negroes in the Watts area) toward the Negro middle class and the leadership it has produced."

King was further quoted as stating that the Negroes' fight is for "dignity and work, and this is the reason why the issue of police brutality looms so high. The slightest discourtesy on the part of an officer of the law is a deprivation of the dignity [that] most of the residents of Watts came North seeking."

King was further quoted as stating, "There is a unanimous feeling among Negroes that there is police brutality." King added that while most Negroes want Police Chief Parker removed he had not heard any recommendations for a replacement for Parker.

A source, who has furnished reliable information in the past, advised on August 20, 1965, that at his press conference on that date King had also stated that he felt that the underlying cause of the riots in Los Angeles were basically economic and grew out of the depths of despair of the Negro. This source further advised that the riots in Los Angeles were of national significance and that while these riots constitute a "crisis" for the nonviolent movement he still felt that the majority of people in the Watts area maintained an attitude of nonviolence.

. . . advised on August 20, 1965, that King and his aide, Bernard

Lee, departed Los Angeles at approximately 3:05 P.M. on the afternoon of August 20, 1965, by Delta Airline Flight 804, which was due to arrive at Atlanta, Georgia, at 9:52 (on the same date).

UNITED STATES GOVERNMENT
Memorandum

TO: DIRECTOR, FBI   DATE: 9/3/65

FROM: SAC, LOS ANGELES (100-106670)

SUBJECT: MARTIN LUTHER KING, JR.
              SM-C

              00: ATLANTA

Enclosed herewith for the Bureau, Atlanta and New York is one Xerox copy each, for information, of a "Statement by Dr. Martin Luther King, Jr. on Arrival in Los Angeles, August 17, 1965."

New York is furnished a copy inasmuch as this statement appears to be primarily the five-point program suggested by Bayard Rustin as set forth in a New York radiogram to Director, Atlanta and Los Angeles dated 8/27/65 captioned CIRM IS-C.

Statement by Dr. Martin Luther King, Jr. on Arrival in Los Angeles
August 17, 1965

I have come to Los Angeles at the invitation of a number of concerned individuals and major organizations that have been, like myself, deeply involved in the struggle of civil rights and human dignity.

Let me say first of all that I profoundly deplore the events that have occurred in Los Angeles in these last few tragic days. I believe and have said on many occasions that violence is not the answer to social conflict whether it is engaged in by white people in Alabama or by Negroes in Los Angeles. Violence is all the more regrettable in this period in light of the tremendous nonviolent sacrifices that both Negro and white people together have endured to bring justice to all men.

But it is equally clear, as President Johnson pointed out yesterday, that it is the job of all Americans "to right the wrongs from which such violence and disorder spring." The criminal responses [that] led to the tragic outbreaks of violence in Los Angeles are environmental and not racial. The economic deprivation, social isolation, inadequate

housing, and general despair of thousands of Negroes teeming in Northern and Western ghettos are the ready seeds [that] give birth to tragic
expressions of violence. By acts of commission and omission none of
us in this great country has done enough to remove injustice. I therefore
humbly suggest that all of us accept our share of responsibility for these
past days of anguish.

I should like to state in quite more specific terms why I make this
journey in the interest of reconciliation and future cooperation between
the races.

First, I have come to minister to the thousands of innocent Negro
people who have done no wrong or who have [not] thought in any way
to use violence, yet whose community has been disrupted by rioting,
the destruction of institutions they daily need, and many of whom have
lost their work. This has been for them, not merely the hardship spring-
ing from the disruption of their physical community; it has been a
spiritual disaster deepening their despair and hopelessness.

Secondly, I have come to minister to the small degree that I can—to
those who have been involved in the rioting. Our Christian effort must
be to redeem them and to leave no stone unturned, despite their guilt,
to help them find a useful place in building a good society in which
they can share as equals. In this connection I shall, as a first step, seek
to visit with them in prison and to urge officials to find ways for them
to help reconstruct the damage they have done.

Thirdly, I would like to confer with the many segments of the white
community that have been the staunch allies of the Negro people in
our struggle. Surely if millions of Negroes across this country are dis-
mayed, deeply hurt, and bewildered by these past few days, it stands
to reason that our white friends are also. The strength of the Negro-
white alliance for justice will be maintained only if we are in constant
dialogue, understanding past mistakes, evolving new programs, and providing ways and means to avert any such recurrence of violence.

Fourthly, I would like to work with the local leadership of Los
Angeles in proposing programs for the eradication of those problems
relating to housing, schools, jobs, and police behavior that were directly
or indirectly related to the disorder.

Fifthly, if the local leadership feels that it will be helpful, I am
prepared to sit with them in discussions with the public officials on the
role and responsibility of governments and to evaluate with them a
program that will eliminate such future occurrences in Los Angeles or
in any other city of our nation.

WASH DC

FBI CHICAGO
955 PM CST URGENT 2/24/66 JLV
TO DIRECTOR (100-106670)
FROM CHICAGO (100-35356)

MARTIN LUTHER KING, JR., SM-C

REMYTEL TODAY.
LOCAL NEWS MEDIA REPORTING CIVIL RIGHTS GROUPS
LED BY KING CONTINUED WITHOUT INTERFERENCE RENOVA-
TION OF WEST SIDE "SLUM BUILDING" AT ONE THREE TWO
ONE SOUTH HOMAN [*sic*] AVENUE, CHICAGO. FURTHER
LOCAL JUDGES, LAWYERS AND REAL ESTATE OFFICIALS
BLASTED AS ILLEGAL THE ACTION OF KING IN ASSUMING
WHAT THEY CALLED "TRUSTEESHIP" OF BUILDING. USDC
JUDGE JAMES B. PARSONS QUOTED IN PART AS STATING "I
DON'T THINK IT IS LEGAL; IT IS THEFT." ALSO "I AM NOT IN
AGREEMENT WITH CIVIL DISOBEDIENCE OR THE FLOUTING
OF GOOD LAWS. THIS IS A REVOLUTIONARY TACTIC."
LATE BULLETIN REPORTED COUNTY PUBLIC AND DEPART-
MENT WILL WITHHOLD RENT PAYMENTS FOR TWO RELIEF
FAMILIES IN BUILDING IF CIVIL RIGHTS GROUPS WHO HAVE
"ASSUMED TRUSTEESHIP" OF BUILDING REFUSE TO TURN
THE RENTAL MONEY OVER TO BUILDING OWNER.

UNITED STATES DEPARTMENT OF JUSTICE

FEDERAL BUREAU OF INVESTIGATION

Chicago, Illinois
March 5, 1966

MARTIN LUTHER KING, JR.

. . . advised the Chicago Office of the Federal Bureau of Investigation
(FBI) that Doctor Martin Luther King, Jr., president, Southern Christian
Leadership Conference (SCLC), arrived in Chicago at 12:05 P.M., March
2, 1966, accompanied by Reverend Bernard Lee, aide to King. King

and Lee arrived in Chicago from the Atlanta Headquarters of the SCLC and indicated to police representatives at O'Hare Airport that they planned to return to Atlanta on March 4, 1966.

... advised that his information concerning King's itinerary reflects that he was to spend the afternoon of March 2, 1966, in meetings with representatives of his SCLC staff here in Chicago, was to attend an early evening social reception on Chicago's north side, and subsequently to continue with staff meetings for the remainder of the evening. There was no information available concerning contemplated activities on the part of King for March 3–4, 1966.

... advised that his information concerning King's activities as of this time was to the effect that King has been ill for several days with a severe cold and has participated in no scheduled activities of any kind. . . . advised that there was no information available which reflected that King, under a doctor's care, would leave Chicago on March 4, 1966.

... above, advised that Dr. King departed Chicago at approximately 4:00 P.M. on this date, from O'Hare Airport, en route to Atlanta. Just prior to King's departure, he is reported to have taped an appearance on *Kup's Show*, a local television conversation program, to be shown during the early morning hours on March 6, 1966, at Chicago ...

In monitoring of the television program, *Kup's Show*, . . . it was observed that Dr. King appeared for approximately fifty minutes . . . General discussion took place concerning the local civil rights campaign of King. It was stated at the inception of the program that King had been ill recently and had interrupted his recuperation to make this television appearance.

King had stated during the program in response to a series of questions from the moderator, generally as follows:

He had brought the SCLC campaign to Chicago because of the urgent problems of racial injustice here. King felt that there was more such injustice now in the large northern cities than in the south, and Chicago, with its vast slums and ghetto areas, represents the classic example of the economic, educational, social, and human problems of the northern Negroes.

A second reason given by King for concentrating on Chicago was the existence here of the Co-Ordinating Council of Community Organizations (CCCO), a grouping of local civil rights organizations, experienced and effective, and the lack of such an organization or organizations in other large northern cities. Consequently, the SCLC, initially upon its arrival in Chicago, was able to utilize the services of the CCCO as a nucleus of local support and utilize the already existent facilities of this group. King continued that the civil rights movement generally has a strong emotional attachment to Chicago because so many Chicago people, both lay and clergy, have activated themselves in the past in the southern civil rights movement.

King advised that issues that will be points of concentration in Chicago are those of employment, schools, and slums, which he described as not just housing conditions, but general conditions of economic exploitation. He emphasized that the SCLC campaign was not an anti-Daly campaign, this is a reference to Chicago's Mayor Richard J. Daly. King welcomed Daly's efforts and programs [that] were in any way directed toward the removal of conditions [that] serve to exploit and inhibit the activities and well-being of the Negroes in Chicago.

Regarding the recent remark attributed to him to the effect that in order to get things done, tensions in Chicago must be raised, King explained that by this he meant that history generally reflects that change has never come without creative tension. He felt that situations must exist, or be created, to make people examine issues [that] they would rather ignore, then recognize that something must be done to change or rectify these situations. He likened this condition to a boil [that] is often concealed, but when brought to a head, is subsequently lanced or cleaned, then heals itself. The tensions [that] he referred to were not intended to be interpreted as an indication of violence and any situations [that] are created in Chicago would be nonviolent type situations.

King believed that it was possible that more northern Negroes than southern Negroes were receptive to violent tactics to improve their conditions, but he believed the great mass of Negroes rejected this approach. He felt the nonviolent movement could succeed in Chicago and stated that all local civil rights leaders of stature have rejected violence as a tactic to be utilized in solving the Negro's problems. Regarding his recent meeting with Elijah Muhammad, identified as the leader of the Nation of Islam, he recalled that since he had started coming to Chicago some time ago, it had been his practice to meet with all types of people representing all types of groups. His meeting with Muhammad was in response to invitations given him in the past by Muhammad but which he had never been able to accept. He stated that he had no illusion about the reality of a joint program of any kind with Muhammad's organization but felt that he had the responsibility, as the leader of a nonviolent movement, to visit with Muhammad to see if there were any possible areas in which the two could cooperate in a manner [that] would be beneficial to the Negro people. King had no explanation for Muhammad's subsequent severe attacks on him, in which King had been referred to as a "lover of white people," but was not in any way concerned by such attacks. He stated that it was his feeling that the philosophy of Muhammad's organization was understandable, since it was based upon the frustrations long suffered by the Negro people, but felt that to substitute a black tyranny for a white tyranny was simply to replace one evil with another. He noted that what he is striving for is freedom for all, both black and white, as individuals and reiterated his belief that American society as constituted today possesses the tools to make integration work. He concluded that the philosophy of Muhammad was not realistic, that the Negro was unmistakably a part of America and has contributed in great measure toward making this country what it is today.

King's attention was then called to the assumption of the "trusteeship" of a slum building on Chicago's west side, a trusteeship [that] his organization, the SCLC, had assumed, together with several local civil rights groups. He was asked for comment concerning the serious criticisms leveled at him by many elements in Chicago subsequent to this activity.

King stated that this is a problem similar to many [that] he has faced in the South. He noted that his organization feels sincerely that they are obligated to engage in activities that in such instances are not legal in a strict sense, but represent moral issues [that] cannot be avoided. He stated that insofar as this particular building was concerned, he and his organization had been faced with the making of a moral decision growing out of an immoral situation. He noted that the tenants in this particular building, many with very young children, had had no heat, light, or water for days, plaster was falling from the building walls, and the building was infested with rats. The tenants here had tried numerous ways to get help, but had been unable to get any relief for these conditions. He stated that his organization felt the moral responsibility to provide immediate help for these people and he personally as well as others in his organization were willing to go to jail if necessary as a result of their actions. King agreed that it was possible his action here might not be perfectly legal, but stated that it is his position that along with property rights goes the responsibility to maintain property in decent, livable conditions for human beings.

King denied that he was making any effort to bring disunity to the community. He praised the local Chicago Police Department for its past patience in dealing with civil rights problems and concluded that the

Negroes, through legislative activities, have made great strides toward equality through the past several years. . . .

The March 5, 1966, edition of the *Chicago Sun-Times*, a daily Chicago newspaper, contained an article concerning the slum building at 1321 South Homan [*sic*] Avenue . . . John B. Bender, age 81, had filed a civil suit on March 4, 1966, against King. . . .

Bender's attorney stated that Bender agreed with the objectives and intentions of King but felt that the law was just as important as civil rights and the objectives of King could only be accomplished under the jurisdiction of the court.

UNITED STATES DEPARTMENT OF JUSTICE

FEDERAL BUREAU OF INVESTIGATION

New York, New York
March 9, 1966

Martin Luther King, Jr.
Security Matter-C

On March 4, 1966, the Public Information Department of the Educational Broadcasting Corporation, 304 West 58th Street, New York City, the operators of WNDT, Channel 13, released a schedule of program [that] [indicated] . . . Martin Luther King would be interviewed on the subject of Vietnam . . . by Arnold Michaelis . . . a noted television producer. . . .

Hereafter follows a resume of King's remarks as heard by Special Agents of the Federal Bureau of Investigation, who observed the show on the night of March 8, 1966:

King, in opening the thirty-minute television show, said that war was considered a social evil [that] has ominous possibilities for the total destruction of mankind. In Vietnam, King said "we" (the United States) have taken a stand against people seeking self-determination. He said there is wrong on both sides and that the wrong on "our" side (the United States) should not be ignored.

King noted that Premier Diem (a former Premier of Vietnam, who was slain) came into power and as a result of oppressive measures the Viet Cong came into being. He said the United States watched the war escalate during the following years. He said that "we" (the United

States) must accept the fact that communism is with "us," adding, however, that he had a great philosophical opposition to communism.

King said he felt at one time war could be a "negative good," in that it could block the spread of a negative evil force, like Hitler, for instance. He said he then arrived at a "pacifism" stage and concluded that war could no longer serve as a negative good because of its destructive capabilities.

He said the United States must go through a reevaluation of its entire foreign policy, and said that sectional concerns must be transformed into ecumenical concerns. He said "we" must have disarmament. He said it is a case of nonviolence or nonexistence.

Furthermore, King said "we" must recognize that the world must live together. It (the world) must become one in terms of brotherly concern. Whatever affects others directly concerns "us" (the United States) indirectly, he said.

King noted that Hitler in *Mein Kampf* also talked about peace. He said too often "we" think of peace as a goal we seek rather than as a means by which "we" arrive at that goal. King said "we" (the United States) talk about world peace in lofty terms, but we are using war to get there.

In answer to a question by Michaelis as to what he would do if he was authorized to speak for the United States, King said he would depend more on moral power than on military power. He said the United States must do something to create an atmosphere for negotiations, must make some good-faith moves.

President Johnson, he said, was not a "warmonger" as he inherited a great deal of the problem. He said if the United States was in favor of unconditional talks, it should make moves to lessen tensions and also stop the bombings in Vietnam.

He said if the United States was willing to negotiate, there was no point in saying that it would not negotiate with the Viet Cong. If the United States could get rid of its pride, he said, it would not hurt morally or militarily to pull out of Vietnam. France, he said, pulled out of Algeria without winning a military victory and it did not damage its position.

King said he was not calling for unilateral withdrawal from Vietnam but instead, had called for negotiations. He said the United States would not pull out, but said events had reached the point where all sides must give a little.

Hanoi and China have been recalcitrant about negotiating. In that regard, he said he was concerned about interpretations being placed on

Chinese statements and felt that if the United States would make it clear that it wanted to negotiate and was not seeking to destroy Vietnamese life and property, something would happen whereby negotiations would be possible for the United States. He said the United States had once before turned down an offer to negotiate.

In commenting on the effectiveness of the United Nations, King said there could not be a real United Nations until the largest nation in the world (China) was in it.

He said there was a need for leadership at this time. In amplifying, King said the administration (the Johnson administration) states that polls show support for its policies. He said, however, that policies should not be molded as a result of what polls reportedly reflect.

He said it was difficult for leaders to break out of their official "molds." The ultimate test of a leader, according to King, is not where he stands in a moment of convenience but, instead, where he stands in a moment of crisis. As an example, he noted the action of President Lincoln (in his Emancipation Proclamation).

When asked if he would go to see Ho Chi Minh or to China, King said he had not gone that far yet. He said he had talked to President Johnson about Vietnam on two occasions and made known his strong convictions.

In concluding his remarks, King said that although he had convictions regarding Vietnam, it did not mean that he was disloyal to the United States.

UNITED STATES GOVERNMENT
Memorandum

TO: Mr. W. C. Sullivan   DATE: 5/9/66

FROM: Mr. F. J. Baumgardner
           <u>MARTIN LUTHER KING, JR.</u>
           SECURITY MATTER-C

As you are aware, we have obtained considerable information identifying Martin Luther King as . . . however, for public consumption, King endeavors to create the image of a substantial member of the clergy and a faithful and devoted husband and father.

In this regard, the New York office made available a tape of an interview by Hugh Downs of Martin Luther King on the NBC *Today* show which took place on 4/18/66. Excerpts of this interview are set out below which indicate his hypocritical attempts to further his public image as a respected member of the clergy.

In answer to a question by Downs about loose sex relations and problems of the youth and what King thought the clergy could do about this, King responded in part: "Well, I think the clergy and the church should plunge right into this problem and deal with it, in what I consider an intelligent moral manner. In the past, too often the church has taken a kind of prohibitive attitude on the whole question of sex, a hush-hush attitude, rather than trying to honestly discuss sex and deal with the problems surrounding it. I think the only answer is for the church through its channels of religious education and other methods to bring this issue out into the open and reaffirm once more that what God creates is good and that it must be used properly and not abused. I think it is also necessary to bring out at this point that sex is basically sacred when it is properly used and that marriage is man's greatest prerogative in the sense that it is through and in marriage that God gives man the opportunity to aid him in his creative activity. Therefore, sex must never be abused in the loose sense it is often abused in the modern world."

Handwritten at the bottom of this page—and initialed "H"—is the notation: "This is positively nauseating coming from a degenerate like King."

Statement by
Dr. Martin Luther King, Jr.
Atlanta, Georgia
Tuesday, April 25, 1967

On Saturday of last week there appeared an article in several prominent newspapers which reported on several groups and individuals urging that I become a candidate for the Presidency of the United States in the 1968 elections. I must confess that I was quite surprised by these sentiments and find it very hard to take them seriously. I understand the stirrings across the country for a candidate who will take a firm principled stand on the question of the war in Vietnam and the problems of the poor in urban ghettos, but I must also add that I have no interest in being that candidate. I have come to think of my role as one [that] operates outside the realm of partisan politics raising the issues and through action create the situation [that] forces whatever party is in power to act creatively and constructively in response to the dramatic presentations of these issues on the public scene. I plan to continue that role in hope that the war in Vietnam be brought to a close long before the 1968 elections and that this present Congress finds both the courage and the votes to once again move our nation toward a truly great society for every citizen.

It is understandable that this war is tending to create a fluid political situation. Should this fantastically unwise and futile war continue to escalate toward World War III, and perhaps humanity's extermination, and should the campaign for racial equality be further starved, rebuked, and forgotten, our country inevitably will be facing national disaster. Such circumstances may well cause profound and broad-based political realignments and make relevant an independent candidacy. But even so, I do not conceive of this as my role.

I reiterate, I have no interest in any political candidacy and I am issuing this statement to remove doubts of my position on this subject.

UNITED STATES GOVERNMENT

FEDERAL BUREAU OF INVESTIGATION

New York, New York
July 25, 1967

Communist Infiltration of the
Southern Christian Leadership
Conference (SCLC)
Internal Security-C

On July 24, 1967, a confidential source, who has furnished reliable information in the past, advised that Stanley Levison, New York advisor to Martin Luther King, Jr., furnished a press release to Dora McDonald, secretary to King, pertaining to the racial situation in Detroit, for release by King. The text of this release, as furnished by Levison, is as follows:

"As the flames of riot and revolt illuminate the skies over American cities there is an intense desire to restore normality. Normality means that Negroes should cease looting stores while the white society resumes looting Negro lives. While no one should condone antisocial acts of Negroes nor [sic] should white America rationalize its destruction and depredations of its black minorities. The storm warnings have been posted a hundred times far in advance but those who have the power to create solutions have created trivialities and diversions. If it is wrong for Negroes to loot and burn, it is even a more horrible wrong for white armed forces to shoot to kill for larceny. This is an example of the moral degradation, hypocrisy, and confusion seeping through society [that] ultimately must destroy its positive values. I do not think we are helpless; we are only acting helplessly. I should like to offer a single proposal that I am convinced will be as effective as it is just. Every single outbreak without exception has substantially been ascribed to gross unemployment particularly among young people. In most cities for Negro youth it is greater than the unemployment level of the Depression '30s. Let us do one simple, direct thing—let us end unemployment totally and immediately. In the Depression days the nation was close to prostrate on the brink of bankruptcy. Yet, it created the WPA to make millions of jobs instantly available for all existing levels of skill. The jobs were tailored to the man, not the man to the job, in recognition of the emergency. Training followed employment, it did not precede it and become an obstacle to it. What we did three decades ago during an economic holocaust can easily be done today in the comfort of prosperity. I propose specifically the creation of a national agency that shall provide a job to every person who needs work, young and old. White and Negro. Not 100 jobs when 10,000 are needed. Not some cheap way out. Not some frugal device to maintain a balanced budget within an unbalanced society. I propose a job for everyone, not a promise to see if jobs can be found. There cannot be social peace when a people have awakened to their rights and dignity and to the wretchedness of their lives simultaneously. If our government cannot create jobs, it cannot govern. It cannot have white affluence amid black poverty and have racial harmony. The turmoil of the ghettos is the externalization of the Negroes' inner torment and rage. It has turned outward the frustration that formerly was suppressed agony. The Negro knows that a society that is able to plan intercontinental war and interplanetary travel is able to plan a place for him. It is callous refusal to be just and civilized the society is driving a wedge of destructive ailenation into the hope of harmony. Tranquility will not be evoked by pious words. To do too little is as inflammatory as inciting to riot. Desperate men do desperate deeds. It is not they who are irrational but those who expect injustice eternally to be endured. I am convinced that a single dramatic, massive proof of concern that touches the needs of all the oppressed will ease resentments and heal enough angry wounds to permit constructive attitudes to emerge. I regret that my expression may be sharp but I believe literally that the life of our nation is at stake here at home. Measures to preserve it need to be boldly and swiftly applied before the process of social disintegration engulfs the whole society."

UNITED STATES DEPARTMENT OF JUSTICE

FEDERAL BUREAU OF INVESTIGATION

San Francisco, California
August 11, 1967

MARTIN LUTHER KING, JR.

On August 10, 1967, at the Fairmont Hotel, San Francisco, California, Dr. Martin Luther King, Jr. addressed a convention of the National Association of Real Estate Brokers, which is composed of Negro members of the real estate profession throughout the country. King spoke to approximately 370 delegates and his speech was later televised over KQED, San Francisco.

Dr. King's topic was "Turning Neighborhoods into Brotherhoods," and had three main points: (1) The Evil of Racism; (2) Poverty in the United States; (3) The War in Vietnam.

Racism:

King discussed the historical roots of racism beginning with slavery, talked about the Emancipation Proclamation, and then discussed the Negroes' present situation, stating that there has never been any real commitment by the white people concerning "black equality." He said racial injustice is "black man's burden and white man's shame." He stated that the roots of racism are very deep in this country and said "the plant of freedom has grown only a bud, not a flower."

Poverty:

In discussing poverty, King talked about the world situation, India's poor people, Negro unemployment, that 50 percent of the Negroes in the United States were in substandard housing conditions, that in ghettos Negroes pay more for less, that Negro schools are inadequate, and that Negro children were trapped with no way out of poverty. He stated that whites move to the suburbs and ignore the Negroes. Sometimes, he said, Negroes have given up because they cannot support their families and in trying to escape they turn to dope and alcohol.

Riots are partly a result of these intolerable conditions. However, riots are self-defeating. He stated his motto is not "Burn Baby Burn, but Build Baby Build, Organize Baby Organize." One cause of riots, he announced, was the nice, gentle, timid, moderate, who is more concerned about order than justice and who is always trying to delay progress. He also lashed out at the middle-class Negroes "who have forgotten the stench of the black waters" and have abandoned their responsibility.

He stated another cause of riots is Congress who is hypercritical and insensitive, and more anti-Negro than anti-riot. He blamed the State Legislatures for refusing to pass fair housing bills, labor unions for keeping Negroes out of unions, and the white clergy for remaining silent. He stated a destructive minority can destroy the majority.

He stated that President Johnson is more interested in winning the war in Vietnam than in winning the war against poverty here at home and Congress is more concerned with rats than Negroes.

America, King said, has plenty of money to solve its problems, but it needs a will and for the Negroes, a massive program like the GI Bill of Rights.

Vietnam War:

King stated that the Vietnam War was now more serious than anything else in the world. He deplored this war for wasting national resources and destroying lives and society. He said the war has isolated the United States morally and politically, and scarred the image of this nation. The war has directed attention away from civil rights.

The United States has built a climate of violence in the world that is contagious. The United States is fighting against freedom in Vietnam and refuses to recognize the Vietnam fight for independence. The United States is not fighting communism, it is fighting a nationalist movement. He said that if KY [sic] were in the United States he would be called an "Uncle Tom" for fighting against his own people.

King said the United States should admit it made a mistake in Vietnam. He said one of President Kennedy's finest moments was admitting, after the Bay of Pigs invasion, that the United States had made a mistake. Therefore, "I call on President Johnson tonight to say to the nation and the world that we have made a mistake in Vietnam." King said the war must stop or the United States is risking being transformed into an inferno "that even Dante couldn't imagine."

In summation of his three main points, King urged his audience to continue to move forward in these areas and ended by saying, "If you can't fly, run; if you can't run, walk; if you can't walk, crawl; but by all means keep moving."

The following report on the Washington Spring Project is excerpted from a Federal Bureau of Investigation analysis of Martin Luther King, Jr., dated March 12, 1968.

Since 1956, Martin Luther King, Jr., has occupied a prominent role in the drive for equal rights for Negroes in the United States. During this critical period in our nation's history, much has depended on him as the individual Negroes in great numbers have looked to [him] for leadership in their drive to achieve equality. Much depends on him still in these times when racial tensions have created an atmosphere of fear and foreboding among many Negroes and whites alike. The course King chose to follow at this critical time could have momentous impact on the future of race relations in the Untied States, and for that reason this paper has been prepared to give some insight into the nature of the man himself as well as the nature of his views, goals, objectives, tactics and the reasons therefore.

Washington Spring Project

Martin Luther King, Jr., President of the Southern Christian Leadership Conference (SCLC), has stated publicly that he and 3,000 of his followers will march on Washington, D.C. this spring. He has announced that he will lead a massive civil disobedience campaign that will disrupt the normal course of business and, in fact, close down the nation's capital. He originally announced this project on August 15, 1967, in Atlanta, Georgia, on the occasion of the tenth anniversary of the SCLC.

King predicted that this massive civil disobedience will be more effective than riots. Concerning civil disobedience, King declared, "To dislocate the function of a city without destroying it can be more effective than a riot, because it can be longer lasting, costly to society, but not wantonly destructive."

King has referred to this campaign as the "Washington Spring Project" and the "Poor People's March," which is reportedly being staged to pressure Congress into passing legislation favorable to the Negro. It is King's contention that the government of the United States does not move until it is confronted dramatically. To add to the dramatic confrontation, King has boasted [that] he and his entourage are coming to Washington to stay; that his followers will conduct sit-ins, camp-ins, and sleep-ins at every government facility available including the lawn of the White House. He has bragged that he will fill up the jails of Washington and surrounding towns.

Black Nationalist Terror

One serious danger in the confrontation lies in the proposed action of the black nationalist groups, which plan to attempt to seize the initiative and escalate the nonviolent demonstrations into violence.

King has met with black nationalists and attempted to solicit their support. Stokely Carmichael of the Student Nonviolent Coordinating Committee (SNCC), an extremist Black Nationalist organization, has conferred with King. Carmichael endorses the objectives of King and advises he will not oppose or interfere with the "Washington Spring Project's" plans for nonviolence. However, he also states his role will be governed by what SNCC decides.

King is aware of the possibility of violence because one of his aides proclaimed recently to the press, "Jail will be the safest place in Washington this spring." However, in spite of this potentially explosive situation, King continues his plans. He adroitly uses this possibility as a lever to attempt to pressure Congress into action by warning that the "Washington Spring Project" may be the last chance in this country for peaceful change with respect to civil needs.

Strong Communist Influence

Another complicating factor in the picture is the degree of communist influence on King. One of King's principal advisors is Stanley David Levison. Ostensibly only a New York City attorney and businessman, Levison is, in fact, a shrewd, dedicated communist. Levison has spent the major part of his life advancing communist interests.

Levison gravitated to Martin Luther King, Jr., in 1956. He has been as dedicated in his support of King as he has been in advancing communist goals. He has actively involved himself in fund-raising drives for King, served as his legal counsel in certain matters, suggested speech material for him, discussed with King demonstrations in which King was involved, guided him in regard to acceptance or rejection of various public appearances and speaking commitments, and helped him with matters related to articles and books King has prepared.

Levison edited most chapters of King's new book entitled "Where Do We Go From Here; Chaos or Community?" Levison wrote one chapter of this book and the publisher's representative complained to King and Levison that it was obvious certain sections of the book were written by different individuals.

Stanley Levison had told Clarence Jones, another advisor to King, that under no circumstances should King be permitted to say anything without their approving it. Levison also informed Jones that King is such a slow thinker he is usually not prepared to make statements without help from someone. Levison is actively participating in the planning for King's "Washington Spring Project."

Explosive Situation

The combined forces of the communist influence and the black nationalists advocating violence give the "Washington Spring Project" a potential to be an extremely explosive situation.

UNITED STATES GOVERNMENT
Memorandum

TO: Mr. W. C. Sullivan   DATE: March 29, 1968

FROM: G.C. Moore
          COUNTERINTELLIGENCE PROGRAM
          BLACK NATIONALIST-HATE GROUPS
          RACIAL INTELLIGENCE
          (MARTIN LUTHER KING)

PURPOSE:
To publicize hypocrisy on the part of Martin Luther King.

BACKGROUND:
Martin Luther King has urged Negroes in Memphis, Tennessee, to boycott white merchants in order to force compliance with Negro demands in the sanitation workers' strike in Memphis.

When violence broke out during the march King led in Memphis on 3-28-68, King disappeared. There is a first-class Negro hotel in Memphis, the Hotel Lorraine, but King chose to hide out at the white-owned and -operated Holiday Inn Motel.

RECOMMENDATION:
The above facts have been included in the attached blind memorandum and it is recommended it be furnished a cooperative news media source by the Crime Records Division for an item showing King is a hypocrite. This will be done on a highly confidential basis.

Enclosure

DO AS I SAY, NOT AS I DO

Martin Luther King, during the sanitation workers' strike in Memphis, Tennessee, has urged Negroes to boycott downtown white merchants to achieve Negro demands. On 3-29-68 King led a march for the sanitation workers. Like Judas leading lambs to slaughter King led the marchers to violence, and when the violence broke out, King disappeared.

The fine Hotel Lorraine in Memphis is owned and patronized exclusively by Negroes but King didn't go there from his hasty exit. Instead King decided the plush Holiday Inn Motel, white owned, operated, and almost exclusively white patronized, was the place to "cool it." There will be no boycott of white merchants for King, only for his followers.

UNITED STATES DEPARTMENT OF JUSTICE

FEDERAL BUREAU OF INVESTIGATION

New York, New York
April 1, 1968

Martin Luther King, Jr.
Security Matter-C

A confidential source, who has furnished reliable information in the past, learned on March 29, 1968, that on that date, Stanley Levison and Martin Luther King, Jr., discussed the position which King has found himself in as a result of the violence that occurred in Memphis, Tennessee, on March 28, 1968, at the time when King led a march through downtown Memphis. King told Levison that he feels they have to face the fact that, from a public relations point of view and every other way, "we are in serious trouble." He referred to the Washington, D.C., Spring campaign, known as the Poor People's Campaign, and said as far as it is concerned it is in trouble. King noted that it will be much more difficult to recruit people for the Washington campaign now because they (the Southern Christian Leadership Conference) (SCLC) are recruiting nonviolent people and these people will hold back if they think they will be in a campaign that is going to be taken over by violent elements. King stated that this is not a failure for the SCLC because it has enough of a program to affirm its position but that it is a personal setback for himself.

King continued [by saying] that persons such as Roy Wilkins (Head of the National Association for the Advancement of Colored People) and Adam Clayton Powell, and Negroes who are influenced by the press, will now feel that he, King, is finished, that his nonviolence is nothing, that no one is listening to it. King reiterated that they had a great-public relations setback as far as his image and leadership are concerned.

Levison attempted to dissuade King from his point of view stating that it would be true only if King accepts "their" definition. He added that he felt it is a profound error King is making.

King noted that he did not accept it himself but that others will. Levison retorted that people would accept it for a few days, but, if events prove otherwise, will not accept it.

King noted that events will not prove otherwise unless they think soberly through this period. He said that somehow he had to reaffirm what the press will refuse to affirm. He referred to the Memphis incident stating that they all know it was just a few people who were involved. He added that it was a failure of the leadership in Memphis. King informed Levison that persons who were responsible for the violence came to see him on the morning of March 29, 1968. He said these persons were fighting the leadership in Memphis, the men who ignored and neglected them, the men who would not give them any attention, who ordered their telephones cut off. King added that he had no knowledge of all this, that the persons responsible for the violence were too sick to see that what they were doing during the violence was hurting him, King, more than it could hurt the local preachers.

King related that he was so upset and shocked over the Memphis violence that he was going to announce a personal fast as a means of appealing to the Memphis leadership, as well as those who participated in the violence, to come to him in a united front to take up the "cudgel" and get on with the movement. He said he felt this kind of spiritual move would be a way of unifying the movement, of transforming a minus into a plus. He added that he feels their Washington campaign is doomed.

Levison attempted to convince King that his reasoning was not correct. Levison said he was concerned over the "trap" King was placing nonviolence in because King was saying that he must have 100 percent adherence to nonviolence, which is an impossibility.

King commented that they could not get 100 percent adherence but that they must face the fact that a riot broke out in the ranks of the march, that "these fellows," in the line of march, would jump out, do something, and then come back and hide within the group. King said he is a symbol of nonviolence and that the press is not going to say what Levison said. He said the symbol will be weakened and it will put many Negroes in doubt. He said he must do something that is a powerful act to unify forces and refute the press.

Levison stated that if it has this result he would agree but that he is bothered by the idea that King would be accepting the logic of the press that if King can control 99 percent, and not the 1 percent who are violent, he is a failure. He said they must find a way in which they do not accept this, otherwise King will never be able to do anything unless he always spiritually reaches a level where he hypnotized every Negro alive.

King questioned how he could say that they can control the planned demonstrations in Washington, D.C., and at the same time conclude they are going to have 1 percent violence.

Levison counseled that King can say that he can control his followers and is not undertaking to control everybody else. He said King could take the position that his followers are nonviolent and will do what they must do.

They agreed to discuss the matter in depth at a meeting in Atlanta, Georgia, in King's church office on the morning of March 30, 1968.

The same source advised on March 31, 1968, that on that date Stanley Levison commented on the meeting held in Atlanta, Georgia, on March 30, 1968. Levison's comments included the following:

At the Atlanta meeting they examined the whole Memphis incident and came up with a new approach. "We are going back to Memphis. We are going to prove that you can have mass action in the streets." Martin Luther King had decided not to go back to Memphis and not to go to Washington (for the Poor People's Campaign). It was the determination of the (SCLC) staff that changed King's thinking. King is going back to Memphis on Tuesday (April 2, 1968), and there will be a big march on Friday (April 5, 1968). The Memphis incident was caused by "a handful of kids" and it could have been controlled by "our guys" (the SCLC) had they been there.

He, Levison, made the point that they could not let "a couple of kids," keep "mass action" from being their weapon.

As for controlling the Washington, D.C., demonstrations, King knows he can control the youth. What has to be done is go to the high schools and tell them what the establishment wants them to do. Once they grasp this there is no chance of anything happening. What they (the SCLC) are afraid of in Washington is a double cross from Stokely Carmichael and the answer to that is that "our job" (the SCLC) is not to stop violence but to be nonviolent themselves. "Our position" is that "we" are going to go on because to be able to march in the streets is "our most important tool" and are not going on the streets because it may start violence. "Why do we have to be afraid of riots? It is their problem not ours."

The Atlanta meeting was good because it shows how much militancy there is in the SCLC.

On April 4, 1968, about six o'clock in the evening, on the balcony outside Room 306 of the Lorraine Motel in Memphis, Tennessee, Martin Luther King, Jr., was assassinated.

ADAM CLAYTON POWELL, JR.

(1908–1972)

Adam Clayton Powell was many things. A dissident and a radical on some issues, he was capable of adopting the pose of a reactionary on others. Widely hailed as a leader of "the race" and sometimes feeling the burden of that unfair and ultimately silly if not inherently racist nomination, he thought most often only of himself. His legacy was in some ways honorable, enduring, proud. But he is also remembered as the con man, the silk-suited preacher, the politician who only traded in cash and who seemed to spend more time boozing and womanizing in Bimini or stocking the bar for his next yacht cruise in the Mediterranean than in affecting policy. Where Gunnar Myrdal had called the race issue America's dilemma, Powell's biographer called his subject a one-man American dilemma. There was no dilemma for J. Edgar Hoover. His FBI agents tracked Powell through it all, opening both a subversive file and a criminal file and doing their best to spread everywhere the ample dirt uncovered.

Born on November 29, 1908, in New Haven, Connecticut, Powell grew up in New York claiming a Cherokee lineage for his grandmother and an (illegitimate) Schaefer brewing lineage for his mother. His father, pastor of the Abyssinian Baptist Church, dabbled in real estate and took the family on frequent vacations to the best resorts in Maine and Canada. (The Powells passed for white.) Educated at Colgate and Columbia, Powell took his divinity degree in 1935 from Shaw University. Elected to the New York City Council in 1941, Powell created a newspaper in 1942 (the *People's Voice*), and then was elected to Congress three years later. (He represented the Sixteenth District from the Seventy-Ninth to the Eighty-Seventh Congress and then the Eighteenth District from the Eighty-Eighth to the Ninety-First Congress.)

Perhaps his biggest early controversy arose when the Daughters of the American Revolution refused to rent Constitution Hall to his wife, the singer and pianist Hazel Scott. When Bess Truman ignored her predecessor's example (Eleanor Roosevelt had resigned from the DAR in protest of its refusal to rent the hall to Marian Anderson), Powell said "from now on there is only one First Lady, Mrs. Roosevelt; Mrs. Truman is the last." The Harry S. Truman White House responded by soliciting an FBI report on the brash freshman congressman.

Powell emerged a formidable figure in Congress (as chair of the Committee on Labor and Education) and in Harlem (as successor to his father's church). By some estimates, including President Lyndon B. Johnson's, he had played a role from 1961 through 1966 in the passage of more than fifty bills; and the Abyssinian congregation of some 70,000 was thought to be the world's largest. Yet he only dared venture into New York incognito, determined to ignore court orders to pay a $155,785 libel judgment from a suit initiated in 1960 by Esther James, a Harlem widow. He had called her, on television, a "bag woman" for corrupt New York City police officers. In 1967, the House of Representatives stripped Powell of his chairmanship and barred him from taking his seat pending an investigation. A special committee subsequently concluded that he was not only contemptuous of the New York courts but had misused congressional funds. On March 1, the full House voted 301 to 116 to eject him.

Ultimately, some eighty judges in ten different courts would have something to say about constitutional questions revolving around the basic issue of whether the House of Representatives had the authority to put Powell out for defying judicial edicts to pay Mrs. James. He won some, lost others. After a successful reelection campaign in November 1968 and a favorable Supreme Court ruling, he returned to Congress on January 3, 1969, only to see the House strip his seniority and impose a $25,000 fine. This time, the Supreme Court refused his request for a hearing. Battling cancer and an opposition group that had formed in Harlem, Powell failed to receive the Democratic party's nomination in the 1970 primaries. It made no difference that his original and now decade-old charge of widespread police corruption had been vindicated. Two years later, on April 4, 1972, Powell died.

Powell's autobiography, *Adam by Adam* (1971) is thin and ultimately disappointing. There is also a modest collection of his public words, Mwalimu I. Mwadhifu, ed., *Selected Speeches, Sermons, and Writings of Adam Clayton Powell, Jr., 1935–1971* (1971). On Powell's difficulties in the 1960s, Andrew Jacobs, Jr., wrote *The Powell Affair: Freedom*

Minus One (1973). Also valuable are Neil Hickey's, *Adam Clayton Powell and the Politics of Race* (1965); Alexander E. Curtis's, *Adam Clayton Powell, Jr.: A Black Political Educator* (1971); Claude Lewis's, *Adam Clayton Powell* (1990); and Charles V. Hamilton's first-rate biography, *Adam Clayton Powell, Jr.: The Political Biography of an American Dilemma* (1991).

June 29, 1942

[Bureau Deletion]
Special Agent in Charge
New York, New York

Re: REVEREND CLAYTON POWELL, JR.
INTERNAL SECURITY-G.

Dear Sir:

From time to time the Bureau has received information from your Field Division reflecting strong indications that the captioned individual is linked with the Communist party. [Bureau Deletion]
. . . In view of the strong indications of communist affiliations on the part of Powell, you are requested to immediately institute a discreet investigation of this individual. Your investigation should be conducted with a view of ascertaining background information of Powell, his connections and affiliations, radical activities into which he has entered and his connection with the Communist party. It is pointed out in view of Powell's reported ministerial capacity, his prominence in Harlem and his political activity, your investigation must necessarily be of a very discreet nature. This matter should be given your immediate attention and an investigation report submitted in the near future.

Very truly yours,

John Edgar Hoover,
Director

Memorandum

DATE: July 10, 1942

RE: ADAM CLAYTON POWELL, JR.

HISTORY AND BACKGROUND

Adam Clayton Powell, Jr., was born in New Haven, Connecticut, November 29, 1908, the son of Reverend Adam Clayton Powell and Nattie (Fletcher) Powell. Shortly after his birth, Adam Clayton Powell, Sr., became pastor of the Abyssinian Baptist Church in New York City and the family then moved to New York City.

Adam Clayton Powell, [Jr.,] received a Bachelor of Arts degree in 1930 from Colgate University and received a Master of Arts Degree in 1932 from Columbia University. In 1938 the degree of Doctor of Divinity was conferred upon him by Shaw University. He became the Assistant Pastor of the Abyssinian Baptist Church in 1929 and in 1936, when his father retired, he became Pastor of the Church. The Abyssinian Baptist Church is 133 years old, the oldest Negro congregation in the North, and one of the largest Protestant congregations in the United States. It has a membership of 14,635 and operates on an annual budget of $4,200.00 Many of the sermons Powell delivers to his congregation have been published, and he has also written editorials for the *New York Post* in 1934 and the *Amsterdam News* in 1936 and 1938.

Concurrently with his religious activities, Powell has been active in Harlem Negro organizations. He has been Chairman of the Coordinating Committee for Employment, a group of 200 Negro organizations, and this committee has been instrumental in conducting picket campaigns for better hospitalization and for social reforms in Harlem. Powell organized a picket line before the New York World's Fair Executive Offices in 1939 and succeeded in raising the number of Negroes employed at the World's Fair from 200 to 732. In the spring of 1940, the Coordinating Committee staged a bus strike, which resulted in an increase in Negro crows. Powell plans picket lines and boycotts on the Telephone Company and on the Board of Education in order to obtain further employment of Negroes in the Telephone Company and in the colleges of New York.

The *Daily Worker* for February 11, 1939, commented on the appointment of Powell as a member of Local School Board District 12 for a period of five years. The newspaper article further states that he is enrolled as a member of the American Labor party and is head of the Citizen Committee on Employment.

The *Washington News* for November 13, 1941, in a United Press dispatch states that Powell had been elected to the New York City Council.

LABOR ACTIVITIES

Available information reflects that Powell was one of the signers of a letter sent to the National Convention of Railway Employees Department of [the] A.F. of L. who were meeting at Chicago in 1938. This letter appealed that action be taken to eliminate from the constitutions of affiliated unions clauses discriminating against Negroes.

It is reported that during April, 1941, he was the Chairman of the Strike Committee, which called a strike against the Fifth Avenue Coach Company and the New York City Omnibus Corporation to force employment of Negroes as mechanics and bus drivers. The *Daily Worker* for April 11, 1941, states that 2,000 people attended a mass meeting at the Abyssinian Baptist Church in connection with this strike. The article further states that Powell, speaking before 5,000 at the Golden Gate Ballroom on April 7, 1941, said that all promises from the Coach Company and Omnibus Corporation must be in writing and in proper legal form.

The *New York Times* on April 29, 1938, comments that the Coordinating Committee for Employment was headed by Powell and that its purpose was to picket and boycott companies discriminating against the Negroes.

The *Daily Worker* for May 23, 1938, hails the victory of the Coordinating Committee for Employment in forcing the Consolidated Edison Company to back down from "its notorious anti-Negro employment policy." [It also] states that Powell would lead the mass picket line outside Governor Whalem's World's Fair Building in protest against Negro discrimination by the World's Fair Corporation.

It is reported that the Trade Unions Committee of New York City held a rally on behalf of Powell on October 29, 1941, and endorsed his candidacy at this time.

ATTITUDE TOWARD WAR PRIOR TO JUNE 1941

Testimony given before the Dies Committee reflects that in 1934 Powell was a member of the National Executive Committee of the

American League Against War and Fascism and that in 1935 he was a member of the National Bureau of the American League for Peace and Democracy.

Available information reflects that on April 23, 1938, Powell sent a letter to House Chairman Sam McReynolds protesting the decision not to have open hearings on the Neutrality Act. This source advises that the letter was sent by Powell in the name of his congregation and stated that peace-loving Americans should have the opportunity to express themselves on such a vital matter.

It has been reported that Powell was on the New York Council of Keep America Out of War as of September 25, 1940. . . .

In the *Daily Worker* for May 27, 1941, 160 leading Negro Americans flayed the defense program as a sham and accused the Administration of fostering a war drive. This article cited discrimination against Negroes in the defense program and stated that the Negroes of America wanted peace and equality. Powell was one of those signing as the initiating group.

[Bureau Deletion]

ATTITUDE TOWARD WAR SUBSEQUENT TO JUNE 1941

[Bureau Deletion]

In a release by Russian War Relief, Incorporated, to all newspapers on March 25, 1942, it was stated that Powell would speak at the New York City Conference of the Russian War Relief, Incorporated, on April 11, 1942. . . .

Available information reflects that Powell was a speaker at the rally held by the Japanese-American Committee for Democracy on April 15, 1942, at the Hotel Diplomat, New York. . . .

The *Daily Worker* for May 16, 1942, reflects that Powell was a speaker at a mass victory rally [that] took place at New York University during May, 1942. He is quoted as follows: "We are waging a people's war with a people's army for a people's peace and the key to victory can be learned from the Chinese people, who are fighting a people's war. Let us demand a regiment of American people, Negro and white alike, fighting a people's war, so that democracy the world over shall become a reality."

The *Sunday Worker* for June 14, 1942, states that Powell was a speaker at an anti-discrimination mass meeting held on June 12, 1942, in Park Palace, New York City. He is quoted as follows: "Despite efforts of certain people, the common people may win at this anti-Hitler

war this year. The death blow to the old world ended with the accord signed by the United States, the Soviet Union, and Great Britain.''
[Bureau Deletion]

Powell is reported to have been a sponsor for the American Rescue Ship Mission to Spain. The purpose of this mission allegedly was to save Spanish refugees. . . .

Available information reflects that Powell was a member of the Executive Committee of the New York Conference of Inalienable Rights and was a sponsor of the emergency meeting called in February, 1941, to combat legislation against free speech and the rights of labor. The New York Conference for Inalienable Rights reportedly had communist affiliations. . . .

Testimony given before the Dies Committee listed Powell on the National Advisory Board of the American Youth Congress, which was reported to be dominated by the Communist party. . . .

The candidacy of Powell for the New York City Council was endorsed by the *Daily Worker* on October 30, 1941, and by the *Sunday Worker* on November 2, 1941. . . .

James W. Ford, writing in the *Daily Worker* of November 23, 1941, hailed the election of Powell as a victory for democracy and for anti-Hitler forces. . . .

The *Daily Worker* for November 15, 1941, editorially commented on the election of Powell as a victory for the anti-Fascist coalition.
[Bureau Deletion]

It is reported that Powell is a vice president of the National Association for the Advancement of Colored People. . . .

[Bureau Deletion]

. . . In an editorial by Powell in the *People's Voice*, on October 31, 1942, he stated in regard to the coming election that the ''daily trouble'' for this year's political campaign is Layle Layne and Benjamin Davis, Jr. In regard to Benjamin Davis, Jr., who ran on the Communist party ticket for the office of Congressman at Large for the State of New York, Powell stated: ''Ben Davis deserves the vote of every Negro. He comes from a great Georgia family. His education left him head and shoulders above the usual run-of-the-mill congressmen.'' He further stated, ''The Negro vote is so important that major political parties nominate a Negro for the position of Congressman at Large, instead of nonentities that are running. My vote goes to Ben Davis, Jr.'' In another section of this editorial, Powell states as follows: ''It is time that the Negroes participated in the political scene as members of the democracy, not just as Negroes. This is the one reason I have always given

credit to the Communist party, because they have the courage to run Negro people in national, state, and county elections.''
[Bureau Deletion]
. . . The *People's Voice* dated October 3, 1942, carried an editorial by Powell in his ''Soap Box'' column, in which he stated:

> ''The attack by Martin Dies on Mary McLeod Bethune is the last straw. Dies has already won infamy as an international jack-ass, but today, with your permission, let us omit the jack. Any low cracker scum like Dies who will dare to point his finger at a great American woman like Dr. Bethune deserves to be publicly purged. Dies is no good, never has been any good, and never will be any good. The sooner he is buried the better. He is one of the few people in history whose body has begun to stink before it dies. Dies is Public Skunk #1. There is only one place fit for him to live and that is Hitler's outhouse.''

The article goes on to relate that the National Federation for Constitutional Liberties has a 64-page booklet on Martin Dies [that] everyone should read; that Dies works hand in glove with the Nazi Fifth Column in the United States and that his tactics are the same as Goebbels's. In the last paragraph of this editorial, Powell states as follows:

''We demand that Congress impeach him and that the FBI investigate him, and that the President of the United States have him arrested immediately as an enemy agent. There is not and never has been one Fascist agent in America whom Dies has not shielded, worked with, protected, investigated, and whitewashed. The death of Dies is just as important as the death of Hitler. Fritz Kunze of the German American Fund supported Dies's request for more money from Congress. Polley, Silver Shirt Leader, told Congress that he founded his organization on Dies principles. The Ku Klux Klan of Oklahoma City issued a special pamphlet praising Dies. The Axis needs Dies today but we don't. To hell with him.''
[Bureau Deletion]

Memorandum

Philadelphia Quartermaster Depot
Philadelphia, Pennsylvania

TO: Officer in Charge   December 2, 1943

SUBJECT: Inter Racial [Sic] Agitation

RE: Agent's visit to a meeting given at the Peniel Methodist
             Church, 20th and Jefferson Street, Philadelphia, Pa. on
             Sunday, 28 November 1943, to witness an address given
             by A. Clayton Powell, Jr. Councilman of New York City,
             Pastor of the Abyssinian Baptist Church, and editor of the
             People's Voice, a New York publication.

. . . Powell spoke on the subject, "White Man's War, Black Man's
Peace." Powell stated in substance that the Negro church in America
would be a stronger organization in the postwar period than what it is
today and at the conclusion of this war, the Negro church will be able
to build by leaps and bounds . . . that we are on the threshold of a new
world—the old world is dead; that in the new world no race can dominate over other races because of their color, and no race can survive
on the basis that they have lived in the old world. Even the church of
the old world has gone and the church that will live in tomorrow's new
world can only live on its contributions to all people's regardless of
race, creed, color, or national origin; that in 1940 this was called a
white man's war, but five million Chinese voices cried out that this is
not a white man's war after we Chinese have been fighting for five
years and have lost millions of men; that we who have been exploited
by the Japanese are not going to allow you to call this a white man's
war.

   After the voice of protest came from the Chinese people, the newspaper editors, writers, commentators, etc., called it the War for the Survival of Western Culture. When this was heard by India, millions of
voices in India arose in protest stating that all of the culture of the
Western World was found in the East; that western culture is the off-
spring of eastern culture. They then tried to call it a Christian war, but
the souls of three million slaughtered Jews spoke out from the grave
and said, "This cannot be called a Christian war when the international
gangsters like Hitler, Tojo, and Mussolini have inflicted death and hu-

miliation upon the Jewish people of the world. They then said that they would call this a War to Make the World Safe for Democracy and at that time, thirteen million Negro voices arose and said, "You cannot deal this death blow for we will never have a free world until all men are equal."

Continuing, Powell stated in substance that the Negro has done more to bring about the passing of the old world than any other group in America for from 1800 to 1920 Negroes have worked and helped build America and participated in all the wars; they have given their lives for a supposed democracy while three thousand Negroes were lynched in America and five thousand died in race riots . . . when Rome was bombed, the Catholic voices protested and the Arch Bishop [sic] of Florida cried out "Save Rome." But, Powell stated in substance, where were the Catholic voices and this same Arch Bishop's [sic] voice when Negroes were being lynched, segregated, and Jim crowed; that this kind of religion is called Churchianity and not Christianity. If Christianity is going to be saved, it will be saved by the Negroes for as long as the churches in the South preach race hatred and mob violence, there will be no Christianity in the churches of America. . . .

Continuing, Powell stated in substance that there can be no peace as long as the Negroes enjoy second class citizenship . . . that unless Negroes and whites can join together, live and die together, we might as well get ready to fight another war. There should be no differences between the two groups; that last week in Baltimore, Attorney General Biddle made the statement before the Negro Bar Association that riots were coming; that at Vassar College, Dr. Ruth Joyce Kennedy of Texas stated, "The acid-test is whether white and black can intermarry;" that these statements are an indication of a changing world for any time a liberal or any other white person from Texas would suggest intermarriage we must realize that we are living in a different age; that out of one blood Jesus Christ created all men. . . . [He said] there is a new white man and a new Negro; that there is more practice of Christianity in [the] trade unions of the CIO then there is in the Irish Catholic Church; that when he spoke at the Willow Run plant to sixty thousand people in Detroit, all of whom were union men, he saw sixty thousand people, white and black, working side by side and everyone being paid on what he did, not on what his color was; that in Alabama, the state where [neither] the stars and stripes nor the Constitution are represented, trade unions elect Negroes as members of the board, and Negroes and whites sit in offices at desks alongside of each other; . . . [but] that a

Negro cannot even enter a white church in the South unless he has a broom in his hand.

Continuing, Powell stated in substance that ... the illiterate Negro and the illiterate white know as much about what we are fighting for as compared to Roosevelt and Churchill. It['s] the same [for] a Negro walking down the streets of Representative Rankin's home as [it is for] a Jew walking down the streets of Berlin. What are we fighting for? In Boston, which is the Cradle of Democracy, the worst anti-Jewish feeling exists today; that Jewish boys were beaten by boys and girls of the Christian Church; that ... we must not allow ourselves to be turned against any other minority group particularly the Jews ... that we, as Negroes, must not permit other people to turn us against the Jews because one Jew may make a derogatory statement.... We must also remember Judge Goldstein who recently resigned from the New York Bar Association because they refused to accept a Negro attorney's membership.... Let no statement by any individual or group provoke you, for these are the tactics of the Fascist anti-Negro groups who help to create race hatred and who want you to hate people like the Jews; these forces were responsible for the riots [that] took place in Birmingham, Detroit, Harlem, and other cities throughout the country and they will continue to spread anti-Negro and anti-Jewish propaganda for the purpose of starting other riots; we don't need to riot; that's what they want.

The new Negro and the new white man must join hands and enter upon the threshold of this new world together to show that there is a new Negro and a new white man and this reflected in the recent election in New York City where a Negro communist, Ben Davis, was elected to the office of City Councilman, and a lawyer, Judge Rivers, was elected to the highest bench in New York City's courts with a salary of $17,000 per year; that the new white man and the new Negro of New York City did not vote for these individuals because they were Negroes nor because one was a communist, they voted for them because they were good men.

Memorandum

TO: Mr. Ladd   DATE: March 6, 1953

FROM: Mr. Rosen

SUBJECT: Unknown Subject
           ADAM CLAYTON POWELL, JR. [Bureau Deletion]
           Victim Civil Rights
           Information Concerning
           Extortion

SYNOPSIS

Congressman Adam Clayton Powell, Jr., New York City, forwarded to the Bureau by letter dated February 27, 1953, four communications received by him in Washington, D.C. Three of these were anonymous and were contained in envelopes postmarked Scotch Plains, New Jersey, on February 20, [or] 24, 1953. The other date in the postmark is obliterated. Powell believes these were sent by the same person. They refer to Powell as a "Nigger." They state that if he ran for Mayor of New York City he would be defeated; that Powell, like all Niggers, doesn't want any laws that interfere with Niggers and all refer to "Powell and his stinkers." There appears to be no threat in these letters. The fourth letter dated February 20, 1953, on the stationery of the Hotel Pierre, New York City, is signed [Bureau Deletion]. Copies of the three anonymous letters forwarded to the Department for an opinion as to whether violation exists over which Bureau had jurisdiction or whether Postal authorities should handle. Copy of letter from [Bureau Deletion] forwarded to New York Division for investigation as to possible violation [of] Civil Rights Statute. Acknowledgement to Powell of his letter of February 27, 1953.

Memorandum

TO: Mr. Nichele   DATE: November 8, 1955

FROM: [Bureau Deletion]

SUBJECT: CONGRESSMAN ADAM C. POWELL (D-NY)

The *National Guardian* for October 24, 1955, on page one, carries a story entitled "20,000 Unionists in N.Y. Protest the Till Lynching." This article reflects that white and Negro trade unionists jammed a city block in New York's garment center for one and a half hours on October 11 in a mass rally to protest the lynching of Emmett L. Till in Mississippi. The meeting condemned the not-guilty verdict in the murder trial at Summer, Mississippi, last month. The article indicates that Congressman Powell, apparently a speaker before the rally, was applauded when he said that "no crisis facing America is more serious than the crisis of racism." Among other things, Powell proposed (1) A delegation to the White House to demand that a special session of Congress investigate violence in Mississippi and (2) A delegation to J. Edgar Hoover "on the problems of the FBI in Mississippi," because its "native" agents are mistrusted by Negroes.

Bufiles reflect that we have conducted no investigation of Powell. Files do reflect he has been affiliated with numerous front organizations some of which have been cited by the attorney general. On several occasions has requested information from Bureau files and was advised of the confidential nature of them. Correspondence with him has been put on a "black letterhead basis."

It is to be noted that on October 14, 1955, (three days after above rally) Powell's secretary telephonically contacted the Bureau and advised that the Congressman wanted to see the Agents who went to Mississippi to investigate the matter of depriving votes to Negroes or wished to speak with someone familiar with what those agents were doing in Mississippi. The Secretary, [Bureau Deletion] was advised that the Bureau had conducted no investigation in the murder of Emmett Till, and it was suggested that the Congressman may wish to inquire through the Department of Justice.

It is further noted that we learned through the Criminal Division of the Department that Congressman Powell had an appointment with the Chief of the Civil Rights Section in the Department on October 19, 1955.

Memorandum

TO: Mr. Mohr   DATE: January 13, 1960

FROM: C.D. DeLoach

SUBJECT: ADAM CLAYTON POWELL, JR.
           (D.-New York)

Congressman Powell called at 5 P.M. today and in my absence spoke with [Bureau Deletion] in my office.

Powell said we probably were aware he was putting out the names
of the numbers racketeers in Harlem and added that quite a furor has
been stirred up as a result. He wanted to know what agency had jurisdiction with respect to the gambling stamp tax and [Bureau Deletion]
advised him the Internal Revenue Service had authority in this area.

Powell said he wanted to mention also that he had received a couple
of local telephone calls [that] were threatening in nature and had also
received several threatening letters. He said that, of course, everybody
in Congress gets such calls and letters from time to time and that he
was not particularly perturbed and added that local authorities in New
York had been advised. He said that both the home of his assistant
minister and his church were under police guard at the present time.
The Congressman said he was aware the Bureau had jurisdiction in
extortion matters and said that he would like to have both the Bureau's
number here in Washington and in New York in case any threats were
made to him [that] would come within FBI jurisdiction. [Bureau Dele-
tion] furnished both telephone numbers and Powell said he would keep
them in his wallet in case of emergency.

The above is for information.

*A handwritten notation by the Director on this memorandum reads;
"alert our N.Y. office as Powell is a terrific publicity seeker."*

Memorandum

TO: MR. ROSEN   DATE: March 28, 1961

FROM: A. J. MC GRATH

SUBJECT: ADAM CLAYTON POWELL
              MISCELLANEOUS - INFORMATION CONCERNING

This memorandum is being submitted to set forth information available concerning the tax case against Congressman Adam Clayton Powell
(D-N.Y.). He was indicted on 5/8/58, on charges of income tax evasion
and went to trial on 3/8/60, which ended in a hung jury on 4/22/60.

Newspaper accounts reflect Congressman Adam Clayton Powell was
indicted on three counts of income tax evasion in the Southern District
of New York on 5/8/58. The first count of the indictment charged
Powell with aiding in [the] filing of a false return for his wife, jazz
pianist Hazel Scott, for the year 1951. The second count charged Powell

with willfully attempting to evade a large part of the income tax due by Hazel Scott. The return showed Scott owed $590, whereas the tax actually amounted to $1,900. The third count charged Powell with attempting to avoid taxes owed by him and Scott in a joint return for 1952. Powell claimed their net income for 1952 was $5,252, and no tax was due, whereas it was alleged their joint net income was $8,952 on which there was a tax of $1,663. This indictment was returned by a federal grand jury which first commenced looking into the tax affairs of Powell in December, 1956.

During the twenty-two months from return of indictment on 5/8/58, to the date trial commenced on 3/8/60, there were numerous delays in setting the trial date. Some delays were sought by government attorneys and some by Powell's attorney, Edward Bennett Williams. The trial lasted five weeks, went to the jury on 4/21/60 after two of the three counts of the indictment were dismissed by the Judge, and resulted in a hung jury on 4/22/60. There is no indication the indictment has been finally disposed of to date.

It is noted Powell also has encountered considerable difficulty with the members of his staff and has received widespread publicity in this regard. Two of his staff secretaries were convicted for income tax evasion. Mrs. Hattie Freeman Dodson, a secretary, served seven months for evading $5,000 in taxes and illegally collecting $2,000 in refunds. Acy Lennon, another secretary, was sentenced to a year and a day in prison for dodging $1,700 in taxes. In addition, in February of this year the newspapers discovered that Powell had raised the salary of his secretary from $3,074 to $12,974. His secretary is his present wife, the former Yvette Marjorie Flores, who Powell married on 12/15/60.

The information set forth in this memorandum is based on newspaper accounts contained in the Bureau files, as the Bureau has not conducted any investigation concerning Powell's tax case.

On this memorandum the Director has handwritten the following notation: "We should keep alert re: Powell & his activities which may involve him in Federal violation of the law."

Memorandum

TO: MR. A. ROSEN   DATE: June 5, 1961

FROM: [Bureau Deletion]

SUBJECT: REPRESENTATIVE ADAM CLAYTON POWELL, JR..
           (D-New York);
           REPRESENTATIVE JAMES ROOSEVELT
           (D-California)
           NAME CHECK REQUESTS

SYNOPSIS

Previous memoranda L'Allier to Belmont set forth that name check requests received from Civil Service Commission (CSC) concerning captioned persons who have been designated to attend International Labor Organization Conferences scheduled June 7–20, 1961, Geneva, Switzerland. This memorandum concerns Powell, Roosevelt is being handled separately. . . .

No applicant or security-type investigation conducted by FBI concerning Powell. Has been involved in various Bureau investigations re: possible kidnapping of son; receipt of threats; allegations of bribery of Powell; impersonation of Powell; and most recent allegations that Powell for money offered to use influence in current Administration on behalf of former President of Haiti. No prosecution developed in any of forgoing matters. All details of latter allegation recently referred to Department. Powell tried on income tax evasion charges 1960; all counts eventually dismissed.

Prior to late 1940s Powell [was] extremely active in communist front organizations and causes of all types. [There is] no evidence [that] Powell ever [was a] member of Communist party; however, [he] associated with Communist party functionaries and campaigned for their election to public office. Operated publication *People's Voice* in New York City from 1942 until 1946 when he severed all connections at reported advice of Negro political leaders to withdraw from all left-wing groups in order not to hurt future political chances. In 1944 [he] publicly described his paper as a Lenox Avenue edition of *Daily Worker*. Files indicate [he is a] member of five and active in connection with eighteen organizations designated pursuant to EO 10450. Various publicity given Powell re kickbacks from former employees, tax evasion convictions of former employees; and Powell's praise in 1959 of Castro's government in Cuba. In 1953 and 1955 Powell mentioned FBI in criticism of civil rights matters. In December, 1960, Powell's secretary contacted Bureau to ask Director to serve on committee honoring Powell; request declined.

DETAILS:

... It is noted that Powell alone is the subject of approximately 3,000 references in Bureau files.... The file review revealed Powell to have been a member of several organizations designated by the attorney general pursuant to Executive Order 10450. Inasmuch as Powell failed to list membership in these organizations on the Form 86 submitted to CSC, the possible violation of Fraud Against the Government statutes is being referred to the attorney general. It is to be noted that the Department has not authorized prosecution in any case [that] does not involve membership in the Communist party.

BACKGROUND

Powell was born in New Haven, Connecticut, 11-29-08. His parents, shortly after Powell's birth, moved to New York City where Powell's father became Pastor of the Abyssinian Baptist Church. Powell attended Colgate University from which he received a B.A. degree in 1930 and Columbia University from which he received his M.A. degree in 1932. In 1934 the degree of Doctor of Divinity was conferred upon him by Shaw University and in 1947 he received the degree of Doctor of Laws [sic] from Virginia Union University. Prior to Powell's graduation from college in 1929 he served as manager of his father's church. Later he became Assistant Pastor and in 1936 when his father retired, Powell became Pastor. The Abyssinian Baptist Church is reported to be one of the oldest Negro congregations in the North and one of the largest Protestant congregations in the United States. Powell was the first Negro Councilman to be elected in New York City, having taken that office in 1941. In 1944 he was elected to [the] United States Congress and has served that body since that date. He is presently Chairman of the House Education and Labor Committee. In 1956 Powell lost the support of certain Democratic leaders in New York City when he supported President Eisenhower for reelection. According to Powell, he crossed party lines at that time because of the civil rights issue.

Powell married Isabelle Geraldine Washington on 3-8-33. They were divorced in November, 1944, and he married singer and pianist Hazel Scott in August, 1945. He subsequently divorced Miss Scott and on

12-15-60 married his current wife, Yvette Marjorie Flores, who also serves as his secretary.

No arrest record identifiable with Powell was located in the files of the Identification Division.

INVESTIGATION INVOLVING POWELL:

No application or security-type investigation has been conducted concerning Powell although Bureau files contain voluminous references concerning his activities over the years.

On 7-14-56 Powell notified the press that a possible attempt had been made that date to kidnap his son, Adam Clayton Powell III, born 7-17-46. Powell was interviewed on 7-15-56 and advised an unknown male caller had on 7-14-56 telephoned his residence and said, he, the caller, had been instructed to pick up Powell's son. The housekeeper answering the telephone advised the caller she would not release the boy and the incident was closed. No information was developed [that] would identify the caller in this matter.

Powell has frequently received letters and telephone calls of a threatening nature and on several occasions, after notifying the press, has referred them to the Bureau. No information [that] would identify the originators of the letters and calls referred to date has been developed.

In 1958 Powell was indicted on charges of tax evasion, which case went to trial 3-8-60. Two counts of the three-count charge were dismissed and the third count resulted in hung jury 4-22-60. On 4-13-61 the remaining count was dismissed at the government's request. This entire matter was handled by the Internal Revenue Service.

Memorandum

TO: MR. BELMONT   DATE: July 16, 1962

FROM: C. A. EVANS

SUBJECT: ATTACK BY COMMUNISTS ON HOME OF
           CONGRESSMAN ADAM CLAYTON POWELL,
           IN PUERTO RICO

[Bureau Deletion] telephoned. She advised she had received a telephone call from Congressman Adam Clayton Powell who wanted to speak to AG. When he was unable to do this he consented to leave a message with [Bureau Deletion].

The Congressman said that the communists in Puerto Rico had attacked his home there, apparently yesterday (Sunday, 7/15). Several hundred dollars' worth of damage was done. The Congressman further said that this attack had been reported to the head of the FBI in Puerto Rico, "a man by the name of Bishop," who expressed "laconic views." The Congressman did clarify this remark.

[Bureau Deletion] said she passed the Congressman's message from our San Juan office on 7/16/62. There was picketing in front of the home of Congressman Powell on 7/15 by members of the Puerto Rican Independence Movement. There was a counterdemonstration by pro-statehood picketers. Minor clashes between the groups were halted by police action.

At 9:05 A.M., 7/16/62, Congressman Powell's wife telephoned the SAC at San Juan and reported that about 1 o'clock in the morning a small group of unknown persons threw rocks on the porch of her home and broke a window. She said she was alone in the house with their child and was frightened. She desired protection for the night of 7/16 in case there were further similar activities. She had not notified the police. She was told that the FBI could not provide such protection, but that we would inform the police. She said she was going to telephone her husband.

ACTION BEING TAKEN:

A memorandum is being prepared for the AG, advising him of the nature of the disturbance at the house of Congressman Powell, the facts surrounding Mrs. Powell's call to our SAC, and the fact that she was informed properly that the FBI cannot provide such protection, but that we would notify the police, which was done.

Memorandum

TO: Mr. Wick   DATE: January 10, 1967

FROM: M. A. Jones

SUBJECT: [Bureau Deletion]
           MEETING WITH THE DIRECTOR
           JANUARY 10, 1967

Per prior arrangements, [Bureau Deletion] was introduced to the Director at 10:00 A.M., today, by SA [Bureau Deletion].

During a very cordial meeting, the Congressman stated the purpose of his visit was to assure the Director that he was 100 percent behind Mr. Hoover in the dispute with Bobby Kennedy and that the great majority of the Congress solidly backed the Director. [Bureau Deletion] stated he had no use for Bobby, who was evidently lying in this matter, and the thing that really "grated" him, [Bureau Deletion] was that Bobby was attacking the integrity of the Director and the Bureau.

... The Director reviewed Bureau policies regarding wiretapping and use of electronic devices, including the restricted use, and how Bobby had insisted such techniques be used in criminal matters. Mr. Hoover stated the proposal to use wiretaps and electronic devices under court orders is a difficult one for us to fight, as we try out cases before Federal judges; nevertheless, there are many untrustworthy Federal judges, including some in the District of Columbia, whom we would not want to have knowledge of particular installations [Bureau Deletion]. . . .

The Director noted Bobby had once wanted him to accept Negro Agents regardless of qualifications and of his flat refusal to do so, and that we have Agents of many races, creeds and colors, but all meet high Bureau standards. Mr. Hoover reviewed our aim in civil rights investigations to be impartial and unbiased. . . . The Congressman agreed with the Director that our investigations in the South have had a most salutary effect in reducing violence. [Bureau Deletion].

[Bureau Deletion] mentioned that the Adam Clayton Powell affair was disturbing to him because Powell was attempting to trade on the color of his skin and was doing a great disservice to legitimate civil rights causes. [Bureau Deletion] stated that if a white Congressman had done what Powell had done, he would be thrown out of the House bodily and would be criminally prosecuted. He stated he and his colleagues would, beginning this afternoon, push for withholding Powell's seat until a complete investigation was made and then attempt to bar him permanently. [Bureau Deletion] doubted they would be able to accomplish this objective as it was beyond the point the Administration and the House leadership wanted to go. The Director stated he certainly agreed with the Congressman's views on Powell. . . .

Memorandum

TO: Mr. DeLoach   DATE: March 29, 1967

FROM: A. Rosen

SUBJECT: CONGRESSMAN ADAM CLAYTON POWELL; ET AL.
           FRAUD AGAINST THE GOVERNMENT-
           CONSPIRACY

On the afternoon of 3/28/67, we received a lengthy memorandum from Assistant Attorney General Vinson requesting a sweeping investigation to develop all pertinent facts surrounding possible false claims for several hundred air trips by staff members of the House Committee on Education and Labor, Congressman Adam Clayton Powell and others (not identified) with no official Congressional connection. In addition, [an] investigation was requested concerning possible payroll abuse in the employment by the Committee of Congressman Powell's wife and concerning Congressman Powell's alleged false accounting for use of counterpart funds on foreign travel. (Counterpart funds are foreign exchange currency owned by the United States for use abroad.)

The Department's request is based on information set forth in reports and hearings of two Congressional committees.[*] Department has advised that bulky files and exhibits relating to these reports are available for review in the Fraud Section of the Criminal Division.

The Department's memorandum sets forth that the possible irregularities in this matter are centered in three areas. The first is the improper use of Committee funds of some $20,000 for air travel by Congressman Powell, his aides, and others while not on Congressional business. It is indicated that during the last three Congresses there were 451 airline tickets involved in this allegation [that] were purchased with Government credit cards.

The second allegation involves Powell appropriating some $28,000 of public funds for his personal use by putting his wife, Y. Marjorie Flores, on the committee payroll as a clerk when in fact she performed no official duties and was not present in Powell's Congressional district or his Washington, D.C., office.

The third involves Powell's having filed reports with a Congressional

---

[*The Conclusions of the Special Subcommittee on Contracts in its report dated January 3, 1967, and the Findings of the Select Committee Pursuant to House Resolution 1, which were submitted on February 23, 1967, follow this memorandum.]

committee [that] reported substantially lower sums for expenditures of counterpart funds used by him and his aides on trips abroad between 1961 and 1964.

The Department's memorandum notes that the Congressional hearings have established that Powell was aware of the alleged abuses but the Government must clearly ascertain whether Powell, in approving specific trips or certifying specific vouchers for payment, was acting with full awareness of the situation; knowingly and willfully falsified material facts, and knowingly presented fraudulent claims under the Bureau's jurisdiction.

The requested investigation will, of course, require that at the outset detailed review of the bulky files and exhibits in possession of the Department be made for pertinent information concerning the allegations and identity and location of witnesses to permit the development of and setting out of leads. The investigation necessarily will also include detailed interviews with all former and present members of the staffs of Powell and the House Committee on Education and Labor and Powell's wife. It will include reviews of appropriate Congressional Committee records, airline records, and interviews of airline personnel. After all investigation is completed consideration will be given to the advisability of interviewing Congressman Powell.

ACTION BEING TAKEN

We are preparing a communication to be sent to Washington field office today forwarding the Department's request. Washington field is being instructed that as many Special Agents as feasible and practical are to be assigned to afford this case immediate, continuous, and top-priority attention. Washington field is also being instructed to respond to any press inquiries that may be received with "no comment" and that if any interviewee inquires as to the reasons for the investigation, the interviewee is to be advised that the investigation is being conducted at the request of Assistant Attorney General Fred M. Vinson, Jr., of the Department of Justice.

This case will receive extremely close supervisory attention at the Bureau to assure that the investigation is thorough in all respects and is completed at the earliest possible date.

Conclusions
of Special Subcommittee on Contracts
and
Findings
Select Committee Pursuant to House Resolution 1

On January 3, 1967, the Special Subcommittee on Contracts of the
Committee on House Administration, House of Representatives, issued a
report of special investigation into expenditures during the 89th Congress
by the House Committee on Education and Labor and the clerk-hire status
of Y. Marjorie Flores (Mrs. Adam Clayton Powell). The report took into
consideration an investigation conducted by the Subcommittee Staff and
Hearings before this Subcommittee on December 19, 20, 21, and 30, 1966.
The Subcommittee in substance concluded that:

(1) Representative Powell and Miss Corrien A. Huff, a staff employee
of the Committee on Education and Labor, used assumed names on many
airline flights purchased with Committee credit cards, thus deceiving the
appropriate authority as to the number of trips made.

(2) The deceptive practice of using names of staff employees on airline
tickets not used by said employees appears to be a scheme devised to
conceal the actual travel of Representative Powell, Miss Huff and others,
so as to prevent questions being raised as to whether they were on Committee business.

(3) One staff member, Mrs. Emma T. Swann, was favored with personal
vacation trips, the transportation being purchased with Committee airline
credit cards and the cost thereof charged to the contingent fund.

(4) Representative Powell placed on the staff of the Committee on Education and Labor one Sylvia J. Givens who had been hired for the express
purpose of doing domestic work for him when he traveled, as well as for
performing clerical work in his committee offices.

(5) Persons with no official connection were provided travel by Representative Powell, transportation procured through Committee airline credit
cards and paid for from the contingent fund.

(6) Failure of staff members, allegedly on official business, to submit
vouchers for travel expenses and subsistence raised questions as to whether
such travel was actually on Congressional business.

(7) A presumption was raised that Y. Marjorie Flores (Mrs. Adam Clayton Powell) was receiving compensation as a clerk for Representative Powell contrary to the law. The Committee concluded that she was not
performing the services for which she was compensated, in Mr. Powell's

offices in the District of Columbia, the State of New York, or the district which he represented, as required by Public Law 89–90, 89th Congress.

(8) All vouchers for payment of travel costs of the Committee bore Mr. Powell's signature certifying said vouchers to the committee on House Administration for payment from the contingent fund.

When the 90th Congress met to organize on January 10, 1967, the right of Congressman Powell to be sworn in and be seated was referred to a Select Committee pursuant to House Resolution 1, which on February 23, 1967, submitted its report. The report incorporated by reference the report, exhibits, and hearings of the Special Subcommittee on Contracts. The findings of the Select Committee were substantially the same as the conclusions of the Special Subcommittee on Contracts. Specific findings mention in the report include:

(1) As a Member of Congress, Mr. Powell wrongfully and willfully appropriated $28,505.34 of public funds for his own use from July 31, 1965, to January 1, 1967, by allowing salary to be drawn on behalf of Y. Marjorie Flores as a clerk-hire employee when, in fact, she was his wife and not an employee in that she performed no official duties and further was not present in the State of New York or in Mr. Powell's Washington office, as required by Public Law 89–90, 89th Congress.

(2) As a Member of Congress, Mr. Powell wrongfully and willfully appropriated $15,683.27 of public funds to his own use from August 31, 1964, to July 31, 1965, by allowing salary to be drawn on behalf of Y. Marjorie Flores as a clerk-hire employee when any official duties performed by her were not performed in the State of New York or Washington, D.C., in violation of House Resolution 294 of the 88th Congress and House Resolution 7 of the 89th Congress.

(3) As chairman of the Committee on Education and Labor, Mr. Powell wrongfully and willfully appropriated $214.79 of public funds to his own use by allowing Sylvia Givens to be placed on the staff of the House Education and Labor Committee in order to do domestic work for him in Bimini, the Bahama Islands [sic] from August 7 to August 20, 1966; and in that he failed to repay travel charged to the committee for Miss Givens from Miami to Washington, D.C.

(4) As chairman of the Committee on Education and Labor, Mr. Powell on March 28, 1965, wrongfully and willfully appropriated $72 of public funds be ordering that a House Education and Labor Committee air travel card by used to purchase air transportation of his own son (Adam Clayton Powell III), for a member of his Congressional office clerk-hire staff (Lillian Upshur), and for personal friends (Pearl Swangin and Jack Duncan), none of whom has any connection with official committee business.

(5) As chairman of the Committee on Education and Labor, Mr. Powell willfully misappropriated $46.16 of public funds by giving to Emma T. Swann, a staff receptionist, airline tickets purchased with a committee credit card for three vacation trips to Miami, Florida, and return to Washington, D.C.

(6) During the chairmanship of the Committee on Education and Labor, in the 89th Congress, Mr. Powell falsely certified for payment from public funds, vouchers totaling $1,291.92 covering transportation for other members of the committee staff between Washington or New York City and Miami, Florida, when in fact, the chairman (Mr. Powell) and a female member of the staff had incurred such travel expenses as part of their private travel to Bimini, the Bahamas.

(7) As chairman of the Committee on Education and Labor, Mr. Powell made false reports on expenditures of foreign exchange currency to the Committee on House Administration.

UNITED STATES DEPARTMENT OF JUSTICE

FEDERAL BUREAU OF INVESTIGATION

Report of: [Bureau Deletion]
Office: Washington, D.C.
Date: April 10, 1967
Field Office File #: 46-8853
Title: CONGRESSMAN ADAM CLAYTON POWELL; Y. MARJORIE FLORES; SYLVIA J. GIVENS; CORRINE A. HUFF; EMMA T. SWANN; TAMARA WALL; UNKNOWN SUBJECTS;
Expenditures by the House Committee on Education and Labor
Character: FRAUD AGAINST THE GOVERNMENT
          CONSPIRACY

SYNOPSIS:
   Criminal Division, Department of Justice, advised of discrepancy between the State Department reports and reports filed by Adam Clayton Powell, Corrine A. Huff, and Tamara Wall concerning expenditures of counterpart funds. Investigation requested to determine requirements for reporting expenditures and significance of reports to operations of Congress. Chief Clerk, House Administration Committee (HAC), advised that expenditures of counterpart funds by Congressmen and employees is covered by Section 502 (b) of Mutual Security Act of 1954. Initially, there

was no limitation on amounts expended. Chairmen of Committees submit letter to U.S. Department of State (USDS) reporting identity of individuals traveling abroad along with requests that counterpart funds be made available. Maximum of $50 per day exclusive of transportation costs are furnished. Individuals submit record of expenditures to their Chairman who summarizes information for HAC. HAC does not audit reports but merely passes information on for printing in Congressional Record. Counterpart funds under control of Treasury Department; however, USDS handles administration of funds, but performs no audit functions. Law, according to sources contacted, provides no penalty for failure to file report on expenditures for travel abroad nor for the accuracy of reports. Reports filed by Powell, 1961 to 1964, generally omitted travel expense amounts.

DETAILS: AT WASHINGTON, D. C. (RE: COUNTERPART FUNDS)

Mr. Fred M. Vinson, Assistant Attorney General, Criminal Division, United States Department of Justice, by letter dated March 27, 1967, to the Director, FBI, enclosed copies of the reports and hearings of both the Special Subcommittee on Contracts, Committee on House Administration, 89th Congress, and the Select Committee pursuant to House Resolution One, 90th Congress. Mr. Vinson requested [an] investigation to develop all pertinent facts surrounding claims for travel both by House Committee on Education and Labor and non-Committee personnel, possible Committee payroll abuses, and accountings for expenditures while on foreign travel. He further requested that all instances of apparent irregularity, as reviewed in the two Committee reports and hearings, should be thoroughly explored as well as any other instances of questionable activity that examination may disclose.

This report contains only the results of [the] investigation relating to the use of counterpart funds. In the regard, the Criminal Division letter requested that inquires be made to determine the requirments for reporting these expenditures and the significance of these reports to the operations of Congress.

The report of the Select Committee submitted February 23, 1967, included a finding that "as Chairman of the Committee on Education and Labor, Mr. Powell made false reports on expenditures of foreign exchange currency to the Committee on House Administration." According to the report, the Select Committee ascertained from the Department of State that, as Chairman of the Committee on Education and Labor, Mr. Powell received from the State Department in 1961, 1962, 1963, and 1964 reports as to the amounts of expenditures of foreign exchange currency in United States funds he made while abroad during these years, as well as similar expenditures made by Miss Corrine Huff and Miss Tamara Wall in 1962. Subsequently, as Chairman of the Committee of Education and Labor, Mr. Powell filed with the Committee on House Administration reports listing substantially lower sums for these expenditures, which were then published in the Congressional Record. The amounts received and the amounts reported are as follows:

Year	Amounts Received By Adam Clayton Powell	Amounts Reported By Adam Clayton Powell
1961	$5,771.21	$3,283.37
1962	$4,300.04	$1,544.00
1963	$1,080.60	$ 721.21
1964	$2,457.59	$1,353.71
	Amounts Received By Tamara Wall	
1962	$3,526.30	$1,653.00
	Amounts Received By Corrine Huff	
1962	$2,998.38	$1,741.50

Memorandum

TO: Mr. DeLoach   DATE: April 13, 1967

FROM: A. Rosen

SUBJECT: CONGRESSMAN ADAM CLAYTON POWELL; ET AL.
           FRAUD AGAINST THE GOVERNMENT
           CONSPIRACY

This is to provide a current summary of the investigation being conducted in captioned matter. The three items of investigation requested by the Criminal Division 3/28/67, are set out below with a brief statement as to results of investigation to date.

(1) Improper use of some $20,000 of Congressional Committee funds by Congressman Powell, his aides, and others while not on congressional business. Some 400 airline tickets are involved in this matter [all of] which

were purchased with Government credit cards. Travel was principally between Washington, D.C., to New York City, and Washington, D.C., to Miami. Some of this travel was performed under assumed names, and identity of actual travelers is unknown. In other cases the travelers had no official congressional connection.

Voluminous records and exhibits were accumulated by congressional committees during investigation of this matter over a four-month period. These records have been under daily review by as many Agents as possible for necessary background information and identity and location of pertinent witnesses. This review has now been completed. Washington field is assembling this information and setting out numerous leads 4/14/67, to develop full facts as to what persons actually performed the travel, whether travel was on committee business, and whether Powell culpably involved in this improper use of committee funds. To check this item out thoroughly, extensive investigation will be required in Washington, D.C., New York City, and Miami, Florida.

In one instance at a social gathering Powell instructed his clerk to purchase four tickets to New York in the names of committee members, but for actual use of three of his friends and his son, Adam Clayton Powell III, age 20. These persons were not congressional employees. New York has been instructed to interview them to determine if this travel involved official business.

(2) Personal use of some $28,000 of public funds by Powell [that] were obtained by putting his wife on the committee payroll when, in fact, she performed no official duties.

San Juan office is presently making arrangements to interview Mrs. Powell to establish that she performed no work for Powell subsequent to 7/31/65. Independent investigation is also being conducted to establish this point. Original payroll checks are being obtained from Treasury Department for Laboratory examination to definitely establish that Mrs. Powell's endorsements on these checks were forged prior to deposit to Congressman Powell's bank account. Investigation also being conducted in attempt to ascertain ultimate disposition of proceeds of Mrs. Powell's salary checks.

(3) False accounting by Powell and two of his aides as to use of counterpart funds for foreign travel. (Counterpart funds are foreign exchange currency owned by the United States for use abroad. Congressmen under specified circumstances are provided counterpart funds for per diem and transportation expense abroad.) With regard to this item, the Department asked that we establish reporting requirements as to these expenditures and significance of these reports to the operations of Congress.

Investigation of this item has established that foreign missions of [the]

State Department furnish these funds to congressmen and render an accounting of funds used. Annually individual congressmen submit reports to the committee chairman and then a consolidated report of the full committee is inserted in the Congressional Record. No audits of these reports are made and the law under which these funds are made available provides no penalty for failure to file a report or for filing an inaccurate report on expenditures for travel abroad.

ACTION

Washington field (which has eleven agents assigned to this case) and auxiliary offices have been instructed that all leads in this matter are to [be] handled forthwith and given top-priority attention in every respect. You will be kept advised of pertinent developments as they occur.

UNITED STATES DEPARTMENT OF JUSTICE

FEDERAL BUREAU OF INVESTIGATION

Report of: SA [Bureau Deletion]
Date: 5/2/67
Office: Washington, D.C.
Field Office File #: 46-8853
Bureau File #: 46-55707
Title: CONGRESSMAN ADAM CLAYTON POWELL
Character: FRAUD AGAINST THE GOVERNMENT
                CONSPIRACY

SYNOPSIS
Travel Analysis

Conclusions of Special Subcommittee on Contracts and findings of Select Committee Pursuant to House Resolution 1 set forth. House of Representatives officials unable to make available original vouchers or bank records without authorization in [the] form of House Resolution. Folder relating to travel by Committee on Education and Labor staff members filed in Powell's office; however, Clerk of House of Representatives advised subpoena directed to Powell would be necessary to obtain records. Schedule set forth showing travel from February, 1965, to August, 1966 between New York or Washington, D.C. and Miami, Florida, for which no claims for sustenance were made by staff members. Vouchers used to pay air travel charges set forth. Six individuals whose names appear on tickets as travelers to Miami have denied this travel. Ten individuals who would be knowledgeable concerning purpose of these trips and the identity of travelers have either declined to be interviewed or could not be located for interview. The schedule shows that the majority of trips to Miami were related to travel to Bimini. Official of Committee on House Administration stated his Committee was deceived when vouchers indicated certain travel was performed when, in fact, travel was performed by someone other than the name appearing on airline tickets. He also expressed the opinion that Congressman Powell and his staff members had no authority to travel to Bimini or to Miami with Bimini being [the final] destination. He cited House Resolution 94, which states in part that funds authorized are for expenses incurred for Committee on Education and Labor activities within the United States. ME T. [sic] Swann, former receptionist for the Committee, testified that she made no trips on Committee business but that on three occasions Powell provided her with tickets for vacation trips from Washington, D.C. to Miami. She stated that one trip took place in January, 1966, but she could not recall dates of two trips in 1965. Review of flight insurance applications disclosed she applied for insurance 7/1/65, 7/30/65, and 1/1/66. Airline tickets charged to Committee totaling $461.16 and bearing her name were used on same dates. INS and air taxi records indicate she traveled to Bimini on these trips. Her name appears on other tickets for travel to Miami. Airline ticket charged to Committee in amount of $133.14 for travel to Miami on 2/14/66 showed Mr. E. Swann as traveler. Flight insurance application dated 2/14/66 located in name of Francis C. Swann. Air taxi manifest indicates Francis C. Swann traveled to Bimini 2/15/66. Emma T. Swann and her husband, Francis C. Swann, who was not a Committee employee, declined to be interviewed. On 5/31/66, Corrine A. Huff transferred from Committee staff to Powell's clerk-hire staff; however, on 7/17/66, airline ticket in amount of $56.28 and bearing her name was used for travel from Miami to Washington, D.C. According to official of Committee on House Administration, Huff was not authorized to travel and this was an improper charge. Although this was the only ticket to Miami bearing Huff's name, INS and air taxi records list her name indicating 17 trips to Bimini. Unable to locate Huff for interview. Adam Clayton Powell's name appears on airline tickets indicating three trips to San Juan, Puerto Rico, between January and September, 1965, ten trips to Miami, and about 20 trips between Washington, D.C. and New York. No sustenance claimed for these trips. INS and air taxi records list his name indicating 17 trips to Bimini. Louise M. Dargans, former Chief Clerk, Committee on Education and Labor, testified that on

3/28/65, following instructions received from Congressman Powell, the Committee air travel card assigned to her was used to purchase four one-way tickets from Washington, D.C. to New York City, totaling $72.00. According to Dargans, the tickets bearing the names of four staff members were used for travel of non-Committee personnel Lillian Upshur, Pearl Swangin, Jack Duncan, and Adam Clayton Powell, III. [Bureau Deletion] Mrs. Dargans, presently employed as clerk, Committee on Education and Labor, declined to be interviewed except in presence of her attorney. Sylvia Jeanne Givens, employed with the Committee on Education and Labor as clerk August 1 to September 9, 1966, stated she performed domestic duties at Congressman Powell's cottage in Bimini for 8/7–21/66. Partial costs of travel furnished to Givens and charged to Committee was repaid by Powell and not included in voucher. Unreimbursed travel costs, $56.39 and payroll costs for two weeks in Bimini, $158.40. Mrs. Eleanor Lee, supervisor for Night Cleaning Force, House of Representatives, referred Givens to Powell after Powell had asked Mrs. Lee to recommend someone to work as a maid in his office. C. Summner Stone, former Special Assistant to Powell, submitted three vouchers between November, 1965 and February, 1966, claiming a total of 12 days per diem at $16 for official business in Miami. INS and air taxi records indicated Stone was in Bimini [for a] major part of [the] three trips. Stone advised he felt justified in filing vouchers since he was on Committee business and his travel to Bimini was at the request of Powell. Alfredo Vidal Chacon, Puerto Rico, was on Committee payroll for the month of April, 1965. He performed no actual work but received check for $536.01.
[Bureau Deletion]

Y. MARJORIE FLORES
(MRS. ADAM CLAYTON POWELL)

Mrs. Powell was on Powell's clerk-hire payroll continuously 1958 through 1966 as a result of clerk-hire appointment form executed 1/4/65 in name of Adam Clayton Powell. Mrs. Louise M. Dargans testified she signed Powell's name to form. On basis of this form, Mrs. Powell's name continued to appear on payroll of Congress and no regular monthly certification was necessary. Seventeen payroll checks issued under name of Y. Marjorie Flores for period 8/1/65 to 12/31/66, in gross amounts of $28,505.34. Fifteen of these checks were mailed to Adam Clayton Powell and two were sent to Mrs. Powell in Puerto Rico. Three of the 15 checks mailed to Powell for the months of August, September, October, 1966, are outstanding. The remaining 12 checks totaling $16,991.69 were deposited to Powell's account at Sergeant-At-Arms Bank. Mrs. Louise M. Dargans testified that at Powell's direction she endorsed Flores' and Powell's names on nine of twelve payroll checks issued subsequent to 8/1/65 that were deposited to Powell's account. Mrs. Powell testified before Select Committee that she performed no work for Powell since July, 1965 and disclaimed endorsement on all checks other than two received by her for November and December, 1966. She stated she received no proceeds of checks received by Powell but admitted that Powell paid utilities for Puerto Rico home and that she received approximately $6,850 in checks during 1965 and 1966, as determined by House Committee investigators from review of Powell's bank account. Of the $6,850, $2,600 represented payments subsequent to 7/31/65, with final check dated 7/12/66. Mrs. Powell declined to be interviewed without presence of her attorney. Seven individuals advised they knew of no work performed by Mrs. Powell subsequent to 7/31/65. Others claimed to have no knowledge of her duties. [Bureau Deletion]

Memorandum

TO:　　　　Mr. DeLoach　　　　　　　　　　DATE: May 5, 1967

FROM:　　　A. Rosen

SUBJECT:　CONGRESSMAN ADAM CLAYTON POWELL, ET AL.
　　　　　　FRAUD AGAINST THE GOVERNMENT
　　　　　　CONSPIRACY

PURPOSE:

　To recommend that attached letter be forwarded to Department pointing out that therefore we can logically proceed further in our inquiry in this matter that testimony of certain uncooperative key witnesses and records not available except by subpoena and House Resolution are necessary. Letter requests [that] we be advised as to plans of Department for securing this testimony and the necessary records.

BACKGROUND:

　By letter dated 3/27/67, the Department requested Bureau investigation into three areas. These were (1) misuse of Congressional Committee funds for personal travel; (2) employment of Mrs. Powell on Congressman Powell's office staff from 7/31/65 to 1/1/67 during which time she allegedly performed no duties and (3) false reports as to expenditures of foreign exchange currency by Congressman Powell and two of his aides. Our investigation into these three items will be completed today, as far as we can logically proceed, with the interview of one potential witness in New York City [who was] not previously available. [The] results of our inquiry as to these three items are as follows:

Misuse of Public Funds for Personal Travel: During 1965 and 1966, some $12,000 in travel expense was charged by Powell's committee for airline trips, principally to New York City and Miami, Florida. Some of this travel was performed under assumed names by both congressional employees and persons with no official congressional connection.

[The Bureau interviewed] various individuals whose names appear on the airline tickets as travelers to Miami or New York but [they] were unable to furnish identities of the actual travelers. Five possible key witnesses regarding this travel flatly refused to be [interviewed by] FBI. Others either have refused to be interviewed except in the presence of their attorney, or have refused to make themselves available for interview after repeated contacts. We have been unable to locate Corrine Huff, Powell's former secretary [Bureau Deletion]

A significant development of our investigation is that in February, 1965, Powell, Corrine Huff, and Emma T. Swann (Powell's receptionist) and Mrs. Swann's husband spent a week aboard a fishing boat [that] was provided by an official of the Southern Conference of Teamsters. The names of Corrine Huff and the Swanns do not appear on any travel tickets during this period but the name of committee employee Aurora Harris does appear. She denies making the travel. Mr. and Mrs. Swann refuse to be interviewed by the FBI. We have been unable to locate Corrine Huff who is possibly in Bimini with Powell.

To complete inquiry of this matter we need various congressional records for handwriting examinations in an attempt to identify the travelers who signed airflight coupons under assumed names. These records can be obtained only by subpoena and House Resolution. The Department has previously been advised by memoranda as to the identities of uncooperative witnesses and records which are needed for completion of this matter. In addition, reports setting out this information have been forwarded to the Department, including a 236-page report of Washington Field Office dated 5/2/67.

Payroll Abuses: This involves salary payments to committee employees who performed no official duties. Mrs. Powell received some $28,000 and reportedly performed no duties after 7/1/65. She declined to be interviewed except in [the] presence of her attorney and by letter dated 4/17/67, we so advised the Department for its consideration in connection with any grand jury action contemplated. Individuals contacted in this matter have no knowledge of Mrs. Powell performing any official duties from 7/1/65 for Congressman Powell.

Mrs. Powell's salary checks were deposited on instructions of Congressman Powell to his account with the Sergeant-at-Arm's office at the Capitol. In attempting to trace out disposition of these funds by Powell, in line with the Department's request, we were advised that these bank account records could not be available except by House resolution. The Department has been advised [of] this situation.

Foreign Exchange Funds: Investigation completed. Failure to fully account for funds advanced of no significance to operations of Congress.

Memorandum

TO: Mr. DeLoach   DATE: June 2, 1967

FROM: A. Rosen

SUBJECT: CONGRESSMAN ADAM CLAYTON POWELL, ET AL.
          FRAUD AGAINST THE GOVERNMENT

In connection with charges in Congress, that the Justice Department was dragging its feet in the investigation of Congressman Adam Clayton Powell, the Director inquired as to whether we have finished our investigation of Powell.

It will be recalled that the Department by letters 3-27-67, initially requested Bureau investigation into three specific areas regarding activities of Powell, namely: (1) Misuse of committee funds for personal travel, (2) Employment of Mrs. Powell on Congressman Powell's office staff during a period when she allegedly performed no duties, and (3) False reports as to expenditures of foreign-exchange currency by Congressman Powell and two of his aides. We pointed out to the Department in letter 5-16-67, and again in letter 5-26-67 (attached), that scope of Bureau's investigation in this case was as specifically defined and requested by the Department in its initial request of 3-27-67. These letters also advised that any additional information as to possible violations outside these areas coming to our attention would be furnished to the Department for its consideration.

As to our investigation of travel irregularities, we are presently being hampered in our primary investigative efforts by the refusal of various key witnesses to talk to us. Further, Congressional records needed to complete inquiry into travel irregularities are not available to us except by subpoena and House resolution. By letter dated 5-5-67, we advised the Department as to the identity of various key witnesses who had refused to cooperate with us, as well as certain House of Representatives records needed for completion of this phase of the case. The Department advised us 5-19-67, that it had negotiations underway to arrange for access by the Bureau to these records. We have not yet received these records, and by letter dated 5-26-67, we advised the Department that we would proceed with [the] investigation as to this aspect of the case upon receipt of the requested records.

Our investigation as to employment of Mrs. Powell has been completed as far as we can go and the Department is presently attempting to secure bank account records of Powell's that are not available to us except by subpoena. These records are needed to trace handling of Mrs. Powell's checks by the Congressman. Various interviews, including Mrs. Powell, have established that she performed no official duties for Congressman Powell from about August, 1965, through January 1, 1967.

With respect to false reports by Powell and two of his aides as to expenditures of foreign-exchange currency, the Department asked that we establish the requirements for reporting these expenditures and the significance of these reports to the operations of the Congress. Our investigation showed that Powell and his two aides submitted reports accounting for only some $10,000 of the $20,140.12 advanced to them. The reports were perfunctorily filed because they were required for publication in the Congressional Record and, congressional sources contacted [said this] had no effect on the operations of Congress. This item of investigation has been completed, and reports have been furnished to the Department. On 5-15-67, we referred an allegation to the Department for its consideration that Congressman Powell received payoffs in connection with labor bills before Congress and kickbacks from a stenographic reporting company in connection with transcripts of testimony of congressional hearings purchased by labor unions. Department by letter 5-22-67, requested investigation of this matter. The persons involved in this allegation have been interviewed and have denied making payments or kickbacks to Powell and disclaim any knowledge of such irregularities. The records of the stenographic reporting company were made available for review on 5-31-67, and Washington Field Office has assigned personnel to expedite completion of examinations of these records by 6-5-67.

ACTION:

All investigation in this case is going ahead as expeditiously as possible with the testimony and records presently available to us. The field has been instructed that any new leads received or developed in this case are to receive same-day handling. The field is being followed closely and you will be advised of pertinent developments.

FBI

DATE: 6/14/67

TO: SACs WASHINGTON FIELD (46-8853) (3 enclosures)
        NEW YORK (46-7233) (12 enclosures)
        NEWARK (6 enclosures)

FROM: DIRECTOR, FBI (46-55707)

SUBJECT: CONGRESSMAN ADAM CLAYTON POWELL; ET AL.
        FRAUD AGAINST THE GOVERNMENT;
        CONSPIRACY; BRIBERY; CONFLICT OF INTEREST

. . . The Criminal Division has requested investigation concerning the possibility that Congressman Powell benefited financially from bills for the benefit of immigrants subject to deportation.

Investigation is to be conducted by New York and Newark. A discussion of the Department's request has been had with the Criminal Fraud Section and the scope of the requested investigation has been altered from that set forth in the enclosed letter. A representative number of the immigrants identified in the lists provided by the Department are to be interviewed, and reports reflecting the results of those interviews will then be reviewed by the Criminal Fraud Section on the Department prior to any determination as to further investigation to be conducted. In view of this, law firms representing immigrants are not to be contacted at this time.

Newark will attempt to locate and interview the six immigrants located in New Jersey. While nine of the immigrants are either deceased or outside the United States, New York will interview a representative number of the ten immigrants with addresses in Manhattan, as well as a representative number of the sixty-four immigrants with addresses in the Bronx, Queens, and Brooklyn. The addresses furnished by the Department are the latest addresses available to INS. While fugitive-type investigations are not to be conducted to locate immigrants whose whereabouts are unknown, New York should attempt to interview a sufficient number of immigrants so that investigative reports will reflect interviews with from 30 to 35 immigrants.

The files reviewed by the Department have been returned to INS, New York City. While it is not believed essential that the files on any of these immigrants be received for information which might assist in the interviews requested, New York may desire to review a small number of those files or to obtain information from INS as the procedure followed by immigrants in having private bills introduced on their behalf. The interviews to be conducted are to be most thorough and should not only develop information as to the financial aspects or fee arrangements but should identify all individuals who had any part to play in the introduction of the private bills. Such individuals would be the persons who informed the immigrant of the possibility that a private bill could be introduced on his behalf and each individual playing any part thereafter.

You will note that the Department requested that the inquiry include a discreet approach to immigrant beneficiaries. This obviously does not mean a discreet investigation, but that the immigrants be approached in a manner [that] will elicit full and complete cooperation and as much detailed information as possible from the immigrants.

New York and Newark are instructed to assign sufficient personnel to this matter to ensure completion by 6/23/67. The necessity for most expeditious and thorough handling cannot be emphasized too strongly. Investigation is to commence upon receipt of this communication and each office is to submit an airtel to the Bureau and Washington Field on a daily basis advising the number of interviews completed, and any significant information furnished by immigrants which would bear upon possible violations of Title 18, U. S. Code, Sections 201 and/or 203.

Since the immigrants may be potential subjects, they should be appropriately advised of their rights. They are also to be advised at the outset that they are being contacted at the request of Assistant Attorney General Fred M. Vinson of the Department of Justice.

UNITED STATES DEPARTMENT OF JUSTICE

FEDERAL BUREAU OF INVESTIGATION

Report of: [Bureau Deletion]
Office: New York, New York
Date: 6/27/67
Field Office File #: 46-7233
Bureau File #: 46-55707
Title: CONGRESSMAN ADAM CLAYTON POWELL; ET AL
Character: FRAUD AGAINST THE GOVERNMENT-CONSPIRACY;
        BRIBERY; CONFLICT OF INTEREST

SYNOPSIS

Immigrants interviewed to date advised they paid fees to attorneys representing them to obtain extensions of the period of time for which they were admitted to the U.S. and/or to have private bills introduced into Congress to accord them permanent resident status in the U.S.; they have no information that anyone other then attorneys received any part of their fees. [The] law firm of Billet and Billet advised that they would advise their clients not to consent to interview unless [an] attorney could be present. Efforts to locate certain immigrants unsuccessful to date.

UNITED STATES DEPARTMENT OF JUSTICE

FEDERAL BUREAU OF INVESTIGATION

Report of: [Bureau Deletion] (A)
Office: Miami Florida
Date: 7/3/67
Field Office File #: 46-3685
Bureau File #: 46-55707
Title: CONGRESSMAN ADAM CLAYTON POWELL; ET AL
Character: FRAUD AGAINST THE GOVERNMENT-CONSPIRACY;

SYNOPSIS

Tycoon Fin-Nor Corp., Miami, advised on 6/28/66 and 7/7/66, they received two phone orders from Congressman Powell, who purchased certain fishing equipment in the amount of $152.95 and $59.67 respectively. Powell paid for the former amount and the latter amount was sent to Powell's office in Washington, D.C., which was subsequently paid by a C. A. Huff check. Juniors Tackle Shop, Miami Beach, requested subpoena prior to any interview. International Game Fish Association possessed no record re Powell, however, stated it is not unusual for individuals to call re size of fish, etc. [Bureau Deletion] skipper of the Teamster's Union vessels *Yellow Rose II* and later, the *Barbara Jo I,* advised in February, 1965, [that] he and his mate [Bureau Deletion] met Powell, Corrine Huff, and Francis Carroll Swann at Chub Cay, Bahamas, where they fished [for] about a week. Powell left Chub Cay aboard John Dunn's vessel *El Pasquado,* for Nassau, noting that Dunn resides in Houston, Texas. [Bureau Deletion] also advised in early July, 1965, at the instructions of Dusty Miller, Southern Conference of Teamsters, he met Powell at Bimini, who allowed Mrs. Carroll Swann to use the vessel *Barbara Jo I* in the Blue Marlin Tournament. Powell and Huff were aboard the *Adam's Fancy,* with [Bureau Deletion] as their mate. [Bureau Deletion] possesses no records re these two trips. [Bureau Deletion] advised he was the mate aboard the *Yellow Rose II* at a time when he and [Bureau Deletion] met Powell and others at Chub Cay. [Bureau Deletion] advised Powell hired him for fishing purposes during 3/9–19/65 to act as mate while Powell, Huff, and Mr. and Mrs. Carroll Swann were fishing in Bimini, noting they all left and returned via Chalk Airlines, Miami. [Bureau Deletion] advised he was aboard the *Adam's Fancy* during the Blue Marlin Tournament in July, 1965. [Bureau Deletion] recalls that Mrs. Swann used the vessel *Barbara Jo I* during this tournament. [Bureau Deletion] advised she was initially accompanied by (FNU) Mitchell and Roy (LNU). Later Carroll Swann accompanied her. U. S. Customs, Miami records reflect *Yellow Rose II* and *Barbara Jo I* arrived Miami from Bimini on 2/16/65 and 7/10/65 respectively.

UNITED STATES DEPARTMENT OF JUSTICE

FEDERAL BUREAU OF INVESTIGATION

Report of: SA [Bureau Deletion]
Office: Washington, D.C.
Date: 1/23/68
Field Office File #: 46-8853
Bureau File #: 46-55707
Title: CONGRESSMAN ADAM CLAYTON POWELL
Character: FRAUD AGAINST THE GOVERNMENT-CONSPIRACY;
    BRIBERY; CONFLICT OF INTEREST:
    THEFT OF GOVERNMENT PROPERTY

SYNOPSIS

C & P Telephone Co. submitted monthly bills to Adam C. Powell's office for calls after 3/1/67. However, [the] House Finance Office never received original certified bills from Powell or triplicate copies from C & P. C & P informed clerk of House in August, 1967, concerning amount of bills incurred. Bills in excess of $4500 have not been paid by Powell or House of Representatives.

An FBI interview re telephone charges was filed on January 3, 1968. In it the interviewee, whose name has been deleted by the Bureau, advises that:

W. Pat Jennings ... had no knowledge of the telephone charges incurred after March 1, 1967, through use of the House member's telephone credit card assigned to Adam C. Powell until the latter part of August, 1967, when they were advised of the outstanding charges by [Bureau Deletion] of the Chesapeake and Potomac Telephone Company (C&P). During this discussion it was made clear to [Bureau Deletion] that the House of Representatives would not pay for any telephone calls made subsequent to March 1, 1967. No bills or summary of charges were presented for payment by [Bureau Deletion] during this discussion.

On or about September 8, 1967, copies of the unpaid telephone calls were sent by Chesapeake and Potomac Telephone Company to the clerk of the House for information only. On September 8, 1967, Jennings directed a letter to Powell advising him the Congress would not pay for telephone calls after March 1, 1967, in accordance with Title 2, United States Code, Section 46F1. This letter also requested Powell to send his check in the amount of $34 for two telephone calls made in February, 1967. Jennings received the check from Powell in the latter part of September, 1967.

[Bureau Deletion] exhibited a letter from Powell to Jennings dated August 28, 1967, in which Powell indicated he was astounded about the telephone charges. The letter also states "I never received the credit card and whoever used it used it 'illegally'."

Re: Adam Clayton Powell;
    Julian Bond;
    Dick Gregory, Appearances
    Black Power Conference,
    University of Michigan,
    Ann Arbor, Michigan
    September 29, 1968

. . . [Bureau Deletion] advised the next speaker was Adam Clayton Powell who began by saying "If all of the FBI or CIA personnel were to leave the building now, over half of those present would leave."

He said the Black Nationalists and young activist whites must walk hand-in-hand [sic] and that 52 percent of the people in the United States today are under 25 years of age. There are leaders willing to die if necessary to turn this establishment around the other way.

Powell said he was discriminated against when censured by Congress and other Congressmen who have done more than himself are still seated.

He said that the young people have proven at the University of California, Columbia University, Florida A&M, and Duke University that they can force change by their demonstrations on each of the college campuses and the young people have already learned that they are and should be through listening to their parents, preachers, priests, who collectively misrepresent facts to them regarding the social ills of our country.

[Bureau Deletion] said that Powell wanted people to know that Black Power is not anti-white, but just true black and is a way you think and feel. He said that black people believe in separation, but he thinks this is not what will help the black race.

Powell ended by saying that "the only man with guts on the presidential scene today is George Wallace and that the black people know where they stand with Wallace and will be better off with Wallace as President.

[Bureau Deletion] said that Bond and Gregory were enthusiastically accepted by the audience, but Powell was not well received. . . .

TELETYPE

TO DIRECTOR
FROM DETROIT (157-NEW)
9-30-68

SPEECH BY CONGRESSMAN ADAM CLAYTON POWELL, JR.,
WESTERN MICHIGAN UNIVERSITY, KALAMAZOO, MICHIGAN
SEPT. THIRTY, INSTANT. RM.
REMYTEL THIS DATE.
[Bureau Deletion] ADVISED POWELL SPOKE BEFORE CAPAC-
ITY AUDIENCE AT UNIVERSITY AUDITORIUM, WESTERN
MICHIGAN UNIVERSITY THIS EVENING. NO DISTURBANCES
OR INCIDENTS.
POWELL SAID HE WOULD MEET OCT. THIRTEEN, NEXT AT
HIS APARTMENT IN NEW YORK WITH BLACK LEADERS TO
DETERMINE WHETHER HE WILL BACK DICK GREGORY FOR
PRESIDENT OR JUST WHOM HE WILL BACK.
POWELL MADE STATEMENT THAT GEORGE WALLACE IS
THE ONLY CANDIDATE WITH "GUTS". HE SAID HUMPHREY
AND NIXON WERE LIKE TWEEDLE-DEE AND TWEEDLE-DUM.
POWELL IS EXPECTED TO DEPART KALAMAZOO AT NINE
THIRTY AM OCTOBER ONE, NEXT.
END.
SVM
FBI WASH DC

Memorandum

TO: Mr. W.C. Sullivan   DATE: April 7, 1969

FROM: G. C. Moore

SUBJECT: ADAM CLAYTON POWELL
          RACIAL MATTERS-BLACK NATIONALIST

This memorandum sets forth information regarding dissemination of
data being developed regarding subject.

Powell is the controversial Democratic Congressman from New York
City. He is a very controversial figure who is widely quoted in the

press. He is presently included in the Agitator Index based on his in-flammatory statements regarding the racial situation and in view of his association with black militants.

Recently he has been making numerous speeches on college cam-puses and he has indicated that he received from $1,500 to $2,000 for each lecture. It is expected that these college and other public appear-ances will continue and that Powell will continue his statements at-tacking the establishment and the U.S. position in Vietnam.

In view of Powell's position as a U.S. Congressman and since he is such a controversial figure, we have instructed the New York office, which is following Powell's activities through established sources, not to disseminate information being developed regarding Powell on a local level. These instructions do not apply to the immediate dissemination of data, such as a threat to Powell's life or other data which by its very nature indicates it must receive immediate dissemination.

Regarding our racial subjects, we normally disseminate information being developed regarding them to the Internal Security Division and the Inter-Division Information Unit of the Department of Justice, Secret Service and the Department of the Army. Since Powell is a key figure in the racial picture and his activities and statements have a bearing on racial activities across the country, it is believed that we should dissemi-nate data being developed regarding Powell to the above mentioned agencies. As mentioned above, Powell's activities are followed through established sources only. Regarding any high-level information being developed we will, of course, consider expanded dissemination to the White House and the attorney general.

Memorandum

TO: Mr. W. C. Sullivan   DATE: February 16, 1970

FROM: [Bureau Deletion]

SUBJECT: ADAM CLAYTON POWELL
           RACIAL MATTERS-BLACK NATIONALIST

During 1/29/70 speech at Ohio State University (OSU), Columbus, Ohio, Representative Adam Clayton Powell, the controversial Demo-cratic Congressman from New York City, stated the Director is the architect of the conspiracy of genocide against the Black Panther Party (BPP), the violence-prone black extremist organization.

Powell's appearance at the University was sponsored by various black student groups. Two thousand five hundred persons heard Powell, evenly divided between blacks and whites. [Bureau Deletion] During his speech, Powell attacked the Nixon Administration, called for an immediate end to the war in Vietnam and claimed capitalism is "on [the] way out."

He claimed there is no justice in U.S. for blacks or the poor. He stated tides of history have been changed by vocal minorities, and he endorsed continued protests by blacks on college campuses. He urged them to become even more militant. He believed the Black Panther party and other black militants are the catalytic agent of hope for blacks in this country.

He claimed there is a conspiracy in U.S. against the Black Panther Party which is headed by the Director. He stated the Director is the architect of the conspiracy of genocide against the Black Panther Party. He emphasized that blacks must realize attacks by police against selected blacks under the guidance of the Director may eventually end up as an attack against all blacks as "that is how Hitler began in Germany.". . .

A. PHILIP RANDOLPH

(1889–1979)

With Chandler Owen, a fellow pacifist and socialist, A. Philip Randolph published the monthly *Messenger* during World War I and as such became one of the first African Americans to attract the FBI's serious attention. In a report released by Congress and entitled *Investigation Activities of the Department of Justice* (1919), J. Edgar Hoover revealed a systematic investigation of "the colored press" centering on "a well-concerted movement" to subvert "the established rule of law and order" by promoting "defiantly assertive" ideas about "the Negro's fitness for self-government," "race consciousness," interest in "sex equality" (miscegenation), and over-all hostility "to the white race." Because the *Messenger* was especially bothersome, Hoover wanted "something ... done" to black journalists such as Randolph because their pronouncements had incited "the Negro elements of this country to riot and to the committing of outrages of all sorts." This particular black man would continue to upset the FBI director for the next half century.

Born in Crescent City, Florida, on April 15, 1889, Randolph studied at Cookman Institute and the City College of New York. In addition to publishing the *Messenger*, he organized an employment agency (the Brotherhood of Labor) and emerged as one of Harlem's best-known soapbox orators. At one street-corner rally, the Justice Department had him arrested on sedition charges for urging blacks not to fight in World War I. (The charges were later dropped.) After the war, he moved away from journalism and increasingly toward labor organizing, heading the Brotherhood of Sleeping Car Porters for forty-three years beginning in 1925 and winning recognition in 1937 from the Pullman Company. He supported United Mine Workers chief John L. Lewis when he left the

AFL and formed the CIO, and emerged during World War II as perhaps the most powerful black leader in the nation.

The occasion of Randolph's emergence was the mid-1940 organization of a March on Washington Movement to pressure the government into granting blacks a fair share of the emerging defense-industry jobs. The Franklin D. Roosevelt administration, however, saw Randolph as little more than a crude blackmailer. At a time when the nation needed stability and unity, in the administration's view, the March on Washington Movement threatened violence unless the president granted a series of demands: that the National Labor Relations Board deny protections to discriminatory unions; that Civil Service halt its practice of screening applicants on the basis of race; that companies found to discriminate not be given defense contracts; and that discrimination be abolished in the armed forces and all training programs for defense workers and civil servants.

President Roosevelt sent his wife, Eleanor, and New York Mayor Fiorello La Guardia to convince Randolph to call off the proposed march. When that failed, he met with Randolph on June 18 in the White House and told him that an executive order applying only to Negroes would enrage the Poles and Irish and every other ethnic group who would demand similar treatment. The President also predicted rioting if the March on Washington actually took place, adding that this would create a backlash against the civil rights effort. But Randolph held firm. He returned to New York and continued organizing the movement— until summoned once more to the oval office. This time, the president caved. He issued Executive Order 8802 prohibiting discrimination in defense industries and establishing a Fair Employment Practice Committee. Although Roosevelt ignored the demand to desegregate the armed forces, Randolph recognized a victory when he saw one and called off the March.

Randolph nonetheless kept the March on Washington Movement alive, threatening a demonstration every spring for the remainder of the war. But there would be no more concessions, only a constant FBI surveillance. Hoover's men wiretapped the movement's telephones, recruited informants at the going rate of forty dollars a month, and generally spied on March organizers and supporters wherever they could be found. Randolph's insistence that the movement be kept free of leftist taint, moreover, had no effect on the FBI. Hoover also sent a steady stream of intelligence to Roosevelt, taking every occasion to make his point about Communist party dreams of converting the all-black March on Washington Movement into an all-Red affair. From Franklin and

Eleanor Roosevelt on down, no administration official questioned the bureau's methods in gathering such information or the underlying assumption that those who crusaded for racial justice in a manner deemed irresponsible were legitimate subjects of federal surveillance.

Twenty years later, Randolph would help organize another March on Washington in the face of White House opposition. This one not only took place in August 1963 but served as the forum for Martin Luther King's greatest speech. In that decade and in the years thereafter, Randolph also presided over the Negro American Labor Council and the A. Philip Randolph Institute. In 1964, Lyndon B. Johnson awarded him a Presidential Medal of Freedom. By that time, he was already revered as the civil rights movement's senior statesman—remembered, in NAACP leader Roy Wilkins's words, as the "tall, courtly black man with Shakespearean diction and the stare of an eagle [who] had looked the patrician Roosevelt in the eye—and made him back down."

With high-blood pressure and a heart condition, Randolph spent his last years at a more controlled pace. On May 16, 1979, he died at his modest, sparsely furnished New York apartment. To read about Randolph's early career, see Theodore Kornweibel, *No Crystal Stair: Black Life and the* Messenger, *1917–1928* (1975); and William H. Harris, *Keeping the Faith: A. Philip Randolph, Milton P. Webster, and the Brotherhood of Sleeping Car Porters, 1925–1937* (1977). Biographies include Jervis Anderson's, *A Philip Randolph: A Biographical Portrait* (1973); and Paula F. Pfeffer's, *A. Philip Randolph* (1990).

FEDERAL BUREAU OF INVESTIGATION

Instructions Received from Special Agent in Charge Edward J. Brennan
Report made at: New York, N.Y.
Date when made: Sept. 16, 1922
Period for which made: Sept 6th to 16th, 1922
Report made by: [Bureau Deletion]
Title and character of case: RE: THREATENING LETTER &
                              HUMAN HAND: Sent by KKK

FACTS DEVELOPED AT NEW YORK, N.Y.:
    The Bureau office was called on the telephone September 6th, 1922, by one Philip, who stated he would like to see an Agent concerning a human hand that had been sent to him by mail on the afternoon of September 5th, 1922, at 1:30 P.M. with a letter signed "K.K.K."

Agent called on Mr. Randolph, who stated that he had no idea who sent him the hand, unless it was one of Marcus Garvey's followers. He felt the letter was written by a Negro and said that during the convention, Garvey, in one of his speeches said he would not be responsible if Randolph and Owen (Randolph's partner) lost a hand or a foot.

Agent then called on and interviewed [Bureau Deletion] who received the package from Randolph, and he informed Agent that he had turned the hand over to the National Examiner. [Bureau Deletion], and the letter and wrapper in which the hand had been received, had been turned over to [Bureau Deletion] Post Office Inspector.

Agent called on and interviewed [Bureau Deletion] who turned the wrapper and letter over to Agent so same could be Photostatted. Agent also called on [Bureau Deletion], but found him out; however, his assistant [Bureau Deletion] stated that it was a hand of a Negro and in his opinion it had been cut off some time, but could not say how long.

The Superintendent of mails at Station "J" interviewed the carrier and he remembered leaving the package for Randolph. P.O. Inspector [Bureau Deletion] will send the wrappers and letter to New Orleans to see if he can locate the sender.

On September 6th, Randolph called the Bureau office and informed Agent that he had just received another letter from New Orleans, which he turned over to Agent, who in turn gave [it] to [the] Inspector [Bureau Deletion] of the Post Office.

Memorandum

DATE: [July 1942]

RE: A. PHILIP RANDOLPH

A. Philip Randolph, also known as Asa Philip Randolph, president of the International Brotherhood of Sleeping Car Porters, American Federation of Labor, was born on April 15, 1889, at Crescent City, Florida, the son of a Negro Methodist minister.

Randolph, upon completing his primary education, went to New York City and worked as a laborer, waiter, and for five years was employed as a porter by the Consolidated Edison Company of New York City. During this period he attended classes at the College of the City of New York and studied political science, economics, and philosophy.

Randolph joined the Socialist party in New York City and in line with socialist theories began to work against discrimination directed towards the Negro race. It has been stated that Randolph believes race discrimination stems from the economic abuses of capitalism and that he joined the Socialist party because it advocates unconditional social, political, and economic equality for Negroes. His views in this regard are expressed in the following quotation from his writings:

> "We do not accept the doctrine of old, reactionary Negroes that the Negro is satisfied to be himself. We desire as much contact and intercourse—social, economic, and political—as is possible between the races. This is not because of our belief in the inferiority or superiority of either race, but because of our recognition that the principle of social equality is the only sure guarantee of social progress."

Randolph, together with Chandler Owen, founded *The Messenger*, a monthly magazine, in 1917. This magazine advertised itself as a "journal of scientific radicalism." *The Messenger* at that time was described as the best edited, best printed, best financed, and the most radical of all the radical publications in America. Also during this period this magazine was reported to be the Russian organ of the Belsheviki [sic] in the United States and the headquarters of revolutionary thought.

The influence of *The Messenger* is said to have been demonstrated in 1917 when over twenty-five percent of the Negro voters in a New York election supported the socialist ticket. During the period of World War I *The Messenger* continued to print and advocate radical teachings. The following is an excerpt from an issue during that period:

> "Civil liberty in the United States is dead. Civil liberty for the Negro, however, was dead even before the war, killed by the combination of a hypocritical North and an unregenerate South who colluded to sweep from the Negro his last vestige of liberty. We repudiate and condemn any pretense at opposition to Jim Crowism, segregation, and all forms of discrimination which does not accept the principle of social equality, since it is upon the fallacious theory of inequality and radical inferiority that all these evils are established and continued."

The Messenger exhorted the Negro people to take an active militant part in preventing abuses to members of their race and in the August,

1919 issue [advised] the Negroes to protect themselves by "shot and shell and fire." It stated further:

> "This may sound rather strange talk for the pacifist editors of *The Messenger*, but we are pacific only on matters that can be settled peacefully. It is his (the Negro's) business to decide that just as he went 3,000 miles away to fight for alleged democracy in Europe and for others, that he can lay down his life honorably and peacefully for himself in the United States."

The Messenger endorsed the INN movement and defended the Bolsheviki form of government setup in Russia. The February, 1919, issue carried an article entitled "We Want More Bolsheviki Patriotism." This article stated: "We want no landless patriots in a country of almost unlimited lands. We want no patriot talking about my country, not a foot of whose land he owns. We want a patriotism [that] practices that any man who protects the country's flag shall be protected by that flag. We want a patriotism not streaked with race, color, or sex lines. What we really need is a patriotism of liberty, justice, and joy. This is Bolshevik patriotism, and we want more of that brand in the United States."

The Messenger was suppressed during World War I and Randolph's radical activities led to his arrest in Cleveland, Ohio, on August 10, 1918, by Agents of the Department of Justice, at which time he was charged with violating the Espionage Act.

During 1918, Randolph was a candidate for Assembly from the Nineteenth District, New York City, on the Socialist party ticket. At that time *The Call*, the official publication of the Socialist party stated: "The new Negro is here and there will be many more of them to enrich the socialist movement in the United States."

Randolph became an instructor at the Rand School of Social Science in New York City and in 1921 he again sought public office in New York on the socialist ticket aspiring to the Office of Secretary of State.

In 1925 Randolph and a group of Pullman Company porters met in a recreation hall in Harlem and founded the Brotherhood of Sleeping Car Porters. Randolph was elected president and general organizer of the union. His publication *The Messenger* shortly thereafter advertised itself as "The official organ of the Brotherhood of Sleeping Car Porters."

Randolph, at the fourth annual convention of the Brotherhood of Sleeping Car Porters held in 1936, stated that he advocated the formation of a Farmer Labor party and pledged active support to the Committee of Industrial Organization which at that time was sponsoring the drive to organize the steel industry. In addition, this convention went on record as opposing fascism and war and all segregation and "Jim Crowing" in the trade union movement. The delegates demanded justice for the sharecroppers and freedom for Tom Mooney, Angelo Herndon, and the Scottsboro Boys.

Randolph in 1936 was chairman of the Norman Thomas for President Committee and the same year was elected national president of the National Negro Congress. In addressing this congress he stated:

"The Negro in politics, industry, education, and his entire social life, is faced with a decisive and imperative challenge to develop and fashion a new and powerful instrumentality with which not only to arouse and fire the broad masses to action in their own defense, but to attack the forces of reaction that seek to throttle black America with increasing 'Jim Crowism,' segregation, and discrimination."

Randolph served as chairman of the May Day Parade in New York City in 1937. The *Daily Worker* in commenting on this parade stated:

"May Day, 1937, is united May Day. As last year, the Socialist and Communist parties have joined with the Progressive trade unions, the garment workers, the furriers, the painters and the shoe workers to carry on the tradition of a glorious, militant, class parade on Labor's own holiday. The importance of this unity cannot be too greatly stressed; for this one day, the disagreements between the various sections of progressive and revolutionary labor are laid aside and a common front presented to the world."

On August 7, 1937, the American League Against War and Fascism staged a "March For Peace" in New York City, at which time Randolph was listed as one of the officers handling the march.

In September, 1937, Randolph announced the Brotherhood of Sleeping Car Porters had signed a contract with the Pullman Company which, he stated, was the first contract a Negro labor union had ever signed in American history. Commenting further, he stated:

"We have won complete representation rights; minority rights; the eight-hour day; and a $2,000,000 annual wage increase for porters, attendants, and maids. Under this agreement we now represent every class of worker on the Pullman cars except the conductors."

In 1937 Randolph was in favor of retaining the CIO unions in the American Federation of Labor and he stated:

"I consider the suspension of the CIO unions ill-advised and introduced a resolution against it in the last American Federation of Labor convention. I opposed the suspension because I thought it would make future trade union unity more difficult."

In May 1938, Randolph was active in the "Co-ordinating Committee For Employment" which advocated the equal employment of Negroes in the local government and utility systems in New York City.

James W. Ford, the notorious Negro communist leader and one-time Vice Presidential candidate on the Communist party ticket, stated in October, 1938, "Another rich experience in my life which I value very highly is my contact and friendship with A. Philip Randolph. Randolph has now become the outstanding labor leader among the Negroes in America."

Ford, in discussing the role of the Negroes in the 1938 election in New York City, stated that Randolph would be an asset in the United States Congress not only for his own people, but to America as a whole.

Randolph, at the American Federation of Labor convention at Houston, Texas, in October, 1938, described the American Labor party of New York as "one of the most effective political agents in American politics and largely responsible for the election of that great Liberal, Mayor La Guardia."

Randolph appeared on the speaker's platform with Norman Thomas and other prominent radicals as the May Day Rally held by the Socialist party, Workmen's Circle and Social Democratic Federation on April 30, 1939, at the Hippodrome in New York City.

On February 11, 1940, Randolph and Norman Thomas were among the sponsors of a rebel bloc within the American Youth Congress, which Lewis Conn, director of the new group, stated was opposed to concentration camp cultures of Russia, Germany, Italy, and other dictator countries. Conn appealed for the support of all "progressive non-communist young people united in the conviction that democracy can live only if it meets human needs."

The Third National Negro Congress was held at Washington, D.C. April 26–28, 1940. Randolph, who had been national president of the organization, walked out and denounced the National Negro Congress as a communist-controlled organization.

Randolph, in addressing the fifteenth anniversary convention of the Brotherhood of Sleeping Car Porters in September, 1940, stated:

"We reject the communist program as a solution of the problems of the Negro, because it is the negation of Democracy. We condemn all communist front and transmission belt organizations as a peril to the constructive and sound program of the Negro people, since they seek only to serve the cause of the Communist party, which is only concerned about the success of the foreign policy of Soviet Russia."

Randolph in 1940 advocated the reelection of Presidential Roosevelt as conductive [sic] to the best interests of the Negro people. He was sharply rebuked by the Communist party for this stand and the *Daily Worker* for September 30, 1940, stated:

"A recent statement by the bogus socialist, A. Philip Randolph, that the interests of the Negro people demand the reelection of President Roosevelt will be sharply refuted in a major election campaign address by James W. Ford, communist candidate for Vice President. Ford will show that the interests of the Negro people, as well as those of the masses of white workers, do not lie in the election of either national candidate of the two major parties, but in the unity of both Negroes and whites under the leadership of the Communist party."

Plans were laid for the march of 100,000 Negroes to Washington, D.C., in July, 1941, to protest against Negro discrimination. This march was canceled by Randolph upon the request of President Roosevelt. Shortly thereafter the President issued Executive Order 8802 which provided for the establishment of the Fair Employment Practice Committee.

Numerous Negro communists, including James Ford, supported the March on Washington Movement in 1941 and were keenly disappointed when Randolph called off the march. On June 17, 1941, Ford in the *Daily Worker* stated:

"Roosevelt has been smoked out with belated and vague promises against Jim Crow in national defense industries. Without a doubt the Roosevelt Administration sanctioned the proposed March on Washington July 1st, headed by A. Philip Randolph with the hope that by throwing out a few sops, the Negro people would be pacified and stop demanding too much. That is the intention of the Roosevelt statement. But the maneuver is not working out as planned. Negro people throughout the country are determined, and are preparing to go to Washington to make their demands heard. They are determined to secure more real demands.

Following the decision of Randolph to call off the March on Washington in 1941, the March on Washington Movement was kept alive and the organized setup was kept intact. Information was received from a confidential source on April 4, 1942, that Randolph did not believe the demands of the Negroes had been realized under the President's order and that he was again laying plans for an additional march on Washington.

Randolph stated in an article appearing in the newspaper *PM* for April 9, 1942:

"The slogan of the 'March on Washington' movement, which is backed by the Negro preacher, teacher, social service worker, trade unionist, doctor, lawyer, and the man in the street is 'Winning democracy for the Negro is winning the war for democracy.' Negroes feel that they have fully earned their rights, and they are not in any mood to beg for them. They have paid for them with blood and tears and a quarter of a thousand years of unrequited toil."

Memorandum

DATE: [May 1944]
SYNOPSIS: [March on Washington] and Co-Chairman of National
            Council to Establish a Permanent [Fair Employment Prac-
            tice Committee]. He recently declined to run for Congress
            against Reverend A. C. Powell, Jr.; On 5/2/44, Randolph
            received the Clendenin Award of the Workers Defense
            League for distinguished service to labor.

DETAILS:

PERSONAL HISTORY

A. Phillip Randolph, also known as Asa Philip Randolph, was born on April 15, 1889, at Crescent City, Florida, the son of a poor Negro clergyman in the African Methodist Church. He studied at Cookman

Institute, Jacksonville, Florida, and then traveled to New York City where he took courses at the City College of New York. He has had a succession of varied jobs as a waiter on the Fall River Line, as an elevator operator, as a porter for Consolidated Edison. In 1915 Randolph married a colored woman, name unknown, in this city and has been married to her ever since. In 1917 the subject and Chandler Owen launched *The Messenger* a monthly magazine with the subtitle ''The Only Radical Negro Magazine in America.''

Because of his militant stand against World War I, Randolph was arrested in June, 1918 in Cleveland by the Department of Justice but was released after a few days in the City jail. Randolph was an instructor at one time at the Rand School of Social Sciences in New York. In 1921 he ran as a socialist candidate for New York Secretary of State and at one time for Congress and the Assembly.

In 1925, even though he had organized a union of Elevator Operators in 1917 in New York City, and had participated in organizational campaigns among motion-picture operators and garment trade workers, he still considered himself a writer and editor rather than a labor organizer. In August, 1925, Randolph was elected President and General Organizer of the Brotherhood of Sleeping Car Porters. Shortly after this time the masthead of *The Messenger* [was] changed to read ''The Official Organ of the Brotherhood of Sleeping Car Porters.''

In August, 1937 A. Philip Randolph succeeded in signing a contract with a Pullman company giving the Pullman employees $2,000,000 in pay increases and guaranteeing them shorter hours with pay for overtime. As the head of the only all-Negro union (Brotherhood of Sleeping Car Porters) with the international charter from the American Federation of Labor, which officially condemns race discrimination but twenty of whose unions draw the color line, Randolph challenged the delegates at the AF of L National Convention in November to tackle the problem. He was not answered. Randolph is still considered a socialist although not an ''orthodox Marxian.''

In his book *New World A-Coming,* Pay Ottley refers to the subject as follows:

> ''The ticklish job of advancing Negroes' causes today is mainly in the hands of two veterans, Walter White and A. Philip Randolph; together they work in easy association from New York headquarters.''

Ottley refers to Randolph as the "most self-effacing of public men."
He describes him further as:

"Tall, dark and broody [sic]. Free from scheming or duplicity. Honest to the point of being almost naive, he has nonetheless achieved
a position of great strategic importance at a crucial moment in Negro
world history. He is unique among Negro leaders in that he is neither
preacher, educator, nor a rabble-rousing politician; but a labor organizer. His present leadership of Negroes seems to be based on this
somewhat nationalistic statement. 'The old policy of defending Negroes' rights is well nigh bankrupt and is of limited value,' Randolph
declared. 'Fundamental rights do not mean a thing if you can't exercise them.' He stated, 'The solution then is for the Negro to take the
offensive and carry the fight for justice, freedom, and equality. No
minority group exploited and discriminated against can win its rights
on the defensive.' "

Perhaps the real clue of his attitude today is revealed in his resignation from the National Negro Congress because, as he stated:

"It was dominated by the Communist party and thus by white
people."

Randolph believes that only in periods of great social upheaval can
Negroes make fundamental gains. It was a year before the present conflict that he [threw] in his lot with power politics and formed the Negro
March on Washington Movement to mobilize Negroes nationwide for
a demonstration in Washington if the need should arise. This movement
excluded communists. The Left attacked Randolph when he made an
early declaration that only solidarity can save the black and white workers of America and their solidarity must be composed of black, white,
Jews, Gentiles, Republicans, Democrats, socialists and communists.
Randolph explained his position in this manner:

"The March on Washington Movement is an all-Negro movement
but it is not anti-white. We believe that Negroes need an all-Negro
movement just as Jews have a Zionist movement and Catholics have
an all-Catholic movement of which only workers are members. The
purpose of the March on Washington Movement is to stress definitely
and emphasize that the main and basic responsibility for effecting the
solution of the Negroes' problem rests upon Negroes themselves."

In the month of June, 1942 Randolph rallied 20,000 Negroes in a mass demonstration held at Madison Square Garden to protest discrimination in industry and the Armed Services.

Late in the summer of 1940 with war threatening, Randolph, Walter White, and Chaning Tobias, a Negro YMCA executive, conferred with President Roosevelt on the status of the Negro in the Armed Services and war industry. This meeting was instrumental in obtaining greater employment and alleviating discrimination to some extent.

In early 1941, Randolph called for a Negro march on Washington. In the midst of the mobilization campaign he told Ottley, then a Negro newspaper man:

"The administration leaders in Washington will never give the Negro justice until they see masses,—ten, twenty, fifty thousand Negroes on the White House lawn."

Buses were hired, trains were charted, and a demonstration of 50,000 Negroes was planned to take place on July 1, 1941. Thousands of dollars were spent, Negro press and pulpit played a decisive role in stirring up sentiment, and those official couriers, the Pullman porters, carried the word to Negro communities throughout the country.

Fiorello La Guardia, Mayor of New York, together with other prominent national and local figures pleaded with Randolph and White to call the march off but they were politely refused. Four days before the crucial day Randolph, White, and others were called to Washington where they agreed to call off the march at the request of Government officials in order to give them more time to study the situation. As a result of this intended march on Washington the Negroes gained for themselves the famous Executive Order 8802 and created the Committee on Fair Employment Practices.

ACTIVITIES

The files of this office were reviewed by the reporting agent in regard to the subject and the following information was obtained concerning him:

A May Day Rally was held by the Socialist party on April 30, 1939. The announced speakers at this meeting were Norman Thomas, Israel Knox, George Backer, and A. Philip Randolph.

The files reflected that in 1935, local conferences of the National Negro Congress were held in various cities in the United States. In

February, 1936, the first NNC conference was held in Chicago with representatives from all parts of the country. At that time the Party planned to use and did use a liberal Negro, one A. Philip Randolph, present National Director of the MOWM, as head of the organization. However, every effort was made by the Communist party to maintain control of the organization. A. Philip Randolph bitterly criticized the activities of the Communist party in this organization and at the Third National Negro Congress held in Washington, D.C. in April, 1940, he was accused of being a ''Red baiter'' and was overwhelmingly defeated. Dr. Max Yergan was elected to succeed Randolph. Yergan was formerly an instructor at the City College of New York and was removed in 1941 because of participation in Communist party activities.

According to information in the New York Field Division Files the MOWM was founded by A. Philip Randolph and an anti-communist group that split off from the National Negro Congress in the fall of 1940. This group decided to plan a march on Washington in order to present the grievances of the Negro to government officials and for the abolishment of discrimination.

It is reported that in June 1941 Randolph called off the March on Washington at the request of government officials in order to give them time to study the matter and make recommendations. Although the organization setup was retained, no further activity was reported until early in 1942, when, according to reports, Randolph's group expressed dissatisfaction with the Negro's position, and again decided to use the organization as a pressure group to demand equal democratic rights for the Negro.

The March on Washington Movement held its first meeting in Madison Square Garden [on] June 16, 1942, attended by approximately 20,000 Negroes. At this meeting A. Philip Randolph introduced the following eight-point program for the organization:

1. We demand in the interests of national unity the abrogation of every law which makes a distinction in treatment between citizens based on religion, creed, color, or racial origin. This means an end to Jim Crow in education, in housing, in transportation and other social, economic, and political privileges, and especially we demand in the capital of the nation an end to all segregation in public places and in public institutions.
2. We demand legislation to enforce the 5th and 14th Amendments, guaranteeing that no person shall be deprived of life, liberty, or property without due process of law, so that the full weight of the

national government may be used for the protection of life and thereby may end the disgrace of lynching.

3. We demand the enforcement of the 14th and 15th Amendments, and the enactment of the Pepper Poll Tax Bill so that all barriers in the exercise of the suffrage are eliminated.

4. We demand the abolition of segregation and discrimination in the Army, Navy, Marine Corps, Air Corps, and all other branches of national defense.

5. We demand an end to discrimination in jobs and job training; further we demand that the F.E.P.C. be made a permanent Administration agency of the United States government and that it be given power to enforce its decisions based on its findings.

6. We demand that federal funds be withheld from any agency [that] practices discrimination in the use of such funds.

7. We demand Negro and minority group representation on all Administrative agencies so that these groups may have recognition of their democratic right to participate in formulating policies.

8. We demand representation for the Negro and minority racial groups on all missions, political and technical, which will be sent to the peace conference, so that the interests of all people everywhere may be fully recognized and justly provided for in the postwar settlement.

It should also be noted that A. Phillip Randolph at the inception of the National Negro Congress became the national president, and resigned from this organization in 1939 because of his opposition to its communistic policies. Subsequent to that time it has been reported that Randolph has taken a stand in direct opposition to the communists. He has stated publicly that the cooperation of the Communist party would be a "kiss of death" for any organization in America. It is further noted that, according to report of Special Agent L. Byron Lockhart, dated October 1, 1942, at Detroit, Michigan entitled: "March on Washington Movement, Internal Security," at the national conference of this organization held in Detroit, September 25, and 27, 1942, the representatives at this meeting adopted a resolution that the March on Washington Movement is opposed to cooperation from the Communist party or any Communist Front organizations, although the resolution was not to be construed as an opposition to the heroic fight of Russia.

The national headquarters of the March on Washington Movement are located in the Hotel Theresa, 2084 Seventh Avenue, New York

City. A. Philip Randolph is the national director, and Lawrence M. Ervin is president of the New York branch of this organization.

The files reflected that the Negro Trends of July 29, 1943, state that there were no new developments during the past week regarding Negro activities. The Communist party still continues to attack the March on Washington Movement. James W. Ford, Negro, and member of the National Committee of the Communist party, in his statement attacked A. Philip Randolph for his statement explaining why white persons are excluded from the MOWM to avoid communist infiltration. The Randolph statement was as follows:

"We don't want communists in the organization for the reason that they penetrate such movements for the sole purpose of dominating them in the interests of the Soviet Union. We cannot have the Negro fighting for his rights subject to the political influence that may exist in Russia."

Ford stated that by no stretch of the imagination can it be said that communists and the Communist party have or hope for a monopoly in the fight for Negro rights. He accused the MOWM of being against the war effort.

The files of the office reflect in the Negro Trends of August 12, 1943, that A. Philip Randolph, presiding over a meeting of the March on Washington Movement on August 4th, 1943, at the Harlem Branch of the YMCA, stated that he was in conference with a number of civic leaders in Harlem, and that it was contemplated that a delegation would be sent to Mayor La Guardia to present the following recommendations:

(1) A Negro Police Inspector and a Negro Police Captain be installed in Harlem.
(2) The appointment of two Negro policemen for every white policeman to serve in the Harlem area.
(3) The establishment of a Race Relations Committee of the Board of Education.
(4) Courses in Negro history to be offered in public schools.
(5) The Mayor to appoint as one of his personal secretaries a member of the Negro race.
(6) Causes of race riots to be investigated and the results published.
(7) The Mayor or the President issue a proclamation abolishing discrimination in the armed forces.

(8) A recommendation to Governor Dewey to form a New York State Race Relations Committee.

Mayor La Guardia was criticized by Randolph for not making the results of the investigation of the 1935 riots public.

The files of this office reflected that A. Philip Randolph, International President of the Brotherhood of Sleeping Car Porters, 217 West 125th Street, Room 301, New York City, reported to the Criminal Division, November, 1943 that he was denied his constitutional right of free speech by O. H. Perry, Sheriff of Shelby County, Tennessee, William Gerber, District Attorney General, Shelby County, Tennessee, Charles Crabtree, County Attorney, Joseph P. Boyle, Police Commissioner, and County Commissioner, F. W. Hale. Mr. Randolph alleged that this group of officials coerced and intimidated a group of Negroes in Memphis to cancel a speaking engagement of Randolph's for November 7, 1943, at the Mount Nebo Baptist Church.

A Philip Randolph, International President of the Brotherhood of Sleeping Car Porters, was interviewed by Special Agent E. Earl Jennings and the reporting agent in regard to the violation of his civil rights. Mr. Randolph prepared a typewritten statement concerning this matter which was signed by him on May 1, 1944, at his office. The original of this statement is being retained in the files of this office.

The files reflect that Confidential Informant ND-119, whose identity is known to the Bureau, advised this office that the subject, together with several other prominent Americans of all races and creeds, attended a conference in Washington on February 20, 1943, in regard to the Fair Employment Practices Committee. The conference was called by Paul B. McNutt, War Man-Power Commissioner. The purpose of this meeting was to strengthen and revise the F.E.P.C.

On March 21, 1943, Confidential Informant ND-119 advised this office that the subject was a speaker at Mother A. M. E. Zion Church, 140 West 138th Street, New York City, in a discussion: "Related Problems of War And Peace." At this time Randolph stated:

"The people today are thinking globally. They are drawing a sharp comparison between totalitarianism and democracy. Totalitarianism means complete suppression of all human rights. Democracy maintains and increases the rights and privileges of the people. Democracy is preferable. The Negro wants to see United Nations win the war, however, the war may be won in Europe and Asia and lost in New York and Georgia.

"The imperialism of Britain is no better than the imperialism of Hitler. Destruction of imperialism is essential to the preservation of democracy. There must be democracy at home as well as abroad. Negroes have never been free. My organization has always sympathized with India and its struggle for freedom. We sent telegrams to Winston Churchill demanding the release of India's leaders and for freedom for India. We must at all times support the movement for freedom for people all over the world.

"Negro soldiers are discriminated [against] and segregated by our own government. Our Negro airmen are sent to a Jim Crow school in Tuskegee, Alabama. They have the disadvantage of working and training in unison with other racial groups. The Red Cross segregates Negro blood. Negroes cannot be officers in the Navy. Negro women cannot join the WAVES and the SPARS. Negroes on every hand are the victims of indescribable injustice. Paul B. McNutt called off the hearing on discrimination in the railroad industry arranged by the F.E.P.C. This will mean that the Negroes now employed on Southern railroads will shut off trains in the South. At peak there were 6,950 Negroes employed on Southern R.R. The number has declined to 2,400 and these face elimination. Negroes have been shot off trains in the South.

"The F.E.P.C. came about as a result of our plans to march on Washington. We postponed it because we felt that it was advisable at the time but this does not mean that we are not going to march. Racial tension is widespread. Injustice and discrimination is evident everywhere. The National Conference called in Chicago in May will take up the question of time and arrangements for a march on Washington.

"There are people in the North as well as in the South who would rather lose this war than to give the Negro his rights.

"The National Conference will also project a national civil disobedience nonviolent campaign to take place simultaneously with the Conference.

"It will be worked out in minute detail for every part of the country so that there can be no mistake as to what we mean and what we do. I shall personally take part in this campaign. I would not ask anyone to do something that I would not do. Our campaign will differ from the campaign in India because the campaign there is aimed at breaking down the British civil authority. Ours is a protest against injustice and violations of the rights of loyal American citizens. It is an action [against] laws and conditions that violate civil rights.

Director, FBI   DATE: July 14, 1944

SAC, New York

FOREIGN-INSPIRED AGITATION AMONG
THE AMERICAN NEGROES
NEW YORK FIELD DIVISION
INTERNAL SECURITY

Under the auspices of the A. Philip Randolph Educational Fund, a luncheon meeting was held on July 12, 1944, at the Hotel Delmonico, 502 Park Avenue, New York City, at which Mr. A. Philip Randolph reported on his observation on racial tension following a two-month tour of the United States.

. . . The following excerpts present the substance of the speech of Mr. Randolph, as reported by Agent Brower.

Opening his fifty-minute speech with a remark that he believed "The question of race to be the central historical, social question of these times," he emphasized "Even the strikes taking place today are not designed to change the social order. They are not revolutionary in their purposes. They are strikes to raise wages, that is the ordinary objective. However, the areas [sic]) which we do have disturbances are the areas of racial intolerance. . . . Now in this country we are confronted with the problem of the treatment of people of our color in the Armed Forces. I have covered much of the country and I haven't found a single Negro who is satisfied with his treatment in the Armed Forces. Whenever you raise the question of democracy and freedom, they talk about discrimination not only in the Army here but in England, Africa, and in the southeast section of the world, wherever they are." He cited as an instance the recent incident in Texas where a party of Negro soldiers were denied admission to a dining car, while later a group of Nazi prisoners were given the privilege of the diner and other comforts. "When you talk to Negroes throughout the country they tell you frankly they do not believe democracy is coming; that the war is not being fought for freedom at all, but for the maintenance of white supremacy. . . . We know if the Axis powers win, democracy will die, but it doesn't follow that if the United Nations win, democracy will live. . . . I visited St. Paul, Seattle, Portland, Oakland, Los Angeles, San Francisco, Salt Lake City, Denver, St. Louis, Chicago, and Buffalo, before returning to New York City. I found areas where tension was on the increase."

Then he described as areas of tension housing, transportation, recreation, and employment conditions. "Housing is undoubtedly one of the centers where we may face repercussions. We are aware of what happened in Detroit. Wherever the Government establishes housing, there is also the segregation pattern [that] goes along with the housing project. This is done by our Government. . . . I have gone to the projects on the West Coast and where they live in the general project they are confined to specific streets or specific sections, and not integrated in the other group. This is a source of discontent, and expressions of hostility can be heard everywhere among them. . . . Some very careful thinking and planning has to be done about this situation in order to avoid race riots in this area of housing."

With regard to transportation, Randolph said that the Negroes are making a drive for opportunity to work as motormen and conductors of street cars and especially was this true in Los Angeles. They were meeting strenuous opposition and soon there is to be a hearing on this question. "I have been told they are beginning to lay off workers in the shipyards and there is a layoff in the production of airplanes and in various forms of shipbuilding. There will be a time when we have a larger supply than we really need; the Negroes, the last to be hired, will be the first to be fired, and so they are going to be more constantly striving for jobs on the street railroads. . . .

"The third area of racial irritation is recreation. All down the coast where the people are seeking relief from heat, Negroes find themselves especially restricted to certain areas. The younger Negroes are going out of the places set aside for them and moving to the places generally used by the public. In various places they have had conflicts. These conflicts have not spread as yet in the form of race riots but as summer goes on there is the possibility of race riots breaking out. The riot in Detroit began in July, a year ago, when people were seeking relief from the heat. . . . There will be something happening unless some prophylactic measure is taken."

Randolph also deplored the attitude of the Police with respect to association of whites and blacks, citing as an illustration the practice employed in some sections where the Police discovered a white woman and a Negro man walking down the street together. He said, "Evidently you are not going to be able to control that situation so you may expect some sort of trouble unless there is an educational program carried on by the City Department with respect to this situation. As the Police are not anthropological and know nothing about causes of racial tension and have their own concepts of superiority and inferiority of race . . . and I am afraid it is going to be productive of quite some trouble.

"In the field of employment, that is one of the most serious areas. When the war is over and the bottom falls out of our economy, then there is going to be this struggle for survival, and the Negroes are always the victims of delayed employment and premature employment ... Consequently this question of employment is a serious issue that confronts us."

He then discussed briefly the work of the FEPC and the efforts to secure the $500,000 appropriation to carry on the work of the committee. He mentioned that the struggle for a permanent FEPC will probably come to a head in August when the respective Senate and House Committees had decided to hold hearings on the measure. . . .

Assistant Attorney General T. Vincent [deletion]inn June 28, 1948
Criminal Division

Director, FBI

A. PHILIP RANDOLPH
TREASON
(Your reference 1467-51-202, NAF)

Reference is made to your memorandum of May 19, 1948, referring to the statements made by Randolph when he testified before the Senate Committee on Armed Services, March 31, 1948. You requested that an investigation be instituted to determine if the statements made by Randolph constituted treasonous activity on his part.

Since the alleged treasonous activity of Randolph is based upon statements made by him during his testimony before the Senate Committee on Armed Services, the transcript of his testimony before this Senate Committee has been examined and two photostatic copies of his testimony from pages 635 to 69, inclusive of his testimony before the Committee on Armed Services for the date of March 31, 1948, are enclosed herewith. . . .

I shall appreciate being advised of your opinion as to whether the statements made by Randolph constitute a violation of the treason statute. In the event that any additional investigation is desired, I would like to be advised.

UNIVERSAL MILITARY TRAINING

Hearings Before The Committee On Armed Services
United States Senate
Eightieth Congress
Second Session
On
UNIVERSAL MILITARY TRAINING
March 17, 18, 22, 23, 24, 25, 29, 30, 31
April 1, 2, and 3, 1948

STATEMENT OF A. PHILLIP RANDOLPH, NATIONAL TREASURER OF THE COMMITTEE AGAINST JIM CROW IN MILITARY SERVICE AND TRAINING, AND PRESIDENT OF THE BROTHERHOOD OF SLEEPING CAR PORTERS, A.F. of L., NEW YORK CITY

... *Mr. Randolph*: Mr. Grant Reynolds, national chairman of the Committee Against Jim Crow in Military Service and Training, has prepared for you in his testimony today a summary of wartime injustices to Negro soldiers, injustices by the military authorities, and injustices by bigoted segments of the police and civilian population.

The fund of material on this issue is endless, and yet, three years after the end of the war, as another crisis approaches, large numbers of white Americans are blissfully unaware of the extent of physical and psychological aggression against and [the] oppression of the Negro soldier.

Without taking time for a thorough probe in these relevant data, a probe which could enlighten the Nation, Congress may now heed Mr. Truman's call for universal military training and selective service, and in the weeks ahead enact a Jim Crow conscription law and appropriate billions for the greatest segregation system of all time.

In a campaign year, when both major parties are playing cynical politics with the issue of civil rights, Negroes are about to lose the fight against Jim Crowism on a national level. Our hard-won local gains in education, fair employment, hospitalization, housing are in danger of being nullified, being swept aside, Mr. Chairman, after decades of work, by a federally enforced pattern of segregation.

I am not beguiled by the Army's use of the word "temporary." Whatever may pass in the way of conscription legislation will become permanent, since the world trend is toward militarism. The Army knows this well. In such an eventuality, how could any permanent Fair Employment Practices Commission dare to criticize job discrimination in private industry if the Federal Government itself were simultaneously discriminating against Negro youth in military installations all over the world?

There can be no doubt of my facts. Quite bluntly, Chairman Walter G. Andrews of the House Armed Services Committee told a delegation from this organization that the War Department plans segregated white and Negro battalions if Congress passes a draft law.

The *Newark Evening News* of March 26, 1948, confirmed this is a Washington dispatch based on official memoranda sent from Secretary Forrestal's office to the House Armed Services Committee. Nine days ago when we called this to the attention of the Commander-in-Chief in a White House conference, he indicated that he was aware of these plans for Jim Crow battalions. This despite his civil rights message to Congress.

We have released all of this damaging information to the daily press, to leaders of both parties in Congress, and to supposedly liberal organizations. But with a relative handful of exceptions, we have found our white "friends" silent, indifferent, even hostile.

Justice Roberts, who provided you last week with vigorous testimony on behalf of the President's draft recommendations, is a trustee of Lincoln University in Pennsylvania, a prominent Negro institution. Yet for nearly four months, Mr. Roberts has not shown us the courtesy to reply to letters asking his support for antisegregation and civil rights safeguard in any draft law.

Three days after the *Newark Sunday News* embarrassed Congressman Harry L. Towe in his home district by exposing his similar failure to acknowledge our correspondence, Mr. Towe, author of the universal military training bill in the House, suddenly found time to answer letters [that] had been on his desk since December.

This situation, this conspiracy of silence, shall I say? has naturally commanded wide publicity in the Negro press. I submit for the record a composite of newspaper clippings. In my travels around the country I have sounded out Negro public opinion and confirmed for myself the popular resentment as reflected by the Negro press.

I can assure members of the Senate that Negroes do put civil rights above the high cost of living and above every other major issue of the day as recently reported by the *Fortune* opinion poll, I believe. Even more significant is the bitter, angry mood of the Negro in his present determination to win those civil rights in a country that subjects him daily to so many insults and indignities.

With this background, gentlemen, I reported last week to President Truman that Negroes are in no mood to shoulder a gun for democracy abroad so long as they are denied democracy here at home.

In particular, they resent the idea of fighting or being drafted into another Jim Crow Army. I passed this information on to Mr. Truman not as a threat, but rather as a frank, factual survey of Negro opinion.

Today I should like to make clear to the Senate Armed Services Committee and, through you, to Congress and the American people that passage now of a Jim Crow draft may only result in a mass civil disobedience movement along the lines of the magnificent struggles of the people of India against British imperialism.

I must emphasize that the current agitation for civil rights is no longer a mere expression of hope on the part of Negroes. On the one hand, it is a positive, resolute outreading for full manhood. On the other hand, it is an equally determined will to stop acquiescing in anything less. Negroes demand full, unqualified, first-class citizenship.

In resorting to the principles and direct action techniques of Gandhi, whose death was publicly mourned by many members of Congress and President Truman, Negroes will be a serving a higher law than any passed by a National Legislature in an era in which racism spells our doom.

They will be serving a law higher than any decree of the Supreme Court, which in the famous Winfred Lynn case evaded ruling on the flagrantly illegal segregation practiced under the wartime Selective Service Act. In refusing to accept compulsory military segregation, Negro youth will be serving their fellow men throughout the world.

I feel qualified to make this claim because of a recent survey of American psychologists, sociologists, and anthropologists. The survey revealed an overwhelming belief among these experts that enforced segregation on racial or religious lines has serious and detrimental psychological effects both on the segregated groups and on those enforcing segregation.

Experts from the South, I should like to point out, gentlemen, were as positive as those from other sections of the country as to the harmful effects of segregation. The views of these social scientists were based on scientific research and their own professional experience.

So long as the armed services propose to enforce such universally harmful segregation not only here at home but also overseas. Negro youth have a moral obligation not to lend themselves as world-wide carriers of an evil and hellish doctrine.

Secretary of the Army, Kenneth C. Royal, clearly indicated in the

New Jersey National Guard situation that the armed services do have every intention of prolonging their anthropologically hoary and untenable policies.

For 25 years now the myth has been carefully cultivated that Soviet Russia has ended all discrimination and intolerance, while here at home the American communists have skillfully posed as champions of minority groups.

To the rank and file Negro in World War II, Hitler's racism posed a sufficient threat for him to submit to the Jim Crow Army abuses. But this factor of minority group persecution in Russia is not present as a popular issue, in the power struggle between Stalin and the United States. I can only repeat that this time Negroes will not take a Jim Crow draft lying down. The conscience of the world will be shaken as by nothing else when thousands and thousands of us second-class Americans choose imprisonment in preference to permanent military slavery.

While I cannot with absolute certainty claim results at this hour, I personally will advise Negroes to refuse to fight as slaves for a democracy they cannot possess and cannot enjoy.

Let me add that I am speaking only for myself, not even for the Committee Against Jim Crow in Military Service and Training, since I am not sure that all its members would follow my position. But Negro leaders in close touch with GI grievances would feel derelict in their duty if they did not support such a justified civil disobedience movement, especially those of us whose age would protect us from being drafted. Any other course would be a betrayal of those who place their trust in us. I personally pledge myself to openly counsel, aid, and abet youth, both white and Negro, to quarantine any Jim Crow conscription system, whether it bear the label of universal military training or selective service.

I shall tell youth of all races not to be tricked by any euphonious election-year registration for a draft. This evasion, which the newspapers increasingly discuss as a convenient way out for Congress, would merely presage a synthetic "crisis" immediately after November 2d when all talk of equality and civil rights would be branded unpatriotic while the induction machinery would move into high gear. On previous occasions I have seen the "national emergency" psychology mow down legitimate Negro demands.

From coast to coast in my travels I shall call upon all Negro veterans to join this civil disobedience movement and to recruit their younger brothers in an organized refusal to register and be drafted.

Many veterans, bitter over Army Jim Crow, have indicated that they will act spontaneously in this fashion, regardless of any organized movement. "Never again," they say with finality.

I shall appeal to the thousands of white youth in schools and colleges who are today vigorously shedding the prejudices of their parents and professors. I shall urge them to demonstrate their solidarity with Negro youth by ignoring the entire registration and induction machinery.

And finally, I shall appeal to Negro parents to lend their moral support to their sons, to stand behind them as they march with heads high to Federal prisons as a telling demonstration to the world that Negroes have reached the limit of human endurance, that, in the words of the spiritual, we will be buried in our graves before we will be slaves.

May I, in conclusion, Mr. Chairman, point out that political maneuvers have made this drastic program our last resort. Your party, the party of Lincoln, solemnly pledged in its 1944 platform a full-fledged congressional investigation of injustices to Negro soldiers. Instead of that long overdue probe, the Senate Armed Services Committee on this very day is finally bearing testimony from two or three Negro veterans for a period of 20 minutes each. The House Armed Services Committee and Chairman Andrews went one step further and arrogantly refused to hear any at all.

Since we cannot obtain an adequate Congressional forum for our grievances, we have no other recourse but to tell our story to the peoples of the world by organized direct action. I do not believe that even a wartime censorship wall could be high enough to conceal news of a civil disobedience program.

If we cannot win your support for your own party commitments, if we cannot ring a bell in you by appealing to human decency, we shall command your respect and the respect of the world by our united refusal to cooperate with tyrannical injustice.

Since the military, with their southern biases, intend to take over America and institute total encampment of the populace along Jim Crow lines, Negroes will resist with the power of nonviolence, with the weapons of moral principles, with the good-will weapons of the spirit; yes, with the weapons that brought freedom to India.

I feel morally obligated to disturb and keep disturbed the conscience of Jim Crow America. In resisting the insult of Jim Crowism to the soul of black America, we are helping to save the soul of America. And let me add that I am opposed to Russian totalitarian communism and all its works. I consider it a menace to freedom. I stand by democracy as expressing the Judean-Christian ethic. But democracy and Christianity must be boldly and courageously applied for all men regardless of race, color, creed, or country.

We shall wage a relentless warfare against Jim Crow without hate or revenge for the moral and spiritual progress and safety of our country, world peace, and freedom.

Finally let me say that Negroes are just sick and tired of being pushed around and we just do not propose to take it, and we do not care what happens.

Thank you very much.

Senator Morse: Mr. Randolph, I want to question you a bit on your proposal for civil disobedience. Up until now refusal to serve in the military forces of this country in time of national emergency has been limited as far as one's psychological attitudes are concerned, to conscientious objections to war, the participating in war.

It is based upon the legal theory of freedom of religion in this country that if one's religious scruples are such that in good conscience he cannot bring himself to participate in war, which involves the taking of human life, our Government has protected him in that religious belief and we have our so-called exemption on the grounds of conscientious objection.

Now, this proposal of yours—I am not one to minimize your testimony—your proposal is not based upon conscientious objection in the sense that the American law has recognized to date, am I not right about that?

Mr. Randolph: That is correct.

Senator Morse: But your proposal, and put me straight on this, your proposal is really based upon the conviction that because your Government has not given to you certain social, economic, and racial protection from discrimination because of race, color, or creed, you feel that even in a time of national emergency, when your Government and the country itself may be at stake, you are justified in saying to any segment of our populace, whether it is the colored group or, as you say in your statement, the white group too, with like sympathies, that under those circumstances you would be justified then in saying, "Do not shoulder arms in protection of your country in this national emergency?"

Mr. Randolph: That is a correct statement, Mr. Senator.

I may add that it is my deep conviction that in taking such a position we are doing our country a great service. Our country has come out before the world as the moral leader of democracy and it is preparing its defense forces and aggressive forces upon the theory that it must do this to protect democracy in the world.

Well now, I consider that if this country does not develop the democratic process at home and make the democratic process work by giving the very people who they propose to draft in the Army to fight for them democracy, democracy then is not the type of democracy that ought to be fought for and, as a matter of fact, the policy of segregation in the armed forces and in other avenues of our life is the greatest single propaganda and political weapon in the hands of Russia and international communism today.

Senator Morse: I understand your position, Mr. Randolph, but for the record I want to direct your attention to certain basic legal principles here, that I want to say most kindly, are being overlooked in your position. I want to discuss your position from the standpoint of a couple of hypothetics and relate them to certain legal principles to which I think you ought to give very careful consideration before you follow the course of action [that] you have indicated.

Let us assume this hypothetical. A country proceeds to attack the United States or commits acts [that] make it perfectly clear that our choice is only the choice of war. Would you take the position then that unless our Government granted the demands [that] are set out in your testimony, or most of the demands set out in your testimony, that you would recommend a course of civil disobedience to our Government?

Mr. Randolph: In answer to that question, the Government now has time to change its policy on segregation and discrimination and if the Government does not change its policy on segregation and discrimination in the interests of the very democracy it is fighting for, I would advocate that Negroes take no part in the army.

Senator Morse: My hypothetical assumes that up to the time of the emergency set forth in my hypothetical, our Government does not follow in any degree whatsoever the course of action that you recommend.

Mr. Randolph: Yes.

Senator Moses: So the facts of the hypothetical then are thrust upon us and I understand your answer to be that under those circumstances even though it was perfectly clear that we would have to fight then to exist as a country, you would still recommend the program of civil disobedience?

Mr. Randolph: Because I would believe that that is in the interest of the soul of our country and I unhesitatingly and very adamantly hold that that is the only way by which we are going to be able to make

America wake up and realize that we do not have democracy here so long as one black man is denied all the rights enjoyed by all the white men in this country.

Senator Morse: Now, facing realistically the hypothetical situation and the assumption that it has come to pass, do you have any doubt then that this Government as presently constituted under the Constitution that governs us would necessarily follow a legal course of action of applying the legal doctrine of treason to that conduct? Would you question with me that that is the doctrine [that] undoubtedly will be applied at that time under the circumstances of my hypothetic?

Mr. Randolph: I would anticipate nationwide terrorism against Negroes who refuse to participate in the armed forces, but I believe that that is the price we have to pay for [the] democracy that we want. In other words, if there are sacrifices and sufferings, terrorism, concentration camps, whatever they may be, if that is the only way by which Negroes can get their democratic rights, I unhesitatingly say that we have to face it.

Senator Morse: But on the basis of the law as it now exists, going back to my premise that you and I think and know of no legal exemption from participation in military service in the defense of our country other than that of conscientious objection on religious grounds, not on the grounds in which you place your civil disobedience, that then the doctrine of treason would be applied to those people participating in that disobedience?

Mr. Randolph: Exactly. I would be willing to face that doctrine on the theory and on the grounds that we are serving a higher law than the law [that] applies the act of treason to us when we are attempting to win democracy in this country and to make the soul of America democratic.

I would contend that we are serving a higher law than that law with its legal technicalities, which would include the group [that] fights for democracy even in the face of a crisis you would portray, I would contend that they are serving a higher law than that law.

Senator Morse: But you would fully expect that because the law of treason in this country relates to certain specific overt acts on the part of the individual that what he considers to be this spiritual or moral motivation in order to seek a social objective over and above the law of America entitles him to as it then at that time exists on the books, that there would not be any other course of action for our Government to follow but indictments of treason?

Mr. Randolph: May I add something there, Mr. Senator?

Senator Morse: First, do you agree with me that that would be certain to follow?

Mr. Randolph: Let me add here in connection with that that we would participate in no overt acts against our Government, no overt acts of any kind. In other words, ours would be one of nonresistance. Ours would be one of noncooperation, ours would be one of nonparticipation in the military forces of the country.

I want you to know that we would be willing to absorb the violence, to absorb the terrorism, to face the music and to take whatever comes and we as a matter of fact, consider that we are more loyal to our country than the people who perpetuate segregation and discrimination upon Negroes because of color or race.

I want it thoroughly understood that we would certainly not be guilty of any kind of overt act against the country but we would not participate in any military operation as segregated and Jim Crow slaves in the Army.

Senator Morse: I think you will agree with me that this is not the time and place for you and me to argue the legal meaning of aiding and abetting the enemy. However, if you refresh your memory of treason cases, as I have here been doing, sitting here this morning, I would only point out to you most kindly that the legal concepts of aiding and abetting, are flexible concepts that can be applied to the behavior of an individual or group of individuals [who] in effect serve the enemy in time of war to the endangerment of the rest of the people of our country.

Furthermore, and I know you are aware of the fact, any such program as you outline would not be a passive program but would be one that would be bound to result in all sorts of overt actions you could not possibly control, but for which you who sponsored it would, as a matter of law, be fixed with the proximate cause of the conduct and, therefore, would be legally responsible for it.

Mr. Randolph: I recognize that fact just as for instance a union may call a strike. The union does not promote the violence but the forces that are opposed to the union may create the violence.

Well, now, in this instance we are definitely opposed to violence of any kind; we are definitely opposed to any overt acts that would be construed in the form of violence but, nevertheless, we would relentlessly wage a warfare against the Jim Crow armed forces program and against the Negroes and others participating in that program, that is our position.

Now, I do not believe the law up to the present time has been faced with such conditions as to enable to envisage these principles. In other words, American jurisprudence has never been faced with this kind of condition and consequently its definition of treason could not possibly take in the type and nature of action [that] we propose in civil disobedience. But, however the law may be construed we would be willing to face it on the grounds that our actions would be in obedience and in conformity with the higher law of righteousness than that set forth in the so-called law of treason.

Senator Morse: I appreciate that the procedure would require the United States Supreme Court to render a final decision as to the application of the legal principles I have discussed here this morning. I would say most kindly and most sincerely that I have no doubt in my mind that under the circumstances of my hypothetical case there is only one decision that could be handed down and that is that the law of treason would be applicable.

Now, Mr. Chairman, I am through with this line of questioning. I felt it necessary to raise these questions. I know Mr. Randolph and I know the fight he has put up for social justice in support of the principles that he believes to be right. I think he knows me, at least I think he knows that I sincerely believe in fighting for putting into effect in America the civil-rights guaranties of the Constitution which for too long have not been put into effect in their full meaning, but that both parties have been too frequently political professionals rather than those who would put it in the form of political action.

I do want to say with all the sincerity that I possess that I do not think the proposal that you offer is the way to establish full civil rights in America.

Senator Baldwin: I know it is a custom of politicians to testify to their sincerity and their deep belief in the cause of equality of civil rights under the Constitution and I do not make any profession of that kind at all although I do believe that is what we have to achieve and I think my record as Governor of the State of Connecticut will bear out that when I was in the position to advance that cause, I gave it all the assistance that it was in my power to give.

I would like to join with what Senator Morse said in questioning the wisdom of the course [that] you say that you are going to follow. It does seem to me that there is a marked difference in the position [that] you take and the position that Gandhi took. You are seeking to assert your point of view with reference to what should be done about civil rights and I am not questioning now whether your point of view about that is correct or incorrect, but it does seem to me that you are using a method to do it that might very well involve you in complications such as has been suggested by Senator Morse; that you might find yourself up against the possibility of a charge of treason because one of the duties of citizenship is to bear arms against an enemy when called upon to do so.

The refusal to do so, whether it is passive, inactive, or just non-compliance, is nevertheless a refusal and that might involve serious consequences.

However, whether you choose to follow that course or not is a matter for your own decision but I wanted to go on further and say in connection with it that in my humble judgment that sort of activity and that sort of point of view in the long run is apt to do more harm, to harm your cause, and our cause if you want to call it that, of trying to achieve equality of rights under the Constitution, than is to advance it and that is the reason why I would suggest to you and question your wisdom in taking such a position.

Mr. Randolph: Well, I fully appreciate your point of view and I have some knowledge of your record as a Governor and so forth but the Negroes have been the victims of such intense discrimination and segregation in two wars that they have reached their limit of their endurance when it comes to going into another Jim Crow army to fight another war for democracy, a democracy that they have never gotten, and there is no indication they will get unless they take some actions themselves which is different from the ordinary procedure with the view to awakening the conscience of America to the realization that a fight for democracy is a fight with its fingers crossed.

We believe that this form of procedure is for the benefit of this country and in the interest of America because it is taking the position of an ostrich to assume that there is no raging storm of resentment in the soul of Negroes today against Jim Crowism.

In all the talks I have had, talking with many Negroes, I have not found one Negro who believes that Negroes ought to fight for democracy in another Jim Crow army, not one, from the top of the bottom.

I am giving you the facts and the truth about the state of mind of the Negro throughout the country.

Something has to be done to stop America going on its hypocritical course of professing one thing and practicing another. If the Negroes, who are the most downtrodden in the country, have got to do it then that is the history as put upon them, that responsibility and obligation and the Negroes must not shirk the responsibility. I believe they have to face it because by doing it they will do American democracy the greatest service that it has ever had from the foundation of our country.

I am greatly concerned about our democracy because I do not believe that America with its present policy on segregation and Jim Crowism will be able to stop the march of the hordes of communism throughout the world. I am sure it cannot. America cannot rely upon material power alone, it cannot rely upon the atomic bomb alone, great armies and great navies and great air forces. America has to rely upon the force of the spirit. America has to do something that will convince the world that it is sound at heart; that it believes in democracy.

Why, in the various world councils when America talks, it is laughed at because the people of the world, especially the darker races, feel that it is pure hypocrisy; that this democracy [that] we have here is shoddy and that it is a farce. Consequently, we colored people within America are not making any great sacrifice when we point out to America that it is willfully wrong and that we are willing to suffer to help America get right.

I think that is our obligation and I fully appreciate the legal aspect that was set forth by Senator Morse and I certainly am aware of his sincerity in fighting for the cause of civil rights.

I listened to his statement over the radio the other night which was masterly, able, brilliant, and sincere but Senator Morse has never felt the sting of Jim Crow and I believe he stands in a class himself. No white man here has felt the sting of discrimination and segregation, Jim Crowism.

As a matter of fact, I believe any one of you men would raise hell in America if you felt the indignities and injustices that are suffered in America. Right here in Washington, the Capital of the Nation, a Negro cannot go to a restaurant and get a sandwich, cannot go to a theater. Do you mean to say that a democracy is worth fighting for by black men which will treat them that way?

We have to face this thing sooner or later, and we might just as well face it now.

PAUL ROBESON

(1898–1976)

While J. Edgar Hoover clerked at the Library of Congress and took night law classes, Paul Robeson was a campus god at Rutgers University. Six-foot three-inches tall and 240 pounds in his prime, he lettered in baseball, basketball, and track, and won all-American honors in football. In the classroom, he earned a Phi Beta Kappa key and membership in Skull and Cap. In the decades to come, he would turn campus celebrity into international celebrity as an artist of stage and screen—being best remembered as a singer for "Ol' Man River" in the musical *Show Boat* and as an actor in the role of *Othello*. He brought his powerful bass-baritone to the political stage as well, emerging as one of the nation's most important and outspoken dissidents. His left-leaning politics led him to support but never join the American Communist party, and his opposition to the cold war led in 1952 to a Stalin Peace Prize. To many in that time, he was a subversive whose life journey took a downward angle from all-American to un-American. To others, he was a twentieth-century renaissance man with the courage to speak out against the emerging global rivalry between the United States and the Union of Soviet Socialist Republics. Hoover's FBI in particular and the American government in general took the former view.

Born in Princeton, New Jersey, on April 9, 1898, Robeson was the son of an escaped slave. A brilliant student by any definition, he left Rutgers with his degree in 1919 and headed for Harlem and Columbia University Law School. Upon graduating in 1921, however, he embarked on a career in the theater, making his first Broadway appearance a year later and also receiving an invitation to appear in London. In New York, he joined the Provincetown Players, a Greenwich Village group, and subsequently starred in *All God's Chillun Got Wings, The Emperor Jones,* and *Porgy & Bess.*

340

He gave his first concert in 1925, singing a collection of spirituals, and for the next fourteen years spent most of his time abroad. His first appearance as Othello came in 1930 on a London stage. Most trips back to America involved commitments to appear in films. (In all, he made eleven movies, including *Show Boat*.) The 1930s saw several visits to the Soviet Union and a conversion to socialism. He even sang for the Republican troops and the International Brigades battling Franco and fascism in the Spanish Civil War.

Controversy arose during the cold war, particularly when he questioned President Harry S. Truman's civil rights commitment and supported Henry Wallace's Progressive party challenge to Truman in the 1948 elections. Most controversial of all were his remarks in 1949 at the World Peace Congress in Paris, where he compared the pervasiveness of American racism with what he considered to be the absence of any racial prejudice in Stalin's Russia. He was a relentless critic of the cold war and attendant militarization of American society.

FBI Director Hoover responded by pressuring the House Committee on Un-American Activities (HUAC) and other Red-hunting committees to subpoena Robeson. More often than not, they obliged and over the years paid Robeson the highest tribute by institutionalizing his name into their proceedings. During the height of the so-called McCarthy-era blacklists, for example, HUAC got in the habit of asking "unfriendly" witnesses whether they owned any Paul Robeson phonograph records. In and of itself, an affirmative answer became an official sign of communist sympathies. HUAC often accommodated black men and women, moreover, with a double-standard Red-hunt. Rarely requiring black witnesses to name names (that is, inform on friends and associates), HUAC usually settled for a denunciation of Robeson. African Americans, as *Nation* editor Victor Navasky later pointed out, were called upon not to degrade themselves but their star.

For its part, the FBI tapped Robeson's telephone, opened his mail, and even tried to find out if he was having an affair with Lord Louis Mountbatten's wife. Hoover was particularly interested in a rumor that Lady Mountbatten had "a huge naked statute of Paul Robeson in her home"—a prurient, voyeuristic interest that always seemed to surface when the director set his sights on a black man. It made no difference whether it was Robeson and "a huge naked statue" or the earlier White Slave Traffic Act pursuit of Marcus Garvey or the later effort to prove that Martin Luther King, Jr., was nothing more than "a tom cat."

Following the Peekskill, New York, riot of 1949, in which veterans' groups and assorted right-wing thugs attacked the crowds arriving for an outdoor concert, Robeson found himself on the fringes of the blacklist. Hounded by congressional committees, the IRS, and the State Department, his income dropped from some $100,000 in 1947 to $6,000 in 1952. He became, in effect, an unperson. Even his name disappeared from the all-America rolls. Never one to take things without a fight, he sued the State Department to get his passport back (having lost it for refusing to sign the then-required non-communist oath). When the department returned it with the case still pending, he left the country for tours of Britain and Australia. He would not perform again in New York until 1958, the same year that the Supreme Court held in a related case that the government had no right to withhold a passport based on a citizen's beliefs and associations.

Chronically ill for the last fifteen years of his life, Robeson died a virtual recluse on January 23, 1976, at the Chester Spring, Pennsylvania, home of his sister. His work lives on in albums and films; in his book, *Here I Stand* (1960); and in such compilations as Dorothy Butler Gilliam's *Paul Robeson Speaks: Writings, Speeches, Interviews, 1918–1974* (1978). Martin Duberman has also written a fine biography, *Paul Robeson* (1988).

FEDERAL BUREAU OF INVESTIGATION

This case originated at: New York City
Report made at: New York City
Date when made: 12/8/42
Period for which made: 11/17,18,19/42
Report made by: [Bureau Deletion]
Title: PAUL ROBESON
Character of case: Internal Security–C

SYNOPSIS OF FACTS:
Robeson born April 9, 1898, Princeton, New Jersey. Attended Rutgers College on scholarships, receiving B.A. degree in 1919. Attended Columbia, afterwards receiving LL.B. Member of American Peace Mobilization, Citizens Committee to Free Harry Bridges, and International Labor Defense Committee, 1942, and other similar organizations. Signed petition for Browder's release in 1942. Traveled abroad extensively. Sent his son to school in the USSR, because he thought boy could grow up normally there. Information from confidential informants pertaining to subject set out.

DETAILS:

The investigation in this case is predicated upon the fact that it appears that Paul Robeson is a member of a number of communist front organizations.

[Bureau Deletion] advises that at a dinner [that] he attended on [Bureau Deletion] at [Bureau Deletion] During the conversation [that] followed, informant advises that the following remarks were made:

Hudson mentioned the WPA folk song collection, which was shelved by the reactionaries when war broke out. Hudson said he had heard some of the records [that] were made and observed that Robeson should somehow get access to this material. To this Robeson is said to have replied that he has contacts in the Library of Congress and will try to get this material and adopt it to the cause.

At this point Robeson told how he sang a simple version of "John Henry" at the Ford meeting. He stated that all the listeners were very much impressed. It is to be noted that Hudson remarked that "John Henry" will become the battle song of the party and observed that it will replace the religious angle of the Negro spiritual within the correct appeal for the masses. . . .

It was related by [Bureau Deletion] that . . . Robeson told how his father, a minister, died when he, Paul, was six years old; that they were living in New Jersey at the time, and Robeson practically became an orphan from the death of his father. He stated that his father was born in North Carolina in 1843 and escaped from slavery at the age of fifteen via the underground system; that he went to Philadelphia, where he married a free Negress. Robeson said that his mother's family looked down on his father's people as they were a poor Carolina type that scratched out an existence after the Civil War. Robeson stated, however, that after his father's death the Carolina branch were the people who practically kept him from starving by sending a meager assortment of foodstuffs to him. He explained that this and the Spanish trouble, coupled with the refugee struggle of Austria, influenced his present stand and caused him to see his duty to the struggling poor of his race as well as other races. [Bureau Deletion] advised that Robeson remarked something to the effect that "Most people don't realize this, as they think of me as an All-American football player and a great and rich singer." Robeson also said that it might be a good idea to put this struggle of his life before the Negro people.

[Bureau Deletion] advised that on the evening of March 23, 1942, at a dinner party given by the Spanish Aid Committee at The Biltmore Hotel, New York City, in honor of Paul Robeson, Negro singer, Robeson had made the greatest and longest speech of his career. [Bureau

Deletion] states Robeson had been introduced as the greatest anti-fascist of today and that Robeson in turn had stated the keynote of the dinner by stating the "The greatest anti-fascist, Earl Browder [American Communist Leader; Presidential Candidate 1936, 1940], is in jail." It is to be noted that [Bureau Deletion] advised that the success of this dinner was indicated by the money contributed at the meeting by those attending, which was in the amount of $10,000.

[Bureau Deletion] advises [Bureau Deletion] arrangements had been made for a meeting on April 2, 1942, at 3:30 P.M., at the apartment of Helen Bryant, 317 Fourth Street, New York City. The meeting was attended by Alexander Trachtenberg and the following Negroes: Max Yergan, James Ford, Roy Hudson, Paul Robeson, and Edward I. Aronon, who are members of the Citizens Committee to Free Earl Browder. The purpose of this meeting, according to [Bureau Deletion] was to draft a letter in connection with the Free Earl Browder Campaign. Robeson's personal stationery was used in sending this letter to approximately three hundred individuals, the majority of whom were located in Washington, D.C. [Bureau Deletion]

From [Bureau Deletion] it was ... learned that "The Negro and Justice—A Plea for Earl Browder" is a pamphlet written by Dr. Max Yergan and Paul Robeson, published by the Citizens Committee to Free Earl Browder, 1133 Broadway, New York, in November, 1941. This pamphlet contains the speeches delivered by Robeson and Yergan at a mass meeting at Madison Square Garden on September 29, 1941, under the auspices of the Citizens Committee to Free Browder.

[Bureau Deletion] has submitted information in regard to the motion picture, *Native Land.* From this source it was learned that this motion picture is receiving copious reviews in the New York press. It advises that *Native Land* is obviously a communist project. It is produced by the Frontier Films, which is a communist instrumentality; it is directed by Paul Strand (communist) and Leo Hurwitz who has many communist connections. The commentary is written by David Wolff, is spoken by Paul Robeson, an avowed communist, and the music is by Marc Blitzstein, communist songwriter. It is noted that this picture, which was filmed over the last three years, purportedly includes scenes that portray violations of civil liberties in the United States. The informant advises that the picture deals with the struggle of the American pioneers with fascism, the struggle of labor unions against company spies, and the gallant fight against Hitler. . . .

An examination of the report of Special Agent [Bureau Deletion] dated November 14, 1942, at New York City, entitled "Congress of

American Soviet Friendship,'' at pages 22 and 23 reveals the following information pertinent to subject:

At the mass rally "Salute to our Russian Ally" held at Madison Square Garden on Sunday afternoon, November 8, 1942, with Paul Robeson representing the entertainment field, Paul Robeson was dramatically introduced to the crowd, when all the lights were extinguished and it was stated that the next person to be heard would be "the voice of the anti-fascist." At this time, spotlights were directed on the stage, bringing Robeson into view. He stated, "I am an anti-fascist. I am American. I am a Negro.'' Robeson proceeded to read a letter [that] had been written by a twenty-seven-year-old Red Army soldier who stated that he was continually marching westward for freedom. Robeson stated he did not know the fate of the soldier who wrote this letter, but the mere fact that he had written the letter made him "my friend and yours.'' PR then sang two songs, namely, "His Motherland'' and "From Border to Border,'' each of which was sung partly in English and partly in Russian. It is noted that the ovation given to Robeson at the time of his introduction and at the conclusion of his musical offering was perhaps the most voluminous of the afternoon.

The following is an extract from *Who's Who in America,* volume 20, for the year 1938–39:

Paul Robeson, born Princeton, New Jersey, April 9, 1898; B.A. Rutgers College, 1919; LL. B. Columbia, 1923; married Eslanda Cardoza Goode, August 17, 1921. Concert tour, Europe, 1926–28; concert tour of Europe, 1931–38; Russia, 1936. Star of feature part in motion picture *Emperor Jones, Show Boat, King Solomon's Mines,* and others. Member of Phi Beta Kappa, Alpha Psi Alpha, and Sigma Tau Delta. Picked by Walter Kamp as all-American in 1918. Home: 19 Buckingham Street, London, England; Address: Metropolitan Bureau, 113 West 57th Street, New York City.

The following is an extract from *Current Biography,* dated 1941, found on pages 716 and 717:

When Robeson left Columbia he was taken into the office of Louis W Stotesbury, a Rutgers man and a prominent New York lawyer. He has made films for British as well as American producers, having for a long time made his home in England because he found less race prejudice there than in the United States.

The racial problem is one that Robeson has studied thoroughly. It is racial discrimination as much as his own acting ability that caused him to give up his career as a lawyer. He sent his son (in 1921 he married Eslanda Cardozo Goode) to school in the USSR because he thought the boy could grow up normally there, and in January, 1941, Robeson with four other Negroes and five whites, [sued] a San Francisco restaurant, because, they asserted, they had been refused admission. Robeson also frequently speaks out on political issues in which he feels his race is deeply involved. In the summer of 1940 he was opposing conscription, speaking for peace—later, urging all Negroes in the industry to join the United Automobile Workers of America in their Ford organizing drive. Even later, speaking and singing at benefits for aid to Britain, China, and the Soviet Union, he has been called irradical [sic].

FEDERAL BUREAU OF INVESTIGATION

This case originated at: New Haven, Conn.
Report made at: New Haven, Conn.
Date when made: 12/18/43
Period for which made: 10/26, 27/43; 11/19, 23, 27/43
Report made by: [Bureau Deletion]
Title: Eslanda Goode Robeson, also known as Mrs. Paul Leroy Robeson and Essie Robeson
Character of case: Security Matter–C

SYNOPSIS OF FACTS:
  Subject was born on 12/15/1896 at Washington, D.C. The subject, a colored woman, received a B.S. Degree from Teachers College at Columbia University in 1920 and later worked in the surgical pathological laboratory at Presbyterian Hospital in New York City. She married the renown [sic] Negro actor and singer Paul Robeson. She has traveled throughout the world with her husband and son, and while living in England she attended the University College in London, 1933–1935 where she studied anthropology. She also resided in Russia with her husband and son for some time during the 1930s. Since 1941, the subject has resided at Enfield, Conn. She is presently studying part time at the Kennedy School of Missions at the Hartfors [sic] Seminary Foundation. Subject has visited Africa and India and is a personal friend of Nehru, Indian National Congress Leader. Recently she entertained the Pandit sisters, nieces of Nehru, at her Enfield, Connecticut home. Informants advise the Subject corresponds with Nehru and other prominent persons and that she receives communications from the U.S.S.R. Embassy at Washington, D.C. Subject is vitally interested in the matter of racial discrimination and is opposed to race segregation. She subscribes to and receives the *Daily Worker* and the *Worker*.

She recently attended a reception at the U.S.S.R. Embassy, Washington, D.C. with her husband and son. Description set forth.

SAC, New York City
J. Edgar Hoover-Director, Federal Bureau of Investigation

PAUL ROBESON;
INTERNAL SECURITY-C

Under date of November 28, 1942, Confidential Informant [Bureau Deletion] of the Indianapolis Field Office furnished that Office with a report covering conversation he had with [Bureau Deletion] at that time. [Bureau Deletion] told the informant that he is himself an active Communist party member [Bureau Deletion] and that Paul Robeson was a Communist party member and that he had joined the party after a professional tour in England. On this tour Robeson met a man by the name of Henry Pollet (phonetic), who was believed to have converted Robeson to the party. [Bureau Deletion] further claimed that upon Robeson's return to the United States he donated his entire earnings from this trip in the amount of $300,000.00 to the Communist party. . . .

This informant referred to above is a paid informant who is considered reliable by the Indianapolis Field Office.

FEDERAL BUREAU OF INVESTIGATION

This case originated at: New York, New York
Report made at: New York, New York
Date when made: 7/25/45
Period for which made: 3/23,24,24; 4/23; 5/1,2,23/45
Report made by: [Bureau Deletion]
Title: *CHANGED:* PAUL ROBESON, was John Thomas
Character of case: Internal Security-C

SYNOPSIS OF FACTS:
Subject continues to be active in Council on African Affairs and is working for communist front organizations. Subject is reported to be a member of the CPA under name of John Thomas by informant of this office.

REFERENCE:
Report of Special Agent [Bureau Deletion] New York, 12/8/42.

DETAILS:
Subject is carried as a Key Figure in the New York Field office.

The title of this case is being changed in order to reflect the additional alias of the subject, John Thomas, inasmuch as Confidential Informant [Bureau Deletion] whose identity is known to the Bureau, advised Special Agent [Bureau Deletion] on April 27, 1944, that subject's CPA name was John Thomas.

A Confidential Informant [Bureau Deletion] whose identity is known to the Bureau, reported that Paul Robeson, on February 28, 1941, spoke at a memorial dinner for the Veterans of the Abraham Lincoln Brigade at Manhattan Center, New York City. Informant advised that the subject said the present war was an imperialistic conflict and was harmful to the people from every point of view. The subject is reported as having said that only in a world where the people's government existed, such as in one-sixth of the world, could there be real peace and democracy. Informant further pointed out that the subject was made an honorary member of the Abraham Lincoln Brigade and stated when given the pin of membership "It is the proudest moment of my life and I'll always wear the pin."

Confidential Informant [Bureau Deletion] whose identity is known to the Bureau, reported on April 17, 1944 that [at] the birthday party of Paul Robeson on April 16, 1944 at the 34th Street Armory, the subject spoke and said that he had "Traveled all over the world and has learned that not only Negroes were suffering, but that refugees whom he had met, had provided to his satisfaction that all races were suffering in one part of the world or another." Further the subject is reported to have said that freedom could not be obtained in this country while people were oppressed in other countries. The subject further said that the liberated people of the Soviet Union were enjoying the rights and privileges of freedom. In this connection, Confidential Informant [Bureau Deletion] advised that Robeson asserted that a comparatively limited few persons controlled the destinies of the people and that the 150 million people in Africa could not be held down. . . .

In the *Sunday Worker* of April 16, 1944, in the article written by Samuel Putnam, there appears a story concerning the subject's life and progress and it quoted Robeson as saying about his first visit to the USSR, "How can I describe my feelings upon crossing the Soviet border. All I can say is that the moment I came there I realized that I had found what I had been seeking all my life. It was a new planet—a new constellation. It filled me with such happiness as I have never before known in my life."

FEDERAL BUREAU OF INVESTIGATION

This case originated at: New York, New York
Report made at: New York, New York
Date when made: 4/5/46
Period for which made: 3/20,21,22,25,26/46
Report made by: [Bureau Deletion]
Title: Paul Robeson, with alias John Thomas
Character of case: Internal Security-C

SYNOPSIS OF FACTS:
  Robeson continues to support communist front programs, lending his presence and influence to various meetings sponsored by known front groups. He continues as Chairman of the Council on African Affairs. Information set out reflecting Max Yergan, known active communist front leader among Negroes and Executive Director of the Council on African Affairs, is very close to subject and exerts considerable influence over his front activities, arranging for his appearances, etc. Information set out reflecting subject is sought after by known communists and utilizes his presence in various parts of the country while on concert tour to lend his prestige to front meetings in these localities. He has urged suppressing of *Uncle Tom's Cabin* at communist instigation, supported actors in argument over their appearance before meeting of Joint Anti-Fascist Refugee Committee, and politically supported Michael Quill, pro-communist, and Benjamin J. Davis, Jr., communist, in 1945 city elections. He strongly praised the Soviet Union before a meeting of the National Council of American-Soviet Friendship.

Memorandum

TO: Mr. Jack D. Neal   DATE: July, 30, 1946
             Chief
             Division of Foreign Activity Correlation
             State Department
             Washington, D.C.

FROM: John Edgar Hoover, Director-Federal Bureau of
             Investigation

SUBJECT: PAUL ROBESON

It has been learned from a reliable confidential source that Paul Robeson addressed a meeting of the Waterfront Section of the Communist party on June 26, 1946, at New York City. At this meeting Robeson reportedly accused Army officers and State Department officials of open collaboration with the Nazis and Fascists in Czechoslovakia, declaring that he knew this to be true because he accompanied these officers and officials in Czechoslovakia while making a tour of Europe just after the termination of World War II.

Following are some of the entries under the heading "Activities in Connection with Various Communist Front Organizations" in a Bureau memorandum dated May 9, 1947.

The *Daily Worker* of February 13, 1945, reports that Robeson spoke at a meeting of the Joint Anti-Fascist Refugee Committee at the Ambassador Hotel in Los Angeles, California, at which time $17,000 was raised. In his speech he is quoted as having said, "We are standing at the cross-roads of history. Something is wrong when such Fascists as Hearst are allowed to mislead and misinform the American people. The American people do not entirely understand that we can have fascism here unless we learn to use our productive resources for the benefit of all people. We can't wait for fascism to die out and the oppressed peoples of the world will not wait. We must understand that we have already entered a changed world. We must have those 60 million jobs that [Henry] Wallace [Vice President to Franklin Delano Roosevelt] speaks of. We must clean out our own fascists."

The Pittsburgh *Courier* of October 27, 1945, carried an article which pointed out that Robeson was the thirtieth recipient of the "Spingara

Medal'' annual award for outstanding achievement, presented by the NAACP. In his acceptance speech before several hundred notables in the Biltmore Hotel in New York, he voiced a frank and pronounced preference for Soviet principles, economic, political, and social. He said, ''The Soviet Union can't help it as a Nation and people if it is in the main stream of change.'' He warned against the rebuilding of fascism, restoration of monarchies, and restoration of their estates to collaborators. He pointed out that the Russians have shown what backward peoples can accomplish in one generation of endeavor. He said, ''Full employment in Russia is a fact and not a myth and discrimination is nonexistent.''

The *Seattle Star* of February 12, 1946, reported an interview with Robeson in which he said his son, Paul, Jr., attended school in Russia from the 8th through the 13th year. He said, ''My son is definitely the product of Soviet education.'' He continued and said, ''I am well satisfied. The Russian standards are extremely high.''

The *People's Voice* of October 19, 1946, ... reported that [Robeson] was a witness before the Tenney Joint Legislative (California) Commission on Un-American Activities in Los Angeles, California, on October 7, 1946. When asked if he thought Russia in 1917 was the ideal country in which to test marxism, he said, ''No, I think the best country to test the principles of Marxism might be the America of today. Russia in 1917 was too poor.'' He said he was not a communist but that ''. . . as a Negro'' he was ''inevitably attracted to the Anti-Fascist Movement . . .''

The *Daily Worker* of October 11, 1946, in reporting this same information quoted Robeson as having told Senator Tenney that the existence of his Committee was evidence of the fact that fascism still lives. He was asked if he was a communist. He replied that he characterized himself as an anti-fascist. He said that he was not a communist, but that he would choose it over the Republicans, explaining that ''in my association with communists throughout the world, I have found them to be the first people to die, the first to sacrifice, and the first to understand fascism.''

The *People's Voice* of February 1, 1947, on page 2, carried an article in which it was stated that Robeson had told reporters in St. Louis, Missouri, that he was leaving the theater and the concert stage for the next two years to ''talk up and down the nation against race hatred and prejudice.'' The article pointed out the Robeson marched at the head of a picket line with about thirty members of the St. Louis Civil Rights

Congress in front of the American Theater in St. Louis, Missouri, to protest its racial segregation practice.

The *Los Angeles Times* of March 17, 1947, pointed out that Robeson's concert at the Philharmonic Auditorium on the Saturday night before, followed the pattern of those set by him in recent years in that it was [part] recital and part political action. The article pointed out that from the remarks made by Robeson it was apparent that he had no intention of changing his routine. It added, "Those who pay to hear his eloquent singing will also have to endure his politicking."

Hedda Hopper in her column "Looking at Hollywood" in the *Los Angeles Times* of March 20, 1947, said "When Paul Robeson sang the communist 'People's Battle Song' here and dedicated it to Gerhardt Eisler, some members of his audience walked out. Why one remained is beyond me. To sit idly listening to a man abusing the precious heritage of freedom given us by our Constitution in flaunting the preachings of our most dangerous enemy is inviting disaster. When such people as Robeson are attacked they scream 'persecution' and 'fascism—the obvious dodge that our Red brethren attempt when cornered by people whom they've goaded out of lethargy. Yet they believe it perfectly right that they be allowed to attack the very foundations of our country—simply because one of our principles provides freedom of speech."

In the *Newsweek* magazine for May 12, 1947, on page 29, under an article entitled "Pecan From Pravda," the following information appears concerning Robeson:

"Paul Robeson: Affiliated with American Committee for Democracy and Intellectual Freedom, China Air Council, American League for Peace and Democracy, American Peace Mobilization, Artists' Front to Win the War, Citizens' Committee for Harry Bridges, Joint Anti-Fascist Refugee Committee, Medical Bureau and North American Committee to Aid Spanish Democracy, National Council of American—Soviet Friendship, National Federation for Constitutional Liberties, National Negro Congress, New Masses, New Theater League, New Dance League, New Theater, Southern Conference for Human Welfare, Soviet Russia Today, Veterans of the Abraham Lincoln Brigade, American Youth for Democracy, International Labor Defense, the Abraham Lincoln School, and the Washington Committee for Aid to China."

The following activities of the subject were reported for the period 1948–49.

On March 10, 1948, the Honolulu Office of the FBI advised that Paul Robeson arrived at Honolulu on that date and was greeted by a number of prominent local communists. While in Hawaii, he visited the islands of Kanai, [sic] Malokai, [sic] Lanai, and Maui, giving a total of fifteen public concerts on the islands. At a press conference prior to his departure for the United States on March 21, 1948, Robeson declined to state whether or not he was a communist, but remarked that as far as he knew "The Communist Party is a legal party." Robeson said he was a real socialist and a "strong Wallace man," but one who "goes beyond Wallace's thinking on progressive capitalism." He also indicated that if there were a strike or a shooting, he would be "on the union's side."

The *New York Post and Home News* on April 5, 1948, reported that Max Yergan, Executive Director of the Council on African Affairs, charged Paul Robeson, as Chairman of the said organization, with part of "a communist plot" to seize the Council was not a communist group as such. He had been attacked by the Robeson faction in the Council for being a Red baitor, the paper reported.

According to the *Herald Tribune* of April 7, 1948, Robeson, replied to the charge of Max Yergan mentioned above by stating "You can't fight the struggles of Africa by being non-partisan or being a Red baitor—someone has to point out that things are not beautiful here in America, in Africa, and other parts of the world. If that makes me a communist, then I'm proud to be one."

The *New York Post and Home News* on April 16, 1948, reported that Robeson, who had been campaigning for Henry Wallace [Progressive Party Presidential candidate] in Columbus, Ohio, was asked by George Lawrence, Managing Editor of the *Ohio State News,* the Negro weekly, whether or not he was a communist, to which Robeson replied "It is none of your damn business." the subject stated, according to the newspaper account, "The last person in the world I would expect to ask that question would be a Negro and a representative of the Negro press. This is no longer a matter of communism. It's a matter of civil rights." Robeson accused "big money men" of "fascist activities" and asked "who could blame a Negro for being a communist or anything?"

Testifying before the committee against the Mundt-Nixon anti-Communist bill on May 31, 1948, Robeson, according to the New York newspaper *PM,* after telling the committee he thought members of the Communist party had done a magnificent job in America, declined to state, in answer to a question Senator Homer Ferguson (Michigan) asked, whether or not he was a communist. He said he would go to jail before he said whether he was a communist. He also failed to tell the Committee whether he would fight for the United States in the event of a war with Russia.

The *Daily Worker* issue of June 3, 1948, reported that five thousand people picketing the White House on the same date in protest against inaction on civil rights legislation, were led by Paul Robeson and Benjamin J. Davis, New York City Communist Councilman. The pickets were a part of a delegation of seven thousand from nineteen states organized by the Non-Partisan Delegation in Washington for Civil Rights legislation and the committee for Democratic Rights. This group opposed the Mundt-Nixon Bill and pressed for passage of anti-lynching, anti-poll tax, and fair employment practices legislation. When questioned by a reporter concerning his being a member of the Communist party, Robeson replied, ''The question has become the basis of the fight for civil liberties, and until that fight is won, I refuse to answer it. That is the only reason I have for not answering.

Confidential Informant [Bureau Deletion] on [Bureau Deletion] reported that, according to Max Yergan, former Executive Director of the Council on African Affairs, Mary McLeod Bethune, member of the Executive Committee of the COAA, stated that Paul Robeson sought her support in his controversy with Yergan over Communist party control of the Council, and that during an interview with her stated ''My money, shoes, clothes—everything—belongs to the Communist party and I am willing to fight anyone who opposes them.''

According to the *Daily Worker* of October 11, 1948, Paul Robeson, on the previous Saturday, returned from a two-week Southwide Third-Party campaign tour. On being interviewed, he stated that the Negro people, no matter what anyone might say, cannot move into the Democratic party in the South because ''the Democratic party there—as well as the Dixicrat—is the white supremacy party.'' He stated that ''with the proper work by the Progressive party, the Negro people should form the bulk of the party's membership in the South.''

The *Daily Worker* of October 20, 1948, reported that the wives of the ''Hollywood 10'' were sending an emissary to the Women Fight Back rally [that] was to be held at the Manhattan Center, New York City, on October 25, 1948. The rally was one of a dozen to be held throughout the country in large cities to protest the deportation of alien communists. Paul Robeson was scheduled to speak at the rally. The ''Hollywood 10,'' referred to above, were the group that refused to answer the question concerning their alleged membership in the Communist party before the House Committee on Un-American Activities.

According to the *Daily Worker* of January 24, 1949, in an article written by Joseph North, Robeson attended the trial of the twelve Communist party leaders on January 23, 1949, shaking hands with each of them. He reportedly stated to North, "I came here because I, too, am on trial." Robeson also stated to North that he attended not only as a citizen but as Co-Chairman of the Progressive Party, as a leader of the Civil Rights Congress, and a Chairman of the COAA. . . .

The *World Telegram* issue of April 20, 1949, reported that at the communist-sponsored world Peace Conference in Paris Paul Robeson declared that the focal point of world fascism is the United States and that President Truman's program for African development meant "new slavery" for millions of Negroes. Robeson reportedly brought the eighteen hundred delegates to the conference to their feet with a call for "a fight for friendship with Russia." He then stated that American Negroes never would go to war for the United States against Russia.

The *New York Post and Home News* on April 22, 1949, reported that a concert given by Paul Robeson in Stockholm, Sweden, April 21 turned into a political row. The trouble, according to the said paper, started when Robeson sang a Russian anthem. The first verse, sung in Russian, was greeted quietly; however, when he sang the second verse in English, which most of the audience understood, a demonstration started, which for a time drowned out the singer. Anti-communists whistled loudly and many left the hall in protest. Pro-communists answered with loud cheers and frantic applause. Following the anthem, Robeson stepped to the microphone and told the audience he could no longer draw the line between his art and his political convictions. He said he wanted universal peace, but above all peace with the Soviet Union.

Translated from the Polish

Trybuna Ludu
June 2, 1949

**Negroes in the Ranks of the World Front in its Fight
for Peace and Progress**

by Paul Robeson

I come to you as a representative of progressive America. The America of Henry Wallace and twelve valiant Communist leaders, who are being persecuted today for their affiliation with the American labor class. I greet you in the name of the American workers, since I, too, am one of them. As a fourteen-year-old boy I worked on the farm. When I was fifteen I worked as a stable boy, later as a shipbuilder, then at docks and hotels, working hard to obtain some money to continue my education in a world full of prejudices. My father was a slave, and my cousins and their children are still working on tobacco and cotton plantations, fighting hard to earn a living. That is why I am devoting all that I possess, all my faculties and energy to the fight for a better tomorrow.

The progressive camp is gaining strength in America

I must state that today the strength of the progressive camp in America is greater than during the elections in 1948. Proof of this may be the continuous wave of strikes, which even the union leaders rightists, and devotees of the capitalists, are unable to check. The American nation is beginning to realize that Wallace was justified when he demanded during the 1948 elections cooperation with the USSR and national democratic countries and a type of peaceful economy which would not be a threat to the world. While the American trusts earn thousands of millions on so-called "American aid"—its costs are paid, on a par with European nations, by the American taxpayer—by the poorly dressed American. That is why the camp for peace and progress is increasing daily in the United States. Despite the policy of reactionary leaders of the AFL and CIO, steadily increasing numbers of workers and entire labor unions are voicing their disapproval of the present policy of governing classes. The Transporters' Union of the Western Coast, the Elections' Union, the Smelters' Union in copper foundries, and many union organizations of miners, textile, and leather industry workers are announcing their support of the progressive forces.

Today we are waging a difficult fight in the United States. But our entire history consists of long battles, waged in defense of our democratic tradition. Jefferson, Lincoln, Roosevelt—they all fought against reactionary forces in our country. This fight must bring us permanent, positive results, just as it is doing for the entire world.

One of the problems that is confronting America today is the so-called Negro problem. Even this problem is connected with the fight for peace and progress, not only in America but throughout the world. I would like to stress that the Negro problem is only one phase of the labor problem. Ninety-five percent of the Negroes in America and other countries are laborers. The emancipation fight of the Negroes is closely connected with the fight of the labor class, because discrimination against Negroes is a desire to ensure cheap labor. That is why the majority of the Negroes—except those few who are in the service of the imperialists and are enacting in Negro society the same role that the rightist union leaders are enacting in the entire labor movement—is in the camp for peace and progress.

Ask the Negro workers from the cotton plantations in Alabama, the sugar cane plantations in Louisiana, the tobacco districts of the South, the banana plantations of the West Indies, the African peasants who have been deprived of land in South Africa, and ask all the Negro inhabitants of the African continent if they want to fight for peace and cooperation with the Soviet Union and national democratic countries. Ask them whether they desire friendship with the Soviet Union where the definition ''backward colored nations'' is just a hollow sound, where former colonial nations within the Soviet structure were able during one generation to rise to an incredible level of cultural and economic development. Ask the Negroes whether they want to join these forces of peace, or if they will allow themselves to be hurled into the abyss of a new war in the interests of those who are denying them the elementary rights of citizenship. Ask them if they desire to join the modern slave dealers, or whether they desire to fight for peace and progress. Obviously they will fight for peace and progress.

The imperialists are gazing at Africa

The imperialists are turning their rapacious stares more frequently and more regularly on the African continent. In their search for cheap labor and crude iron, they are seeking new bases in Africa and the West Indies, after their ignominious defeat in China. American capital is striving to stretch its control over South Africa just as it did over the Philippines. Financial occupation and capitalistic control—this is their way of building a colonial empire.

Africa at the present time is a fragment of the extensive plans of the exploiters.

It is the duty of every progressive individual to fight against these plans, and to explain to the colonial nations that under these conditions the supposed benefits of the gradual industrialization of their countries is nothing else but the imposition of new forms of slavery and exploitation.

Colonial nations are natural allies of European and American workers in the fight for peace.

Trust will be victorious.

The imperialists presently are endeavoring to occupy Western Europe and deprive it even of its shadow of economic freedom. In Western Germany they prefer to cooperate with posthumous Hitlerites than with progressive forces. This is all a part of our common fight.

But I am convinced that the reign of capitalism and imperialism will end, just as it ended in Soviet Russia and in national democratic countries and as it is presently ending in China, thanks to the splendid victories of the National Army.

NY10-25857
REFERENCE: Bureau file 100-12304
                    Report of SA [Bureau Deletion] 7/16/49 at New York

DETAILS:
The *New York Times,* issue of June 20, 1949, reported that Paul Robeson "at a welcome home rally for him attacks trial of Red leaders here." The article further reflected that the "communist sympathizer" told a cheering crowd at the Rockland Palace, 155th Street and 8th Avenue, New York City, on June 19, 1949, that he "loved the Soviet people more than those of any other nation."

This article further reflected that Robeson on June 16th had returned from a four-month tour of Europe and the Soviet Union. Robeson is reported to have said in his speech at the rally that he "loved the Soviets because of their suffering and sacrifices for us, the Negro, the progressive people, the people of the future of this world." Robeson referred to the eleven communist leaders as "brave fighters for my freedom whose struggle is our struggle." He declared "that if the defendants were not freed all Americans can say good-bye to civil liberties, and especially the Negro people can say good-bye to any attempt to secure civil liberties."

In the above article it was reported that the meeting was held under the auspices of the Council on African Affairs, of which Robeson is co-chairman. The following individuals were also listed as having spoken at the meeting: Benjamin J. Davis, Jr., Representative Vito Marcantonio, and Dr. W. E. DuBois. [sic]

The *New York Post and Home News,* issue of July 14, 1949, reported that Manning Johnson had testified before the House Committee on Un-

American Activities in Washington, D.C., on the above date. Johnson, an admitted former member of the Communist party National Committee, had testified that Paul Robeson "had been a member of the Communist party for many years." Johnson stated that Robeson "has illusions of grandeur and that Robeson is desirous of becoming the black Stalin and the Communist party is encouraging that." The article further reflected that Johnson had stated that he had been a member of the Communist party up to 1940 and that "during my years of communist membership I frequently met Paul Robeson in Party Headquarters, going or coming from meetings with top communist leaders." Johnson advised that these Communist party leaders with whom Robeson had associated were Earl Browder, William Z. Foster, Jack Stachel, and J. Peters. Johnson stated that Robeson's party membership has been kept secret from rank and file communists.

The Following entries concern the Peekskill incident, which occurred on September 4, 1949, at a concert featuring the subject.

The *Daily Worker,* issue of September 6, 1949, reported that "an emergency committee of prominent progressive and labor leaders yesterday demanded the arrest and trial of all individuals and officials guilty of fomenting or aiding the Peekskill outrages." The following individuals were reported to have participated in the formation of the above committee: Paul Robeson, Howard Fast, C. B. Baldwin, Leon Strauss, and Benjamin J. Davis.

Memorandum

TO: Director, FBI   DATE: March 16, 1950

FROM: SAC, St. Louis

SUBJECT: ESLANDA GOODE ROBESON wa.
           Mrs. Paul Robeson, Sr.
           SECURITY MATTER -G

On [Bureau Deletion] of known reliability, submitted a report to SA [Bureau Deletion] dealing with Informant's attendance at a meeting held at [Bureau Deletion] Centennial Christian Church, Aubert at Fountain Park Avenue, St. Louis, Missouri, at 8 P.M. on 3-13-50 which was addressed by Eslanda Goode Robeson under the auspices of The Division of Work of the Centennial Christian Church.

The subject of her talk was a report on the Women's International Democratic Federation Council in Moscow and Peking.

Mrs. Robeson stated that she represented the Women's International Democratic Federation Council, the African Council in the United States, and the Progressive party. She stated at the beginning of her speech that she was not a communist and understood very little about communism.

Mrs. Robeson told of her visit to Moscow, Russia, to attend a meeting of the Women's International Democratic Federation Council. . . . She stated that in Moscow the people told her that they thought that Paul Robeson was married to a Negro, and she assured them that she had been married to him for twenty-nine years. (It was noted that in this connection informant pointed out that Mrs. Robeson is very light skinned and appears to be almost white.) She stated the people in Moscow didn't know what a Negro was and why she was traveling about when she should be home protecting her husband. She assured people that while some hoodlums tried to kill her husband in Peekskill, she felt certain that thousands of loyal progressive Americans would take good care of him. She assured the people that the mob in Peekskill really didn't wish to kill her husband but rather wanted to silence him, and that she pointed out that the only way this would be accomplished would be to kill him. . . .

Mrs. Robeson also spoke of her recent visit to China, and she stated that she and the other delegates who accompanied her wondered how they would be received in China after American bombs had been dropped from American planes killing thousands of Chinese. She pointed out that she and the other delegates were cheered wherever they went . . . as friends. She stated that the people's government in China had won the war and that the United States appeared rather foolish by not extending recognition to the new Chinese government. She added the prediction that this would come to pass within the next month.

She stated that the Chinese women had done a great deal for the new government and consequently they were now treated like women and not like cattle. She stated that schools were appearing throughout China, and all China was learning to read. She declared that some delegates [from] Africa attended the conference in China. She spoke at some length on the African situation. She pointed out that delegates from both Africa and India reported that colonialism was dead and buried as the people were tired of being exploited. . . .

On several occasions she stated that the Negro was not a citizen in the United States and therefore he cannot be called a disloyal citizen if he is not in fact a citizen. She also referred to the "Iron Curtain" on several occasions insinuating that this phrase was a piece of fiction built up in the United States. . . .

Director, FBI   July 31, 1950
SAC, New Haven
ESLANDA GOODE ROBESON, aka
SECURITY MATTER (C)
Bufile 100-12304

PAUL ROBESON
SECURITY MATTER (C)

For the information of the Bureau and the New York Office and for possible referral by the Bureau of certain of this info to U.S. Naval authorities, there is being set forth below certain info [that] was voluntarily furnished to a Special Agent of this office by [Bureau Deletion] in which city the Robesons maintain a residence known as "The Beaches." [Bureau Deletion] has requested that her identity be protected and not disclosed to any outside sources.

[Bureau Deletion] exhibited to the Agent two Air-Mail postal cards which were received on 7/25/50 by Mrs. Eslanda Goode Robeson, wife of Paul Robeson, addressed to "The Beaches, Enfield, Connecticut." The cards were as follows:

1. Post card postmarked Valdes, Alaska, July 22, 1950. (Front of this card is a commercial aerial photo of the Port of Valdes, Alaska.) A message written in pencil appears on the correspondence side of the card as follows: "Mrs. Robeson—Here's a card for your collection. [Bureau Deletion] Seattle, Wash."

2. Post card postmarked Seward, Alaska, bearing cancellation date of July 22, 1950. (This card contains a commercial aerial photograph of Seward, Alaska.) The handwritten message on this card as follows: "Dear Mrs. Robeson—I'm on the SS Aleutian. I'll try to send you a postcard from every port we hit. (Signed) [Bureau Deletion]

It is believed that the Bureau may desire to furnish the above information to the appropriate Naval authorities. . . .

[Bureau Deletion] further informed that Pearl Buck, noted author, corresponds weekly with Mrs. Robeson from Perkasie, Pennsylvania, under the name of Mrs. Richard Walsh. [Bureau Deletion] stated that Pearl Buck has been very friendly with the Robesons for years and has recently been collaborating with Mrs. Robeson on some book Pearl Buck is writing.

[Bureau Deletion] also advised that Mrs. Robeson sends newspaper clippings to Pandit Nehru (India) every week and she receives mail from the Indian Government. . . .

Activities of the subject selected from reports in news media and by FBI informants for the period January 1950 to December 1952 follow.

[Bureau Deletion] of known reliability, furnished a pamphlet entitled "The Negro People and the Soviet Union" by Paul Robeson, published in January 1950, in which Robeson stated:

"I am deeply grateful for this opportunity to join more than half the people in the world in celebrating a great anniversary. Yes, with fully half of humanity—and even this is an underestimation. For it would be a mistake to assume that this 32nd anniversary of the Union of Soviet Socialist Republics is an occasion of joy and pride and thanksgiving only for the eight hundred million people who live in the Soviet Union and the People's Democracies of Eastern Europe and China.

"True, these eight hundred million, as direct beneficiaries of the establishment of the Soviet Union and of its policies of struggle for peace and democracy, are rejoicing because of the new promise of a fuller and richer life for all, which they enjoy because they live in the Soviet land or in countries of the People's Republic, Mao Tse-tung.

"The Soviet Union is the friend of the African and West Indian peoples. And not [an] imperialist wolf disguised as a benevolent watch-dog, and not Tito disguised as a revolutionary, can convince them that Moscow oppresses the small nations. Africa knows the Soviet Union is the defender and champion of the rights of all nations—large and small—to control their own destinies.

"The Soviet Socialist program of ethnic and national democracy is precisely the opposite of the Nazi, fascist, South African, and Dixiecrat programs of racial superiority. . . .

"I am and always will be an anti-fascist and a fighter for the freedom and dignity of all men. We anti-fascists—the true lovers of American democracy—have a tremendous responsibility. We are not a small band—we are millions who believe in peace and friendship. If we mobilize with courage, the forces of world fascism can and will be defeated—in Europe, in Africa, and in the United States. . . ."

The *Daily Worker* issue of June 12, 1950, page 2, column 1, reported that on June 10, 1950, Paul Robeson spoke at the National Labor Conference for Negro Rights, which was held in Chicago on June 10 and 11, 1950.

The following are excerpts from the speech made by Robeson at the meeting of the National Labor Conference for Negro Rights held in Chicago:

"And so, even today, as this National Labor Conference for Negro Rights charts the course ahead for the whole Negro people and their sincere allies, it sounds a warning to American bigotry and reaction. For if fifteen million Negroes, led by their staunchest sons and daughters of labor, and joined by the white working class, say that there shall be no more Jim Crow in America, then there shall be no more Jim Crow!

"If fifteen million Negroes say, and mean it, no more anti-Semetism, then there shall be no more anti-Semetism!

"If fifteen million Negroes in one voice demand an end to the jailing of the leaders of American progressive thought and culture and the leaders of the American working class, then their voice will be strong enough to empty the prisons of the victims of America's cold war.

"If fifteen million Negroes are for peace, then there will be peace!

"And behind these fifteen million are 180 million of our African brothers and sisters, 60 million of our kindred in the West Indies and Latin America—for whom, as for us, war and the Point Four program would mean a new imperialist slavery.

"In every subject land, in every dependent area, the hundreds of millions who strive for freedom have set their eyes upon a new star that rises in the East—they have always chosen as the model for their conduct the brave people and stalwart leaders of the new People's Republic of China. And they say to our atom-toting politicians, 'Send your guns and tanks and planes to our oppressors, if you will! We will take them away from them and put them to our own use! We will be free in spite of you, if not with your help!'

"Your tasks, then, are clear. The Negro trade unionists must increasingly exert their influence in every aspect of the life of the Negro community. No church, no fraternal, civic, or social organization in our communities must be permitted to continue without the benefit of the knowledge and experience [that] you have gained through your struggles in the great American labor movement. You are called upon to provide the spirit, the determination, the organizational skill, the firm steel of unyielding militancy to the age-old strivings of the Negro people for equality and freedom.

"On the shoulders of the Negro trade unionists there is the tremendous responsibility to rally the power of the whole trade-union movement, white and black, to the battle for the liberation of our people, the future of our women and children. Anyone who fails in this does the Negro people a great disservice.

"And to the white trade unionists present—a special challenge. You must fight in the ranks of labor for the full equality of your Negro brothers; for their right to work at any job; to receive equal pay for equal work; for an end to Jim Crow unions; for real fair employment practices within the unions as well as in all other phases of the national life; for the elimination of the rot of white spremacy notions which the employers use to poison the minds of the white workers in order to pit them against their staunchest allies, the Negro people—in short, for the unbreakable unity of the working people, black and white, without which there can be no free trade unions, no real prosperity, no constitutional rights, no peace for anybody, whatever the color of his skin. To accept Negro leadership of men and women and youth; to accept the fact that the Negro workers have become a part of the vanguard of the whole American working class. To fail the Negro people is to fail the whole American people."

The *Daily Worker* issue of June 30, 1950, page 3, column 4, reported that the Civil Rights Congress sponsored a meeting at Madison Square Garden, New York City, on June 28. . . .

On [Bureau Deletion] Confidential Informant [Bureau Deletion] furnished a copy of the speech made by Robeson at the above Civil Rights Congress meeting. In his speech, Robeson charged that, "Every means of communication, every organ of prestige, beginning with the President himself has been telling us these last two days that the future welfare of the American people is somehow tied to the fate of a corrupt clique of politicians south of the 38th parallel in Korea—But we have come together to say that the American people will not be stampeded; that the efforts to fan the cold war into a flaming inferno of world-wide destruction are doomed to failure. . . .

"Today above all it means hands off Korea.

"For American intervention in Korea is the culmination of a wicked and shameful policy which our government has ruthlessly pursued with respect to the colonial peoples of the world. . . .

"I have said before and say it again that the place for the Negro people to fight for their freedom is here at home—in Georgia, Mississippi, Alabama, and Texas—in the Chicago ghetto and right here in New York's Stuyvesant Town.''

The *Daily Worker* issue of August 4, 1950, contained an article entitled, ''Rule Robeson Passport NG.'' The article reported that the State Department has canceled Robeson's passport to prevent his leaving the country. It was reported that the State Department stamped Robeson's passport record ''null and void'' a week ago after he had refused to surrender it at the request of the State Department. This action was reportedly taken because the State Department does not consider Robeson's travel abroad ''in the interest of the United States.''

Informant also furnished a copy of a news release from the Council on African Affairs dated August 4, 1950. The news release was a ''statement to the Council on African Affairs concerning the invalidation of the passport of Paul Robeson.'' The Council charged that the invalidation of Robeson's passport ''is another blatant example of the Administration's efforts to silence the demand of Negro Americans for their full rights as citizens. We are confident that American Negroes and all fighters for human rights throughout the world will denounce the banning of Paul Robeson from traveling abroad not only in defense of his personal rights as an American citizen but also in defense of the universal freedom of art and for the sake of the democratic rights of all people against police state tyranny.''

Masses and Mainstream issue of January 1951, contained an article entitled, ''Our People Demand Freedom.'' This article presents extracts from speeches made by William L. Patterson, National Executive Secretary of the Civil Rights Congress, and by Paul Robeson. Robeson's speech was a recorded message sent by him to the Second World Peace Congress [in] Sheffield, England.

''The life and struggles of this outstanding American of the nineteenth century afford me great inspiration as I find myself separated from you by the edict of the United States State Department. You may be assured while I remain in the United States a victim of the detestable program of house arrests initiated by our government, while I cannot be in your midst among many friends from all parts of the world, as had been my custom in years past, I do not remain quietly or to live a life of ease.

''I remain in the United States as [Frederick] Douglas returned to it, and in his words, 'for the sake of my brethren.' I remain to suffer with them, to toil with them, to endure insult with them, to undergo outrage with them, to lift up my voice in their behalf, to speak and work in their vindication and struggle in their ranks for that emancipation which shall yet be achieved by the power of truth and of principle for that oppressed people. And so today at this World Peace Congress we move forward in the best traditions of world democracy, representing as we do the hundreds of millions throughout the world whose problems are much the same. We are peoples of all faiths, all lands, all colors, of all political beliefs, united by the common thirst for freedom, security, and peace.

"Over here our American press and commentators and politicians would discourage these basic human aspirations because communists adhere to them as well as others. Now I have seen the liberty-loving people and peace-seeking partisans in many parts of the world, and though many of them are not, it is also true that many are communists. They present a new way of life in the world, a new way that has won the allegiance of almost half the world's population. In the last war they were the first to die in nation after nation. They were the heart of the underground anti-fascist movement, and city after city in Europe displays monuments to their heroism. They need no apologies. They have been and are the solid core of the struggle for freedom. And today in America we proudly fight to free the eleven leaders, the communist leaders, of the American working class, as well as many others who suffer bitter persecution. In this struggle for peace and a decent life, I am sure that we shall win. One simple reason why we shall win is that our friends are so much more numerous than our enemies. There are millions and millions all over the world who are determined never to give up the fight for freedom, decency, equality, abundance, and peace."

The *New York Amsterdam News* of May 17, 1952, page 41, columns 3 and 4 contain an article captioned "Frisco Mayor, Board Ban Robeson Concert." This article stated that San Francisco last week became the latest city to ban Paul Robeson, noted baritone, in his current concert tour of American cities. It further stated that when the board of trustees, spurred by Mayor Elmer Robinson, voted to deny the singer permission to sing in the opera house, San Francisco joined Oakland, California, and Seattle, Washington, as cities which have refused to allow the singer to sing.

The mayor was quoted as follows: "It's time to quit compromising with the communists. I don't say Robeson should be banned from singing in San Francisco—that is up to those who have halls to hire. But I don't believe that Robeson should be permitted to sing at the tombstone of those who gave their lives for this kind of government that they believe in and Robeson opposes.

Confidential Informant [Bureau Deletion] of known reliability, advised concerning the activities surrounding a concert given by Paul Robeson in Milwaukee, Wisconsin, on May 29, 1952. The Informant reported [Bureau Deletion] Robeson stated that one thing he wanted to destroy was fear in the minds of our presses that he was a communist. "The question is not whether Paul Robeson is a communist or not—if that were true and they could prove it, they would have already hauled me before a Congressional Committee or court." Robeson stated, according to the Informant, "many times I have offered to go before any committee and present my feelings to qualify my stand. Yes! I have stated that I liked what I saw in Soviet Russia during my visits there. The great transfiguration of a people that was shown and that had taken place between my first visit in 1936 and my last visit in 1947, makes me like what I saw. For that reason I educated my son there. But the real core of my fight is not political but is based on the sympathy and love of my people and all colored people of the world. I am determined to strike down all 'Jim Crowism' and second-class citizenship wherever I find it. The only thing we must concern ourselves with is Negro liberation to full citizenship in all the world and world peace."

The New York edition of the *Pittsburgh Courier* of June 14, 1952, page 19, column 6 carried an article captioned "Robeson Will Sing in Street if Necessary." This article stated that the American House in St. Paul canceled a contract for the singer's appearance there after "veteran and civic organizations protested on the basis of Robeson's alleged political activities."

The *Daily Worker* issue of December 19, 1952, page 3, columns 2–5, contained an article entitled, "Robeson Wins Stalin Poaco Prizo, Hailed as Leader of Negro People." This article stated in part, "Moscow, Dec, 21-Stalin Poaco prizes were awarded on Premier Joseph Stalin's 73rd Birthday today to seven persons, including Paul Robeson, great American singer and people's leader, who was hailed as 'the standard bearer of the oppressed Negro people.' " This article continued, "The prizes for 'strengthening peace among nations', were established on Stalin's 70th birthday. They bring the winners awards of 100,000 rubles each ($25,000 at the official exchange rate of four rubles to the dollar)."

FEDERAL BUREAU OF INVESTIGATION

Reporting Office: Miami
Office of Origin: New York
Date: 6/22/56
Investigation Period: 6/1,14/56
Report Made By: [Bureau Deletion]
Title of Case: PAUL ROBESON
Character of Case: INTERNAL SECURITY - C

SYNOPSIS:

[Bureau Deletion] advised during 1936 while on world tour she met Paul Robeson in Moscow, Russia, at International Hotel. Robeson, during conversation with [Bureau Deletion] and others, allegedly said, "I am a communist and have come here to stay—I'm never going back—I'm tired of being pushed around over there (America)—I'm a communist and I can come out in the open over here—There's no such thing as freedom in the USA." Later in 1936 while in London, [Bureau Deletion] again saw Robeson and during conversation Robeson allegedly said, "I'm going back to the USA, but I will not give up my work, for I still believe in the cause." [Bureau Deletion] was unwilling to furnish a signed statement, but says she is willing to testify as to the above conversations she had with Robeson. [Bureau Deletion] described as "living in another world" and "a psychopath."

August 29, 1957

RE: PAUL LEROY ROBESON

Reference is made to previous communications containing information concerning captioned individual. The following additional data is furnished for your information.

Robeson currently resides at 16 Junel Terrace, New York City, and is self-employed as a concert singer. His public appearances in the last several years have been confined primarily to the United States in view of the denial of the United States Department of State to grant him a passport for travel abroad. It may be noted, however, that the United States Department of State recently removed the restrictions on any travel Robeson may contemplate to countries in the Western Hemisphere for which a passport is not generally required.

The San Francisco Chronicle, *San Francisco, California, final edition, issue of February 5, 1958, contained an article captioned, "Paul Robeson—More Music Than Politics." In this article it was stated:*

"Paul Robeson has always been one of the most emotional of singers and about the last person you would expect to hear talking about music in terms that might send an advanced musicologist back to his reference books.

"Returning to the concert circuit after six years of singing in churches and informal recitals, the 59-year-old bass will appear at the Oakland Auditorium Sunday afternoon. And after a lunch with Robeson last week at the Whitcomb Hotel—and a conversation loaded with such technical terms as 'pentatonic scale' and tritone intervals'—I could hardly help being convinced that he is more interested in musicology than in politics.

"After his Oakland appearance, Robeson plans to tour the U.S. and Latin America, and, if his passport restrictions are removed, he will go back to England (where he may do *Othello*), Europe, and the Soviet Union. He was frank on his feelings toward Russia. 'They are making great strides under great difficulties,' he said. 'But the United States has also greatly advanced in the field of race relations.

" 'I am sorry now that I quit the concert stage because of politics. It happened six years ago in St. Louis when I was singing in a non-segregated hall across the street from a segregated theater that I had picketed with the NAACP the same afternoon. I told the audience I would stop singing until these two things were reconciled. They are not yet, but I see now that I should have gone on with my work.'

" 'There is a whole new generation for me to perform before,' said Robeson. 'Any "politics" in the future will be in my singing. A friend was shocked when I told him the only speeches Sunday would be Shakespeare and Shelley. Then I will sing French, Russian, Yiddish, and Chinese folk songs along with Negro spirituals. the audience can draw its own conclusions.' "

Memorandum

TO: Mr. L. V. BOARDMAN DATE: February 11, 1958

FROM: Mr. A. H. BELMONT

SUBJECT: PAUL LEROY ROBESON
             INTERNAL SECURITY - C

BACKGROUND:

Robeson is a noted Negro concert singer who has long been a controversial figure due to his consistent support of communist and related
front causes and his outspoken praise of the Soviet Union. He was
chairman of Council on African Affairs (cited by the attorney general)
until its dissolution in 1955. The State Department has refused Robeson
a passport since 1950 for failure to answer questions concerning CP
membership; however, the State Department has recently lifted the ban
on travel by Robeson to countries in the Western Hemisphere where a
passport is not generally required. Robeson, his wife, and his son are
current Security Index subjects of New York Office. His son, Paul, Jr.,
was recently elected to the New York State Communist Party Board.

Robeson authored a book *Here I Stand* published February 3, 1958.
He states he was assisted by noted Negro writer, Lloyd L. Brown, who
is believed identical with Lloyd Louis Brown, a current member of the
CP National Committee [Bureau Deletion]. The book was published by
Othello Associates (apparently affiliated with Othello Recording Com-
pany, a company controlled by Robeson in the handling of his re-
cordings), and available to date only in Jefferson Book Shop, New York
City, which deals in communist and front group literate [sic].

REVIEW AND ANALYSIS:

Robeson emphasizes his dedication to winning freedom of Negro
[sic] and explains purpose of book to discuss meaning of fight for
Negro freedom and means of securing such freedom. In so doing, he
seeks to explain his current political viewpoint in an effort to set the
record straight.

Robeson claims current controversy concerning him originated with
"Big White Folks" who he describes as his persecutors and real "Un-
Americans." He shows contempt for these people and in turn expresses
concern for the Negro as well as the common people, i.e. working class,

foreign born, nationality groups, Jewish people, middle class progressives, and people in arts and sciences.

Robeson emphasizes his basic views have not changed for years. He claims he voiced friendly sentiment for Soviet Union and Afro-Asian nations several years ago and has seen no reason to change his views in the face of a cold war and "McCarthyism." He alleges his sentiment for Soviet Union and Afro-Asian nations is founded in their support of "colonial liberation movement" as well as their support of the Negro people throughout the world. He claims the Soviet Union in world affairs has been an important factor in this regard and cites as an example how the Soviet Union blocked "Western Imperialists" from retaking the Suez Canal from Egypt. Robeson charges that his warm feeling for the Soviet Union has, according to Washington officials, made him a part of an "international conspiracy." He emphatically denies ever having been a part of an "international conspiracy" or knowing anyone who is. (At no time does Robeson deny present or past CP membership). He claims his refusal to testify before legislative committees is based upon the unconstitutional nature of committee inquiries. He describes the House Committee on Un-American Activities (HCUA) as the "Un-American Committee."

With reference to his passport case, he charges that the State Department's refusal to grant him a passport is arbitrary. He claims there is no evidence to support Government charges and alleges his passport refusal is based upon his concern for the Negro rights. In general, he attempts to put across the point that his support of Soviet Union and Afro-Asian policy concerning colonial liberation movement and racial equality has been misinterpreted as Un-American activity. He frequently criticizes the State Department and United States Government concerning both domestic and foreign policy in this regard. He continuously emphasizes the alleged lack of racial discrimination in Europe and Asian countries as contrasted to the United States.

At one point Robeson expresses his conviction in scientific socialism as an advancement to a higher stage of life and as being superior to "capitalistic imperialism." He does not elaborate further on this matter; however, he does comment at one point about the "new China" (Red China) in a favorable light and also emphasizes that the "communists of the world denounce racism."

Robeson admits he has never hesitated to associate with nonconformists and radicals, and in this regard points out his long association with Ben Davis, current national CP functionary. He points out the mutual interest of himself and Davis in regard to the fight for Negro freedom.

He goes on to describe the Smith Act convictions as unconstitutional and likewise denounces the Walter-McCarran Act.

The majority of Robeson's comments deal with his views concerning Negro inequality in the United States. He denounces segregation and its advocates. He proposes coordinated mass Negro action built around strong Negro leadership to cope with the current crisis. He suggests a central fund, concerted Negro support of already existent organizations such as the National Association for the Advancement of Colored People, and the exertion of influence of the Negro in Labor Unions.

In concluding, Robeson compliments the Soviet Union on the launching of the Sputnik and describes it as a step toward world peace.

OBSERVATIONS:

Robeson's book appears to be directed to the Negro reader for whom it will undoubtedly have appeal. He attempts to analyze the world racial situation from the standpoint of the Negro and apparently attempts to incite the Negro into a form of concerted action for the purpose of fighting for Negro equality. It would appear, however, that Robeson's attempts to explain and justify his political views, as related to his discussion of the racial question, is obviously an attempt to influence public opinion in the United States and abroad to his favor for the purpose of influencing the State Department to issue him a passport. It is noteworthy that Robeson evades any specific reference to the CP, USA, and fails to provide any argument regarding his alleged support of CP, USA, and front group causes other than his previous association with the Council on African Affairs.

It is noted the Robeson's book contains no reference to the FBI and likewise contains no new information of intelligence value to Bureau.

RECOMMENDATION:

None. For Information.

The following activity re: the subject in 1958 is excerpted from a comprehensive Bureau report.

Activity of the Communist Party Concerning the Distribution of Robeson's Book. Here I Stand

[Bureau Deletion] advised on [Bureau Deletion] that at the Southern California CP District meeting held on March 9, 1958, at Los Angeles, California, it was reported that the CP in that area, through its leaders, stated that it is very important that they support Paul Robeson's book and that they should utilize Robeson while he is on the Pacific Coast.

[Bureau Deletion] advised on [Bureau Deletion] that at a CP meeting held in Chicago on [Bureau Deletion] Claude Lightfoot, a member of the National Committee of the CP, USA, stated that this book must be sold in every store in the south side of Chicago and he desired every person present to pledge to sell at least ten copies.

Lightfoot stated to read Robeson's book is to be convinced that the Marxist stand that Robeson has taken on the Negro question is the correct position.

[Bureau Deletion] advised on [Bureau Deletion] that a meeting of the [Bureau Deletion] CP was held on [Bureau Deletion] at [Bureau Deletion] New York City. The informant stated that Benjamin Davis, New York State CP Chairman, was the featured speaker at this meeting and he described the recently published book of Paul Robeson as "a magnificent weapon, a magnificent cultural and political event." He stated that this book would be a weapon for the CP to go through in the fight for civil rights and for peace and to wake up the whole campaign for Robeson to get his passport.

Davis stated that there were 100,000 copies of this book in print and that 25,000 were to be distributed in the New York area. He stated that it was the duty of each club and section to take as many of these books as possible and see that they were sold and distributed widely.

[Bureau Deletion] advised on [Bureau Deletion] that it was announced at a meeting of the CP Harlem Tenants Club on [Bureau Deletion] that the first edition of Paul Robeson's book had been sold out.

[Bureau Deletion] advised on May 28, 1958, that [at] a meeting of the Industrial Board, Industrial Division, New York State CP, held at Adelphi Hall, 74 Fifth Avenue, New York City ... one of the speakers described Robeson's book as "a manifesto of the Negro people." The speaker stated that Robeson's book is the formula for the accomplishment of the alliance between the Negro people and the labor movement. The goal of the Communist party is to guarantee the sale of 100,000 copies of Robeson's book primarily in the Negro community. The Industrial Division of the CP has a goal of 40,000 books.

Activity in Connection with Robeson's
60th Birthday Celebration

The Worker of April 27, 1958, page 6, column 3, contained an article written by Robeson's wife, Eslanda Robeson, captioned, "How World Greeted Paul Robeson." This article stated:

"Throughout seven long years of persecution Paul Robeson has been sustained by the knowledge that many people in many places, near and far, have continued to respect him and remain steadfastly loyal to him as an artist and as a man.

"These people, whose number runs into hundreds of millions, have assured Paul from time to time that they consider him a great artist and a courageous human being. They have been indignant because the U.S. Department of State continues to deny him his right to travel, preventing them from hearing him sing and act. They have, upon occasion, arranged trans-Atlantic telephone concerts in order to hear his 'live' voice.

"This year, friends, neighbors, colleagues, and admirers all over the world decided to honor Paul Robeson by celebrating his 60th birthday (April 9th). Formal and informal Paul Robeson Birthday Committees were organized in Australia, Bulgaria, Ceylon, China, Ecuador, England, France, Germany, Hungary, India, Japan, Mexico, Norway, Poland, Sweden, Switzerland, the USSR, and the USA.

"On or about April 9th these Committees held concerts, meetings, radio and television programs in which distinguished academicians, scientists, theater, and film personalities took part. Together with many groups and individuals, they sent Paul Robeson cables, telegrams, letters, cards, and presents for his birthday. These continue to pour in more than a week after the birthday.

"Telephone calls and greetings came to our home from Accra, Armavir, Azerbaijan, Berlin, Bombay, Brooklyn, Bucharest, Budapest, Calcutta, Detroit, Kalinin, Kazan, Kiev, Kingston, Leningrad, London, Los Angeles, Mexico City, Moscow, New Delhi, New Haven, New York, Odesa, Peking, Paris, Port-au-Prince, Prague, Reykjavik (Iceland), Rostov, San Diego, Sofia, South Norwalk, Stalingrad, Stockholm, Sydney, Tashkent, Tiflis, Tokyo, Ulan Bator, (Mongolia), Vienna, Vilnius, Warsaw, Washington, D.C., and many other places. [Bureau Deletion]. . . .

Activity in Connection with Foreign Travel

The *New York Times* issue of June 26, 1958, page 22, column 4, contains an article captioned, "Robeson to Leave for Britain Soon," by Louis Calta. This article is set forth as follows:

"Paul Robeson, who for the last eight years has been denied a passport, will be able to leave for London within a fortnight to fulfill stage, concert, and television commitments there.

"News of the actor-singer's imminent departure was made known yesterday by his lawyer, Leonard B. Boudin. Mr. Boudin said that officials of the Passport Office of the State Department in Washington informed him yesterday morning that the document would be 'issued to Mr. Robeson as quickly as possible or in about five days.'

"Mr. Robeson's plans include discussions with British producers about a London presentation of *Othello,* with himself in the title role, and conferences with Harold Davison, Ltd., a theatrical, band, and concert agency. He last appeared on the London stage in 1936 in a play called *Toussaint L'Ouverture.* . . ."

The Passport Office, Department of State, advised in June, 1958, that Paul Robeson was being issued Passport Number 1145187 to travel to Europe for the purpose of singing and acting.

The *New York Times,* late city edition, section 1, page 8, column 5, dated July 11, 1958, contained the following article captioned, "Robeson Off to Europe After 8-Year Battle." The article is set forth as follows:

"Paul Robeson, who had been barred for eight years from leaving the country because he refused to sign a noncommunist affidavit for a passport, left for London yesterday to start a series of concerts.

". . . Mr. Robeson said he would give concerts in Europe, including Czechoslovakia and the Soviet Union.

"Mr. Robeson was asked if he planned to stay abroad. He replied: 'This is my land. My grandfather and father were born here, too, and I don't plan to leave it.' "

The *New York Times,* late city edition, issue of August 16, 1958, page 10, contained an article captioned, "Robeson in Moscow." This article is set forth as follows:

"Singer Welcomed at Airport
on Arrival for Tour

"London, Aug. 15 (Reuters)

"Paul Robeson, American singer, arrived with his wife, Eslanda, in Moscow by air today, Tass, the Soviet news agency said.

"At the Vnukovo Airport near Moscow he was met by his Moscow friends, leaders of the Soviet Peace Defenders Committee, artists, musicians, and journalists. He was welcomed by Nikolai A. Mikhailov, Soviet Minister of Culture.

"After the throng began to applaud, Mr. Robeson dropped his two suitcases and hat to clap his hands in time with the welcomes—a Slavic custom.

"Mr. Robeson will give concerts in Moscow, which he last visited nine years ago, and in various cities of the Central Asian republics, Tass said.

"The singer is expected to give his first concert Sunday at Moscow's Palace of Sports, which seats 14,000. He will fly to Paris after two weeks of engagements, but is expected to return later for a tour of Soviet cities."

The *New York Times,* late city edition, August 18, 1958, page 6, contained an article captioned, "Robeson in Russia, Cites Soviet Amity." This article is set forth as follows:

"Moscow, Aug. 17 (AP)

"Paul called on the Soviet people today to fight for freedom. He did not specify what freedom or for whom, but he spoke and sang in general terms of man's right to be free.

" 'When I read in America about the Sputnik,' he told a concert audience here, 'my thoughts went out to my friends, the peoples of the Soviet Union whose minds and hands have created this miracle, opening up to mankind the boundless expanse of the cosmos'....

The *New York Herald Tribune,* late city edition, issue of August 30, 1958, page 7, contains an article captioned, "Khrushchev Sees." This article is set forth below:

"Moscow, Aug. 29 (UPI)

"Soviet Prime Minister Nikita S. Krushchev had a 'friendly and cordial talk' with American singer Paul Robeson in the Crimean resort of Yalta, the Moscow radio reported today.

"Mr. Krushchev, who is on a vacation, met Mr. Robeson and his wife, Eslanda, in the Nizhnyaya Oreanda health sanatorium. Mr. Robeson sang for the Soviet pioneers at the Artek camp the same evening in a performance attended by Mr. Krushchev....

TRANSLATION FROM GERMAN
Neue Zeit (New Time)
April 27, 1961

My Plans—Fight for Freedom:
Our Moscow correspondent Henrik Gurkow spoke with the
world-famous singer Paul Robeson about his last journeys.

The famous peace fighter and artist Paul [Robeson] will come to
Rostock for this year's Baltic Sea Week. Our Moscow correspondent
talked with [him] during his stay in the Soviet metropolis.

The telephone rang constantly. All wanted to speak with [him]; all
wanted to welcome him in their homes. Enterprises and schools, the
editorial offices of the newspapers and theaters called. He smiled and
clapped his hands in astonishment. He wanted to be everywhere; however, this was unfortunately impossible. Even in the Soviet Union,
where science really accomplishes wonders, the day cannot be prolonged. Twenty-four hours—this is too little time!

We sit in his room which he had reserved in the Hotel "Sovi-
etskaya." Paul speaks—energetically and clearly—in the manner peculiar to him. This man and indifference are two poles which exclude
each other. In the so well-known, inimitable tone of his voice lies
sincere warmth when he talks about his impressions in Moscow, but
also bitterness and scorn when he thinks of those who still have not
conquered for themselves the right to human dignity; when he sees
before his eyes the life of the Africans, of the Australian aborigines,
and of the Negro of America.

MEETINGS WITH THE PUBLIC

[Robeson] stated: "Now I am on the road without having any definite
aim. I simply wanted to say 'hello' to my Soviet friends. Of course,
quite a number of friendly meetings took place. One of them was the
visit to 'Izvestia.' I was particularly glad to meet the young generation
of Soviet journalists. I sang a few songs and then we talked to each
other for a long time: about the struggle of the Soviet youths for peace,
about their participation in the construction of communism, about their
successes in the work in the new territories. We also discussed music,
Negro spirituals and jazz. As you see, our discussions covered a lot
of territory."

Paul talked about his visit to the Great Theater and expressed his approval of the "Ballad about the Soldier." He said: "Of course, I also visited the University of the Friendship Between Nations. I wanted to meet the students from the African countries and also the youths of Asia and South America. The young men and women as the representatives of different nations will not only take with them from Moscow excellent technical knowledge, but also the feeling of respect for each other. The university fulfills a noble task. The words of the rector had gladdened me very much, who praised the important role of my wife at the execution of this task."

I asked: "Your last goal was Australia? Did a starring performance lead you there?"

[Robeson] replied: "This was not the only reason. You see, during such a trip my appearances as artist combine with the work of the political human being who represents the world peace movement. I gave a few concerts. However, in the true sense of the word this is not the correct designation. I call the appearances, within the framework of a public event, meetings with the public. During such meetings I sing, read verses, and discuss the questions of music; in particular, of popular music."

ONE INVITATION AFTER THE OTHER

"In Australia and New Zealand the people know me from Gramophone records and films which are twenty to thirty years old. Now they want to see and hear me. I gave four concerts; it could have been fourteen."

[Robeson] suddenly became very serious and said: "One thing has embittered me. On the fifth continent I encountered a phenomenon which I have experienced in Africa and America: racial discrimination in the most loathsome form. If we compare the situation of the Maoris—of the aborigines in New Zealand—with the situation of American Negroes from northern states, we can call the situation simply terrible in which they and the Australian aborigines [exist]. Here open extermination is effected. Here the public opinion in the world must go to work and say a serious word.

"I intend to return to Australia. I shall make films and give concerts. The proceeds shall benefit the aboriginal population languishing in poverty. I already did that in Africa, and now I want to repeat it once more in Australia."

"Would you tell us something about other plans in the near future?"

Paul replied: "The next plans are closely connected with the invitations [that] I received from some socialist countries. During the first summer weeks I shall be in the German Democratic Republic and in Hungary. Then I wish to go to Ghana and, if possible, also to Guinea and other countries of West Africa. Furthermore, I received an invitation from Cuba. However, it will be difficult for me to find the time for everything."

ALSO IN THE USA

[Robeson] continued: "Meanwhile in the USA wide circles have ceased to fear a visit of my concerts. I have again conquered the American public. This is not only important to myself, but likewise to numerous colored artists who were oppressed by any means. All had to be shown that those have lost who wanted to silence me. However, I am standing on my feet again and singing."

[Robeson] concluded his report as follows: "In England and Scotland the public welcomed me like a good acquaintance. I thank my success in England partly to my appearance in the Shakespeare Memorial Theater in Stratford-on-Eavon (sic). Here I had to accept the role of other. To be sure, many Americans came to Stratford. They were apparently embarrassed that an American actor, who is not permitted to appear in America, plays in England; and then not only on an ordinary stage, but on the stage of the Shakespeare Theater, which has the best actors of various English-speaking countries at its disposal. There is no greater honor for an actor than to appear there.

"The role of Othello is the biggest one [that] I played as an actor. For the rest of my life I want to use my energies completely for the struggle for Africa's freedom, for the freedom of the American Negroes and of the Australian aboriginal population—for the freedom of all who suffer from oppression."

When we said good-bye to each other, I felt in the firm handshake of this wonderful man [to be] a confirmation of his words.

Following is an excerpt from a report on the subject's activities in 1963:

ROBESON'S ALLEGED BREAK WITH THE SOVIET UNION

A Chicago publication called the *National Insider* dated January 6, 1963, on page 7, set forth an article entitled "Paul Speaks—This Is

My Story." In this article, Paul is alleged to have made the following statements.

"I was a communist for a long time. I wasn't forced into it. I did it of my own free will because of certain convictions I had. And at times I have also been a socialist and a fascist.

"I am ashamed of being a fascist, but not of being a socialist or communist. I only regret what these philosophies led me to do.

"I was young when I first told the world I was a communist, and when I first moved to the Soviet Union—young, not in years, but in ideas. The young are always rebelling against social injustices . . . and they are always impatient to achieve the perfect society. Age does not always bring wisdom, and just because I was a grown man does not mean I was mature.

"Even if I had been more mature in those days, I would probably have rebelled against the same thing: the injustice suffered by my people. But my approach would be different. I would have tried to improve the Negro's lot by staying within the framework of American government, rather than trying to overthrow the government and replacing it with communism—an ideology that promises much, but does very little."

"I am not making excuses, nor am I saying that I completely reject Communism today. I feel each philosophy has an element of good in it—some more than others. But there is a certain amount of good in Communism, and a certain amount of evil in a Republic."

"I told the world I was a communist, and it made me proud at first. But in the end, it ruined my life."

This article further narrated [sic] that Paul sang [an] "illegal song" while giving a recital in Russia and, as a result, he was "punished." He was not to give any more concerts for eight months and the money taken in at his last concert was to be given to the State. [Paul] allegedly stated that this was a very small thing, but it was one of the many things that led him toward disenchantment with the Soviet Union.

The *National Insider,* January 13, 1963, on page 15, continued the story and set forth the following statements attributed to Paul:

"I left the Soviet Union as you know. I have not rejected all the basic communist philosophy, nor have I rejected all the socialist philosophy. But this should only go to point up one of the strengths of democracy. A man must be free to voice his opinions, even if they are in opposition to the government. Remember, to voice them is one thing, this is the thing I am saying—to try to forcefully put them into effect is another.

"I don't reject communism or the dream of a classless society. But I reject the Soviet Union's type of communism, and I think that if ever my people and other minorities become completely free and equal, it will happen in this country, and under this system, before it will happen in the U.S.S.R. . . ."

BAYARD RUSTIN

(1910–1987)

If Bayard Rustin did not operate behind the scenes exactly, he was never well known outside of the civil rights movement. Apparently content to concentrate on organizing and to let others seek glory, he remained a background figure his entire political life. This is immensely surprising given personal eccentricities that only can be described as flamboyant and considering the FBI's efforts to make him famous. For J. Edgar Hoover, Rustin was a perfect specimen for exposure. Rustin's five years as a card-carrying communist and his commitment to pacifism (to which he was so strongly devoted that he opposed American entry into World War II) provided a history that could be used to smear the movement if it were widely known just how important a role he actually played in the struggle for racial justice. He was also homosexual, a committed socialist, and an ex-con to boot. Other movement people, including the NAACP's Roy Wilkins and to some extent Martin Luther King, Jr., imagined Hoover drooling at the prospect of detailing Rustin's politics and sexual orientation. But the bureau never quite did the damage that it hoped to do (for reasons that remain largely inexplicable), and Rustin remained near the movement's center for more than thirty years.

Born the last of nine children on March 17, 1910, into a Quaker community in West Chester, Pennsylvania, Rustin was a fine athlete (track and tennis) and student (class valedictorian in high school). He studied at Wilberforce University, Cheyney University, and the City College of New York, and made ends meet during the Depression decade by exploiting his considerable musical talents. (He sang backup for Leadbelly in city cafes and went on the road with Josh White.) City College and Harlem also introduced him to the New York radicalism of the 1930s, and in 1936 he joined the Young Communist League. With pacifist ideals proving stronger than Marxist-Leninist doctrine, he resigned in June 1941 when Germany invaded the Soviet Union. After Pearl Harbor, a conscientious objector claim earned twenty-eight months in Lewisburg Penitentiary when he turned down his right to Quaker war duty in a hospital. He served as race relations director of the Fellowship of Reconciliation from 1941 through 1953, and in 1947 he helped organize the first freedom ride (the Journey of Reconciliation). He also served briefly as a field secretary for the Congress of Racial Equality; head of the Free India Committee (where he was arrested more than once for picketing outside the British Embassy in Washington); and executive secretary of the War Resisters League. He was capable of putting together a coalition almost overnight and sending it off to protest the Korean War or the bomb or anything else.

In the 1950s, Rustin hung out at the White Horse Tavern in Greenwich Village, drinking and singing with Dylan Thomas and Norman Mailer, among others, and generally immersing himself in the emerging beat culture. An arrest on a morals charge in Pasadena, California (he was picked up in the back of a parked car with two other men) led to his resignation from the Fellowship of Reconciliation and a sad break with A. J. Muste, the nation's most prominent pacifist. During the Montgomery, Alabama, bus boycott, he arrived in town unannounced and quickly won the confidence of Dr. King. By 1960, however, King had broken with Rustin, a break precipitated when New York Congressman Adam Clayton Powell, Jr., made a thinly veiled threat to blackmail the bus boycott hero by exposing Rustin's homosexuality.

Rustin's greatest contribution to the movement came in 1963 when he emerged as the organizing genius behind the March on Washington. King and Wilkins wanted him out, but his longtime mentor, A. Philip Randolph, wanted him in and held firm. Rustin's most controversial contribution followed a year later when he helped organize the New York City school boycott. He also headed the institute that bore Randolph's name; chaired the executive committee of the Leadership Conference on Civil Rights; and sat on the Notre Dame board of trustees. He died on August 24, 1987, leaving behind scattered writings, including *Down the Line* (1971) and *Strategies for Freedom* (1976), and the legacy of an amazingly nimble political and personal life that frustrated J. Edgar Hoover in five different decades. That life awaits a proper biography.

FEDERAL BUREAU OF INVESTIGATION

This case originated at: [Bureau Deletion]
Report made at: [Bureau Deletion]
Date when made: [Bureau Deletion]
Period for which made: 4/26,28/43
Report made by: [Bureau Deletion]
Title: BAYARD RUSTIN
Character of Case: Custodial Detention - C

SYNOPSIS OF FACTS:

Bayard Rustin, colored, Field Secretary of the Fellowship of Reconciliation, alleged to have advocated immediate freedom of India, no matter what the effect might be on the allied cause. Subject also stated there was not one case of Japanese espionage in California or Pearl Harbor, and that unless the Negro problem was intelligently handled there would be a revolution. No credit or criminal record. Check of city directories for 1931 to 1942 negative.

DETAILS:

This investigation is predicated upon a letter received from the Providence Field Office advising that the subject, colored, Secretary of the Fellowship of Reconciliation, advocated the immediate freedom of India, no matter what the effect might be on the allied cause. He stated England had been exploiting India for so long that the former had lost all moral consciousness and fibre, and that the country is paying only lip service to the cause of India's freedom, because of military necessity. Rustin also advocated the immediate release from concentration camps of 72,000 Japanese now confined there. In this connection, he stated dogmatically that the Toland report to Congress had shown definitely that there had not been one case of Japanese espionage either at Pearl Harbor or in California, that J. Edgar Hoover had concurred in this and said that there had been but 40,000 suspect Japanese in the whole United States up to the time of the Roland report. The Japanese, incidentally, he said were fighting a logical war—a psychological one also—and that there was after all no difference between that country's attack on Pearl Harbor and our own on Casablanca. He further stated that the Negro and Jewish problem must also be solved, and warned that unless the Negro problem was intelligently handled, there would shortly be a revolution. Rustin also remarked that all the papers, except the *New Republic* and the *Nation* pander to their advertis[ers] and are, therefore, not reliable news agencies; that this is a capitalistic war, and that our leaders have no consciousness of the part of the people in this struggle. Rustin called upon his audience to do something about it. [Bureau Deletion] Subject had spoken at a meeting, which meeting was held under the auspices of the Fellowship of Reconciliation. [Bureau Deletion].

[Bureau Deletion]

BAYARD RUSTIN   February 13, 1957

Rustin is an ardent pacifist and is considered to be a foremost Negro exponent in the U.S. of the doctrine of "passive resistance." He is an orator of national prominence and has delivered lectures at various universities and pacifist meetings throughout the U.S. and in India. He has been active in numerous picket lines, demonstrations, and other agitation against military conscription and racial segregation. He has been arrested on several occasions for activities in the above connection. Since 1942 he had been active as a field representative for the Fellowship of Reconciliation, and he is currently the Executive Secretary of the War Resisters League, an international pacifist organization. In these capacities he has traveled extensively throughout the U.S., giving speeches condemning the use of force in solving the world's problems [Bureau Deletion].

Rustin was born March 17, 1912, [sic] at West Chester, Pennsylvania, and was educated at Wilberforce University and the City College of New York. According to his own admission, he was a member of the American Student Union (cited as a communist front by the House Committee on Un-American Activities) in 1939, but withdrew in 1940 to embrace the Quaker religion. [Bureau Deletion] Selective [Bureau Deletion] Service records.

Rustin was investigated by the Bureau for Selective Service Violation in 1943–1944, when he refused to comply with the provisions of the Act on grounds of alleged conscientious objection. During the course of this investigation, agents of the New York Office observed Rustin acting as chairman of a pacifist meeting in New York City on February 12, 1943, during the course of which he urged men in the audience to come out on the stage and burn their draft cards. . . . [Bureau Deletion] Rustin pleaded guilty on February 17, 1944, to an indictment charging violation of the Selective Service Act and was sentenced by the U.S. District Court, New York City, to three years imprisonment on that date. After serving in Lewisburg, Penitentiary, Rustin was conditionally released on June 11, 1946. . . .

On October 25, 1946, Rustin was reportedly arrested by the [Bureau Deletion] Police Department for violation of Section 722 of the Penal Code (offering to commit a lewd or indecent act). The disposition of this arrest is not known. . . .

Rustin was one of twelve individuals, both Negroes and whites, who left New York City in April, 1947, on a so-called "journey of reconciliation" through the southern states, the purpose of which was to test racial discrimination laws. On April 17, 1947, Rustin was arrested at Asheville, North Carolina, for violating a segregation ordinance and received a sentence of court costs. An article in the *Amsterdam News* of July 5, 1947, reported that Bayard Rustin, Negro, was convicted and fined costs at Chapel Hill, North Carolina, for sitting with a white man on a public bus. The arrest reportedly took place during an interracial bus trip through the South by the Fellowship of Reconciliation. [Bureau Deletion]

The *Washington Star,* August 30, 1948, reported from New York City that Bayard Rustin, 33, colored, of West Chester, Pennsylvania, led a group of pickets outside a high school in Manhattan where registration for selective service was then taking place. The pickets were protesting racial segregation in the armed forces and urged youths not to register. (25–203164A)

The Police [Bureau Deletion] Department reported on [Bureau Deletion] September 2, 1948, that Rustin on that date was arrested on a charge of disorderly conduct in connection with a meeting to protest registration for the draft. The disposition of this arrest is not known. [Bureau Deletion]

The American Consul General at Bombay, India, reported to the U.S. State Department on February 2, 1949, concerning the unfavorable impression made by Rustin during a six-week lecture tour through India in December, 1948 to January, 1949. It was noted that Rustin spoke very unfavorably and in an inflammatory manner regarding racial conditions in the U.S. and his public appearances and statements were highlighted and given an anti-American slanting [sic] in the Indian press. It was suggested by the Consul General that an attempt be made to have some prominent American Negro "of recognized reputation and balanced judgment," tour India to counteract the unfavorable impression made by Rustin. [Bureau Deletion]

Rustin was one of twelve persons arrested in Washington, D.C., on October 4, 1949, for picketing the French Embassy. The picket line was sponsored by the War Registers [sic[League and the Fellowship of Reconciliation. The disposition of this arrest is not known. . . . [Bureau Deletion]

On January 21, 1953, Rustin, according to his fingerprint record in the Bureau's Identification Division, was arrested by the Police Department [Bureau Deletion] for investigation as a suspected sexual pervert. He was turned over to the Sheriff's Office [Bureau Deletion] and charged on January 22, 1953, with "lewd vagrancy," on which charge he was convicted and sentenced to sixty days in the county jail.

[Bureau Deletion] Made available a leaflet of the "Committee for Justice to Puerto Ricans." Bayard Rustin is identified on this leaflet as a member of the Committee, which was then soliciting $50,000 for the defense of Puerto Ricans in connection with investigations of the terroristic attack on the U.S. Congress by members of the Nationalist Party of Puerto Rico.

Bayard Rustin reportedly was one of twenty-nine persons arrested on June 15, 1955, in New York City for deliberately refusing to take cover during a Civil Defense mock air raid. Rustin and eighteen others of the persons so arrested were convicted on December 23, 1955, of a violation of the New York State Civil Defense Code in the above connection. . . . [Bureau Deletion]

In connection with the organization for War Resisters [sic] League, of which Rustin is Executive Secretary, the Bureau's files disclose that we have conducted intermittent investigations of this organization's activities since 1940 and have found it to be a purely pacifist organization.

The foregoing is a summary of information identifiable with Rustin in the Bureau's files and includes representative items of information [that] are typical of numerous other activities of Rustin as set forth in the Bureau's files.

FBI

AIRTEL

TO: SAC, New York [Bureau Deletion]

                                              Date: October 4, 1963

FROM: Director, FBI [Bureau Deletion]

SUBJECT: COMMUNIST PARTY, USA
                NEGRO QUESTION
                COMMUNIST INFLUENCE IN
                RACIAL MATTERS [Bureau Deletion]
                [Bureau Deletion]

As you are well aware it is our immediate responsibility to not only take every available measure in determining communist efforts to exploit the racial situation and the extent of the party's influence among the Negro people, but also to take necessary steps to neutralize and frustrate the party's endeavors. To ensure that we are making [every] effort to meet these responsibilities, the Bureau is currently considering the possibility of installing technical-type coverage on the activities of Bayard Rustin.

Rustin, who has admitted past Communist party affiliation and who was a principal in the 8/28/63 March on Washington, continues to maintain a leadership position in the current Negro struggle for civil rights. The *New York Herald Tribune,* in its issue dated 3/14/63, indicated that Rustin was secretary to Martin Luther King, Jr., from 1956 to 1960. As of 11/1/62 Rustin was Assistant Secretary for the Southern Christian Leadership Conference. . . .

The New York Office after carefully considering all aspects of this matter including the daily activities of . . . Rustin, should furnish the Bureau its comments and recommendations as to establishing technical coverage (technical and/or microphone surveillances). Information from New York should include a complete firm picture of the situation on which the Bureau can base an unqualified decision. [Bureau Deletion] A request for authorization should be included along with New York's recommendations if technical-type coverage appears feasible and advisable by the New York Office. [Bureau Deletion]

Memorandum

TO: Attorney General   DATE: October 28, 1963

FROM: John Edgar Hoover, Director

RE: COMMUNIST PARTY, USA
           NEGRO QUESTION
           COMMUNIST INFLUENCE IN RACIAL MATTERS
[Bureau Deletion]

[Bureau Deletion]
Bayard Rustin resides at Apartment 9J, 340 West 28th Street, New York, New York. Rustin, who was the Deputy Director of the August 28, 1963, March on Washington, continues to participate in the current Negro struggle for civil rights. According to a confidential source who has furnished reliable information in the past, [Bureau Deletion] also commented recently, [Bureau Deletion] that the Negroes are now willing to know what the Communist party has to say and to welcome whatever support the communists can give "in this new stage, which is how to break the resistance of the Dixiecrats and how to stop the McCarran Act."
In order to obtain further information concerning the plans of the CPUSA relating to influence in racial matters, it is requested that authority be granted to place a technical surveillance on the residence of Bayard Rustin or on any future residence to which he moves. . . .

Memorandum

TO: Mr. W. C. Sullivan   DATE: February 11, 1964

FROM: Mr. J. F. Bland

SUBJECT: BAYARD RUSTIN

According to a Washington News Service item dated 2/10/64 Bayard Rustin said that both the Republican and Democratic National Conventions this summer would be picketed by civil rights demonstrators. The Director asked for an up-to-date summary on Rustin.
Bayard Rustin was born 3/17/12 at West Chester, Pennsylvania. He studied at Wilberforce University and the College of the City of New York but received no degree. He is on the Reserve Index. He was a

member of the Young Communist League (YCL) from 1936 to 1941 and has stated that his Quaker religion caused him to drop YCL activities. Another reason he has given was that after the Nazi attack on Russia, the YCL accepted racial segregation in the armed forces. Rustin was sentenced in 1944 to three years [of] confinement for violation of the Selective Service Act. He was arrested on a homosexual charge in 1953 and was convicted after he entered a plea of guilty. Rustin attended the 16th National Convention of the Communist Party, USA (CPUSA), in 1957 as one of eight so-called noncommunist observers. He was secretary to Martin Luther King, Jr., head of the Southern Christian Leadership Conference (SCLC), from 1956 to 1960 and in 1962 was assistant secretary of the SCLC. He was deputy director of the 8/28/63 March on Washington and was extremely active as an organizer. During the past year Rustin has been in frequent contact with leaders in the civil rights movement as well as some national leaders of the CPUSA.

Rustin, with other leaders of the Negro movement, including Martin Luther King, attended an SCLC meeting in the mountains of North Carolina in mid-January, 1964, and on 1/23/64 he stated that the March on Washington office was being closed the following day and that he would be at the War Resisters League office. This is a well-known pacifist organization with which Rustin has been connected for many years. Rustin also stated that he had been offered two jobs: one as Project Secretary for the National Association for the Advancement of Colored People, which he planned to reject, and the other as special assistant to Martin Luther King, Jr., which he planned to accept. He would have an office in New York and would be in charge [Bureau Deletion] of direct action projects. [Bureau Deletion]

Memorandum

TO: Mr. W. C. Sullivan   DATE: February 12, 1964

FROM: Mr. J. F. Bland

SUBJECT: BAYARD RUSTIN

In connection with a memorandum dated 2/11/64, which is attached, concerning Rustin, it was stated that Rustin was arrested on a homosexual charge in 1953 and was convicted after he entered a plea of guilty. The Director asked ''Where?''

Rustin was arrested 1/21/53 by the [Bureau Deletion] Police Department while Rustin was in company of two male adults whom he propositioned to engage in oral sodomy, Rustin taking the active part. He entered a plea of guilty to the vagrancy-lewd [sic] charge and on 1/22/53 was sentenced to serve sixty days in the Los Angeles County Jail. Following his conviction, he was turned over to the Sheriff's Office, [Bureau Deletion] on 1/22/55.

ACTION:
For the Director's information. . . .

UNITED STATES DEPARTMENT OF JUSTICE

FEDERAL BUREAU OF INVESTIGATION

New York, New York
April 13, 1964

Re: Communist Party, United States
of America - Negro Question
Communist Influence in
Racial Matters [Bureau Deletion]
[Bureau Deletion]

The *Rockland County Journal-News,* a daily newspaper in Nyack, New York, April 10, 1964, issue, contains an article captioned, "Red Desire to Submerge Civil Rights Goal Seen." The article reports the appearance of Bayard Rustin at a meeting of the National Council of the Fellowship of Reconciliation at its Upper Nyack branch headquarters, on April 9, 1964.

According to the article, Rustin announced that a meeting of national civil rights leaders is being sought by A. Phillip [sic] Randolph (President, Brotherhood of Sleeping Car Porters, American Federation of Labor—Congress of Industrial Organizations), to discuss the emergence of Malcolm X's philosophy, white taxpayers groups, and the influence of totalitarian groups within the Negro movement.

According to the article . . . Rustin referred to communist infiltration when he said, "as (the Negro revolt) moves North a group of communists move in, partially out of a vacuum and a need for new organization". . . .

"I am opposed to the communist movement. There is no ultimate principle or position in their movement," Rustin told reporters after his address. Rustin said he learned firsthand of the communists' desire to submerge the goal of social justice as a former member of the "Youth Communist League" before and after the end of World War II. . . .

Rustin also discussed the possibility of a fast in Washington by the Reverend Martin Luther King in protest of the Senate's handling of the controversial civil rights bill. Revealing that King was "definitely interested" in the move, Rustin said "no single act would be better." He said it would do more than a million letters could. . . .

Rustin predicted that the masses of Negroes would never follow Malcolm X because of his program and methods.

Of the rights struggle, Rustin said it could not be successful until the churches, labor unions, and other groups realize that the Negro situation is part of the whole sphere of social problems affecting the nation. He pointed to the millions of impoverished people, automation, and unemployment. "They must speak out vigorously demanding public assistance and public works. The government has the moral obligation to put people back to work if the private sector of the economy can't," Rustin declared.

The *New York Herald Tribune* issue of August 14, 1963, page 7, column 1, contains an article captioned "Thurmond Assails a Leader of March." The article stated that, in answer to charges by Senator Strom Thurmond, Bayard Rustin admitted joining the Young Communist League (YCL) in 1936. Rustin also reportedly stated that he broke completely with the YCL in June, 1941. . . .

UNITED STATES DEPARTMENT OF JUSTICE

FEDERAL BUREAU OF INVESTIGATION

New York, New York
July 28, 1964

[Bureau Deletion]
Communist Party, USA
Negro Question
Communist Influence in Racial Matters [Bureau Deletion]

[Bureau Deletion] the Reverend Martin Luther King, Jr., President of the Southern Christian Leadership Conference (SCLC) and Bayard Rustin conferred on that date. King sought Rustin's advice as to what his role should be as a leader in the nonviolent revolution in relation to the riots in Harlem and Rochester, New York. In this regard, King said Mayor Wagner of New York City desired to discuss the situation with him tomorrow night (July 27, 1964). King said he had set a tentative date to meet the mayor for July 27, 1964, but was not certain it was the correct thing to do in view of the situation. Rustin told him that the situation in New York was quiet at that time. . . .

Rustin told King that he had appeared on a national television program on that date (July 26, 1964). He said the program on the National Broadcasting system was participated in by James Farmer (National Director of the Congress on Racial Equality) (CORE), Cleveland Robinson (Secretary-Treasurer of District 65, Retail, Wholesale and Department Store Union, American Federation of Labor—Congress of Industrial Organizations, AFL-CIO), and a representative of the National Association for the Advancement of Colored People (NAACP). Rustin said everyone took the position that Mayor Wagner had been derelict in the performance of his duties.

Rustin, [Bureau Deletion] expressed the opinion that there was a serious problem concerning King's meeting with Mayor Wagner, unless King could be critical, as all other leaders maintained that he was not doing enough. Rustin also felt that King should be free to make a statement to the press following the meeting, otherwise he (King) would really be in a "box." King said he agreed with Rustin and felt that he should be free to criticize the mayor, and tell the press that he told Mayor Wagner that he thought the demands of the Negro community were just demands and that he [Wagner] needed to act on them immediately. Rustin told King that he should say something similar to the following: "Law and order do not exist in a vacuum; to the degree that you have justice—to that degree can law and order be maintained, and where justice is nonexistent frustration will break out in some form, either Negroes being unjust to themselves, preying on themselves, using violence on themselves or someone else, and the root of the problem is to get rid of the situation." Rustin said King should "urge Mayor Wagner to face the housing, school, and job problems, and that many Negro leaders in New York City were united in seeing these as the major problems. Rustin said that anything short of this would spoil King's image. King said that Rustin was exactly right and that he just wanted to be sure that their positions coincided since the mayor had talked about having an off-the-record conference. Rustin told King that he should not do that (have an off-the-record conference) and [said that King] definitely should be free to make a statement to the press in which he could urge the mayor to move on much more housing, to integrate the schools and to find jobs for the unemployed. King asked Rustin's opinion as to what else was needed by him at that time, to which Rustin replied he would have to give some serious thought to the matter.

[Bureau Deletion], King and Rustin considered the feasibility of King making an appearance and speech to end the violence in New York City, as he had done in some southern communities. King said he felt it would be a mistake because some of the groups might be determined to repudiate/him and he would not get a chance to speak. To this Rustin agreed and said, "They are dangerous dogs who will lash out at anything."

UNITED STATES DEPARTMENT OF JUSTICE

FEDERAL BUREAU OF INVESTIGATION

New York, New York
July 30, 1964

Communist Party, United States
of America - Negro Question
Communist Influence in Racial Matters [Bureau Deletion]

[Bureau Deletion] Bayard Rustin conferred with an unidentified male on that date. Rustin remarked that "we" (Reverend Martin Luther King, Rustin, and others) were with Mayor Wagner of New York City from 10:00 P.M., July 27, 1964, until 2:30 A.M., July 28, 1964, and from 1:00 P.M., July 28, 1964, until early evening, July 28, 1964.

Rustin said the mayor had agreed to go to Washington, D.C., on Monday (August 3, 1964) to request ten million dollars to aid people in the ghetto (Harlem). Rustin said "we" have convinced the mayor that he should report that the problem (riots in Harlem) was economic; therefore he is trying to find 1,500 jobs by Monday for young Negroes in the ghettos. . . .

Another point under negotiation with the mayor, Rustin said, is the establishment of a civilian commission to investigate alleged cases of police brutality. Rustin said this proposed commission would be comprised of Negroes, Puerto Ricans, and whites. He said, however, that Police Commissioner Murphy was fighting this to the bitter end.

Rustin was asked by the unidentified male why Mayor Wagner had asked King to come to New York City. Rustin answered that Mayor Wagner could not negotiate with the Negro leaders in New York because they were "stupid and crackpots"; furthermore, Rustin said Wagner wanted the "umbrella" of King's name in the negotiations. He said some Negroes in Harlem were screaming that King had no right to come to New York because conditions here were none of his business.

[Bureau Deletion] Rustin and Martin Luther King had conferred during the night. King inquired if Rustin had heard any results of the conference between the mayor and Police Commissioner Murphy. Rustin replied, "Murphy is impossible; this indicates to me that they are putting up a real fight." King said the mayor was still meeting with the commissioner, and that he (King) had been requested by the mayor to stand by. King said it was urgent that "we" meet with him.

As regards any agreement reached between the mayor and him, King said several problems were involved, namely: his (King's) fear of criticism from Harlem Negro leaders, and the possibility that he would be placed in the role of "Uncle Tom." Rustin agreed that King should not be placed in the role of a negotiator.

King was of the opinion that the Harlem leaders would agree to certain issues if they did not think that he had proposed them and agreed to them in the conference with the mayor. In continuing their conference, King was of the opinion that there should be a press conference on July 29, 1964. To this Rustin suggested that King's press conference should be held in Harlem, possibly at A. Philip Randolph's (office of A. Philip Randolph, President, Brotherhood of Sleeping Car Porters, American Federation of Labor—Congress of Industrial Organizations, AFL-CIO, at 217 West 125th Street, New York, New York) to show the people that the conference is at the seat of the problem. Rustin told King that he should stay out of the Harlem "mess" and that he, Rustin, would get a group of leaders to give him (King) a vote of confidence and thank him for coming to New York. Rustin said King should state during the conference the following: that he talked for hours with the mayor, bringing to his attention the relationship between the economic problems and the disorder; that he urged the mayor to contact the governor of New York and the federal government as a symbol of how this problem should be handled nationally; and that he (King) had been urged to go to other cities in this regard, including Rochester, New York. Also King was told by Rustin to state that his job had been completed, and it was up to the leaders (Harlem) to reap whatever benefit they could from the approach he had taken with the mayor, and that he (King) assumed they would be negotiating. Whatever "comes out," Rustin said, everybody knows, would be the result of what he (King) had done. In this way, Rustin told King, he would not have to recommend it, accept it, or be there when it is accepted.

UNITED STATES DEPARTMENT OF JUSTICE

FEDERAL BUREAU OF INVESTIGATION

New York, New York
August 6, 1964

Communist Party, United States
of America - Negro Question
Communist Influence in Racial Matters [Bureau Deletion]
Internal Security - C

On August 5, 1964, a confidential source, who has furnished reliable information in the past, advised that Bayard Rustin and Reverend Martin Luther King, Jr., were in contact on that date. King asked if Rustin had done any thinking on what needs to be done to dramatize the finding of the boys (the finding of the bodies of the three Mississippi civil rights workers). To this, Rustin advised King to send a telegram to the National Council of Churches, to the National Council of Bishops of the Catholic Church, and to the Board of Rabbis, requesting them to declare this Sunday (August 9, 1964) as a day of repentance. . . .

Rustin posed the question as to how repentance should be brought about, concluding that members of these religious groups should repent, not by feeling sorry for them (the civil rights workers) but instead, by dedicating themselves to the eradication of all the vestiges of segregation and discrimination and by rededicating themselves to work for the freedom and justice of all men.

Rustin, according to the source, urged King to call a press conference for that evening (August 5, 1964) at which time he should read the telegram.

During their conference, King and Rustin also considered matters relating to the forthcoming Democratic National Convention (August 24, 1964, in Atlantic City). Rustin in this regard said he had been unable to ascertain what the Student Nonviolent Coordinating Committee (SNCC) and the Congress of Racial Equality (CORE) intend to do "around" the convention.

Rustin told King that he was trying to avoid getting him (King) involved in something (demonstrations) [that] could alienate all "our friends." Rustin said if they (SNCC and CORE) have any demonstrations and civil disobedience, regardless of what the situation is, all the labor people, all of "our friends in the Democratic party, and that is where all of our white friends are, and that is where most of the money comes from that we receive from white people, there is going to be a terrific squabble." Rustin concluded: "All of Walter Reuther's people (Walter Reuther, Vice President of the American Federation of Labor—Congress of Industrial Organizations) (AFL-CIO), and Helstein's people (Ralph L. Helstein, President of United Packinghouse, Food and Allied Workers) and most of the people we know, are very distressed over the way things are opening up."

UNITED STATES DEPARTMENT OF JUSTICE

FEDERAL BUREAU OF INVESTIGATION

New York, New York
August 14, 1964

[Bureau Deletion]
Communist Party, United States
of America - Negro Question
Communist Influence in Racial Matters [Bureau Deletion]

[Bureau Deletion] Bayard Rustin and the Reverend Martin Luther King, Jr., were in conference on that date. According to the source, King told Rustin that he had talked with Lee White (Special Assistant to President Johnson) last night and was informed by him that the President was tied up today and tomorrow (August 13–14, 1964), and wondered if he could confer with him (King) on the phone. King said after thinking about it, he believed "this" was important enough that he talk to President Johnson face to face and not over the phone.

It is noted that on August 7, 1964, [Bureau Deletion] advised that Bayard Rustin and King conferred on that date, and King was advised to send a telegram to President Johnson requesting a meeting with him for this week. The purpose of the meeting, the telegram stated, was to consider the moratorium on demonstrations and the possibility of further conflict in urban centers. . . .

In continuing their conference, King said he had the impression that he (President Johnson) was not only trying to avoid the issue, but also avoid meeting him face to face for fear that it would get back to the South that he (the President) was dealing with him.

King, [Bureau Deletion] thought he (the President) was trying to avoid meeting him in Washington, where the press would let the nation know he was meeting with him. He said this was the reason he (the President) first proposed they meet in New York. This, King said, made him a little sensitive.

Rustin told King that his position was correct for two reasons: because he would not derive any satisfaction over the telephone; and secondly, because "those young people must know you are putting up a fight for them."

King apprised Rustin that he was told by Lee White that possibly the President would see Joe Rauh (Counsel to the United Auto Workers, American Federation of Labor-Congress of Industrial Organizations) on Monday or Tuesday (August 16–17, 1964). . . .

King instructed Rustin to contact Lee White and let him know his (King's) feelings; let the President know that he feels this is "downright avoiding him and the issues." Furthermore, King was of the opinion that the matter was so important the President should deal with it himself rather than through some assistant. King said that President Johnson should know that he does not like it, adding that if "we" do not wage a fight "they" will just run over us in the next two months. "Lyndon Johnson," King said, "needs the Negro vote. He feels that we have no way to go but we can certainly stay home."

[Bureau Deletion] advised on August 13, 1964, that Bayard Rustin and Lee White, Special Assistant to President Johnson, were in conference on that date. [Bureau Deletion] Rustin told White that the Reverend Martin Luther King, Jr., had talked with Rustin and other Negro leaders in New York City and that there was a sense of distress because King was asked to see the President not only on his own behalf but on behalf of a number of others. Rustin continued that King had very definitely gotten the impression that the President did not want to see him in Washington. . . .

Rustin asked White to talk to King again. Rustin continued [by saying] that almost all of the men who were involved in this moratorium signing (against demonstrations) feel that they are in a very peculiar position and that someone should talk with the President. Rustin added that Mr. Joseph Rauh was one of the persons who had urged King to see the President. Rustin went on to say that the leadership does not choose to pass on to the President their point of view through Mr. Rauh. Rustin again stated that it would be a good thing if White again talked to King.

White commented that this was especially true if that is the feeling in King's mind that the President is trying to avoid him. . . .

UNITED STATES DEPARTMENT OF JUSTICE

FEDERAL BUREAU OF INVESTIGATION

New York, New York
August 25, 1964

[Bureau Deletion]
Communist Party, United States
of America - Negro Question
Communist Influence in Racial Matters [Bureau Deletion]

[Bureau Deletion] Bayard Rustin, Martin Luther King, Jr., (President of the Southern Christian Leadership Conference) and Andrew Young (Executive Assistant to King) were in contact on that date. They took the opportunity to consider the Democratic National Convention (opening in Atlantic City, New Jersey, August 24, 1964) and whether Rustin thought King should attend.

Rustin advised King that he should appear tomorrow (August 22, 1964) at 2:00 P.M. and put up a fight to get them seated (Freedom Democratic Party delegates from Mississippi). After that, Rustin opined, it seemed that King might be in a position that he might not want to be in. In explaining to King and Young just what he meant, Rustin said that in the event President Johnson did something unacceptable to the "left youngsters," they would demonstrate . . . and if King were there, they would expect him to join them, and should he refuse, the press would ask for an explanation. Regardless of what King might say, Rustin said, it would be interpreted by them (the youngsters) as harmful to their efforts. He said King should not be in that position, and that one way to prevent it was to leave tomorrow (August 22, 1964) after his appearance.

In continuing, Rustin said if King were in Atlantic City and something should happen, people like Walter Reuther (President of the United Auto Workers and Vice President of the American Federation of Labor-Congress of Industrial Organizations, (AFL-CIO) would ask his support in stopping the "youngsters" from doing "kookie things." For that reason, Rustin said, he (Rustin) would not go to the Convention.

[Bureau Deletion] Rustin told King and Young that he had been called by "youngsters" in Atlantic City, New Jersey, requesting that he call King and ask him to telegram Attorney General Robert Kennedy and request his support (in seating the delegates from the Freedom Democratic party). In this regard, Rustin advised King to do whatever he could to strike a blow for freedom.

King, Rustin said, should make his appearance at the meeting of the Credentials Committee on August 22, 1964, then he could return to New York City, to Atlanta, Georgia, or go any place he desired to go. In the event King desired to return to the Convention he could consider going on Monday or Tuesday, Rustin stated, provided there was to be a peaceful demonstration to seat the delegates. In this regard, King said he had been assured by James Farmer of the Congress of Racial Equality (CORE) that demonstrations would be peaceful. To this, Rustin said Farmer did not have control of CORE, therefore, he could not control what happened. Rustin said this was because Farmer had given his "left wing" such freedom to do what they wanted, that nobody paid any attention to him.

Furthermore, Rustin said that CORE had sent the biggest "kook" down to Atlantic City to organize demonstrations. According to the source, Rustin identified this person as Herb Callender (Chairman of the Bronx chapter of CORE).

Rustin told Andrew Young that he should attend the Convention to act as King's representative. This, Rustin said, would permit people to relay requests and messages to King through Young, who could then inform them that King was unavailable due to an accident. Rustin said King's injury might be the most fortunate thing to ever happen to King. King said he was using a crutch in order to get around. This prompted Rustin to advise King to go to Atlantic City on a crutch. By doing that, Rustin said, the people from the Student Nonviolent Coordinating Committee would interpret it as a great token.

With regard to King's appearance before the Credentials Committee, Rustin told him that Joseph Rauh (counsel to the United Auto Workers and counsel to the Freedom Democratic party) would expect him to talk for about fifteen minutes. Rustin told King to make a real emotional appeal for the Freedom Delegates and to read a statement [that] Andrew Young had prepared. The following is in essence what was contained therein:

"That no state had gone to such extremes to prevent participation of Negro citizens in political life as the state of Mississippi," and enumerated such things as "literacy tests, economic reprisals, police intimidation, and church burnings," to support the allegation, and said that "as a consequence, citizens of that state had come to the Convention in a moral appeal for recognition and representation in the Democratic party. The seating of the delegation from the Freedom Party has political and moral significance far beyond the borders of Mississippi or the halls of the Convention, for there the very idea of representative government is at stake." In conclusion, the statement urged the seating and recognition of the Freedom Democratic party delegates.

Rustin, [Bureau Deletion] was highly complimentary of the statement, but instructed Young to add the following: "that to all who love democracy and freedom, nothing was so symbolic as whether the right decision was made to seat the delegates."

. . . [Bureau Deletion] advised on August 22, 1964, that Bayard Rustin was in contact with one Cortland (ph) on that date. Rustin told Cortland that Martin Luther King was going to appear before the Credentials Committee of the Democratic party on that date, to present his testimony.

Rustin said King was also willing to send a telegram to Attorney General Kennedy (seeking his moral support in seating the delegation from the Freedom Democratic party). In light of that, Cortland read the following telegram which was to be sent in the name of King to Kennedy:

"Four years after the Convention in which your brother took up the fight for full civil rights throughout the United States, we call upon you to carry that fight forward by voicing your support for the Mississippi Freedom Democratic Party. Your experience as Attorney General has made you the man in the country who is most aware of the moral imperative to support the Mississippians in their serious effort to change the human condition. Your voice on this issue would carry a great moral and political weight in favor of a democratic decision on the floor of the Convention. Your statement of support will encourage all who work for the liberal cause in both the North and the South."

Rustin approved the statement and told Cortland to release it from the office of the Freedom party in Atlantic City, New Jersey, when the right opportunity arose.

[Bureau Deletion] during a meeting of the National Board, CP, USA, Benjamin J. Davis remarked that, "Rustin calls me constantly—openly."

[Bureau Deletion] Bayard Rustin contacted Benjamin J. Davis on those dates, and sought his advice as to how he could escape from a speaking engagement to which he was committed. On the latter contact, Davis told Rustin that he was working on his request and had contacted friends who had contacts with the group to which Rustin was to speak.

[Bureau Deletion] Benjamin J. Davis was National Secretary of the CP, USA.

The *New York Times,* Monday, August 24, 1964, page 27, column 4, reports that Benjamin J. Davis, National Secretary, CP, USA, died in New York City on Saturday night, August 22, 1964.

UNITED STATES DEPARTMENT OF JUSTICE

FEDERAL BUREAU OF INVESTIGATION

New York, New York
September 29, 1964

Communist Influence in Racial Matters [Bureau Deletion]
[Bureau Deletion]

[Bureau Deletion] Bayard Rustin (the organizer of the March on Washington, August, 1963) was in contact on that date with an unidentified woman. [Bureau Deletion]

Rustin told the woman that he also had a meeting at the A. Philip Randolph Institute (A. Philip Randolph, President of the Brotherhood of Sleeping Car Porters, American Federation of Labor—Congress of Industrial Organizations, AFL-CIO). In that regard, he said he spoke with two men from the office of George Meany (President, AFL-CIO), who were very interested in the A. Philip Randolph Institute (Washington, D.C.). In view of Meany's interest, and the fact that he (Meany) was prepared to say that the AFL-CIO was willing to give $10,000, many other unions would fall into line, Rustin said.

Continuing, Rustin said "they" wanted him to proceed vigorously to try to get the tax exemption (for the A. Philip Randolph Institute) because "they" said at the "present time" Rustin was very high on both President Johnson's and Humphrey's list as a result of his work at Atlantic City (during the National Democratic Convention). In view of that, Rustin said, he spoke to Joseph Rauh (Vice President of the Americans for Democratic Action, ADA, and General Counsel to the

United Auto Workers, AFL-CIO), who said he was prepared to push the tax exemption through the Department of Justice. . . .

[Bureau Deletion] advised that Rustin was in contact with an unidentified woman on that date. Rustin related that he had recently talked with Dr. Logan (Dr. Arthur Logan, Chairman of the Board of Directors of the Haryou-Act), who informed him that he (Rustin) was being considered for an appointment to the Board of Directors of Haryou-Act.

It should be noted that Haryou-Act is a combination of Harlem Youth Opportunities Unlimited and Associated Community Teams, whose purpose is to fight juvenile delinquency in Harlem. [Bureau Deletion]

Bayard Rustin was in contact with an unidentified male on that date. . . . Rustin said he would write a statement endorsing Johnson (President Lyndon B. Johnson), which King would use under his own name.

Rustin then talked about the A. Philip Randolph Institute, and in this regard, listed the names of the following, who he said would be advisors: Roy Wilkins (Executive Secretary, National Association for the Advancement of Colored People, NAACP); Martin Luther King, Jr., (President of the SCLC); Whitney Young (Executive Secretary, National Urban League), as well as others. Rustin said it was very important that the public see that those civil rights leaders were aligned with the Institute. . . .

UNITED STATES DEPARTMENT OF JUSTICE

FEDERAL BUREAU OF INVESTIGATION

Cleveland, Ohio
Bayard Rustin

The *Cleveland Plain Dealer,* a local daily newspaper of general circulation in the Cleveland area, in its issue of November 3, 1964, advised that "Bayard Rustin, civil rights leader, who directed last February's school boycott in New York City, will speak Friday at the City Club of Cleveland."

[Bureau Deletion] member of the City Club of Cleveland, advised on [Bureau Deletion] that he attended the City Club Forum at which Bayard Rustin spoke, and that Rustin presented his views in a fair manner, stating that all the Negroes wanted was equality of opportunity and protection under the law.

[Bureau Deletion] stated that in response to a question of what he thought of the Black Muslims, Rustin commented that the Black Muslims have given up all hope of the Negro bettering himself; that the Black Muslins are the lowest segment of the Negro community; that Malcolm X's claim to being able to rehabilitate prostitutes, narcotic addicts, and drunks is a hoax on the Negro people. [Bureau Deletion] advised that Rustin was also asked about the activity of communists in the civil rights movement, and he replied that communists have no place in the civil rights movement; that they are very sharp and must be watched at all times. . . .

The *Cleveland Press,* daily newspaper of general circulation in the Cleveland area, in its issue of November 6, 1964 . . . reported that:

"In an interview before his speech, Rustin said:

"We'll be returning to the streets in ever greater numbers now that the election is over. This time, however, we must broaden the participation to include many more whites, and we must concentrate on economic measures and not so much on public accommodation.

"The right to use accommodations doesn't mean anything for the Negro if he doesn't have the money to use them.

"If President Johnson is really interested in creating the Great Society he speaks of, then he should welcome the Negro's return to the streets.

"If there had been no Negro demonstrations for jobs, there would be no war on poverty by the Johnson Administration.

"If there had been no Negro demands for school integration, there would have been no great debate on establishing 20th-century education in this country to supplant the 19-century system we have.

"If there had been no Negroes in motion, there would have been no ecumenical religious movement concerned with social issues.

"The Negro alone has been the catalyst in advancing social progress."

UNITED STATES DEPARTMENT OF JUSTICE

FEDERAL BUREAU OF INVESTIGATION

New York, New York
November 13, 1964

Communist Influence in Racial Matters [Bureau Deletion]
[Bureau Deletion]

[Bureau Deletion] Bayard Rustin (Organizer of the March on Washington, D.C.) was in contact on that date with an unidentified woman.

During their contact, Rustin was asked why he was not in London, England. He replied that he had planned to go to London on that date, but said he had waited too long to apply for his passport, and due to the holiday (Veterans Day), it was not processed. He said the passport office was closed but that "Frank Montero, who works for United Nations Ambassador Adlai Stevenson," arranged to get the office open (New York Passport Office) but nothing could be done since the Washington Passport Office was closed. He said he had tickets (airline) for tomorrow (November 12, 1964) and planned to go then.

[Bureau Deletion] Rustin also conferred with Peggy Duff of London, England (Executive Director of the Campaign for Nuclear Disarmament) on November 11, 1964. . . .

Duff, [Bureau Deletion] said there was nothing new on the Archbishop of Canterbury matter. Rustin asked if she thought he could take care of all the matters on Friday so that he would be able to return to New York on Friday night. Duff said she thought he could accomplish everything in one day.

[Bureau Deletion] Bayard Rustin and Andrew Young (Executive Director of the Southern Christian Leadership Conference, SCLC) were in contact on that date, during which time they discussed the fact that confusion had arisen in London over Martin Luther King's trip to London in December, 1964. The confusion, according to the source, arose over the fact that the Archbishop of Canterbury desired to receive King, but due to King's affiliation with the Baptist Church, there was opposition to him greeting King.

It was agreed during their conference that Rustin would go to London on Wednesday, November 11, 1964, to try to clarify the confusion.

[Bureau Deletion] Rustin was in contact on that date with Frank Montero. . . . Rustin said there was a possibility that President Johnson might come to New York to attend an affair on King's return from receiving the prize. . . .

With regard to King's trip to Europe to receive the Nobel Prize, Rustin told Montero that he (King) would probably meet with the Archbishop of Canterbury and Prime Minister Wilson while in London. Rustin asked Montero if he did not think that "our people" (United States Embassy) in London should do something (apparently alluding to King's visit there). Montero replied in the affirmative, adding, however, that "we have a stuffy Ambassador there by the name of Bruce, but it may be possible."

[Bureau Deletion] Bayard Rustin was in contact with Dr. Ralph Bunche on that date. Rustin related that he was in touch with Martin Luther

King on November 10, 1964, during which time King said he would accept United Nations Secretary U. Thant's invitation to dinner on December 4, 1964.

Bunche told Rustin that he would also like to hold a dinner party in King's honor. The party, Bunche said, would be composed of about eighteen to twenty people and would be held at his home on the evening of December 3, 1964.

[Bureau Deletion] Rustin was in touch with Andrew Young, during which time Rustin relayed to Young that King's presence was desired at a dinner by Secretary U. Thant on December 4, 1964, and at a dinner by Dr. Ralph Bunche on December 3, 1964. According to Young, King will be present at both dinners.

UNITED STATES DEPARTMENT OF JUSTICE

FEDERAL BUREAU OF INVESTIGATION

New York, New York
November 13, 1964

Re: Communist Influence in Racial Matters [Bureau Deletion]

[Bureau Deletion] Bayard Rustin, on that date, contacted Tom Kahn, who is a friend and associate of Rustin. Rustin stated that he had finally gotten his passport which, he said, had been held up all day. Rustin further stated that he had gotten the White House, the Democratic National Committee, and Roland (phonetic), (who was not further identified), working on it. According to Rustin, Roland had determined that the passport was being held up because of Congressional investigation. Kahn inquired if they were investigating Rustin, and Rustin replied that apparently they were because of the March on Washington. Rustin made the statement that he "would just love to be investigated."

Rustin indicated that he wanted to get the matter of the passport cleared up because of the other trip to Oslo, Norway, with Martin Luther King, Jr., (President of the Southern Christian Leadership Conference, who is to receive the Nobel Peace Prize in Oslo, Norway, in December, 1964). Rustin also stated that Lee White (White House Assistant) "really went to bat" for him in order to get the passport. . . .

UNITED STATES DEPARTMENT OF JUSTICE

FEDERAL BUREAU OF INVESTIGATION

New York, New York
November 17, 1964

Re: Communist Influence in Racial Matters [Bureau Deletion]

[Bureau Deletion] Rustin and Andrew Young (Assistant to King) were in conference on that date. Their contact, the source said, was to permit Rustin to relate to King through Young the results of his trip to London, England, on November 12, 1964, to make preparations for King's visit in December, 1964. Rustin said Prime Minister Wilson will be in New York City on the same day that King will be in New York (on December 3, 1964,) permitting a meeting between them. Rustin said he (the Prime Minister) had desired that King go to London earlier but knew that he could not make it in view of his (King's) earlier commitments.

Rustin, in enumerating the commitments of King in London, listed the following:

On Sunday, December 6, 1964, [he] will preach in St. Paul's Cathedral; on Monday, December 7, [he] will attend a mass meeting in one of the large halls in London to raise money to be divided between King's work in the South and the work being done in South Africa; [he] will also meet with the Archbishop of Canterbury on Monday, December 7, and with the Chief Rabbi of Great Britain, and at 4:30 P.M., on the same date, he will meet with Cabinet members and with members of the House of Lords.

Rustin told Young he thought there would be tremendous enthusiasm about King's visit, and said preparations over there were in very capable hands. He said he had completed a first draft on things he thought King should include (in his remarks). . . .

On November 10, 1964, [Bureau Deletion] Rustin, Martin Luther King and Andrew Young were in contact. Rustin took the opportunity to inform them that United Nations Ambassador Stevenson desired to give a reception for King on the night of December 4, 1964. He said the tentative time for the affair is between the hours of 6:00 P.M. and 8:00 P.M. King said this would be suitable to him.

King said that after having learned of his schedule of events in London, that he preferred to curtail some of his activities so that he will not be worn out when he arrives in Oslo, Norway. Rustin advised him to adhere to his commitment with the Archbishop of Canterbury since he met with the Pope a short time ago.

UNITED STATES DEPARTMENT OF JUSTICE

FEDERAL BUREAU OF INVESTIGATION

New York, New York
November 18, 1964

Communist Influence in Racial Matters [Bureau Deletion]

[Bureau Deletion] Bayard Rustin (organizer of the March on Washington) was in contact with Frank Montero of the United States Mission to the United Nations on that date. Montero said, "This thing (reception in honor of Martin Luther King to be given by United Nations Ambassador Adlai Stevenson, December 4, 1964) is really going to be a big deal because they have decided at a staff meeting that they will have Rusk (Secretary of State Dean Rusk) there (at the reception) as well as all the foreign ministers."

Montero said he would make reservations for the King party to fly to London, England, on the night of December 4, 1964, following the reception. He said the reservations would have to be aboard a BOAC (British Overseas Airways Corporation) flight [that] leaves New York at 10:00 P.M. Rustin, at Montero's request, said the following people would be in the party: King, Andrew Young (right-hand man to King), Bernard Lee (personal Secretary to King), Reverend Ralph Abernathy (Treasurer of the Southern Christian Leadership Conference), and Dora (Dora McDonald, secretary at Southern Christian Leadership Conference headquarters, Atlanta, Georgia).

Rustin said that Coretta King, the wife of Martin Luther King, Jr., would fly to London, England, on a different flight because they never travel together on the same plane.

Memorandum

TO: Mr. W. C. Sullivan   DATE: December 17, 1964

FROM: Mr. F. J. Baumgardner

SUBJECT: MARTIN LUTHER KING, JR.
           SECURITY MATTER-COMMUNIST

Special Agent in Charge Rodney, New York Office, telephonically furnished the following information at 8:45 A.M. today (12/17/64).

[Bureau Deletion] Rustin related the following to two acquaintances, Rochele Horowitz and Tom Kahn. Rustin said that when he was in Oslo, Norway, with King, he was called down by the police at 4:30 A.M. one morning because the police had caught a prostitute coming out of the room of A. D. King (brother of Martin). A. D. King attempted to hide when the police came by running into Martin's room. The police accused the prostitute of stealing money, but she claimed she was paid by the occupant of A. D. King's room. Rustin claimed that he talked the police out of arresting the prostitute in order to avoid besmirching King's reputation (presumably Martin's). Rustin also claimed that members of Martin Luther King's entourage had naked girls running up and down the corridors of a hotel where they stayed and were bring [sic] white prostitutes to their rooms. . . . [Bureau Deletion]

Memorandum

TO: Mr. W. C. Sullivan   DATE: August 5, 1965

FROM: Mr. F. J. Baumgardner

RE: MARTIN LUTHER KING, JR.
        SECURITY MATTER-COMMUNIST

[Bureau Deletion] informed of a conversation between Bayard Rustin and Harry Wachtel, advisers of King with subversive backgrounds, concerning King's position on Vietnam. Rustin proposed having King write President Johnson stating that he was happy to have had a chance to talk with the President about Vietnam. Rustin's idea is to have King also write to Ho Chi Minh* and thus King would be instrumental in negotiations concerning Vietnam. According to Rustin's plan, King could later at a public affair, read the letters he had written to the two leaders and thus cast an image of King as a great moral leader. Wachtel said that before he agreed with Rustin's idea, he wanted to have a conference call with King.

*President of Communist North Vietnam.

[Bureau Deletion]

UNITED STATES DEPARTMENT OF JUSTICE

FEDERAL BUREAU OF INVESTIGATION

New York, New York
August 10, 1965

RE: Communist Infiltration of the
    Southern Christian Leadership
    Conference (SCLC)
    Internal Security - C

A confidential source, who has furnished reliable information in the past, advised on August 8, 1965, that Martin Luther King (President of the SCLC) and some of his advisors, specifically Bayard Rustin (Organizer of the March on Washington), Harry Wachtel, and Andrew Young (Executive Director of the SCLC), conferred on that date. Their conference, according to the source, was devoted exclusively to the convention of the SCLC, which opens in Birmingham, Alabama, on August 9, 1965, and run through August 13, 1965.

King, in opening the conference, said the real purpose in conferring with his advisors, was to decide which resolutions would be presented at the convention and which would be most newsworthy. This prompted all to agree that the one dealing with the Vietnam conflict would be most newsworthy, especially since King is being questioned continuously on this issue.

It was agreed that Rustin should be the individual to handle the questions dealing with Vietnam. In order to do this, Rustin will work on a statement dealing with the question, write a memorandum on the question, and prepare an open letter to the President, to the Premier of the Soviet Union, and to the heads of all countries involved in the Vietnam conflict. The letter will be written in the name of King and will state that he writes as a Nobel Peace Prize recipient and as an advocate of nonviolence, and as such, urges negotiations to end the conflict.

Rustin, in declaring his position, said the civil rights movement was not ready to speak to the world on Vietnam, but that King could speak as an individual, thereby getting the impact of the civil rights movement behind him. In that way, Rustin said, the other civil rights leaders could not criticize King for speaking out on the matter.

The letters to the various world leaders should go out on Thursday, Rustin said, but in the case of President Johnson, he should receive a telegram first, followed by the letter. . . .

Memorandum

TO: Mr. Mohr   DATE: September 22, 1965

FROM: J. J. Cooper

SUBJECT: 16TH ANNUAL LAW ENFORCEMENT INSTITUTE
            UNIVERSITY OF MARYLAND
            BAYARD RUSTIN, LECTURER

SAC Tully, Baltimore, telephonically advised [that] he learned on 9/21/65 that Bayard Rustin, a controversial Civil Rights leader with an alleged sex perversion, criminal, and communist background, has been scheduled to lecture at captioned Institute which is held annually on the campuses of the University of Maryland for law enforcement in the District of Columbia, Maryland, and Virginia areas. Rustin is to speak at the College Park campus on October 12, 1965, and will give the same lecture the next evening at the Baltimore campus. He allegedly will discuss "Today's Civil Rights Movement."

Article captioned "Convicted Sex Pervert and Civil Rights Leader to be Police Lecturer" in the 9/16/65 issue of the *Maryland Monitor* reported Rustin's scheduled appearances at the Institute. Article . . . identifies sponsors of the Institute as the University of Maryland, Maryland Law Enforcement Officers, Inc., Metropolitan Police Department, Maryland Municipal League, United States Park Police, Maryland State Police, and police agencies in Maryland and Virginia. Article contains background information regarding Rustin's alleged criminal record (selective service and morals convictions), communist affiliations and civil rights activities. According to the article, Rustin's participation at the

Institute was arranged by [Bureau Deletion], Administrative Office, University of Maryland, who said Rustin was asked to speak to local and state police "to present the other side."

SAC Tully stated the Advisory Committee of the Institute was not consulted regarding the invitation allegedly extended Rustin [Bureau Deletion]. The Committee met in May of this year to discuss the agenda for the 16th Session which is to include lectures on Natural Law vs. Human Law, Sociology in Law Enforcement, Alcoholism, Computer Science, Criminal Abortion, Battered Child Syndromes, and Due Process in Criminal Interrogation. [Bureau Deletion] Training Division, is scheduled to lecture at the Institute on 12/14–15/65 on Due Process in Criminal Interrogation. No mention was made of Rustin at the meeting of the Advisory Committee, and heretofore all speakers arranged for by the University of Maryland have been acceptable to law enforcement.

SAC Tully stated he has already briefly discussed Rustin's possible appearance before the Institute with Colonel Carey Jarman, head of the Maryland State Police. Tully said City of Baltimore Police Department, Maryland State Police, Baltimore County Police and Metropolitan Police Department personnel constitute a substantial percentage of attendees at the Institute, [Bureau Deletion].

[Bureau Deletion] He stated there is limited information in Baltimore files regarding Rustin and he would like to have public source information on the Subject to be made available to those law enforcement executives on a confidential basis as corroboration to the allegations in the newspaper article.

Memorandum

TO: Mr. Mohr   DATE: September 23, 1965

FROM: C.D. DeLoach

SUBJECT: 16TH ANNUAL LAW ENFORCEMENT INSTITUTE
         UNIVERSITY OF MARYLAND
         BAYARD RUSTIN, LECTURER

Reference is made to the memorandum from Mr. Casper to you dated 9/22/65 in captioned matter. . . .

DEVELOPMENT:

[Bureau Deletion] today, ASAC George W. Hall of the Baltimore Office, advised [Bureau Deletion] had stated that Associated Press is carrying a story quoting Dr. Donald Deppe this afternoon as saying he extended the invitation to Rustin and that he had "talked to the FBI concerning Rustin and the Federal organization said it saw no reason why Rustin could not speak at the University."

Mr. Hall said today's afternoon edition of the Baltimore *Evening Sun* carries an article written by Donald Bremner, which quotes Dr. Deppe as stating, "We asked the Justice Department whether he (Rustin) is on any subversive list and they said they saw no reason why we could not invite him." Deppe is quoted further in this story as saying speakers at the University must sign the Maryland Ober Loyalty Pledge (in effect stating "I am not a communist," etc.). According to the quote, Rustin had been sent the Pledge in a letter and Deppe opined that if Rustin refuses to sign, the invitation might be cancelled. The story also says Rustin in a telephone conversation with reporter Bremner denounced the loyalty oath at the school and [said] that he would not sign it. [Bureau Deletion]

UNITED STATES DEPARTMENT OF JUSTICE

FEDERAL BUREAU OF INVESTIGATION

New York, New York
December 19, 1966

Re: Stokely Carmichael

[Bureau Deletion] that Stokely Carmichael and Bayard Rustin debated on December 14, 1966, at Hunter College, New York. The topic of debate was the future of the Negro Movement for Civil Rights.

Carmichael and Rustin both agreed that if the Negro did not get what he thinks he is entitled to, there will be more riots and insurrections.

Carmichael said there are two types of "blocks" against the Negro, mainly the individual block where an individual makes up his own means of obstructing the Negro's advances for civil rights. Second is the institutional block as exemplified by discrimination against the Negroes in schools, ... discrimination in housing by landlords and the power regime [that] hinders the Negro cause.

Carmichael's estimate of the progress of integration was that of merely a "filtering off" of the Negroes [that] are "accepted" into the white society such as "college guys or professional men"—these are the ones who manage to leave the ghettos and enter the white society.

Carmichael then defended "black power" as a means for the Negro to gain self-esteem and prestige through economic means or through whatever means necessary that is available. According to Carmichael, insurrection was also a means to gain civil rights.

Bayard Rustin, during the debate, was more conservative in his approach to civil rights. Rustin explained [that] the Negro must align himself to the power regime and by this way secure his rights through aligning himself with the majority. According to Rustin, the Negro must work with the "white power" structure for mutual gain.

Rustin further stated that unemployment in the ghettos is going up by leaps and bounds caused by automation and union discrimination. Unemployment, states Rustin, is what breeds insurrection and not the direct contact between the white and the Negro. Unemployment and the "ghetto situation" states Rustin, are what breeds [sic] insurrection, it's the feeling of depression.

[Bureau Deletion] advised on December 16, 1966, that a debate between Stokely Carmichael and Bayard Rustin on the topic of "black power" versus the "Freedom Budget" was held at Hunter College on February 14, 1966, at New York City.

Carmichael, when introduced on the stage, began counting the microphones in order to "see which one belonged to the CIA." He then proceeded to tell the audience that the Student NonViolent Coordinating Committee (SNCC), and his concept of "black power," is "to control the community by the inhabitants, control—politically, economically, and socially." He said no one can support a racist country that "enjoys the sweat that comes from our brothers in South Africa, Latin America, and Vietnam." This very same government, states Carmichael, promotes injustice by supporting apartheid in South Africa. Carmichael said the "Freedom Budget" is not a step forward for it "automatically supports the war in Vietnam."

Carmichael accused President (Lyndon B.) Johnson of being hypocritical when he said that Negroes could help themselves by joining their local Democratic parties and yet said Carmichael, "that man did not repudiate the racists of his own party, giving as an example Senator Eastman and Ross Barnett."

Bayard Rustin called upon the people, both black and white to unite around his "Freedom Budget." Rustin further stated "we must not keep the whites guessing or wondering whether they will be welcome into our program." He said as Negroes "we cannot succeed alone for we are only 10 percent of the population." He said the only way it could work is if we act together, both Negro and white. He then challenged Carmichael to show him in "A, B and C" his program for lifting the Negro. Carmichael answered by saying it was his organization, SNCC, that founded the Mississippi Freedom Democratic party. Carmichael then challenged Rustin on why he and A. Philip Randolph (of the Railroad Porters Union) supported President Johnson in the 1964 election.

Rustin replied by saying he supported "President Johnson because he was the lesser of two evils," and though he took a position on President Johnson in 1964, today "it is somewhat modified." Carmichael replied by saying that it is about time for this country to say we do not vote for evil men, that "this is a racist society and the country is racist from the top to the bottom, from left to right."

Later on in his speech, Carmichael said that the political system in this country is outdated and that we need new forms. He stated "if you can't control the politics, you can't control the economy." He further stated that President Johnson must stop the civil rights movement because it is a threat to this great society. . . .

UNITED STATES DEPARTMENT OF JUSTICE

FEDERAL BUREAU OF INVESTIGATION

New York, New York
July 24, 1968

Southern Christian Leadership
Conference (SCLC)
Racial Matters

[A confidential] source learned on July 21, 1968, that on that date Bayard Rustin contacted Stanley Levison. . . . Rustin, confidentially, told Levison that [Ralph] Abernathy had recently contacted him on two occasions on one of which he asked Rustin to intercede with Norman Cousins (Editor of the *Saturday Review*) to get an invitation for Mrs. Abernathy to an important conference of women which Cousins was putting on in New York City on July 23, 1968. Rustin stated that

Abernathy noted that he, Rustin, was a friend of Cousins and that Mrs. Abernathy, the first lady of civil rights, must be present, but has not received an invitation. Rustin told Levison that he did contact Cousins and arranged the invitation for Abernathy's wife.

Levison felt that this placed Mrs. Abernathy in an awkward position because Coretta King is the featured speaker.

According to the source, Rustin alluded to the recent Poor People's Campaign sponsored by the SCLC and the mass march on Washington, D.C. on June 19, 1968, in support of the campaign. Rustin told Levison that he would like to tell Levison the inside story of what happened during the brief period he was head of the mass march and the real reason he left this post. Rustin did state that certain persons, whom he did not name, tried to set up a committee in which they once used the march on Washington as a means of dropping Abernathy and putting Coretta King in his place. He added that they even had the labor leaders in Memphis involved in it and that they threatened to attack him if he did not go along. Rustin said this was going to be done over the heads of the SCLC Board and that one of the most important people involved was Andy (Young, SCLC Executive Vice-President). Rustin explained that he obtained this from someone he described as very important but whom he did not name. . . .

Levison . . . added that one of the key problems is that Abernathy, the press, and others keep talking about how loyal the staff is to Abernathy when, in fact, they are disloyal. He said only Martin Luther King would have had the prestige to tell the SCLC staff that Rustin was going to speak whether they liked it or not. . . .

Rustin mentioned that SCLC was designed as an extension of the most dynamic personality of the century but, if the SCLC is to continue as an effective organization, it has to be totally restructured. He said that without a strong, disciplined staff it will fall apart. . . .

According to the source, Levison and Rustin discussed SCLC personalities who could take over the SCLC with Levison stating there is no one other than Coretta King and that she will not take it over.

Rustin mentioned that everywhere he goes he is asked by all classes of Negroes why he does not try to influence Coretta King to take over the SCLC and make something of it. Levison added that this includes the white middle class also. . . .

Later the same date, the source learned that Levison told Coretta King of his contact by Rustin. . . . He warned that, as long as Abernathy has the approach that his wife is the first lady of civil rights, Coretta has a problem with him because Coretta is the first lady of civil rights, not Abernathy's wife. He related that Rustin mentioned that everyone he comes in contact with, from the lowest Negro to the highest, raises the question why Coretta King does not take over [the SCLC]. He said that, therefore, to pit his wife against Coretta when people are pitting Coretta against him is an absurdity. . . .

Memorandum

TO: Mr. DeLoach   DATE: December 12, 1968

FROM: A. Rosen

SUBJECT: BAYARD RUSTIN
           NAME CHECK MATTER

PURPOSE:

To advise that a name check request has been received from the Civil Service Commission (CSC) regarding Rustin, who is being considered as a consultant for the Division of Research and Publication, National Foundation on the Arts and the Humanities (NFAH) and to recommend reports containing background information regarding Rustin be disseminated to CSC.

BACKGROUND:

The CSC has submitted to the Bureau a name check request for Bayard Rustin, who is being considered for employment as a consultant in the Research and Publication Division of the National Foundation on the Arts and the Humanities. The name check request indicates Rustin would be paid at a rate of $50 per day. The name check request indicates Rustin currently resides at 340 West 28th Street, New York City, and that he was born March 17, 1910. He is currently employed as Executive Director, A. Philip Randolph Institute; [he was the] organizer of the 1963 March on Washington; former Special Assistant to Dr. Martin Luther King, Jr.; and was the First Field-Secretary for Congress of Racial Equality.

Considerable investigation has been conducted concerning Rustin and our files indicate that Rustin has admitted he joined the Young Communist League in 1936 and claims he broke with this organization in June,

1941. Rustin has been convicted for sodomy and violation of the Selective Service Act.

[Bureau Deletion]

Memorandum

TO: Director, FBI   DATE: March 4, 1969

FROM: SAC, MIAMI

SUBJECT: BLACK NATIONALIST MOVEMENT RM
          (ANTI-SEMITISM)

Enclosed for the Bureau ... [is] a blind memorandum dated and captioned as above.

Bayard Rustin, well-known Negro civil rights activist and Executive Director of the A. Phillip Randolph Institute, writing in the February 8, 1969 issue of the *Amsterdam News,* a Negro newspaper published in New York City (NYC), warns against the continuance of hostility between Negro and Jew and quotes a previous statement he made on the subject in which he said it would be a great tragedy if either group used prejudice against the other. . . .

The February 7, 1969, edition of the *Miami Times,* a Miami, Florida, weekly newspaper published mainly for Miami Negro communities, contained an editorial by Bayard Rustin captioned, "On Blacks and Jews". . . .

Bayard Rustin Speaks
ON BLACKS AND JEWS:
By Bayard Rustin

Two years ago, in response to a growing trend of hostility between Negroes and Jews, I wrote that "it would be one of the great tragedies of Negro and Jewish experiences in a hostile civilization if the time should come when either group begins using against each other the same weapon (of prejudice) [that] the white majorities of the West have used for centuries to crush and deny both of them their sense of humanity." Events have made these words even more relevant today. Jewish leaders have spoken to the Jewish conscience about these developments, and it is with a sense of urgency that Negro leaders must now address their own communities.

I am sure I need not explain to Negroes why anti-Semitism, as a form of prejudice, is morally wrong. Certainly Negroes have seen as clearly as any people in history how prejudice can brutalize and oppress. They have seen how bigots can stereotype a race and deny the dignity of a people because they have neither the courage to recognize that dignity nor the wisdom to understand it. And certainly Negroes must know that if an atmosphere of vilification and condemnation is permitted to develop, that they themselves will be its chief victims. It is in this sense that the anti-Semitism of some Negroes is not only morally wrong but strategically suicidal.

I have written before that anti-Semitism is an outgrowth of frustration, that because Negroes have been obstructed in their fight for full equality, there have been some who in their despair have attacked those very people who have been the closest allies of the Negro struggle— namely, the Jews. To understand this, however, is not to condone it. Nor is it to ignore the politically disastrous effect that anti-Semitism will have on Negroes, for if it is permitted to gain a foothold, it will be the first step in the disintegration of the liberal Catholic-Jewish Protestant coalition on which Negroes have had to depend for the passage of civil rights legislation and other measures for social and economic justice.

Up to now the distinguishing—and most distinguished—feature of the Negro struggle for social equally has been its moral authority. On the basis of this authority we have been able to appeal in our struggle to the great American documents such as the Declaration of Independence and the Constitution as the moral and legal foundation of our demands. The emergence of anti-Semitism not only undermines the basis of this appeal, but it makes a travesty of a movement that has been the conscience of this nation.

I appeal to the Jewish community not to permit the anti-Semitism of a small, unrepresentative minority in the black community to drive them out of the struggle for social justice and democracy. And I emphasize that this is in their interest for if the overall struggle for democracy breaks down, then Jews—a minority themselves, like Negroes—will inevitably suffer. The central problem, as some Jewish leaders have pointed out, is that racism is unavoidable when there is no democratically viable alternative for dealing with social and economic injustice.

And I appeal to the Negro community, that just as we call on Jews to continue their dedication to democracy and social equity, that we pledge not to ignore or excuse any manifestation of anti-Semitism in the black community and to combat it vigorously wherever it appears. I urge this not for the sake of Jews or Negroes, but for the sake of the preservation of the democratic values which Jews and Negroes must share—values we must all share in the ultimate hope of a liberated mankind.

Memorandum

TO: Mr. Mohr   DATE: November 21, 1969

FROM: Mr. N.P. Callaham

SUBJECT: BAYARD RUSTIN

Jay Howe, Clerk of our House Appropriation Subcommittee, telephonically contacted the writer this afternoon and stated that Chairman Rodney had just learned of Rustin's being appointed to the Board of Trustees at Notre Dame University and was most concerned at this development. Howe stated [that] the Chairman had requested that he call the Bureau to see if it would be possible to get any details concerning the arrest of Rustin on a sodomy charge, which the Director had mentioned at a previous hearing during his appropriations testimony. Howe indicated he felt the Chairman wanted to take this matter up with some clergy friends of his to see what . . . could be done about removing Rustin from his recently appointed post.

Attached is a copy of a reprint from the Director's 1967 appropriation testimony dealing with Bayard Rustin, which was given on the record. In addition, there is attached a thumbnail sketch of Rustin, which was brought up to date on 11/5/69 by the Domestic Intelligence Division, which sets forth the specifics with regard to Rustin's conviction in California in 1953 on a charge of sex perversion (sodomy). Also attached for information is a copy of the FBI criminal record of Rustin.

The thumbnail sketch indicates that on the occasion of Rustin's arrest in California on the sex charge he admitted a previous arrest on the same charge in New York City in 1946. Attempts were made to verify Rustin's arrest in New York City in 1946 without success.

RECOMMENDATION:

It is recommended that the attached copy of the excerpts from the Director's 1967 appropriation testimony and the thumbnail sketch on plain bond unwatermarked paper be furnished to Rodney and that he be given the identification arrest record. . . .

Excerpt from the Director's 1967 appropriations testimony reads as follows:

Bayard Rustin

At the University of Maryland last year, at a law enforcement institute held for police officers of Maryland, Virginia, and Washington, D.C., the university invited Bayard Rustin to be one of the speakers. Bayard Rustin was convicted for [sic] sodomy, a violation of the Selective Service Act and was an admitted member of the Young Communist League. Such a selection was not to the credit of the university.

Mr. Rooney: I intended to ask you about him. Was he convicted on his own plea of guilty to the crime of sodomy?

Mr. Hoover: He was. He admitted sodomy. He was apprehended in Pasadena, California.

If they wanted a man to speak on civil rights they could have invited Roy Wilkins of the NAACP, who is a reputable man, or some other responsible racial leader. But to pick out a man who has such a bad background was wrong.

(Discussion off the record).

November 20, 1975
Bayard Rustin
340 West 28th Street
New York, New York 10001

Federal Bureau of Investigation
Washington, D.C.
Federal Bureau of Investigation
201 East 69 Street
New York, New York

Gentlemen:

It has come to my attention that the Federal Bureau of Investigation has maintained an extensive dossier on my political and private life during the past thirty years.

I request, under the freedom of information act, that the Federal Bureau of Investigation make available to me all records maintained by your agency with respect to me.

This request is made upon you pursuant to Title 5 United States Code, S.552 et seq.

Thank you for you prompt attention herein.

Sincerely yours,

Bayard Rustin

Certified Mail.

Return Receipt Request

November 25, 1975
Federal Bureau of Investigation
201 East 69th Street
New York, New York 10021

Mr. Bayard Rustin
340 West 28th Street
New York, New York 10001

Dear Mr. Rustin:

This is in reply to your letter of November 20, 1975, which makes request for records identifiable with you under the Freedom of Information Act. Your letter was addressed to both the Washington, D.C., and New York Offices of the Federal Bureau of Investigation (FBI).

In the event you are not aware, the Privacy Act of 1974, Title 5, United States Code, Section 552a, became effective on September 27, 1975. Pursuant to a ruling by the United States Department of Justice, the Privacy Act is now the primary method by which the Federal Bureau of Investigation is processing requests from individuals, seeking access to United States Government records identifiable with the requester. I believe this statute would apply to your request.

On Wednesday, August 27, 1975, regulations under the Privacy Act applying to requests for access to the Federal Bureau of Investigation Central Records System were published in the Federal Register, at page 38769. For your information, I am quoting these regulations, as follows:

"*Record Access Procedures:* A request for access to a record from the system shall be made in writing with the envelope and the letter clearly marked 'Privacy Access Request.' Include in the request your full name, complete address, date of birth, place of birth, notarized signature, and other identifying data you may wish to furnish to assist in making a proper search of our records. Also include the general subject matter of the document or its file number. The requester will also provide a return address for transmitting the information. Access requests will be directed to the Director, Federal Bureau of Investigation, Washington, D.C. 20535.''

Based on the above quoted regulations, I regret that the Federal Bureau of Investigation will be unable to begin processing your request until it is resubmitted in complete form. If you desire to resubmit your letter request, please prepare a new letter addressed to the Director, Federal Bureau of Investigation, Washington, D.C. 20535. Please designate your letter as a ''Privacy Access Request'' and include in your letter your date of birth, place of birth, and a notarized signature. This necessary information to establish your identity was not included in your letter of November 20, 1975.

At the present time, I will advise [the] Federal Bureau of Investigation Headquarters, Washington, D.C., of your letter of November 20, 1975, and of this reply.

Very truly yours,

J. Wallace La Prade
Assistant Director in Charge

ROY WILKINS

(1901–1981)

Roy Wilkins was one of the few civil rights leaders to have a bona fide relationship with the FBI and J. Edgar Hoover. Because Wilkins shared with Hoover an obsession with communism and a hatred for Martin Luther King, Jr., Hoover was able to use this NAACP leader in his campaign to damage if not destroy the larger movement to which both Wilkins and King belonged and gave so much. Most often, this effort consisted of Hoover passing on Wilkins's derogatory remarks about King to executive branch officials. Hoover's efforts to promote factionalism among black leadership and then report that factionalism to high-ranking government officials clearly affected the course and nature of the civil rights movement. To measure that effect, however, is no easy task. The bureau's files speak for themselves only for what they tell us about Hoover's priorities; these files do not clearly detail the priorities of Roy Wilkins.

Wilkins understood factionalism early on. Born in St. Louis, Missouri, on August 30, 1901, and reared in the St. Paul, Minnesota, home of an aunt and uncle, he edited the weekly *Kansas City Call* after graduating from the University of Minnesota. Walter White brought him to the NAACP's national office in New York in 1931 as assistant executive secretary, with the specific mission of helping to control the bothersome editor of *The Crisis,* W. E. B. Du Bois. Wilkins started fast, organizing a telegram protest campaign after Will Rogers used the word "nigger" in his premier NBC radio broadcast. (Bowing to the pressure, Rogers switched to the slightly more acceptable word "darky.") In 1934, after a Du Bois editorial that radically contradicted the NAACP's integrationist message, Wilkins was named editor of *The Crisis.* Thereafter, he wrote and spoke widely, serving as a consultant to the War Department and the American delegation at the founding conference of the United Nations in San Francisco. He also chaired the National Emergency Civil Rights Mobilization. When Walter White died in 1955, Wilkins was unanimously appointed NAACP executive secretary (executive director after 1965). In 1977, he retired.

Wilkins solidified his stature in the 1960s as a voice of moderation. He never quite embraced direct-action protest; he frequently criticized the tactics and strategies of other civil rights leaders and groups (particularly the students active in the movement and the SCLC gang of Baptist preachers); he condemned the advocacy of violence and all forms of black power and black nationalism; he supported the use of United States troops both to quell the decade's major riots and to fight the civil war in Vietnam. Both Hoover's FBI and the White House considered him "a responsible Negro leader," and it was a reflection of his status that President Lyndon B. Johnson was always calling on the telephone or sending a summons for an oval office conclave. In person, LBJ would slide his chair so close that his knees rubbed against Wilkins's. On the phone, Wilkins recalled, the President once "dropped whatever issue that it was that preoccupied him, practically in mid-sentence, and said, 'I'm always calling you. Why don't you call *me* more often?' "

Wilkins died on August 4, 1981, shortly after finishing his autobiography, *Standing Fast* (1982), which includes fascinating and generally candid comments about the men of power he rubbed knees with from Franklin D. Roosevelt to Richard M. Nixon. But there is little candor on the subject of the substantive fund-raising rivalries and assorted petty jealousies that lay at the root of his dislike of Martin Luther King, Jr. And there is no candor whatsoever on the subject of the FBI. If he met and spoke with bureau executives even more frequently than oval office occupants and staff, one gets no sense of this from his memoir. His biographer will be well advised to make extensive (and careful) use of the bureau's files as they comprise the only extant record of that relationship.

Memorandum

TO: Mr. Mohr   DATE: February 25, 1960

FROM: C. D. DeLoach

SUBJECT: ROY WILKINS, EXECUTIVE SECRETARY
          NATIONAL ASSOCIATION FOR THE ADVANCE-
          MENT OF COLORED PEOPLE (NAACP)
          20 WEST 40TH STREET
          NEW YORK 18, NEW YORK

Pursuant to instructions, I met with Mr. Wilkins 2–24–60. He desired
to express his appreciation to the FBI for the continuing good cooperation between the Bureau and the National Association for the Advancement of Colored People (NAACP). He asked that his comments be
conveyed to the Director and was assured that they would be
immediately.

Mr. Wilkins conceded there were a number of communists in the
NAACP. He stated he could not prove this and actually was unaware
of their identity. He strongly emphasized that communists were not in
control of any of their chapters and would be booted out if enough
proof could be obtained on them. He pointed out that the Los Angeles
NAACP branch was at present composed of "extremists" and that he
feared the activities of this group very much. He stated that administrative steps were being taken to rid the Los Angeles branch of this group
of "extremists" and he sincerely hoped that within the next several
years conditions would improve. He advised [that] he did not want to
mention any names at this time but would keep in close touch with us
in the event this group became too strong in their demonstrations.

I took the liberty of expressing the Director's appreciation to Mr.
Wilkins for his support of the FBI and the fact that he had mentioned
us very favorably on a number of occasions in his speeches. I told him
the Director deeply appreciated the very favorable resolution passed by
the NAACP at its last convention in New York. Mr. Wilkins stated he
and Irving Ferman had engineered this matter.

I told Mr. Wilkins that as he well knew considerable pressure had
been put on the FBI by minority groups to make available to the public
FBI reports in the Mack Charles Parker case. He was told that the FBI
had withstood all types of disadvantages in order to solve this case
against great odds. However, not withstanding this fact, we have never

received adequate credit for the great work done. I told Mr. Wilkins that actually we had received a number of letters containing insults to our actions in this case and particularly as to why our reports were not made available to the public. I explained in some detail why it would be wrong under our democratic system of government to expose these reports.

Mr. Wilkins indicated that he was well aware of the above-mentioned problem. He stated he would take every step to remedy this situation and intended seeing to it that the FBI go the credit it deserved in the Mack Charles Parker Case.

Wilkins was most cordial throughout and indicated he would keep in touch with us from time to time.

ACTION:
For information.

While Roy Wilkins was never the subject of an official investigation conducted by the Bureau, references to him appear throughout the FBI files. These references were at various times culled and placed in the Wilkins file as a record of his activities. A sampling of such references follows:

. . . Roy Wilkins gave an address on "The Negro and Democracy" at the open forum held in Portland, Ore. on 11–1–42. Wilkins speech dealt with the Negro minority in the U.S. emphasizing the Negro situation in wartime. During a question period Wilkins stated that Negroes did not want to violate any given rights by securing labor legislation but only wanted an even break.

. . . The *Worker* on 3–28–43 carried an article on page 1, section 1, entitled: "Harlem Angry at Press Smear, Sees Tie-up with Southern Reaction," which charged that a "smear" campaign was being directed towards Negroes in Harlem by the Metropolitan press. According to the article Roy Wilkins, Assistant National Secretary of the NAACP, had joined with Ben Richardson, Benjamin Davis, and other prominent Negro leaders in proposing that a concerted campaign against the press be organized by civic and labor organizations throughout the city. The article quoted Wilkins as stating that the press campaign against Negroes in Harlem was "linked to the action against labor and post war plans. It is part of the movement to see that the little people don't get too uppity and the Negro people are part of the little people." Wilkins also pointed out that the press stories about Harlem were picked up throughout the country especially in the South where they were used as a weapon against the movement for Negro rights.

... [Bureau Deletion] advised that Roy Wilkins was the principal speaker on 8–11–44 at the Fifth Annual Meeting of the South Carolina conference of the NAACP held June 11, 12, 1944 at Sumter, S.C. Wilkins reviewed the history of the Negro, relating how the Negro has always been disregarded as a personality both physically and politically. He stated the day of persecution for the Negro was terminating. He extolled the efforts of the NAACP on behalf of the Negro and criticized political figures of the State of South Carolina for their dogmas on white supremacy. He stressed the fact that the Negro in South Carolina was still practically a slave to the white man. Wilkins emphasized the fact that the Negro did not desire to acquire his lawful rights through revolution but by lawful court procedure.

... During the week of Feb. 25 to March 3, 1945, the Negro press reported that Roy Wilkins, Assistant Secretary of the NAACP, spoke before members of the Welfare Victory Committee of Welfare Center 40, 270 Elton Ave., Bronx, N.Y., in celebration of Negro History Week (date not given). Wilkins denounced the treatment of American Negro soldiers in the South and compared their position with the German and Italian prisoners of war, who he stated received better treatment than the Negro soldiers.

An editorial in the July 1946 issue of *The Crisis,* the Negro publication edited by Roy Wilkins, contained the following statement: "Our guess is that the Klan will grow for a brief time and die. There will be more condemnation and prosecution than there was after the last war, but the doom of the Klan lies in the fact that the Negro, organized labor, and the world are much more than 25 years ahead of 1920. The Klan is too stupid and too late to accomplish its announced purpose."

... According to press reports of the 39th Annual Conference of the NAACP held in Kansas City, Mo., June 22–27, 1948, Roy Wilkins made the following statement in his keynote speech: "Anyone who speaks up for his rights or who does not follow the beaten path is likely to be called a communist." Wilkins urged the delegates not to be intimidated by the cry of communism. He further stated that Negroes do not want a totalitarian state in America, either of the right or the left; they wanted democracy and would speak and work for it with every weapon in their command.

... The *Daily Worker* of 1–24–49 carried on page 7, Abner W. Berry's column, "As We See It" under the subtitle, "NAACP Leaders Praise Jersey Justice." The leadership of the NAACP was condemned by Berry for its action in opposing cooperation with the Civil Rights Congress and other organizations [that] were active in defending the "Trenton Six" murder case. The article quoted a telegram sent by Roy Wilkins, Acting NAACP Secretary, from the National Office to the Trenton branch NAACP. Wilkins's wire stated [that] the CRC was not an organization with which the NAACP cooperated and the Trenton branch was instructed not to cooperate or to participate in a rally in Trenton, N.J. on Jan. 28, which was to [be] addressed by Paul Robeson.

The *Greenwich Times,* Greenwich, Conn., on 12–8–50, carried an article entitled: "NAACP Told Negro Soldiers in Korea Being Victimized." The article was an account of the address made by Roy Wilkins, Administrator for the NAACP, on 12–7–50 at the Eighth Anniversary Dinner of the Greenwich branch of the NAACP. In his address, Wilkins stated that the Negro soldier in Korea was being discriminated against and victimized. Wilkins spoke of the problem of race relations as the "number-one problem before our country and the western world." He pointed out [that] the people of India, Asia, and Africa wanted to know how Democracy worked in regard to the treatment of Negroes in the U.S. as compared to the Soviet Union. He also discussed race discrimination in education, transportation, and the armed services and attacked Republican opposition to FEPC.

. . . [Bureau Deletion] The city edition of the *NY Times,* 1/1/60, carried an article captioned "Rights in Racial Extremism Worries Harlem Leaders." The article stated that Roy Wilkins had stated that the Temple of Islam was no better in its racial creed than the Ku Klux Klan. Wilkins had also stated "We also feel that any cult which seeks to make a minority believe that it can solve its problems through racial hatred is misleading the people and spreading destruction."

On 11/7/60, [Bureau Deletion] advised that according to the records of the [Bureau Deletion], the following African nationalist groups were active in New York City: United African Nationalist Movement; United Sons and Daughters of Africa; The Order of Dumballah Hwedo; African Nationalist Pioneer Movement; International Committee in Defense of Africa. These groups had certain beliefs in common, and they referred to the NAACP as a "black body with a white head." Men like Roy Wilkins were called "tools of the white man" and were referred to as "Uncle Toms."

. . . The *New York Amsterdam News* a New York weekly newspaper, of 1/20/62, reported that the Leadership Conference on Civil Rights would stage a mass mobilization of civil rights leaders throughout the country to Washington, D.C., in early March, 1962, to seek bipartisan support behind certain civil rights bills. Roy Wilkins, Chairman of the Leadership group and Executive Secretary of the NAACP, stated, according to this article, that this year's mobilization would not seek to have a large mass of people but to have a wide cross section of representation from all parts of the country, "to show that we don't agree with the Kennedy Administration's civil rights position." Wilkins said the Leaders Conference represented sixty national organizations.

[Bureau Deletion] advised that she attended the press conference conducted by James H. Meredith in Memphis on 11/10/62, in the office of A. W. Willis, Jr., a Memphis Negro attorney. She stated that when someone from the "Commercial Appeal" asked Meredith if he had written the story about himself in the recent issue of the *Saturday Evening Post,* he evaded an answer at first but finally said he had written it.

[Bureau Deletion] pointed out that it was common hearsay [sic] knowledge that Roy Wilkins, National Secretary of the NAACP, wrote the story.

The *Worker* of 12/2/62 contained an article entitled "Negro Leaders Back Africa's Liberty Fight," which reported that almost 100 of the nation's Negro leaders, meeting in Harriman, N.Y., over the weekend, adopted a program of action to aid the newly independent African states. This meeting, which was called American Negro Leadership Conference on Africa, was called by six Negro leaders including Roy Wilkins, executive secretary, and president [of the] Negro American Labor Council.

The program embodied seven resolutions dealing with South Africa, South West Africa, Portuguese Africa, the Central African Federation, the Congo, and Kenya and the issues of equal participation of Negro Americans in U.S. programs in Africa.

On 12/17/62 the Washington Capital News Service reported that a group of Negro leaders, including Roy Wilkins, and Martin Luther King, Jr., were scheduled to confer with President Kennedy at the White House, on 12/17/63, to urge a greater role for Negroes in U.S. African policies. This group was critical of the State Department for not placing more Negroes in the Foreign Diplomatic Service, particularly in the critical areas of Africa.

. . . On 5/10/63 the Savannah Office furnished information relative to a conference of the Southern Police Institute, University of Louisville, Ky. (Date not given)

[Bureau Deletion] advised that he thought the conference was helpful and said the Chiefs of Police were divided into groups and each group had the opportunity to question NAACP and CORE officials as to their respective problems. It was [Bureau Deletion] impression that Roy Wilkins, NAACP official, was well received, but the CORE official, James Farmer, made no friends with the group because he advocated violence, if necessary, on the part of his group to achieve their objectives.

[Bureau Deletion] advised that the overall impression he gained at the conference was to remind the Police Chiefs of their oath taken to uphold the dignity of the law and protect minority groups.

... [Bureau Deletion] advised that an NAACP demonstration would possibly take place in Biloxi, Miss., during the weekend of June 8 and 9, 1963, to protest segregation of certain beaches and swimming facilities in the Biloxi area. [Bureau Deletion] was unable to furnish any details regarding the number of individuals who might participate in this demonstration.

The radio broadcast of Drew Pearson on Sunday evening, 6/30/63, was received through a NYC station at 6:00 P.M. Pearson stated that Roy Wilkins (Executive Secretary of the NAACP) had told Justice Department officials that his headquarters gets an average of one telephone call every five minutes from Negroes throughout the country who want instructions on how to organize demonstrations.

... The 7/16/63 issue of the *New York Journal—American* contains an article entitled "The Negro View: 'Now or Never'—Leadership 'Disunity' Grows Graver." This article was the third in a series by Negro Author Louis E. Lomax, which disclosed the increasing friction among Roy Wilkins, James Farmer, and Martin Luther King, leader of the NAACP, CORE, and SCLC, respectively. Who would get the credit for holding mass demonstrations and to whom well-wishers should send their money, were at the root of the "current" crisis. In a speech in Virginia, Wilkins claimed the NAACP was doing all the work and footing the bills while other organizations including CORE and King, were making all the noise and grabbing the headlines. He advised the people not to send money to the [sic] CORE and Rev. King but to the NAACP.

FEDERAL BUREAU OF INVESTIGATION

July 25, 1963

Granville W. Reed, Program Assistant, Chicago Branch, National Association for the Advancement of Colored People (NAACP), 431 South Dearborn Street, made available a prestamped postcard. This card was addressed to the "National Association for the Advancement of Colored People, 431 S. Dearborn, Chicago, Illinois." The postmark was cut off but appeared to have been mailed on July 15, 1963. This card was handwritten in blue ink and stated "ATTENTION! All NAACP members! If your head, Roy Wilkins, wants to live beyond Sat. 7/20 he had better leave the country. I warn you I make no empty threats!" This card was signed "K.P."

This card also contained additional printing [that] read "RECEIVED JULY 16 1963." Reed stated that this stamp was placed on the card when it was received in the mail.

Reed stated that this card was received in the regular morning mail delivery this date. He stated that several people in the office have handled the card and he also had copies of the card made.

Reed could furnish no suspects. He stated that his office has not received any crank letters to his knowledge and he only recalls that approximately one month ago, Reverend Carl A. Fugua, the Executive Secretary, received a package [that] contained a dummy bomb. This matter was turned over to the local police. He stated that he also recalls that a number of months ago his office received a crank telephone call but does not recall the contents of this call.

Reed stated that he has notified [Bureau Deletion] about this matter. He was advised that he should notify them if he felt that protection was needed.

On July 17, 1963, [Bureau Deletion] advised SA [Bureau Deletion] that he had checked his records and found the following persons with the initials of K.P.

[Bureau Deletion] On July 17, 1963, [Bureau Deletion] telephonically advised that he had been assigned the case involving the postcard received by the NAACP. He stated that he would contact the Chicago Office of the FBI should he develop any information concerning this card.

By report dated July 19, 1963, the FBI Laboratory advised that the postal card was searched in the Anonymous Letter File with negative results. Also no indented writing was found.

By report dated July 22, 1963, the Latent Fingerprint Section of the Identification Division advised that an examination of the postal card disclosed eight latent fingerprints of value.

Roy Wilkins, Executive Secretary of the National Association for the Advancement of Colored People (NAACP), was interviewed at his office, 20 West 40th Street.

He said he had previously been informed by SA [Bureau Deletion] that a postcard had been received at the office of the NAACP at Chicago, Illinois, which threatened his life. He had in his possession a facsimile of this postal card which had been sent to him by his Chicago office.

He said he had no suspects and did not know who might use the initials K.P.

He was informed that protection could not be afforded him by the Federal Bureau of Investigation (FBI). He was told that the nature and contents of the threat had been brought to the attention of the New York City Police Department and that if he desired protection, he should contact that department. He had not contacted the New York City Police Department as of the time of the interview.

Mr. Wilkins said he did not inform his wife of the receipt of the threat as he did not want to unduly alarm her. He said his wife is employed on the staff of the Commissioner of Welfare, City of New York. She is director of Community Relations and is employed in the offices of New York City Department of Welfare, 250 Church Street, on the 14th floor. The telephone number is DI 4-8700, extension 615.

Mr. Wilkins pointed out [that] he had attended a convention of the NAACP in Chicago, and he had left Chicago on July 7, 1963, traveling to Charleston, South Carolina. He had stayed in Charleston, South Carolina, a short time and then traveled by train to New York, arriving at noon, July 8, 1963.

TELETYPE

TO: DIRECTOR   DATE: DECEMBER 5, 1963

FROM: SAC NEW ORLEANS

UNKNOWN SUBJECT

THREATS AGAINST ROY WILKINS, EXECUTIVE SECRETARY, NAACP.

ERNEST NATHAN MORIAL, PRESIDENT NEW ORLEANS CHAPTER, NAACP

TELEPHONICALLY INFORMED THIS DATE ROY WILKINS IS SCHEDULED TO SPEAK AT MUNICIPAL AUDITORIUM, NEW ORLEANS, EIGHT PM DECEMBER FIVE, NEXT. MEETING BEING SPONSORED BY NEW ORLEANS CHAPTER OF THE NAACP.

MORIAL RELATED THAT MRS. MARCELLA JACKSON, SECRE-

TARY NEW ORLEANS CHAPTER, OF NAACP, HAS INFORMED
HIM, MORIAL, OVER THE PAST SEVERAL DAYS SHE HAS RE-
CEIVED TWO OR THREE LOCAL TELEPHONE CALLS, WHICH
SHE BELIEVED [sic] HAVE BEEN MADE BY THE SAME ANONY-
MOUS CALLER TO THE EFFECT THAT WE DO NOT NEED ROY
WILKINS HERE AND HE IS GOING BACK HOME LIKE JACK
KENNEDY. MORIAL STATED HE IS ATTEMPTING TO CONTACT
[BD] CONCERNING THESE CALLS, HOWEVER, HE IS NOT PLAN-
NING TO ASK HIM FOR ANY POLICE PROTECTION FOR WIL-
KINS HE WILL LEAVE SUCH A DECISION UP [BD].

MORIAL STATED WILKINS ITINERARY AS KNOWN TO HIM
AS FOLLOWS—ARRIVING NEW ORLEANS EVENING DECEM-
BER FOUR INSTANT, VIA COMMERCIAL AIRLINES FROM NEW
YORK VIA STOP OFF AT WASHINGTON D.C. IDENTITY OF AIR-
LINES OR TIME OF ARRIVAL NEW ORLEANS NOT KNOWN.
WILL NOT BE NET [sic] AT AIRPORT.

STOPPING AT HILTON INN, KENNER, LOUISIANA, WHERE
WILL REMAIN THROUGH EARLY MORNING DECEMBER SIX,
NEXT, AT WHICH TIME WILL DEPART COMMERCIAL AIRLINES
FOR LOS ANGELES, CALIFORNIA, DURING DAY AND EVENING
OF DECEMBER FIVE, NEXT. MORIAL STATED HE WOULD BE
WITH WILKINS WHO IS SCHEDULED TO MAKE SPEECHES AT
XAVIER UNIVERSITY, TEN AM, DILLARD UNIVERSITY TWO
PM, AND TULANE UNIVERSITY THREE PM. AT ONE PM HAS A
NEWS CONFERENCE WITH PRESS AT CLAVER BUILDING IN
CONFERENCE ROOM OF BUILDING. ALL NEW ORLEANS.

[BD] HAS ADVISED THAT AT APPROXIMATELY TEN THIRTY
AM ON DECEMBER THREE, LAST, SHE RECEIVED AN ANONY-
MOUS LOCAL TELEPHONE CALL FROM A MALE WHO SHE
CONSIDERED BY HIS VOICE TO BE A MATURE MALE. CALLER
ASKED IF HE WAS TALKING TO THE NAACP. WHEN ADVISED
THAT IT WAS, THE PERSON SAID, "GO HOME ROY, WE DON'T
NEED YOU DOWN HERE, YOU WILL GO HOME LIKE JACK
KENNEDY." THIS SAME PERSON CALLED AGAIN AT ABOUT
TWO PM. HE ASKED THE SAME QUESTION, IF HE WAS SPEAK-
ING TO THE NAACP AND WHEN TOLD HE WAS, REPEATED EX-
ACTLY THE SAME STATEMENT AS HE HAD DURING THE
MORNING AND THEN HUNG UP. [BD] SAID THIS SAME PER-
SON CALLED AGAIN AROUND TEN FIFTEEN AM, DECEMBER
FOUR INSTANT AND WENT THROUGH THE IDENTICAL ROU-
TINE HE HAD DONE TWICE THE PREVIOUS DAY.[BD]

Memorandum

TO: Mr. Mohr   DATE: November 27, 1964

FROM: C. D. DeLoach

SUBJECT: ROY WILKINS, EXECUTIVE SECRETARY
NATIONAL ASSOCIATION FOR THE ADVANCE-
MENT OF COLORED PEOPLE (NAACP)
APPOINTMENT 11/27/64, FBI HEADQUARTERS
WASHINGTON, D. C.

Roy Wilkins, Executive Secretary for the NAACP called me from New York at 12:55 P.M. today. He stated that he had to fly down to Washington to see me immediately. He asked if I had any available time. He apologized for attempting to arrange an appointment on [what] he termed a "holiday weekend." I told him the "holiday weekend" made no difference to us and that despite his unwarranted statements concerning the Director and the Bureau I would sit down and talk to him.

Wilkins arrived at 4:00 P.M. He stated that he was greatly concerned. He made reference to the Director's Loyola speech last Tuesday, 11/24/64, in which the Director had made reference to "sexual degenerates" in pressure groups. Wilkins stated he personally knew about whom the Director was talking, although many other Negroes did not know. [Bureau Deletion]

Wilkins stressed the fact that he was not seeing me as an emissary but stated he had some influence on King but not much. He added that there were others within his movement who had greater influence and that perhaps together some pressure could be brought on King. Wilkins then added that he hoped that the FBI would not expose King before something could be done.

I interrupted Wilkins at this point. I told him that the Director, of course, did not have in mind the destruction of the civil rights movement as a whole. I told him the Director sympathized with the civil rights movement as exemplified in the Director's supervision of the FBI's many brilliant accomplishments in this field. I added, however, that we deeply and bitterly resented the lies and falsehoods told by King and that if King wanted war we certainly would give it to him. Wilkins shook his head and stated there was no doubt in his mind as to which side would lose if the FBI really came out with all of its ammunition against King. I told him the ammunition was plentiful and that while we were not responsible for the many rumors being initiated against King, we had heard of these rumors and were certainly in a position to substantiate them.

I told Wilkins that inasmuch as he was attempting to hold out the fe[elers] of peace he should know a few positive facts of life. He asked what I meant. I told him my point was that he was attempting to prevent the FBI from exposing King, certain highly placed informants of ours had tipped us off to absolutely reliable information that King had organized a bitter crusade against the Director and the FBI. I told Wilkins these longstanding and well placed informants had advised us that he had contacted people in various parts of the United States to get them to send telegrams to the President, the Attorney General, and the FBI asking for Mr. Hoover's retirement or resignation. I told Wilkins that King had also encouraged telegrams to be sent advising the FBI of laxness in the investigation of civil rights matters. I asked Wilkins how in the hell could he expect the FBI to believe his offers of friendship and request for peace when King was at this time attempting to ruin us. Wilkins merely hung his head and stated [that] he had no idea that King was carrying on such a campaign. He stated that this upset him greatly and made him all the more determined to initiate action to remove King as soon as possible.

[Bureau Deletion] Wilkins diverted from the subject of the conversation to spend some time in explaining that he had also noted communist influence in the civil rights movement in Mississippi. He stated that the cry of "Down with the Proletariat" was getting to be the battlecry of the militant Negro allegations of laxness on the part of the FBI. He mentioned that the Negroes have been led by King and Bayard Rustin to believe that the FBI could do nothing right; consequently, the FBI's solution of civil rights cases made little impression upon some Negroes in the civil rights movement.

Wilkins stated he was wrong in his criticism of the Director. He admitted that he was attempting to accomplish, in a mild manner, a division between the battle of the Director and King and any phases of the battle [that] would reflect upon the civil rights movement. He stated he has a hard time controlling his 32-man Board of Directors, particularly since King is a member of this board. He then added, "We [are] hurting," and something must be done.

Wilkins told me that he will be lecturing in California most all of next week. He stated that before he leaves for the coast he will attempt to see King, along with other Negro leaders and tell King that he can't possibly win any battle with the FBI. [Bureau Deletion] He stated he may not have any success in this regard; however, that he is convinced that the FBI can easily ruin King overnight. [Bureau Deletion] I told Wilkins this, of course, was up to him; however, I wanted to reiterate once again most strongly, that if King wanted war we were prepared to give it to him and let the chips fall where they may. Wilkins stated this would be most disastrous, particularly to the Negro movement and that he hoped this would never come about. I told him that the monkey was on his back and that of the other Negro leaders. He stated he realized this. We then shook hands and he left to return to New York.

ACTION

It is suggested that the attached letter be sent to the President in connection with the above conversation.

UNITED STATES DEPARTMENT OF JUSTICE

FEDERAL BUREAU OF INVESTIGATION

Cincinnati, Ohio
March 16, 1965

RE: ROY WILKINS
    EXECUTIVE SECRETARY OF NAACP

The *Journal Herald,* a daily morning newspaper of general circulation published in Dayton, Ohio, published the following article on page 35 of the final edition on March 13, 1965. The article under caption "Wilkins Stresses Need for Fair Housing Here" stated as follows:

"Roy Wilkins, executive director of the National Association for the Advancement of Colored People (NAACP) urged Daytonians to fight for a strong state fair housing bill and a local fair housing ordinance with teeth last night in an address at Tabernacle Baptist Church.

Satirically referring to Dayton as a 'little paradise,' he stressed the need in Dayton for fair housing.

'You have a problem here,' he declared.

'And I hope you're not going to let anyone frighten you out of an ordinance or maneuver you into a bad or weak law.

'It's better to have no law at all than one with absolutely no teeth.'

His statements about the Dayton's housing situation brought applause from the 4,450 Negroes and whites in the audience.

'But watch those housing laws. Keep in touch with the state legislature,' he warned.

'You're getting along pretty well in Dayton with your school board in eliminating de facto segregation,' he added. 'It's nothing to crack your heels about, but at least you're moving.'

While praising Rev. Martin Luther King's Selma, Ala., actions, he warned that Negroes should not criticize President Lyndon Johnson for not 'going to Selma and fighting with his bare hands.'

'That's not his job,' Wilkins declared. 'He has not remained silent. His stand on voting rights is clear. His outrage over Selma is evident in his sending his emissaries to Alabama along with the attorney general and the FBI. That's what he has an administration for.'

Wilkins, who delivered an emotional address full of descriptions of the recent Selma beatings by state police, drew several responses from the audience.

'That's right, it's true,' Negroes commented aloud.

He said the NAACP has scheduled two new programs for the South this summer, including a Mississippi project and citizenship training clinics.

'Colored people must learn to become better, more efficient citizens all over the country,' he said.

He forthrightly placed some blame for the Negro's second-class citizenship in the laps of the Negroes.

'There isn't one large corporation in this country that isn't crying for Negroes,' he declared. 'They will hire any good secretary if she's not as black as coal and [doesn't] look like a locomotive after a wreck.'

'Don't ever lump all white people together. Do for them what you ask of them—see them as people and individuals, not as just white people.'

He stressed the reality of unity of white and Negro in the Selma situation, referring to last Sunday's violence as 'Selma Sunday.'

Echoing King when he spoke in Dayton two months ago, Wilkins reminded the Negroes that 'We've made progress, but we've got a long way to go.'

'I think there will be a new civil rights law that will provide for federal registrars, state and local elections and will abolish literacy tests,' he added.

He pointed out the greatest task for the Negro today is to 'analyze the obstacles ahead of us.'

'How are you going to fight the Gov. George Wallaces and the Sheriff Jim Clarks?' he asked. 'What kinds of minds are these?'

He said he has been invited to speak at a memorial service for Rev. James Reeb, the Boston Unitarian minister who died in Selma Thursday after being beaten by whites.

'He had the old-fashioned religion,' Wilkins said. 'That kind of religion isn't fashionable any more. People just count their money and try to figure out how they can get ahead now.'

Some of the subject's activities reported for the period of April-May 1968 follow:

At a press conference in NYC on 4/8/68, Roy Wilkins explained that the NAACP was distributing antiviolence stickers across the country, one of which read "Hot Head, Hot Lead, Cold Dead."

The *New York Times* issue of 4/9/68 quoted Roy Wilkins as saying "millions of Negroes in this country" were opposed to violence and rejected what he said was the "shrill" contention of militants that they were taking over the Negro community. Wilkins stated that Dr. Martin Luther King, Jr., would be "outraged" by the disorders following his assassination. He acknowledged that New York's militant Negroes "have chosen to be good citizens" cooperating with Mayor John Lindsay in his efforts to keep NYC calm.

According to the *Evening Star* dated 4/3/68, Washington, D.C., Roy Wilkins, in a speech before the National Press Club in Washington on 4/3/68, warned that black militants who called for violence and separatism were actually playing into the hands of white racists and were causing officials in some cities to give police departments "blank checks" to buy heavy weapons. He then displayed several stickers being passed out by the NAACP, whose slogans pertained to nonviolence.

The *Washington Afro-American* dated 5/7/68, Washington, D.C. newspaper, reported that Wilkins, after a visit to the White House in early May, stated that he saw "no immediate danger of the whole colored American population going off on a violence kick."

UNITED STATES DEPARTMENT OF JUSTICE

FEDERAL BUREAU OF INVESTIGATION

New York, New York
June 28, 1968

Jamaica Rifle and Pistol Club,
Incorporated (JRPC)

[Bureau Deletion] advised on June 16, 1968, that Herman Ferguson and Arthur Harris, members of the JRPC, were found guilty by a New York, Queens County Supreme Court jury on June 15, 1968, charged with conspiracy to commit murder in the first degree in plotting to assassinate civil rights leaders Roy Wilkins, Executive Director of the NAACP, and Whitney M. Young, Jr., Executive Director of the National Urban League.

According to [Bureau Deletion] Justice Paul Balsam, presiding, has not set a date for sentencing. The maximum penalty Justice Balsam could impose would be seven years imprisonment.

The key witness for the prosecution was Edward Howlette, a Negro Detective, NYCPD, who infiltrated the Revolutionary Action Movement (RAM), a subgroup organized by Ferguson, state [Bureau Deletion]

According to [Bureau Deletion] Defense Attorney Gene Ann Condon failed to put Ferguson or Harris on the witness stand or call other witnesses after she heard in private, tape recordings obtained by the NYCPD containing conversations between Ferguson, Harris, and others dealing with the conspiracy to assassinate Roy Wilkins and Whitney M. Young, Jr.

POSSIBLE RACIAL VIOLENCE [IN] MAJOR URBAN AREAS
San Francisco, California Area.

On July 1, 1969, Bobby Seale, Chairman of the BPP [Black Panther Party], gave a press release by reading the text of a telegram received from Roy Wilkins, Executive Secretary for the NAACP.

Wilkins' telegram read as follows:

"I am desirous of exploratory conference with officers of militant group and particularly with you as chairman of the Central Committee of the Black Panther Party. Do not desire public meeting at this time. Certainly cannot arrange trip to West Coast before late July account prior commitments. At this time my desire to explore areas of possible agreement and disagreement is purely an administrative one on my own authority as Chief Executive Officer of NAACP. It is official, of course, but not binding nor does it have the formal endorsement of my Board of Directors. I simply feel very strongly that present situation of our race requires trying to reach some common ground and arrival at some sort of strategy that will be effective even if used in only a few areas. I may be in error and there is not unanimous support even among my immediate co-workers on staff, but I fell [sic] I must try. I hope we may continue the effort to arrive at a mutually satisfactory meeting date and place late in July or early in August. /s/ Roy Wilkins, 1072 Lynch Street after July 7, 790 Broadway New York.''

It should be pointed out during the time this telegram was sent, the NAACP was conducting its national convention in Mississippi.

Seale stated he sent Wilkins a telegram on June 30, 1969, stating the Central Committee would meet with Wilkins on July 4, 1969, at a public meeting in DeFremery Park, Oakland, California, in connection with a rally and picnic originally scheduled.

Seale state[d] it [was] obvious that Wilkins [did] not want to meet with the people and that he is separated from the black community, [that] if Wilkins was really concerned he would have accepted a public meeting.

MALCOLM X

(1925–1965)

Much of the force behind the charge that the FBI (or the CIA) assassinated Malcolm X is the result of historical projection. Gunned down before the black power movement rose and in the midst of a philosophical transformation that had already begun to soften his message, Malcolm became larger in death than in life. In life, of course, he was widely known and widely feared. In death, his legacy grew to almost mythical proportions—and not only in America's urban ghettoes. His legacy also grew in the mind of J. Edgar Hoover's FBI. While he lived, Malcolm was never more than the bureau's secondary target in the Nation of Islam. The primary target was always Elijah Muhammad, and the things the bureau did to worsen the break between Malcolm and Muhammad were routine. Fanning the flames of factionalism within any and all dissident groups was an institutionalized part of Hoover's security-state responsibilities. In the case of the so-called Black Muslims, the difference was that a target ended up dead.

The FBI has blood on its hands not because any one special agent or group of agents bought the gun that killed Malcolm or otherwise served as direct accomplices. The FBI is guilty because their federal police force pushed on knowing that murder was a possibility and further that their own efforts to exacerbate tensions made it that much more likely. If the bureau scarcely understood these Muslims, it knew enough before and after the assassination to understand that Elijah Muhammad had more than a few followers unstable enough to do anything to protect the good name of the self-proclaimed Messenger of Allah. In the years after Malcolm's death, moreover, fratricide continued—including the execution of seven rival Hanafi sect Muslims in the former Washington, D.C., home of basketball star Kareem Abdul-Jabbar, himself a Hanafi Muslim. Of the seven, five were children. All were shot or drowned. Through it all, the FBI kept trying to divide and conquer.

What the FBI did was horrible enough short of actual participation in any assassination. What could be more disgraceful than a government trying to manipulate for its own interests those Muslim leaders and followers who didn't care about their own lives or the life of anyone else? Those holy warriors who could fire point blank at the black shining prince or look through clear tap water into the terrified eyes of the nine-day-old baby they were drowning in a bathroom sink?

Malcolm X understood violence long before he dropped his "slave name" and added the "X" (and eventually the formal Muslim name of El-Hajj Malik El-Shabazz). Born Malcolm Little in Omaha, Nebraska, on May 19, 1925, the seventh of eleven children, his father was a Baptist preacher and an organizer for Marcus Garvey's Universal Negro Improvement Association. After racists drove the family out of Omaha, the Littles settled in Lansing, Michigan, where Malcolm's father was murdered (probably by Ku Klux Klan-style thugs). When his family fell apart soon thereafter, Malcolm dropped out of school and began a career in the Boston and Harlem worlds of numbers running, drugs, prostitution, and burglary. Arrested in 1946 for burglary and larceny, he received an eight-to-ten-year sentence.

Like many of Elijah Muhammad's followers, Malcolm converted in prison—the first in an extraordinary series of personal transformations. Ordained a minister in the Nation of Islam after being paroled in 1952, he quickly became one of Muhammad's favorites and was placed in charge of the Harlem mosque. He was the sect's most effective and electrifying evangelist, who most clearly articulated the message of self-defense against white racism by any means necessary. While Martin Luther King, Jr., was establishing himself in the American mind as the prince of nonviolence, Malcolm was building a reputation as the prince of violence. Among other things, he was perhaps the most sought-after speaker on the nation's campuses and spoke frequently to packed lecture halls and auditoriums at Harvard and other elite universities. Gradually, the Muslim hierarchy grew jealous and plotted against the man whose star shined brighter than that of the Messenger himself. In December 1963, after Malcolm created an uproar by saying the assassination of President John F. Kennedy was a case of "chickens coming home to roost," Muhammad suspended him. Malcolm left the Nation of Islam in 1964 deeply disillusioned with Muhammad (having learned of the Messenger's habit of impregnating the young Muslim sisters who served as his secretaries).

In the last two years of his life, Malcolm organized a Muslim Mosque, Inc., in Harlem and an Organization of Afro-American Unity with chapters scattered across the country, and even several chapters in Europe and Africa. Following a *haji* (pilgrimage) to Mecca in spring 1964, Malcolm converted to orthodox Islam and condemned Elijah Muhammad as a ''racist'' and a ''faker.'' Upon returning to New York, death threats flew about and at least one attempt was made on his life. The assailants were never identified, though Malcolm believed them to be messengers of the Messenger. On February 14, 1965, another assault team firebombed his Queens home and fled unidentified into the night. Malcolm, his wife Betty, and four daughters were asleep inside at the time. Death came a week later, on February 21, when addressing followers at Harlem's Audubon Ballroom. While two of the three Black Muslims subsequently convicted of murder were probably innocent, the best evidence indicates that five renegades from the Newark, New Jersey, mosque carried out the assassination as an act of Muslim vengeance

For Malcolm's life, the best source remains *The Autobiography of Malcolm X* (1965), as told to Alex Haley. The book also served as the basis for the Spike Lee film *X* (1992). Also valuable are books by George Breitman, ed., *Malcolm X Speaks* (1965) and *By Any Means Necessary* (1970); and Steve Clark, ed., *Malcolm X Speeches: February 1965* (1992). The latter is projected as the first volume of the collected speeches and writings. Other useful books include Breitman's *The Last Year of Malcolm X* (1967); Hakim Abdullah Jamal, *From the Dead Level* (1972); Peter L. Goldman, *The Death and Life of Malcolm X* (1979); John Henrik Clark, ed., *Malcolm X: The Man and His Times* (1990); David Gallen, ed., *Malcolm X: As They Knew Him* (1992); and Edward R. Leader, *Understanding Malcolm X: His Controversial Philosophical Changes* (1992). Michael Friedly, *Malcolm X: The Assassination* (1992), is a measured account of that topic. Karl Evanzz, *The Judas Factor: The Plot to Kill Malcolm X* (1992), emphasizes a federal government conspiracy. The best study of the Nation of Islam remains C. Eric Lincoln, *The Black Muslims of America* (1959).

FEDERAL BUREAU OF INVESTIGATION

This case originated at: Detroit
Report made at: Boston
Date when made: 5/4/53
Period for which made: 3/20;4/1,3,6/53
Report made by: SA [Bureau Deletion]
Title: MALCOLM K. LITTLE, was Malachi Shabazz; [sic]
"Rhythm Red" Little; "Detroit Red" Little; Jack Carlton
Character of case: Security Matter-C; Security Matter-MCI

SYNOPSIS OF FACTS:
   Subject resides at 4336 Williams Street, Inkster, Michigan. Subject claimed in June, 1950, that he was a communist and during September, 1952, he indicated membership in the Muslim Cult of Islam.

DETAILS:
   This investigation was predicated upon information received from [Bureau Deletion] Norfolk, Massachusetts, to the effect that the Subject [Bureau Deletion] had written two letters that included comments on communism.

BACKGROUND
Birth
   [Bureau Deletion] the Subject was born May 19, 1925, in Omaha, Nebraska, and is a citizen by virtue of his birth.
Employment
   Information received from Boston Informant [Bureau Deletion] of known reliability, reflects the Subject is presently unemployed.
Residence
   [Bureau Deletion] Subject resides at the home of his brother at 4336 Williams Street, Inkster, Michigan.
Military Service
   [Bureau Deletion] Massachusetts State Prison, Charlestown, Massachusetts, advised Subject's Selective Service status had been verified by prison authorities during the late 1940s and information obtained from Selective Service records reflected Subject was registered with Local Board No. 59, New York, New York, and classified 4-F.
Status of Health
   Information received from [Bureau Deletion] reflects Subject is under

a doctor's care at the present time. The nature or extent of his illness is not known.

Criminal

[Bureau Deletion] Subject was sentenced to serve eight to ten years on a charge of breaking and entering in the nighttime and that he began this sentence February 27, 1946. [Bureau Deletion] Subject was eligible for parole May 29, 1951, but was denied parole at that time.

On September 23, 1953, [Bureau Deletion] Norfolk Prison Colony, Massachusetts, stated Subject is a former inmate and had been paroled in care of Michigan parole authorities on August 7, 1952.

The following record was obtained from [Bureau Deletion] Massachusetts State Board of Probation, Boston, Massachusetts, the central repository for all arrest records in the Commonwealth of Massachusetts:

Date Offense	Court	Disposition
11/30/44 Larceny	Roxbury	3 months House of Correction SS 11/30/45-Filed
1/15/46 Carrying firearms	Roxbury	M.R.ss 1/15/47-Filed
1/16/46 Larceny Breaking & Enter.	Quincy	1/2-Grand Jury
2/27/46 Larceny Breaking & Enter.	Middlesex Superior	8–10 years. State
2/27/46 Larceny Breaking & Enter.	Middlesex Superior	8–10 years State
2/27/46 " " " "	" " " "	
2/27/46 Conspiracy, Break. and Entering	Middlesex Superior	Filed
4/10/46 B & E., Larceny	Norfolk	6–8 years SP conc.
3/7/46 B & E., Larceny	Newton	Dismissed
8/7/52 Paroled 4 5/4/53	State Prison	

Credit

The records of the Credit Bureau [Bureau Deletion] contained no reference to Subject.

COMMUNIST PARTY ACTIVITIES

The Communist party has been cited by the attorney general of the United States as coming within the purview of Executive Order 9835.

[Bureau Deletion] several excerpts from letters written by Subject. [Bureau Deletion] these excerpts were not quotes but rather notes jotted down [Bureau Deletion] on the contents of these letters.

On June 29, 1950, the Subject mailed a letter.

Editors Note. *The file indicates that an unidentified source copied out sentences from this letter. In one of them Malcolm states, "I have always been a Communist." In World War II, Malcolm says he attempted to enlist in the Japanese Army with the result that he will now never be drafted into the U.S. Army. He adds that it's not difficult to convince anyone that he's crazy since everyone has always said he was anyway.*

In January, 1952, [Bureau Deletion] Subject had been visited by [Bureau Deletion] a member of the Crispus Attucks Club of the American Youth for Democracy. The AYD has been cited by the attorney general of the United States as coming within the purview of Executive Order 9835.

There is no further information concerning the Subject's communist activities in Boston.

MUSLIM CULT OF ISLAM

[Bureau Deletion] the Muslim Cult of Islam, which is also known as the Allah Temple of Islam, is a religious cult whose members regard Allah as their supreme being and claim to be the direct descendants of the original race on earth. The members fanatically follow the teachings of Allah as interpreted by Elijah Muhammad, the "true prophet of Allah" entitled titular head of the Muslim Cult of Islam in the United States, and believe that any civil law [that] conflicts with the Muslim law should be disobeyed. The members disavow their allegiance to the United States and pledge their allegiance only to Allah and do not consider it their duty to register for Selective Service or to serve in the United States Armed Forces as they cannot serve two masters. According to the teachings of Elijah Muhammad and the cult's ministers, the members of a minority race in the United States are not citizens of this country but are merely slaves of this country and will continue to be slaves until they free themselves by destroying non-Muslims and Christianity in the "War of Armageddon."

[Bureau Deletion] Muslims known to him either shave their hair or wear goatees.

According to records [Bureau Deletion] the Subject wears chin whiskers.

DESCRIPTION

The following description of the Subject was obtained from the records [Bureau Deletion]

Name	MALCOLM K. LITTLE, was Malachi [sic] Shabazz; "Rhythm Red"; "Detroit Red"; Jack Carlton
Date of Birth	May 19, 1925 Omaha, Nebraska
Race	Negro-mulatto
Sex	Male
Residence	4336 Williams Street, Inkster, Michigan
Height	6' 3½"
Weight	180 lbs.
Build	Slender
Hair	Black
Eyes	Brown
Complexion	Light
Scars & Marks	1" scar from right eye to nose; ½" scar below left elbow
Peculiarities	Confirmed user of marijuana; wears chin whiskers and mustache
Employment	Cut Rate Department Store 8940 Oakland Avenue Inkster, Michigan (Presently unemployed)
Marital Status	Single
Nationality	American
FBI No.	4282299
Social Security No.	376 16 3427

FEDERAL BUREAU OF INVESTIGATION

This case originated at: Philadelphia
Report made at: New York
Date when made: 9/7/54
Period for which made: 8/24,25,27/54

Report made by: SA [Bureau Deletion]
Title: MALCOLM K. LITTLE, was Brother Malcolm X
Character of case: Security matter-MCI

SYNOPSIS OF FACTS:

[Bureau Deletion] the subject attended meetings of the MCI, Temple No. 7, NYC, during January, 1954. [Bureau Deletion] subject was a tour leader for the NYC Temple No. 7 at the Chicago Convention of the Cult in February, 1954. [Bureau Deletion] subject was in attendance at Temple No. 7 and was enthusiastically going over the teachings of the cult. [Bureau Deletion] the subject has openly spoken against the "white devils" and has encouraged greater hatred on the part of the cult towards the white race. [Bureau Deletion] that the Subject resides in Philadelphia and rents a room at 25-35 Humphrey Street, East Elmhurst, Queens, New York when he is in the city.

FEDERAL BUREAU OF INVESTIGATION

This case originated at: New York
Report made at: Philadelphia
Date when made: 11/18/54
Period for which made: 10/12,21,29;11/3,4,8,10/54
Report made by: SA [Bureau Deletion]
Title: MALCOLM K. LITTLE, was Brother Malcolm X
Character of case: Security matter-MCI

SYNOPSIS OF FACTS:

Subject resides at 25-35 Humphrey Street, East Elmhurst, New York. [Bureau Deletion] Minister of MCI Temple at Philadelphia and New York; has made numerous speeches at MCI meetings indicating a knowledge of the aims and purposes of the MCI; attended numerous meetings of MCI at Philadelphia during period March, 1954, to present.

The subject spoke at a meeting of the MCI [Bureau Deletion] and stated that he was being followed by the FBI and had been questioned by them because they are frantic to stop the teaching of Islam. Little stated that there is nothing that the FBI could do to stop the spreading of the message that the white man is the devil and the black man is God.

FEDERAL BUREAU OF INVESTIGATION

This case originated at: New York
Report made at: New York
Date when made: 1/28/55
Period for which made: 11/3,4,8,18,19,22,23,29;12/
                        1,3,6,9,13,20,23,27,28,/54;
                        1/3,10,11,14,17,21/55
Report made by: SA [Bureau Deletion]
Title: MALCOLM K. LITTLE, was Brother Malcolm X
Character of case: Security Matter-MCI

BACKGROUND
Birth
  [Bureau Deletion] of the Bureau of Vital Statistics, Douglas County, Health Department, 1201 South 42nd Street, Omaha, Nebraska, made available file A39357 which reflects that Malcolm Little was born at the University Hospital, Omaha, Nebraska on May 19, 1925. The parents were listed as Early Little, who was born in the State of Georgia, and Louise Norton Little, who was born in the West Indies. Both parents, as well as the subject, were listed as of the Negro race and at the time of the birth were listed as residing at 3448 Pinkney Street, Omaha, Nebraska.
Education
  [Bureau Deletion] the subject had indicated he had eight years in an elementary school and had three years of high school as of July 15, 1943.
Service in the Armed Forces
  [Bureau Deletion] Malcolm Little had registered at Local Board 59 of New York City on June 1, 1943, while residing at 2460 Seventh Avenue, Apartment 31, New York City. [Bureau Deletion] on October 25, 1943, the subject was found mentally disqualified for military service for the following reasons: psychopathic personality inadequate, sexual perversion, psychiatric rejection. Subject was classified 4F on December 4, 1944.
Residence
  On January 10, 1955, the subject stated he resides at 25-35 Humphrey Street, East Elmhurst, Queens, New York, at the home of Curtis and Susie Kenner.
Employment
  [Bureau Deletion] the subject was a full-time minister of the New

York Temple No. 7 of the Muslim Cult of Islam (MCI) at New York City and at Philadelphia, Pennsylvania.

[Bureau Deletion] the subject is a minister of the MCI Temple No. 7, 102 West 116th Street, New York City, and was devoting his full time to the MCI.

Information Concerning the Muslim Cult of Islam (MCI)

[Bureau Deletion] the MCI, also known as the Temple of Islam and the Allah Temple of Islam, is an organization composed entirely of Negroes, which was reportedly organized around 1930 in Detroit, Michigan. The national leader and founder is Elijah Muhammad, who claims to have been sent by Allah, the supreme being, to lead the Negroes out of slavery in the United States.

Members fanatically follow the alleged teachings of Allah, as interpreted by Muhammad, and disavow allegiance to the United States. Members pledge allegiance only to Allah and Islam and believe any civil law [that] conflicts with Muslim law should be disobeyed. The cult teaches that members of the dark-skinned race cannot be considered citizens of the United States since they are in slavery in this country, and, therefore, must free themselves by destroying non-Muslims and Christianity in the "War of Armageddon." For this purpose, the cult has a military branch called the Fruit of Islam (FOI) composed of all-male, able-bodied members, who participate in military drill and judo training.

Members of the cult also believe that they are directly related to all Asiatic races, and any conflict involving any Asiatic nation and a Western nation is considered a part of the War of Armageddon, in which the Asiatic nation will be victorious.

Meetings and speeches made by the Subject at
MCI Meetings, Temple No. 7, which is presently
located at 102 West 116th Street, New York City

[Bureau Deletion] at a meeting of the MCI Temple No. 7, New York City, [Bureau Deletion] the Minister Malcolm Little was the main speaker. Little spoke on the lines of racial hatred, always referring to the white race as being "the white devils." Little compared President Eisenhower to Pharaoh of Egypt in the biblical days and compared Elijah Muhammad of Chicago, Illinois, to Moses. He stated that Elijah Muhammad is going to lead the "black race" out of slavery in the United States as Moses did the "Jews" in Egypt. Little stated that President Eisenhower is nothing more than a Pharaoh of the United States and is keeping the "black man" in slavery in the United States. Little stated that the Muslims do not allow any "white devils" in this temple. They just allow their own kind to meet and the Muslim Temple is only for Negroes.

[Bureau Deletion] Malcolm Little was the principal speaker at the meeting [Bureau Deletion] at which time Little expounded upon the origin of the white race, stating that it was created by Yacob and it took six thousand years to create the "white devil." Little stated this was obtained by breeding the white-skinned and yellow-skinned races and that when the black-skinned babies were born they were killed off and it took six thousand years to accomplish the creation of the present-day "white devil."

During this meeting Little explained that the guards of the Temple are soldiers in the army and that when the war is started these guards are duty-bound to see all churches are destroyed. Little made the statement that they would chop your head off too if you do not believe in the teachings of Islam. Little stated that the members are "fools" if they put on the uniform of the "white devil's army."

Little stated, however, he was not telling them not to do so, [Bureau Deletion] it was indicated from the theme of Little's talk that it would not be along the Muslim lines for an individual to serve in the armed forces of the United States.

[Bureau Deletion] in regards to the overthrow of the government, Malcolm Little had made statements to the effect that it was expected that the Negro race would be the rulers of the world and it had been indicated that the white man's rule in the United States would end with the year 1955. [Bureau Deletion] they continuously referred to the Battle of Armageddon and that it had been explained that this Battle would be between the "black man" and the "white man."

FEDERAL BUREAU OF INVESTIGATION

Interview of MALCOLM LITTLE on

January 10, 1955
New York, NY

In an interview on January 10, 1955, Malcolm Little advised SAs [Bureau Deletion] and [Bureau Deletion] that he resides at 25-35 Humphrey Street, East Elmhurst, Queens, New York, at the home of Curtis and Susie Kenner.

The subject readily admitted membership in the MCI Temple No. 7, New York City, but would not admit that he was the minister or teacher of Temple No. 7, New York City. Subject would not admit that he was affiliated with the MCI Temple in Philadelphia, Pennsylvania, nor would he admit membership in the Detroit and Boston Temples.

The subject was uncooperative in this interview. He refused to furnish any information concerning the officers, names of members, to furnish doctrines or beliefs of the MCI, or family background data on himself.

The subject stated that he believes in all the teachings of Elijah Muhammad of Chicago, Illinois, and that Elijah Muhammad was his leader and that he considered Elijah Muhammad superior to all. Subject considered the "Nation of Islam" higher and greater than the United States government. He claimed that Allah is God, the supreme being, and that Elijah Muhammad is the greatest prophet of all, being the last and greatest Apostle.

When questioned concerning alleged teachings of racial hatred of the MCI, he stated they do not teach hatred but the truth, that the "black man" has been enslaved in the United States by the "white man" and that no one could dispute it. Little stated that the "black man" has died for the "white man" all over the world. He described the "black man" who respects the United States government as "Uncle Tom" in that they have considered the white man and his government first and placed themselves in a secondary position.

When subject was questioned concerning whether he would serve in the United States armed forces and if he would defend the United States against an attacking enemy he would not answer. He stated that no one could look in the future so he contended that he would not know what he would do if the above events would happen. The subject would not answer as to whether he considered himself a citizen of the United States.

When asked if he considered the MCI a government as well as a religion the subject would not answer. When asked if he considered himself and the Negro race in slavery in the United States by the white man, the subject remarked that you would have to only read the history books in the library to know that they are in slavery.

When he was questioned concerning the War of Armageddon, he remarked that the Bible states this will be when God destroys the devil. When asked how the MCI was going to participate in this war, he would not answer. When asked what the FOI and military training was for, he stated this was to teach the members to be upright and righteous. Subject claimed that Muslims are peaceful and they do not have guns and ammunition and they do not even carry knives.

The subject did, however, admit that during World War II he had admired the Japanese people and soldiers and that he would have liked to join the Japanese Army at that time. The subject claims to have never been a member of the Communist party or the American Youth for Democracy or to have known anyone who was associated with it.

The American Youth for Democracy and the Communist party have been designated by the attorney general of the United States pursuant to Executive Order 10450.

FEDERAL BUREAU OF INVESTIGATION

Reporting Office: New York
Office of Origin: New York
Date when made: 4/23/57
Period for which made: 5/11,15,18,19,22,25,28/56
Report made by: [Bureau Deletion]
Title: MALCOLM K. LITTLE, was
Malcolm X; Malcolm X Little
Character of case: Security Matter-NOI

SYNOPSIS:
[Bureau Deletion] subject is official minister of NOI Temple No. 12, Philadelphia, Pa. [Bureau Deletion] subject continues to be minister of NOI Temple No. 7, NYC. [Bureau Deletion] believes Little is No. 2 or No. 3 man in NOI. Activities of subject in various United States cities set forth. Subject resides at 25–46 99th Street, Elmhurst, New York, and has no employment other than duties in NOI.

ACTIVITIES OF MALCOLM LITTLE IN
CHICAGO, ILLINOIS

[Bureau Deletion] at a meeting of the Fruit of Islam (FOI), Temple No. 2, Chicago, Illinois, held at the Temple of Islam, 5335 South Greenwood Avenue, Chicago, ... the subject stated that there had recently been a meeting of the National Association for the Advancement of Colored People in New York City, which was attended by over twenty thousand persons, who listened to Mrs. Eleanor Roosevelt. Little stated that Mrs. Roosevelt told those present at the meeting that there are many more dark people in the world than white and it was time for Americans to wake up to this fact. Little also declared that Tallulah Bankhead also spoke at this rally on the deplorable treatment and persecution of the colored race in the South, especially in the state of Alabama.

Little told the group that this government (United States government) sends troops all over the world to protect the rights of smaller nations, but refuses to send troops into the South to protect the rights of black Americans. He stated that the only solution to the race problem in America was Elijah Muhammad.

[Bureau Deletion] Minister Malcolm of New York City spoke at a meeting of the Chicago Temple of the NOI. . . .

Little called upon the American Negro to form his own government in the United States and told the congregation that southern white men had murdered the Negro's father and raped the Negro's mother. He stated that at this time there were two steps set forth by Elijah Muhammad separating the Negro from the white man. The first step was for the Negro to drop the white man's name and the second step was for the Negro to drop the white man's religion, Christianity. Little went on to advise that he first met Elijah Muhammad in prison and embraced Muhammad's teachings while serving a ten-year sentence. He related that as a Christian he had committed various wicked acts, but since he had become a Muslim, he had lived a new and religious life. . . .

ACTIVITIES OF MALCOLM LITTLE IN
DETROIT, MICHIGAN

[Bureau Deletion] a regular meeting of Detroit, Michigan Temple No. 1 [Bureau Deletion]. He stated that the guest speaker was Malcolm Little, Minister of Temple No. 7, New York City. By selecting several words and combining various roots in a manner to produce words or combinations of words, [Little] attempted to prove that the government of America was evil.

To illustrate this point, Little used two words: *demon* "which means devil," and *krasy*, which according to Little is Greek and means government. Little dropped the letter *n* from the word *demon*, thereby producing *demo*. He then indicated that the Greek letter *k* is represented in English by the letter *c*. Therefore, the Greek word *krasy* becomes *crasy* when translated into English. By combining the two words *demo* and *crasy* he produced the word *democracy*.

[Bureau Deletion] Little then added "his syllogistic reasoning" and stated that the word meant devil government.

[Bureau Deletion] he then continued to pursue the Muslim line of reasoning, which states that all white people are devils and their government is a devil government. Little said that this is why the United States is identified with the concept of democracy more than any Caucasian civilization.

OFFICE MEMORANDUM

UNITED STATES GOVERNMENT

TO: DIRECTOR, FBI (100-399321)   DATE: 7/2/58

FROM: SAC, NEW YORK (105-8999)

SUBJECT: MALCOLM LITTLE
             SM-NOI

ReBulet 5/20/58, which states that in view of Little's increasing activities in the affairs of the NOI on a national level, the Bureau desires that the NYO consider him for designation as a key figure.

The NYO after due consideration believes that Little should be designated a key figure in view of his extensive activity as Minister of Temple No. 7, 102 West 116th Street, New York City.

It is noted that Temple No. 7 has approximately three to four hundred members and that in his capacity as minister, Little is the leader of Temple No. 7.

In addition, Little travels to various temples throughout the United States and at meetings of these temples has made numerous speeches [that] are violent in nature wherein he attacks the United States and the white race.

UACB, the NYO is designating Little a key figure and is placing this case in a pending inactive status.

The NYO will continue to follow Little's activities and will submit a report within six months from the date of reBulet.

SAC, New York (105-8999)   July 15, 1958
Director, FBI (100-399321)
MALCOLM LITTLE
INTERNAL SECURITY — NOI
   reBulet 7/2/58.
The Bureau agrees with your designation of Little as a key figure. You will be furnished up-to-date Security Index cards on him separately.

Inasmuch as Little has been designated a key figure, you should obtain and forward to the Bureau a current photograph of him as well as suitable handwriting specimens.

You should carefully review that part of Section 87D of the Manual of Instructions relating to key figures.

UNITED STATES DEPARTMENT OF JUSTICE

FEDERAL BUREAU OF INVESTIGATION

Report of: SA [Bureau Deletion]
Office: NEW YORK
Date: 19 MAY 1959
File Number: New York 105–8999   Bureau file 100–3999321
Title: MALCOLM K. LITTLE
Character: INTERNAL SECURITY-NOI

NOI ACTIVITY AND STATEMENTS MADE
BY SUBJECT

In Buffalo, New York

On February 12, 1959, [Bureau Deletion] stated that a meeting of the MTI in Buffalo, New York, was held February 11, 1959, at the above address. [Bureau Deletion] stated Malcolm X was the speaker and he spoke as follows:

   The Messenger wants everyone to do something for himself and
   to stop waiting for the white man to do everything for the Negro.
   He urged those in attendance to develop businesses so that the Negro

could become self-dependent. He urged the followers of Elijah Muhammad not to break any of the white man's laws, pointing out that these laws must be obeyed. He stated that the Messenger did not want his followers to break any laws of the white race. The black man and the black woman should not mix with the white race because the white race is the enemy.

At Cleveland, Ohio

On February 18, 1959, [Bureau Deletion] furnished information concerning a meeting of the MTI No. 18, held February 15, 1959, at 11005 Ashbury Avenue. [Bureau Deletion] stated Malcolm X from New York spoke as follows:

The so-called Negroes are so lazy that they are willing to suffer anything rather than go to work. When we find a brother who is lazy we put him out of the brotherhood. Laziness in Islam is a sin. Any man that does not work in Islam is no good.

At New York, New York

On February 9, 1959, [Bureau Deletion] furnished information concerning a meeting of the NOI in New York on February 8, 1959. [Bureau Deletion] stated that Malcolm X spoke as follows:

Self-preservation is the first law of nature, preservation of family and preservation of people as a race.

The wars of 1914 and the Second World War have weakened the white race. God bless Japan for bombing Pearl Harbor. We should thank them. The only way Japan was conquered was through the atom bomb. The third and last war is the fight between the nations and the white race.

On March 26, 1959, [Bureau Deletion] furnished information concerning a meeting of the NOI in New York on March 22, 1959. [Bureau Deletion] stated Minister Malcolm asked if there were any representatives from the FBI or any detectives or cops present. [Bureau Deletion] stated a member of the police force identified himself. Malcolm welcomed him and stated that he wished more would come and visit the temple. Malcolm also stated that the officer should report that they are law-abiding people and they do not teach their people to love "white folks.'' Malcolm further stated ''man, you should arrest them. We were kidnapped. We were not brought here on the queen Mary or the Mayflower.''

On March 31, 1959, [Bureau Deletion] furnished information concerning a NOI meeting held in New York, March 29, 1959.

[Bureau Deletion] stated Minister Malcolm spoke and stated the sooner the so-called American Negro realized that what is wrong with us is not the color of our skin or the texture of our hair, but rather the condition of our minds and take steps to rectify this condition, the sooner we can have a race of which to be proud. Malcolm stated that the Negroes should sit and wait without violence because the white man will destroy himself.

UNITED STATES DEPARTMENT OF JUSTICE

FEDERAL BUREAU OF INVESTIGATION

Report of: SA [Bureau Deletion]
Date: 11/17/59   Office: New York
File Number: New York 105-8999   Bureau: 100–399321
Title: MALCOLM K. LITTLE
Character: INTERNAL SECURITY—NOI

Synopsis:
Malcolm Little is the Minister of NOI temple No. 7, NYC. . . . In July, 1959, Little took a trip to the Middle East and Africa as Elijah Muhammad's ambassador. . . .

Trip Abroad

On July 27, 1959, the file of Malcolm Little at the Passport Office, Department of State, was reviewed and disclosed the following information:

Passport number 1595569 was issued to Malcolm Little, known as Malik El-Shabazz, on May 27, 1959. This passport was marked ''not valid'' for travel in the following areas under control of authorities with which the United States does not have diplomatic relations: Albania, Hungary and those portions of China, Korea and Vietnam under communist control.

Regarding his travel plans, Little stated that he intended to depart from the United States at the Port of New York City on June 5, 1959, via air transportation, for a proposed length of stay abroad of two weeks in order to visit the United Kingdom, Germany, Italy, Greece, United Arab Republic, Saudi Arabia, Sudan, Lebanon, Turkey, and "others" for the purpose of attending the annual sacred Moslem Pilgrimage Rites at the Holy City of Mecca (Saudi Arabia) being held from June 9, 1959, to June 16, 1959.

Little answered "no" to questions in the application asking: "Are you now a member of the Communist party?" and "Have you ever been a member of the Communist party?"

[Bureau Deletion] Elijah Muhammad, national leader of the NOI, appeared at the St. Nicholas Arena, New York City on July 26, 1959.

[Bureau Deletion] prior to the speech by Elijah Muhammad, Minister Malcolm X of the NOI Temple No. 7, New York City, spoke. Among his other remarks, Malcolm X told of his recent trip to the Far [sic] East.

Malcolm X stated that he had just returned from the Far [sic] East. He stated he did not speak with Nasser but saw him. He stated that he was well accepted by Muslims and that the Muslims in Egypt and Africa are blacker than he. He stated he was well entertained and squired around due to the fact that he was a Muslim. He stated he was taken on a cruise in a boat in forbidden territory. [Bureau Deletion] he did not furnish more details concerning this.

[Bureau Deletion] Malcolm X stated that in Egypt, he became very ill and as a result was not able to go to Mecca.

[Bureau Deletion] Little stated that he could have gone to Mecca but he felt he should return to New York for the visit by Elijah Muhammad.

SAC, New York (105–7809)   June 1, 1960
Director, FBI (25–330971)
NATION OF ISLAM
INTERNAL SECURITY—NOI

Rerep SA [Bureau Deletion] dated 5/17/60, at New York captioned "Malcolm K. Little."

[Bureau Deletion] a movie was shown which "was about FBI intelligence, how they work with the local police, and their training, and their lab." Bufiles are negative concerning previous receipt of this information.

From the description in rerep, the film allegedly shown strongly re-
sembles *A Day with the FBI,* which is an eighteen-minute color film
dealing basically with the working of the FBI Laboratory, its cooperation with local law enforcement agencies, and illustrates science in
crime detection. A copy of this film has been previously furnished [sic]
your office.

Promptly review the files of your office [Bureau Deletion]. If this
film was charged out or loaned to someone outside the Bureau that
individual should be interviewed to determine where the film was [Bu-
reau Deletion] and whether this film was loaned by that individual to
another, or otherwise out of his possession. In tracing this film back to
an individual or individuals beyond the one to whom the film was
charged out or loaned, same should be interviewed unless the files of
your office contain information [that] would make such an interview
inadvisable. If such is the case, notify the Bureau, setting forth the facts
why you deem the interview inadvisable and submit your recommendations [as to] whether the Bureau should or should not grant authority
for such an interview. You should also advise the Bureau [as to] the
steps taken by your office to develop complete identification of this
film [Bureau Deletion]. In the event you took no action and it is now
determined the film is identical with the Bureau's film, explanation of
all personnel involved should be obtained and submitted to the Bureau,
together with your recommendation for administrative action.

UNITED STATES DEPARTMENT OF JUSTICE

FEDERAL BUREAU OF INVESTIGATION

Report of: [Bureau Deletion]
Date: 11/17/60   Office: New York, New York
File Number: New York 105–8999   Bureau File No: 100-399321
Title: MALCOLM K. LITTLE
Character: INTERNAL SECURITY-NOI

Synopsis:
Subject resides [at] 23-11 97th St., East Elmhurst, Queens, NY, is the
Minister of NOI Temple No. 7, NYC, and is considered one of the
national leaders of the NOI. . . . One source believes subject desires to

take over the NOI on death of Elijah Muhammad and that he also is considering running for public office, possibly U.S. Congress. Subject contacted Cuban Premier Fidel Castro while latter [was] in NYC, during September, 1960, to attend the UN General Assembly.

Subject's Contact with Cuban Premier
FIDEL CASTRO, at New York, New York,
September, 1960

[Bureau Deletion] advised on September 21, 1960, that in conversation with subject on that date, subject stated that he had visited with Castro for approximately thirty minutes in his Hotel Theresa room. The source advised that Little stated that during his visit he told Castro, in reference to Castro himself, that usually when one sees a man whom the United States is against, there is something good in that man. To this Castro replied that only the people in power in the United States are against him, not the masses. Little further expressed the opinion that any man who represented such a small country that would stand up and challenge a country as large as the United States must be sincere.

[Bureau Deletion] further stated that Little denied that the meeting with Castro was prearranged and Little further stated that the NOI was not allied with Castro or with any foreign power on earth. Little stated that the NOI was allied with God in whom they believe, hence, they cannot be affiliated with communism since it is atheistic.

[Bureau Deletion] stated that in explaining his reason for the visit, Little stated that he was on a committee [that] was formed to meet and greet any of the African delegates to the United Nations when they came to Harlem, and when he heard that Castro had moved to a hotel in Harlem, he felt that as a representative of this committee he should greet Castro. Little also stated he was the only member of the committee available at the time of the visit, hence, he went to the meeting with Castro accompanied by three NOI members and two members of the Negro press.

UNITED STATES DEPARTMENT OF JUSTICE

FEDERAL BUREAU OF INVESTIGATION

Report of: [Bureau Deletion] Office: New York, New York
Date: 5/17/61
Field Office File No. 105–8999   Bureau File No.: 100–399321
Title: MALCOLM K. LITTLE
Character: INTERNAL SECURITY-NOI

Contact with the KKK

The KKK has been designated by the attorney general of the United States pursuant to Executive Order 10450.

[Bureau Deletion] advised on January 30, 1961, that certain Klan officials met with leaders of the NOI on the night of January 28, 1961, in Atlanta, Georgia. One of these NOI leaders identified himself as Malcolm X of New York, and it was the source's understanding that Malcolm X claimed to have a hundred seventy-five thousand followers who were complete separationists, were interested in land and were soliciting the aid of the Klan to obtain land. During this meeting subject stated that his people wanted complete segregation from the white race, and that land obtained would be occupied by them and they would maintain their own businesses and government. Subject further stated that the Jew is behind the integration movement, using the Negro as a tool. Subject was further quoted as stating that his people would do anything to defend their beliefs and promote their cause and in his opinion there would be violence some day. Subject was further quoted as saying at this meeting that if one of his people went against their teachings, he would be destroyed. Subject also stated that if his people were faced with the situation that the white people of Georgia now face, that traitors, meaning those who assisted integration leaders, would be eliminated.

UNITED STATES DEPARTMENT OF JUSTICE

FEDERAL BUREAU OF INVESTIGATION

Report of: [Bureau Deletion] Office: New York, New York
Date: 11/16/62
Field Office File No.: 105–8999   Bureau File No.: 100–399321
Title: MALCOLM K. LITTLE
Character: INTERNAL SECURITY-NATION OF ISLAM

Subject's Activities Following the
Los Angeles Shooting Incident

Outlined below are the activities of the subject on behalf of the NOI following a shooting incident on April 27, 1962, between Los Angeles NOI members and the LAPD in Los Angeles, California, at which one NOI member was killed, several wounded, and a number arrested. Also set forth are activities by the subject as a result of this incident in concert with various Los Angeles groups who protested alleged police brutality against the Negro population there.

Subject attended and conducted funeral services held at 5606 South Broadway, Los Angeles, California, on May 5, 1962, for NOI member Ronald Stokes who was killed on April 27, 1962, in a shooting incident between Los Angeles NOI members and the LAPD.

The May 10, 1962, edition of the *Los Angeles Herald Dispatch* also contained an article [that] reflected that on May 4, 1962, in the Statler-Hilton Hotel, Los Angeles, California, subject had held a press conference relative to the shooting on April 27, 1962, of seven Los Angeles NOI members, one of whom (Ronald Stokes) died.

The article reflected that subject's opening statement was that "... Seven innocent unarmed black men were shot down in cold blood by Police Chief William J. Parker's Los Angeles City Police." The article continued that subject referred to the incident as "one of the most ferocious, inhuman atrocities ever inflicted in a so-called 'democratic' and 'civilized' society," and subject referred to the death of Stokes as a "brutal and cold-blooded murder by Parker's well-armed storm troopers."

This article went on to say that according to the subject, the official version of the incident which was related in the "white press" was that the Muslims were engaged in a gun battle with police provoked by the Muslims. Subject ridiculed this article saying that the Muslims obey the law religiously and he further ridiculed the "white press" for helping Chief Parker "suppress the facts."

Also during this conference, the subject refused to clarify how one of the white policemen was shot, stating that he was acting on the advice of the attorneys of the Muslims who were accused and arrested for assault.

The May 17, 1962, edition of the *Los Angeles Herald Dispatch* contained an article [that] reflected that a Los Angeles Coroner's Jury inquiring into the death of Ronald Stokes on April 27, 1962, at the hands of the LAPD, ruled that it was "justifiable homicide under lawful performance of duty and in self-defense." The article further indicated that only the police officers testified and that the nine Muslims who were arrested at the scene refused to testify and left the hearing after being advised that they were not required to testify if they thought their testimony might incriminate them.

This same article quoted the subject as saying after hearing the above verdict that Stokes's death was "a murder in cold blood" and that the Muslims "despaired of getting justice" and would pray to "God that he gives justice in his own way." The article went on to say that in response to questions the subject stated that Muslims obey the law, do not carry firearms, and are never the aggressors but if attacked have their God-given right to defend themselves.

The May 24, 1962, edition of the *Los Angeles Herald Dispatch* contained an article [that] reflected that a protest rally against police brutality was held in Los Angeles on May 20, 1962, at the Park Manor Auditorium which was sponsored by the "County Civic League," the latter being described in the article as an independent organization dedicated to the protection and preservation of the black community.

The article reflected that the subject spoke at this meeting and is quoted as saying ". . . Not a Muslim but a black man was shot down." The article indicated that the subject reiterated the importance of not letting religious, political, social, or economic differences divide the blacks. He further stated, according to the article, "For you're brutalized because you're black and when they lay a club on the side of your head, they do not ask your religion. You're black, that's enough."

The June 6, 1962, edition of the *Los Angeles Herald Examiner* contained an article [that] reflected that news media of Southern California

were asked by Los Angeles Mayor Samuel W. Yorty to publicize statements made by the subject at an NOI meeting in Los Angeles, California. The article indicated that Mayor Yorty, during a press conference
in his office, played a tape recording of the NOI meeting which included
a speech by the subject during which the latter said in regard to the
crash of a jet airliner in Paris, France, in which all the passengers
were killed:

> I would like to announce a very beautiful thing that has happened.
> As you know, we have been praying to Allah. We have been praying
> that he would in some way let us know that he has the power to
> execute justice upon the heads of those who are responsible for the
> lynching of Ronald Stokes on April 27.
>
> And I got a wire from God today (laughter) wait, all right, well
> somebody came and told me that he really had answered our prayers
> over in France. He dropped an airplane out of the sky with over 120
> white people on it because the Muslims believe in an eye for an eye
> and a tooth for a tooth (cheering and applause).
>
> Many people have been saying, "Well, what are you going to
> do?" And since we know that the man is tracking us down day by
> day to try and find out what we are going to do so he'll have some
> excuse to put us behind his bars, we call on our God. He gets rid
> of 120 of them in one whop. But thanks to God, or Jehovah or Allah,
> we will continue to pray and we hope that every day another plane
> falls out of the sky (cheering and applause). I want to just let you
> understand this.
>
> Whenever you read in the paper or hear on the television about
> accidents in which these good, blessed, blue-eyed people have lost
> their lives, you can say amen, for that's God's work. God knows
> you are cowards; God knows you are afraid; God knows that the
> white man has got you shaking in your boots. So God doesn't leave
> it up to you to defend yourself.
>
> God is defending you himself. They don't know what makes those
> airplanes come down; they start looking for mechanical failure. No,
> that's godly; that's "divine failure."

Following the playing of the above recording the article indicated
that Mayor Yorty stated that he did not believe that Malcolm X or the
black Muslims had the support of the Los Angeles Negro community
and urged that wide publicity be given to this statement of Malcolm X
so the public could understand the threats of this philosophy.

AIRTEL

TO: DIRECTOR, FBI (25-330971)   February 4, 1963

FROM: SAC, WFO (100-22829)
             NATION OF ISLAM
             IS-NOI

During a simultaneous release of a filmed interview on radio and television stations WMAL, Washington, D. C., on 2/3/63, at 7:00 P.M., Malcolm X, New York City, described as the official spokesman for the black Muslims and Minister of Muhammad's Mosque, No. 7, New York City's Harlem District, made some comments as follows:

The honorable Elijah Muhammad teaches that the black man is closer to God and is actually superior physiologically, psychologically, socially, and numerically.

The religion of Islam eliminates drunkenness, dope addiction, vice, immorality, smoking, drinking, stealing, lying, cheating, gambling, and disrespect for womanhood.

Regarding violence, Muslims are taught to obey the law, respect the law and to do unto others as "We would like them to do unto us," but that after having religiously obeyed the law, the Muslims are within their rights to defend themselves when attacked.

Muslims are never involved in riots and are never involved in violence unless attacked.

Elijah Muhammad has never advocated the overthrow of the government. If the black man cannot go back to his own people and his own land, Elijah Muhammad is asking that a part of the United States be separated and given to the Muslims so they can live separately. Elijah Muhammad is the only man the white people can deal with in the solving of problems of the so-called Negro, as Elijah Muhammad knows his problems.

Communism does not support the Muslim ideology.

The FBI spends twenty-four hours daily in attempting to infiltrate the Muslims and after Muslim meetings are held, the FBI goes from door to door asking about the meetings. The FBI goes far beyond its duty in the "religious suppression" of the Muslims.

The NAACP has existed for fifty-four years, during which period it has always had a white man as President. Malcolm believes that the organization is not developing leadership among the black people or it is practicing discrimination.

There is a group of Muslims in every Negro community.

Financial support from the white people is not desired, but would be accepted because it would represent what the white "forefathers" robbed from the black "forefathers" during the 310 years that the Negro spent in bondage while working without pay for the white people.

The above interview was conducted by Matthew Warren and Malcolm La Place, reporters for WMAL News.

Mr. W. C. Sullivan   February 4, 1963

[BUREAU DELETION]

NATION OF ISLAM
INTERNAL SECURITY-NOI
MALCOLM X LITTLE
INTERNAL SECURITY-NOI

My memorandum 2/1/63 advised a scheduled program called *Black Muslim* would be presented at 7 P.M., Sunday, 2/3/63 on Channel 7, WMAL Television, Washington, D.C. "Black Muslims" is the term used by the news media in referring to the Nation of Islam (NOI). WMAL, the *Evening Star* (a Washington, D.C., daily newspaper) station, advised that one of the reasons they were presenting the program was because they felt it presented Malcolm X and the "Black Muslims" in a "bad light."

During the program Malcolm X did refer to the FBI [re. infiltration, harrassment, religious suppression].

We have many occasions where they [The FBI] have tried to threaten and frighten Negroes from becoming Muslims, but it doesn't work. Today they have a new Negro on the scene and the more harassment and threats the FBI or the police or anyone gives toward Islam or toward the Negro, it only makes us grow that much faster.

OBSERVATIONS:

In carrying out our responsibilities in the security field [Bureau Deletion]. However, the statements concerning harrassment and threats are absolutely false and are additional examples of wild untrue statements made to influence the Negro.

The program did not put Malcolm X or the "Black Muslims" in a "bad light." The "answers" given by Malcolm X were not questioned. He was allowed to expound the NOI program in such a way that he created interest in the NOI. This is another example of the effect of publicity concerning the NOI. While it was intended to have an adverse effect, it created interest in the organization [that] was out of proportion to its importance.

RECOMMENDATION:
It is recommended that we continue to follow the approved policy of taking no steps which would give them additional publicity.

DIRECTOR, FBI (100-439895)   March 13, 1963

SAC, CHARLOTTE (100-4273)

NATION OF ISLAM
IS-NOI

[Bureau Deletion] made available to SA [Bureau Deletion] a recording of the speech made by Malcolm X Little at the Hi-Fi Country Club in Charlotte, N. C., on 1/30/63.

[Bureau Deletion]
Hearing the actual speech of Malcolm X enables the listener to discover the type of argument and logic employed by a hate peddler. The resulting effect is clearly heard in the background of this particular tape.
[Bureau Deletion] The listener can hear audience reaction in the background as Malcolm X stimulates his listeners to the release of their prejudices, grievances, and wishes. Some of the content of the tape underlines the inhibitions and repressed attitudes of a segment of Negroes in general and of Charlotte Negroes in particular. These bitternesses are easily identified on the tape through crowd outbursts as Malcolm X underlines some of the causes of Negro unrest.
This taped speech [Bureau Deletion] shows clearly how Malcolm X unites the individuals into an emotional entity, how he achieves rapport, reaches common understanding and responsiveness as he fuses individuals into a unit.
It is interesting to listen to the method of using statements of fact to set a favorable state of mind as he interweaves easy catch phrases of hate into the content of his speech. He continually throws irritants into an atmosphere of growing disapproval of the white race.
Malcolm X uses his skill as a speaker to direct [the] emotions and hatreds of his audience toward white people whom he sets up as a scapegoat for Negroes, described by him as a people severed from their racial heritage.

UNITED STATES DEPARTMENT OF JUSTICE

FEDERAL BUREAU OF INVESTIGATION

Report of: [Bureau Deletion] Office: New York
Date: 11/15/63
Field Office File No.: 105-8999   Bureau File No.: 100-399321
Title: MALCOLM K. LITTLE
Character: INTERNAL SECURITY-NATION OF ISLAM

Animosity Between Subject and
the Family of Elijah Muhammad

On several dates during March, April, and May, 1963, [Bureau Deletion] advised that there continued to be a feeling of hostility and resentment between subject and members of Elijah Muhammad's family.

According to [Bureau Deletion] this animosity was particularly aggravated by an article [that] appeared in an April edition of the *New York Times* to the effect that subject overshadowed Elijah Muhammad, and was taking over the NOI from Elijah who was ill.

In May, 1963, [Bureau Deletion] advised that this animosity has apparently quieted down during this month since subject had written an apologetic letter to Elijah Muhammad and Elijah had told subject that they should not be divided but should work together.

Statements and Activities Relative
to Racial Matters

The May 17, 1963, edition of the *New York Times* contained an article datelined Washington, D.C., May 16, 1963, which reflected that subject attacked President Kennedy for the manner in which he dealt with the Birmingham racial crisis. Subject claimed that President Kennedy's statement to Alabama editors in a recent meeting with them, that failure of the nonviolent movement for Negro rights might spur Negro extremist groups such as the Black Muslims, indicated that President Kennedy did not want Negroes treated right because it was right, but because the world was watching.

The May 25, 1963, edition of the *New York Amsterdam News* contained an article [that] reflected that in an interview with subject at Washington, D.C., subject had attacked Martin Luther King, Jackie Robinson, and Floyd Patterson as unwitting tools of white liberals. Subject claimed that the lesson of Birmingham is that "Negroes have lost their fear of the white man's reprisals and will react today with violence, if provoked."

On June 13, 1963, [Bureau Deletion] advised that subject had been instructed by Elijah Muhammad not to take part or assist the NAACP or any other Negro organization in their demonstrations for civil rights.

On [Bureau Deletion] 1963, [Bureau Deletion] advised that in subject's speech at the NOI Bazaar held at the Boston Arena, Boston, Massachusetts, on August 17, 1963, subject had informed the audience that Elijah Muhammad and the NOI are in no way supporting or participating in the March on Washington being held by civil rights groups in Washington, D.C., on August 28, 1963. During this speech subject warned that the March would probably end in a bloodbath, and no Negro should be foolish enough to participate.

At an FOI meeting held in Muhammad's Mosque No. 7, New York City, on August 19, 1963, subject informed those in attendance that any members of the NOI who participated in the March on Washington on August 28, 1963, would be given ninety days out of the mosque. Subject further stated that if any member belonged to a union [that] required them to participate in the March, they had better "get sick."

DATE: December 6, 1963
TO: Chief, U. S. Secret Service
FROM: John Edgar Hoover, Director
SUBJECT: NATION OF ISLAM
            INTERNAL SECURITY-NOI

[Bureau Deletion] had confirmed reports that Malcolm X Little, Minister of the Nation of Islam (NOI) Temple in New York City, and leading NOI spokesman, had been suspended from the NOI on December 4, 1963, by Elijah Muhammad for expressing joy over the death of President Kennedy.

Malcolm X Little, who spoke at a rally held by the NOI in New York City on December 1, 1963, stated that the late President Kennedy had been "twiddling his thumbs" at the slaying of South Vietnamese President Ngo Dinh Diem and his brother, Ngo Dinh Nhu. Little added that he "never foresaw that the chickens would come home to roost so soon." He also stated, "Being an old farm boy myself, chickens coming home to roost never did make me sad; they always made me glad." Elijah Muhammad, National Leader of the NOI, was scheduled to speak at this New York rally but canceled his appearance out of respect to the death of President Kennedy and instructed NOI members to make no comments concerning the assassination of the President.

The NOI is an all-Negro, anti-white, semi-religious organization which advocates complete separation of the races and teaches extreme hatred of all white men.

FEDERAL BUREAU OF INVESTIGATION
Interview of Malcolm Little on
February 5, 1964
New York, NY

Malcolm Little advised he is generally known as Malcolm X and resides at 23-11 97th Street, Queens, New York City. He stated that until sometime in December, 1963, he was the Minister in charge of the Nation of Islam (NOI) Mosque in New York City. In December, 1963, he was suspended by Elijah Muhammad from his duties. He would not say the reason for his suspension or its duration. He stated that any comment on this would have to come from Elijah Muhammad.

He stated that his suspension from duties caused him to reappraise his loyalty to the NOI and Elijah Muhammad. He stated that because of his suspension, he is now more firmly devoted to Elijah Muhammad than ever. He pointed out that his suspension proves that the rules of the NOI apply to everyone equally. He stated he is in no way bitter towards Elijah Muhammad and that anything that might have caused his suspension was entirely his own fault and he could blame no one else.

He stated that the NOI cooperates with the United States government more than any other Negro organization in that the NOI stops members from smoking, drinking, and committing crimes and many other things which result in a benefit to the United States government but which the government is unable or unwilling to do itself. Because of this, the NOI is the only group that really benefits the Negroes. He pointed out that other Negro groups do not have a program [that] will benefit the Negro and eventually the Negro will realize this. He stated that when the Negro realizes that the government, white people and so-called Negro leaders are not really helping the Negro or obtaining for the Negro the things which he wants or should have, then the Negro will start helping himself to these things. He did not care to explain this except by stating that at that time there could be a great deal of trouble.

He stated that the so-called Negro leaders are incompetent to lead the Negroes and stated that Bayard Rustin, who was a leader of the one-day school boycott in New York City on February 3, 1964, is nothing but a homosexual. He furnished no other information on either Rustin or any other person he considered a Negro leader. He reiterated that he is cooperating with the government in view of the principles of the NOI but to suggest any other means of cooperation was an insult to his intelligence. He stated the teachings of the NOI are public and are well known to the government. He stated he had no information concerning membership of the NOI, either as to numbers or names and even if he did have such information, he was not disposed to furnish it to the government.

He stated that he would have no objection to being contacted by the Federal Bureau of Investigation regarding demonstrations or other public affairs contemplated by the NOI. He stated he realized that in the past the NOI has been blamed for a number of incidents with which they were, in fact, not involved. He stated he would be most willing to be contacted in order to clear up any such possible misunderstandings.

UNITED STATES DEPARTMENT OF JUSTICE

FEDERAL BUREAU OF INVESTIGATION

Report of: [Bureau Deletion]   Office: New York
Date: 6/18/64
Field Office File No. 105-8999   Bureau File No. 100-399321
Title: MALCOLM K. LITTLE
Character: INTERNAL SECURITY-MUSLIM MOSQUE, INCORPORATED

SYNOPSIS:
Subject continues to reside at 23-11 97th Street, East Elmhurst, Queens, New York, and is founder and leader of the Muslim Mosque, Incorporated (MMI), with headquarters in the Hotel Theresa, New York City. Subject was a National Representative of the Nation of Islam (NOI) and Minister of NOI Mosque No. 7, New York City, until temporarily suspended by NOI leader Elijah Muhammad on 12/4/63, for remarks made by the subject on 12/1/63 concerning the assassination of former President Kennedy. The suspension was originally for ninety days, but was made indefinite in early March 1964, allegedly because of a power

struggle within the NOI between the subject and NOI officials. . . . Subject broke with the NOI on 3/8/64, and on 3/2/64 publicly announced the formation of the MMI, an organization with Islam as its religious base and a political, economic, and social philosophy of black nationalism. The subject outlined the ultimate aim of the MMI as the separation of races and the return of the Negro to Africa. The current aim is to work with civil rights groups to improve conditions of Negroes in the United States, although the subject opposes integration. As MMI spokesman, subject claims Negro struggle should no longer be nonviolent, and he urges Negroes to practice self-defense if and when attacked. He also suggested on 3/12/64 the formation of rifle clubs by Negroes for self-defense in areas where Negroes are not protected by the government. Subsequently, the subject denied he was promoting or organizing Negro rifle clubs, only suggesting that it was legal to own rifles and shotguns and Negroes should do so to protect themselves and their homes, if necessary. He also urged Negroes to vote in order to control their own community politically. . . . His relationship with some Negro civil rights leaders [is] set out along with comments by other Negro civil rights leaders who apparently reject him. . . . Also set forth is information on alleged threat against his life and association with sports figures. Efforts by NOI in New York City to evict him from his residence are also set forth. . . .

BREAK FROM THE NOI

Break by Subject

The March 9, 1964, edition of the *New York Times* contained an article on page 1 which reflected that on March 8, 1964, Malcolm X publicly announced that he had broken with Elijah Muhammad and the NOI due to his continued suspension and that he would organize a politically oriented "black nationalist party."

On March 12, 1964, special agents of the FBI attended a press conference held by Malcolm X in the Park Sheraton Hotel, 7th Avenue and 55th Street, New York City. At this press conference Malcolm X passed out a copy of the public statement he issued on March 8, 1964, concerning his break with the NOI [and] a copy of the telegram he sent to Elijah Muhammad on March 11, 1964.

Editor's note. *In the telegram Malcolm emphasizes that he has not left the Nation of Islam of his own free will and that he has in fact submitted to pressures both from Captain Joseph in New York and from national officials. His present course of action, Malcolm feels, will help to preserve the unity of the Nation of Islam and the faith of Muhammad's followers. Malcolm then states that he has never criticized Muhammad or his family to the press and continues with an acknowledgment of Muhammad as his "leader and teacher," to whom he gives "full credit for what I know and who I am."*

On March 9, 1964, from 10:00 to 10:30 P.M., Malcolm X appeared on the news commentary and interview program *The World at 10,* over TV station WNDT, Channel 13, New York City, where he was interviewed regarding his split with the NOI. Malcolm X explained that he was suspended (on December 4, 1963) for disobedience to Elijah Muhammad as the result of his remark on the assassination of President Kennedy, since Elijah Muhammad had previously told him not to comment on the assassination. He stated the suspension was originally for ninety days, but he recently learned that the suspension would be for an indefinite time.

The March 14, 1964, edition of the *New York Amsterdam News*, a Negro weekly newspaper published in New York, New York, on page 1, contained an exclusive interview by that paper with Malcolm X concerning his break with the NOI and the formation of the MMI.

In this interview, Malcolm X charged that NOI headquarters in Chicago had been waging a power struggle against him that led to his suspension in December, 1963. The article quoted Malcolm X as stating "they forced me to take the stand I am taking because I had to find a way to circumvent the forces in the movement that opposed me and at the same time to expedite Mr. Muhammed's program as I understand it."

This article reflected that Malcolm X's announcement to split with the NOI and form his own group was brought on by a letter he received on March 5, 1964, from Elijah Muhammad, informing him that he was to remain on suspension for an indefinite time.

Reaction of NOI Officials

The March 10, 1964, edition of the *New York Journal American,* a daily newspaper published in New York, New York, contained an article on page 1 [that] reflected that NOI leader Elijah Muhammad, in

Phoenix, Arizona, was on the verge of tears when he heard of subject's break with the NOI and he declared, "I never dreamed this man would deviate from the NOI. My people are adapted to peace. They believe in peaceful solutions."

The March 28, 1964, edition of the *Chicago Defender*, a daily newspaper published in Chicago, Illinois, contained an article on page 1 captioned "Hit Malcolm X As Judas." This article indicated that Philbert X, NOI Minister in Lansing, Grand Rapids and Flint, Michigan, and a brother of subject, denounced subject as a traitor for breaking with the NOI and forming his own group. Philbert X stated he had brought his brother into the NOI ten years ago and he claimed subject's actions were caused by "resentment" over the suspension given him by Elijah Muhammad. He described subject's new organization as "dangerous," and he denounced subject as a Brutus, Judas, and Benedict Arnold. He added that subject would do anything to gain mention and news coverage.

AFFILIATION WITH THE MUSLIM MOSQUE, INCORPORATED

On March 12, 1964, special agents of the FBI attended a press conference by subject in the Park Sheraton Hotel, New York City, from 11:00 A.M. to 1:00 P.M. which was attended by approximately sixty representatives of the press. At this press conference subject publicly announced the formation and incorporation of his new organization named "Muslim Mosque, Incorporated."

On March 16, 1964, [Bureau Deletion] New York County, New York, New York, advised that on that date a Certificate of Incorporation was filed for the MMI pursuant to Article IX of the Religious Corporation Law of the State of New York. The certificate was filed under number 2330 for 1964. The certificate was executed on March 9, 1964, notarized on March 10, 1964, and filed on March 16, 1964, by Edward W. Jacko, Jr., attorney at law, 217 West 125th Street, New York City.

The certificate reflected that on March 9, 1964, in conformity with Section 192 of the Religious Corporation Law, a meeting to decide for incorporation was held at 23-11 97th Street, Queens, New York. Present at this meeting were Malcolm X Little, who presided, Earl Grant, and James M. K. Warden. At this meeting it was decided to incorporate and the name chosen was "Muslim Mosque, Incorporated." It was also decided at this meeting that there would be no less than three nor more than twenty-one trustees, and the meeting then proceeded to elect Little,

Grant, and Warden as its trustees to serve until the first Sunday of March, 1965. On that date a second election of trustees would be held, and thereafter a new election of trustees would be held on the first Sunday of each calendar year. The certificate further indicated that the principal places of worship were to be in the borough of Manhattan, New York County, New York.

[Bureau Deletion] that James X (Warden) is a former FOI Lieutenant of NOI Mosque No. 7, New York City. In March, 1964, he went over to Malcolm X's new organization, the MMI, and he is Malcolm X's Chief Assistant.

The above incorporation record of the MMI set forth is purposes as follows:

(a) To provide a suitable place of worship for its members and others in accordance with the Islamic Faith.

(b) To maintain a house of study for the advancement of the Islamic Faith and Religion.

(c) To stimulate interest among the members in the formation, maintenance, and the teachings of the Islamic Faith.

(d) To publish textbooks, pamphlets, brochures, and to solicit, collect, and in other manners raise funds for the hereinabove and hereinafter enumerated purposes.

(e) To work for the imparting of the Islamic Faith and Islamic Religion in accordance with the accepted Islamic Religious principles.

(f) To purchase, lease, acquire, sell, and mortgage improved or unimproved real property and any interest therein.

(g) The foregoing clauses shall be considered both as objects and purposes, and it is hereby expressly provided that the foregoing enumerated specific objects and purposes shall not be held to limit or restrict in any manner the powers of this corporation, but that this corporation shall be entitled to enjoy all the powers that a religious corporation may have under and by virtue of the Laws of the State of New York.

RELATIONSHIP WITH CIVIL RIGHTS ORGANIZATIONS AND LEADERS

The March 11, 1962 edition of the *New York Journal American*, on page 2 contained an article [that] reflected that James Farmer, National Director of CORE, and Whitney Young, Head of the National Urban League, downgraded the influence in the Negro community of Malcolm

X and other black supremacists. They stated that the goals of Malcolm
X did not mesh with the overall civil rights effort since the latter is
pledged to integration and not separation, and their modus operandi
is nonviolence.

The March 15, 1964, edition of the *New York Herald Tribune*, a
daily newspaper published in New York, New York, contained an article [that] reflected that Dr. Martin Luther King of the Southern Christian
Leadership Conference denounced the suggestion of Malcolm X that
Negroes form rifle clubs to defend themselves as "a grave error" and
an "inefficient and immoral approach."

The March 21, 1964, edition of the *New Crusader*, page 5, quotes
New York Congressman Adam Clayton Powell as saying that Malcolm's plan to arm Negroes is "totally and completely wrong." He
predicted failure for Malcolm since he [Malcolm] is dedicated to separation, while the entire civil rights movement is for desegregation.

The April 26, 1964, edition of the *New York Herald Tribune* contained an article on page 10, relative to the racial situation, by former
professional baseball player Jackie Robinson. In a prelude to the article,
Robinson was described as a "loud and influential voice in the Negro
battle for equal rights," who is bitterly opposed to the forces fighting
civil rights legislation in Congress, and equally opposed to irresponsible
Negro leadership and tactics.

In the article, Mr. Robinson wrote that he could not understand why
the national "white" press, in reporting on civil rights and racial matters, persisted in "glorifying on their front pages the very persons they
condemn in their editorials."

Mr. Robinson cited Malcolm X as an outstanding example of this
reporting and he then made the following comments on Malcolm X:

> ... Malcolm has big audiences, but no constructive program. He
> has big words, but no records on deeds in civil rights. He is terribly
> militant on soapboxes on street corners of Negro ghettos. Yet, he
> has not faced Southern police dogs in Birmingham as Martin Luther
> King has done, nor gone to jail for freedom as Roy Wilkins and
> James Farmer have done, nor brought about creative dialogue be-
> tween business and civil rights leaders as Whitney Young does daily.
>
> In fact, here is a man who has been exposed and disowned by the
> very organization [that] he had so eloquently espoused—the Black
> Muslims. In spite of all this, Mr. X receives more publicity in na-
> tional media than is given to all the responsible Negro leaders we
> have mentioned above. . . .

MISCELLANEOUS

Alleged Threat Against Subject's Life

The March 21, 1964, edition of the *New York Amsterdam News* contained an article on page 50 [that] reflected that subject claimed that officials at NOI Mosque No. 7 had tried to persuade NOI members that he was insane after his suspension in December, 1963. After these NOI officials believed they had turned enough NOI members against him, subject alleged that they sent a brother out to kill him in cold blood during February, 1964, but because truth was stronger than falsehood the brother did not believe the charge and instead of killing him told him of the plot and of the actions of NOI officials. Subject claimed that when he demanded an opportunity to refute these charges before NOI Mosque No. 7 his request was refused.

[Bureau Deletion] had no information to indicate that an attempt was ever made or contemplated against the life of subject by members of the NOI, and that subject had never made such a complaint [Bureau Deletion].

Association with Sports Figures

The January 25, 1964, edition of the *New York Amsterdam News* contained an article on page 1 that subject and his family were in Miami during the past week, vacationing as the guests of heavyweight Boxing Contender Cassius Clay.

The February 1, 1964, edition of the *New York Amsterdam News* contained a photograph on page 1 of subject, his wife Betty, and their three daughters sitting together with Cassius Clay in Miami, Florida.

The March 20, 1964, edition of the *New York Herald Tribune* contained an article on page 6 [that] reflected that subject was in Miami Beach, Florida, presumably to attend the heavyweight boxing championship fight between Cassius Clay and Sonny Liston.

The March 9, 1964, edition of the *New York Post* contained an article on page 4 [that] reflected that subject, who had broken with the NOI, had stated that he would not take Cassius Clay with him out of the NOI. The article indicated that subject was generally accredited with Clay's joining the NOI.

The March 10, 1964, edition of the *New York Journal American* contained an article on page 1 [that] reflected that Cassius Clay indicated he would not leave the NOI to follow subject.

The May 18, 1964, edition of the *New York Post* contained an article on page 4, datelined "Accra, Ghana." This article indicated that the allegiance of Cassius Clay to rebel Muslim leader Malcolm X seemed to be over. The article indicated that during the separate African tours of subject and Cassius Clay they met in Morocco on April 17, 1964, and Clay made the following remarks concerning subject:

"Man, did you get a look at him? Dressed in that funny white robe and wearing a beard and walking with a cane that looked like a prophet's stick? Man, he's gone so far out he's out completely." Then, turning to Herbert Muhammad, the son of Elijah Muhammad, who is accompanying Clay on his African tour, Clay stated, "Doesn't that just go to show that Elijah is the most powerful? Nobody listens to that Malcolm anymore."

Efforts by NOI to Evict Subject from Residence

As reflected in Section 1, Part A, above, subject resides with his family at 23-11 97th Street, East Elmhurst, Queens, New York.

[Bureau Deletion] advised that after Elijah Muhammad learned subject had broken with the NOI on March 8, 1964, he instructed [Bureau Deletion] to tell subject that he must give up his residence, which is owned by the NOI.

[Bureau Deletion] advised that [Bureau Deletion] sent the following letter under date of March 10, 1964 to subject:

Dear Brother Malcolm,
    You have several items such as letters, Mosque film, Negro documents, etc., relative to the Muslims and their affairs . . . [T]he laborers and believers hereby request your cooperation in turning these items over to Muhammad's Mosque No. 7 immediately. Also you are residing in a building which was purchased by Muhammad's Mosque No. 7 for the use by a laborer as designated by the leader and teacher, the honorable Elijah Muhammed, who may serve in ministerial capacity or whatever position he places them. As you no longer hold this position we the laborers and believers request that you vacate premises located at 23-11 97th Street, East Elmhurst 69, New York, upon receiving this letter. Upon a call to Captain Joseph arrangements can be made to have personal items belonging to the Nation of Islam picked up. This letter will also serve notice your car insurance is in Muhammed's Mosque No. 7. We are requesting that you discontinue using the name of Muhammad's Mosque or the

Nation of Islam for your personal effects. . . . If you continue to use the Nation's name on your car then the Mosque will have to take possession of the car, which we do not want to do because this car is your personal property. . . . This letter also serves notice that Muhammed's Mosque No. 7 will discontinue handling expenses on utilities at said 23-11 97th Street.

[Bureau Deletion] Landlord and Tenants Proceedings, Civil Court of the City of New York, Queens County, 126-06 Queens Boulevard, Queens, New York, advised that eviction proceedings were filed by Muhammad's Temple of Islam Incorporated (NOI) On April 8, 1964, and are filed under index number L&T 4845 for 1964. Subject answered on April 13, 1964, and a hearing was set on April 17, 1964. This hearing was postponed until May 26, 1964, and postponed again until June 3, 1964. [Bureau Deletion] made the papers in the file available.

Subject's answer and counterclaim was filed by the law firm of Sutton and Sutton, 135 West 125th Street, New York City.

On June 3, 1964, [Bureau Deletion] advised that the trial on the above matter scheduled for that date had been postponed to June 15, 1964. . . .

FEDERAL BUREAU OF INVESTIGATION

Reporting office: NEW YORK

Office of origin: NEW YORK

Date: 1/20/65

Investigative period: 12/1/64–1/15/65

Report made by: [BUREAU DELETION]

Title of case: CHANGED
MALCOLM K. LITTLE aka
M. Khalil

Character of case: IS-MMI

The title of this case is marked "Changed" to add the alias of M. Khalil used by the subject when he registered at the Hilton Hotel, NYC, on 1/2/65.

AFFILIATION WITH THE MUSLIM MOSQUE, INCORPORATED
(MMI)

Efforts to Discredit NOI
Leader Elijah Muhammad

On June 8, 1964, Malcolm X, in attempting to make arrangements
with [Bureau Deletion] Columbia Broadcasting System (CBS) Television, New York City, to provide the full story of the illegitimate children of Elijah Muhammad on a film interview, told [Bureau Deletion]
that there are six women involved. Malcolm said all are former members of Muhammad's secretarial staff who have had illegitimate children
by him since 1956 or 1957. According to Malcolm two of these women
have had two children and one of the two women at that time was
pregnant with a third child of Muhammad's. Malcolm claimed that the
real reason for his split with the NOI was that when he heard of these
indiscretions, he told NOI officials who had in turn told Elijah Muhammad in a manner that made it look like he was "stirring up things"
instead of trying to resolve them. Malcolm X told [Bureau Deletion]
that his life is at stake because he poses a threat to the NOI since
public revelation of this information would cause NOI members to desert Elijah Muhammad. On the same date, [Bureau Deletion] received
a telephone message for Malcolm X from an anonymous caller who
said "Just tell him he is as good as dead."

On [Bureau Deletion] 1964, [Bureau Deletion] advised that at an
MMI public rally held in the Audubon Ballroom, New York City, on
June 7, 1964, Malcolm X, in answer to a question from the audience,
stated that Elijah Muhammad was the father of six illegitimate children.
He claimed the NOI covers this up and would even murder to keep it
quiet. Malcolm indicated that he had learned this from Elijah's son,
Wallace Muhammad.

On June 12, 1964, Malcolm X was the guest on the program *Conversation for Peace* over radio station WEEI, Boston, Massachusetts. During the program, he stated that the real reason for his break with the
NOI was due to a moral problem. He then told the story of several
teenage NOI members who went to work for the NOI since 1957, and
became pregnant. It was always assumed that a non-Muslim male was
involved since no one ever stood with the girls when they were brought
before the temple to stand charges for their actions. In February, 1963,
according to Malcolm X, he learned that Elijah Muhammad was the

father of these children and that he talked to Muhammad about it and the latter admitted it. In October, 1963, Malcolm said he was informed by Elijah's son, Wallace, that it was still going on and he then realized that he could no longer represent Elijah Muhammad. Malcolm indicated that Elijah Muhammad had children by six of his secretaries.

[Bureau Deletion]

It is to be noted that since June, 1964, Malcolm X and the MMI have attempted to publicize the illegitimate children of Elijah Muhammad through various news media. Malcolm X has been successful in getting the story on several radio programs during interviews, but a fear of a libel suit has apparently kept such publicity at a minimum. However, representatives of various news agencies have advised Malcolm that they could publicize it if the women involved instituted legal action against Elijah Muhammad.

AFFILIATION WITH THE ORGANIZATION OF AFRO-AMERICAN UNITY (OAAU)

On June 30, 1964, [Bureau Deletion] advised that Malcolm X sent [a] telegram on that date to Dr. Martin Luther King, Southern Christian Leadership Conference at Saint Augustine, Florida, and also to [Bureau Deletion] the Student Nonviolent Coordinating Committee at Philadelphia, Mississippi, where both of the above were engaged in activities and demonstrations on behalf of the civil rights movement. [Subject advised King that if federal government will not send troops to King's assistance, then on King's word "we will immediately dispatch some of our brothers there to organize our people into self-defense units among our people and the Ku Klux Klan will receive a taste of its own medicine. The day of turning the cheek to the human brute beasts is over."]

An OAAU-sponsored public meeting was held on December 13, 1964, at New York City, attended by about five hundred people.

The featured speaker was OAAU Chairman and MMI leader Malcolm X. He devoted most of his speech to the Congo situation, claiming that the United States is responsible for the situation there because of its support for the Congo Premier Moise Tshombe. Malcolm X charged that it was the United States who was hiring white mercenaries for

Tshombe and these white mercenaries described by Malcolm X as "hired killers" are the ones who are killing innocent Africans.

Malcolm X also spoke on Mississippi and indicated that the struggle for independence by Africans was synonymous with the struggle for freedom by Afro-Americans in the United States. Malcolm X also stated that the Federal Bureau of Investigation cannot stop the murders in Mississippi so "they" would have to take care of it. He did not elaborate further on what "they" would do other than to remark in jest that he would pay a reward of $1,000 to anyone who would "get" the sheriff and his deputy who were recently released after being arrested for killing three civil rights workers. . . .

BREAK FROM THE NATION OF ISLAM (NOI)

On June 4, 1964, Malcolm X appeared on Radio Station WDAS, Philadelphia, Pennsylvania, and was asked why he left the Nation of Islam. Malcolm stated that Wallace Muhammad, son of Elijah Muhammad, is the one who really told him what was going on and told him to wake up and leave the organization. He said he learned from Wallace Muhammad that Elijah Muhammad, NOI leader, fathered six illegitimate children by women who were secretaries at the NOI in Chicago. He said two of the women went to Phoenix and were put up in a motel in that city. Two other women were from Detroit. Malcolm stated that John Ali, National Secretary of the NOI, is currently running the NOI. He said Elijah Muhammad's sons had him go to Phoenix so that John Ali could run the organization. All members of the NOI were told to have absolutely nothing to do with Malcolm. Malcolm said John Ali is running the organization (NOI) for one purpose and that is to get all the money out of it that he possibly can.

An article in the June 26, 1964, issue of the *New York Post*, a local New York newspaper, captioned "Malcolm X to Elijah; Let's End the Fighting." This article states:

> Malcolm X today called for an end to the three-month dispute which has split the black Muslim movement in Harlem.
> In an open letter to Elijah Muhammad, he urged an end to hostilities which threaten to flare into open warfare between the two groups, his dissidents and the parent body headed by Elijah. He called for unity in solving the problems of Negroes in Mississippi, Alabama, Georgia, and other parts of the South.

"Instead of wasting all this energy fighting each other," he wrote, "we should be working in unity with other leaders and organizations in an effort to solve the very serious problems facing all Afro-Americans."

He asked Elijah Muhammad how, since the Muslims did not resort to violence when they were attacked by "white racists" in Los Angeles and Rochester, N. Y., they could justify declaring war on each other.

Malcolm X's statement came on the heels of an announcement by Muhammad's followers that they had received a "tip" from one of Malcolm's followers that plans were being made to assassinate Elijah Muhammad when he arrives at Kennedy International Airport Sunday morning.

Malcolm X, reached at his Boston hotel, denied that he or his followers were plotting to kill the Muslim leader. "I'm surprised at the accusation," he said. "No Muslim would think of assassinating Muhammad. He has never been in any danger in his life.

"We don't have to kill him. What he has done will bring him to his grave." ...

ALLEGED THREATS AGAINST MALCOLM X

At New York

The *New York Herald Tribune*, a local New York daily newspaper, dated June 16, 1964, contained an article captioned "Eight Guards, Thirty-two Police for Malcolm X." In this article it is stated that the police and guards were guarding Malcolm X because of anonymous telephone tips to the wire service and a newspaper that Malcolm would be shot if he appeared in court for an eviction trial. Malcolm is quoted as saying, "There is no people in the United States more able to carry out this threat than the Black Muslims. I know; I taught them myself."

Malcolm X contacted the New York City Police Department on July 3, 1964, and advised them that he was returning home alone in his car at 11:30 P.M. the same date and stopped in front of his home at 23-11 97th Street, East Elmhurst, New York, when two unknown Negro males approached his car and touched the door, at which time he sped away, drove around the block and returned to his residence and the two unknown Negro males were nowhere in sight.

A police guard was placed in front of Malcolm's home until 4:00 P.M., July 4, 1964. It is believed that the complaint of Malcolm X was a publicity stunt since he apparently notified the wire and news service as well as the police department about the incident.

Malcolm X was contacted on July 5, 1964, [Bureau Deletion], who advised Malcolm that orders to kill him, Malcolm, have come from Chicago and that witnesses can be furnished if Malcolm wants to take the NOI to court.

At Boston, Massachusetts

On June 12, 1964, [Bureau Deletion] Boston, Massachusetts, advised that at approximately 1:40 P.M. on the same date [Bureau Deletion] had received an anonymous phone call concerning Malcolm X. The caller stated that "Malcolm X is going to be bumped off."

[Bureau Deletion] advised that police were sent to guard Malcolm X who was appearing on a radio program, [at] station WEEI at 182 Tremont Street, Boston, Massachusetts from 2:10 P.M. until 5:00 P.M. and at 10:00 P.M. the same date Malcolm X was to appear on radio station WMEX, Boston.

Malcolm X appeared on the *Jerry Williams Radio Program* on WMEX, Boston, from 10:00 P.M., June 12, 1964, to 1:00 A.M., June 13, 1964. Williams introduced Malcolm X as the former spokesman for Elijah Muhammad and the Muslims. He stated he understood several threats had been made on Malcolm's life that day and Malcolm stated that several threats had been made on his life during the last five months. Malcolm then remarked that recently on a radio program in Chicago known as *Hot Line*, John Ali, National Secretary of the Muslims, had been asked by a telephone caller if it was true that Muslim movement was trying to kill Malcolm X. According to Malcolm, John Ali replied that they were trying to kill Malcolm X and that he should be killed.

FOREIGN TRAVEL OF MALCOLM X

To Africa, April 13, 1964
through May 21, 1964

On May 21, 1964, Supervisor John Adams, Immigration and Naturalization Service (INS), John F. Kennedy (JFK) International Airport, New York, advised that Malcolm X Little, Passport Number C294275, using the name Malik Elshabazz arrived in the United States at 4:25 P.M., aboard Pan American flight 115 from Paris, France.

On July 13, 1964, [BUREAU DELETION] furnished an itinerary
[for] Malcolm X during his trip to Africa which indicated the following schedule:

April 13, 1964	He departed the United States for Cairo, Egypt.
April 14 to	In Cairo, United Arab Republic, Beirut, Lebanon
May 5, 1964	and Saudi Arabia, where he completed pilgrimage to Mecca.
May 6, 1964	In Lagos, Nigeria.
May 8, 1964	In Ibadan, Nigeria.
May 10, 1964	In Accra, Ghana.
May 18, 1964	Morocco.
May 19, 1964	In Algiers
May 21, 1964	Returned to the United States.

At Ibadan, Nigeria

[Bureau Deletion] made available on May 27, 1964, a copy of the
newspaper *Pilot*, datelined Ibadan, Nigeria, dated May 8, 1964, [which]
contained an article of an interview with Malcolm X. According to this
article Malcolm X stated "United States Peace Corps [members] are
spies. They are missionaries of neocolonialism and although white
American Peace Corps [members] were dangerous enough to invoke
protest from any country they were operating, Negro American Peace
Corps [members] were more dangerous and objectional." This article
also stated that Malcolm X remarked that the "Negroes in [the] Peace
Corps were being used by the American Government to place a wedge
between American Negroes and Africans with views toward ending
[the] concept of Africanization of Negroes." ...

At Accra, Ghana

[Bureau Deletion] advised on June 11, 1964 that Malcolm X arrived
in Accra, Ghana on May 11, 1964. He was not officially invited to
Ghana by the Ghanaian Government but came at the invitation of the
"Marxist Forum," a new student organization in the University of
Ghana. He did not have an interview with President Nkrumah nor did
the government hold any official reception for him.

During his visit, Malcolm spoke to the Association of Ghanaian Journalists and gave a lecture at the University of Ghana entitled "Will
Africa Ignite America's Racial Powder Keg?" He also spoke before

the students of Kwame Nkrumah's Ideological Institute and to an informal group of Parliament members.

malcolm emphasized the following basic themes during his tour to
Ghana:

1. The Negroes were stolen from Africa and forced to forget their
culture and traditions, yet they never have been accepted into American society.

2. The Christian religion has been used to oppress Negroes and encourage them to accept an inferior position.

3. Force is the only possible way to achieve equality.

4. The United States is the "master of imperialism" without whose
support other imperialistic nations could not exist.

5. White America is guilty of dehumanizing the American Negro and
putting him to death as a human being.

6. If America is not interested in human rights in America, how can
she be interested in human rights in Africa? The American Government
should not send the Peace Corps to Africa, they should send them to
Mississippi and Alabama.

7. The only difference between apartheid in South Africa and racism
in the United States is that "white South Africa preaches and practices
segregation, the United States preaches integration and practices
segregation."

On May 23, 1964, Malcolm X appeared on *Kup's Show,* Channel 7-
TV, Chicago, Illinois.

Malcolm said he arrived in Cairo about three in the morning and his
inability to speak Arabic plus his American passport made him automatically suspect. So he was taken from the group that he originally started
out from Cairo with and placed in a compound [that] has been built
there in Jedda which houses all of the incoming pilgrims, and he thought
about ninety thousand came in this year by plane alone. He was put in
this place and he had to admit he was worried because he couldn't
communicate. And he stayed there about twenty hours and he was in
a haram (phonetic) which is a two-piece towel outfit. Your waist from
the belt downward is wrapped in one towel and from the waist upward
in another. And after being in this particular plight for about twenty
hours, he recalled that Dr. Schwarbe (phonetic) from New York had
given him a book that had been sent to him by Abdarakman Azam
(phonetic). The name of the book is *The Eternal Message of Muhammad.* So [Malcolm] called his son [who] came to the place where he
was and used his authority to get him released, get [his] passport. He

took him to his home where he met Azam Parsha (phonetic), and he gave him his suite at the Jedda Palace Hotel and the next morning he was visited by the son of Prince Faisal (phonetic), Muhammad Faisal (phonetic). He informed him that he was to be a state guest so that the remaining twelve days that he was in Arabia, he was a guest of the state. They ... placed a car at his disposal, gave him a guide—a mua-lam (phonetic), and a chauffeur and made it possible, after going before the highest committee of the court, for him to travel back and forth between Mecca and Jedda and Medina almost at will. He was given the highest honor and respect and hospitality that a visitor could receive anywhere.

On [Bureau Deletion] 1964, [Bureau Deletion] furnished a copy of a letter written by Malcolm X from Jedda, Saudi Arabia, dated April 20, 1964, which stated that during his pilgrimage to Mecca, he observed many white persons who displayed the spirit of unity and brotherhood that he did not believe could ever have existed based on his previous American experience. He stated that America needs to understand Islam because it is the one religion that erases the race problem from society. He also stated that if whites and non-whites would accept Islam they would become changed people since it removes racism, and all members thus automatically accept each other as brothers and sisters. He went on in the letter to state "you may be shocked at these words coming from me" and he added that his pilgrimage has taught him that if Islam can replace the spirit of true brotherhood in the hearts of whites he has met there, it can also remove the "cancer of racism" from the heart of white America.

Travel to Africa from July 9, 1964 to November 14, 1964

On July 6, 1964, Malcolm X, using the name Hajj Malik El-Shabazz with passport number C294275, purchased a one-way ticket to Cairo, Egypt via London, England. He was scheduled to depart from JFK International Airport, New York, on July 9, 1964, aboard Trans World Airlines (TWA) flight 700, due to arrive in London, England, 7:30 A.M., July 10, 1964. He was scheduled to depart London, England, 3:30 P.M., July 11, 1964, aboard United Arab Airlines, flight 790 to Cairo, Egypt. Malcolm failed to make return reservations or airline bookings when he arrived in Cairo for his return trip to the United States.

At Cairo, Egypt

The *New York Times*, dated July 14, 1964, captioned "Malcolm X in Cairo Says He'll See African Leaders." This article, datelined Cairo, July 13, states:

Malcolm X the black nationalist leader said today that he had come to attend a meeting of the council of ministers of the Organization of African Unity as an observer. He arrived yesterday.

He said he intended to acquaint African heads of state "with the true plight of America's Negroes and thus show them how our situation is as much a violation of the United Nations human rights charter as the situation in Africa and Mongolia.

The *New York Times*, dated August 13, 1964, contained an article captioned, "Malcolm X Seeks UN Negro Debate—He Asks African States to Cite United States Over Rights." This article, datelined Washington, August 12, states:

The State Department and the Justice Department have begun to take an interest in Malcolm X's campaign to convince African states to raise the question of persecution of American Negroes at the United Nations.

The Black Nationalist leader started his campaign July 17 in Cairo, where the thirty-three heads of independent African states held their second meeting since the Organization of African Unity was founded in Addis Ababa fourteen months ago. . . .

Malcolm also warned the heads of the African states that their countries would have no future unless the American Negro problem was solved. . . .

Asserting that the Negro problem is not one of civil rights but of human rights, Malcolm said:

If United States Supreme Court Justice Arthur Goldberg a few weeks ago, could find legal grounds to threaten to bring Russia before the United Nations and charge her with violating the human rights of less than three million Russian Jews—what makes our African brothers hesitate to bring the United States Government before the United Nations and charge her with violating the human rights of 22 million African-Americans?

We pray that our African brothers have not freed themselves of European colonialism only to be overcome and held in check by American dollarism. Don't let American racism be "legalized" by American dollarism.

Malcolm argued that "if South African racism is not a domestic issue, then American racism also is not a domestic issue."

The Black Nationalist, who quit the Chicago-based Black Muslim movement led by Elijah Muhammad to form his non-sectarian Organization of Afro-American Unity, said it was the intention of his group in coalition with other Negro groups "to elevate our freedom struggle above the domestic level of civil rights."

At Addis Ababa, Ethiopia

[Bureau Deletion] advised on 10/6/64 that on 10/3/64 Malcolm X, during a three-day visit to Addis Ababa, addressed the open student assembly of the university college at the invitation of the University College Student Union. There was an estimated audience of five hundred to six hundred persons consisting primarily of Ethiopian students and others consisting of faculty members and outside visitors.

After a flattering and enthusiastic introduction by a student leader ("known throughout Africa as a man standing for principle, truth, and justice") Malcolm X presented a rather surprisingly low-keyed lecture which stressed two major purposes of his safari in Africa: 1) to remain away from the U.S. until after the election in order to avoid making the decision as to whether he (and presumably American Negroes in general) would be devoured by "a fox or a wolf"; and 2) to attempt to persuade the independent African nations to haul the U.S. before the UN on charges of being "unable or unwilling" to give the American Negro his civil rights.

Malcolm X's speech employed clever distortions of truth to lead to distorted conclusions—e.g., when World War II started, the U.S. was not taking Negroes into the army or navy for fear they would learn to use weapons against whites. The tone of the speech reflected Malcolm's assertion at the beginning that he had just concluded two months of "quiet rearrangement" of his "thinking" in Cairo. He was not nearly so emotional as he sometimes has been in the past, nor did he lay himself open to traps as often as he is sometimes prone to do.

The audience response was good, with several interruptions for applause, particularly during his attacks on the United States' effort in Africa.

Following Malcolm's speech the student moderator felt compelled to note that of course African students don't believe that United States aid comes "out of human kindness." The four questions from the audience were rather bland, but did permit Malcolm to develop the theme that while Goldwater was a rather open racist, Johnson ("the fox") was more subtle, but that the latter's record during thirty years in Congress was also that of a racist. In discussing the coming election, he stated that the American people don't govern, that southern-dominated congressional committees control under the seniority system and it is they "who send military equipment to Tshombe."

In answering the final question, he emphasized the relative unity between himself and such leaders as Martin Luther King, saying that their differences were primarily differences of method rather than goals. "The main difference is that he doesn't mind being beat up and I do."

At Lagos, Nigeria

[Bureau Deletion] advised on 11/6/64 that Malcolm X visited Lagos for the second time on October 29, 1964. He previously visited Lagos in May, 1964.

On his arrival on October 29, 1964, he held a press conference. Malcolm X was quoted as saying that he was "touring Africa to better acquaint himself with the problems facing the continent so that he could tell his people at home about these problems, factually and in detail." Malcolm X said that "one of the greatest problems facing Africa was internal squabbling" and continued, "in East Africa it is the Africans against the Asians, and in West Africa, it is the Moslem against Christians, and all these are fed by outside force."

At Conakry, French West Africa

[Bureau Deletion] advised on 11/14/64 that Malcolm X left Conakry by plane on November 13, 1964. He was "GOG Guest" and carried a visitor's visa. He visited the hospital ship *SS Hope* twice accompanied by a GOG interpreter and took pictures. He was enthusiastic about "Project Hope," saying "it was the best United States project he had seen in Africa and especially commended integration aboard ship."

Return to United States from African Tour on 11/24/64

[Bureau Deletion] New York City, advised on November 24, 1964, that passenger manifest list of TWA flight 801, Paris, France, contained the name "Shabazz." This flight was scheduled to arrive at JFK International Airport, 6:00 P.M., November 24, 1964.

MISCELLANEOUS

On September 4, 1964, [Bureau Deletion] Rome, New York, furnished the following information to SA [Bureau Deletion].

[Bureau Deletion] stated that on September 1, 1964, he visited the office of Alexander Palmer Haley, a Negro writer and newspaper correspondent at 414 West Dominick Street, Rome, New York, on an official matter. According to [Bureau Deletion] Haley advised he had just completed a book he had written concerning Malcolm X Little. [Bureau Deletion] Haley indicated he had been in contact with Malcolm X on more than one occasion in regard to this writing, and that he, Haley, and Malcolm are to share in the royalties expected from this book.

OPINION OF THE DEPARTMENT OF STATE

A. Re. MALCOLM X

By letter dated September 2, 1964, J. Walter Yeagley, Assistant Attorney General, Internal Security Division, Department of Justice, advised that Malcolm K. Little aka Malcolm X, in the course of his recent tour of the Middle East and African countries, has reportedly been in communication and contact with heads of foreign governments urging that they take the issue of "racialism" in America before the United Nations as a threat to world peace.

Mr. Yeagley indicated that since such activities could conceivably fall within the provisions of the Logan Act, and are moreover deemed to be inimical to the best interests of our country and prejudicial to our foreign policy, the Department of Justice requested the Secretary of State to make appropriate inquiries of our embassies in the Middle East and Africa for any pertinent information concerning Malcolm X's alleged contacts and communications with heads of foreign governments.

Mr. Yeagley expressed concern over the fact that Malcolm X's activities abroad indicate a possible violation of the Logan Act.

B. Re MMI

By letter dated September 28, 1964, Mr. Yeagley advised that if evidence is available [that] will establish the MMI has been or is receiving funds from any Arab or African government, or is acting at the order, request, or under the direction of the foreign government, it may be obligated to register under the Foreign Agents Registration Act.

FBI

DATE:2/4/65

AIRTEL

TO:　　　　　DIRECTOR, FBI (100-399321)

FROM:　　　SAC, CHICAGO (100-33593) (P)

SUBJECT:　MALCOLM K. LITTLE, aka IS-MMI (OO: New York)

Re Chicago teletype to Director dated 1/29/65.

Referenced teletype stated that Malcolm X was to appear on *Kup's Show*, a TV panel-type discussion, on 1/30/65 in Chicago.

Kup's Show is a local TV show televised over WBKB-TV, Chicago, from approximately 12:15 A.M. to 3:00 A.M. on Sunday mornings. This show was televised on 1/31/65 but was taped on 1/30/65 P.M. at studios of WBKB-TV, Chicago. Irving Kupcinet, Chicago newspaper columnist and TV moderator, conducts the show.

The following is the transcript:

KUPCINET: Malcolm, you know you've changed a lot since your first appearance on this show some years ago. At that time you were sort of a stormy individual and you hated all whites you said.

MALCOLM: I've gotten older.

KUPCINET: Now you have a different attitude completely and you told me that your religious experience in Cairo has changed your attitude and your outlook.

MALCOLM: Well, as a Muslim, since I left Elijah Muhammad's Black Muslim movement—I should say since they put me out 'cause that is what they did—I have had a chance to do some traveling and travel does broaden your scope, and as a Muslim whose religion is Islam, as it is practiced and taught in the Muslim world, I realize that it is impossible to call oneself a Muslim, to call one's religion Islam and at the same time judge a man by the color of his skin. . . .

KUPCINET: This poses two very interesting things. In other words, you no longer believe as Elijah Muhammad has been quoted as saying that all white men are devils. You have changed everything.

MALCOLM: If Elijah Muhammad says that all white men are devils, then you have the King of Arabia, King Faisal, who is white. He is the keeper of the Holy City of Mecca and many other Arabs, in Egypt, in Algeria, and in other places. They are from all appearances white.

KUPCINET: Now this poses a second problem I would like to get your opinion on. Of course, you may be biased because you no longer are a member of the so-called Black Muslims, but is the Black Muslim a religion or not, because this is coming up in a case in Chicago where a prisoner in Stateville converted from Roman Catholicism to Black Muslim and demanded to be allowed to practice his religion in jail. The warden denied this because he said the Black Muslims were not a bona fide religion. How do you feel?

MALCOLM: I want to answer that with this explanation first. Number one: no one can use me against Elijah Muhammad or against the Black Muslim movement. On the other hand, anything that Elijah Muhammad says or does, or the Black Muslim movement says or does, which I feel is against the best interest of the black community, then I will attack it myself, but I won't attack it because someone sics me on it. . . . Islam teaches that belief in all of the prophets, especially Muhammad ibn Abd Allah, who was born and died in Arabia fourteen hundred years ago and the Muslim believes that Muhammad of Arabia was the last prophet, the last messenger, whereas Elijah Muhammad teaches that Muhammad of Arabia was not a prophet, but an enthusiast, and that he, himself, Elijah, is the prophet, so that . . . what Elijah Muhammad is teaching is diametrically opposed to the principles of Islam and the Muslim world itself, the religious officials at Mecca and other religious officials and those at the top authority on Islam theology, totally reject what Elijah

Muhammad teaches as being any phase, even of Islam. On the other hand, what he is teaching can be easily defined as a religion, but it cannot be labeled Islam ... and I think that if the penal authorities were farsighted enough to permit the religion of Islam, real Islam, true Islam, to be taught in prison by qualified Islamic religious leaders as they let Judaism, Catholicism, and the Protestant religions be taught there, then many of the people that are in prison would not be misled like I, myself, was because there is a vacuum in this country where Islam is concerned ... and in that vacuum, it is easy for any phony or faker to come along with a concocted, distorted product of his own making, and say that this is Islam.

KUPCINET: Are you by inference saying that Elijah Muhammad is a faker and a phony?

MALCOLM: If Elijah Muhammad really believed in the same God that I believed in—I believed in Elijah Muhammad stronger than he believed in himself. I believed in his God more than he did and I was not aware of this until I found he was confronted with a crisis in his own personal moral life and he did not stand up as a man. Anybody could make a moral mistake, but when they have to lie about it and will be willing to see that murder is committed to cover up their mistake not only are they not divine, they are not even a man. ...

KUPCINET: Are you trying to tell us that there has been an attack on your life because of your withdrawal from the Muslim religion?

MALCOLM: I have had several.

KUPCINET: You have?

MALCOLM: And just thanks to Allah, so far I have been successful. I believe that when you are a black man born in this particular society, you are faced with certain dangers already. You get used to it and plus the stand that I took when I was in the Black Muslim movement was uncompromising. I defended an indefensible position. Anyone that defends an indefensible position as I did—they must have believed in it.

UNITED STATES DEPARTMENT OF JUSTICE

FEDERAL BUREAU OF INVESTIGATION

New York, New York
February 16, 1965
Malcolm K. Little
Internal Security—Muslim Mosque, Incorporated

[Bureau Deletion] New York City Police Department (NYCPD), advised the New York Office of the Federal Bureau of Investigation (FBI) on February 14, 1965, that early that morning Malcolm X's home was destroyed by a fire.

On February 14, 1965, a conference was held at the 114th Precinct, NYCPD, at 23-16 30th Avenue, Queens, New York, with Special Agents (SAs) of the FBI, [Bureau Deletion] Detective District, New York City, [Bureau Deletion] New York City, concerning the burning of the residence of Malcolm X, 23-11 97th Street, East Elmhurst, Queens, New York, leader of the MMI and the OAAU.

[Bureau Deletion] stated that the first alarm was received by telephone at 2:46 A.M. February 14, 1965, from [Bureau Deletion] East Elmhurst, Queens, New York. [Bureau Deletion] later interviewed by the fire department, stated she was awakened by the noise of glass breaking. She looked out the window and saw a round hole in Malcolm X's living room window, and the room was in flames. [Bureau Deletion] stated she saw no one near Malcolm X's residence at that time.

[Bureau Deletion] advised that the second alarm was sounded by [Bureau Deletion] Queens, New York, a cab driver who, with an unidentified passenger, noticed a bush burning in front of Malcolm X's residence. [Bureau Deletion] said he put the bush fire out and while doing so, he heard glass breaking twice. He stated he then looked along the side of the house, and saw a fire in the rear of the home. He then stated he knocked at the front door of Malcolm X's home and at the same time, heard voices inside. He then knew that they were awake so he ran to set off the fire alarm.

[Bureau Deletion] said that from the time he first saw the bush fire in front of the home to the time the fire department arrived, he neither saw nor heard any person or vehicle leaving the area.

[Bureau Deletion] stated the fire engines arrived at Malcolm X's home at 2:50 A.M. on 2/14/65. He stated the fire was confined to the living room area, with smoke and water damaging areas of the home. He stated Malcolm X, his wife and four children, ages six months to six years, escaped through the back door and were in the back yard when the fire apparatus arrived.

[Bureau Deletion] stated that an investigation conducted by the New York City Police and Fire Departments disclosed the following:

Investigation of Fire

1. The bushes and front of the home on the right side of the front steps were scorched.
2. The fire was confined to the living room only.
3. The rear bedroom window was broken, the ground and fence in the vicinity of the broken rear window were scorched.
4. The venetian blind on the broken rear window was closed and down, and was scorched at the bottom, although there was no evidence of fire in the rear bedroom.

Evidence Obtained at Scene of Fire

1. The bottom ⅛ part of a whiskey bottle containing gasoline was found in the enclosed front porch. The glass of the bottle was scorched, although there was no evidence of a fire in the front porch area.
2. A quart whiskey bottle filled with gasoline was located standing upright on the dresser in the rear bedroom where Malcolm X's other daughters slept. This bottle had a screw cap which was intact and did not have rags attached to it.

It is noted that all firemen who entered Malcolm X's home during the fire were interviewed and all stated they did not place the bottle on the dresser.

3. A broken neck of a whiskey bottle with a scorched cloth wick attacked to the neck of the bottle was located in the rear of the said home at approximately 15 feet from the house and near the bedroom with the broken window and scorched ground and fence.
4. A broken neck of a whiskey bottle and shoulder of a whiskey bottle which matched the neck section was found in the center of Malcolm X's bedroom. A piece of cloth soaked with gasoline but unscorched was on the bedroom floor a few feet from the broken whiskey bottle. No evidence of a fire could be located in this bedroom.

The youngest daughter, age six months, slept in a third bedroom opposite Malcolm X's room.

No evidence of bottles could be located in the living room where the fire was confined, but according to [Bureau Deletion] there was evidence that gasoline was used in the living room fire.

[Bureau Deletion]

The investigation by [Bureau Deletion] and [Bureau Deletion] determined that Malcolm X stated he awoke himself and discovered the fire and that his wife, Betty, stated that she awoke him and then grabbed their children and left their home through the rear door.

Malcolm X, after the fire, and during the interview, showed no emotion or anger and actually laughed when he was asked who he thought may have burned his home.

Malcolm X left his family with friends, returned to his home after the fire was put out, secured some clothing and recording tapes and left about 9:00 A.M. for a meeting in Detroit....

UNITED STATES DEPARTMENT OF JUSTICE

FEDERAL BUREAU OF INVESTIGATION

New York, New York
February 16, 1965

Organization of Afro-American Unity
Internal Security—Miscellaneous

[Bureau Deletion] OAAU held a public rally from 8:15 P.M. to 10:15 P.M., February 15, 1965, at the Audubon Ballroom, Broadway and 166th Street, New York City. Approximately six hundred persons were in attendance. There was extensive press coverage of the rally.

The meeting was opened by MMI Assistant Minister Benjamin X Goodman who made a few introductory remarks and then introduced the featured speaker, OAAU and MMI leader, Malcolm X Little.

Malcolm X talked at length on the firebombs [that] were thrown into his house in the early morning of February 14, 1965, destroying the house. He was quite angry and upset that the incident had placed his wife and daughters in danger and he angrily accused the NOI of doing it on the direct orders of NOI leader, Elijah Muhammad. He ridiculed the suggestion by the NOI that he set the fire himself and claimed that he knew absolutely nothing about his being evicted from the house on February 15, 1965, based on a court action by the NOI, until he heard it on the radio on February 15, 1965.

Malcolm X then claimed that a conspiracy exists between the NOI and the Ku Klux Klan that is not in the best interest of the black people. He alleged that both the NOI and the Klan have agreed to leave each other alone and that the Klan has offered land in North Carolina to the NOI for the latter's "separate state" for Negroes plan. Malcolm X also implied that Elijah Muhammad and his NOI are sympathetically linked with George Lincoln Rockwell and his American Nazi Party.

FBI

DATE: 2/19/65

AIRTEL

TO:		DIRECTOR, FBI

FROM:		SAC, CHICAGO (100-35635)

SUBJECT:	NATION OF ISLAM
		IS—NOI

Re Philadelphia teletype to Director, Chicago and New York dated 2/16/65, entitled "Organization of Afro-American Unity, is—miscellaneous."

Referenced teletype reflected a meeting of the OAAU was held on 2/15/65, at [the] Audubon Ballroom, in New York City; that Malcolm Little was the main speaker and alleged that while he was active in the NOI in 12/60, he attended a meeting with [Bureau Deletion] of Elijah Muhammad's Mosque [Bureau Deletion] and KKK officials at [Bureau Deletion] home in Atlanta for the purpose of negotiating for land for Elijah Muhammad to set up a separate state in Georgia or in South Carolina. Little further alleged that George Lincoln Rockwell and his American Nazi Party and KKK and Elijah Muhammad were connected.

Regarding Malcolm's allegations concerning the meeting with officials of the KKK in Atlanta in 1960, attention is directed to report of SA [Bureau Deletion] dated 4/14/61. Pages 44 and 45 carry information reflecting [that] Elijah Muhammad spoke at [the] Magnolia Ballroom in Atlanta, Georgia, on 9/11/60. Pages 96 and 97 set forth information regarding a meeting between Malcolm Little and [Bureau Deletion] with KKK leaders at Atlanta in late [Bureau Deletion] This is apparently the meeting Little was referring to.

Regarding Little's allegations that Muhammad is connected with the American Nazi Party, attention is directed to the report of SA [Bureau Deletion] dated 4/24/62. Pages 122 through 125 set forth information regarding an appearance by George Lincoln Rockwell at the Annual Muslim Convention held at Chicago, Illinois, on 2/25/62, and also sets forth information regarding Muhammad's comments regarding Rockwell and his associates. Attention is also directed to report of SA [Bureau Deletion] dated 10/24/62. Page 132 sets forth information regarding alleged cooperation between the American Nazi Party and the NOI.

FEDERAL BUREAU OF INVESTIGATION
U. S. DEPARTMENT OF JUSTICE
COMMUNICATIONS SECTION

FEBRUARY 18, 1965
TELETYPE
SENT BY CODED TELETYPE
FBI NEW YORK
7-16 PM URGENT 2-18-65 DAE
TO DIRECTOR -10- 100-399321
FROM NEW YORK 105-8999
MALCOLM K. LITTLE, AKA IS-MMI.

RENYAIRTELS AND LHM-S DATED FEB. SIXTEEN, SIXTY FIVE CAPTIONED AS ABOVE AND OTHER CAPTIONED OAAU, IS-MISC.

AT NINE AM FEB. EIGHTEEN, SIXTY-FIVE MALCOLM X OFFICIALLY EVICTED FROM HIS RESIDENCE TWENTY THREE-ELEVEN NINETY-SEVENTH ST., EAST ELMHURST, QUEENS, NY, AT WHICH TIME REGINALD THORPE, MARSHAL OF CITY OF NEW YORK TURNED RESIDENCE OVER TO [BUREAU DELETION] NOI MOSQUE NUMBER SEVEN, NYC. MALCOLM X MOVED BELONGINGS FROM RESIDENCE AT ONE AM FEB. EIGHTEEN, SIXTY-FIVE. [BUREAU DELETION] ADVISED FEB. EIGHTEEN, SIXTY-FIVE MALCOLM X NOW RESIDING AT THIRTY FOUR-FIFTY ONE HUNDRED TENTH ST., EAST ELMHURST, QUEENS, NY WITH MMI MEMBER.
SND AND PLS HOLD . . . .

FEDERAL BUREAU OF INVESTIGATION
U. S. DEPARTMENT OF JUSTICE

COMMUNICATIONS SECTION

FEBRUARY 22, 1965
TELETYPE
FBI PHILA
1-58 PM URGENT 2-22-65 RM
TO DIRECTOR /100-399321/ AND NEW YORK/105-8999/
NEW YORK VIA WASH
FROM PHILADELPHIA /100-39918/
MALCOLM K. LITTLE, AKA IS-MMI.

RE NEW YORK TELETYPE 2-21-65.

[BUREAU DELETION] THEY POSSESSED NO INFO ON KILL-
ING OF SUBJECT OR ATTEMPT TO RETALIATE BY HIS FOL-
LOWERS. THEY WILL IMMEDIATELY ADVISE THIS OFFICE
SHOULD THEY OBTAIN INFO CONCERNING ABOVE

[BUREAU DELETION] WAS AT RALLY NEW YORK CITY
WHEN MALCOLM X WAS KILLED. . . .

FEDERAL BUREAU OF INVESTIGATION

Interview of SA [BUREAU DELETION] on
February 24, 1965
Philadelphia, PA.

[Bureau Deletion] was at the rally in New York City on February
21, 1965, at the Audubon Ballroom, where Malcolm X was killed.
This meeting was sponsored by the Organization of Afro-American
Unity (OAAU).

[Bureau Deletion] arrived at the ballroom [as] Benjamin X was
speaking. Malcolm X was not in sight. About 3 P.M. Malcolm X appeared on stage right and walked to the podium. Benjamin X then left
the stage.

Malcolm X gave the Muslim greeting, "As Salaam Alaikem," and
then said "Brothers and Sisters." At this time a Negro male, wearing
a three-quarter-length black leather coat, pushed his chair back, stood
up, and said to the Negro male sitting on his left "Get your hand out
of my pocket."

The Negro male who stood up was very dark complected, slender
build, about 5'10" tall, weighing 160 pounds, age in the late twenties,
lean face, with medium length straight hair.

This man then pushed his coat back and produced an object [that] looked to be metallic and raised his arm. At this point, people from the audience, which consisted of about four hundred individuals, began jumping to their feet. Malcolm X told everyone to "take it easy."

The next thing [Bureau Deletion] was that [Bureau Deletion] heard about four gunshots, which were fired in rapid order, and which sounded like they came from a semiautomatic pistol.

[Bureau Deletion] then fell to the floor and [Bureau Deletion] believed [Bureau Deletion] blood on Malcolm X's face. While lying on the floor about five minutes later [Bureau Deletion] heard at least ten or eleven more gunshots, which sounded like they came from the same type [of] gun mentioned above and from the same location.

While still lying on the floor and immediately after the last burst of gunfire, [Bureau Deletion] [saw] a man from the waist down walk [Bureau Deletion] loading a gun clip [Bureau Deletion] believed this clip to be smaller than a .45 caliber clip but could not be more specific. [Bureau Deletion] did not believe this man to be the one wearing the black leather jacket, as his hands appeared to be those of a light-skinned Negro.

This man wore brown or cordovan-colored shoes and had medium-sized feet. [Bureau Deletion] he could furnish no further information regarding the murder of Malcolm X, as the scene was, by this time, "utter confusion."

[Bureau Deletion] possessed no information concerning any plans of retaliation by the followers of Malcolm X or any other individuals.

[Bureau Deletion] did not know who shot Malcolm nor did he see any firearms. [Bureau Deletion] it appeared to him there was a definite lack of security at this rally. In addition, [Bureau Deletion] there did not appear to be enough guards in the front of the hall nor any guards near the exits.

[Bureau Deletion] the Audubon Ballroom is rectangular shaped, with exits at the left center side and left rear side. He said that chairs were set up in rows for the audience to sit in, with aisles on either side and an aisle down the middle. [Bureau Deletion] the podium behind which Malcolm X stood was directly in front of the center aisle.

[Bureau Deletion] The man who stood up, mentioned above, sat about in the middle of the left row of chairs, about three rows [Bureau Deletion] and about four rows from the front row of chairs.

[Bureau Deletion] that Malcolm X was the leader of the OAAU and Muslim Mosque, Inc., (MMI).

SAC, New York (105-8999)   2/25/65
Director, FBI (100-399321)
MALCOLM K. LITTLE
INTERNAL SECURITY—MMI

In view of the subject's death, his name is being removed from the
Security Index at the Bureau and you should handle accordingly in
your office.

Submit an appropriate memorandum noting his death, for dissemination at the Bureau.

ATTENTION [Bureau Deletion]

Cancel SI cards.

UNITED STATES DEPARTMENT OF JUSTICE

FEDERAL BUREAU OF INVESTIGATION

New York, New York
March 12, 1965

Malcolm K. Little
Internal Security—MMI

On February 21, 1965, at 3:10 P.M. [Bureau Deletion] advised that
Malcolm X had just been shot in the Audubon Ballroom, New York
City, while addressing an OAAU public rally. [Bureau Deletion] that
Reuben X Francis, one of Malcolm's officers, fired back at those shoot-
ing at Malcolm X. [Bureau Deletion] a Negro male (later identified as
Talmadge Hayer) was captured outside the Audubon Ballroom immedi-
ately after the shooting.

[Bureau Deletion] advised on February 21, 1965, that at approximately 3:10 P.M., this date, he received a call at the station that a
homicide was committed at the Audubon Ballroom, 564 West 166th
Street, New York City.

He stated that Patrolman [Bureau Deletion] New York City Police
Department, advised the same date that Malcolm X, Negro, male, age
39, of Suite 128, Hotel Theresa, 7th Avenue and 125th Street, New
York City, while on the stage of the Audubon Ballroom, was shot and
killed by unknown persons. Patrolman [Bureau Deletion] stated that
Malcolm X was pronounced dead on arrival by [Bureau Deletion] at

Vanderbilt Clinic, Presbyterian Hospital at 168th Street and Broadway, New York City, on February 21, 1965. [Bureau Deletion] stated that the Police Department determined that the shooting of Malcolm X occurred at about 3:10 P.M., February 21, 1965.

On February 21, 1965, [Bureau Deletion] and [Bureau Deletion] both of the [Bureau Deletion] advised that Malcolm X was shot that afternoon during a rally of the OAAU at the Audubon Ballroom. They stated that [Bureau Deletion] was on patrol on Broadway when he heard shots coming from the Audubon Ballroom. He immediately proceeded in that direction where he saw people coming out of the said ballroom shouting that Malcolm X had been shot. Others were shouting "Don't let him get away." [Bureau Deletion] at that time arrested person identified as Thomas Hagan as he was running out of the ballroom. When arrested, Hagan (true name Hayer) had in his pocket a .45-caliber automatic clip containing four rounds. Hayer had been shot in the left leg.

[Bureau Deletion] further stated on February 21, 1965, that the Police Department obtained two witnesses immediately after the shooting, namely [Bureau Deletion] both freelance reporters and photographers of [Bureau Deletion].

[Bureau Deletion] stated that [Bureau Deletion] and [Bureau Deletion] gave statements in which they say they saw Hayer with a gun in his hand while Malcolm X was on the stage speaking. They said Malcolm X suddenly called out "Hold it" and after this, [Bureau Deletion] dropped to the floor and did not actually see Malcolm X shot, but stated before they dropped to the floor, they saw Hayer with a gun in his hand pointing it towards Malcolm X. The next thing they saw was Hayer trying to run out of the ballroom with a gun in his hand. According to [Bureau Deletion] as Hayer ran out, one of Malcolm's group shot three times at Hayer with an automatic pistol. Hayer did not have the pistol on him when he was arrested outside the ballroom.

[Bureau Deletion] also stated that [Bureau Deletion] who was sitting in the front row in the Audubon Ballroom was shot in the foot during the shooting spree in which Malcolm X was shot. He also stated that [Bureau Deletion] was also hit during the shooting spree in the ballroom and both [Bureau Deletion] and [Bureau Deletion] were treated at Columbia Presbyterian Hospital, New York City.

[Bureau Deletion] later advised that the police found a 12-gauge sawed-off double-barrel shotgun manufactured by J. C. Higgins, model 1017, also bearing the number 5100. The police advised, upon examination, that the shotgun had been fired and left at the scene.

At approximately 7:45 P.M., on February 21, 1965, [Bureau Deletion] advised that Hayer was being detained in the prison ward at Bellevue Hospital, under guard. He stated that Hayer had one bullet in him which entered his left thigh and shattered the thigh bone. He stated the hospital plans to put Hayer's left leg in traction and [said] that the bullet would stay in the leg for about two weeks until such time as the bone would be healed enough to permit an operation.

On February 21, 1965, [Bureau Deletion] New York, contacted the office of the Federal Bureau of Investigation (FBI) at New York City and stated that he had one of the pistols used to kill Malcolm X. [Bureau Deletion] was at that time in [Bureau Deletion] and asked that Bureau Agents meet him at the [Bureau Deletion] address as soon as possible. [Bureau Deletion] when contacted the same date by Agents of the FBI, [Bureau Deletion] was in the back of the Audubon Ballroom, the same date, to hear Malcolm X speak. He stated that he is a member of the OAAU. He said Malcolm X was just introduced and began to speak when some people began to scream somewhere about eight rows from the front of the auditorium. He said people in that area began to move away and Malcolm X put up his hands as though to quiet the people down and was heard to say "Keep your seats." Just then, [Bureau Deletion] shots rang out, but [Bureau Deletion] could not see who was doing the shooting. After the shots were fired [Bureau Deletion] the persons shooting headed for the exit. Some of the people in the audience tried to stop them by throwing chairs at them or in their way. At this time, two of Malcolm X's men were shooting at the assailants as they were trying to leave the ballroom. [Bureau Deletion] said the two men involved in the shooting passed him, but as the other two men involved were running towards the exit, one turned to fire back at Malcolm X's men. As this man then turned to run through the exit, [Bureau Deletion] threw a "body block" into him knocking him down the stairs, at which time, this person dropped a .45-caliber pistol. [Bureau Deletion] picked up the gun and attempted to shoot the man he knocked down as he was running down the stairs, but the gun jammed and he ran out of the building. [Bureau Deletion] said he checked the gun and noticed that three rounds were still in the clip. [Bureau Deletion] then turned over to Special Agents of the FBI a .45-caliber automatic pistol, serial number 335055, containing a clip with three rounds of ammunition.

At 10:15 P.M., February 21, 1965, [Bureau Deletion] came to the office of the FBI, at which time, they were furnished a .45-caliber automatic pistol, which was obtained by Agents of the FBI from [Bureau Deletion].

[Bureau Deletion] stated that Hayer, who was arrested immediately after shooting Malcolm X, has been charged with homicide and that Reuben X Francis, a member of Malcolm X's group, was charged with felonious assault and possession of a deadly weapon.

[Bureau Deletion] also stated that the Police Department has a witness who identified Francis as the person firing back at assailants of Malcolm X. He said Francis was believed to have fired a shot which struck Hayer in the leg. He said Francis is suspected of being the person who fired a .32-caliber pistol, which has never been recovered by the Police Department. [Bureau Deletion] stated that it is estimated that up to four persons may [have been] involved in the killing of Malcolm X.

[Bureau Deletion] further advised that an autopsy performed on Malcolm X reflected that he had ten bullet wounds in his chest, thigh, and ankle plus four bullet creases in the chest and thigh. The autopsy located one nine-millimeter slug and one .45-caliber slug, and several shotgun pellets in the body of Malcolm X.

[Bureau Deletion] said that when the Police Department examined the Audubon Ballroom after the shooting they found a sawed-off double-barrel shotgun wrapped in a green suit coat. In the suit coat pocket was found a key for a Yale lock, a package of camel cigarettes, and an empty eyeglass case bearing the optometrist name "M. M. Fine, Main Street, Flushing." The shotgun contained two discharged Remington express shells, single 0 buckshot shells, and there were indications that the gun was recently fired.

[Bureau Deletion] also stated that in the ballroom were found three .45-caliber shells and slugs, six nine-millimeter shells and two slugs, and three .32-caliber slugs and 10 pieces of lead, presumably fired from the shotgun.

The FBI Identification Division, on February 22, 1965, identified prints of the person arrested in the shooting of Malcolm X as Talmadge Hayer, who up until then, was known to the Police Department only as Thomas Hagen. Identification records reflect that Hayer, FBI #142496F, is a male, Negro, born March 16, 1942, at Hackensack, New Jersey, last known residing at 347 Marshall Street, Paterson, New Jersey. [Bureau Deletion]

[Bureau Deletion] that Malcolm X arrived at the Audubon Ballroom, February 21, 1965, in a white 1965 Cadillac. Malcolm X was surrounded by his bodyguards and was then escorted into the front corridor of the Audubon Ballroom and then to the stage. When Malcolm X began to speak, a disturbance occurred between two men. Up in the front near the stage, Malcolm X's bodyguards started to move towards the two men causing a disturbance, when Malcolm X said "Hold it." Without hesitation, two men occupying the front seats, left side, middle aisle, looking towards the stage, got into a crouched position and fired several shots in the direction of Malcolm X. The fire "spitting" from the guns "crashed" into the chest of Malcolm X and he fell backwards as if knocked down by a sudden powerful force. Still in the crouched position, the gunmen hastily moved toward the exit in the back of the hall, stepping over persons who were laying on the floor. It is believed that approximately twenty shots in all were fired during the shooting.

[Bureau Deletion] reviewed a photograph of Talmadge Hayer and identified him as one of the persons who shot and killed Malcolm X on February 21, 1965, at the Audubon Ballroom.

[Bureau Deletion] advised on that date Hayer's fingerprints were found on the clip of the .45-caliber pistol that was picked up by [Bureau Deletion] at the Audubon Ballroom the day Malcolm X was killed and turned over to the FBI.

On February 26, 1965 [Bureau Deletion] Norman 3X Butler, 661 Rosedale Avenue, Bronx, New York, was arrested at 3:00 A.M., same date, by the New York City Police Department, as one of the assassins in the killing of Malcolm X on February 21, 1965. [Bureau Deletion] said that three witnesses including [Bureau Deletion] placed Butler in the Audubon Ballroom at the time that Malcolm X was shot and he was identified as one of the persons who actually shot at Malcolm X.

[Bureau Deletion] a photograph of Norman 3X Butler, who was arrested by the Police Department for the killing of Malcolm X as one of the persons who participated in the shooting of Malcolm X at the Audubon Ballroom..

On February 27, 1965, [Bureau Deletion] advised that [Bureau Deletion] identified Talmadge Hayer and Norman 3X Butler, both now in the custody of the New York City Police Department, as assassins in the killing of Malcolm X. Butler was arrested in January 1965, for shooting a Correctional Officer who broke away from the NOI and, at the time he was arrested for killing Malcolm X, he was on $10,000 bail.

[Bureau Deletion]

[Bureau Deletion]

[Bureau Deletion]

[Bureau Deletion] identified Norman 3X Butler from photographs as the man who was sitting [Bureau Deletion] and said. "Get your hands out of my pocket" in the Audubon Ballroom, just before Malcolm X was killed. [Bureau Deletion] cannot recognize Thomas 15X Johnson from photographs as being in the Audubon Ballroom on February 21, 1965.

On March 4, 1965, [Bureau Deletion] stated that as of this date, Hayer, Butler, and Johnson, all arrested for the killing of Malcolm X, have refused to furnish any information other than their names and ages.

On March 8, 1965, [Bureau Deletion] advised that [Bureau Deletion] was interviewed by the New York City Police Department on the same date. According to [Bureau Deletion] stated that he saw Hayer shoot Malcolm X and also observed Butler and Johnson in the Audubon Ballroom the day Malcolm X was killed. [Bureau Deletion] saw Johnson run out the side exit after the shooting.

[Bureau Deletion] stated that Johnson, when arrested, denied being in the Audubon Ballroom on February 21, 1965. [Bureau Deletion] stated that [Bureau Deletion] after the shooting, he picked up the shotgun used to kill Malcolm X and gave it to Rueben X Francis. He said he also picked up a German Luger pistol and gave it to another person to hold until the police arrived.

[Bureau Deletion] stated that the German Luger was never turned over to the Police Department and this gun could probably account for the nine-millimeter slug in Malcolm's body. [Bureau Deletion]

On March 10, 1965, [Bureau Deletion] advised that the [Bureau Deletion] in conducting interviews of persons, particularly MMI members who were present in the Audubon Ballroom when Malcolm X was shot, seem to have the same "clear cut" story that they were in the ballroom when Malcolm X was shot and when the shots rang out they fell to the floor and never got a look at the assassins. [Bureau Deletion] stated that the Police Department learned that [Bureau Deletion] of the MMI in New York City, has instructed members of the MMI and the OAAU to cooperate with the Police Department but only say that they fell on the floor when the shooting started and cannot identify the person who shot Malcolm X.

[Bureau Deletion] said the [Bureau Deletion] is now shifting their investigation towards officials of the MMI [Bureau Deletion]. In reference to [Bureau Deletion] stated that information has been received that [Bureau Deletion] also was one of Malcolm X's bodyguards the day he was shot, and has been seen in the Harlem area "dressed to kill," "wearing one-hundred-dollar suits" and a "pocket full of hundred dollar bills" since the death of Malcolm X. [Bureau Deletion] said that [Bureau Deletion] has no visible means of support at this time.

[Bureau Deletion] also stated that on March 10, 1965, the New York County Grand Jury handed down first-degree murder indictments in the killing of Malcolm X on February 21, 1965, against Talmadge Hayer, Norman 3X, Butler and Thomas 15X Johnson.

TELETYPE UNIT

MARCH 11 1966

ENCODED MESSAGE

FBI NEW YORK
1/43 P URGENT 3-11-66 JAM
TO DIRECTOR /4/ 100-399321
FROM NEW YORK 105-8999 1P
MALCOLM K. LITTLE, SM-MMI
  NEW YORK STATE SUPREME COURT JURY FOUND TAL-
MADGE HAYER OF PATERSON, NEW JERSEY, NORMAN THREE
X BUTLER AND THOMAS FIFTEEN X JOHNSON OF NEW YORK,
GUILTY OF FIRST DEGREE ON MARCH ELEVEN NINETEEN
SIXTY SIX FOR THE MURDER OF MALCOLM K. LITTLE COM-
MONLY KNOWN AS MALCOLM X.
SENTENCE SCHEDULED FOR APRIL FOURTEEN NEXT.
  LETTER FOLLOWS.
  COPY OF INSTANT TELETYPE BEING SENT TO NEWARK BY
MAIL.
CORR TIME SHD BE 143 PM
END
2-HL
FBI WASH DC

FBI

DATE: 4/14/66

AIRTEL

TO: DIRECTOR, FBI

FROM: SAC, NEW YORK

SUBJECT: MALCOLM K. LITTLE aka SM-MMI

On 4/14/66, [Bureau Deletion] NY County, NYC, advised that on this date, NY County Supreme Court Judge Charles Marks sentenced Norman Butler, Thomas Johnson, and Talmadge Hayer to life imprisonment for the murder of Malcolm Little, commonly known as Malcolm X.

It is noted that a person sentenced to life imprisonment for murder in the first degree in NY County must serve a minimum of 26 years, 8 months before they can be eligible for parole.

Index

512